With best wishes to a
respected colleagues
           Graham

MODERN MARRIAGE

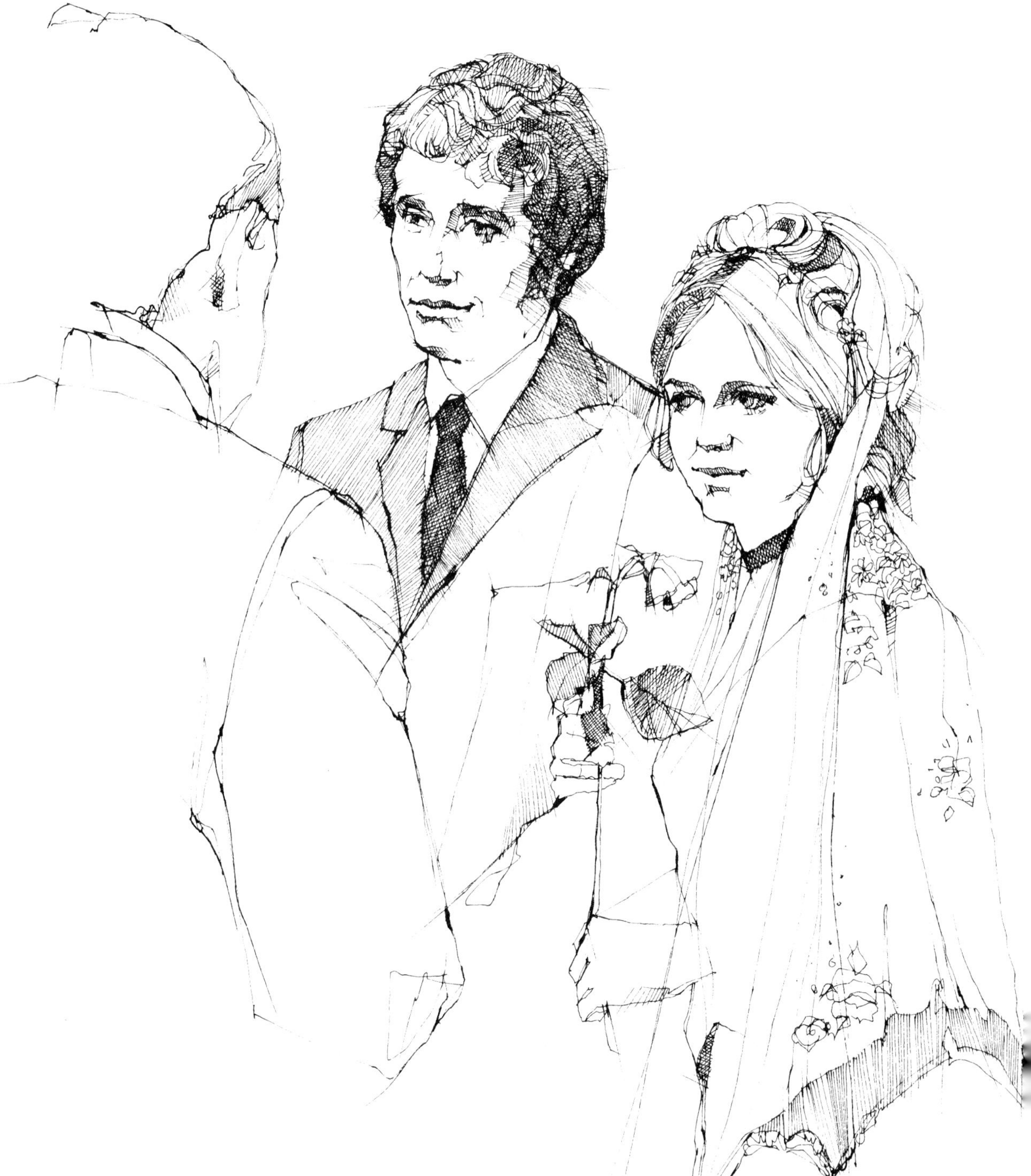

MODERN MARRIAGE

Eighth Edition

Henry A. Bowman
Department of Sociology
The University of Texas, Austin

Graham B. Spanier
Division of Individual and Family Studies
and Department of Sociology
The Pennsylvania State University

McGraw-Hill Book Company

New York   St. Louis   San Francisco   Auckland   Bogotá   Düsseldorf
Johannesburg   London   Madrid   Mexico   Montreal   New Delhi
Panama   Paris   São Paulo   Singapore   Sydney   Tokyo   Toronto

MODERN MARRIAGE

Copyright © 1978 by McGraw-Hill, Inc. All rights reserved. Formerly published under the title of MARRIAGE FOR MODERNS, copyright © 1974, 1970, 1965, 1960 by McGraw-Hill, Inc. All rights reserved. Copyright 1954, 1948, 1942 by McGraw-Hill, Inc. All rights reserved. Copyright renewed 1970, 1976 by Henry A. Bowman. Printed in the United States of America. No part of this publication may be reproduced, stored in a retrieval system, or transmitted, in any form or by any means, electronic, mechanical, photocopying, recording, or otherwise, without the prior written permission of the publisher.

1234567890VHVH783210987

This book was set in Century Schoolbook by Black Dot, Inc. The editors were Lyle Linder, Janis M. Yates, and James R. Belser; the designer was Joseph Gillians; the production supervisor was Leroy A. Young. The frontmatter and part-opening illustrations were done by Cheryl Cooper; new drawings were done by E. H. Technical Services.
Von Hoffmann Press, Inc., was printer and binder.

Library of Congress Cataloging in Publication Data

Bowman, Henry Adelbert, date
    Modern marriage.

    Editions 1-7 published under title: Marriage for moderns.
    Includes bibliographies and index.
    1. Marriage.   I. Spanier, Graham B., joint author.
II. Title.
HQ734.B76   1978   301.42   77-10089
ISBN 0-07-006802-X

To My Wife
Lucille Bowman

To the Memory of My Grandmother
Rose Spanier Fox

Contents

Preface   XV

PART I   MEN, WOMEN, AND AMERICAN MARRIAGE

Chapter 1   Marriage in a Changing Society   3
The Centrality of Marriage   4
Marriage and Its Alternatives   5
Marriage and Social Change   6
Ethnocentrism in the Study of Marriage   7
Research and Individual Decision Making   8
Terms to Be Learned   9
Selected Readings   9

Chapter 2   Males and Females: What They Are and Why   11
Sexual Socialization, Sex, and Gender   12
    Development of Sex-Object Preference | Development of Gender Identity | Development of Gender Roles | Acquiring Sexual Skills, Knowledge, and Values | Development of Dispositions to Act in Sexual Contexts
The Difference between "What Should Be" and "What Is"   13
How Different Are We?   15
    Puberty | Sex Drive | Orgasm and Sexual Performance | Some Differences in Sexual Socialization
What Causes Similarities and Differences?   22
    Determiners in the Cells | Physiological Processes | Glands | Culture and Experience
Birth and Death Rates   26

VIII Contents

Conclusion	28
Terms to Be Learned	28
Selected Readings	29

Chapter 3 Marriage Alternatives and Variations — 33
Families and Households — 35
Singleness — 36
  Factors beyond Conscious Control | Homosexuality | Factors Subject to Conscious Control | Repudiation of Marriage
Cohabitation: An Alternative before Marriage — 38
  Cohabitation As a Temporary Matter of Convenience or Choice | Trial Marriage | Cohabitation As a Permanent Alternative to Marriage | Common-law Marriages
Communes — 45
  The Diversity of Communes | Prospects for Communal Living
Group Marriage — 48
Homosexual Marriage — 50
Single Parenthood — 51
Terms to Be Learned — 52
Selected Readings — 53

PART II MARRIAGE PREPARATION AND PARTNER SELECTION

Chapter 4 Socialization for Marriage: Love and Dating — 59
Why Do People Marry? — 60
Love — 61
  Falling in Love | Multiple Loves | Misconceptions Concerning Love | Love and Infatuation | Questions for Self-evaluation
Dating in America — 71
  Dating: Its Definition and Functions | Dating and Social Change | A Continuum of Experience | Qualities of a Date | The Impact of Physical Attractiveness | The Rating and Dating Complex | The Principle of Least Interest | The Trends toward Early and Steady Dating
Terms to Be Learned — 81
Selected Readings — 81

Chapter 5 Premarital Sexual Behavior and the Sexual Revolution — 83
Is There a Sexual Revolution? — 84
  The "Revolutionary" Kinsey Studies
Premarital Sexual Intercourse — 87
  What Are the Recent Trends? | Summary of Research Findings | Sexual Standards | Male and Female Orientation | Methodological Problems
Sexual Socialization and Premarital Sexual Behavior — 97
Freedom of Choice — 98
Double Standard — 99
Goal Orientation — 99
Do Males or Females Need Sexual Intercourse? — 100
Effect on the Relationship between Man and Woman — 100
Petting — 102

IX
Contents

The Problem of Risk	**103**
Consequences for Females	Consequences for Males	Pressure to Marry in Case of Acknowledged Paternity	Premarital Intercourse with Inadequate Protection	Reasons for Inadequate Protection	Frequency of Premarital Pregnancy	
Risk of Venereal Disease	**109**
When to Seek Medical Attention	
Conclusion	**112**
Terms to Be Learned	**113**
Selected Readings	**114**
Chapter 6 Preparation through Choice	**117**
Principles Governing Mate Selection	**118**
Choosing a Marriage Partner	**119**
Qualities of a Marriage Partner	Background Factors	Sexual Attraction	Physical Health	Hereditary Traits	Common Interests	Standards of Behavior	Economic Elements in Selection of a Partner	"Likes" and "Opposites"	Choosing a Partner like One's Parent	Length of Acquaintance	Some Developmental Theories about Marital Choice	Reasons for Poor Choice of Marriage Partner	Parental Objections	
Engagement	**131**
How Long Should Engagement Be?	Engagement As Transition	Rings, Pins, and Other "Ornaments"	Questions to Be Discussed during Engagement	Telling about Oneself	Broken Engagement	
Terms to Be Learned	**137**
Selected Readings	**138**
Chapter 7 Partner Selection and Mixed Marriages	**139**
Mixed Marriage	**140**
The Marriage Rate	**141**
Propinquity	**142**
Age	**142**
Age at First Marriage	Age and Marital Stability	Age Difference	
Nationality	**145**
Race	**146**
Family Background and Social Class	**148**
Social Class and Marital Stability	
Education	**150**
Education and Marital Stability	
Intelligence	**151**
Mate Selection Differentials	**152**
Previous Marital Status	**153**
Religion	**154**
Trends in Interfaith Marriage	What Are the Options?	Catholic–non-Catholic Marriage	Preparing for Catholic–non-Catholic Marriage	Jewish–non-Jewish Marriage	Religion and Marital Stability	
Conclusion	**163**
Terms to Be Learned	**164**
Selected Readings	**164**

Contents

PART III MARRIAGE IN PROCESS

Chapter 8 Launching Marriage — 171
Law — 172
  The Capacity to Marry | Void and Voidable Marriages | Waiting Period | Health Certificate | License | Officiant | Residency | Change in Status | Proxy, Shipboard, and Alien Marriages | Premarital Pregnancy | Interracial Marriage | Remarriage after Divorce | Reciprocity | Antenuptial Contracts | "Marriage Contracts"
Marriage Readiness — 177
The Wedding — 178
  The Wedding Ceremony | Marital Adjustment Implied | Is Marriage Dissoluble?
Wedding Customs — 180
The Transition from Singleness to Marriage — 183
College Marriages — 186
  Number and Composition of Student Population | Status | Grades | Spouse's Mobility | Attitude of Parents | Finances | Reversal of Role | Wife's Responsibilities | Academic Pressures | Making College Marriage Successful
Terms to Be Learned — 191
Selected Readings — 191

Chapter 9 Marriage and the Social Climate — 193
Changes in American Marriage — 195
  The Role of the Husband | The Role of the Wife
Gainfully Employed Married Women — 200
  Problems Growing Out of Married Women's Gainful Employment | Effect of Working Wives on Marriage Relationships | Effect of Working Mothers on Children
The Position of Women in Modern America — 206
  The Women's Liberation Movement
The Position of Men in Modern America — 210
  The Men's Liberation Movement
Other Factors in the Social Situation — 211
  Legislation | Lack of Preparation for Marriage | Obscurantism | Premarital Romance and Sex | Lack of Serious Attitude | Stereotypes | Publicizing of Failure
Terms to Be Learned — 214
Selected Readings — 215

Chapter 10 Making Marriage Meaningful: Marital Adjustment and Interaction — 221
Marital Quality and Marital Stability — 222
Conflict Is Normal — 225
  Conflict Resolution
Marital Adjustment over the Family Life Cycle — 226
  Measuring Marital Adjustment
An Understanding of Personality and Behavior — 228
  All Behavior Has Causes | Some Aspects of Behavior | Perspective | Tremendous Trifles | Focal Points

Contents

Important Aspects of Marital Functioning	**238**
Use of Money	Use of Leisure Time	Motivation	Acceptance		
Communication	Fear	Domination	Overdependence	"Homeopathic	
Remedies"	Tension	In-laws	Law of Diminishing Returns	Principle of	
Least Interest	
Terms to Be Learned	**249**
Selected Readings	**250**

Chapter 11 Sex in Marriage — **253**

Sex and Marriage	**254**
The Nature of Sex	**255**
An Understanding Attitude toward Reactions	**255**
Mutuality	Male-Female Differences in Reaction	Rights and Duties		
Success and Failure	Understanding Each Other	
Sexual Adjustment	**261**
Fear of Pain	Pelvic Examinations and Premarital Counseling		
The Husband's Responsibility	
Sexual Response	**265**
Similarities and Differences	Other Considerations	Periodicity		
Premenstrual Syndrome	
Marital Sexuality	**275**
Frequency	Marital Adjustment and Sexual Adjustment	
Extramarital Sex	**276**
Swinging	
Sexual Dysfunctions	**281**
Sexual Dysfunctions in the Male	Sexual Dysfunctions in the Female		
Treatment of Sexual Dysfunction	Conclusion	
Terms to Be Learned	**286**
Selected Readings	**287**

PART IV FROM MARRIAGE TO THE FAMILY

Chapter 12 Birth Control and Fertility — **293**

Requirements for Means of Birth Control	**294**
Understanding Birth Control	**295**
Menstrual Cycle	
Methods of Contraception	**298**
Oral Contraceptive Pills	Side Effects	Oral Contraceptives and	
Thromboembolic Disease	Other Benefits of Oral Contraceptives	The	
Mini-pill and Progestins	Intrauterine Contraceptive Device (IUD or	
IUCD)	Diaphragm	Condoms	Spermicides	The "Safe Period" or "Rhythm"		
Incomplete Intercourse (Withdrawal)	Douching	The Morning-after	
Pill (DES)	Other Forms of Contraception	Sterilization	The Effective-	
ness of Conception Control	Trends in Contraceptive Practice	
Infertility	**318**
Artificial Insemination	**321**
Abortion	**323**
Types of Abortion	The Nature of the Fetus	The Rights of the	
Man	Other Effects of Liberalized Abortion	Methods of Inducing Abortion		
The Future of Abortion	

Adoption   330
Terms to Be Learned   332
Selected Readings   333

Chapter 13   Pregnancy and Childbirth   335
Determiners of Heredity   336
    Chromosomes and Genes | The Gametes
Organs and Processes in Reproduction   338
    The Production of Sperms | The Production of Ova | Fertilization | Parthenogenesis | Development of the Fetus | Duration of Pregnancy | Fetal Protection and Food and Oxygen Supply | Maternal Impressions | Gender Determination
Signs of Pregnancy   352
    Presumptive Signs | Positive Signs
Tests for Pregnancy   355
Childbirth   355
    Lactation | Multiple Births
Rh Factor   371
Choosing an Obstetrician   375
Pregnancy and the Couple's Adjustment   376
Terms to Be Learned   378
Selected Readings   379

Chapter 14   Child Rearing and Family Living   381
Trends in Parenthood   383
Family Size and Family Interaction   384
Transition to Parenthood   387
Child Rearing   388
    Children's Needs
Education for Sexuality   398
    Nature and Objectives | Bodily Exposure | Children's Questions | Vocabulary | Masturbation | Education for Sexuality Is Unavoidable
Family Development   403
Terms to Be Learned   405
Selected Readings   405

PART V   BEYOND MARRIAGE

Chapter 15   Marital Dissolution   411
The Nature of Divorce   413
Definitions   414
Marital Dissolution in Historical Perspective   415
Marital Dissolution in Cross-cultural Perspective   415
American Divorce Rates   416
    Factors Affecting the Rate | Duration of Marriage before Divorce | Differentials in Divorce Rates
Divorce and Children   423
    Effects of Divorce upon Children
Divorce Law   424
    The Adversary (Fault) System | Who Files for Divorce? | No-fault Divorce | The Future of Divorce Law

Contents

Annulment	429
Separation	429
Child Support and Alimony	430
Postdivorce Adjustment	430
Remarriage	431
Terms to Be Learned	433
Selected Readings	433

Chapter 16 Marriage and Family Counseling — 435
Who Should Visit a Counselor? | When Should Counseling Be Sought? | What May Counseling Be Expected To Accomplish? | Types of Counseling | The Nature of Marriage and Family Counseling | The Counselor | How May Competent Counselors Be Located? | Training of Marriage and Family Counselors | Some Basic Principles | Premarital and Postmarital Counseling | The Responsibility of the Prospective Counselee

Terms to Be Learned	443
Selected Readings	443

Epilog — 445

Appendix   Marriage and Divorce Laws in the Fifty States — 447

References — 455

Indexes — 479

  Name Index

  Subject Index

Preface

Social change is a continuous process. As with other aspects of social life, there has been dramatic social change in marriage, the family, and sexual behavior—the topics discussed in this text. Similarly, there has been significant change in how these subjects are taught, and in the backgrounds and experiences of the students who study these subjects. The eighth edition of *Modern Marriage*, formerly *Marriage for Moderns*, has been prepared with an awareness of and appreciation for such change.

This book has a unique history. It was first published in 1942, earlier than any marriage and family textbook currently on the market. But a textbook, like the phenomena it discusses, must "evolve" to meet changing circumstances, knowledge, and points of view. Otherwise, it soon loses touch with student concerns and needs. This eighth edition has been revised substantially to provide students both with a sound knowledge base necessary to understand the complexities and challenges of marriage and with information which may be useful for marriage preparation.

Perhaps the change which will be noticed first by those familiar with previous editions of the book is the addition of a second author. The preparation of the eighth edition has been an active collaboration of two individuals who differ in age by forty-five years. This was an unusual, yet intellectually fruitful circumstance. This collaboration has been personally rewarding for both authors and has resulted in a book which we believe has much to offer. This edition combines recent, important research findings with revised discussions of issues relevant to marriage education. In addition, to illustrate points, we have incorporated examples of actual problems and experiences revealed in teaching and in marriage and family counseling.

We believe the text is at the threshold of a new period of growth. We hope that instructors in marriage and family courses will recognize this as they peruse this new edition. This growth is symbolized, in part, by a change in the book's title, which has been suggested by some readers and reviewers of previous editions.

In this edition, much new material has been added. New insights and points of view have been introduced. Topics such as "the sexual revolution," partner selection, mixed marriage, birth control and abortion, the similarities and differences between men and women, preparation for marriage, sex in marriage, and marital interaction and adjustment have been reexamined. The book has been completely reorganized, and new chapters have been added covering dating and love, marriage alternatives and variations, marriage and family counseling, and marital dissolution. In addition, a new introductory chapter has been included.

The book is addressed primarily to college and university students who are currently in the process of thinking about, considering, or planning for marriage. We realize, too, that many of our readers are already married, some will not marry at all, and some of today's college students are in their thirties or forties or beyond.

The authors have taken the position that present-day freedom of choice permits each individual to choose his or her own values and way of life. This does not indicate that the authors are without personal values. Rather, it indicates our expectation that students will work out their own value structure regardless of what a textbook says. Food for thought is preferable to an attempt at indoctrination.

An effort has been made to clarify the meaning of "sex," "sexuality," and "gender." Using these terms appropriately has emerged only recently as a consideration in social science. Also, throughout the text the authors have made every effort to resolve the problem of the use of the masculine pronoun as the indefinite pronoun.

At times such usage may make for what seems like awkward expression to the reader. We believe that in the long run, however, attention to language used in marriage and family textbooks will facilitate the removal of traditional barriers which have tended to portray males and females in an inappropriate, rigid fashion.

We wish to express our gratitude to Janis Yates, Lyle Linder, and James Belser, of the McGraw-Hill Book Company, who have been especially helpful throughout the process of publishing this book. Joanne Nicholson and Robert Casto have made valuable contributions to the eighth edition through their indispensable assistance in manuscript and book preparation. We thank the secretarial staff of the Division of Individual and Family Studies at The Pennsylvania State University, under the supervision of Diane Bernd, for typing the manuscript.

Our primary objective has been to present the reader with a view of the realities of marriage—its history and future, its problems and rewards, and its traditions and alternatives. If *Modern Marriage* continues to meet student needs, our goal will have been realized.

Henry A. Bowman
Graham B. Spanier

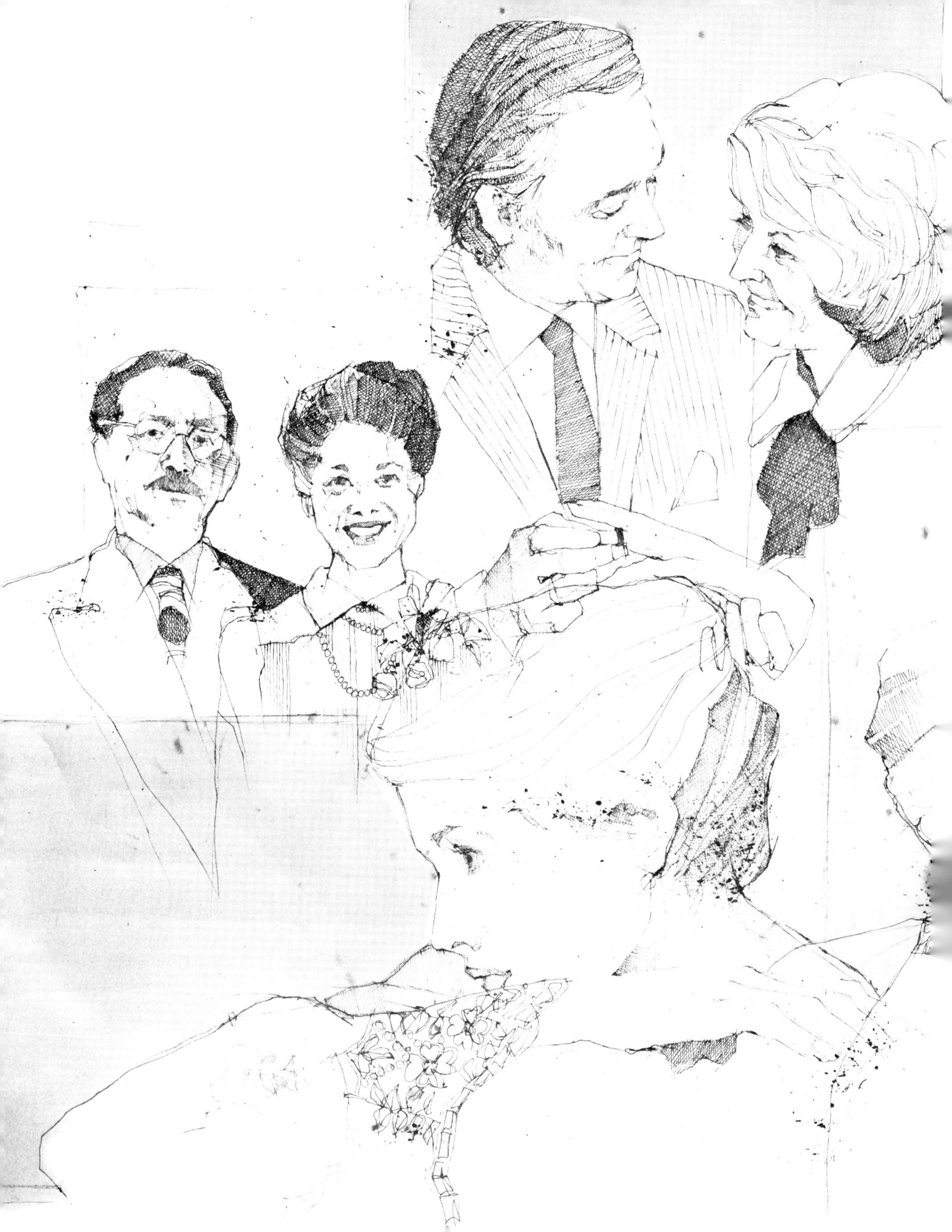

Part I
Men, Women, and American Marriage

Chapter 1

Marriage in a Changing Society

Marriage is among the most highly valued forms of human association. All societies have designed socially approved ways in which males and females bond together. Similarly, every society provides ways for units of closely related individuals to share legal, economic, and affectional responsibilities and rewards. Societies call the male-female bond *marriage*, and the unit of related individuals, in which children are produced and reared, is known as the *family.* In modern America, marriage eventually attracts more than nine out of ten adults (U.S. Bureau of the Census, *Statistical Abstract*, 1976).

Marriage has taken many forms throughout history and from society to society. In some societies, an individual may have two or more spouses simultaneously. *Polygamy* is the general term which describes these unions. There are two forms of polygamy. *Polygyny*, the more common, involves one husband and more than one wife. *Polyandry* involves one wife and more than one husband. There are also a few examples of *group marriage*, a union of three or more males and females, although this has never been the dominant marriage form in any society. Of course, the marital form with which we are most familiar is *monogamy*, which involves one male and one female. In America, where both custom and law determine the conditions under which we marry, monogamy is the usual practice.

THE CENTRALITY OF MARRIAGE

The centrality of marriage in America can hardly be disputed. Children are socialized for marriage from early childhood. Virtually all children, if asked, will say they intend to marry. Such responses should not be unexpected, since television, school books, motion pictures, and the example presented by their parents suggest to them that marriage is expected. The mass media continue to confirm the centrality of marriage as the child matures. In America, where couples typically marry because they are in love, the great amount of attention devoted to love, romance, sex, and marriage has a powerful influence on individuals of all ages.

In some societies, marriages are arranged by the parents, and the young persons who are involved in the union have little say in the matter. Such a practice seems highly unusual to most young Americans contemplating marriage, since a marriage based on love cannot be created by individuals other than those in love. But marriage has different meanings for different people. In societies where marriage is arranged by parents, the marriage ceremony has the very important function of bringing two families together as much as it brings two individuals together. Since the parents and other family members have much at stake in the marriage, they take a greater role in finding mates for their children than American parents do. Definitions of love between potential spouses may also vary from culture to culture. In America, love usually has a strong romantic component. However, some cultures may consider love to be primarily a feeling of commitment, companionship, or security. Thus, in arranged marriages, love is expected to develop after the wedding, rarely before.

The modern American system of dating, courtship, and marriage is different from that of many primitive, less industrialized societies. The process leading to marriage has also changed considerably over the years. Many of these changes, which we shall discuss later, have come about because of the increasing importance of the marriage relationship. Although parent-child, sibling, peer group, and employee-employer relationships are considered important to most persons, it is the marriage relationship which captures our greatest interest. Only in rare cases do persons marry because they want to have children, or terminate a relationship because they are unable to. Most couples eventually do have children, but their primary motivation to marry is more likely to center on the rewards and satisfactions they expect to receive from a love-based marriage.

There are some good explanations why marriage has become increasingly important in America and why it is the focus of many high school, college, and university courses. As our society has become more modern, technological, and urbanized, it also has become more impersonal. The mobility of thought created by television and telephones, and the mobility of people created by automobiles and airplanes has made America a fast-paced, forward-looking country. In a given day, most of us encounter dozens or even hundreds of persons. Contrast this with the society of the colonial Americans or the society of the post–Civil War farmer. In these time periods, one was unlikely to encounter anyone other than family members in a given day. The impersonality fostered by our contact with hundreds of persons whom we will never really know has made marriage an even more important place for us to develop the close personal relationships most of us need.

Thus, marriage has taken on a greater role in the emotional gratification of its partners (Winch, 1971). This important function was always a part of marriage in America, but one could argue that it will become increasingly important. Contrast this emerging function with others which are declining in the family. The socialization and education of children, for example, occur more and more outside the home. The increase in preschools and day care among young children, college and university education among young adults, and the great deal of peer group interaction during childhood and adolescence reflect a trend which began several decades ago, when the family started to shift the socializing-educational function from the home to the public schools.

Similarly, the family's religious function has gradually shifted from the home to religious schools and churches. We have transferred the protective function from the man of the house, who in colonial days was required to have a rifle if he owned property, to state and local police forces who are specially trained for this role. We have seen a shift in the economic function, which many years ago was firmly rooted in the family by virtue of the dominance of agriculture and the family farm. Now, most persons make their living away from their home. Even the recreational function has moved outside the home as we have increasingly come to rely on leisure opportunities created by a modern society: campers, spectator sports in grand facilities, golf courses, racquetball courts, tennis clubs, swimming pools, ten-speed bicycles, snowmobiles.

The decline in the socializing-educational, religious, economic, protective, and recreational functions of the family has not influenced modern American marriage as much as the demands placed on it by the increase in the affectional, emotional gratification role. We expect a lot from marriage. The inability of many couples to meet this expectation undoubtedly contributes to our very high divorce rate.

MARRIAGE AND ITS ALTERNATIVES

Our need for close affectional ties has traditionally led Americans to marry. This is easy to understand, since marriage was the one clearly sanctioned relationship in which it was permissible to have sexual intercourse, live together, and have children. Americans no longer are uncompromisingly tied to the traditional system of dating, courtship, marriage, and childbearing. Although most of us eventually marry, the routes we take in getting there are considerably more varied than at any time in recent American history. The need for close affectional bonds with members of the opposite gender still seems to dominate much of our premarital, marital, and postmarital interaction. For example, despite suggestions from some parents to the contrary, adolescents often prefer a succession of steady dating partners to "playing the field" during their dating years. Couples who are not yet married often live together. Many married persons develop affectional ties with persons other than their spouse. Even couples who recently have been divorced are likely to remarry within surprisingly short periods following the final divorce decree.

Marriage is the most common type of lasting union between men and women, and it

Men, Women, and American Marriage

is the focus of this book. But any treatment of marriage must acknowledge that not everyone marries, and among those who do, many divorce. Among those who do not marry, a range of alternatives is available: cohabitation with persons of the same or opposite gender, communal living, or single living. Any of these alternatives might involve children. Among those who do marry, there is an option not to have children, although most couples do. And among those who marry and divorce, remarriage may follow. Marriage is not now and never was a simple institution. It involves many possibilities and options for its participants. Consequently, this book considers the various possibilities within and outside of marriage. We also consider the processes leading to marriage; the decisions couples face before marriage; the way in which we are prepared for marriage; the immense challenge marriage poses for those who undertake it; the adjustments we make in our lives as a result of marriage; the experience of childbearing and child rearing; and the consequences of marriages which are unsuccessful.

MARRIAGE AND SOCIAL CHANGE

Husbands and wives come together to form a unit, while retaining their individual identities. Exhibit 1-1 illustrates that this marital unit is part of a larger family unit, which may include the couple's children as well as the couple's parents, in-laws, and other relatives. The family in which we are raised is called the *family of orientation*. The family that we develop after marriage is called the *family of procreation*. Our families are part of an even larger social context, which includes important reference groups, friends, employers, the mass media, and a wide range of laws, social norms, and influences which govern our be-

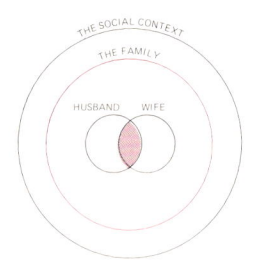

Exhibit 1-1 Marriage in its social context.

liefs, behaviors, and experiences. The character of married life and preparation for it have changed in recent years as changes in the social context have occurred.

We live in a time of change. Although marriage is still quite normative, Americans are becoming increasingly willing to accept a person's right to remain single. Some individuals are apparently choosing to remain single, since there has been a decrease in the number of persons eventually marrying (Glick and Norton, 1973). There has been a dramatic increase in the number of persons living together without marriage (Macklin, 1974). It appears that most cohabiting persons eventually marry, although future marital partners are only sometimes the persons with whom they have cohabited.

Marriages begun in recent years are almost as likely to fail as to succeed. The United States divorce rate is the highest of all modern nations; it is now as high as it has ever been in the history of the country (U.S. National Center for Health Statistics, 1976). Glick and Norton (1973) conservatively estimate that 30 to 40 percent of marriages contracted since 1940 will end in divorce. Furthermore, nearly half of all marriages (including remarriages) involving persons 25 to 30 years old in 1975 are projected to end in divorce (Glick and Norton, 1976). If we include couples who remain married, but are very unhappy with their situation, it is no exaggeration to suggest that perhaps the majority of all marriages will not work out well. The increase in divorce has been accompanied by an increase in the remarriage rate (Glick and Norton, 1973). Almost 50 percent of Americans are remarried within three years of their divorce (Glick and Norton, 1976). This propensity to remarry suggests that most couples are not rejecting marriage or the family, but rather their particular partner. Marriage appears to be here to stay, but additional changes may be required if it is to continue to attract large numbers of individuals.

Other changes are noteworthy. Dating is still a fundamental part of marriage preparation, but it is changing in character. Dating is becoming less formal, with females taking a greater role in initiating dating activities. Many couples meet and develop their relationships through group activities.

Sex outside of marriage is increasingly common. Recent studies indicate that most males and females have coitus before marriage (Spanier, 1978). The increase in premarital sexual behavior has been particularly pronounced among women. Although use of effective methods of contraception has increased among both married and unmarried women (Westoff, 1976), the increase in contraceptive use among unmarried women has not kept pace with the increase in sexual behavior. Consequently, there has been a growing number of abortions performed for unmarried women, the illegitimacy rate has increased among young women, and large numbers of women continue to marry after becoming pregnant. There is also recent evidence to suggest that the extent of extramarital sexual involvements is increasing, particularly among women (Levin and Levin, 1975; Bell and Peltz, 1974).

Among married women, more effective use of contraception has allowed for better family planning (Westoff, 1976). The United States birth rate has recently reached an all-time low (U.S. Bureau of the Census, *Current Population Reports*, 1976). Women are wanting and actually are having fewer children, and increasing numbers of couples are deciding to have no children at all. These and other changes in reproduction and childbearing have provided married women with greater freedom to further their education and pursue careers. There are now more women working than ever before, with approximately half of all adult married women in the labor force (U.S. Department of Labor, Bureau of Labor Statistics, 1976).

The changes cited above undoubtedly encourage some married couples to change their life-styles. There is no sure way of predicting the future, but we can say with some certainty that marriage will continue to change. Adaptation to change is a fundamental part of human life. Marriage has adapted to the world around it through decades of sweeping social change, and there is no reason to believe that it will not continue to do so.

ETHNOCENTRISM IN THE STUDY OF MARRIAGE

Ethnocentrism is the tendency to think that one's own group or society is superior. It also refers to the belief that one's way of life is the appropriate or preferable way. Americans are often considered ethnocentric since most of us are relatively isolated from persons of different cultures and their ways of life. This isolation may cause us to have a very narrow view of marriage. Hence, from time to time throughout this book, we shall mention some fascinating customs, rituals, and daily practices of the members of different societies. We should note, however, that our primary interest is in marriages of North America. Accordingly, we shall rely heavily on information obtained about marriage in the United States. Unless otherwise noted, it can be assumed that we are writing about individuals, marriages, and families in America.

RESEARCH AND INDIVIDUAL DECISION MAKING

No two marriages are alike. This simple fact makes it impossible for any student of marriage to be able to answer with certainty what will make one marriage succeed and another fail. Researchers have been asking that question for over fifty years, and hundreds of studies have been conducted to gain some insight into it. Answers are only beginning to emerge. If we could come up with a master plan for marriage or a formula for success, several things might happen. First, marriage education courses could be initiated in all schools, and students receiving an A would live happily ever after. Marriage counselors would have a 100 percent success rate, and books with every imaginable formula for success, which now adorn bookstores and newsstands, would no longer be sold. Such an occurrence is fantasy. We live in a world where human behavior cannot be predicted with perfect accuracy.

As we learn more about human behavior, however, we are able to make better predictions about individuals and their marriages. We are now moving along this continuum of understanding. We know, for example, that persons tend to marry other persons who are similar to themselves in social backgrounds. We know that marriages involving a premarital pregnancy have a greater likelihood of failure than marriages that do not. And we know that the quality of marital relationships tends to deteriorate during the first several years of marriage. These findings from research studies have a way of being interpreted by uncritical students as imperatives. Any good social scientist, including those who came up with the above findings, would caution students against such rigid conclusions.

Research involves large numbers of respondents from studies with diverse samples of individuals with different social histories. Whereas research findings from physics or chemistry will almost always be invariant, findings from sociology, psychology, or human development cannot always be used as a basis for individual decision making. For example, a pilot knows that an airplane will stay in the air because air passing below and above the wing will create a pressure differential which will keep the plane aloft. This principle, which is always true, is called *Bernoulli's theorem.* If it weren't always true, no pilot would ever start a plane.

Let us return to our examples from marriage research. Although it is true that premarital pregnancy may create circumstances for the couple which make them more likely candidates for divorce, it is not true that all couples with a premarital pregnancy will divorce. Indeed, some will have very good marriages. Similarly, some persons marry outside of their race, religion, or educational level, even though the majority do not. And some marriages improve over time, even though the research shows that most do not.

The difference between the physical and the social sciences is that of *determinism* and *probabilism.* Determinism means that one event is always determined by a sequence of clearly defined causes. Probabilism means that an event may or may not be determined by other causes. Individual variation and a person's motivation are involved. The probabilistic model of the social sciences allows us, within limits, to pattern our lives the way we want, to make our own decisions, and to make things happen differently for us if we are motivated to do so.

Marriage in a Changing Society

As a textbook for an academic course on marriage, our first concern must be with factual material which is important for understanding the nature of modern marriage. We realize the variability of human relationships, however, and feel it is important to emphasize that our information can only be as good as the research allows. Readers must always consider how findings from different studies and the trends discovered from investigation of large numbers of persons can be related to individual experiences, decision making, and planning.

TERMS TO BE LEARNED

Special and technical terms used in the text which may be new to the student or the meaning of which may previously have been unclear are included at the end of each chapter. They are terms which the student should know in order to understand the discussion in the text. He or she should also know them in order to understand what is read in other books and in popular magazines. The underlying assumption is that an individual can think only as clearly as vocabulary permits.

birth rate
cohabit (cohabitation)
coitus
communal living
courtship
dating (date)
determinism (deterministic)
ethnocentrism (ethnocentric)
extramarital

family
family of orientation
family of procreation
family planning
gender
group marriage
marriage
monogamy
normative

peer group
polyandry
polygamy
polygyny
probabilism (probabilistic)
reference group
sibling

SELECTED READINGS

ARIES, P.: *Centuries of Childhood: A Social History of Family Life*, Random House, Inc., New York, 1962. A social history of childhood and the family based on the author's interpretation of art, clothing, games, and other historical evidence.

GLICK, PAUL: "A Demographer Looks at American Families," *Journal of Marriage and the Family*, vol. 37, pp. 15–26, 1975. Marriage, fertility, divorce, living arrangements, kin network ties, and changes in these are examined in terms of demographic data.

GOODE, WILLIAM J.: *World Revolution and Family Patterns*, The Free Press, New York, 1963. The effects of industrialization on the family; the trend toward egalitarianism; the meaning of changing family patterns; dating and premarital sexual intercourse; divorce; women's rights.

GOUGH, K.: "The Origin of the Family," in R. F. Winch and G. B. Spanier (eds.): *Selected Studies in Marriage and the Family*, 4th ed., Holt, Rinehart and Winston, Inc., New York, 1974. Compares and contrasts social organization among humans and other primates, focusing on the evolution of the family system.

NYE, F. IVAN, AND FELIX BERARDO: *The Family: Its Structure and Interaction*, The Macmillan Company, New York, 1973. Analysis of family behavior through the use of sociological research findings and key sociological concepts.

QUEEN, S. A., AND R. W. HABENSTEIN: *The Family in Various Cultures*, 4th ed., J. B. Lippincott Company, Philadelphia, 1974. "Combines the comparative and the historical approaches" to the cross-cultural study of family systems.

WINCH, ROBERT F.: *The Modern Family*, 3d ed., Holt, Rinehart and Winston, Inc., New York, 1971. A text which deals with structure and functions of the family.

——— **AND GRAHAM B. SPANIER** (eds.): *Selected Studies in Marriage and the Family*, 4th ed., Holt, Rinehart and Winston, Inc., New York, 1974. Readings in the sociology of marriage and the family.

Chapter 2

Males and Females: What They Are and Why

That the human race is composed of two types of beings—male and female—is one of the fundamental facts of life. It is a fact that at first glance may seem too obvious to mention. Yet whether a person is male or female is usually the first thing we want to know about a newborn child, and it is among the first observations we make about those with whom we come in contact. Out of this fact of sexual *dimorphism* (two forms) grows much of the world's beauty in art, literature, drama, and human relations. Out of it, also, grow some of life's most trying problems, most bitter disappointments, and deepest hurts.

Males and females exhibit not only relevant differences but also important similarities. Furthermore, there is disagreement as to what the similarities and differences are and what causes them, as well as which should be changed and how change may be brought about. There is, of course, agreement on the presence of average differences in height, size, muscular strength, presence or absence of a beard, and similar readily observable characteristics. There is agreement also on some, but not all, similarities. The only major differences on which there is universal agreement are the female's ability to menstruate, become pregnant, give birth, and lactate (secrete milk), and the male's ability to produce sperm, discharge seminal fluid, and impregnate.

SEXUAL SOCIALIZATION, SEX, AND GENDER

Sex is defined as anything connected with genital stimulation, sexual gratification, reproduction, and the behavior that accompanies such stimulation, gratification, and involvement. Kissing, petting, coitus, and masturbation, for example, are considered forms of sexual behavior and are referred to in this book by the term "*sex*" and its derivatives, *sexual* and *sexuality*. Sexual behavior discussed within a particular social or contextual domain—for example, premarital, marital, or extramarital sexual behavior—refers to those acts (physically acted out, or mentally acted out in the case of fantasizing) which usually involve another individual (imagined or real), and which center upon sexual gratification.

We shall use the term *gender* to mean the attribute of being male or female. *Gender identity* and *gender role*, for example, refer to the qualities of maleness or femaleness, masculinity or femininity, or roles and behaviors understood or performed with reference to the individual's identity as a male or female. This chapter, then, deals primarily with the male and female genders and the differences between them.

Sexual socialization is the process of becoming sexual, taking on a gender identity, learning gender roles, understanding and relating to the variety of sexual behavior, and generally learning the knowledge, skills and dispositions that allow a person to function sexually in a given culture. Sexual socialization, then, is the entire developmental process that forms the basis of our sexuality, our masculinity or femininity, and our maleness or femaleness.

There are five components of sexual socialization (Spanier, 1978):

Development of sex-object preference This component involves the way in which an individual learns to direct his or her sexual interest toward persons of the same or other gender. Research is not clear on the relative contributions of biological and social-psychological influences in determining how we become sexually attracted to males or females, but it is likely that the socialization experiences that we have in childhood and adolescence are important in determining what our sexual orientation will be as adults. Most persons are *heterosexual*, meaning that they are attracted sexually to persons of the other gender. A small, but significant portion of the population is to one degree or another *homosexual*, meaning that they are sexually attracted to persons of the same gender. Most individuals are exclusively homosexual or heterosexual throughout their entire lives, but many persons have both types of experiences at different times in their lives.

Development of gender identity This component involves the process by which an individual comes to identify himself or herself as a male or female. The social definition given to the child at birth customarily follows from the anatomical gender of the child, but one really acquires gender identity through a lengthy process during the first several years of life. Individuals come to understand, internalize, and adapt to their definition as male or female. When a person comes to believe that he or she has a gender different from what his or her anatomy would suggest, the individual is called a *transsexual*. A transsexual, then, is a person who believes he or she is trapped inside the wrong kind of body. A male-to-female transsexual is someone who has a male's anatomy, but who believes he (she) is a female. A female-to-male transsexual is someone who has a female's anatomy, but who believes she (he) is a male. There is a complex surgical procedure which in many cases can change a person's external genitals to conform to what he or she really wants. Clinics that specialize in such surgery are called *gender identity clinics* and can be found affiliated with some medical schools. Psychological and legal counseling is usually provided along with the medical treatment, which also involves hormonal treatments. The phenomenon of transsexuality is quite rare in the population as a whole, but several hundred such operations have been performed during the past twenty years.

Transvestism is sometimes confused with transsexualism and homosexuality. Transvestites are persons (more often males than females) who enjoy dressing up as a person of the other gender. They may receive sexual pleasure from such cross-dressing, and they may or may not be homosexual besides. Technically, however, homosexuality, transsexualism, and transvestism are three distinct variations of the customary sexual socialization process, although some scientists have identified background characteristics and experiences which these individuals share in common.

Development of gender roles This component involves the process by which individuals (1) learn to define roles as "masculine," "feminine," or unrelated to gender-linked distinctions and (2) conceptually affiliate with and behaviorally perform these roles. We shall discuss these terms in more detail later in this chapter.

Acquiring sexual skills, knowledge, and values This component means acquiring information about sexuality, internalizing it, and attaching meaning to it. This process includes the value formation which will influence an individual's behavior in sexual contexts. A later chapter will discuss education for human sexuality, which is part of this component, more fully.

Development of dispositions to act in sexual contexts This component involves the individual's motivation process, which leads to specific sexual behavior. Included is how values, knowledge, and skills, under the influence of certain stimuli (pleasurable sensations, peer or partner pressure to act sexually, "sexual drives," etc.), lead to specific sexual behavior. This component, then, is the link between "what is in one's head" and "what one does."

THE DIFFERENCE BETWEEN "WHAT SHOULD BE" AND "WHAT IS"

Perhaps no topics have generated as much controversy, emotion, and interest during the past decade as have sex and gender differences, male-female roles, and the women's liberation movement. There is little doubt that significant change is occurring in America with regard to male-female relationships. A major part of this change has been the emergence of interest among social scientists in the study of gender roles and sexual socialization. There is, however, one very troublesome aspect of such important social change. The difficulty centers upon the difference between "what exists" and "what should be." These distinctions are easy to understand at a theoretical level but more difficult to separate in our day-to-day lives, since we all have some very strong beliefs about what sorts of behavior and characteristics are appropriate for males and females.

For example, we might make the observation, which is supported by a great deal of data, that males are more active in all forms of sexual activity than are females (e.g., sexual intercourse, masturbation, homosexual relations, childhood sex play). Some persons may feel very strongly that this distinction does not or should not exist. We don't really know whether it *must*, but we have established through research that the difference does now and probably has always existed (Kinsey et al., 1948, 1953; Carns, 1969, 1973; Spanier, 1973; Zelnik and Kantner, 1972).

Another example is perhaps more subtle. We are aware, of course, that women are more likely than men to take primary responsibility for child rearing. They more often leave their jobs after the birth of the first child and tend to spend more time with their children than fathers do. The fact that women have taken a greater role in child rearing has led many to believe that they are more suited for it. In other words, many Americans have come to believe that it is a biological, social, or cultural imperative that women take the primary responsibility for child rearing. There is, however, no real evidence to suggest that this is an activity which must be performed primarily by women. Persons who believe that men should take a greater or even the primary role in child rearing may find it difficult to accept this long-standing cultural tradition. We must nevertheless realize that although these traditions may account for the practice more than biological imperative, the differences do exist, and this fact must be a starting point for social change. There is little doubt that fathers could take a more active or even primary role in child rearing. But it should be clear that there is a difference here between "what exists" and "what could or should exist." In this book we primarily consider what we know to exist in modern America. Readers will have ideas about what should be different and what possibilities for change exist. Such opinions and speculations are valuable, and they may serve in part as a basis for future social change.

Before leaving the subject of our last example, let us consider the history of this basic traditional difference between males and females. Only in recent generations has it been technically possible for the typical woman to separate the functions of childbearing and child rearing. Of course, only women can bear children. But as recently as a hundred years ago, women were much more tied to homemaking and child-rearing activities than they are now. First of all, most Americans were engaged in agriculture. Before modern machinery was available, a great deal of strength was required to do most of the farm work. A division of labor was thus created which put the man in the field and the woman in the home, where she could cook, sew, and tend to the children. With only so many hours in a day to do what had to be done, a division of labor along gender lines was the solution. Furthermore, there were less effective methods of contraception available than we know today, and families tended to be larger than they are now. Consequently, women then were more likely than modern women to be pregnant or have young children. Finally, virtually all children were breast-fed, whereas today the majority of women bottle-feed their children. Breast-feeding naturally tied them to their young children and prevented them from working outside the home.

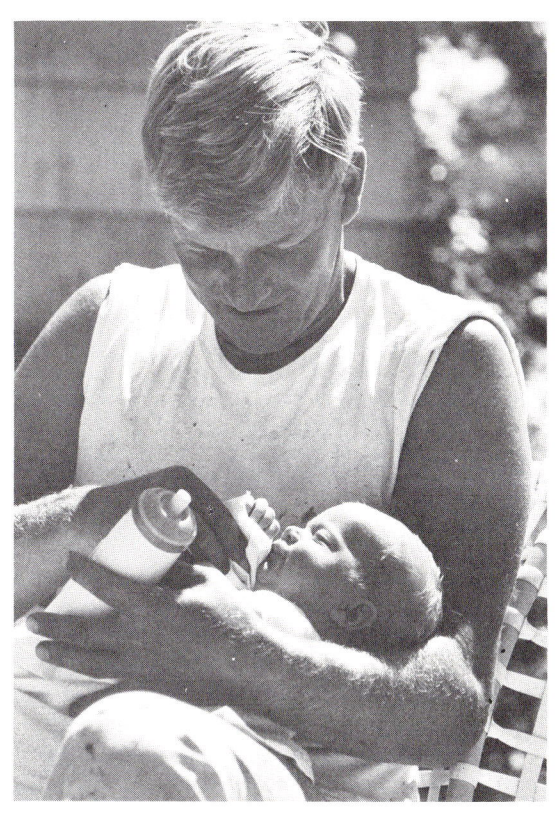

Modern society allows us to separate childbearing from child rearing. While only females can bear children, men are now able to participate in tasks such as feeding infants. (Christa Armstrong, Rapho/Photo Researchers)

With industrialization came hundreds of jobs that did not rely on strength. Contraception gave modern women better control over their reproductive behavior, and nursery schools, day care centers, and bottle feeding permitted women to leave the home and work, if they so desired. In 1975, there were more women in the labor force than at any time in previous history. Over half of all adult women were working; 45 percent of married women were in the labor force; and more than a third of women with children under 6 years of age were working (U.S. Department of Labor, 1976).

HOW DIFFERENT ARE WE?

Biologists specializing in human development have observed that males and females are indistinguishable until several weeks after conception. The development of their reproductive systems is actually more similar than different. It is true that the combination of chromosomes that a fertile male and female contribute to conception is established when the sperm and egg meet, but during the first few weeks of prenatal development, all embryos have a pair of potential gonads (sex glands, such as ovaries and testes) and two sets of reproductive tubes and ducts. Under the impact of various stimuli, mainly hormonal in nature, one set of gonads and tubes advances, while the other regresses. It is not until the seventh week of development that we begin to see the emergence of distinguishable males and females (Tauber, Haupt, and Fassel, 1970). Thus, every part of the male reproductive system has a counterpart in the female reproductive system and vice versa, even though the functions and appearances of these organs will be quite different as the individuals mature.

This basic example of both the similarity and difference of males and females is only a part of a multitude of overlapping attributes in the two genders. We find this overlap of similarities and differences not only in biological characteristics, where they are most obvious, but also in social and psychological characteristics. Allowing for diagrammatic oversimplification, a comparison of the characteristics of males and females as groups can be depicted by Exhibit 2-1, while a comparison of the characteristics of one male and one female is illustrated by Exhibit 2-2.

Men, Women, and American Marriage

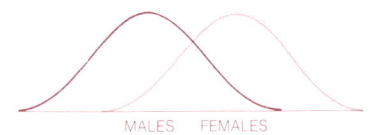

Exhibit 2-1 The overlap of the characteristics of males and females as groups.

Anthropologists have demonstrated, through their research into other cultures, that no task, social personality trait, or behavior has been found that is exclusively characteristic of males in some cultures and exclusively characteristic of females in other cultures. Warfare was universally a male activity in primitive times, but today even warfare involves females (e.g., the Israeli Army). There appear to be no universal gender-related behaviors other than those associated with reproduction. Thus, the ways we think of males and females, the roles they perform, and masculinity and femininity are to a large extent determined by our socialization—in short, by the customs and traditions of our culture and the way in which they are learned by us.

There are two ways in which one may better come to understand males and females. The first involves scientific data establishing "natural," inborn, innate attributes. Research is gradually providing such data. The other way involves being aware of similarities and differences as they are exhibited by individuals in our culture, regardless of whether they are innate or acquired. Research is also helping us to understand this area better.

Exhibit 2-2 The characteristics of males and females as individuals.

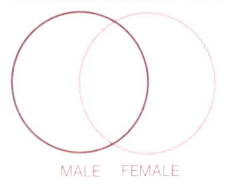

We shall not attempt a complete inventory of all similarities and differences between the genders. In fact, at the present stage of knowledge such an inventory is impossible because so much remains to be learned. There are numerous items on which research studies do not agree, and a great many attributes are conditioned by culture and are not fixed, but change as culture changes. Also, not every individual conforms to the average or stereotype of the group.

There are differences between males and females in physiology, anatomy, hormonal balance, genetic and hereditary characteristics, sexual response, and in social-psychological behaviors. Men are, on the average, able to move faster, jump higher, reach further, and strike harder; they are generally taller and stronger. Men have more of their height in their arms and chest, whereas more of a woman's height is in her abdomen, partly because of the uterus and the necessity of accommodating a fetus. Women have broader hips and relatively large thigh muscles to support them. If any of these differences would suggest the superiority of men, there are other differences which suggest the superiority of women. Baldness, congenital deafness, color blindness, and hemophilia are gender-linked defects which are found almost exclusively in men. Women live eight years longer than men, on the average (U.S. Bureau of the Census, *Statistical Abstract*, 1976). There are hundreds of studies showing differences in personality traits (Maccoby and Jacklin, 1974). Men are more likely to have college and graduate degrees, although women are more likely than men to finish high school (most dropouts are males), and there are still significant occupational differences between men and women. Men have more prestigious jobs, are found in greater numbers in the professions, and make more money, even at the same jobs (U.S. Bureau of the Census, 1970). Yet despite all of these

Males and Females: What They Are and Why

While differences between males and females are not as great as many think, these extreme examples remind us that men tend to be bigger and stronger while women tend to be smaller and more graceful. (United Press International)

differences, there are more similarities than differences between men and women, an important point to remember.

The traditional demand in American culture that a man must be demonstrably successful in whatever he undertakes or in what society expects of him—whether it be occupation, sports, sexual intercourse, or what not—places the male in a vulnerable position that makes failure in any of these areas threatening. Women have been placed in a similar position relative to getting married and having children. As the trend toward equal employment opportunity continues and the blending of gender roles goes on, one wonders whether women will become subject to the same expectation of success that is now typical of men.

It is often said that women are more emotional while men are more intellectual, that men reason while women feel. When one witnesses some of the intellectual achievements of some women, however, and observes some of the failures of some men, one is prone to doubt this assumed difference in intellectual and emotional behavior. The difference between men and women is not that the former reason while the latter feel; it is one of type of emotion expressed and degree of freedom in expression.

The common and uncritical assumption is that men have greater freedom than do women. In some respects this is true. Men may move about more freely, are supervised less carefully, and are in some ways freer to determine their own behavior. In other ways, however, men have less freedom than women do. There are standards of manliness to which men are in a measure expected to adhere. Women are freer to express such emotions as fear, pity, sadness, and affection for persons of the same gender. A man may feel like crying, but he may not do so for fear of being called "sissy." He may be petrified with fright, but he must put on a bold front to avoid being classified as a coward. In some respects, also, men are so overlaid with traditional restrictions and inhibitions as a result of training that they not only do not express such emotions freely but often come to experience them to a lesser degree.

Puberty

At puberty a child's sex organs, which have remained more or less quiescent, begin to function in more nearly adult fashion. During the same period, secondary changes take place. A boy's voice changes. His muscles increase in size. His shoulders broaden. Pubic hair appears. What was previously only an unimpressive fuzz becomes a shaveable beard.

In a girl, the breasts develop. Owing to fat deposits, what were angularities become more esthetic lines. Pubic hair appears. The pelvis broadens, and the girl is prepared for childbearing. But, although there are instances of extremely early motherhood, there is evidence to suggest that in many cases a girl does not immediately become fertile when she reaches the *menarche*, that is, when she begins to menstruate (Montagu, 1946; Riley, 1959; Wilkins, 1965; Wharton, 1967). Some investigators, however, question this and believe that in many girls, fertility typically is established just prior to the first menstrual period (Greenhill, 1960). The earliest authenticated case of motherhood is that of Lina Medina of Peru, who began to menstruate at the age of 8 months; became pregnant at age 4 years, 10 months; and had a 6½-pound boy by Cesarean section (a surgical procedure to remove the baby from the uterus) at age 5 years, 8 months (Jolly, 1955).

In addition to adjusting to the physical changes that occur at puberty, the child must adjust to emotional changes and learn to live with the new attitudes and new subjective experiences that spring up within the young person. Also, since girls on the average reach puberty earlier than boys, there is a period in which many girls are both more mature and taller than boys of the same chronological age. The situation creates problems for both genders. It is at this period that some girls begin to prefer older boys.

In both genders the release of sex cells begins (sperms in the male, ova in the female). In the boy there is the secretion of seminal fluid, which is stored in the seminal vesicles and constitutes an internal stimulus or readiness to respond to sexual stimulation. Puberty is announced in part by the discharge of this fluid during sleep. These nocturnal emissions, or "wet dreams," are a normal occurrence in the male. Typically they are marked by pleasurable sensations (orgasms) and are accompanied by sexually colored dreams (as compared to romantic dreams). In such a dream the boy sees a girl's body or parts of girls' bodies or has contact with a girl's body, or something similar. In the girl puberty is marked in part by the first menstruation.

Most children reach puberty at about their twelfth to fourteenth year, but in exceptional instances girls have menstruated much earlier. Some girls do not begin to menstruate until their late teens or early twenties. A few never do, and their condition is termed *amenorrhea*.

Sex Drive

Generally speaking, a man's sex drive is characterized by greater urgency than a woman's. A woman's sex drive may be as strong as a man's when circumstances are favorable and she is aroused; but sex drive does not have the same priority in a woman as in a man. Men are more compulsive with regard to sex; and sexual interest is more nearly ever-present. Women's interest is less compulsive and more likely to be periodic; and women are more likely to have inhibitions. As a group, women can get along more comfortably with less sexual release than men can. There are more women than men who have little or no interest in sexual intercourse. We do not know how much of the difference in sex drive is determined by hormonal balance versus socialization, but both are undoubtedly involved to some extent.

In their ability to respond sexually, women vary over a wider range than men do. Men tend to cluster around the average. Bardwick (1970) mentions the "all-or-none phenomenon in males." Women exhibit more extremes. "There is great variation in both the intensity and the duration of female orgasmic response, while the male tends to follow standard patterns of ejaculatory reactions with less individual variation" (Masters and Johnson, 1966). There is a natural brake put on the male in that his ability to repeat ejaculation of seminal fluid within a brief time span depends upon the rapidity with which his glands can secrete that fluid and he can be resensitized to sexual stimulation. Since a woman's response is not dependent upon any such secretion and ejaculation, she may, in some cases, have a series of climaxes far surpassing the number of her partner's climaxes. This means that the most responsive women are more responsive than the most responsive men. Woman's "physiological capacity for sexual response infinitely surpasses that of man" (Masters and Johnson, 1970).

But there are differences in the timing of response in individual acts of sexual intercourse. Men's response in intercourse tends to be more rapid and more spontaneous. Women's response tends to be slower and less spontaneous. These two differences between the genders—one, rapidity of arousal and spontaneity of response; the other, capacity for repeated response—are sometimes confused.

Orgasm and Sexual Performance

Ours has become a very orgasm-conscious society in recent years. There are dozens of books at newsstands and bookstores prepared to instruct us as to how we can improve our sex lives. Much of the attention in these books is directed to the satisfaction of the female through orgasm. Females have become increasingly concerned about their ability to have or recognize orgasms. Males are increasingly concerned about whether or not their partner has one. Since Masters and Johnson (1966) published their findings that women were capable of multiple orgasms, many persons have erroneously concluded that this response was characteristic of most women. It is not. Furthermore, many women do not have orgasmic responses until well into a sexual relationship with a given male, perhaps not for months or years. Other women find that they are able to have orgasms immediately from the beginning of a sexual relationship. Still other women are able to have orgasms through masturbation or manual manipulation by males, but not through sexual intercourse. These are all common variations of female sexual response.

It is possible for a woman to enjoy sexual intercourse without having orgasm. Many women do regularly. Others do occasionally. It is also possible for a woman to pretend to have an orgasm, but this is a form of deception which many individuals find undesirable (Masters and Johnson, 1975). Some women do so for the sake of their partner. A man's sexual enjoyment, however, is not entirely tied to his partner's sexual response, although this varies from person to person. Most men will have orgasm-ejaculation and find sexual intercourse pleasurable regardless of their partner's response. Our society has put a great deal of pressure on men to perform sexually, however. A man may be considered a failure if he cannot bring his partner to orgasm. But he is likely to feel more of a failure if he is unable to obtain an erection himself (impotence) or if he is unable to wait a sufficient length of time before ejaculation (premature ejaculation). These problems, when they exist, are evident to both partners. The pressures on males and females alike to perform sexually contribute greatly to sexual problems. We shall discuss these problems in more detail in Chapter 11.

There is an important difference between the genders which needs both to be understood and to be kept in mind when the relative freedoms and pressures of men and women are compared. Men more readily separate sex and love, while women are more inclined to combine them (Bardwick, 1971). This is one of the important differences between males and females. It means, among other things, that men and women approach sexual behavior from somewhat different points of view or orientations. We shall discuss this difference more fully later. Failure to understand and appreciate it is a frequent contributor to unsatisfactory sexual relationships.

Some Differences in Sexual Socialization

At puberty boys and girls meet a fork in the road of development that is the point of departure for some of the later differences in sexual attitudes and behavior. The changes which occur at this time further sharpen the differentiation between the genders, lead to increased sexual attraction, and establish more firmly the individual's identification with his or her own gender. To some degree these processes are already under way before puberty is reached, not only through anatomy but also through names, clothes, social groups, and differential treatment and expectations. Generalizing and recognizing the fact of variation in both groups, the genders may be described as on pp. 21–22. Whether these differences are culturally or biologically determined is not our immediate concern.

One of the differences between the genders very difficult for both to understand is the difference in interest in visual experience. Males are typically interested in seeing females—the more the better, both numerically and anatomically. They tend to want to see female bodies with as little concealment and as much exposure as possible. They are interested in pictures of female bodies, as evidenced, for example, by the multiplicity of magazines devoted to such pictures to be found on newsstands. Millions of copies of such magazines are sold monthly. The females in the pictures are essentially anonymous; male readers are usually not concerned about their identity.

Females, on the other hand, are ordinarily less interested in seeing the nude male body. They are less interested in seeing pictures of the nude male body for the erotic value of such pictures. There are magazines containing pictures of males to be looked at by females, but the males are mostly conventionally clothed romantic figures, movie stars, singers, or similar persons. There are also

Males and Females: What They Are and Why

MALE	FEMALE	MALE	FEMALE
1 Considerable interest in sex.	1 Less interest in sex, but this is changing.	physically pleasurable, frequent; may produce guilt in some.	sions, but may have sexual dreams. Some experience orgasms in sleep.
2 Much discussion of sexual activities, less of romantic activities.	2 Less discussion of sexual activities, more of romantic activities.	6 Masturbation practically universal, usually beginning in the teens.	6 Masturbation at some time by majority, but not universal; frequency less.
3 Sexual sensitivity and response spontaneous. 　a Little or no learning needed for response. 　b Accumulation of seminal fluid constitutes internal stimulus. 　c Tend to cluster around mean; less variation; relatively few unresponsive.	3 Sexual sensitivity and response less spontaneous. 　a More learning needed for response. 　b Nothing equivalent to accumulation of seminal fluid. 　c Wider range of variation; many unresponsive; some more responsive than males.	7 Premartial sexual intercourse: 　a More males engage in. 　b More frequent by those who engage in. 　c More males initiate. 　d Begin earlier. 　e Less emotional involvement likely. 　f Less likely to feel guilty about first sexual experiences.	7 Premartial sexual intercourse: 　a Fewer females engage in. 　b Less frequent by those who engage in. 　c Fewer females initiate. 　d Begin later. 　e More emotional involvement likely. 　f More likely to feel guilty about first sexual experiences.
4 Pleasurable sexual experience (orgasm): 　a Frequent. 　b Tends to occur often. 　c Typically starts early in life. 　d Practically all have orgastic experience at some time. 　e Experiences orgasm plus ejaculation. 　f Lesser orgasm capacity; can achieve orgasm and ejaculation less frequently in limited time span.	4 Pleasurable sexual experience (orgasm): 　a Less frequent. 　b Often long periods between instances of sexual activity. 　c Typically starts later in life than among males. 　d Some never have such experience during entire life. 　e Experiences orgasm; nothing equivalent to ejaculation. 　f Greater orgasm capacity if responsive; can reach orgasm frequently in limited time span.	8 Imagination relative to sex: 　a Nocturnal sexually colored dreams common; sometimes accompanied by orgasm and ejaculation. 　b Sexually colored daytime fantasies more common. 　c Romantically colored daytime fantasies common.	8 Imagination relative to sex: 　a Nocturnal sexually colored dreams less common; rarely accompanied by orgasm. 　b Sexually colored daytime fantasies less common. 　c Romantically colored daytime fantasies common.
		9 Tactile sensations (touch): 　a Responds more quickly to being touched by other gender especially in genital area.	9 Tactile sensations (touch): 　a Responds less quickly to tactile sensations. Often resists being touched in genital area.
5 Nocturnal emissions practically universal;	5 Nothing equivalent to nocturnal emis-	10 Is reared with less	10 Is reared with con-

MALE	FEMALE
emphasis upon modesty.	siderably more emphasis upon modesty.
11 Nothing equivalent to menstruation.	11 Menstruation.
12 More readily separates sex and love.	12 More inclined to combine sex and love.
13 Much interest in visual experience. Great interest in seeing pictures of nude females. Considerable erotic value	13 Less interest in visual experience. Considerable curiosity likely, but less erotic value in the experience.

magazines with pictures of scantily clad male athletes. Others show pictures of nude males to be looked at by male homosexuals. But until recently there has been no widely read publication for females similar to the many for males featuring pictures of nudes of the other sex. In 1972, one of the national women's magazines for the first time featured a photograph of a nude male. Following this, several wide-circulation magazines featuring pictures of nude males were launched. But even now, several years after the first one, the number of such publications is small in comparison with the number of corresponding publications for men. Whether this will prove to be an experiment or the beginning of a new trend remains to be seen.

There is evidence to suggest that there is a difference in the way males and females respond to erotic movies. A male is more likely to see a female in a film as a sex object, while a female is more likely to identify with a female in a film and fantasize being in the picture herself, sought by a male. This difference is sometimes expressed as "I want to have" compared with "I want to be" (Money and Tucker, 1975).

This difference in interest in seeing the nude body of a member of the other gender is important, because obviously two persons of opposite gender participate in the same sexual relationship. The combination of this difference in modesty plus the difference in urgency of sex drive may create a problem for a couple unless understood, or previously experienced, by both parties.

WHAT CAUSES SIMILARITIES AND DIFFERENCES?

Determiners in the Cells

Each human being begins life as a single cell. This cell is the result of the fusion of two other cells—one from the mother, one from the father—and contains within it the determiners (*genes*, *chromosomes*) of the individual's hereditary traits as well as the determiners of gender.

When the original cell divides into two, these two into four, and so on until in the fully grown person there are trillions of cells, the determiners of gender pass into each of the new cells in the same combination as found in the first one. The only exception to this are the cells which determine the gender of the new individual, in which only one of the pair of determiners of gender is found. In a sense, a person is male or female through and through. All the body cells are male or female, as the case may be.

This fact is actually not so all-important as it may seem at first glance. As Money says (Winokur, 1963), "The presently observable chromosomal differences between male and female are such that by themselves and in isolation from other variables of sex they bear no relationship at all to the development of gender role and identity." Many factors operating after the new individual is formed may alter development by affecting the way in which inborn characteristics, physiological processes, and experience within environment react upon one another. But the fact remains that all cells, with that one exception, have the same genetic constitution, the same determiners; and because of this the individual has a tendency to fall on one side or the other of the gender fence.

Physiological Processes: Glands

Both sexual and individual similarities and differences are produced in part by the way the body functions, by the physiological processes that occur, and by the way an individual reacts to stimuli. One of the chief factors in determining such processes is the glandular setup. In many important respects we are what our glands make us.

One pair of glands, the secretions of which play an important role in making us what we are, is the sex glands (gonads—ovaries in the female, testes or testicles in the male). As we mentioned at the beginning of this chapter, early embryos are genitally undifferentiated; they develop similar structures (Money and Tucker, 1975; Oliven, 1974; van Niekerk, 1974). The combination of chromosomes typical of male (XY) or female (XX) is the first link in a chain reaction. If the combination is typical of the female, the embryo develops ovaries. Embryonic ovaries secrete no hormone. If, however, the combination is typical of the male, the embryo develops testes. Embryonic testes secrete *androgen* (male hormone) and are developed earlier than ovaries. In other words, the individual will develop into a female, or at least develop female body structure, unless there are active testes secreting androgen, which causes the individual to develop into a male. "Male features appear only if testicular masculinizing factors impose masculinity and push back femininity" (Jones, Jr. and Scott, 1971). This is not the same, however, as saying that all embryos are female, as some persons assert. In the early embryo, two separate anatomic systems exist, the Wolffian (male) and the Muellerian (female). Under the influence of hormones, at a critical point in prenatal development, "one system proliferates . . . into functional organs of one sex, and the other regresses to a vestigial state" (Money, 1974).

When a baby is born with some male genitals and some female genitals, or when the baby has some genitals which are indistinguishable, undeveloped, or missing, the condition is called *hermaphroditism*. Parents of hermaphrodites must make a decision as to whether they intend to raise their child as a boy or girl. Once having made that decision, surgery can be useful in helping the child to establish a gender identity. Later, hormonal treatments may be used to help the development of appropriate secondary sex characteristics. Research has suggested that the social definition given to a hermaphrodite at birth is more critical in determining gender than the child's chromosomal, hormonal, or gonadal sex (Money and Erhardt, 1972). Gender identity appears to become clearly established by the time a child has reached the age of 4 or 5, and is extremely difficult to change after this time (Money and Erhardt, 1972).

When by accident or for medical reasons the sex glands are removed from a human male (castration), profound changes occur. Such a person is termed a *eunuch*. If the person is young at the time, he fails at the age at which puberty normally occurs to develop the typical characteristics of men. Voice remains high-pitched. Beard and body hair do not appear in normal amount. Muscles have a tendency to be flabby, and weight usually increases. The genital organs fail to develop normally, and, of course, the person is sterile. Male aggressiveness often fails to appear. If the glands are removed later in life, masculine traits change somewhat, and characteristics such as those mentioned above appear. In addition, the sexual impulse and interest in the opposite gender decrease considerably or may disappear entirely (Bremer, 1959;

Charny, Suarez, and Sadoughi, 1970). In short, the person may become "neuter." Equally important changes occur when the ovaries are removed from females (the operation is termed *ovariectomy* or *oophorectomy*).

The hormones which play so important a part in masculinizing the male are normally found in smaller quantity in the female. On the other hand, the hormones which play so important a part in feminizing the female are normally found in smaller quantity in the male. Thus, maleness or femaleness is in part a result of hormonal balance and may vary in degree as that balance varies.

The effects hormones produce are relative to the character of the tissues and organs on which they act, and these, in turn, are basically male or female. There is even evidence suggesting that "part or parts of the central nervous system are masculine or feminine, depending on the sex of the individual" (Young, Goy, and Phoenix, 1964; Money and Ehrhardt, 1972; Levine, 1973).

Maleness and femaleness, masculinity and femininity, constitute a continuum. A continuum connotes differences of degree rather than simply "all or none." Maleness is not the same as masculinity, nor femaleness the same as femininity, though there is an overlap of terms as well as an overlap of anatomy and behavior. Generally speaking, "maleness," "femaleness," "masculinity," and "femininity" all connote something positive; none represents merely a lack of its paired opposite.

Masculinity and *femininity* connote a certain relativity. Neither could exist were it not in contrast to the other, just as there could be no long without short, no up without down, no light without dark. Neither masculinity nor femininity would be possible if there were one gender instead of two. Masculinity and femininity also connote not only the objective existence of a combination of attributes, but also a degree of reciprocity, a relationship. A woman is feminine not only because she exhibits certain characteristics per se, but also, and perhaps more importantly, because she has the ability to make men interpret her and respond to her in a certain way. The converse is true of a man and masculinity. Masculine and feminine characteristics vary with individual and societal expectation. But the one thing which transcends culture and cannot be permanently removed is that aspect of complementarity which provides the genders with a mutual look in each other's direction.

Culture and Experience

"Masculine" and "feminine" apply to learned behavior, as suggested above. Because of genetic constitution (determiners in the cells), anatomy, physiology, and hormones, typically each individual, as indicated earlier, begins life more or less "leaning" in the direction of masculine or feminine behavior, as the case may be. Such biological factors "lower the threshold" so that "it takes less of a push" to learn *some* behavior, and they "raise the threshold" so that it takes "more of a push" to learn *other* behavior. Culture tends to "reinforce and maximize sexual differences" (Money and Tucker, 1975). But with a few exceptions, biological factors do not by themselves determine such behavior. Biological factors present opportunities for and impose limitations upon what is learned with respect to gender roles.

Each individual is born into a cultural framework which from birth onward determines to a considerable extent the manner of life, the direction of development, and the definition of what the person is expected to do and become, depending upon gender classification. "Sexuality is a dimension of personality (being male or female) expressed in every human act" (Masters and Johnson, 1970).

It is because of this fact of cultural framework within which the individual develops and the fact that culture varies among peoples, even among groups within a people, and with the passage of time, that males or females do not exhibit identical behavior the world over or through time among a given people. Definitions of masculinity and femininity differ as culture varies and changes. For example, in this country slenderness for women is considered to be more attractive than larger size, but in some countries a buxom woman more nearly meets the ideal. In the United States feminine modesty demands that in public a woman conceal her genital anatomy; in some countries she must cover her face.

When life conditions change, alterations in behavior may ensue. For example, during World War II the balance between males and females was upset because so many young men were in military service and hence unavailable to women in their home communities. As a result, many women became quite "unfeminine" in the degree to which they became aggressive in taking the initiative in arranging dates and altered their standards as to acceptable appearance and manners of men. In present-day America the population is so large and so varied, and our culture is changing so rapidly (though not at a uniform rate in all respects or in all subgroups), that there is considerable difference of opinion as to what standards of masculinity and femininity are acceptable.

But whatever the differences developed or permitted, in every known culture there are generally understood and expected means, such as clothing, hair styling, ornamentation, names, and terms of address, for readily distinguishing between the genders. In this country today, it is interesting to note that when some of the means, such as clothing, hairstyling, ornamentation, etc., for readily distinguishing between males and females have been replaced by similarities, there has been a revival of beards and mustaches, as conspicuous a means as possible for readily distinguishing male from female.

Some experience is sexually colored; some is not. From infancy boys and girls are subjected to different educative processes and different expectations. Their games and toys are different and reflect their future adult roles. The stories they read or hear tend to have a masculine or feminine coloring. The standards set for them by their parents and by society at large differ. There is a selection of experience so that different environmental factors act upon the two genders. Each is encouraged to do certain things and prohibited, or at least strongly discouraged, from doing others. Each has restrictions on freedom but in different ways. Girls are given more protection, and they grow to expect it. Boys are allowed more independence, and they grow to take it for granted as a masculine prerogative. As the individual grows older, this process of selection, like other aspects of culture, becomes increasingly internalized; each experience conditions the person further so that screening of new experiences becomes more and more a matter of one's own choosing rather than having to be left to the discretion of others, as in the case of the young child.

The differences in standards of behavior set up by the group are expressed in exaggerated fashion in the old nursery rhyme: "What are little boys made of? Snips and snails and puppy-dog tails. And what are little girls made of? Sugar and spice and everything nice." "He's a real boy," says the proud father, implying that there is a standard of "boyness" and that his son is living up to that standard. The half-shocked mother who says, "Boys will be boys," implies that being a boy is different from being a girl. The words "tomboy" and "sissy" show that there are rather well-defined roles of behavior even for children and that deviation from those roles is not socially approved. In short, each gender tends to learn to act as it is expected to act. Maleness and femaleness, masculinity and femininity are cores around which the structure of personality develops. An individual is born male or female, but he or she learns to be masculine or feminine, as the case may be, according to the cultural patterns of society.

In assessing the contribution of various factors to the sexual and gender development and behavior pattern of the individual and in classifying individuals of confused gender, seven criteria or "variables of sex" (J. L. Hampson, 1964) are employed:

1 Chromosomal sex—the genes and chromosomes.

2 Gonadal sex—the presence, structure, and function of testes or ovaries.

3 Hormonal sex—the quantity and proportion of "male" and "female" hormones.

4 Internal reproductive structures—the presence or absence of internal organs other than testes or ovaries.

5 External genital morphology—the structure of external genital anatomy.

6 The sex of assignment and rearing—the designated sexual classification of the child at birth and whether the child was reared as a boy or as a girl.

7 Gender role or psychologic sex—the individual's sexual behavior and attitudes toward classification and expected role; everything the person says, thinks, or does to indicate status as a male or female. "Gender role is not an innate endowment, but rather is built up gradually during the course of growing up as a consequence of the planned and unplanned life experiences which a child encounters and transacts. The earliest years of life appear to be the most critical ones. . . . Of all the variables of sex . . . the best predictor of the gender role of an individual is the *sex of assignment and rearing*" (J. G. Hampson, 1964).

At birth, so far as gender role and identity are concerned—that is, whether the individual will be masculine or feminine—the individual is "bi-potential." (This does not mean bisexual.) The final, but not the only, determiner of gender role and identity is experience within a given culture, especially the way an individual is reared owing to that individual's classification at birth. Gender identity is established very early in life; most investigators say within the first four or five years, and perhaps earlier. As suggested earlier, the individual is born male or female but becomes masculine or feminine. Gender role is learned, but this does not mean that either the masculine or the feminine role can be learned equally readily by either gender. Being born male or female, the stage is set for the selectivity of an individual's experience and, to some degree at least, the predisposition of his or her response to cultural expectations (Hampson, 1965; Sears, 1965; Young, 1965; Stoller, 1968; Dewhurst and Gordon, 1969; Green and Money, 1969; Josselyn, 1970). Culture "condenses already existing tendencies into authoritative guiding images; it does not freely invent them without regard to reality" (Bednarik, 1970).

No one factor—inborn traits, physiological processes, or experience—is sufficient alone to determine individual or gender differences. They all react one upon the other, making the individual as well as the group the product of both nature and nurture.

BIRTH AND DEATH RATES

There are more males than females among babies born alive. The rate averages about 105 boys to 100 girls in the United States (U.S. Bureau of the Census, *Statistical Abstract*, 1975). Fluctuations occur from year to year, but there are always more boys than girls at birth. It has been estimated that for every 100 female conceptions, there are between 120 and 180 male conceptions. Thus, the ratio of 105 males to 100 females at birth suggests that most spontaneous abortions (miscarriages) are of males.

There are also more males among babies

born dead. More males die in infancy. In fact, the death rate for males exceeds that for females at all ages (U.S. Bureau of the Census, *Statistical Abstract*, 1975), from the prenatal period through old age. "This sex differential for mortality is not limited to the United States. . . . Excess mortality for men is almost universal" (U.S. Department of Health, Education, and Welfare, *Monthly Vital Statistics Report*, 1971). Men are more subject to hazardous occupations, dangerous leisure-time activities, and warfare. Most major diseases strike down more males than females. There are two and one-half times as many male suicides as female suicides, and three times as many male as female homicide victims (U.S. Bureau of the Census, *Statistical Abstract*, 1975). The average expectation of life is about eight years greater for women than for men (U.S. Department of Health, Education, and Welfare, *Monthly Vital Statistics Report*, 1976).

The typical white male and female live to be 72 and 80 years old, respectively. Blacks do not live as long. The average black male and female live to be 65.5 and 73.5, respectively. Life expectancy has changed dramatically in this century, however. In 1900, white males and females had a life expectancy at birth of 46.6 and 48.7 respectively. Black males and females had life expectancies of only 32.5 and 33.5. These figures showing the difference between 1900 and the present also suggest to us that marriages of earlier generations rarely lasted as long as some marriages do now. Before the turn of the century, couples married later and died earlier. Thus, we might wonder whether married couples in earlier generations would have envisioned the possibility of most marriages being expected to last forty or fifty years.

The result of the combined operation of these birth rate–death rate factors is that at younger ages there are more males than females in the population. In the middle twenties for whites, and in the mid-teens for blacks, the sex ratio—that is, the number of males per 100 females—drops below 100 and remains so for every older age (U.S. Bureau of the Census, *Current Population Reports*, 1975). In 1975 just over 51 percent of the population was female, just under 49 percent male (U.S. Bureau of the Census, *Current Population Reports*, 1976). There were more than 5 million more females than males.

The sex ratio of the entire population has

Exhibit 2-3 How long do males and females live?

Life table value and age	Total	White Male	White Female	All other Male	All other Female
Expectation of life:					
At birth	71.3	68.4	76.1	61.9	70.1
At age 21	52.2	49.6	56.7	44.1	51.7
At age 65	15.3	13.2	17.3	13.1	16.2
Percent surviving from birth:					
To age 1	98.2	98.2	98.7	97.0	97.5
To age 21	96.8	96.5	97.8	94.6	96.2
To age 65	72.9	67.5	82.2	51.0	68.1
Median age at death	75.3	72.0	79.8	65.5	73.5

Source: Life Tables: 1973. Vital statistics published by the U.S. Department of Health, Education, and Welfare, 1975.

shown a steady decline since 1910 and is now 94.9 (U.S. Bureau of the Census, *Statistical Abstract*, 1975). Out of each 100,000 of each sex born alive, approximately 53,700 males as compared to 73,118 females survive to the proverbial "three score and ten years." By age 80 there are almost twice as many female as male survivors (U.S. Department of Health, Education, and Welfare, *Vital Statistics of the United States*, 1975). The longer life expectancy of women, combined with the tendency of women to marry men older than themselves, results in the fact that there are about five times as many widows as widowers (U.S. Bureau of the Census, *Statistical Abstract*, 1975).

This is an interesting situation in view of men's traditional image as the stronger gender. When it is a question of living long, living well, and withstanding the vicissitudes of existence, men must yield the place of honor to women. Men are stronger, but women are more durable.

CONCLUSION

One often hears the questions: Are men and women equal? If not, which is inferior and which superior? Taken as it stands, the first question is unanswerable. Equal in what respect? Two things cannot be just equal; they must be equal with respect to a given set of qualities. Even then the answer depends in part on the connotation of "equal." As we have seen, males and females exhibit both similarities and differences. Some of these are biologically determined and are innate. Some are culturally determined and are subject to change. In the last analysis, both genders are necessary for the continuation of human life (except insofar as reproduction by cloning or some similar artificial process may some day be utilized).

With respect to some of the most fundamental and important differences, the genders are complementary, that is, neither alone is complete. Together they may form a functioning unit. To speak of males and females as complementary does not suggest that one be a satellite of the other; that they be diametrically opposite in all traits; that one merely corrects the deficiencies in the other's personality; or that the wife direct all her energy toward furthering the occupational success of her husband. It implies a recognition of similarities and differences between men and women and a utilization of this recognition for the furtherance of common ends.

TERMS TO BE LEARNED

amenorrhea
androgen
biological imperative
bipotential
castration
chromosome (chromosomal)
cloning
complementary (complementarity)
congenital
continuum

counterproductive
cultural framework
cultural imperative
culture
dimorphism
ejaculation
embryo (embryonic)
erection
erotic (eroticism)
eunuch
female (femaleness)

feminine (femininity)
fertility
gender identity
gender role
gene (genetic)
genital
gonad (gonadal)
hemophilia
hereditary
hermaphrodite (hermaphroditism)

Males and Females: What They Are and Why

heterosexual (heterosexuality)
homosexual (homosexuality)
hormone (hormonal)
internalized
lactation (lactate)
male (maleness)
marital
masculine (masculinity)
masturbation (masturbate)
menarche
menstruation (menstruate)
morphology
neural
nocturnal emission
nurturant (nurture)
oophorectomy
orgasm (orgasmic capacity)
ovariectomy
ovary
psychologic sex
puberty
rate (birth, death)
reciprocity
role
semen (seminal fluid)
seminal vesicle
sex (sexual, sexuality)
sex of assignment and rearing
sex ratio
sexual climax
sexual drive
sexual gratification
sexual performance
sexually colored experience
simultaneity
socialization
spontaneous abortions
supplementary
tactile
testicle
testis (testes)
transsexual
transvestism (transvestite)
variables of sex
vestigial

SELECTED READINGS

ALTMAN, DENNIS: *Homosexual: Oppression and Liberation*, Avon, New York, 1973. Cited in Sol Gordon's *The Sexual Adolescent* as "probably the best of the vast number of recently published books about homosexuality."

ASTIN, HELEN S., ALLISON PARELMAN, AND ANNE FISHER: *Sex Roles: A Research Bibliography*, National Institute of Mental Health, Rockville, Md., Department of Health, Education, and Welfare Publication No. (ADM) 75-166, 1975. (Paperback.) Abstracts of 456 items regarding sex differences, development of sex roles, cross-cultural overviews, historical accounts of status of the sexes, theory of the process of socialization, methodological issues.

BALSWICK, JACK O., AND CHARLES W. PECK: "The Inexpressive Male: A Tragedy of American Society," *The Family Coordinator*, vol. 20, no. 4, pp. 363–368, October 1971. Inexpressiveness in males is culturally produced. Boys are taught that expressiveness is inconsistent with masculinity. Inexpressive males are of two types: cowboys (John Wayne) and playboys (James Bond).

BARDWICK, JUDITH M.: *Psychology of Women*, Harper & Row, Publishers, Incorporated, New York, 1971. (Paperback.) The author says that "there are fundamental psychological differences between the sexes that are, at least in part, related to the differences in their bodies" and that "these constitutional dispositions are responded to differently by a particular culture according to the values of that culture."

————— (ed.): *Readings on the Psychology of Women*, Harper & Row, Publishers, Incorporated, New York, 1972. (Paperback.) The development of sex differences, sex roles, and the "motive to avoid success" in women are discussed.

—————, **ELIZABETH DOUVAN, MATINA S. HORNER, AND DAVID GUTMANN**: *Feminine Personality and Conflict*, Brooks/Cole Publishing Company, Belmont, Calif., 1970. (Paperback.) Each chapter is written by a psychologist and addresses some problem associated with the status of women. Discusses the nature of female sexuality, women's conflicts over their sexuality, relationship between femininity and achievement, masculine and feminine ego styles.

CHAFETZ, JANET SALTZMAN: *Masculine/Feminine or Human? An Overview of the Sociology of Sex Roles*, F. E. Peacock, Publishers, Inc., Itasca, Ill., 1974. (Paperback.) An analysis of the nature of stereotyped sex roles, how they develop and are transmitted to children, what their implications, values, and costs are. The author examines emerging trends that may possibly undermine traditional sex roles and "allow for the emergence of a society of *humans* whose lives are based on achieved rather than ascribed characteristics."

CONNELL, ELIZABETH B., JOSEPH W. GOLDZIEHER, AND ELEANOR Z. WALLACE: *Hormones, Sex and Happiness*, Cowles Book Company, Inc., Chicago, 1971. A nontechnical discussion of the various hormones and their roles, with special emphasis on sexual development and function, menstruation, pregnancy, infertility, contraception, and sex differences.

FASTEAU, MARC FEIGEN: *The Male Machine*, McGraw-Hill Book Company, New York, 1974. A discussion of the effects of the male-role stereotype on men's behavior, sexuality, personalities, expectations, attitudes, and relationships with each other and with women. Cultural pressure on men to prove their masculinity and to succeed in competition. Men as husbands, as fathers, in sports, at work; men and violence.

GOLDBERG, STEVEN: *The Inevitability of Patriarchy*, William Morrow and Company, Inc., New York, 1973. Author maintains that hormonal differences between the sexes result in greater aggression in males, that socialization conforms to this difference but does not produce it, and that this male aggression makes patriarchy, male dominance, and male attainment of high-status roles and positions inevitable in all societies. He is very critical of feminist assumptions and analyses.

GOSLIN, D. A. (ed.): *Handbook of Socialization Theory and Research*, Rand McNally, Chicago, 1969. Important collection of papers dealing with socialization from a variety of disciplinary perspectives.

GREEN, RICHARD: *Sexual Identity Conflict in Children and Adults*, Basic Books, Inc., New York, 1974. Report of a study of feminine boys and masculine girls, plus adults who have conflict over their sexual classification. Discusses the possible factors that contributed to their condition. Raises questions about the influence of prenatal experience, hormones, family experiences, etc., in the production of sex differences in temperament and behavior.

HAMMER, SIGNE (ed.): *Women: Body and Culture, Essays on the Sexuality of Women in a Changing Society*, Harper & Row, Publishers, Incorporated, New York, 1975. Essays explore some of the ways in which body and culture affect the sexual life of women in our culture.

HOFFMAN, M.: *The Gay World*, Basic Books, Inc., New York, 1968. A study of the male homosexual community in the San Francisco Bay Area; written for the layman.

HUTT, CORINNE: *Males and Females*, Penguin Books, Inc., Baltimore, 1972. (Paperback.) Author says, "I make no apology for stating the case for the biological bases of psychological sex differences." Made observations on preschool children. "The evidence strongly suggests that at the outset males and females are 'wired up' differently." Says social factors operate on already well-differentiated organisms.

HYDE, JANET SHIBLEY, AND B. G. ROSENBERG: *Half the Human Experience: The Psychology of Women*, D. C. Heath and Company, New York, 1976. (Paperback.) Objective discussion of the psychology of women, similarities and differences between the sexes, black women, female sexuality. Includes a lengthy bibliography.

LEWIS, EDWIN C.: *Developing Woman's Potential*, Iowa State University Press, Ames, Iowa, 1968. (Paperback.) Gender differences in personality, abilities, and roles; and factors causing them. Cites numerous studies.

LIPMAN-BLUMEN, JEAN: "How Ideology Shapes Women's lives," *Scientific American*, vol. 226, no. 1, pp. 34–42, January 1972. Based on a study of over 1,000 college women showing that a woman's life goals, particularly her educational and occupational aspirations, are guided by the type of sex-role ideology acquired in childhood.

MACCOBY, ELEANOR EMMONS, AND CAROL NAGY JACKLIN: *The Psychology of Sex Differences*, Stanford University Press, Stanford, Calif., 1974. Discussion of a great many differences (and assumed differences) and similarities between the sexes and what causes them. The authors utilize available research findings. This book includes an annotated bibliography of over 1,400 research studies.

MILLER, JEAN BAKER (ed.): *Psychoanalysis and Women*, Brunner/Mazel Publishers, New York, 1973. "What do women want and need? What is their basic nature and how does it evolve?" Presents "a view of women which differs from the commonly known psychoanalytic formulations."

MONEY, JOHN, AND ANKE A. EHRHARDT: *Man & Woman, Boy & Girl*, The Johns Hopkins University Press, Baltimore, 1972. (Paperback.) A comprehensive discussion of the nature and development of gender identity.

———, **AND PATRICIA TUCKER**: *Sexual Signatures: On Being a Man or a Woman*, Little, Brown and Company, Boston, 1975. Discussion of sex differences and what causes them. Nontechnical. What are the actual differences, what are the cultural stereotypes?

SHERMAN, JULIA A.: *On the Psychology of Women*, Charles C Thomas, Publisher, Springfield, Ill., 1971. A survey of empirical, psychological studies of the female life cycle. Discusses the psychology of women, biology and psychology of sex differences, female sexuality; a critique of the Freudian theory of feminine development.

WEINBERG, M., AND C. J. WILLIAMS: *Male Homosexuals*, Oxford University Press, New York, 1974. Examines the problems and adaptations of male homosexuals in the United States, the Netherlands, and Denmark; the authors collected survey data and also studied the milieu occupied by their respondents.

YORBURG, BETTY: *Sexual Identity: Sex Roles and Social Change*, John Wiley & Sons, New York, 1974. How and why sexual identity and sex-typed role conceptions develop and vary relative to culture and other factors.

Chapter 3
Marriage Alternatives and Variations

Are marriage and the family dying? On the basis of much of what is said in the mass media, one would think so, but all social scientific evidence is contrary to this conclusion. More than nine out of every ten Americans eventually marry. This marriage rate is among the highest in the world. As Exhibit 3-1 indicates, the proportion of persons eventually marrying has increased during the past several decades. Furthermore, our high divorce rate, which might otherwise be an indication of the decline of marriage, is to a considerable extent overshadowed by our high remarriage rate. When 30 percent of all divorced persons are remarried within a year of their divorce and almost one-half within three years (Glick and Norton, 1976), there is good reason to believe that divorcing individuals are rejecting only their particular spouses—not marriage.

Despite the popularity of marriage and the realization

Exhibit 3-1 Proportion ever married, by sex and age: 1910, 1974

Age group	Proportion Ever Married 1910	1974
Males		
20-24	25.1	43.0
25-29	57.2	77.4
30-34	74.0	89.2
35-44	83.3	91.7
45-54	88.9	94.1
Females		
20-24	51.7	60.4
25-29	75.1	86.9
30-34	83.9	93.2
35-44	83.6	95.1
45-54	91.5	95.8

Source: U.S. Bureau of the Census, *Statistical Abstract of the United States: 1975* (96th edition). Washington, D.C.: Government Printing Office, 1975.

that this life-style is the norm in America, we must be aware that for a significant minority of our population, there is a range of alternatives to and variations of traditional marriage which have some appeal. There appears to be an interest in alternatives even among those who marry. Some persons may choose an alternative to marriage during one part of their life, while choosing marriage during another part. We must also realize that there are probably more variations *within* marriage than there are outside of marriage. A married couple may have children or not; they may live with other married couples in a large household or alone; they may limit their sexual relations to each other or may allow extramarital sex; and they have the option of a dual worker marriage, a traditional marriage with the husband as breadwinner and the wife at home with the children, or they may have a role reversal with the wife working and the husband at home. Thus, there is a multitude of variations within marriage as well as alternatives outside of it.

What do the terms *alternative life-styles* or *alternatives to marriage* suggest? In a heterogeneous population, a pluralistic society such as ours, not every person or group subscribes to the same way of life. This has been true in the United States for some time. Communal societies; polygamous marriage; group marriage; males having wives and mistresses simultaneously; extramarital sexual relations; unmarried persons living together (either with or without the intention of marrying); and other life-styles all have historical precedents. Although they have received increased attention recently, none of these is new. What is new, perhaps, is a growing acceptance—and tolerance—of these life-styles and sometimes a recommendation of them as a solution to certain problems of living.

The term *alternatives* could imply that certain life-styles are substitutes for conventional marriage or that there are various choices, one of which is marriage. There is a shade of difference in these two interpretations. The former sets up conventional marriage as a base from which other alternatives are variations. The latter suggests freedom of choice among all alternatives. At this point in American social development the former interpretation is probably more widely applied.

We have long accepted intercultural differences in life-styles. If the members of an Israeli kibbutz want to have a communal living arrangement, we can accept that people's right to do so. If the Eskimos want to have wife lending, that is acceptable to us. If the Todas, a tribe of Southern India, want to have polyandry, that is their privilege. Now, perhaps, we are coming to a similar acceptance of intracultural differences. We have become more flexible in interpreting possible threats to the established mores. "Live and let live" is increasingly characterizing our approach to life.

Among the alternatives to and variations within marriage which we shall discuss are lifelong singleness; cohabitation as a lasting alternative to marriage, as a temporary matter of convenience or choice, or as a "trial marriage"; communal living; group marriage; homosexual marriage; and single parenthood.

We cannot assume that the practices of the majority necessarily meet the needs of a specific minority. Neither can we assume that the practices of a specific minority will necessarily eventually meet the needs of the majority. Whether a given life-style represents a step toward general practice or whether it represents the meeting of the needs of a small, temporary, peripheral group or whether it is an experiment, only time will tell. It is sometimes assumed, not only by the individuals involved but also by outside observers, that every seeming innovation in a small group represents the point of the wedge of social change. If we learn anything from history, we learn that many such apparent innovations either remain as the life-styles of small minorities or are gradually phased out.

Sometimes it is assumed that it is the form of a given life-style that determines its success or failure, that the solution to the problems of one style is the adoption of another. It is not only the form (or structure) that is important; it is also the people in it that will determine whether a given way of life will succeed or fail. People who are failures in, or discontented with, one type of relationship will not automatically become successes in, or contented with, another just because it is different.

Since the focus of this book is the study of and preparation for marriage, only brief attention will be given to alternatives to marriage. The reader is referred to the Selected Readings for this chapter for further discussion of these alternatives.

FAMILIES AND HOUSEHOLDS

What is a marriage? A family? The study of alternatives to conventional marriage is a challenging and sometimes controversial one for social scientists. Part of the difficulty in researching this topic is that there is not agreement about just what constitutes a marriage or family relationship.

Terms like "marriage" and "family," which we use every day, can evoke much discussion among scholars, and agreement over definitions may be difficult. Most would agree with the general definition that *marriage* is a formal and socially recognized union between persons of opposite gender. A *nuclear family*, the most basic and common family unit in America, consists of a husband-father, wife-mother, and offspring. Alternative forms of marital or family relationships, then, are variations of or substitutes for traditional marriage or nuclear families. Winch (1974a) uses the term *domestic family* to refer to a family living in a single dwelling unit. A domestic family, therefore, could be a single adult or more than one adult who may or may not be legally married, with or without children, who perform many of the functions traditionally thought of as familial.

Sociologists have tended to look at families in terms of their *structures* and their *functions*.

▶ We can say that to qualify as a family . . . a social group must present differentiated positions, the relations among which bear designations of kinship. For example, a set of three actors bearing the designations of husband-father, wife-mother, and offspring would be recognized as a complete nuclear family. . . . This is a *structural* definition, and it leads to information answering such questions as to the make-up of the modal family of a society or of a sub-societal category.

▶ We can impose the requirement that to qualify as a familial system a social group must be engaged in one or more activities we recognize as familial, e.g., sexual gratification, reproduction, child-rearing. . . . This is a *functional* definition. A consequence of the functional definition is that we bring under scrutiny social systems not otherwise thought to be within the field of the family (Winch, 1974a).

If we think of a family as a social group consisting of a husband, a wife, and children who carry out certain activities, what do we call a social group where there are no children? One parent? Or where there are all of the "required" persons but where certain traditional functions are not carried out? Winch (1974a) argues that there may be different groups that some would consider families in which traditional familial functions are present but where structures are different (communes or group marriages, for example). Some groups who meet the structural definition of the family may be lacking function. This is characteristic, for example, of families on the verge of dissolution. There is also one other criterion which has traditionally been used to define the family—common residence. The term "household" can be used to designate this common residence. But this is a limiting part of a definition of the family, since there may be some family structures which take up more than one household. Other cultures have been known to have families which live in more than one household (Eastern and tribal societies have a diversity of residential patterns), and very closely knit extended families in modern America fall within a definition of the family.

In looking at alternatives to traditional marriage, we must first consider the way in which individuals live together in households. Between 1960 and 1970, there was an eightfold increase in the number of household heads who were reported as living apart from relatives while sharing their living quarters with an unrelated adult "partner" (roommate, friend, cohabitant) of the opposite gender (Glick, 1975). United States census data indicate that although most persons are found in households consisting of nuclear families, an increasing number of persons can be found in other types of living arrangements. In 1970, 143,000 "unmarried couples" were reported in the census. There are an unknown number of persons living in communes and group marriages, although their numbers are thought to be rather small. There are a large number of families with one parent absent. In the most typical case, the husband is more likely to be absent than the wife, but both types of single-parent families exist. In 1975, 12.9 percent of white families and 42.7 percent of black families with children under 18 had only one parent.

The most common of the alternatives to marriage is singlehood. In 1974, there were almost 24 million single adults in the United States, 17 percent of the population (U.S. Bureau of the Census, *Statistical Abstract*, 1975). About half of these single persons eventually are expected to marry, but many will not. The number of persons remaining single may be greater than anticipated, since data analyzed during the past decade suggest the possibility of a slight downward trend in the proportion of persons eventually marrying (Glick and Norton, 1973). Let us begin our examination of alternatives to marriage by looking at single persons who never do marry.

SINGLENESS

There are many possible reasons why an individual may not marry. Some of these reasons involve involuntary factors over which the person really has no control. Many of these individuals might have married if circumstances had been different. Other persons voluntarily choose to remain single for a variety of reasons. A person who is single for his or her entire life may actually be involved in any number of different household arrangements. Single persons often share their households with unmarried persons of the same or opposite gender. Sharing living accommodations does not imply, although it does not rule out, sexual relations with a roommate or housemate. Single persons often have active sexual relationships, even though they may not be cohabiting or intending to marry. And, of course, cohabiting couples who are not married are generally single, but we shall discuss cohabitation separately.

Not everyone is suited for marriage. It takes a great deal of wisdom and courage for an individual to recognize that he or she would make a poor marriage partner or would simply find the confines of marriage too limiting. We live in a marriage-oriented society and consequently we do not often realize that not everyone is suited for marriage. Some persons would take issue with such a statement. One could argue that *somewhere* there is a suitable mate for every person. Perhaps. But most marriage and family counselors are able to cite cases where, in their opinion, one or both spouses lack the personal qualities, preparation, motivation, or interest necessary to make marriage work. These characteristics sometimes apply only to the client's current marriage. But in other cases, counselors feel that they are able to cite individuals who would have been unsuitable marriage partners for anyone. This observation does not imply that persons who are unsuited for or not interested in marriage are inferior in any way. Persons may choose a single life-style for very *positive* reasons, in contrast to others who avoid marriage for negative reasons. Our society is sufficiently heterogeneous that single persons choosing to remain single may be able to find satisfaction in this life-style. A man or woman who realizes that marriage is not for him or her and makes life-style decisions accordingly should be commended, rather than ridiculed, since that person is likely to make a better contribution to society than if he or she reluctantly entered into a marriage which ultimately failed. Let us now examine some other specific reasons for singleness.

Factors beyond Conscious Control

Some of the factors that can prevent marriage are the existence of more females than males in the population; the type of community in which one lives; responsibilities which prevent meeting eligible persons; occupational isolation; ignorance of ways of approaching the other gender; too-long delay in earlier years; lack of interest; distorted ideas; disinclination to assume the responsibilities of marriage; disappointment in love; death of a fiancé(e); parental objections; fear of sex or of one's own capacity to "measure up," guilt; or falling in love with a married person.

Homosexuality

Homosexuality itself is, of course, beyond the individual's conscious control. He or she does not decide by simple choice to be homosexual or heterosexual. An individual who is a homosexual may choose to change his or her orientation and cease to be homosexual and, to that end, seek counseling help, but such change is difficult. Homosexuality is not an either-or state. There are degrees and gradations. Some persons are as nearly 100 percent homosexual and others are as nearly 100 percent heterosexual as it is possible to be. But in between the extremes there are many individuals who exhibit a combination of characteristics. Many homosexuals marry persons of the opposite gender, have children, and raise a family. But many individuals with homosexual preference remain unmarried by choice. In recent years, since homosexuals have become freer in identifying themselves and in seeking an end to discrimination, some homosexuals have demanded the right to "marry" each other, and a few have had "wedding" ceremonies. Such arrangements are not marriages in the customary sense of the term and do not have the same legal status, although for some homosexuals they apparently do meet a need.

Factors Subject to Conscious Control

The deliberate choice of celibacy—that is, singleness due to religious vows, as in the case of a priest or nun—is such a factor.

Repudiation of Marriage

A reason for not marrying which has gained some prominence in recent years is the repudiation of marriage as an unnecessary and undesirable relic of a Puritan past, an outmoded and dysfunctional attempt on the part of society to limit the freedom and dictate the life-style of the individual. The feeling is that people should be free to live together without marriage if they so desire. It is claimed that, in the last analysis, a marriage license or certificate is only a piece of paper. It is not so important as the couple's relationship. In fact, marriage may detract from, rather than contribute to, the completeness of the couple's commitment, since marriage places limitations on their love. It is said that the wedding is only an outward form which establishes another outward form, marriage. True meaning is found not in forms but in a relationship. A wedding may satisfy the demands of society, but it does nothing for the couple. If a couple love each other, they do not need a wedding. If they do not love each other, a wedding will not help. The data we presented earlier suggest that only a small number of young persons hold such views.

COHABITATION: AN ALTERNATIVE BEFORE MARRIAGE

Cohabitation—an unmarried male living together with an unmarried female—has become very common in the United States, and it now involves tens of thousands of young persons at any given time. Especially evident on college and university campuses, where most of the research on this phenomenon has been conducted, cohabitation is also becoming widespread in other than college and university settings throughout the country. A 1974 national study of a representative sample of American men between 20 and 30 years of age found that 18 percent of these young men reported having at some time lived with a woman for six months or more without being married to her (Clayton and Voss, 1977). On college campuses, studies have found that as many as half of the students have cohabited for some duration by the time they reach college graduation (Macklin, 1974; Peterman, Ridley, and Anderson, 1974; Lewis and Spanier, 1975). Cohabitation, then, is a widespread phenomenon, particularly among young persons. Most persons who live together outside of marriage, however, eventually do marry, although there are no data available as to how often they marry the persons with whom they have cohabited. Some studies indicate more than half of the persons studied who have cohabited have done so more than once before marriage (Peterman, Ridley, and Anderson, 1974).

Cohabitation may take three distinct forms. First, and most commonly, it may be seen as a temporary matter of convenience or choice—an arrangement which appeals to the persons involved at the moment without any necessary commitment to marriage. Second, cohabitation may be defined as "trial marriage," in which the couple anticipate marriage and wish to "see if they are compatible" or simply to live together until their own personal circumstances are more favorable to marriage. Third, and most rarely, cohabitation may be seen as a permanent and lasting alternative to marriage.

Cohabitation As a Temporary Matter of Convenience or Choice

This is the most common form of cohabitation. It is widespread at colleges and universities, both on and off campus. Many cohabiting relationships are very short-lived, some lasting only a matter of weeks and others lasting several months. It is rare to find a relationship which lasts for more than a year or two on college campuses (the relationship usually dissolves or results in marriage), although it is much more common to find long-term relationships away from universities—in the "real world," so to speak. College campuses appear to have an insulating effect on students. It is possible to live together at college without much negative sanction, whereas such a relationship might be frowned upon and avoided in the student's home town. The majority of students who live together do not tell their parents about the relationship, although they readily tell friends (Macklin, 1974). The fact that students normally do not tell their parents indicates that as common as cohabitation is, it has not received widespread acceptance and may be considered deviant, wrong, or immoral by many Americans.

We are inclined to believe—and the evidence suggests—that this form of cohabitation is likely to increase in the future. Young persons find that there is much to be gained by way of convenience, intimacy, and sharing. The primary rewards they report are the sexual, affectional, and companionship components that are found in many intimate personal relationships. The motivation to live together is essentially what might be expected as a normal extension of the courtship process—namely, the desire to spend increasing amounts of time with a person one wants to be with and/or loves. The reasons couples give for cohabiting, then, center on the intensity of their relationship, the possibility that they may marry, the added convenience of having their belongings together in the same place, or experimentation with a new lifestyle. Many couples gradually drift into such a relationship. They find that they are spending more and more time with each other, sleeping together, eating together, and sharing expenses. They may "find" themselves living together, and one then gives up his or her former residence, or they may make a formal decision to live in the same household. Many cohabiting couples maintain two separate residences, even though they live in one, because of fear that parents or relatives might find that they are cohabiting. Some have special mailing addresses and separate phone numbers.

Many landlords will not rent to cohabiting couples, although the legal validity for such a decision is dubious. Nevertheless, some cohabiting couples find it difficult to rent an apartment or buy a house if their unmarried status is known. In university communities and urban areas, problems are not as great.

Cohabitation is characteristic mainly of the young—persons in their late teens and twenties. There are increasing numbers of individuals in their thirties and forties who are cohabiting, however, particularly after a divorce or separation. Cohabitation has always been more common and better tolerated among persons of low socioeconomic standing. This can be explained by greater family instability, greater difficulty in being able to afford and obtain divorces, regulations cutting back aid for children when a woman with children remarries, and the more liberal acceptance of cohabitation as a life-style. Cohabitation also exists among an often ignored group of individuals—the elderly. Perhaps because we are less inclined to think there is a sexual component to their relationship (a fact which should not always be assumed), there has been less concern about cohabitation among the aged. Three reasons can be cited for this form of cohabitation. The first, and perhaps the most important, is that social security regulations have traditionally discriminated against elderly married couples. Two single elderly persons will receive a greater amount of social security than will an elderly married couple. Marriage, then, decreases the social security pension—an understandable reason for living together without being married. A second reason is that many persons think it is frivolous if elderly parents take a spouse following divorce or widowhood and discourage such unions. A third reason is that some elderly persons simply prefer not to go through the formalities of a wedding. This is the exception rather than the rule, however.

A group of American researchers who study cohabitation have met regularly for several years to compare their findings, plan for future research, and share ideas. At one meeting (Groves Conference on Marriage and the Family, 1974) the following conclusions were drawn:

▶ *Prevalence.* About 30 percent of the undergraduate population studied has experienced at least one cohabiting relationship. There is, however, great variation from campus to campus. Even on campuses where there is not a high prevalence, there is a high acceptance of cohabitation, with many individuals indicating that if the opportunity were available, they would participate.

▶ *Description of cohabitants.* Cohabitants tend to be less religious and to have reference groups and personal values supportive of cohabitation. On campuses where cohabitation is not yet a widespread phenomenon, there is a greater likelihood that participants will be persons who contravene socially sanctioned values. As the phenomenon increases, however, this and other factors are no longer differentiating variables. It is suggested that the variables most predictive of cohabitation are: low perception of social disapproval, low internalized guilt, and high availability of opportunity.

▶ *Why do people cohabit?* Changed attitudes with regard to premarital sexuality, improved contraception, reduction of *in loco parentis* regulations, and the growth of the feminist movement are conducive to cohabitation. The most common reason given by respondents is emotional attachment to the partner. Desire for security, companionship, and convenience are of somewhat lesser importance. These are very similar to the intrinsic and utilitarian reasons for marriage.

▶ *Characteristics of the relationship.* There is no single pattern for cohabitation. The relationship falls somewhere along a continuum from friendship through casual dating, steady dating, quasi-engagement, formal engagement, and substitute marriage, with the majority of cohabiting college students indicating a strong affectionate, exclusive relationship with no specific plans for marriage to that partner.

▶ *Problems experienced.* The main problems identified to date are parental problems, with strong evidence of hesitance to reveal the relationship to parents; emotional problems, particularly problems of jealousy and overdependence; sexual problems, similar to those characteristic of early marriage; and community discrimination, depending on the particular community.

This same group of researchers and scholars made four policy recommendations which are likely to be considered controversial by some. These recommendations are personal opinions, since there is no specific research which strongly suggests that implementation of any of these recommendations is mandatory:

1 Convinced that the decision to cohabit should be an individual one, and that persons should have freedom of choice in the matter, it was urged that consideration be given to rethinking existing laws which discriminate against cohabitation (zoning laws, for example, which may restrict the ability of two unrelated individuals to live in the same dwelling).

2 Colleges, universities, and communities should provide the support services appropriate for a sexually active unmarried population (e.g., interpersonal skill development, relationship counseling, contraceptive counseling, and medical services).

3 There should be an extension of services and an equalization of benefits currently available only to married persons.

4 Because of the increasing numbers of persons involved in this type of relationship and the paucity of available information, priority should be given to research efforts directed toward increasing knowledge regarding cohabitation.

The eightfold increase in cohabitation from 1960 to 1970 suggested by an analysis of census data (Glick, 1975) suggests that cohabitation is not a new phenomenon, but its widespread prevalence is. It is one of the more remarkable trends in modern social life, since few social activities of such great personal significance have accelerated so dramatically in a span of only a few years. There have now been several dozen articles, papers, theses, and reviews written about cohabitation (see Macklin, 1974, 1976; Lewis and Spanier, 1975; Lewis, Spanier, Storm, and LeHecka, 1975), but many of these have not yet made their way into publications that are readily available to the public.

Although it is clear that most cohabitants eventually marry, it is not clear how often they marry the first or a subsequent person with whom they have cohabited. In one study (Macklin, 1974) of about 300 university students, one-third had cohabited. At the time of a three-month follow-up study, 5 percent of these relationships had ended in marriage, 25 percent were at a stage of tentative or formal engagement, 50 percent were still on-going but as yet uncommitted relationships (although a number of these persons were no longer living together due to geographic separation, desire for more freedom, or pressure from parents), and 20 percent of the relationships had dissolved.

The available evidence suggests that cohabitation as a temporary matter of convenience or choice is likely to be with us for some time. It appears to be a normal part of the premarriage process for some individuals and is gaining wider acceptance. It may be many years, however, before a majority of persons will be able to live together before marriage with full approval from parents and the community in which they live. Finally, it should be observed that many persons have no desire to cohabit before marriage. In this matter of choice, as with others, it is important to respect an individual's decision not to participate.

Trial Marriage

Some cohabiting couples have entered into what they consider to be a trial marriage. They intend to marry each other, but first want to make sure they are compatible. This type of relationship may also be considered a logical extension of the courtship process, since it is the couple's final test to determine whether or not they are suited to one another. The compatibility testing may involve sexual, emotional, and economic components, as well as testing their ability to live in the same household with each other in a twenty-four-hour-a-day existence.

Although this form of relationship is conceptually meaningful, many of the same problems that may face other cohabiting couples may be present in a trial marriage. It is possible that the trial marriage truly will not be an adequate test of a marriage relationship, since the commitment to the partner may be different than it might be following marriage, and it has been demonstrated that commitment is a critical variable in the adjustment of both cohabiting and marital relationships (Lewis, Spanier, Storm, and LeHecka, 1975; Dean and Spanier, 1974; Spanier, 1976b). There may be parental, peer, or community sanctions against such an arrangement. A problem might emerge (e.g., sexual adjustment, financial burden, pregnancy, conflict) which might be resolved following marriage but not during a trial marriage, thus prematurely terminating the relationship.

Some couples intend to marry, but any one of a number of circumstances (education, economics, previous marriage) makes immediate marriage impossible or difficult. As a result, many persons live together until the circumstances for marriage are more favorable. There are no research data to help us understand whether persons who have trial marriages are happier after marriage than those who do not have such arrangements. It is probably safe to say that each couple must decide whether living with a future spouse before marriage is advantageous. It is likely that it will enhance the relationships of some couples and will adversely affect the relationships of some others. Family sociologists have always emphasized the importance of knowing as much as possible about one's partner before marriage. Now that premarital sexual behavior is becoming normative, as well as a great deal of intimacy and openness during engagement and extended periods of dating, it follows that cohabitation before marriage or trial marriage are predictable extensions of the courtship process. It must be realized, however, that some persons have religious or moral convictions which argue against such arrangements, and this must be considered along with possible parental disapproval and the other potential disadvantages mentioned above.

Margaret Mead (1966) discusses "marriage in two steps." She mentions "individual marriage," a licensed union with only an ethical, not an economic, obligation. The male would not be required to support the female. "Individual marriage" would be binding on the couple's being committed to each other as long as they wished to remain together, but it would not apply to them as future parents. "Parental marriage," with its own license, ceremony, and kinds of responsibility, and always preceded by individual marriage, "would be explicitly directed toward the founding of a family." This would be marriage that "looked to a lifetime relationship." Individual marriage would be a serious commitment, entered into in public, and validated and protected by law and in some cases by religion, in which "each partner would have a deep and continuing concern for the happiness and well-being of the other." It would give two young people a chance to know each other better than in a brief love affair and "would help them grow into each other's life—and allow them to part without the burden of misunderstood intentions, bitter recriminations, and self-destructive guilt.

"In contrast to individual marriage, parental marriage would be hard to contract." In parental marriage, "each partner would know the other well, eliminating . . . any one of the thousand shocks that lie in wait for the person who enters a hasty marriage with someone he or she knows little about."

The idea of marriage in two steps is intriguing, but one wonders whether it is feasible. If two young people enter an individual marriage before they are well acquainted, what is to guarantee that there will not be complex problems of adjustment, with disappointment and disillusionment, as is possible in any type of marriage? If they dissolve the individual marriage, it could be as traumatic as the breakup of any marriage, especially if one partner wants to dissolve it and the other does not. Mead says that an "individual marriage" would allow a couple "to part without the burden of misunderstood intentions, bitter recriminations, and self-destructive guilt." But by the time such parting occurs, original logic may become dissolved in emotion. If they enter individual marriage knowing that it may be considered tentative, would this be a real test of marriage? Mead assumes that a couple in an individual marriage will not have a child simply because they do not plan to have it. What if they have a child during that marriage and one (or both) of them does not want to go on to the next stage, parental marriage? Will they then have a parental marriage against their will and be ill prepared for it? Is there any basic difference between an individual marriage and the first, childless phase of most marriages?

Cohabitation as a Permanent Alternative to Marriage

Only a small number of cohabitants report that they have rejected traditional marriage and intend always to live together without formally marrying. Couples have found that a permanent living-together relationship often presents legal problems, especially if there are children or if the relationship dissolves. Contrary to popular belief, a couple who live together do not have a "common-law marriage" unless some very special conditions exist—and even then only a few states allow for common-law relationships. (We shall discuss such marriages in the next section of this chapter.) Legal problems may exist in a long-term relationship because our laws have not been designed to accommodate a couple that live together for many years while jointly accumulating property, debts, and other material goods, having children, or earning money. What will such a couple do if the relationship dissolves? Who will take the children, the house, the furniture, the automobile, or the savings? Court precedents have been quite clear. When it cannot be demonstrated that a marriage existed, property, savings, and other material possessions must be divided as if the persons had always been single. Thus, the person whose name is on the deed to the house, the car title, the savings account signature card, or the loan application will have claim to or responsibility for these things. A child will normally be considered the illegitimate offspring of the woman, although an important court precedent (*Stanley v. Illinois*, 1972) gives the natural father certain rights with respect to the child. As has always been customary when paternity can be established, the father may have some financial responsibility should there be an illegitimate child. When both partners have made major purchases and this fact is so registered on a deed or title, there are adequate laws to deal with the termination of the joint ownership. However, when such formal steps have not been taken, the possibility exists that in a time of hostility between the partners, one may wish there were some legal mechanism available to deal with the termination of the relationship.

Couples can avoid potential problems by drawing up a legal contract to protect their rights as unmarried, cohabiting couples, but such contracts are rare. In some jurisdictions formal agreements are emerging, mainly among young, highly educated, middle-class persons who have incomes or personal wealth which they feel need to be protected. Generally speaking, however, our laws are far from accommodating such relationships.

Of course, the legal aspect is only one, perhaps minor, problem for couples intending to permanently cohabit. There may be pressures to marry from relatives, friends, or work associates, or from within the community at large. The couple may find that the society in which they live is not as open to long-term cohabiting relationships as they thought. The ability of a cohabiting couple to adopt this type of life-style will depend on the motives for such a relationship, the support they receive from significant others, and the type of community they live in. University communities tend to be more tolerant of alternative arrangements, and urban areas, by virtue of the greater impersonality, are often more conducive to alternative life-styles.

Is cohabitation as a permanent alternative to marriage likely to become common in the future? We do not think so. First, if it were to emerge as a major life-style, it would need to demonstrate clear advantages over a marriage relationship. The ease of divorce in the United States has made it unlikely that couples would live together instead of marrying simply to avoid the difficulty of a marital breakup. From a social-psychological standpoint, the breakup of any long-term relationship will involve a great deal of anguish and hurt, regardless of the formal legal status. Secondly, the sometimes cited advantage that nonmarital cohabitation allows its participants greater freedom and independence in their life-styles than marriage may be diminishing. There is great diversity within marriage, and couples are finding that they are increasingly able to define their own marriage in a way that is suitable for them.

If cohabitation as a lasting alternative to marriage were to become widespread, our laws would have to change to accommodate such a phenomenon. We might then find that this variant of cohabitation was essentially similar to marriage from a legal standpoint, leaving no advantage to one form or the other. Should this happen, it would only be a matter of semantics as to what we call each of the different forms of relationships.

Common-law Marriages

Thirteen states and the District of Columbia recognize common-law marriages contracted within their borders as valid (Pennsylvania Bar Institute, 1976). Common-law marriages were written into marriage and family laws several decades ago. Since that time several states have done away with laws permitting such relationships. A common-law marriage is one in which a man and woman begin married life without the benefit of a marriage license and legally recognized marriage ceremony. It is a marriage which commences as a result of a decision on the part of the two individuals that they are now married. A common-law marriage is quite distinct from a modern cohabitational relationship in many ways.

Common-law marriages were permitted in the 1800s and earlier because many persons could not afford the time it took to travel by horse and buggy to the county courthouse, which might have been more than a day's journey each way. Distance was much more formidable in those days, and common-law marriage was a mechanism whereby a couple could begin their married life by proclaiming to each other and those geographically close to them that they were married. There was an expectation that the couple would formalize the marriage when a local clergyman or official made the rounds through their community or whenever they could make the journey to the courthouse themselves. In the meantime, however, it was expected that the couple would consider themselves husband and wife and would hold themselves out to the public as such. This meant that the woman would take the husband's last name, they would have joint ownership of property, and they would both have their married names on bank accounts and other official documents. They were, in all public and private respects, married.

When legislation began to replace the Common Law brought from England, there were couples who had been considered married without having had a ceremony, and their relationship continued to be recognized.

Nowadays common-law marriage has outlived its usefulness, and the need for it no longer exists. It comes to light only in unusual cases where, for example, a man dies and a woman unknown to or disliked by other relatives of the man claims to be the man's common-law wife in order to inherit part of the estate. Other cases concern women who claim to have been living in a common-law marriage and are now seeking a divorce settlement from their common-law husband. These cases require that a judge first declare that there was a marriage and then declare that there will now be a divorce.

All common-law marriages must eventually be declared valid by a judge, contrary to myths which state that couples become "automatically" married after so many years living together. All marriages, including common-law ones, must at some time be declared valid by a jurisdiction of the state.

Cohabitation, then, is not common-law marriage, and couples will run into legal problems if they attempt to use only common residence as a basis for establishing marriage. Marriage *intent* at the time the joint residence began, not at a future time, is a basic requirement in determining the validity of a common-law marriage. Both parties must be competent to marry, and they must hold themselves out to the public as married from the time their joint residence began. Cohabitation may work against the possibility of later establishing a common-law marriage, since it is evidence of a "meretricious" (for sexual purposes only) relationship, and this is not sufficient grounds for the validity of common-law marriage (Pennsylvania Bar Institute, 1976).

COMMUNES

One of the alternative life-styles that has been given considerable attention in recent years is the *commune*, or *community*. It is difficult to generalize about communes because they represent such a broad spectrum of different types. Communal societies have been organized at various times throughout a good part of American history. Most of them have been short-lived. A few have continued in greatly altered form. Still fewer have persisted in approximately their original form for more than a few years.

Communes range in size from just a few individuals to several hundred. They have existed throughout the world (the Bruderhof of Germany, the kibbutz of Israel, the Shinkyō of Japan) and throughout history in the United States (the Shakers, Hutterites, Moravians, the Oneida Community). They have never been the dominant family form in any society nor have they existed for any sustained period of time through history. They are, nevertheless, fascinating entities.

The Diversity of Communes

A modern American commune may be defined as "three or more persons among whom the primary bond is some form of sharing, rather than blood or legal ties" (Fairfield, 1971). Modern communes may be classified into six basic types (Fairfield, 1971):

1 *Religious communes* (The City of Light, The Oregon Family, The Lama Foundation), which today commonly profess some mixture of Christianity and various Eastern faiths.

2 *Ideological communes*, which adhere either to socialistic doctrine or to doctrines arising out of behavioral psychology (Cold Mountain Farm, The School of Living).

3 *Hip communes*, which tend to be based on some sort of drug culture and generally have a more or less mystical quality about them (Drop City, Morning Star Ranch, Magic Farm).

4 *Group marriage communes*, which set themselves the task of developing new family styles (Harrad West, The Family).

5 *Service communities*, which are created to provide a total work-recreational environment for disadvantaged persons (Camphill Village, Synanon, The Catholic Worker Farm).

6 *Youth communes*, which usually are composed of college graduates or dropouts who simply wish to share the advantages of group living (Yellow Submarine, Greenfeel).

Communes exist today throughout America, although it is probable that only a tiny fraction of the population is currently involved. There was a proliferation of interest in communes during the late 1960s and early 1970s, and much of this interest has since died. Nevertheless, there are some young persons who would like or intend to either experiment with communal living for a period of time in their lives, or permanently join such a group. Communes of all varieties attempt to embody what social psychologists call "a sense of community" (Kanter, 1973).

An example of a religious commune known to the authors is "Reba Place," a "Christian" community of more than 100 persons of all ages in Evanston, Illinois, which has existed for many years. At Reba Place, some persons work full time in the "community," a street with several houses. Some persons take care of children, while others may do carpentry or household repairs. Many persons work outside the community, but the money they earn is turned over to the community. All purchases and expenditures are decided by a governing group of individuals. There are many hours of fellowship and worship during the week, as this is a central activity in this community.

An example of an ideological community known to the authors is in central Pennsylvania. This commune is founded on the principles of Skinnerian behaviorism, a variant of the sort of life described in B. F. Skinner's book, *Walden Two*. There are seven persons in this commune, including one married couple with a child. All other persons are unrelated. All members must pass an exam and write a paper on behaviorism and then pledge to live according to those principles. For example, if someone is being sloppy, leaving things around the house, and so on, the group will set up a behavior modification program for this person to encourage him or her to clean up. Members work both inside and outside the rural commune, and a formula determines how much of one's outside income is considered communal property and how much is considered personal income, which belongs to the individual.

Some communes exist simply because the members are attracted to the life-style, apart from any set of beliefs. This may be more typical of the *youth* and *hip* communes. But perhaps the most common communal arrangement, which is not mentioned in the list above, is a group of persons who live together temporarily because it is economically advantageous to do so (sharing rent, buying food in larger quantities, etc.). An example of such a commune is a residence in Washington, D.C., just a mile or two from the White House. This urban commune, in a very large three-story house, consists of twelve persons. There are two married couples, one committed but unmarried couple, and six single individuals. The members range in age from 21 to 35. There are no children. All the group have outside jobs in Washington and pay a share of the rent, food, and maintenance. One person has been elected to pay bills and to prepare the work, cooking, and housecleaning schedules. Each individual or couple has a private room, although bathrooms are shared. The group buys their food from a cooperative consisting of several other "economic" communes, and one member must staff the cooperative each week. The sharing in this commune, then, is largely for economic and functional reasons, and when a person leaves, he or she is replaced with a new member who is willing to adopt the life-style—at least temporarily. Many communes exist, then, because the arrangement is attractive and convenient for its participants.

Some communes welcome everybody who comes to them; anyone who wants to stay may do so and share what the members of the commune have. Other communes are selective, either in theory or because they have found through experience that the group cannot continue to function effectively if all types of persons are permitted to join it regardless of what those persons are, what they are seeking, or how they fit into the group.

Some communes are composed principally of persons whose primary motive is escape from the "establishment," the "mass society." Others attract individuals whose motive is to leave one type of life in order to seek another they consider better. A commune may include a variety of types, some well educated (with, in some cases, professional degrees or professional training) and others less educated, as well as individuals of different personality types. A commune may be organized or may lack organization. The members may feel not only that organization is unnecessary but that its lack is a source of pride.

There may be one or more persons in the commune representing authority or leadership either through being chosen for such a function or through having personal qualities and charisma that lead to the emergence of such a role. In other communes there is no one who has any more authority than anyone else. Decisions are made by vote of the entire group, a process that sometimes proves laborious and time-consuming but is democratic, although at other times it leads to inactivity when no decision can be reached.

In some communes there is a plan for work—for doing chores, for cooking, etc. Persons are assigned to jobs according to a schedule. In other communes there is no planning, no scheduling. Everyone is free to do as he or she wishes. There are no requirements, the assumption being that everyone will want to do one's share and the work will get done. In reality such an arrangement often results in work being left undone.

Some communal groups own the property on which they are situated. In some cases they purchased it, and in others the land originally belonged to one member of the group. In still others a group member owns the land and buildings and lets the commune live there.

Some communes are productive and self-sustaining. They raise a good part of their own food, construct buildings, and repair equipment. Some members may be gainfully employed and contribute their earnings, or a portion of them, to the group. In some cases the commune or certain members manufacture salable products. In other communes attempts at productivity have been only partially successful or have failed completely, or the production of salable items has not been tried.

There is a variety of points of view and practices relative to sex and marriage. In some communes there are both married couples and single members. In some, sex is entirely free, and twosomes may pair up as they wish, whether or not one or both are married. In others there is "group marriage" by mutual understanding, although such an arrangement has no status within the law. Some communes are felt by their members to be large "families."

In some communes children are cared for by their natural parents. In some, care of children is scheduled as other tasks are scheduled, while in others the assumption is made that all members of the group are responsible for all children. If, for example, a

Men, Women, and American Marriage

Communal living has always attracted a small number of Americans. Most young adults, however, prefer to marry and establish their own household. (Susan Ylvisaker)

mother leaves for the day, her children will be cared for without previous planning. In some groups males as well as females take an interest in child care.

In some communes each member is free to do as he or she wishes regarding the use of drugs and alcohol. In others the use of drugs, especially, is discouraged or even prohibited.

Prospects for Communal Living

Very few data are available to instruct us about the success of communes. What evidence there is (Kanter, 1973; Berger, Hackett, and Millar, 1972; Roberts, 1971) suggests that most communes tend to be very short-lived. Those that have the greatest chance of surviving are the ones based on a set of beliefs and the ones which have some organization and leadership. It can be argued that the success of a commune should not be determined by the length of its existence. Perhaps a more appropriate indicator is how the relationship enhanced the development of its members. In any case it appears that most of the persons who entered communes in the late 60s and early 70s have since left them. Many have married and live outside a communal setting. Some persons have made a lifelong commitment to communal living and have demonstrated that there can be great satisfaction for some in such a life-style.

GROUP MARRIAGE

A *group marriage*, also referred to as a *multilateral marriage*, consists of three or more persons who consider themselves to be married to at least two other members of the group (Constantine and Constantine, 1971, 1972, 1973; Ramey, 1972). Most group marriages are small, in comparison to many communes. Group marriages usually involve from three to six persons, with three being the most common size. Many group marriages begin as couple marriages, with an additional person or couple being added at a later time. Although group marriages have been known to exist in many cultures throughout history, such arrangements never predominated in any known societies (Murdock, 1949). In the United States today, only a small number of group marriages have been identified, and it is not likely that this alternative to marriage is chosen very often. Nevertheless, there is some research available which has been able to give us some insight into this alternative marriage form (Ramey, 1972; Constantine and Constantine, 1971, 1972, 1973).

In group marriages, it is usually the case that sexual relationships occur, or are at least permitted to occur, between all individuals of opposite gender. In addition, there are sometimes sexual relationships between persons of the same gender. The homosexual relationships which do occur seem to be more common among female pairs. These relationships are less disruptive than male homosexual pairings and have greater acceptance. The characteristic which distinguishes a group marriage from a commune or other alternative to traditional marriage is the greater intensity of bonds between couples, the greater number of such bonds, and the self-definition that within the group there are several "marital" relationships, each equal in intensity to any single marital relationship. A group marriage does not, of course, have any legal status.

The success of group marriages, if measured by their duration and stability, is not great. Most of the group marriages studied begin to falter within a year. This is understandable since such an arrangement, imbedded in a society which is not supportive of such variation, will receive very little social support from outside the household. Furthermore, we are all products of a socialization process which would in only the rarest of cases prepare us for and teach us to accept group marriage. Beyond these social factors which limit the possibility for success, there are, of course, many interpersonal and situational factors which undoubtedly play a part. The adjustment of just two persons is a difficult and challenging task. When there are three, four, or more persons to adjust to a marriage, the complexities can be awesome.

Exhibit 3-2 illustrates some stable and unstable structural arrangements that are found in group marriages. The important feature of such a diagram is not the particular combinations of arrangements which are possible, but the illustration of the possible complexities which can be produced in a group marriage. In a marital relationship with two individuals, there is only *one* relationship. In a marriage where a third individual is added, there are now *three* relationships. The addition of a fourth person adds three more possible relationships, or a total of *six*. And so it goes. As each individual is added, the number of possible relationships increases by several individuals. There are fifteen pair combinations possible in a group marriage of six persons. Thus, the complexity of day-to-day living, jealousy, and sexual commitments can be overwhelming.

One woman who came to one of the authors for counseling had been living in a group marriage for six months. The male and female with whom she was now living had been married for two years before the group marriage began. The woman in counseling, 25, had initially been attracted to the man and they spent increasing amounts of time together. They began having sexual intercourse and fell in love. The man declared that he loved both women and suggested that the two of them get to know each other better. They became friends over a period of three

Some structures that are probably stable.

Some structures that are probably unstable.

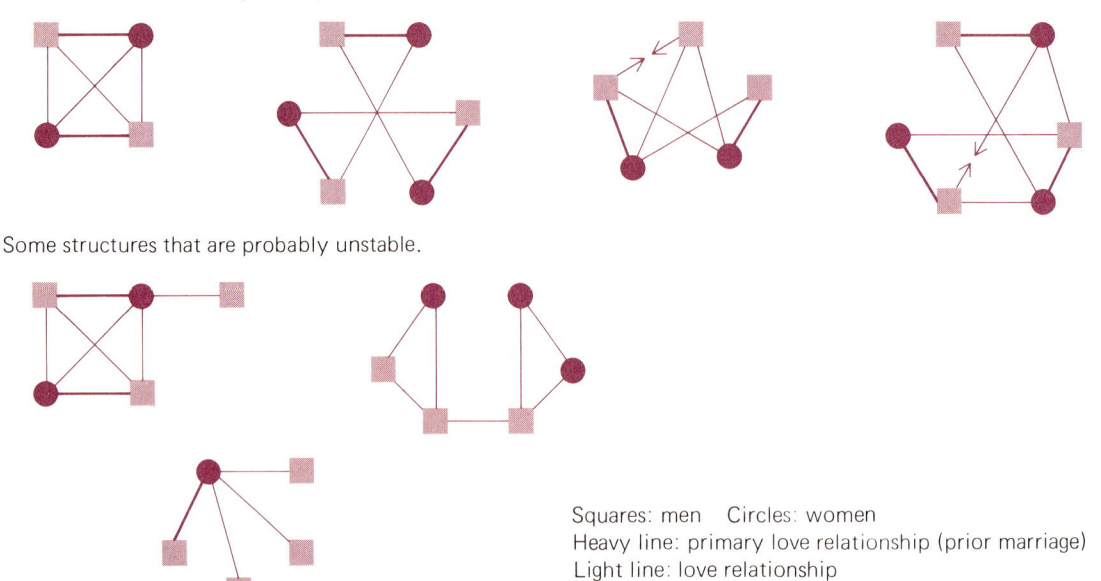

Squares: men   Circles: women
Heavy line: primary love relationship (prior marriage)
Light line: love relationship
Pointed arrows: antagonistic relationship

Exhibit 3-2 Stable and unstable structures of group marriage. (*Source*: Constantine and Constantine, "Where Is Marriage Going?" *The Futurist*, no. 45, April 1970. Published by World Future Society, P.O. Box 30369, Washington, D.C. 20014.)

months. The two women began having sexual relations together, occasionally in the presence of the husband. The woman who was new to the marriage began sleeping over, and eventually she moved in. The two women shared housekeeping responsibilities. The man made most decisions. After six months it was clear that the jealousy between the two women over the attentions of the man became too great to tolerate, and the woman who joined the couple soon left. The original couple had been talking about divorce at the time of the breakup, but the counseling was terminated before it was learned if divorce did occur.

HOMOSEXUAL MARRIAGE

In some quarters today there is a demand for the legalization of the "marriage" of two homosexuals. There is a reason to believe, however, that such a "marriage" would not constitute a valid legal union. In common usage the term "marriage" means a union of persons of opposite gender, and this was undoubtedly the meaning that legislators had in mind when enacting legislation before homosexuality became so visible. Statutes contain such expressions as "husband and wife," "bride and groom." Underlying the demand for homosexual marriage is the assumption that the right to marry without regard to the gender classification or sexual orientation of the parties is a fundamental right of all persons, and the restricting of marriage to only couples of different gender is discriminatory. In 1971, a case was taken to the Supreme Court of Minnesota. In its decision the court said, "We hold . . . that [Minnesota law] does not authorize marriage between persons of the same sex and that such marriages are accordingly prohibited.... We do not find support for ... [the above contentions] in any decisions of the United States Supreme Court" (Kanowitz, 1973). It is highly likely that courts in other states would follow this precedent.

Thus, although two homosexuals may live together as if they were spouses, it is unlikely that their union will be recognized by society in this way. Most individuals who have continuing homosexual relationships and live with their partner are reluctant to acknowledge publicly or even to friends or work associates that their relationship is homosexual. This is understandable, since they might be subject to discrimination, harassment, or misunderstanding as a result. Consequently, most homosexuals who live together and who have ongoing relationships with each other are very discreet about it. Those who wish publicly to marry and be recognized as a legally constituted union are rare individuals.

SINGLE PARENTHOOD

One-fifth of American children under 18 do not live with two parents. There are more than 13 million such children in the United States (U.S. Bureau of the Census, *Current Population Reports*, 1975). Over 30 percent of children under 18 are not living with *both natural parents* (Glick, 1975). The difference between these two percentages can be accounted for by a large number of persons who are living with one natural parent and a stepparent through remarriage. Single parenthood is much more common than most persons realize. It is a circumstance that touches persons of every race, social class, and religious group. It is one alternative to marriage that is rarely entered into by choice. Most single-parent families with school-age children are the result of divorce or separation. A much smaller number may be attributed to widowhood. And an even smaller number are men or women who have kept an illegitimate child or adopted a child and never married.

In 1975, 12.9 percent of white families with children under 18 had only one parent. Twelve percent of these families were headed by males, 88 percent by females. Among blacks, 42.7 percent of families with children under 18 had only one parent. Four percent of these were male-headed families, 96 percent female-headed. As Exhibit 3-3 illustrates, the proportion of families with only one parent present increased dramatically in the five-year period between 1970 and 1975. Among whites the proportion of such families increased 47 percent. Among blacks, the increase was 36 percent. This increase may be attributed to increases in divorce and separation rates and to an increased proportion of never-married parents who are keeping children born out of wedlock (U.S. Bureau of the Census, *Current Population Reports*, 1975).

Single parenthood is a life-style to which few people aspire but which many people eventually experience. If our divorce rates increase, if customs change to permit single persons to adopt children, if the stigma of an illegitimate birth subsides, and if persons become less likely to remarry very soon after a divorce—all changes which many family scholars expect—then single parenthood will increase.

Some attention has been given in the news media in recent years to individuals who do not wish to marry but who do want children. There are no data to suggest that single parents could not be good parents and raise emotionally healthy and well-adjusted children. There is a traditional belief, however, that children in single-parent families are prone to maladjustment, but such thinking is being challenged in contemporary America. Adoption agencies have been reluctant to give children to single persons. There have now been court precedents upholding the legality

Men, Women, and American Marriage

Exhibit 3-3 Persons under 18 years old, by presence of parents, United States: 1975 and 1970 (percent)

	1975			1970		
Presence of parents	Total*	White	Black	Total*	White	Black
Living with both parents	80.3	85.4	49.4	84.9	89.2	58.1
Living with mother only	15.5	11.3	40.9	10.7	7.8	29.3
Separated	4.9	3.0	16.9	3.4	1.7	13.6
Other married, husband absent	0.9	0.8	1.8	1.3	1.1	2.6
Widowed	2.4	1.9	5.1	2.0	1.7	4.2
Divorced	5.5	5.1	8.1	3.3	3.1	4.6
Single	1.8	0.5	9.1	0.8	0.2	4.4
Living with father only	1.5	1.5	1.8	1.1	0.9	2.2
Living with neither parent	2.7	1.7	7.9	3.3	2.2	10.4

*Excludes persons under 18 years old who were heads and wives of heads of families and subfamilies.

Source: U.S. Bureau of the Census, *Current Population Reports*, Series P-20, No. 287, "Marital Status and Living Arrangements: March 1975," December 1975.

of such arrangements, and individual agencies must decide what their policy will be. It is clear that being a single parent has special challenges. There is less opportunity to share child-raising responsibilities with another adult. A single parent must usually work, and this responsibility requires day care facilities for young children. Less time is available with children of all ages, although the quality of the interaction in the time available can be as important as the quantity of interaction. A balance between these two dimensions must be considered.

There is no doubt that single parenthood, whether by choice, by accident, or by circumstances resulting from a broken marriage, poses special problems that dual-parent families do not face. When financial resources are scarce or nonexistent, when single parenthood has been forced on someone or reluctantly chosen, when the parent has little or no time for the child, or when the parent sees the child as an emotional or financial burden, single parenthood can be an unfortunate experience for the adult and a potentially damaging one for the child. Many of these difficulties can be overcome by a dedicated, thoughtful, and loving parent. The ability to afford child care and to provide in other ways for the child certainly contributes to one's ability to handle such a life-style. Single parenthood, like dual parenthood, can be either a positive or a negative experience depending on the individuals involved.

TERMS TO BE LEARNED

alternative life-styles
celibacy (celibate)
charisma
common-law marriage
commitment
commune (communalist, communitarian, community)
compatibility
conventional marriage
domestic family
dual-worker marriage
dysfunctional

Marriage Alternatives and Variations

heterogeneous (heterogeneity)
homosexual marriage
household
individual marriage (Mead)
in loco parentis
intercultural
intracultural
marriage in two steps (Mead)
meretricious
multilateral marriage
nuclear family
parental marriage (Mead)
peripheral
repudiation of marriage
role reversal
spouse
trial marriage

SELECTED READINGS

ALD, ROY: *Sex Off Campus*, Grosset & Dunlap, Publishers, New York, 1969. The author spent eighteen months interviewing 136 couples living together without marriage at fourteen colleges in various parts of the country. He reports the types of students involved, their reasons for living together, problems faced, suggested solutions. Twelve couples tell their own stories.

——: *The Youth Communes*, Tower Publications, Inc., New York, 1970. (Paperback.) The author visited twenty-two communal settlements and reports on his observations regarding what kinds of people communalists are and how they live.

BERGER, BENNETT, BRUCE HACKETT, AND R. MERVYN MILLAR: "The Communal Family," *The Family Coordinator*, vol. 21, no. 4, pp. 419–427, October 1972. Based on an investigation of communes on the West Coast. Discusses the economic bases of communes, ideologies, recruitment, authority and leadership, marital and parent-child relations.

BERGER, MIRIAM E.: "Trial Marriage: Harnessing the Trend Constructively," *The Family Coordinator*, vol. 20, no. 1, pp. 38–43, January 1971. Discusses the concepts of trial marriage, "companionate marriage," "two-step marriage." Historical and anthropological survey.

BERNARD, JESSIE: *The Future of Marriage*, The World Publishing Company, New York, 1972. How each spouse sees marriage differently, the "housewife syndrome," "renewable marriages," changing concepts of extramarital relationships, communes and cooperative households, swinging, group marriage, serial polygamy, the women's liberation movement, the future of marriage.

CARDEN, M. L.: *Oneida: Utopian Community to Modern Corporation*, The Johns Hopkins University Press, Baltimore, 1969. Deals with one of the earliest communal settings known, considering its development and transformation.

CONSTANTINE, LARRY L., AND JOAN M. CONSTANTINE: "Group and Multilateral Marriage: Definitional Notes, Glossary and Annotated Bibliography," *Family Process*, vol. 10, no. 2, pp. 157–176, June 1971. Definitions and operational differences among multilateral marriage, swinging, communes, etc.

—— AND ——: *Group Marriage: A Study of Contemporary Multilateral Marriage*, The Macmillan Company, New York, 1973. Based on nearly three years' research into group marriages and the people in them. The authors embarked on their research after a brief experience in a group marriage.

CROAKE, J. W., J. F. KELLER, AND N. CATLIN: *Unmarrieds Living Together: It's Not All Gravy*, Kendall/Hunt Publishing Company, Dubuque, Iowa, 1974. Based on research done by the authors on cohabitation.

FAIRFIELD, RICHARD: *Communes U.S.A.: A Personal Tour*, Penguin Books, Inc., Baltimore, 1972. (Paperback.) Author visited communes in Europe and the United States. Discusses various types of communes.

FITZGERALD, GEORGE R.: *Communes: Their Goals, Hopes, Problems*, Paulist Press, New York, 1971. (Paperback.) Discusses the people who join communes and why; hopes and objectives; life in communes; sex, marriage, family relationships, child rearing; strengths and weaknesses; future of communes.

GORDON, MICHAEL (ed.): *The Nuclear Family in Crisis: The Search for an Alternative*, Harper & Row, Publishers, Incorporated, New York, 1972. (Paperback.) The family in the present-day communal movement in the United States; group marriage; historical perspective on communal families and experimental family organization.

HART, HAROLD H. (ed.): *Marriage: For and Against*, Hart Publishing Company, Inc., New York, 1972. (Paperback.) Fifteen views of marriage, its functions and dysfunctions in the United States; alternative life-styles; a criticism of Margaret Mead's "marriage in two steps."

HOURIET, ROBERT: *Getting Back Together*, Coward, McCann & Geoghegan, Inc., New York, 1971. Author visited and reports on a variety of communal groups, including one group marriage.

KANTER, ROSABETH MOSS: *Commitment and Community: Communes and Utopias in Sociological Perspective*, Harvard University Press, Cambridge, Mass., 1972. An analysis of communities and utopias founded during the nineteenth century, applying what is learned to the problems and possible contributions of contemporary groups.

KINKADE, K.: *The Walden II Experiment: The First Five Years of Twin Oaks Community*, William Morrow and Company, Inc., New York, 1973. An account, by one of its founders, of a behaviorist community based on B. F. Skinner's Walden II model.

LIBBY, ROGER W., AND ROBERT N. WHITEHURST (eds.): *Renovating Marriage*, Consensus Publishers, Inc., Danville, Calif., 1973. (Paperback.) An examination of various life-styles: monogamy, extramarital sexual relations, comarital sex, group marriage, sexually free marriages, swinging, etc. Some of the contributors depict American marriage as being a tragic failure.

MACKLIN, ELEANOR D.: "Heterosexual Cohabitation among Unmarried College Students," *The Family Coordinator*, vol. 21, no. 4, pp. 463–472, October 1972. Based on a study of "unmarried cohabitation as experienced by female students at Cornell University"; reasons for involvement; nature of the relationship; problems and benefits.

MASSEY, CARMEN, AND RALPH WARNER: *Sex, Living Together, and the Law: a Legal Guide for Unmarried Couples (and Groups)*, Courtyard Books, Nolo Press, Berkeley, Calif., 1974. (Paperback.) Written by two lawyers. Discusses ownership of property, bank accounts, debts, common-law marriage, group living, homosexuals, illegitimacy, legal problems that may arise when persons live together without marriage.

MEAD, MARGARET: "Marriage in Two Steps," *Redbook*, pp. 48–49, 84–85, July 1966. A suggestion for a "new" type of marriage.

MELVILLE, KEITH: *Communes and the Counter Culture: Origins, Theories, Styles of Life*, William Morrow and Company, Inc., New York, 1972. (Paperback.) Author "investigates the communal movement as a form of rebellion against the American middle class" and looks at American culture through the communes. Says that "valuable ideas are being tested in the communes."

O'NEILL, NENA, AND GEORGE O'NEILL: *Open Marriage: A New Life Style for Couples*, M. Evans and Company, Inc., New York, 1972. "Open marriage is expanded monogamy." "The traditional, closed marriage is a form of bondage." Authors suggest individualizing marriage so that each couple can adjust it to fit their needs. They suggest "open marriage" rather than alternative life-styles.

OTTO, HERBERT A. (ed.): *The Family in Search of a Future*, Appleton Century Crofts, New York, 1970. (Paperback.) Alternatives to the American family structure, "progressive monogamy," group marriage, the tribal family, marriage in two steps.

RAMEY, JAMES W.: "Emerging Patterns of Innovative Behavior in Marriage," *The Family Coordinator*, vol. 21, no. 4, pp. 435–456, October 1972. A discussion of free love, swinging, communes, and group marriage as "innovative rather than deviant marriage alternatives."

ROBERTS, RON E.: *The New Communes*, Prentice-Hall, Inc., Englewood Cliffs, N.J., 1971. (Paperback.) Discusses some of the utopian and communalist movements in this country. The author feels that "most communes do not threaten today's society" and that the majority of Americans will never participate in a commune. Discusses the absence of sexual restraint.

ROBERTSON, C. N. (ed.): *Oneida Community: An Autobiography 1851–1876*, Syracuse, N.Y., 1970. An account of the Oneida Community written by the daughter of its founder, John Noyes.

ROGERS, CARL R.: *Becoming Partners: Marriage and Its Alternatives*, Delacorte Press, New

York, 1972. The author's objective is to offer young people something "in some of their pioneering struggle to build new kinds of marriages and alternatives to marriage." The book is based on verbatim reports of people living in a variety of relationships, plus the author's comments. The author is a psychotherapist.

SPECK, ROSS V., JEAN BARR, RUSSELL EISENMAN, EDWARD FOULKS, ARNOLD GOLDMAN, AND JOAN LINCOLN: *The New Families*, Basic Books, Inc., New York, 1972. During three years of research the authors visited dozens of communes. Discusses life in communes, male-female attitudes and relations, what communalists are trying to achieve, who the members are and why they join.

SPIRO, M. E.: *Kibbutz: Venture in Utopia*, Schocken, New York, 1970. The author explores kibbutz life.

SPRAGUE, W. D.: *Case Histories from the Communes*, Lancer Books, Inc., New York, 1972. (Paperback.) In-depth study of individuals who have experienced communal life; verbatim reports; marriage and sexual practices; types of communes; historical development of communes.

WOLF, SUSAN, AND JOHN ROTHCHILD: *The Children of the Counterculture*, Doubleday, Garden City, N.Y., 1975. The authors spent eight months visiting various types of communes to study what happens to children in communal groups and whether they are prepared for life outside the commune.

YANKELOVICH, DANIEL, INC.: *The Changing Values on Campus*, Washington Square Press, New York, 1972. A survey based on 1,244 interviews with students at fifty colleges in 1971. Reports students' attitudes toward marriage, communal living, parenthood, and other topics.

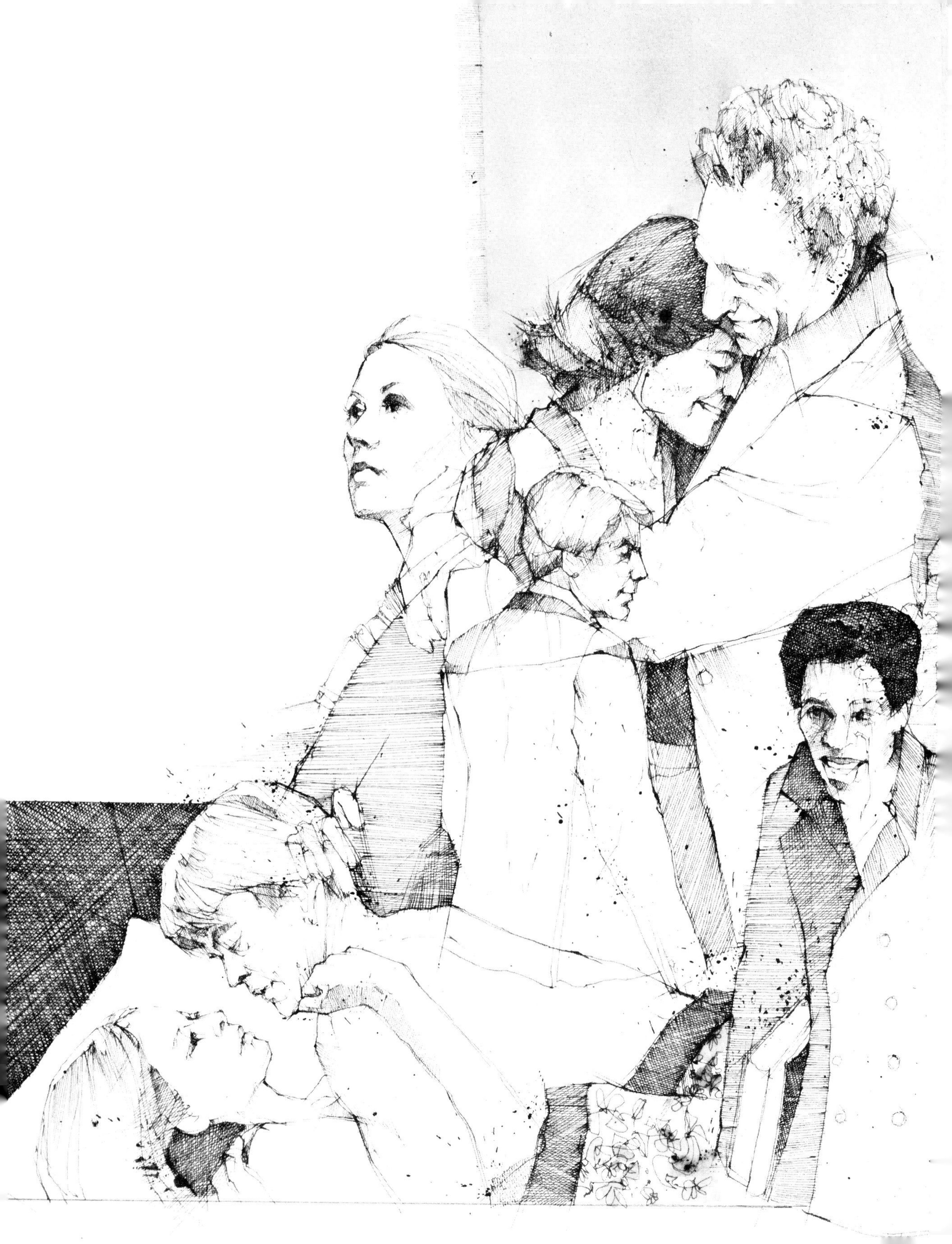

Part II
Marriage Preparation and Partner Selection

Chapter 4
Socialization for Marriage: Love and Dating

Socialization refers to the process by which persons acquire the knowledge, skills, and dispositions that make them more or less able members of their society (Brim, 1966). Socialization for marriage, then, involves the process that prepares individuals for their roles as marriage partners. The development of a love relationship and dating are important parts of marriage preparation in our culture. Marriage is not something that happens automatically. Nor is it the product of inborn behavior patterns or "instincts." Marriage is a social institution which has come to exist in one form or another in every society (Murdock, 1949). Marriage is a cluster of traditions, attitudes, ideas, and social and legal definitions. Whereas lower animals mate, humans both marry and mate. If marriage and mating were the same, there would be no illegitimate children. But the social definitions humans place on marriage clearly separate its importance from that of mating. If, then, humans do not marry instinctively, why do they marry?

WHY DO PEOPLE MARRY?

People marry for a combination of reasons. Many influences from our socialization encourage us to marry. Such reasons as economic security, home and children, emotional security, parents' wishes, escape from loneliness or from a parental home or other disagreeable situation, money, companionship, sexual attraction, protection, notoriety, social position and prestige, gratitude, pity, spite, adventure, and common interests are all possibilities. Law and custom play a part. But perhaps the reason which most motivates a young couple to marry is love.

There are still weddings resulting from pressure—"shotgun weddings"—but these are very rare. There is a growing feeling against forcing a couple to marry, even if there is a premarital pregnancy. A forced marriage gives a child two legal parents but cannot ensure a loving home nor the advantages of having happily married parents. Sometimes when there is neither love nor social pressure a man feels honorbound to marry the mother of their child But such a feeling is hardly a substitute for love and is difficult to sustain throughout marriage.

Parents often exert pressure on their children to prevent them from marrying a given individual. In some cases this pressure is so great that the relationship dissolves and the marriage does not take place. In other cases, however, the more parents object to a marriage, the more determined the young couple become and the more attractive they seem to each other. Some persons marry more quickly than they might if circumstances were different. There are great pressures for some individuals to marry during the early to middle twenties, and some individuals undoubtedly marry more hastily than they should. Graduation from high school, college, or graduate school can be followed by the loss of many potential dating partners from the school setting. When accompanied by the realization that many friends have already married, a transition such as graduation and the change in social life which may follow encourages some individuals to marry prematurely.

In some cases, a person who has been disappointed in love, had an engagement broken, or suffered some similar painful experience, will transfer affection from the first love object to a second, even though the second may be a quite different sort of person and even though he or she has not known the second long enough to be in love with that person. The hurt individual may make a choice before he or she has sufficiently regained the emotional balance necessary to make a wise marriage decision. This is marriage on the rebound.

In the last analysis, people marry because marriage is the most widely accepted social pattern for relationships between males and females. Monogamous American marriage involves a cluster of values which goes far toward meeting the needs of the majority of the people. It is not perfect, but neither is any other social arrangement. Many fail in attempting to work it out, but failure is not uncommon in any human endeavor. Whatever its shortcomings may be, American marriage contains the possibility for males and females to engage in a mutually rewarding relationship. Enduring love; companionship; the security of mutual commitment and concern; that special understanding, closeness, and acceptance that humans can receive from one other person; "the profoundly reaffirming experience of genuine intimacy" (Kennedy, 1972); cooperation in the maintenance of life; parenthood and family living; and similar values continue to attract people to marriage and motivate them to fulfillment in the context of this relationship. This cluster of values of which the individual becomes aware during the socialization process is the basic reason why Americans marry. Many persons achieve what for them is a completely satisfactory marriage. Many fail to achieve a marriage that they can continue to tolerate. But in between these extremes there are millions of Americans who achieve a type of marriage which, though less than ideal, for them is more acceptable than an alternative.

The relationship between love and marriage which Americans have known for several decades now is developing in other parts of the world. Over forty years ago, an American anthropologist observed that "all societies recognize that there are occasional emotional attachments between members of the opposite sex, but our present American culture is practically the only one which has attempted to capitalize on these and make them the basis for marriage" (Linton, 1936). Millions of marriages have been formed and endured on the foundation of a love relationship. Love will continue to serve as the basis for marriage in America; it has become normative in most modern, industrialized nations; and we can expect that the practice will become characteristic of other cultures which are undergoing transition to a participant-run courtship system with marital choice in the hands of the young.

LOVE

If you were to ask a group of married people why they married, it is unlikely that they would enumerate the values mentioned above. Probably the majority of them would say, "Because we were in love." No doubt they would be at least partly correct. They did marry because they experienced a feeling that they interpreted as love. It is difficult, however, to state with any great degree of precision just what the feeling is. We use the term *love* in a great many different senses. You say, for example, "I love my parents," "I love my fiancé," "I love God," "I love my country," "I love animals," "I love ice cream." It is obvious that you cannot love your mother in the same way that you love ice cream. You do not have the same emotional experience with your country that you have with a fiancé.

Love, then, has different meanings depending on:

▶ The background and experiences of the person involved

▶ The nature of the love object (mother, fiancé, activity, object)

▶ The period in the individual's life

▶ The intensity of the individual's attraction to the love object

▶ The importance the individual places on being in love

Some individuals feel that love is such a special feeling that they will purposely use the term in only the rarest of situations. These persons believe that love is reserved for the most special and committed associations. Others fall in love quickly and often. They are able to tell many individuals that they love them. Such variations probably tell us more about the individual than about the nature of love.

Most individuals have been in love once or twice. This applies to college students as well as their grandparents. There is a tendency, which many persons do not recognize, to avoid "promiscuous love." In other words, romantic love is a special feeling which one usually does not have with a large number of individuals. Thus, many young adults will

In America, love is often idealized. Romantic love is the foundation on which most marriages develop. (Ken Heyman)

state in retrospect that the love relationships they had in high school were really not love-based after all. Similarly, adults married for many years will state that the relationships they had with other persons when they were younger did not really involve love. There is a tendency, then, to redefine previous relationships, now terminated, as "infatuation" while defining more current relationships as love.

The romantic love associated with marriage has an obvious sexual element. This is not the same as saying that love is founded entirely on a physical basis, for it is not. Sex involves more than physical response, and love involves more than just sex. But in romantic love, there is a centering of attention on the other person as a focus of sexual interest.

Exhibit 4-1 illustrates the diversity of definitions of love available to us. These definitions range from the philosophical to the hedonistic, from the romantic to the practical. There is also cultural variation. In some societies, romantic love before marriage is prevented or even punished. As Goode (1959) points out, every society develops ways to prevent love from disrupting existing social arrangements. In societies where marriage partners are chosen by parents, romantic love before marriage must be avoided so as to prevent competing influences from other than parentally approved mates.

Despite the variety in our conceptions of love, most persons would agree that love involves *sexual attraction, companionship, caring, and commitment* (Blood, 1969). Such components of love suggest that all forms of love are to some degree based on the needs of the individual (Winch, 1971). This premise allows us to present one especially useful definition of love (Winch, 1971):

Love is the positive emotion experienced by one person in an interpersonal relationship in which the second person either (1) meets certain important needs of the first, or (2) manifests or appears to manifest personal attributes (beauty, skills, status) highly prized by the first, or both.

Falling in Love

Is there such a thing as "love at first sight"? If love is an intense feeling of attraction between two individuals involving commit-

Exhibit 4-1 What is Love?

The profoundly tender or passionate affection for a person of the opposite sex; a feeling of warm personal attachment or deep affection, as for a parent or child; sexual passion or desire, or its gratification; a person toward whom love is felt; beloved person; sweetheart; a personification of sexual affection; affectionate concern for the well-being of others. (Webster's Dictionary)

Love is like God. It's loused up so bad by liars and hypocrites, I can't say it to anyone I care about. (Lipton)

Love is the delusion that one woman differs from another; love is a state of perpetual anesthesia. (Mencken)

Love derives from the efforts of each partner to involve the other, without becoming involved himself. Love emerges when sentiment formation overcomes objectivity. Each partner strives to be like the dating partner's idealized image of him. Each partner assumes behaviors not characteristic of him and what he can not actually achieve in behavior, the partner completes in his imagination. (Waller)

Love may be defined as a strong emotion directed at a person of the opposite sex and involving feelings of sexual attraction, tenderness, and some commitment to the other's ego needs. (Bell)

Love is patient and kind; love is not jealous, or conceited, or proud; love is not ill mannered, or selfish, or irritable; love does not keep a record of wrongs; love is not happy with evil, but is happy with the truth. Love never gives up; its faith, hope, and patience never fail. Love is eternal. (I Corinthians 13: 4-8)

Love is an idealized passion which develops from the frustration of sex. (Wallin)

Love is aim-inhibited sex. (Freud)

It may be defined as a cancerous growth of unknown origin which may take up its site anywhere without the subject knowing or wishing it. (Durrel)

Love is locating the center of your existence in someone else.

ment, companionship, and caring, it surely must develop over time. Falling in love is a developmental process which can be broken down into four stages (Reiss, 1960):

1 *Rapport.* As two individuals get to know each other better and become attracted to each other, a feeling of rapport develops.

2 *Self-revelation.* As the couple become increasingly relaxed and comfortable with each other, they begin to reveal themselves. They talk, do

things together, and do away with the formalities of early interaction.

3 *Mutual dependency.* As we begin to develop more and more habits that center on the other person, mutual dependency is developed. Our partners become the focus of our humor, our frustrations, and our sexual desires.

4 *Personality need fulfillment.* Both partners have emotional and personality needs which they can provide for each other. The more the relationship grows, the more we find ourselves depending on our partner to meet our basic needs.

The wheel theory of love presented in Exhibit 4-2 suggests that we fall in love gradually by moving through the four stages presented. Once we have moved through the four stages, the processes become interdependent, so that all four must be maintained at a sufficiently high level. Of course, just as we fall in love, we can fall out of love. Graphically, this means that the wheel can unwind.

Multiple Loves

Is it possible to love more than one person at a time? Theoretically, we are inclined to believe it is. Many persons report that they have been in love with two persons at once. Such a situation can develop, for example, when, following high school graduation, a love relationship begun in high school continues while a new love relationship begins with a different person in college. Similarly, some married persons develop a second love relationship which competes with their marital relationship. This can be explained if we recognize that the wheel of love development described above is in no way necessarily restricted to one person.

As a practical matter, however, dual love relationships do not commonly occur. There is likely to be little social support for such an arrangement, and dual love relationships may be difficult to manage. As our society has

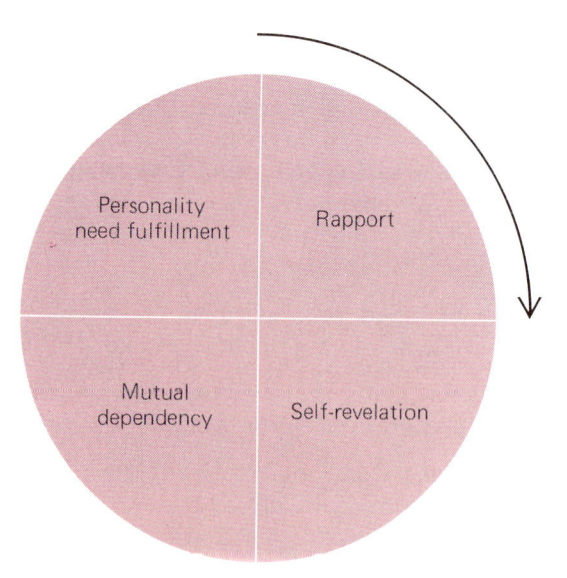

Exhibit 4-2 The wheel theory of love. (Adapted from Reiss, 1960.)

become more impersonal, we have demanded that our male-female love relationships carry much of the burden for making our lives personally meaningful. Thus, these increasingly intimate friendships and marriage relationships bring people closer together both emotionally and in their day-to-day activities. A relationship of such intensity is not likely to succeed for long if another developing relationship begins to fulfill the same needs for the individual. Sooner or later, one or the other of the love relationships will be likely to falter, since the person in the middle will find it difficult to divide his or her time, energy, and attention to both relationships, and since both of that person's partners are likely to want a clear commitment to *their* relationship. Multiple love is possible, but difficult.

Misconceptions Concerning Love

There are a number of common misconceptions concerning love that play a part in our thinking about it and add to the confusion of the individual who is attempting to determine whether what he or she is experiencing is genuine love or one of the counterfeits that often pass for it.

We assume that we fall in love only with our "hearts," but that is not true. We do "fall in love" with our hearts but also, it is hoped, with our "heads." In addition, the process is colored by the traditions, customs, standards, ideas, and ideals of the group in which we live and out of which our attitudes spring.

It would be much better to say that we grow into love. That would be nearer the truth, but it sounds unromantic. Although one may abruptly fall into a condition of violent infatuation, it takes time for love to develop. Love is a complex sentiment. It does not strike suddenly or fall unexpectedly like manna from heaven. It comes only when two individuals have reoriented their lives, each with the other as a new focal point.

Some persons believe that when an individual is experiencing what he or she interprets as love, immediate experience outweighs all other considerations. The person is sometimes expected to lose perspective. Some individuals believe that because they have had sexual intercourse they must be in love. Others claim that because they are in love, sexual intercourse is imperative. These misconceptions go hand in hand with the uncritical assumption that love is largely a physical experience.

Some persons attribute to love an almost unlimited power to offset or eradicate individual shortcomings. The assumption seems to be that if feelings are sufficiently intense, personality traits will affect neither the couple's relationship nor their marriage, or else that undesirable traits will be molded to fit the ideal merely through the healing balm of love. There exists a similar misconception about love's ability to solve problems. Individuals supposedly in love often blithely disregard problems connected with parents, income, pregnancy, employment, the completion of their education, and important sociocultural differences.

Some individuals believe that somewhere in the world is *the* one, the only person with whom they could fall in love and with whom they could find happiness. They are depending upon a kind fate, plus a certain amount of seeking on their own part, to bring the two predestined lovers together. This is a very romantic conception, but it cannot be squared with the facts. We tend to marry individuals with whom we are in love; we tend to fall in love with those whom we date; we tend to date those whom we meet at school, at our places of employment, or by chance in the community; and thus, our acquaintances and dates are persons who live in our community and probably have much in common with us to begin with.

Our model of Prince Charming and the Princess could more accurately be described as follows. Two persons who meet, like each other, are attracted to each other, and begin spending time together, begin to revamp their ideas about an ideal marriage partner to fit the other person, and consequently each has fallen in love with the ideal partner. But before that happened, they might as readily have fallen in love with any one of a number of persons. After the ideals have been revamped and centered on given individuals, however, this fact colors their attitude toward other persons and might make it difficult to fall in love with anyone else.

There is a misconception that when love does come it can be instantly recognized. But some individuals fall in love with persons whom they initially did not like. Conversely, of course, many persons who initially excite, fascinate, or greatly impress us are later forgotten or even disliked by us. We have all experienced initial thrills when meeting someone. Some individuals do lose sleep, eat more (or less), cry, become ecstatic (or depressed), become more motivated to work (or are unable to work), or can think of nothing else but their lover when relationships are formed or are dissolved. But these are almost always temporary conditions. Mature love involves considerably more than these temporary physical states.

Finally, we must add that not all lasting love relationships result in marriage, and not all marriages involve everlasting love. Love has gone from many marriages that continue to remain legally intact, and many persons who might have been happily married will never realize the possibility, since other circumstances have perhaps prevented them from marrying. The song which claims that love and marriage go together like a horse and carriage is only partially correct—you *can* have one without the other.

Love and Infatuation

There is no simple formula for determining the presence of love. It is not possible to state that love has certain characteristics that are distinctly separate from characteristics of infatuation. There do appear to be some tendencies, however, which we would like to present. Love grows, and all growth requires time. Infatuation may come suddenly. "Love at first sight" may be compulsive in nature. The individual may have a strong urge to love someone, and this urge becomes focused on a particular person. What should be expressed as, "This is the individual I must love" is expressed by the person concerned as "This is the individual I do love." Such an urge is not uncommon in adolescence, when new emotions, with which the young person has not yet learned to live and which are largely the result of lack of experience, begin to well up within him or her.

Such "love" may also be an outgrowth of an individual's insecurity or fear that, because of personal unattractiveness or inability to meet members of the opposite gender, he or she may never marry. When someone exhibits an interest, the person becomes convinced that it must be love at first sight.

Of course, many love relationships begin as infatuation, but time and experience undoubtedly have a role in transforming a relationship from infatuation to love. Usually an individual reaches a sound conclusion that he or she is in love after seeing the other person under a variety of circumstances. An individual may become infatuated after seeing the other person in relatively few situations, or even in only one, and reach a premature decision about love. Love grows out of an appraisal of all the known characteristics of the other person. Infatuation may arise from an acquaintance with only one or a few of these characteristics.

When an individual is genuinely in love, he or she is in love with the other person as a total personality; feelings grow primarily out of the relationship with that other person and a total estimate of him or her. An infatuated individual may be "in love with love." Feelings are primarily self-generated and grow only in part out of the relationship with the other person. The other person is a hook on which these self-generated emotions are hung.

An individual in love tends to have a sense of security and a feeling of trust after considering everything involved in the relationship with the other person. An infatuated individual tends to have a blind sense of security based upon wishful thinking rather than upon careful consideration, or the individual may have a sense of insecurity that is expressed as jealousy.

Love leads to idealization, but because the ideal is partly an outgrowth of understanding of and appreciation for the other person, it may be checked against reality without loss. In infatuation there tends to be idealization accompanied by a disregard of reality. A certain amount of idealization may be desirable, for none of us can look at a love object with complete impersonality; but the idealization should be continually checked with reality and not depart so far from it that sight of the real person is lost and a true appraisal is impossible.

Love tends to be more constant than infatuation, which often varies with the "distance" between the couple. There may be greater attraction when they are separated, because they overidealize each other, but less when they are together, because they see each other as they are and are more critical. Or there may be greater attraction when they are together, because of physical appeal that beclouds judgment, and less attraction when they are separated, because physical responses are less intense and they see each other from a different point of view.

Physical attraction is a relatively smaller part of their total relationship when a couple are in love, a relatively greater part when they are infatuated. Allowing for oversimplification, in Exhibit 4-3 the square representing physical attraction is the same in both diagrams. It is a relatively greater part of the square representing infatuation, a relatively smaller part of the square representing love. The reason for this is that infatuation is largely physical attraction, while love is founded on a broader base; the couple in love have a more inclusive relationship, of which physical attraction is only one facet. When a couple are in love, any physical contact that they have is likely to have meaning as well as to be a pleasurable experience in and of itself. It expresses what they feel toward each other.

When love changes, the reasons are usually more or less apparent. Infatuation may change for no apparent reason, but there is usually a lesser commitment to the relationship than is the case between individuals who are in love. Both authors of this text have counseled individuals who have claimed to be in love after very short periods of time. One woman was planning to marry a man she had dated for about two weeks. Although she had a similar experience on three previous occasions, she was confident that this relationship was "different." A person ready to be in love would see what had happened earlier and realize that "this time" could be proved different only by waiting longer to discover how the relationship developed.

Persons who are genuinely in love are concerned about their relationship with their lovers, not just about the contribution of the relationship to their own pleasure. In a healthy love relationship, individuals are alert to possible means of strengthening the relationship, furthering its development, and preserving it.

A couple in love are not indifferent to the effects of postponing their wedding and do not prolong the period of postponement unduly, but they can wait a reasonable time; they do not feel an irresistible urge toward haste. They may think of the period of postponement as one of further preparation so that when it does occur, their marriage will be on a sounder basis than if they married immediately. An infatuated couple often feel an urge toward immediate marriage. Postponement is intolerable to them, and they interpret it as deprivation rather than as preparation. When a couple feel that marriage is so important to

Exhibit 4-3 The relationship between physical attraction and infatuation and love.

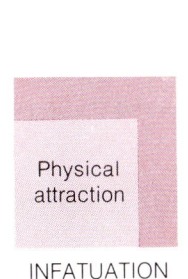

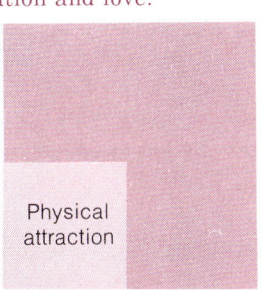

Marriage Preparation and Partner Selection

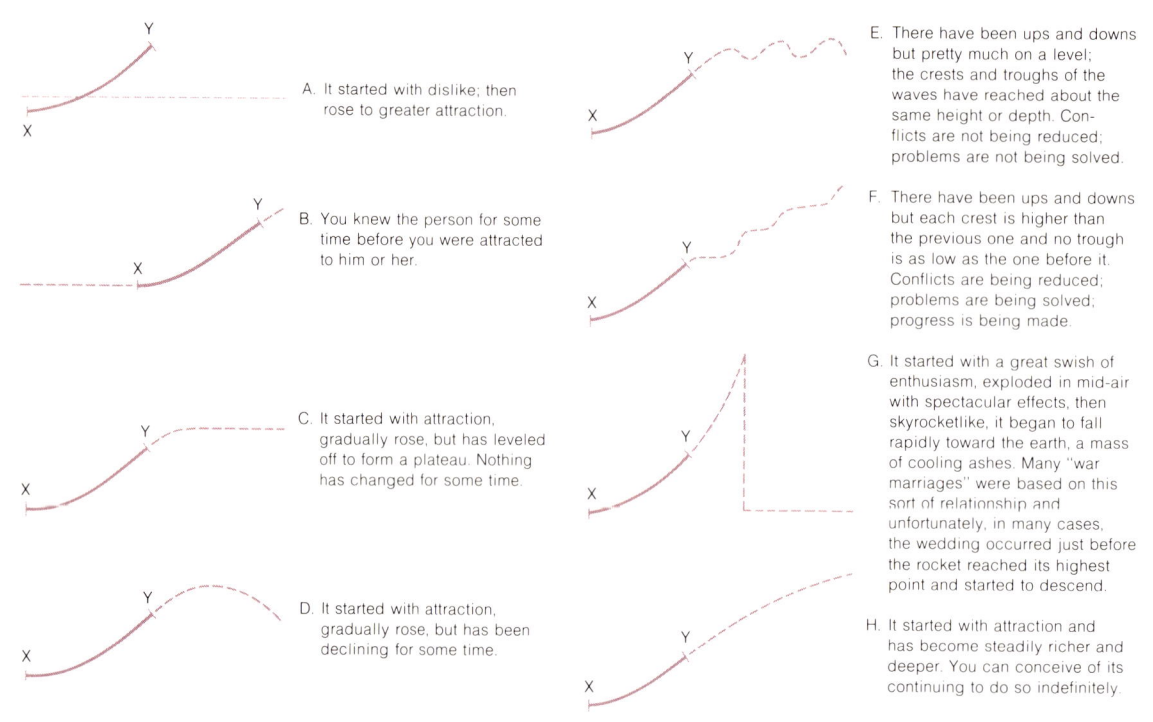

A. It started with dislike; then rose to greater attraction.

B. You knew the person for some time before you were attracted to him or her.

C. It started with attraction, gradually rose, but has leveled off to form a plateau. Nothing has changed for some time.

D. It started with attraction, gradually rose, but has been declining for some time.

E. There have been ups and downs but pretty much on a level; the crests and troughs of the waves have reached about the same height or depth. Conflicts are not being reduced; problems are not being solved.

F. There have been ups and downs but each crest is higher than the previous one and no trough is as low as the one before it. Conflicts are being reduced; problems are being solved; progress is being made.

G. It started with a great swish of enthusiasm, exploded in mid-air with spectacular effects, then skyrocketlike, it began to fall rapidly toward the earth, a mass of cooling ashes. Many "war marriages" were based on this sort of relationship and unfortunately, in many cases, the wedding occurred just before the rocket reached its highest point and started to descend.

H. It started with attraction and has become steadily richer and deeper. You can conceive of its continuing to do so indefinitely.

Exhibit 4-4 Possible changes in a couple's relationship to be considered in diagnosing love. The X-Y portion of each line may look the same as that portion of the others, disregarding the oversimplification. The direction the line will take after point Y can be determined only over time.

them that they cannot wait, they only prove what they do not see, namely, that marriage is too important to be hasty.

Questions for Self-evaluation

The questions listed below are intended as an aid in self-evaluation. They are for the person who has doubts; they are not meant to undermine the confidence of anyone who feels sure. There are no right or wrong answers. One must determine the significance of an affirmative or a negative answer in one's own case and weigh each answer in the light of one's own personality, the other person's personality, and the total relationship. Not all the questions necessarily apply to every person, and there are no criteria by which decisions can be made. "No" answers are not necessarily undesirable in some situations. Being in love cannot be expressed by a mathematical average. Furthermore, a person cannot make love happen by "going through the motions" of the things suggested in the questions; but the answers can aid an individual in analyzing himself or herself to determine whether or not love is present.

▶ Do you like to be in the company of the other person? Do you prefer that person's company to anyone else's?

▶ Is the individual personally attractive to you? Do you feel inclined to apologize for his or her appearance, manners, ideas, conversation, or language?

Socialization for Marriage: Love and Dating

▶ As you look back over your relationship from the first meeting, how has it changed? Which of the diagrams in Exhibit 4-4 most nearly depicts it, and what does this mean in your case? (Notice that all the possibilities may show considerable resemblance to one another in the earlier stages. Only increasing acquaintance over a period of time makes it possible to distinguish among them.)

▶ Do you have common interests? Did you have these interests before you met? Or did you develop them together? Or did you become interested in the other person's interests? If the last is the case, are your interests sincere, or are they a means of being attractive to the other person?

▶ Has enough time elapsed to tell? The sooner after meeting a couple consider themselves in love, the greater the probability of infatuation.

▶ Is there anything more than physical attraction in your relationship? How soon after becoming acquainted did you begin to be affectionate? What proportion of your time is taken up with close physical contact? How intense is such contact? Does it dominate your relationship? Is it characterized by such urgency that it leads you to disregard time, place, circumstances, other people, or appropriateness? Is it preventing the two of you from getting to know each other in a way conducive to the development of love? Is it furthering your total relationship, or are you letting one aspect of your relationship get out of perspective?

▶ Do you love the individual as a person, or do you like merely your feeling about him or her? (Are you "in love with love"?)

▶ Are you attracted to the individual for what he or she is or for what you read into him or her? Have you overidealized the person to the point of blindness, so that you pick out those traits that seem to fit your picture of an ideal spouse and close your eyes to others? Is the individual like an oil painting, attractive because of what is on the canvas, or like a motion-picture screen, reflecting only what is projected onto it?

▶ Does the person "wear well" with your friends and family? You may see qualities that your friends do not appreciate or have not had the opportunity to observe. On the other hand, your friends may be more objective and unbiased; they are not likely to be blind to shortcomings. Your parents may not know the person as well as you do; they may be biased in their appraisal; and they cannot weigh all the subjective elements involved in your choice. On the other hand, however, it is highly likely that your parents have had more experience with marriage than you have.

▶ Are you attracted to the person for what he or she is or for what he or she can give you or do for you?

▶ Over what matters and how frequently do you have conflict? Is the conflict open or suppressed? Is it superficial or fundamental? How do you weather a crisis together?

▶ Do you have any doubts about your love? A certain amount of doubt while love is developing is not unusual. But when the question is whether or not to marry, the old adage, "When in doubt, don't," is apropos. Marrying to escape a doubt-ridden situation does not resolve doubts; it merely puts them out of mind temporarily.

▶ Are you sufficient stimulus for each other when you are together, or do you require external stimuli, such as movies, dancing, or a group of people, to prevent boredom? To what degree is your stimulus for each other limited to purely physical appeal?

▶ In your mind, how does the individual fare in competition with others? As comparisons are made with others, is he or she always at the top of the list? Or are you constantly looking for "greener pastures"?

▶ How readily and how frequently do you publicize what ought to be private? Calling attention to the other person's weaknesses, recounting embarrassing experiences, or disclosing confidential information may indicate a disregard for the feelings of the other party.

▶ What is the relationship between your enthusiasm and the presence or absence of the other person? What is the effect of separation after it is over?

▶ Do you feel that your relationship hangs on a very slender thread and could be easily broken? Does it seem to be constantly threatened?

▶ Do you willingly permit the person to date when you are separated for an extended period? What is the reason for your answer, and what does it mean with regard to your relationship with the other person?

▶ Do you forgive, tolerate, accept, overlook, or resent faults and shortcomings? Do you love the individual "faults and all," or are you holding yourself in check pending the other person's reform?

▶ Have you seen the individual in a sufficient variety of situations and observed enough of his or her personality facets to know that you are in love? An individual may base judgments of another person upon words rather than upon direct observation of behavior. Do you see each other primarily during vacations or weekend visits, when the holiday spirit may generate attitudes and behavior that may be misleading?

▶ If your partner has told you in no uncertain terms that he or she loves you and will love you forever, what part does this certainty play in making you feel that you love him or her? If your partner seems indifferent, has it caused you to confuse love with the "spirit of the chase"? Are you under the pressure of some "test" of love, such as "If you love me, you will do thus and so"?

▶ Do you feel that you love the other person even though he or she does not love you, has mistreated you, has rejected you, or has exhibited qualities clearly unfavorable to marriage? If so, why? What does it mean?

▶ To what extent do you feel identified with this person? Do you think of yourselves as a pair or as isolated individuals? How much do you voluntarily share with each other?

▶ How much are you concerned about the individual's welfare and happiness?

▶ Is there anything or anybody in life that you consider more valuable to you than this other person or that you love more than you love him or her? If so, what or who is it, and what does that fact mean?

▶ Do you have a desire to escape an unhappy home, school, or work situation? Such a desire to escape often "makes the grass on the other side of the fence look greener." Marriage looks like the way out. Under such circumstances, it is easy to confuse infatuation and love.

▶ What has been your reaction to these questions? Have you found it difficult to be honest with yourself? Have you rationalized any of your answers? Have you dismissed the use of such analysis on the assumption that questions cannot help you anyway? Have the questions put you on the defensive, as if you were afraid they would undermine something not fully secure?

The reader may wonder whether there can in fact be genuine love. Doubts about his or her own feelings may have increased. Remember that love that cannot stand the test of twenty-seven questions could never stand the test of twenty-seven years of marriage or, for that matter, even twenty-seven months of marriage.

In many cases, individuals cannot reach a conclusion as to whether or not they are in love. Sometimes the more these individuals try the more confused they become; and the more confused they become, the more they feel impelled to reach a conclusion, until the vicious circle into which they have been placed absorbs a large portion of time, energy, and attention. There is no simple prescription that may be administered to such persons to rid them of the problem that plagues them. Probably the answer is time, and the explanation of their plight is this: They are trying to reach a conclusion by intellectual processes alone, when that conclusion must be based at least in part on a growth process, and growth requires time. An individual's experience up to date in his or her relationship with the other person has contributed certain "data" that form part of the basis upon which a conclusion will eventually be reached. But the "data" are incomplete, and although the individual goes over them, examines them, and "digests" them again and again, he or she arrives nowhere. What is needed is more experience, more contact with and observation of the other person, more "data." This will require time. Since it is indecision that is plaguing him or her, and since any decision will aid in breaking the vicious circle, the individual may "make a decision to make no decision"; that is, he or she may definitely make up his or her mind to suspend judgment until more "data" are available and for the time being stop trying to reach a conclusion.

Putting all that we have discussed up to this point into a nutshell, we may say that two individuals are in love not only when they have certain strong emotional responses to one another and have a particular type of regard for each other. They are in love when their mutual relationship fosters the growth of each individual and is itself likely to increase in depth. They are in love when they begin to merge their patterns of life into one common pattern that will eventually represent a new entity of which each individual is a complementary part.

DATING IN AMERICA

In America today marriage is typically preceded by a period of dating during which young people presumably become acquainted and gradually narrow down the possible choices of marriage partners until a final choice is made. In spite of this practice, however, there is some tendency to separate dating activities from socialization for marriage and to think of them as incidental and, to some extent, as ends in themselves. In modern American society, young persons begin to date at age 14 or 15, on the average, although this is highly variable. Dating sometimes begins before junior high school or as late as post-college. Dating then continues until marriage. Most of us will date several persons before we marry. In some parts of the world the extensive dating experience characteristic of American youth is considered both unusual and immoral. To date a number of persons without a marriage commitment or even an interest in marrying them is considered wrong in many cultures. Our own culture also has a history of restrictive dating patterns. It is only since the turn of the century that Americans have experienced the open, partner-centered, free-choice, and romantically based dating system we now know.

Dating, then, has changed over the years. Two hundred years ago, Americans practiced *bundling*, a part of the courtship system that allowed men to visit potential brides in their home, stay overnight, and cuddle up (sometimes with a board between them) in the same bed to keep warm. The long trip between homes, the cold winter nights in New England, and the shortage of beds made this an acceptable practice for a time, but sex was not expected and actually was considered sinful. Nevertheless, evidence from church records in Massachusetts before the American Revolution indicates that sexual intercourse sometimes took place and in many cases led to pregnancy (Calhoun, 1945).

But bundling was part of a larger courtship system which was actually very restrictive. Until about 1920, dating in America was a carefully regulated, but important social activity. Dating was traditionally closely tied to marriage. Couples who dated were expected to be serious about marriage. In some social circles, it was fully expected that couples who were dating with parental approval were committed and would thus marry. Dating in the twentieth century differs from earlier dating norms in several ways (Mead, 1959):

▶ An introduction of the young man to the young woman by a member of the family is not considered necessary.

▶ There is no chaperone.

▶ There is no commitment or obligation, either public or private, on the part of either the male or the female to continue the relation beyond the actual time of the date itself.

▶ The date is planned by the adolescents themselves, rather than arranged by elders.

▶ Physical intimacies are expected rather than forbidden (with degree of intimacy depending upon length of acquaintance, age, social class, educational level, religious affiliation, and various personality elements).

The automobile, telephone, commercialized amusements, the growth of cities, the shrinkage of dwelling size, the changing status of women, new expectations with regard to marriage, increased leisure time, the emancipation of youth from their parents, greater freedom of association among young people, and a myriad of other factors are making dating somewhat different today. The expansion of the socialization function of the public school system and our social involvements within educational settings undoubtedly also have influenced the changing character of dating and courtship. As noted already, today there is less societal and parental control; this fact puts a new responsibility upon the shoulders of the young persons making their own plans and choices.

Dating sometimes involves much idealizing and wishful thinking. Sometimes promises are made that cannot be kept, and expectations are built up that cannot be fulfilled. Marriage then seems like a let-down. The reason is not that marriage is less interesting or exciting than dating, but that in marriage there is an inevitable impact with reality; and in dating reality may be temporarily obscured by imagination. Much is said about how people change, often for the worse, after they marry. Before marriage the persons may see each other from a favorably biased point of view. Couples may idealize each other, emphasizing their partner's positive attributes. Similarly, individuals may not display some undesirable aspects of their personality. Then after they begin living together each is better able to see the spouse as he or she is, not as he or she was thought to be. This observation is supported by data indicating that of all couples whose marriages end in divorce, more are separated in their first year of marriage than any other yearly period. Fourteen percent of couples who eventually divorce are separated by the end of their first year of marriage (Plateris, 1973).

Much is written and said about failure in marriage. Relatively little is mentioned concerning dating failures except in connection with failure to date or to have a good time. Yet, in a significant sense, many "marriage failures" are in reality "dating failures." These include the failure to allow sufficient time to become acquainted, failure to make intelligent decisions about one's future, failure to correlate values with behavior, and failure to make wise choices. These failures occur before the wedding but may become apparent only afterward. Dating, of course, can be a rewarding activity which enhances the personal growth of the individuals involved and helps them develop a range of social skills which may be useful in relating to members of the opposite gender.

Dating: Its Definition and Functions

Dating is a term we all understand, yet it is difficult to define. Many individuals do not like to use the term at all, since it conjures up images of the very traditional system of courtship in which males were permitted to call females, pick them up, open doors, pay bills, and initiate sexual intimacies. Some persons reject the term because they do not feel themselves to be a part of this traditional system. Although most of these practices are still with us in varying degrees, times have changed with regard to male-female role differentiation in dating relationships. Some young persons will tell their parents that they are "going out" with someone, but to parents who developed their vocabulary a generation earlier they will define the activity as a "date." Whether we use the term "going out," "dating," or some other term, we are interested here in those recreational activities between unmarried males and females which have become the basic foundation of premarital interaction in America.

One writer has described dating as follows (Saxton, 1972):

A "date," as the term is used in our society, is a planned event involving any shared activity between two persons (usually young unmarried persons of the opposite sexes). It may be planned many months or just minutes in advance; it may involve only the one couple or another couple as well, or it may take place within a group. In any case, an event becomes a "date" only when one person (usually but not necessarily the male) asks the other to share in the activity. They then form a paired relation, publicly recognizable, for the duration of the event. The pairing may be loose, casual, and tentative; or it may be highly tenacious and exclusive.

Regardless of the motivation for requesting or accepting a given date, the activity may serve one or more of several important functions (Winch, 1963; Skipper and Nass, 1966):

▶ Dating may be a form of recreation. It provides entertainment for the individuals involved and is a source of immediate enjoyment.

▶ Dating may be a form of socialization. It provides an opportunity for individuals of opposite gender to get to know each other, learn to adjust to each other, and to develop appropriate techniques of interaction.

▶ Dating may be a means of status grading and status achievement. By dating and being seen with persons who are rated "highly desirable" by their peer group, individuals may raise their status and prestige with the group.

▶ Dating may be a form of courtship. It provides an opportunity for unmarried individuals to associate with each other for the purpose of selecting a mate whom they may eventually marry.

Dating and Social Change

New norms governing dating relationships are emerging. Standards are ill defined in this period of transition. Young people must rely upon their own judgments, their own conclusions, their own definitions of objectives, and their own self-discipline more than before. Many of the admonitions of their parents are of the "don't" variety and have their roots in a cultural period somewhat different from the present. Survivors of a previous era cannot be expected to set the standards for our current one. What, then, are some of the new standards which have developed?

More freedom for females Most of us are aware that the dating and courtship system has been a male-dominated one. Men have been expected to call on females, arrange for the activity, provide transportation, and foot the bill. Females have been expected to accept or reject offers for dates, but not initiate them. When they have been permitted to initiate dates, special circumstances such as turnabout dances, sorority formals, or Sadie Hawkins days provided an occasion for the reversal. Just as females have gained more freedom in other areas of their life, so also are females taking a greater role in initiating dating contacts. As some of our traditional stereotypes disappear, females will feel increasingly freer to call a male on the phone, ask him to attend a recreational activity, pay the bill, and initiate sexual intimacies, if desired. We are still a long way, however, from equality in this regard. Despite some claims to the contrary, dating activities are still tied largely to the male's initiative.

Less formality Dating is becoming less formal. Whereas males of a generation ago were expected to call for a date several days or even a week or two in advance, these norms have been relaxed. Couples engage in many more spur-of-the-moment activities and view many of their dating relationships as friendships rather than romantically based encounters. Couples often dress informally and participate in activities which require little planning or expense. Many dating activities such as picnics, walks, talks, campus lectures, studying, tennis, swimming, jogging, or dancing require little planning and little expense and provide good opportunities to get to know the other person.

More group activities Our highly mobile society has made it easy for us to communicate with a large number of persons in a short period of time. Many young married couples met their spouses in the context of a group activity which may have been specially planned or formed on short notice. Parties, exchanges, mixers, and informal gatherings are numerous on college campuses, and it is often within this context that a couple meet, become interested, and eventually form a close relationship. Much of our current dating and recreational activity involves a group of males and females who decide to participate in an activity together. Groups who work together in an office; live in the same fraternity, sorority, or residence hall; belong to the same social club; are members of a racial minority group attending a predominantly white university; or have something else in common may engage in social activities which bring males and females together.

The three changes cited above will, we believe, have some positive consequences for the future of dating relationships. If one reason could be cited as to why some males have been reluctant to ask females out, it is probably their fear of being turned down. All men are familiar with the anxiety that sometimes exists when asking a woman out for the first time. For some males, the anxiety can be so great, and the fear of rejection so powerful, that dating is avoided altogether. An individual's self-confidence and self-concept are both involved in this phenomenon. The greater freedom being experienced by women in initiating dates, the lessening formality of dating relationships, and the possibility of embedding the couple's date in a group situation can reduce much of this anxiety. A male calling for a date a week in advance would almost always interpret a "no" as a firm rejection and a blow to his self-concept. If he now calls and asks the female whether she would like to join a group of individuals who are planning an event, a "no" could be more easily interpreted as a rejection of the activity or a statement about other competing plans, rather than as a rejection of the male. The messages that they communicate to each other may eventually be the same, but the decreased formality and the insulation a group can provide may have some positive functions.

There may also be advantages for females. A generation ago, a female expected to be called several days before an important event. Some females who received a call only the day before an event would claim to be busy even if they were not, because they feared giving the impression that they were waiting for the male's call. They would then spend the evening alone. The new norms which are developing will allow a female greater freedom to accept a late invitation if she is not busy but still wants to participate. Of course, good sense and common courtesy will undoubtedly continue to be important in our participant-run courtship system, but these changes may relieve some of the anxiety previous generations have experienced and allow for greater honesty in dating relations.

A Continuum of Experience

Young people in modern America appear to be in the midst of a transition from our former traditional courtship and dating system to a more open, less formal, and increasingly permissive one. Young persons are dating more than they did just a decade or two ago, and they are likely to have more dating experience before marriage than their parents did (Bell and Chaskes, 1970). In any community or any college campus, we are likely to find a continuum of experience ranging on the one hand from individuals who are still very tied to a formal, male-dominated dating system to individuals who are engaged in relationships where females are as likely to call as are males, where both partners pay their own way, and where the presence of a group initially may mask a given couple's identity as a pair.

Most communities or campuses include significant numbers of individuals at all points along this continuum, depicted in Exhibit 4-5. We suspect that there is a shift occurring from the traditional end to the nontraditional end, but it is clear that it will still be several years before a new norm is established with which a substantial majority of persons are comfortable. For now, we are likely to continue to see considerable variety in male-female roles in connection with dating, sexual standards, a female's freedom to initiate dates, attend social functions unescorted, and pay her own way, and how seriously individuals consider given dating relationships.

Qualities of a Date

The qualities desirable in a husband or wife and those desirable in a date are not necessarily identical. In dating, some of the more superficial and inconsequential qualities may play a prominent role. This difference between "ideal date" and "ideal mate" characteristics is understandable, since the American system of dating relies heavily on first impressions and circumstances surrounding how we meet potential dating partners. When students are asked to list (1) the qualities that they prefer in a date and (2) those that they desire in a husband or a wife, the same characteristics usually appear, but in differ-

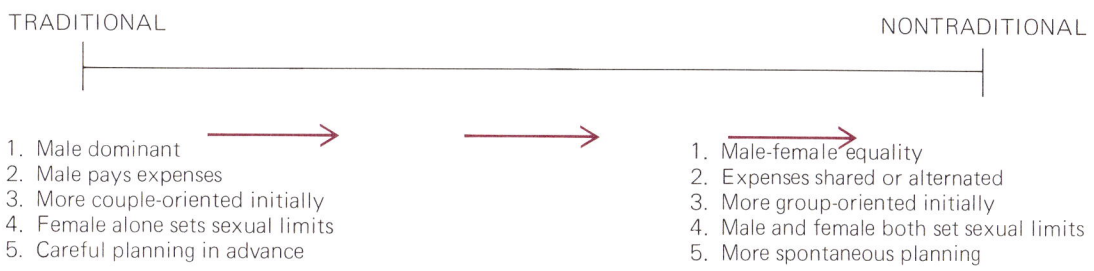

Exhibit 4-5 A continuum of the formality of dating relationships.

TRADITIONAL → → NONTRADITIONAL

1. Male dominant
2. Male pays expenses
3. More couple-oriented initially
4. Female alone sets sexual limits
5. Careful planning in advance

1. Male-female equality
2. Expenses shared or alternated
3. More group-oriented initially
4. Male and female both set sexual limits
5. More spontaneous planning

ent orders. Physical attractiveness seems to be more important in dating than in marriage, whereas occupational stability or compatibility might be more important as marriage considerations.

Somewhere in the myriad of each individual's personal attributes are those traits that will contribute most abundantly to his or her success or failure in marriage. Typically, people do not marry until they have dated each other for a more or less extended period. As a dating relationship progresses and becomes increasingly marriage-oriented, the standard of what constitutes desirable traits in a date may well be reappraised. An individual may consciously begin to ignore those aspects of his or her partner which were important considerations initially and perhaps were unrelated to successful marriage and begin to give more attention to those qualities that are related to that person's notion of an appropriate marriage partner. In this way a person may come to have a more marriage-related dating experience. When such a transition does not occur, an individual may base the choice of a marriage partner on a partially inappropriate set of qualities.

The Impact of Physical Attractiveness

There are few questions as complex as "What attracts two persons to each other?" Social psychologists have devoted much thought to the qualities, characteristics, and processes involved in determining how and why two individuals initially become attracted to each other (Huston, 1974). There can be little doubt, however, that in dating situations, first impressions are important in determining whether or not two individuals are likely to initiate even a tentative relationship. And after taking into account our initial observations about the person's gender, race, age, and perhaps marital status, it is unlikely that any factor is as important as his or her physical attractiveness.

Males and females alike rate physical attractiveness as the most important characteristic in a date (Huston, 1973; Saxton, 1972; Berscheid and Walster, 1972; Walster et al., 1966). Persons arranging blind dates for others are typically asked first what the person looks like. We have all experienced the scene at a party, dance, open house, bar, or other similar social gathering when several individuals "perk up" or even descend on a particularly attractive individual who has just entered. And we often feel a great deal of self-esteem when we have had the opportunity to interact with or date an especially attractive person. Physical attractiveness is something highly valued in our culture.

Our great emphasis on how a person looks is also evident in the mass media. Television commercials continually advertise products designed to enhance our appearance. Television and movie stars are usually especially attractive. And our magazines display picture after picture of men and women who, although largely anonymous to us, can be quite appealing and exciting.

Suppose, for a moment, that you were asked to produce a television commercial for a shaving cream advertisement to appear during an important football game. If you have been told that the producer intends to use an attractive female and asks you to select an appropriate model, would you select a woman who is young or old? Blond or brunette? Tall or short? Slender or chubby? Long- or short-haired? Shapely or flat-chested? Wearing everyday clothes or something sexy? It is likely that in a class of students there will be some consistency of replies to the above choices, although some might differ among racial or other subcultural groups. Our responses undoubtedly reflect cultural stereotypes which we have learned over the years of our socialization.

Our predisposition to appreciate the attractive is, in short, a product of our socialization process, which is certainly oriented to this end. We admire beautiful babies; we constantly tell especially attractive children how pretty, cute, or good-looking they are; we seek out and date the most attractive boys and girls; we elect queens (and increasingly kings) of every variety, ranging from homecoming to local Junior Miss to Miss America; and we have even witnessed young men and women who, with their friends, will give numbered ratings to members of the opposite gender who might wander by.

Of course, what is appealing to one person may not be appealing to another, and many individuals prefer to choose dating partners who are similar to rather than vastly different from themselves in physical attractiveness. Furthermore, many individuals consider factors other than physical characteristics in an overall evaluation of attractiveness. Dress, demeanor, conversational abilities, mannerisms, and "charm" are factors which may be determined on first impression and could be important in an evaluation of attractiveness. Consequently, we find that there is much dating among persons at all levels of physical attractiveness.

Research reveals some important gender differences, however. Girls tend to begin dating earlier, with greater frequency, and have more dating partners than do boys (Bell, 1975). Attractive individuals, boys and girls alike, date more often than less attractive individuals. Girls tend to date males of the same age or older, whereas males tend to date females of the same age or younger. It has been suggested that females are slightly more likely than males to have either a very high or a very low dating frequency (Blood, 1969). This can be explained by realizing that males are more likely to initiate dates, and in doing so will be more likely to ask out the particularly attractive females and less likely to ask out the particularly unattractive females. Since males tend to seek partners more attractive than they are (Berscheid and Walster, 1972; Walster et al., 1966; Huston, 1973), the extremes will be more overrepresented for females.

Research on computer dances, during which male-female pairing could be controlled by researchers, revealed that physical attractiveness outweighed all other variables in determining whether a male asked a female out again (Walster et al., 1966). Such findings should not lead us to believe that looks are all-important, for they are not. But their importance in initial encounters, which may subsequently determine possible dating relationships, should not be underemphasized.

The Rating and Dating Complex

Our discussion of the importance of physical attractiveness may lead some readers to wonder whether dating is not really just a game of sorts. Many years ago it was observed that dating was a game that one had to leave in order to get serious. This notion stemmed from the work of the first sociologist ever to study the dating phenomenon, Willard Waller (1937). In a paper titled "The Rating and Dating Complex," based on his research at The Pennsylvania State University in the late 1920s and early 1930s, Waller suggested that dating was a period of dalliance and experimentation between men and women and was an end in itself. Dating was strictly for the enjoyment of the participants, a form of thrill-seeking essentially unrelated to marriage. Fifty years ago dating was an activity for the privileged few. It was distinct from courtship and involved considerable attention to the status of the dating partners. Waller found that persons in fraternities and sororities tended to date each other and, furthermore, that men in high-status fraternities tended to date females in high-status sororities. When dating did not occur at the same status, men were more likely to date females of lower social status. Penn State, like other colleges then, had six men to every woman. This ratio intensified the competition for the most attractive dates among males and females alike.

Among Waller's findings was that exploitation was more likely to occur when a high-status male dated a low-status female. Sexual favors were more likely to be expected by the male, and females apparently were more likely to grant them. Waller observed that a male's primary goal in dating was sexual gratification, while the female's primary goal was the status of dating the most "desirable" man and the attainment of other symbolic or material rewards that could be gained from the date. While some of us may recognize some of the characteristics of dating Waller described as still applicable today, it is clear that dating has taken on different meanings for many contemporary young persons.

Subsequent research in the 1950s and 1960s failed to support much of Waller's theory (Smith, 1952; Blood, 1955; Reiss, 1965; Christensen, 1958), indicating that dating had taken on new meaning for students a generation later. Nevertheless, some of the elements of dating as a status game appear to remain to this day. There is still a tendency for independents to date independents and "Greeks" to date "Greeks." It still appears to be true that on any college campus students in the "Greek" system are capable of distinguishing high-status versus low-status fraternities and sororities. Furthermore, members of high-status fraternities are more likely to date members of high-status sororities (Rogers and Havens, 1960; Reiss, 1965). These tendencies will probably be less pro-

While dating practices do change, some traditional customs persist. These students traveled in style to their high school prom by dressing in the fashions of the Roaring Twenties and riding in a Bentley and Rolls Royce. (United Press International)

nounced over time, with most persons being less concerned about the social labels placed on their dates.

There is a danger in likening dating to a game. Such analogies give the impression that dating is frivolous or governed by calculating individuals with shady motives. This certainly does not characterize most persons. There are really no winners or losers in the dating game. Some persons are adept at dating; they find it easy to make acquaintances. They ask many persons out and are comfortable on dates. Many of these persons have numerous possibilities for dating partners. Others find dating a struggle and avoid it.

A minority of young persons today are like the college students Waller studied in that they see dating as an activity where "points" are to be accumulated. The majority of young persons today, however, find dating a rewarding activity which may develop important social skills (Blood, 1969):

▶ *Self-expression.* Dating encourages self-confidence, which results in the ability effectively to communicate with persons of the opposite gender.

▶ *Empathy.* Dating provides the opportunity to learn better how to perceive the partner's attitudes and feelings.

▶ *Decision making.* Since dating is an activity involving two persons, it requires individuals to learn to make decisions.

▶ *Commitment.* A decision to have even one date requires some planning and represents an obligation to the other person, if only a temporary one. These obligations enhance our ability to make more lasting commitments later.

The Principle of Least Interest

In most stable dyadic (couple) relationships (dating, marriage, or other), the partners are sufficiently committed to each other and to the continuance of the relationship that both take an active role in maintaining it. However, when one person is less committed (or less interested) than the other, the *principle of least interest* may apply. Willard Waller suggested that in a relationship where a difference of commitment existed, the less interested party would have more power and influence in the relationship. In a dating relationship, this might mean that persons who initially display only marginal interest in the other or who, after the development of a dating relationship, feel that there is no more challenge to it, will have more power, more influence, and a greater role in decision making. In a marriage relationship, as we shall point out later, it might mean that a spouse alway threatening divorce will find the other person giving in more to the least interested party in order to keep the marriage intact.

We have all seen examples of the principle in operation. Many persons find themselves in dating relationships where one member is eager to continue the relationship and the other is no longer interested. The less interested partner may have more influence as a result, while the more interested partner gives in while attempting to keep the other partner in the relationship. Such a situation potentially leads to sexual or social exploitation when the less interested partner expects or encourages favors from the more interested partner.

Some individuals continually find themselves in one role or the other. They may be uncomfortable in that role, or they may enjoy it. For example, many young persons find themselves, at one time or another, in a dating relationship they are not very serious about. They are not eager to continue the relationship, but the other person is. By being less interested, they are in a position of power which they may not relish. They would just as soon have the relationship terminate as see their partner suffering through the termination of the relationship. Eventually the relationship is likely to end. Although some couples continue relationships with highly differential commitment and are happy with such an arrangement, most couples find it uncomfortable and difficult to manage. These relationships are more likely to terminate than those with equal interest and commitment.

The Trends Toward Early and Steady Dating

American youth begin dating earlier today than did the youth of their parents' generation. Most persons begin their dating in junior high or high school and continue to date until marriage. Thus, it would not be uncommon for an individual to date for more than ten years before marriage. Those who begin dating earliest come from the higher socioeconomic groups. They tend to be from small families with parents of higher education and social position (Lowrie, 1961, 1965; Bayer, 1968). The trend toward early dating can be explained by the increasing pressures on young people to develop social graces, become popular with their peers of both genders, and have fun during their adolescent years. These pressures may come from parents, peers, or the mass media, but they are present all around us.

It appears that the trend toward early dating has leveled off in the last decade (Bell and Chaskes, 1970), but we believe it unlikely that the ages at which young persons begin dating will increase. Early dating is something we can expect to have with us for some time. With this in mind, let us raise a few questions about the impact of early dating. How does it relate to age at marriage? Research shows that within the same social class, the earlier dating commences, the more likely early marriage will be (Bayer, 1968).

The social class distinction is important to mention, since individuals from lower socioeconomic groups tend to marry earlier than persons from higher socioeconomic groups. Is early dating related to marital stability? The data indicate that there is no relationship between the age when dating begins and subsequent marital stability (Bayer, 1968). The length of one's dating relationship with his or her future spouse is important, however, since the best adjusted and most stable marriages are those with longer periods of acquaintance, dating, and engagement (Bayer, 1968; Spanier, 1971). In summary, early daters tend to marry earlier, but they do not have significantly greater chances of marital failure. Rather, it is the length of their dating relationship with their spouse which is more important in determining the quality and stability of their marriage.

American youth tend to ignore parental advice to "play the field," "date around," or "not become involved while young." Ours is a culture where security and companionship are important in both dating and marriage relationships. Dating is really not as different from monogamous marriage as it may seem at first glance. Even before dating begins we talk of "boy friends" and "girl friends," "John and Mary sitting in a tree . . . ," or two persons who are "going together." It is not uncommon for junior high students to claim to be going with someone, even though they have not engaged in any activity which could be likened to a date. A steady relationship carries with it some status and security which is prized by those who are involved. Many young persons find little satisfaction in dating numerous individuals, and some find it a hassle. We do not intend to imply that steady dating is good or bad. It is a fact of American courtship that is perfectly understandable.

Steady dating has the drawback, of course, that participants may be limited in their exposure to persons of the opposite gender and may base an engagement or marriage decision on a very narrow field of experience. The norm, however, is for young persons to engage in a series of steady relationships, some quite brief and others of long duration. Ultimately, the typical person has had adequate dating experience through this succession of steady relationships.

There is little doubt that young persons who go steady are more likely to become sexually intimate than those who date casually with a wider range of individuals (Spanier, 1976a, 1976c). In other words, the greater the commitment and emotional involvement in a relationship, the greater the likelihood of sexual intimacy. Many parents suspect that this finding exists and have strong objections to the steady relationships of their children, particularly when they are still in high school. Parents want their children to be popular and attractive, but find themselves in a dilemma. They usually accept their child's decision, although many times reluctantly and not without a struggle.

There is much criticism of steady dating. Participants don't like the term (most prefer "going together" or some other variation), parents tend not to like the possibility of an early marriage and greater sexual intimacy, and many other observers believe that it does not contribute to maximal social development. Steady dating is nevertheless a common and basic part of dating interaction and marriage preparation, serves important social functions, and is likely to continue to be a part of our courtship and marriage system.

TERMS TO BE LEARNED

bundling
empathy
hedonistic
infatuation
instinct
love (romantic)
mate (mating)
principle of least interest
promiscuous (promiscuity)
rapport
rating and dating complex
rebound
social institution
value
wheel theory of love

SELECTED READINGS

ALTMAN, I., AND D. TAYLOR: *Social Penetration Process: The Development of Interpersonal Relationships*, Holt, Rinehart and Winston, Inc., New York, 1973. Intended primarily for individuals involved in the social study of interpersonal relationships, this book examines the dynamics of relationship formation.

BACH, G. R., AND R. M. DEUTSCH: *Pairing*, Peter H. Wyden, Inc., New York, 1970. Written for the nonacademic, this book deals with the formation of couple relationships.

BERSCHEID, E., AND E. WALSTER: *Interpersonal Attraction*, Addison-Wesley, Reading, Mass. 1969. Basic work on interpersonal attraction. Recommended for persons who wish to learn more about this topic.

DOTEN, D.: *The Art of Bundling*, Farrar, New York, 1938. Interesting account of a traditional courtship technique.

EHRMANN, WINSTON: *Premarital Dating Behavior*, Henry Holt and Company, New York, 1959. A "study of the premarital heterosexual activities and of certain associated behavior and attitudes of over one thousand male and female college students."

FROMM, E.: *The Art of Loving*, Harper & Row,

New York, 1956. Examines the different types of love, the nature of love, and the role that love plays in our lives.

GOODE, W. J.: "The Theoretical Importance of Love," *American Sociological Review*, vol. 24, pp. 38–47, 1959. "Views love in a broad perspective, focusing on the structural patterns by which societies keep in check the potentially disruptive effect of love relationships."

HILL, R., AND J. ALDOUS: "Socialization for Marriage and Parenthood," in D. Goslin (ed.): *Handbook of Socialization: Theory and Research*, Rand McNally & Company, Chicago, 1969. Explores various factors within and outside the family affecting the individual's knowledge and understanding of marriage and parenthood.

LEVINGER, G., AND J. D. SNOEK: *Attraction in Relationship: A New Look at Interpersonal Attraction*, General Learning Press, New York, 1972. Theoretical work on social attraction; examines the various evidence for different theories in this area.

MURSTEIN, B. (ed.): *Theories of Attraction and Love*, Springer Publishing, New York, 1971. Papers presented at a symposium of scholars examining attraction, love, and mate selection.

RUBIN, Z.: *Liking and Loving*, Holt, Rinehart and Winston, Inc., New York, 1973. A social-psychological approach to interpersonal attraction; deals with topics such as affiliation, social exchange, person perception, sex roles, prejudice, group dynamics, and intergroup relations.

Chapter 5

Premarital Sexual Behavior and the Sexual Revolution

It does not require very astute observation or very sensitive perception to be aware that something is happening in this country relative to sex. Sex is freely discussed. Censorship of movies has relaxed to the vanishing point. Nudity, sexual intercourse, and masturbation are shown on the screen. Television programs, even commercials, include reference to sex. Many popular magazines heretofore devoted solely to other subjects—for example, women's magazines—devote considerable space to it. Publications showing nude males and females are too numerous to count. Books and articles on a great variety of sexual experiences and techniques, from bona fide research materials to extremes of inaccuracy, are plentiful and readily available. Homosexuality is increasingly accepted, and many homosexuals freely admit their preferences. There are, however, still organizations and persons who insist upon a more traditional morality, oppose sex education in schools, and, if they could, would remove sex from all public discussion.

IS THERE A SEXUAL REVOLUTION?

Whether or not we conclude that there is a sexual revolution depends not only on fragmentary data and all-too-common broad generalizations but also, and very importantly, on the answers to a number of questions. When the term *revolution* is employed, what is being compared with what? Is the reference to changes in attitudes, behavior, incidence of premarital sexual intercourse, cohabitation, freedom of discussion and publication, legal restrictions, homosexuality, acceptance of activities such as oral-genital sex, censorship, moral standards, use of contraception, legalization of abortion—or what? What time period is implied? When did the revolution begin? If we are thinking of changes that have occurred since Puritan days, that is one thing. If we are thinking of changes that have occurred since World War II, that is another. Are we thinking of a long, slow process, such as the Industrial Revolution? Or are we thinking of a sudden occurrence, such as a political or military coup during which one power group takes over control from another power group? What proportion of society must be involved to constitute a revolution?

Perhaps the term *sexual evolution* is more appropriate than "sexual revolution" in describing what has happened and is happening in American culture. The distinction is partly one of definition. Since parts of culture

Sex before marriage has become more widely accepted in recent years. It is not uncommon to see young couples embracing in public (or not so public) places. (Ken Heyman)

are interrelated, sexual changes will occur as other aspects of social life change.

When this change is so dramatic that it creates an imbalance between or threatens the normal evolution of other basic societal institutions, then perhaps a revolution has occurred. But when change is consistent with, follows from, or is compatible with other societal changes, then we can say evolutionary change has occurred. It is undoubtedly this latter form of social change that has occurred with regard to human sexual behavior during the last couple of decades in North America (Spanier, 1978).

Whichever it is—evolution or revolution—it is on a broader base and permeates farther into our total way of life than we might realize. It involves everything we think, know, or do about sex. But there is no conclusive evidence that the evolution has occurred in all areas at the same rate or to the same degree. People adhere to, accept, or resist a multiplicity of ideas, standards, and ways of life. Ours is a diverse society. This is no more apparent in any aspect of American life than it is in the area of sex. Perhaps one of the most important results, if not the most important result, of sexual evolution is the growing, but not yet universal, acceptance of this fact of diversity. Difference is tolerated, even encouraged. Experimentation is looked upon not as a threat to established ways, but rather as a seeking after new and better ways.

In this sense there is a "new morality." It is a morality of freedom of choice rather than a morality of conformity. Of course, freedom of choice necessarily involves definition, limitation, and responsibility, for unless our own freedom of choice is prevented from injuring others and from depriving others of *their* freedom of choice, ultimately freedom of choice ceases to exist; no one has it. Perhaps this is the crux of the problem of the new morality. The solution cannot be found in law, moralizing, preachment, rebellion, rule making, forceful restraint, or indoctrination. The solution can be found only through awareness of available facts, carefully thought-through personal values, and the acceptance of responsibility for one's individual behavior. Unless freedom of choice is based on an understanding of the alternatives from which choice is to be made, it cannot be truly free. The fact that American society is pluralistic does not imply that the individual is without a point of view. It implies only that he or she works out his or her own point of view; one does not accept it ready-made from others.

The "Revolutionary" Kinsey Studies

Alfred Kinsey and his associates at the Institute for Sex Research published what are considered to be the most important, as well as the most controversial, studies on sexual behavior ever conducted. The volumes *Sexual Behavior in the Human Male*, published in 1948 (Kinsey, Pomeroy, and Martin, 1948), and *Sexual Behavior in the Human Female*, published in 1953 (Kinsey, Pomeroy, Martin, and Gebhard, 1953), generated a great deal of discussion in the mass media and the professional literature. Social scientists and statisticians debated the sampling methods, the significance of the findings, and the believability of the study. The public was aghast for many reasons. First, it was the first time a complete study of the sexual lives of thousands of persons had been conducted and published. But more important was that most readers were surprised by many of the data on the variety and extent of sexual behavior before, during, and after marriage of the 16,000 or so persons who were interviewed between 1938 and 1950. Kinsey and his colleagues found that masturbation was nearly universal among males and involved a majority of females. They found that 37 percent of adult men had one homosexual experience to orgasm, and 19 percent of the females had a sexual contact with another female. They found that childhood sex play was much more common than everyone thought, involving 70 percent of all males and 48 percent of all females. Premarital intercourse was experienced by 92 percent of all men and 50 percent of all women. Fifty percent of married men and 26 percent of married women had had extramarital sexual intercourse, and, for males especially, there were more than trivial amounts of sexual contacts leading to orgasm during childhood, in early adolescence, with animals, and with prostitutes.

We do not wish to debate the merits of Kinsey's findings here, nor do we need to review in detail the hundreds of findings which emerged from the research. Rather, it is worthwhile to note that coincidentally with the release of Kinsey's studies and the social changes brought about by the post–World War II period of industrialization, the advent of television, and the proliferation of movies, sexuality became a more open topic for discussion. It is not known how much influence the Kinsey studies had on the emergence of sexuality into the mass media, but they certainly had some impact. Americans became more aware of the extent of some sexual practices and became increasingly willing to talk about them. However, as persons came to talk more and more about sex, many also came to the conclusion that there was actually more and more of it occurring.

Many factors tended to reinforce the belief that the incidence of premarital intercourse had increased. There was an assumption that changes in attitude toward sex must necessarily reflect changes in behavior. Sometimes changes in attitude follow changes in behavior, and sometimes the reverse is true. Sometimes attitude changes without any changes in behavior, and vice versa.

Attitudes toward homosexuality have changed without any demonstrable change in the incidence of homosexuality. Acceptance of a given type of behavior may neither reflect nor produce changes in that behavior.

Freedom of discussion of sex has increased public awareness of various types of sexual activity. But discussion of the phenomenon is not the phenomenon itself. As Reiss (1966b) says, "What has been going on less openly for some decades becomes known and is thought to be new."

The mass media did their share to contribute to the belief that premarital intercourse was increasing. Sex is a marketable commodity, a salable product. The media have not failed to notice this. Kennedy (1972) says, "This is the best-reported revolution in history." The mass media often function like a lens, dissecting out and magnifying small groups and making them appear to be entire populations. Some popular writers are knowledgeable and endeavor to present the facts. Others are more articulate and assertive than they are informed. Some are not aware of many of the studies that have been conducted or what they may indicate, and as a result they are prone to make broad generalizations and draw premature conclusions. Some will write almost anything that will assure sale of their wares.

It appears now that the sexual "revolution" that so many persons thought they were witnessing in the 1950s and early 1960s was really more of a revolution in attitudes, values, and openness about sexuality in the society. There is no evidence to suggest that there was any major shift in actual sexual behavior during those years. There were some studies before Kinsey's, and there have been many since. These studies give us some insight into sexuality and social change. Let us now review these studies and then reexamine the question of changes in premarital sexual behavior over time.

PREMARITAL SEXUAL INTERCOURSE

Most of us are aware that the nature of premarital sexual behavior has changed in the last few years. But this is one area where something more than observation and perception is needed, because, of necessity, both observation and perception are limited. What we need are facts. Are there any known facts? If so, what are they? It is sometimes assumed that the major aspect of the sexual "revolution" is an increased incidence of premarital intercourse. Is such intercourse more widespread, more common than it used to be? What do available research data indicate?

Various studies arrive at different conclusions relative to the incidence of premarital intercourse. With considerable condensation and oversimplification to permit presenting them in tabular form, the findings of available research in premarital sexual intercourse are summarized in Exhibit 5-1.

If at least part of the conclusion regarding the incidence of premarital intercourse is to be based on studies such as these, it behooves us to take a close and critical look at the statistics reported. It must be admitted, of course, that in the area of sexual activity getting facts is extremely difficult. Investigators who have laboriously gathered the reported statistics have made a genuine contribution to understanding. But these statistics do not constitute the last word on premarital intercourse.

The figures presented in these studies represent *cumulative incidence*, that is, the percentage of a given sample that *ever* had premarital intercourse. In those studies in which married persons were included, *ever* means just that, namely, up to the time of marriage. But relative to never-married persons in a study, *ever* means up to the time of the study, because some such persons may have premarital intercourse after the time of the study but before marriage. Some of these figures, then, reflect experience only through junior high school, high school, or college. Compared with cumulative incidence there is *active incidence*, that is, the percentage of a given sample *currently* having premarital intercourse. To aid in clarifying the distinction between cumulative and active incidence, let us apply the concepts to the occurrence of measles. If a large number of people, say, a good-sized college class, were asked whether they had ever had measles, the great majority would probably report that they had. But this, being cumulative incidence, would not indicate that there was a current measles epidemic (active incidence). In a similar way the cumulative incidence for premarital intercourse cannot tell us what is currently going on.

Many of the incidence statistics do not include certain qualifying considerations that are important in evaluating sexual behavior. Such behavior cannot be measured simply by counting the number who report that they are no longer virgins. Ascertaining the percentage of virgins tells us little, if anything, about current sexual practices.

Some studies indicate characteristics of the sample such as age of respondents, class differences, race, whether the subjects were students or nonstudents, what proportion were married, and so on. Other studies do not make these distinctions. College students are not a completely homogeneous group. Those in large urban universities, small colleges, religious schools, private colleges, and so on may exhibit different behavior. Note, for example, the differences indicated by Christensen and Gregg in Exhibit 5-1 for Midwestern and Mountain state students.

Whatever may be the incidence statistics, the nature of the groups, or the methodology employed in various studies, "counting cases" is an inadequate and incomplete way of evaluating premarital intercourse; and compar-

Marriage Preparation and Partner Selection

Exhibit 5-1 Incidence of premarital intercourse as reported by various investigators. (Dates in most cases, except where two studies by the same researchers are compared, are those of publication of the data, since the research often extended over several years.)

DATE	INVESTIGATOR	NATURE OF SAMPLE	PERCENT OF SAMPLE REPORTING INTERCOURSE MALES	FEMALES
1915	Exner	518 college students	36	
1923	Peck and Wells	180 college-level	35	
1925	Peck and Wells	230 college-level	35	
1929	Davis	1,200 college-level		11
		1,000 college-level and high school–level		7
1929	Hamilton	100 male college-level, 100 female college-level	54	35
1934	Dickinson and Beam	350 college-level and high school–level		12
1938	Terman	792 college-level and high school–level (couples)	61	37
1938	Bromely and Britten	470 male college students, 618 female college students	52	25
1938	Peterson	419 college students	55	
1940	Landis et al.	109 college-level and high school–level		23
		44 college-level and high school–level		27
1946	Porterfield and Salley	285 male college students, 328 female college students	32	9
1947	Finger	111 college students	45	
1947	Hohman and Schaffner	1,000 college students	68	
1948	Kinsey et al.	5,300 (total)	92	
		3,471 college-level	67	
1950	Ross	95 college students	51	
1951	Gilbert Youth Research	college students	56	25
1953	Kinsey et al.	5,940 (total)		50
		4,457 college-level		60
1953	Burgess and Wallin	580 males, 604 females	68	47
1953	Clark	113 females given pelvic exam		60
1953	Landis and Landis	600 male college students, 1,000 female college students	41	9
1954	Reevy	139 college students		7
1958	Christensen and Gregg	94 male college students, 74 female college students (Mountain states)	39	10

Exhibit 5-1 (Continued)

DATE	INVESTIGATOR	NATURE OF SAMPLE	PERCENT OF SAMPLE REPORTING INTERCOURSE	
			MALES	FEMALES
		213 male college students, 142 female college students (Midwestern)	51	21
1958	Bell and Chaskes	250 college students		
		(dating)		10
		(going steady)		15
		(engaged)		31
1959	Ehrmann	841 college students	65	13
1960	Kanin	177 wives of college students, with future husband		44
1965	Yankowski	245 males, 255 females	81	57
1965	Robinson et al.	129 male college students, 115 female college students	65	29
1967	Freedman	49 college seniors		22
1967	Elias	5,001 male college-level, 4,514 female college-level (white)	72	53
		1,075 male non-college-level, 1,247 female non-college-level (white)	60	79
		499 male, 494 female (nonwhite)	94	82
1967	Kaats and Davis	239 male college students, 319 female college students	60	41
1968	Christensen and Gregg	115 male college students, 105 female college students (Mountain states)	37	32
		245 male college students, 238 female college students (Midwestern)	50	34
1968	Bell and Chaskes	205 college students		
		(dating)		23
		(going steady)		28
		(engaged)		39
1968	Packard	665 male college students, 728 female college students	57	43
1968	Katz	47 male college students, 39 female college students	36	23
		41 male college students, 39 female college students	39	26
1969	Carns	593 male college students, 584 female college students (national probability sample)		
		freshmen	36	19

Marriage Preparation and Partner Selection

Exhibit 5-1 (Continued)

DATE	INVESTIGATOR	NATURE OF SAMPLE	PERCENT OF SAMPLE REPORTING INTERCOURSE	
			MALES	FEMALES
		sophomores	62	30
		juniors	60	37
		seniors	68	44
1969	Peretti	298 males, 367 females	50	20
1970	Robinson et al.	137 male college students, 158 female college students	65	37
1970	Merit	10,560 male high school students, 11,440 female high school students	18	15
1971	Merit	11,730 male high school students, 11,279 female high school students	22	19
1971	Fujita et al.	163 male college students, 283 female college students	46	31
1972	Eastman	98 male college students, 88 female college students	55	49
1972	Lehtinen	472 male college students, 484 female college students since entering university	67	51
1972	Zelnik and Kantner	4,240 never-married		
		at age 15		28
		by age 19		14
				46
		371 married		60
1973	Sorensen	222 males, 189 females, aged 13–19	59	45
1973	Bell and Balter	2,372 married females		65
1974	Hunt	982 males, 1,044 females, by age 17, eventual		
		college	50	
		noncollege	75	
		by age 17, married		20
		nonmarried		33
		by age 25, married		50
		never married		75
1974	Vener and Stewart	junior high school and high school males and females in 1970 and 1973		
		1970: 989 males, 924 females	28	16
		1973: 937 males, 1,035 females	33	22
		By age 17	34	35
1975	Lubin-Finkle and Finkle	421 male high school students	69	

Exhibit 5-1 (Continued)

DATE	INVESTIGATOR	NATURE OF SAMPLE	PERCENT OF SAMPLE REPORTING INTERCOURSE	
			MALES	FEMALES
1975	Levin and Levin	100,000 females		
		married before 1965		69
		married 1964-1969		81
		married 1970-1973		89
		married after 1973		93
1977	Zelnik and Kantner	1886 never married females (national probability sample)		
		by age 15		18
		by age 16		25
		by age 17		41
		by age 18		45
		by age 19		55

ing incidences in different time periods falls short of "telling the whole story." "Why?" and "What did it mean to the persons involved?" are even more important than "How many?" Sexual intercourse is not a simple uniform experience that may be assumed to be the same wherever, however, and with whatever frequency it occurs.

Actually it may be assumed to be different and highly individualized for each pair of participants. Consider the differences between the following: a commercialized contact in which a male visits a prostitute; promiscuous contacts; two adolescents experimenting; casual contact in which a couple have intercourse hardly knowing each other or with one or both under the influence of alcohol or other drugs; the relationship between two people who share the same permissive point of view and believe that "sex for fun" is ample reason for having intercourse at any time with any acceptable partner; and the experience of a couple in love who plan to marry. There are innumerable variations such as these that make lumping them together in a statistical study, in which items are merely counted, less meaningful. It is difficult, if not impossible, to include and evaluate all such factors in a research study and even more difficult to include them in such a way that differences between the present and the past may be elucidated.

What Are The Recent Trends?

The data show that premarital sexual intercourse has been characteristic of a significant portion of the population from the time of the first studies on the subject. It is obvious through literature that it has always existed in America, although it has never been possible to ascertain precisely how widespread it has been at any given time. Premarital intercourse has always been more common for men than women, indicating that some of the women who do have premarital sexual intercourse account for the sexual experiences of many men. Most women, however, report fewer partners than do men. The best evidence available suggests that there was no significant increase in premarital sexual behavior during the fifty-year period beginning around World War I. Almost every study since the mid 1960s, however, indicates a rather significant and consistent increase since then. The increase applies to both males and females, but it has been more dramatic among females. Virtually all married men in contemporary America have had premarital intercourse, but the experience of females has traditionally been more limited. The "catching-up" phenomenon that can be observed among females is to be expected in a time of greater sexual freedom, women's liberation, and increasing equality between the genders.

In the past ten to fifteen years, then, it appears that the cumulative incidence of premarital sexual intercourse has increased in the United States. This trend can be expected to continue, we believe, since increased equality between males and females will be likely to result in still more similarities in the nature and extent of male and female sexual behavior. It is not likely that females will seek or have as much experience as males in the near future, but the gap may be expected to decrease further. There is some agreement that most of the increase can be attributed to individuals having sexual relations with persons to whom they are emotionally committed or with whom they are in love. A smaller portion of the increase involves individuals having sexual contacts promiscuously or with casual dates (Cannon and Long, 1971). There is other, indirect evidence for the recent trend in premarital sexual behavior. There has been a marked rise in the venereal disease rate, especially among young people; the number of illegitimate births has increased; unmarried women are obtaining more abortions; a growing number of women are requesting oral contraceptives; and the incidence of nonmarital cohabitation has increased dramatically.

Summary of Research Findings

There have been dozens of studies which have given social scientists some insight into the process leading to sexual intercourse before marriage: differences between males and females, blacks and whites, low and high social classes, college students and nonstudents; how sexual experience is related to sexual socialization, sex education, parental influence, religiosity; and the consequences of premarital sexual intercourse for the individual. We cannot review all of these studies, but let us summarize some of the key findings which have emerged from a few recent studies and reviews (Kinsey, Pomeroy, and Martin, 1948; Kinsey, Pomeroy, Martin, and Gebhard, 1953; Ehrman, 1959; Reiss, 1960; Reiss, 1967; Sorensen, 1973; Zelnik and Kantner, 1972; Carns, 1969, 1973; Spanier, 1973, 1976a, 1976c, 1976f; Cannon and Long, 1971). We must point out that not all studies agree; therefore, we shall include findings about which there is some agreement. It must also be noted that these findings are tendencies found in research involving large samples. Not every individual in every study fits the conclusion reported. These statements, then, reflect what exists for a majority, but not all, of the respondents. There is a great deal of variation from person to person.

▶ There are significant differences between males and females. Males tend to have their first sexual experience at an earlier age. Their first partner is more likely to be a pickup or casual date than is a female's first partner. A female's first partner is more likely to be someone to whom she is seriously committed or with whom she is in love. The first intercourse is less likely to be planned among men, and less likely to be discussed if planned ahead of time among men. Men are more likely to report that they enjoyed their first sexual experience than are women. They are less likely to do it again with their first partner, they talk about it sooner, tell more people, and are more likely to receive an approving reaction from the persons they tell. They tell their parents more often than females do. They have a greater frequency, they have more partners before they are married, and they report less guilt about having had sexual intercourse than females do (Carns, 1973).

▶ Every study analyzing racial differences demonstrates that blacks tend to begin sexual intercourse sooner, and more participate before marriage. In a study of a national sample of several thousand females, for example, 40 percent of the white females had had sexual intercourse by age 19, whereas over 80 percent of black females had already had intercourse (Zelnik and Kantner, 1972). Contrary to a widespread belief, however, blacks do not have more sexual partners than whites. About 60 percent of teenage Americans who have had sexual intercourse have had only one partner. Among the 40 percent who have had more than one partner, however, the data suggest that white nonvirgins have sex more frequently than blacks and have more partners (Zelnik and Kantner, 1972).

▶ A number of studies have demonstrated that religiosity—but not religion—is related to premarital sexual behavior. The more religious a person is, the less likely he or she is to have coitus before marriage. Those with weaker religiosity—as measured by devoutness, belief in God, attendance at church services or activities, etc.—are more likely to have premarital coitus. A person's religious affiliation is unrelated to premarital sexual activity. In other words, it does not seem to matter whether one is a Catholic, Protestant, or Jew (Spanier, 1973; Cannon and Long, 1971).

▶ Premarital sexual intercourse begins earlier and is more likely to have occurred among persons of lower socioeconomic groups. In other words, the lower the social class, the higher the cumulative incidence (Kinsey, Pomeroy, and Martin, 1948; Kinsey, Pomeroy, Martin, and Gebhard, 1953; Ehrman, 1959).

▶ Physical attractiveness is related to the incidence of premarital coitus. The most attractive individuals have the greatest number of sexual partners (Kaats and Davis, 1970).

▶ The greater the emotional attachment to a partner, the greater the likelihood that premarital intercourse will occur. A number of studies have demonstrated that dating frequency, emotional commitment to the partner, engagement, love, and length of acquaintance are all factors associated with premarital intercourse. In short, the more involved one becomes with a person, the more likely it is that this involvement will include sexual intercourse (Spanier, 1973, 1976a, 1972c; Reiss, 1967; Cannon and Long, 1971; Ehrman, 1959).

▶ Age is an obvious correlate of premarital sexual behavior. The older one gets, the more years there are in which to have had premarital intercourse. Thus, when age is considered, we find, for example, that individuals who do not marry until they have reached their middle or late twenties have a greater cumulative incidence of premarital intercourse than persons who married in their early twenties. This finding is sometimes misinterpreted, since young persons of today have sexual intercourse more often than young persons of a decade or two ago, and subsequently the passage of time is easily confused with the passage of age.

▶ Education has been shown to be negatively related to premarital sexual intercourse. That is, the higher the level of educational attainment, the less likely a person is to have coitus before marriage. College students have a lower cumulative incidence of sexual intercourse than do high school graduates, who have a lower incidence than persons who have not finished high school. Although the differences appear to be diminishing somewhat in recent years, Kinsey and his associates found that among men, 67 percent of those with a college education had premarital intercourse, whereas 84 percent of those with a high school degree and 98 percent of those with only a grade school education had sexual intercourse before marriage. This difference, however, was not characteristic of the women studied (Kinsey, Pomeroy, and Martin, 1948; Kinsey, Pomeroy, Martin, and Gebhard, 1953).

Sexual Standards

Every person has a sexual standard. This standard may change during a person's life. Individuals often begin with a more restrictive standard—one which instructs us that sex is to be reserved for marriage. Yet one may then develop a new standard, perhaps after falling in love or coming to college, which permits him or her to have sexual intercourse before marriage in certain circumstances. Reiss (1960) differentiates between two types of sex: *Body-centered* sex has its emphasis on the physical nature of sex, and *person-centered* sex has its emphasis on the emotional relationship between the individuals who are engaged in the sex act. Furthermore, *individuals* may be classified according to one of four sexual standards:

1 *Abstinence.* Premarital intercourse is wrong for both men and women, regardless of circumstances.

2 *Permissiveness with affection.* Premarital intercourse is right for both men and women, as long as there is emotional attachment, love, or strong affection.

3 *Permissiveness without affection.* Premarital intercourse is right for both men and women whenever there is physical attraction, regardless of whether affection is present.

4 *Double standard.* Premarital intercourse is considered right for men but wrong for women.

Sociologists have debated whether the double standard or the abstinence standard was dominant throughout modern Western history. Even though it has always been stated, since the emergence of Christianity, that abstinence was the norm, it is certainly true that it was never fully practiced. It is probably correct to say that, until recently, abstinence has been the culturally approved standard, whereas the double standard existed in reality for a significant portion, perhaps a majority, of the population. Today, most young persons adhere to a permissiveness-with-affection standard, although it is likely that the commitment necessary for "affection" has been relaxed somewhat in recent years. The double standard is on its way out, although remnants of it must surely still be around, since male-female differences continue to be evident. The abstinence standard is reported by many young persons, although it appears that this standard is replaced by one of the permissiveness standards sometime before marriage for a majority of American youth. A minority of persons adhere to the abstinence standard, particularly those of strong religious conviction and those under strict parental influence.

The permissiveness–without–affection standard has never been dominant. It probably involves only a small portion of the population, but is undoubtedly increasing. There have been many times in history when young people were accused of advocating "free love" and sexual promiscuity. In the 1950s such persons were called "beatniks" in the mass media. In the 1960s they were called "hippies" and "yippies." In the 1970s, they are known as "freaks." Whatever the term applied, it is incorrect to conclude that young people have ever held one universal standard. And the permissiveness–without–affection standard never ran rampant. There are a variety of sexual standards among American youth, and our society is becoming increasingly willing to allow each individual to choose his or her own standard.

One study of the moral judgments of college students found that there were six categories of sexual philosophy which could be identified on a campus (D'Augelli, 1972). These categories are not really sexual standards, as are those mentioned above, but rather are descriptions of the sexual experiences or potential for sexual experience found in a given setting (D'Augelli, 1972; D'Augelli and Cross, 1975):

1 *Inexperienced Virgins.* These individuals usually have little dating experience until college. Their dating relationships have not been serious or involved. They have not thought much about sex, the relationship they desire, or about themselves. They may be moralistic about sex, although not necessarily. They have a close relationship with their parents and do not want to hurt them. Their sexual experience has usually been kissing, necking or light petting.

2 *Adamant Virgins.* These individuals are set in their idea that intercourse should be saved for marriage: "Virginity is a gift for the spouse" is a predominant theme. However, they may say that premarital intercourse is permissible for others—it is up to the individual. They say that they do not feel guilty about light or heavy petting but say they would feel guilty about going further. They often attribute control to the partner and presently pet with someone special. They do not usually confine themselves to one partner. There is a sense that the marriage license is important in assuring that the partner is the "right" one. Their family or religion is often mentioned as directly influencing their sexual views.

3 *Potential Nonvirgins.* These individuals often say that given the right situation, they would have intercourse. They say that they have not yet been in the right situation and/or have not yet met the right person. They feel that premarital intercourse is morally acceptable, but they have a high fear of pregnancy. They seem to want more security than they have in their present relationships, at least at the point of development in the relationship, and the ideas of commitment of some sort and love are important to them. They seem frustrated by their cautiousness or inconsistency.

4 *Engaged [or Committed] Nonvirgins.* These individuals have had intercourse usually with one person only, although not necessarily. This person is usually considered someone very much loved and may be the fiancé(e). Often, marriage or some future commitment is mentioned, but the important thing in justifying the sexual behavior is the love and commitment to the relationship between the partners. The relationship is described as very close and very important, and the development of that relationship is of high value to them. They usually have discussed sex with their partner. Morality is considered an individual's personal concern.

5 *Liberated Nonvirgins.* These individuals engage in sex in a freer way than others. They have a freer, looser life style and are not interested in the security of the relationship as much as in the relationship itself. Sex within the context of the meaning of the relationship is important, and what is stressed is the agreed-upon meaning for the two partners. The physical act itself is valued for its pleasure. Reciprocal pleasure-giving as well as other reciprocities are important.

6 *Confused Nonvirgins.* These individuals engage in sex without real understanding of their motivation, the place of sex in their lives, or its effects on them. There is usually some ambivalence about having had intercourse under these circumstances, especially if there have been many partners. The relationships between them and their partners gradually terminate. They seem generally confused about themselves and may be characterized as having a diffuse identity. Sex is seen as a pleasure and a need; it also seems to be the means to an end, an attempt to establish relationships.

Male and Female Orientation

There are females who enjoy intercourse for its own sake, just as males do, but there are fewer females who do so than males. Generalizing, the female is more likely to be interested in intercourse when she has a meaningful relationship with the male, especially if she believes that she and he are in love. For example, as a result of his research Reiss (1970a, 1970b) says, "The factor that most decisively motivated women to engage in coitus and approve of coitus was belief that they were in love." "Romantic love led more women than men to be permissive" (Reiss, 1970b). Ehrmann (1959) says that females are more concerned with romanticism, while males are more concerned with eroticism. He states that the difference is "so marked that there are distinct male and female subcultures." Bardwick (1971) says that females tend to engage in sex for love and for the sake of the male. A woman's primary motive for having sexual intercourse "is not the gratification of her own genital sexuality but the gratification of the male and the securing of his love" (Bardwick, 1970). Bernard (1972a) says that females want caresses, tenderness, sexual appreciation, and the interested attention of men, and that "if they had their own way, most would not feel compelled to seek genital sex relations." Reiss and Ehrmann are men; Bardwick and Bernard are women.

Methodological Problems

All studies of premarital sexual intercourse to date entail methodological problems of one sort or another. This is not necessarily an indication of carelessness on the part of the researcher; in many instances it is a built-in limitation of the study of sexual activity. Sampling is a perennial problem in social research. Reference to Exhibit 5-1 will readily indicate the wide range of samples; some samples, for example, were college classes, while others were people living in a given community; sample sizes vary greatly; and there is an overweighting of college students and college-level individuals. College classes are "captive" groups and are hardly random samples, since selection has already occurred when students enter college.

A special type of sampling error may creep into this kind of research. Unless great caution is exercised in designing the method of research, there is the possibility that students most amenable to answering a questionnaire on sex will be those contacted or those who most readily volunteer.

Even the most carefully conducted research studies of premarital sex are unavoidably based upon recall, that is, on the ability and the willingness of individuals questioned to remember and accurately report previous sexual activity. Some individuals are inclined to overreport, some to underreport.

How much credence, for example, can be given to the following report sent to one of the authors by a male student? Shall we interpret it as a statement of fact, a tongue-in-cheek attempt to shock a professor, or boasting by an insecure male who substitutes wishful thinking for reality?

I am a twenty-one-year-old senior. I belong to a social fraternity and maintain a B average. I participate actively in intramural sports and some campus activities. To the best of my knowledge, I have dated 97 girls. (I am excluding those I may have dated only once.) I have had sexual intercourse with 64 of these. Of the 33 others, I have dated 17 of them only twice, 8 three times, 1 four, 3 five, 3 six, and 1 seven times. I had sexual intercourse the first time when I was fourteen years old. The total number of times since then ranges between 950 and 1,100. Frequency has been relatively the same for the past five years, namely, three or four times per week. In the past year, however, intercourse has been limited to the same six girls. I have been pinned during this time; consequently I have not been dating in the general sense of the word. I have generally dated girls from better families. Most of them have been popular students. The most numerous incidents of sexual intercourse with one girl is about 100; the least is eight. I have never had intercourse with a prostitute.

There is not always consistency between what we say we believe we should do, what we actually do, and what we report we do. Years ago C. Wright Mills (1940) pointed out that discrepancies between talk and action constituted the central methodological problem in social science. "Often there is a disparity," he said, "between lingual and social-motor types of behavior." In the last analysis, all studies of premarital sexual intercourse are based on subjective reports, not objective facts. Objective data are not produced by the alchemy of quantifying subjective data.

The studies provide useful insights. They present a more helpful picture of cumulative incidence than of active incidence. The result is that while the picture of cumulative incidence is incomplete, the picture of active incidence is sketchy indeed. Some of the studies document and corroborate what experienced counselors have long suspected.

SEXUAL SOCIALIZATION AND PREMARITAL SEXUAL BEHAVIOR

In recent years there has been a controversy about whether sex education in the public schools encourages premarital sexual behavior. This policy-related question is part of a larger one which social scientists have also been interested in recently: What is the process that eventually leads to premarital intercourse? Do parents play a part? Do the mass media have an influence? Do magazines, X-rated movies, or pornography play a part? What about pressures from friends or dating partners? There are now some research data to help answer these questions (Spanier, 1973, 1976*a*, 1977*a*, 1977*b*).

Data obtained during interviews with a national sample of about 1200 college students were grouped into three categories:

1 Formal sex education—sex education taught within school classrooms, for example in health, biology, physical education, or family relations classes.

2 Informal sex education—sex information obtained from family members, peer groups, or other sources. Examples of informal sex education are a girl who has seen an older man expose himself, two children who are "playing doctor," an adolescent who discovers that touching his or her genitals is pleasurable, and a high school student who reads a *Playboy* magazine.

3 Dating experiences—frequency of dates, degree of closeness to persons dated, total amount of dating experience, and pressures and influences associated with dating.

The findings of the study showed that of all three types of influences, dating experiences were the most influential in explaining the nature and extent of premarital sexual behavior. Persons who had a greater dating frequency, were more emotionally involved with the partners they dated, and had the most extensive dating history had the most active sex lives. Informal sex education experiences were not as strongly related to a person's sexual behavior, and formal sex education was least related of all.

These findings suggested that it is the *context* of the person's involvement at the present time which is most influential. What the person was taught when growing up does not seem to be as important as what is happening in that person's life at the moment. For example, parents who were very strict and conservative about sexual matters and taught their children accordingly did not have as great an influence as the pressures from a current dating partner. Religiosity at present was more important than religiosity while growing up. Attendance in sex education classes did not seem to influence sexual behavior one way or another, regardless of when the course was taken, what kind of class it was, who taught it, and whether coitus or birth control was specifically mentioned. (This finding should allay the fears of some persons critical of sex education.) Exposure to erotic materials was related to greater sexual activity, but it is probable that exposure to erotic materials and sexual behavior are correlated, but not causally related. In other words, they both seem to be an increasingly likely occurrence but one cannot be attributed as the cause of the other. This research suggests that the pressures and influences an individual faces in a given relationship can be powerful enough to outweigh all other teaching to the contrary.

These findings also suggest that many young persons go through a great personal struggle in deciding how to reconcile values acquired from parents and others while growing up with pressures from peers or partners, one's own sexual interest and sex drive, and the expectations that one may perceive exist for sexual performance in a given situation.

How, then, does the process work? It appears that sexual behavior occurs in stepwise fashion. An individual starts with hand-holding. He or she then moves on to kissing, light petting, heavy petting, and finally sexual intercourse. The speed with which one moves through these stages varies from time to time and from person to person, and it depends on one's emotional involvement, pressures from peers and partners, and one's own inclination to advance to the next level. The more time a person spends at one level, the less interesting that activity becomes, and eventually he or she advances to the next. Virtually all couples who have dated for a while kiss each other, but at some point the level of their intimacy advances. There is a complex social-psychological process that determines the rate at which individuals move through these levels. There is a continuous inclination to advance to the next level. Some do so readily. Others prevent themselves from doing so by setting limits on their behavior and adhering to their decision. At some point, then, decisions must be made by the individuals involved about what they feel is appropriate for them.

FREEDOM OF CHOICE

Where does all this discussion leave the reader? Analysis of research findings and of common assumptions may furnish information, provide food for thought, or motivate one to reexamine one's own assumptions. But so far as the reader's own sexual behavior is concerned, the individual still has to make judgments in terms of values and objectives. Even if it were accurately known how many people have premarital intercourse, the reader would still have to make personal decisions. If one concludes that there are forces at work that are beyond control and that will shape attitudes and determine standards for the individual, then the individual has relinquished freedom of choice. Any choice, any decision made, represents a value judgment; it cannot be completely objective. Research may be value-free, but a decision never is. A person who feels something must be done because others are doing it has sacrificed freedom of choice just as much as the individual who refrains from doing something because others have prohibited it.

Students sometimes make generalizations based on limited observations or hearsay. For example, a student says, "All my friends have had premarital intercourse," as if there were a sound basis for generalization. What the individual "knows" about friends' sexual activity is more likely to be what they have reported than what has been observed.

If there is to be freedom of choice regarding premarital intercourse, it must be a choice *among* alternatives, not simply the choice of a given alternative. Some persons think that freedom of choice means only the freedom to *do* something. They forget that it means also the freedom *not* to do that thing. So, when it is suggested that the individual have freedom of choice regarding premarital intercourse, such persons conclude that everyone will choose to have intercourse. But individuals who choose not to have intercourse have exercised freedom of choice, too.

It is part of the nature of human beings to believe in something. One of our continuing problems is to interpret life in terms of meaning. Hence, the individual has the problem of imputing some kind of meaning to premarital intercourse. Sex per se is neither good nor bad, beautiful nor ugly, moral nor immoral. Whether it becomes one or the other of each of these pairs of attributes depends upon how it is used and the meaning imputed to it. The individual has the freedom to choose the type of sexual behavior deemed most suitable. Hence, there can be a commitment to a given pattern of sexual activity. Indeed, there must be a commitment to some pattern of sexual activity since it is humanly impossible to live by all possible patterns simultaneously.

DOUBLE STANDARD

In many aspects of life in this country we are moving toward equality of men and women. In the specifically sexual sphere, however, there are remnants of a double standard. Infidelity is considered by many to be more serious for a wife than for a husband. In cases of premarital pregnancy there tends to be more severe criticism of the woman than of the man. The assumption that males should have more premarital sexual freedom than females is still made by some members of both genders. Some males set up one standard of premarital sexual freedom for themselves, a similar standard for females with whom they have their premarital intercourse, and a standard of premarital chastity for the group of females from which they will choose their wives. Such a position is logically untenable because, if universal, it would result in all females being virgins, in which case no males could have premarital intercourse, or else in all females having premarital intercourse, in which case there would be no virgins to marry. The double standard has always been predicated on the existence of two classes of women; those who do have nonmarital intercourse are either prostitutes or women who have departed from the mainstream of society, and those who do not have intercourse outside of marriage are the "desirable" women whom men wish to marry.

Some individuals interpret present-day practices as movement in the direction of a single standard of premarital sexual freedom for both men and women. Some persons advocate such a standard. Others insist that there should be a single standard of premarital chastity. There is much confused thinking and still more confused assertion on this issue. At some place in the formulation of one's own point of view, each individual must come to some conclusion on this issue if one's philosophy is to be integrated and consistent.

GOAL ORIENTATION

In spite of the fact that some students claim that marriage is no longer necessary or even desirable, and in spite of the fact that some persons choose alternative life-styles, some of which do not involve marriage, most college students expect someday to marry or are already married. We may assume that they want marriage to be successful. What constitutes marital success is determined in part by cultural standards but also in part by the attitudes of the persons involved. At any rate, as already mentioned, it is reasonable to suggest that, in making a decision regarding premarital intercourse, the individuals evaluate it in terms of the most universal objective of marriage which students set for themselves. When this is done, such questions as the following arise: Is premarital intercourse a contribution to the achievement of this objective? Or is it neutral? Or is it an impediment?

Research findings are far from conclusive with regard to the effect of premarital intercourse on marital adjustment (Davis, 1929; Hamilton, 1929; Terman, 1938; Kinsey, Pomeroy, Martin, and Gebhard, 1953; Hamblin and Blood, Jr., 1956; Kanin and Howard, 1958; Kirkendall, 1961). The reasons for this inconclusiveness are the difficulty of getting the data and of separating the variables involved. Premarital intercourse can affect a marriage only insofar as the two persons with their particular attitudes react to it. It is also difficult to determine cause and effect. For example, if more women who have had premarital intercourse than women who have not had such intercourse are sexually responsive in marriage, does this indicate that premarital intercourse increases responsiveness or that responsive women are more likely to have premarital intercourse (Kinsey, Pomeroy, Martin, and Gebhard, 1953)?

Whatever the research findings may be, only the individuals involved can decide whether premarital intercourse fits into the pattern of attitudes and values upon which they expect to build their own marriage. Both successful and unsuccessful couples are to be found among those who had premarital intercourse as well as among those who did not. So the fact of intercourse alone cannot be considered a determining factor.

DO MALES OR FEMALES NEED SEXUAL INTERCOURSE?

The question, "Do males or females want sexual intercourse?" is very different from the question, "Do they *need* it?" The word "need" has a variety of definitions. Sometimes it is used to mean "require"—for example, "I need food." Sometimes it is used to mean "want urgently"—for example, "I need a new car." Which meaning describes sexual drive? Masters and Johnson (1970) say that "sexual functioning . . . has a unique facility that no other natural physiological process . . . can imitate. *Sexual responsivity can be delayed indefinitely or functionally denied for a lifetime*" (Masters and Johnson's italics). Kaplan (1974), a counselor of wide experience, says "A person can survive indefinitely without any sexual release at all." This would seem to put it into a class with "need" for a car rather than "need" for food—in short, to consider it as an urgent want rather than a necessity, a "felt need" rather than an actual need.

Whether one believes that he or she has an actual need or a felt need (an urgent want) for sexual intercourse, this belief is likely to affect decision making. If a person believes he or she has an actual need and that unless this need is met there will be dire consequences, then from this person's point of view seeking intercourse becomes a form of self-preservation. Pressuring a reluctant female to have intercourse because a male needs it becomes, to him, acceptable procedure. If he believes he has an urgent want and failure to satisfy it will not result in dire consequences, then pressuring a female to have intercourse takes on a different color. Perhaps the basic questions are: What controls whom? Who controls what? Does sex control the individual, or does the individual control sex?

EFFECT ON THE RELATIONSHIP BETWEEN MAN AND WOMAN

When intercourse occurs with a prostitute, the relationship between the male and the female is already defined. When the intercourse is over, the relationship is terminated. The relationship is not meaningful and holds little, if any, possibility of becoming so. But when intercourse occurs between two persons who are eligible as marriage partners or who have an emotional response to one another or an emotional investment in each other, the possible effect of the intercourse on the relationship, present or future, becomes a consideration.

In spite of the fact that there is increasing acceptance of premarital intercourse, there are also people who do not accept it. Some men and women still insist on virginity in the persons they marry. Some women accept instances of premarital intercourse with other women on the part of their husbands only with reluctance and the somewhat cynical attitude that "that is the way men are" and women cannot do anything about it. The question is not whether it is justifiable for people to maintain such attitudes. The realistic question is, "Can a person be happy in marriage with an individual who does maintain such attitudes?" Withholding knowledge of premarital intercourse from the other person until after the wedding or having that person learn of it indirectly has been known to be more traumatic than the fact of the intercourse itself because of the reflection on mutual trust.

Kirkendall (1961), in doing research on college males, found that some of them had a poignant regret for having intercourse with one woman and in so doing felt they had let down another woman, for example, a fiancée. Sometimes premarital intercourse tends to separate a couple when they assumed it would strengthen their relationship. In some cases the relationship does seem to be strengthened by intercourse. This may actually occur, or it may be, as Kirkendall (1961) suggests, that the intercourse does not damage a relationship that is already strong.

Sometimes the relationship is one-sided because the male seeks only his own sexual release, with little if any thought for the female and her feelings and frustrations. For her it seems to be all "give" and for him all "take." This depersonalizes a relationship that should be very personal. It seems to the woman that, instead of being wanted for all her personal qualities, she is wanted only because she is female. As one woman said after a fourth man had invited her to spend the night in his apartment, "I was beginning to think that nobody cared about *me*."

The relationship may also be one-sided if the male seeks intercourse to "prove" that he is a "real man." If he actually believes that intercourse is a valid test of manliness, he may feel better after he passes the test, even though he has had no concern for the woman and has considered her only as a means to an end. Surely being a "real man" includes more than the ability to copulate.

As mentioned earlier, females are more apt to combine sex and love, while males more readily separate them. Hence, the female may have intercourse because she feels she loves the male. Therefore, *ipso facto*, since he suggested intercourse, it must indicate that he loves her. She mistakenly assumes that his thinking is the same as hers.

There is still another way in which the relationship may be one-sided. The argument is often advanced that if a woman does not want to have intercourse, a man who loves her and respects her will not expect her to do so. To this a counterargument is sometimes expressed to the effect that if a man wants intercourse, a woman who loves him and respects him and is aware of the male's sexual drive will have it with him for his sake rather than her own. What is overlooked in the counterargument is the fact that the man's restraint and the woman's yielding may involve different "costs" which cannot be equated.

If a woman fears that she will lose a man unless she agrees to intercourse, she may have it, in a sense, voluntarily, but she does not have it freely. If he would give her up as a person because he cannot have her as a sexual partner, how highly does he regard her as a person? How much respect does he have for her feelings? Does he have the sort of attitude toward her that she would want in a husband?

The anticipation of male sexual demands may put a woman so on guard that a barrier is put in the way of what otherwise might develop into a sound relationship. Some women express appreciation for a sense of security in dating. They dislike spending a date uneasily wondering when the man is going to make a suggestion regarding intercourse. They prefer to be able to trust the man so that they may relax, knowing that no such suggestion will be made.

The idea that the man might take some responsibility in this respect seems ludicrous to many male college students. On numerous occasions, in groups of male students and in mixed classes, the authors have asked the question: Why don't men set the sexual limits? The question is sometimes greeted with laughter. Of course, some college males do set sexual limits. But many males have the attitude that any woman who will agree to intercourse is fair prey. They interpret their own responsibility as being limited to going no further than the woman wants them to go. They push her to determine where she draws the line, and then usually they abide by it. But if she is willing to have intercourse, they will.

In a word, all this suggests that the issue facing people today is not only one of freedom versus restriction or of preventing pregnancy, but also one of deciding upon what meaning they want to express through sex and how this may best be accomplished.

PETTING

A discussion of premarital sexual freedom would be less than complete without some mention of petting. There are hundreds of terms that apply to physical contact that stops short of sexual intercourse. None of them is specific. Some are picturesque. Some are geographically so highly localized that they are meaningless to persons from other parts of the country. Take, for example, making out, grubbing, hinking, Russian hands and Roman fingers, making like crickets, going to third base, messing around, playing baseball, feeling up. The great variety of such terms is one sidelight on the widespread distribution and frequency of the activity they are designed to describe and indicates, too, the casualness with which this activity is currently accepted. We shall use the term *petting* because it is probably the most widely understood.

We shall define "petting" as physical contact for pleasure as an end in itself, involving some degree of bodily exploration and arising from sexual desire in one or both parties. In petting there is produced an increased sexual sensitivity and response and an increased tension that can be relieved by intercourse or some substitute. In the absence of relief, the tension has a tendency to persist for a time. When a couple's petting includes parts of their bodies ordinarily not exposed, they not only increase the stimulation of one or both but they redefine their relationship. In a sense, every bodily contact contributes a definition of a relationship.

It is unlikely that anyone is seriously hurt by petting per se. It is so common that, if it were hurtful, there would be a continuous epidemic. This does not mean, however, that there are no questions to be asked about it or that there is nothing to be taken into consideration in making decisions regarding the relationships between the genders.

Petting involves strong emphasis on physical stimulation and response. In a study of approximately 500 college females and 400 college males from two large Midwestern state universities, Kanin (1970) found that when "mutually consented erotic involvement has progressed to the genital petting stage," the male may exert "a forceful attempt to bring his companion to coitus." In other words, when there is genital petting, "college men sometimes use physical force" to get intercourse.

It is not uncommon for the sexual tension generated in petting to be relieved by orgasm for the female and orgasm plus ejaculation for the male, instead of its eventuating in intercourse. This sexual tension may also result in pain in the region of the testes in the male, a condition referred to as *orchialgia* or *testalgia*. It is probably referred pain due to congestion in the prostate gland (Cawood, 1971). Such pain is uncomfortable, but it is not dangerous. It tends to disappear in a short time after the stimulation causing the tension ceases, even in the absence of orgasm-ejaculation. Knowledge of the possibility of such pain on the part of the male who has the prospect of it sometimes is used as a lever to persuade a woman to have intercourse for his sake, especially if she does not understand the nature of the pain and fears that it will be harmful to the male. Under similar circumstances of stimulation without release, some females, too, have discomfort due to congestion and tension in the pelvic region. This condition, called *vasocongestion*, is discussed in Chapter 11.

We may guess that with their different orientations toward sex, males more often than females initiate petting (using the term as we have defined it, namely, as involving bodily exploration). Of course, some women initiate petting. Some college women—even in these days of presumed sexual freedom—ask how petting may be prevented. Why do men always want to pet? Why do women always have to fight men off? Why do men always want to put their hands under a woman's clothing? Why do men always want to unfasten a woman's bra? Some women consider such activities, when initiated by men, a violation of their privacy. Men do not have to contend with the kind of behavior that women may consider a problem, or if they do confront it, they consider it not a problem but an opportunity. The different attitudes of the two genders is something that should be taken into account in a particular situation.

THE PROBLEM OF RISK

Serious questions could be raised about an individual who confused freedom to drive a car with freedom from the possibility of accident while driving. One would hesitate to ride with a person who assumes that accidents happen to other people but cannot happen to him or her, or that accidents happen only when they are planned. It is as shortsighted to disregard the risks in premarital intercourse as it is to build a case against it primarily on the basis of risk.

Life entails risk. Some risk is unavoidable, for example, the risk of inhaling harmful bacteria while breathing. Some risk is practically unavoidable, for example, that involved in travel. Other risks are entirely avoidable, for example, the risk involved in intercourse without contraceptive protection. Each individual has, on the one hand, the problem of reducing necessary risk and, on the other hand, that of deciding how much unnecessary risk he or she is willing to undergo. In doing this the person must reach some conclusion as to what possible price may willingly be paid for what possible gain. Since neither the gain nor the price of premarital intercourse can be accurately predicted in advance, one could prove to be out of proportion to the other—like burning a cathedral to fry an egg. Would the end result be the purchase of complex problems with the currency of pleasure, or the purchase of an enriched relationship with the coin of risk? Or would the risk element not be great enough to be given serious attention?

Risk may be considered in two ways: (1) What is the statistical risk, that is, how frequently is it incurred relative to the frequency of premarital intercourse? (2) What is jeopardized if the consequence does occur, and what can be done about it? The individual's problem is not merely the achievement of the scientist's objective understanding of a statistical analysis of a situation, but also the subjective one of evaluating and assimilating what may be a world-shaking, life-encompassing experience, even though the individual may be only one inconspicuous statistic in the overall picture.

In premarital intercourse both parties assume risk. For the woman, the primary risk is pregnancy.

Consequences for Females

At the present stage of knowledge there is no 100 percent perfect contraceptive. Employed with care and intelligence under circumstances conducive to their most efficacious use and based upon the advice of a physician, the better contraceptives assure a reasonable degree of control of conception. Under circumstances not conducive to careful use—for example, where there is haste, inadequate knowledge, or lack of responsibility; when the contraceptive methods used provide a low degree of effectiveness; or if the contraceptives are purchased on the recommendation of drugstore clerks or magazine advertisements—the risk of pregnancy is ever-present.

Neither contraceptive information nor contraceptive devices alone can prevent conception. Information must be applied. Devices must be put to use. There is a not uncommon assumption, even among professional writers, that with the ready availability of effective contraceptives, especially the pill, the risk of premarital pregnancy is no longer a threat. Assuming that all students know about contraceptives is unrealistic. Assuming that if they did know about contraceptives, they would all put that knowledge to work is equally unrealistic, as we shall see.

Knowledge of effective methods of contraception has been available in this country for some time. Yet American women continue to have hundreds of thousands of unwanted pregnancies each year. Technological advance is not a substitute for human responsibility. One indication of this is the number of college and university couples who have premarital intercourse without, or with inadequate, contraceptive protection.

When a woman has a premarital pregnancy, there are three alternatives open to her:

Marry If she was engaged when the pregnancy started and her fiancé is the father of the child, the situation is as favorable as it could be under the circumstances. If she marries a man whom she would not otherwise marry, the marriage gets an inauspicious start. If she marries a man she knows is not the father of the child and does not apprise him of the fact of pregnancy, in some states the man has ground for annulment or divorce should that fact become known after the wedding. At best such a procedure is a serious form of misrepresentation. A woman may, and in some cases does, marry a man who accepts the child even knowing that he is not the father. If a couple have premarital intercourse when they are not ready to marry, will they be more ready to marry if a pregnancy leads them to marry earlier? There is evidence to suggest that marriages entered in order to camouflage a premarital pregnancy may be more than ordinarily unstable. The divorce rate is more than twice as high for those marriages in which a child is born before the marriage than for those marriages in which childbirth occurs after the wedding. The difference in divorce rates is only slight, however, when conception, but not childbirth, occurred before marriage (Grabill, 1976).

Remain unmarried and have the baby She may keep the baby or place it for adoption.

Have an abortion We shall discuss abortion in a later chapter.

Recent data indicate that among unmarried American adolescent women aged 15 to 19 who become pregnant, 20 percent of these pregnancies end in miscarriage, 38 percent in abortion, 29 percent in out-of-wedlock births, and 14 percent in marriage of the mother-to-be (Jaffe and Dryfoos, 1976).

Consequences for Males

An unwanted pregnancy The greatest risk that a man faces is a possible pregnancy for the female. He may disclaim any involvement with her, but in the typical case, men acknowledge their involvement and are affected by the pregnancy. The female carries the greater burden because, after all, she is pregnant and will usually be considered legally responsible for the child. The man, however, may be faced with the expenses of an abortion, a forced marriage, or a wedding which is quickly moved up. Above all, perhaps, he must at a more personal or emotional level deal with the problem he has had a role in creating. But the consequences for the male may be even more severe.

Accusation of rape by force Most cases of rape are violent acts committed by troubled men. However, cases are not unknown in which a woman voluntarily has premarital intercourse, and afterward, because she feels guilty, or because the fact is discovered, or for some other reason, she claims rape (see Macdonald, 1973). Usually there are no witnesses to premarital intercourse. Hence it is the man's word against the woman's. She may not succeed in making her accusation hold up in court. But even after the fire is put out, so to speak, the odor of smoke remains in the air, and there may be people who still wonder whether the man was guilty and justice miscarried. There may be others who wonder what the woman's ulterior motive was. "There is hardly any accusation so easily made and yet so hard to disprove as that of rape" (Graves and Francisco, 1970).

Accusation of statutory rape Typically, state law specifies an "age of consent." This is the minimum age which an unmarried girl must have reached in order legally to give consent to sexual intercourse. If she is below the age of consent, she cannot legally consent to having intercourse even though she voluntarily says the words agreeing to it. A comparable situation is found in an individual's inability to sign a valid legal contract before age 18 or 21 even though his or her name is on the contract form.

Let us assume that in a given state the age of consent is 16. A physically well-developed 15-year-old girl claims to be 17. A 21-year-old man takes her at her word. She voluntarily has sexual intercourse. Her parents discover this fact and make known her correct age. The man with whom the girl had intercourse is liable to prosecution for statutory rape, which constitutes a felony.

Accusation of paternity If a woman becomes pregnant, any man who has had intercourse with her within a given time span is a possible candidate for an accusation of paternity.

Contrary to common assumption, paternity cannot be unequivocably ascertained by means of blood tests. It is true that blood types are hereditary. Blood tests made upon man or men, mother, and child can ascertain whether a given man could or could not be the father. That is not equivalent, however, to determining that a given man *is* the father. For example, suppose Miss X has a child. She admits having had intercourse with three men, namely, A, B, and C. Blood tests are made on all five persons. The tests indicate that Miss X could not have had that child, with its particular blood type, with A or B. She could have had that child with C. That still does not prove beyond all doubt that C is the father. Miss X may not have mentioned D, with whom she also had intercourse and whose blood type is the same as C's.

Blood tests can establish *nonpaternity* as a certainty, but paternity only as a possibility. The scientific definition of "fact" and the legal definition of "fact" are not the same. The former implies certainty, while the latter implies only "beyond a reasonable doubt." The former is based on proof, the latter on evidence. Therefore, "proof" of paternity may reach a level of probability that is acceptable in a court (Krause, 1971).

Pressure to Marry in Case of Acknowledged Paternity

Pressure to marry in such cases may be "external" or "internal." It may come from parents, fear of gossip, or concern for reputation. Or it may come from a sense of responsibility.

If the couple are engaged, there may be no pressure in the usual sense of the term because they plan to marry anyway. Their problem is relatively simpler, involving only actual or asserted change of wedding date. In some cases, however, marrying earlier than they had expected is a serious upset to a couple's families and to their educational and occupational plans.

If, on the other hand, the couple had not planned to marry, would not be good choices as marriage partners for one another, do not know each other well enough, or are not in love, marriage to camouflage a pregnancy or to give a child a legal father and a name may be damaging to all three persons.

Premarital Intercourse with Inadequate Protection

Eighty percent of sexually experienced never-married females aged 15 to 19 indicated in a recent nationwide study that they had engaged in sexual intercourse at some time without using contraception. About three in ten of them became pregnant. Most carried their pregnancies to term and had illegitimate births. The overwhelming majority indicated that the pregnancy had been unintended, but only 13 percent of them reported that they had used any kind of contraception to prevent it (Shah, Zelnik, and Kantner, 1975). Among sexually active white females between 15 and 19, 11 percent have been pregnant at least once. Among teen-age sexually active black females, 51 percent have been pregnant at least once (Shah, Zelnik, and Kantner, 1975). Sorensen (1973), in a sample of 411 individuals aged 13 to 19, found that 49 percent of the males and 63 percent of the females reported having used no contraceptive at first intercourse. In Shah, Zelnik, and Kantner's (1975) national sample of 4,611 females aged 15 to 19, 28 percent of whom had already had premarital intercourse, 53 percent failed to use contraception the last time they had intercourse.

In one study (Crist, 1971) of 393 sexually active college females it was found that 65 percent used no contraceptive or used one of the least effective methods, namely, rhythm, withdrawal, or douche. In another study (Fujita, Wagner, and Pion, 1971) it was found that of 163 college males and 283 college females, 30 percent of the former and 22 percent of the latter reported no contraceptive use, except rhythm or withdrawal in some cases. In a study of 98 college males and 88 college females it was found that 40 percent generally used no contraceptive or one of the three least effective methods mentioned above (Bauman, 1971). Another report growing out of the same study (Eastman, 1972) mentions that 59 percent of the males and 64 percent of the females had their first intercourse with no contraceptive or used a method of "limited reliability." It is clear from these data that college and university students are often not contraceptively prepared for sexual intercourse.

Reasons for Inadequate Protection

It is not sufficient to point out that pregnancy is a possible unintended consequence of sexual intercourse. We must emphasize that among unmarried persons it is an extremely common consequence. It is an outcome which can be prevented, but often is not. Why?

The authors have counseled dozens of women who became pregnant outside of marriage. Few of these women were contraceptively protected. They report a variety of reasons as to why they did not adequately prepare. Generalizing, we can make the conclusion that many young women feel that it is awkward, presumptuous, and unromantic to be contraceptively prepared for sexual intercourse. In short, sexual intercourse is something that is supposed to happen "naturally" in a romantic context. A woman is reluctant to be asked to have coitus and reply, "Why yes, I was hoping you would ask, and therefore I was fitted for a diaphragm yesterday," or, "Sure—and I'm OK as far as the pill is concerned. I began taking it last month since I expected that our relationship would come to this." Many women feel that the romance is taken out of the situation if they have anticipated it or prepared for it. A woman does not want to appear that she was presuming to have coitus, even though she perhaps was. Since it is the female that gets pregnant, she must be especially concerned about possible pregnancy. The male, however, has a role. Men need to take a more active role in contraceptive preparation. No urge is so great that intercourse could not be delayed an hour or so, or a full day, until contraception is acquired. Many females have the belief that they are not necessarily "bad girls" if they are overcome with passion and have sexual intercourse, but they are "bad" if they are contraceptively prepared for it. We shall discuss contraceptives in Chapter 12.

Studies have brought to light a variety of reasons for which premarital intercourse occurs without adequate contraceptive protection (Lehfeldt, 1971; Sandberg and Jacobs, 1972; Shah, Zelnik, and Kantner, 1973). Among them are ignorance of what contraceptive methods are effective and where to get them; nonacceptance of a method prescribed by a physician because it is thought to be unsafe; objection to contraception on religious or moral grounds; denial that contraception works; irresponsibility; immaturity; willingness to take a chance; emotional disturbance; desire for evidence of fertility or virility; enhancement of sexual pleasure by the thrill of taking risks; availability of abortion; rebellion against society or parents; hostility toward the other gender; diminishment, by contraception, of the possibility of controlling or manipulating the relationship; equation of love with self-sacrifice; a belief that intercourse is sinful and pregnancy is the punishment; a feeling that pregnancy is a gift of love; the belief that sex is for procreation only; unwillingness either to deny oneself or to delay intercourse; a desire of the female to become pregnant to force marriage; an unconscious desire to become pregnant; the feeling that "it can't (or won't) happen to me"; the belief that intercourse is a demonstration of love; the belief that the girl was too young; the belief that intercourse was too infrequent or occurred at the wrong time of the month.

Some of the specific reasons females gave in a recent study for not using contraception are given in Exhibit 5-2.

Tietze (1960), after careful mathematical analysis, wrote, "The probability of conception resulting from a single unprotected coitus would . . . appear to lie between 1 in 50 and 1 in 25." These figures do not suggest that a woman may have intercourse between twenty-four and forty-nine times without the risk of conception. For women individually, the chances are zero or one: Either they get pregnant or they do not. When pregnancy occurs, the odds have suddenly become 100 percent. Every pregnancy results from one act of intercourse. Each time a woman has intercourse without adequate contraceptive protection, she assumes not a part of the risk, but the entire risk of conception. Yet some students think that infrequent intercourse is only a partial risk. Coeds have been known to say, "I didn't do it very often—how could I get pregnant?" (Fujita, Wagner, and Pion, 1971).

Frequency of Premarital Pregnancy

There is no way at present to get a complete and accurate picture of premarital pregnancy. But there are useful statistics giving some indication of frequency. These include such items as the number of babies born alive to unmarried mothers, the number of unmarried women who have abortions, the number of babies conceived before the wedding but born in marriage, and the number of women who report premarital pregnancy regardless of the termination of such pregnancy.

In 1974, there were an estimated 418,100 illegitimate births in the United States (U.S. Department of Health, Education, and Welfare, *Monthly Vital Statistics Report*, 1976). In 1950, illegitimate births constituted 4 percent of all live births (U.S. Bureau of the Census, *Statistical Abstract*, 1975), and in 1974, 13.2 percent (U.S. Department of Health, Education, and Welfare, *Monthly Vital Statistics Report*, 1976). In the period 1962–1970 the illegitimacy rate showed a continual increase. Since 1970 it has declined slightly each year for all age groups except 15- to 19-year-old white women (U.S. Department of Health, Education, and Welfare, *Monthly Vital Statistics Report*, 1976). More than three-fourths of the illegitimate births are to women in the high school and college age range (U.S. Bureau of the Census, *Statistical Abstract*, 1975). It is important to keep

Exhibit 5-2 Unprotected Intercourse among Unwed Teenagers

Reason	Percent of never married sexually experienced women 15 to 19, according to reasons they reported for not using contraception, 1971*
Time of month (persons thought they couldn't become pregnant)	39.7
Low risk (too young to become pregnant, didn't think she could, infrequent intercourse)	31.9
Nonavailability (didn't know about it, wasn't available, too expensive)	30.5
Hedonistic objection (partner objected, sex isn't as much fun if it's used, too inconvenient, just didn't want to use it)	23.7
Want pregnancy (trying to have a baby, didn't mind if she became pregnant)	15.8
Moral/medical objection (believed it was wrong or dangerous, medical reasons)	12.5

*Percentages total more than 100 since respondents could cite more than one reason.

Source: Shah, Zelnik, and Kantner, 1975.

in mind that these figures are for births, not pregnancies.

In cases of premarital pregnancy there is still pressure put upon couples to marry, but not as much as there used to be. Yet there are many premarital pregnancies legitimated by marriage. In the light of the U.S. Supreme Court decision of 1973 to legalize abortion (which will be discussed in a later chapter), the number of these may be expected to change even more than it has up to date. The proportion of live births considered premature has declined recently (U.S. Department of Health, Education, and Welfare, *Monthly Vital Statistics Report*, 1976) and will probably continue to decline as abortion becomes more common. Before the Court decision, it was estimated that about one-fifth of first babies were born to women married less than eight months. When babies born out of wedlock were added to these, the estimate was that one-third of all first babies were conceived outside of marriage (U.S. Department of Health, Education, and Welfare, *Monthly Vital Statistics Report*, 1970). It was also estimated that of women bearing babies within the first eight months of marriage, about one-fourth had attended college for one to four or more years (U.S. Bureau of the Census, *Current Population Reports*, 1971). Another startling finding is that 30,000 young girls under age 15 become pregnant each year in the United States (Jaffe and Dryfoos, 1976).

In a study of marriages in the Midwest, Christensen (1963) compared dates for first births with wedding dates of the parents of the children, making an allowance for premature deliveries. In this study he found that one-fifth of all first births within these marriages were the outcome of conceptions that must have occurred before the wedding.

Let us assume a reasonable degree of validity in the statistics mentioned and others like them. If we (1) combine figures for births recorded as illegitimate, (2) add children born within marriage but conceived before the wedding, (3) assume the addition of an unknown number of premarital pregnancies terminated by abortion before or after the wedding, and an unknown number of such pregnancies ending with miscarriage or a stillborn child, we could conservatively estimate that there are at least one million premarital pregnancies each year. If our figure is even close to correct, we certainly have a problem of major proportions in this country.

The number of children born out of wedlock does not by itself present the entire picture of illegitimacy. In one study made in New York City it was found that more than 20 percent of the unmarried mothers had no prenatal care until the seventh or eighth month, and 17 percent (as compared with 3 percent of married mothers) had no prenatal care at all. In another study, also made in New York City, it was found that the maternal death rate among the unmarried was almost twice as high as among the married. The infant death rate was more than twice as high for children born out of wedlock as for those born in wedlock. Among children born out of wedlock the death rate for those born to mothers who had no prenatal care was $3\frac{1}{2}$ times as high as for those born to mothers who had such care. Almost twice as many children born to unmarried mothers, as compared with those born to married mothers, were premature (Oettinger, 1962).

RISK OF VENEREAL DISEASE

When an infection is transmitted primarily by sexual intercourse it is called a *venereal disease*. There are several common infections of the genital tract which are transmitted through sexual intercourse. Trichomoniasis, herpes simplex virus type 2, vaginal thrush, the "crabs," and prostatitis are common infections of the genital tract that are often transmitted by sexual intercourse with an infected person. These infections induce discharges and/or irritations which are a nuisance and sometimes difficult to treat (Goldstein, 1976). Space does not permit going into detail regarding the organisms that cause these diseases or their symptoms, cures, and effects. Our point of focus will be the risk of contracting one of the two most serious types of venereal diseases, *syphilis* and *gonorrhea*.

Syphilis and gonorrhea are both very contagious. Of reported cases of syphilis, 95 percent are contracted through intercourse, and the other 5 percent are contracted through kissing when there is a cut or scratch in the mucous membrane of the lips or mouth, by oral-genital contact, by prenatal transmission, or by transfusion. Gonorrhea is almost always contracted through sexual intercourse. Reports of contagion by means of bathtubs, swimming pools, and toilet seats are without foundation in fact. It is difficult to get accurate statistics on the incidence of syphilis and gonorrhea because only a proportion of cases are reported. This fact must be kept in mind in interpreting figures indicating changes in incidence. It is possible that part, although by no means all, of any apparent increase in incidence is due to better reporting.

It is estimated that in the twelve-month period ending June 30, 1974, there were 2,700,000 new cases of gonorrhea, although only 874,161 cases were reported. This latter figure was 8 percent higher than the previous year and the greatest number since the Public Health Service started keeping records more than a half century ago. In that same year, 24,728 cases of syphilis were reported, although the American Social Health Association estimated that 80,000 new cases occurred (ASHA, 1975). On the average, about every eleven seconds an American is infected with one of these venereal diseases.

Until about 1969 there seemed to be a downward trend in the rate (cases per 100,000 population) of reported cases of syphilis. Many people were optimistic that the disease had been brought under control. Then in 1970 (ASHA, 1971) an unexpected upturn in the rate was reported, as if a smoldering fire had burst into flame. There is now what may be interpreted as an epidemic. The World Health Organization ranks gonorrhea as the most prevalent communicable disease after the common cold.

This situation is serious any way it is considered. But there are several facts that further complicate it relative to premarital intercourse. For both syphilis and gonorrhea the highest rates are in the 20- to 24-year-old age group. Reported cases of both diseases are about twice as numerous among males as among females. As many as 80 percent of females and a small proportion of males who have gonorrhea are asymptomatic, that is, they have the disease and can transmit it to others, but they themselves show no symptoms of it (ASHA, 1975). Of course, the presence of the disease can be ascertained by laboratory tests. Asymptomatic individuals are generally not aware of the fact that they have gonorrhea. Syphilis may become asymptomatic only after the primary and secondary stages of the disease have passed, and this may be several years after the original infection (ASHA, 1975).

There is a not uncommon tendency to pooh-pooh gonorrhea as being no more serious than, say, a cold. But complications of the disease in women cost the nation millions of dollars annually and account for 175,000 hospital admissions totaling 1,200,000 hospital-patient days. On any given day, an average of 3,200 patients are hospitalized and an estimated 5,750 girls are absent from school

(ASHA, 1975) as a result of gonorrhea infections.

At one time it was thought that penicillin would prove to be the ultimate cure for syphilis and gonorrhea. It is still effective in most cases. But some gonorrhea organisms are becoming partially resistant to it. Other antibiotics are being used with some success, but the final answer has not yet been found (Neumann and Baecker, 1972; Schroeter and Lucas, 1972; Rudolph, 1972).

The only contraceptive that is even partially effective in preventing venereal disease contagion is the condom. Fiumara (1972) mentions conditions (some of which would be likely to make intercourse less than satisfactory) to be met before the condom is effective against gonorrhea: There must be no preliminary sex play involving the genitals before putting the condom on; the condom must be intact before and after use; it must be put on and taken off correctly. Even if all these conditions are met, the condom is more protection against gonorrhea than against syphilis because it does not cover all the areas of the couple's bodies that may come into contact (Hart, 1975). With the increasingly widespread use of contraceptive methods (especially the pill) designed for women, a reasonable guess would be that more men will leave the responsibility for contraception to the woman, and consequently fewer men will use the condom. Some investigators believe that this is now happening and that it is one of the reasons for the rising incidence of venereal infection.

When to Seek Medical Attention

Venereal disease is not only widespread; it affects persons of all races, ages, social classes, and educational levels. It is found on as well as off college campuses. If one is ever in doubt about the possibility of having contracted venereal disease, it is important to seek medical attention from a physician, hospital, public health clinic, university health service, or family planning clinic. Most states have laws which protect the confidentiality of venereal disease treatment, even from parents in the case of minors. The necessity for treatment might come to light either because one has been told by a sexual partner that he or she has venereal disease, because one suspects that the partner might be infected, or because one or more symptoms have presented themselves, as described below.

In gonorrhea, males will usually notice a burning sensation while urinating two to five days after contracting the disease. There may be a yellowish discharge from the urethral opening at the tip of the penis. If the disease is untreated, serious infection of the reproductive system is possible. Females are not usually able to detect symptoms easily. There may be a mild irritation or discharge which a woman may be inclined to ignore, but should not. Sterility is likely to follow after a few months if the infection is not treated, since gonorrhea travels to the cervix, fallopian tubes, and ovaries.

Syphilis has several stages. The incubation period, the time from initial exposure to the appearance of the first disease symptom ranges from ten days to eight weeks, with an average of twenty-one days (Goldstein, 1976). In the primary stage a pimple-like chancre sore appears. Syphilis should be detected and treated when such a sore is recognized. This symptom will disappear in two weeks or so. If it is not treated, a secondary stage occurs during which a rash appears on parts of the body. If the rash ulcerates, it can be highly contagious. The rash may be accompanied by sore throat, fever, headache, falling hair, and other symptoms. After several weeks the secondary symptoms disappear, and latent and tertiary stages follow in which no more visible symptoms appear. Left untreated, syphilis can cause severe damage to the individual ranging from heart disease to blindness.

Although not as serious, herpes simplex virus type 2 (HSV-2) should be mentioned, since it ranks behind gonorrhea as the second most common venereal disease in the United States (Goldstein, 1976). A group of tiny blisters usually form on the tip of the penis or on the scrotum of men, and on the inside of the vagina, on the cervix, and occasionally elsewhere in females. The fluid-filled blisters are painful, can ulcerate, and are sometimes accompanied by other symptoms as well. Symptoms last from one to four weeks and can be dangerous to a fetus carried by an infected mother.

CONCLUSION

The extent of premarital sexual behavior appears to be greater now than at any time in previous American history. It can be assumed that most young people will have premarital intercourse, although for many the experience will include only a future spouse. For others, the experience may include a fiancé(e), other persons with whom the individual has been in love, or persons with whom there was no or only slight emotional attachment. Some persons will still choose to wait until they are married before having sexual intercourse, but among males and females alike such persons are now in the minority. Despite pressures that various persons feel to have sex or not to have sex, it appears that our society is becoming more tolerant of a variety of personal decisions regarding sex before marriage.

It is clear that young people are becoming more aware of contraception and find it more readily accessible; but surprisingly, the increase in contraceptive use has not kept up with the increase in sexual activity. The number of abortions being performed on unmarried women is at an all-time high, many women have illegitimate births before marriage, and in a significant proportion of marriages, the bride is pregnant on the wedding day. As the sexual activity of unmarried men and women increases, the importance of contraceptive preparation will become increasingly important.

Whether or not there has been a sexual revolution is a difficult question to answer. Our answer would depend mainly on how we defined "revolution." We would suggest that we are now in the process of a sexual "evolution"—a gradual change which is consistent with and follows from many of the changes seen in other aspects of American social life. Greater sexual freedom; our increased ability to talk about sex openly; and the freedom to choose a life-style, sexual orientation, sexual partners, and forms of sexual expression are all components of an evolutionary process which is compatible with a changing, progressive, modern society.

Sexual revolution involves more than just an increase in the number of persons having sex at some time before they are married. The quality of sexual relationships, the nature of the involvement between the partners, the freedom of choice involved in deciding to participate, and the meaning the activity has to the participants must all be considered in assessing one's overall sexual experience before marriage. If a revolution were to be completed today, we might expect that the six conditions cited below would be met. These are not conditions which we are advocating, for there are certainly different points of view about whether they should occur. However, we can state that if these conditions were to exist, the nature of sexual experience would certainly be different—perhaps different enough to allow all of us to agree that a revolution had indeed occurred. Whether or not these conditions should be allowed to develop can serve as a basis for interesting contemplation and discussion.

1 Open, but *responsible* discussion of human sexuality in both public and private settings concerning biological, social, psychological, and interpersonal issues. Such discussion would include sex education in the home and in public school settings appropriate for individuals at various stages of the life cycle.

2 Equality between males and females in making decisions regarding sexual behavior and involvement.

3 The ability of all persons to structure their sexual activities in such a way that an individual's values and standards regarding sexual involvement are allowed to conform to that person's behavior, so long as sexual activity with another partner involves mutual consent, without coercion, violence, or physical aggression.

4 Reduction of guilt and anxiety associated with sexual behavior and interaction, resulting in sexuality as a straightforward expression of an individual's love, affection, or physical attraction.

5 The acceptance of an individual's or couple's right to engage in whatever expressions of sexual behavior he, she, or they deem appropriate or desirable, so long as they maintain privacy and respect for their partner, avoid coercion, and refrain from violating the civil rights of any other individual.

6 A change in the sociocultural definitions existing in the society which regard sex as a mysterious, sinful, or solely lustful activity.

The six conditions presented represent an "ideal type," in that it is clear that none of these, let alone all six of them, will ever occur for all individuals in any society. It is reasonable to consider each condition as a continuum on which movement may take place toward or away from the objective stated. As we move toward the objective, or, stated differently, as the values and behavior of more individuals in a society reflect each condition, the society can be said to be going through sexual revolution.

TERMS TO BE LEARNED

abstinence
age of consent
asymptomatic
consenting adults
copulation (copulate)
double standard
empirical
freedom of choice
goal orientation
gonorrhea
herpes simplex virus type 2
homogeneous
illegitimate (illegitimacy)
immoral (immorality)
incidence (cumulative, active)
methodology

moral (morality)
new morality
orchialgia
oral-genital sex
orientation (male, female)
paternity
peer group
permissiveness
petting
pluralism (pluralistic society)
postpubertal
promiscuity
qualitative
quantitative (quantification)
rape

sample (random)
sampling
sexual evolution
sexual responsiveness (responsivity)
sexual revolution
statutory rape
subculture
syphilis
testalgia
urban (urbanized)
value (value-free)
venereal disease
virgin (virginity)

SELECTED READINGS

BANOWSKY, WILLIAM S.: *Sex Isn't That Simple: The New Sexuality on Campus*, Seabury Press, New York, 1974. (Paperback.) Addressed to college students. Human sexuality, its meaning and values, its role in life, differences between male and female, homosexuality, premarital intercourse, "recreational sex," love and commitment, the future of marriage. Author says, "I do not believe that any external authority . . . can determine for students what is appropriate sexual behavior."

———: *It's a Playboy World*, Fleming H. Revell Company, Publishers, Westwood, N.J., 1969. Critical analysis of the playboy philosophy, not only as it is expressed in the magazine *Playboy*, but also in the context of what is happening socially, sexually, and morally in America, where, the author believes, the playboy philosophy is widely accepted as a way of life.

BRECHER, E. M.: *The Sex Researchers*, Signet Books, New York, 1971. The lives and contributions in the area of sexuality by noted experts of their times.

CANNON, KENNETH L., AND RICHARD LONG: "Premarital Sexual Behavior in the Sixties," *Journal of Marriage and the Family*, vol. 33, no. 1, pp. 36–49, February 1971. Also in Carl B. Broderick (ed.): *A Decade of Family Research and Action*, National Council on Family Relations, Minneapolis, Minn., 1971, pp. 25–38. A "review and appraisal of research focusing upon premarital sexual behavior" during the 1960s.

CUTRIGHT, PHILLIPS: "Illegitimacy: Myths, Causes and Cures," *Family Planning Perspectives*, vol. 3, no. 1, pp. 26–48, January 1971. Analysis of illegitimacy: what it is, causes, factors affecting it, what might be done to reduce the rate.

EHRMANN, WINSTON: "Marital and Nonmarital Sexual Behavior," in Harold T. Christensen (ed.): *Handbook of Marriage and the Family*, Rand McNally & Company, Chicago, 1964, chap. 15. An analysis of sexual behavior in the Western world, especially the United States; changes in sexual behavior; differences between male and female. Refers to many research studies.

GAGNON, J. H., AND W. SIMON: *Sexual Conduct: The Social Sources of Human Sexuality*, Aldine Publishing Co., Chicago, 1973. A social learning theory of the development of sexual behavior.

GORDON, S.: *The Sexual Adolescent: Communicating with Teenagers about Sex*, Duxbury Press, North Scituate, Mass., 1973. Written for parents and professionals, with an extensive sex education materials bibliography.

HETTLINGER, RICHARD F.: *Human Sexuality: A Psychosexual Perspective*, Wadsworth Publishing Company, Inc., Belmont, Calif., 1975. (Paperback.) Addressed to college students. Author develops a "philosophy of sexuality." Discusses sex, values on campus, the new sexuality, love and commitment, marriage and the future of marriage, homosexuality, contraception, abortion.

HOFFMAN, HANS. *Sex Incorporated*, Beacon Press, Boston, 1967. "A positive view of the sexual revolution." Discusses "how sex can be incorporated into a total life-awareness."

JUHASZ, ANNE MCCREARY (ed.): *Sexual Development and Behavior: Selected Readings*, The Dorsey Press, Homewood, Ill., 1973. (Paperback.) A book of readings presenting various points of view on sexual development, sexual behavior, changing values and standards, sex on campus, abortion, venereal disease, swinging, changes in the family, and related topics.

KENNEDY, EUGENE C.: *The New Sexuality: Myths, Fables, and Hang-ups*, Doubleday & Company, Inc., Garden City, N.Y., 1972. Analysis of sex in present-day America, premarital intercourse, extramarital sexual relations, homosexuality, masturbation, pornography. Author says American culture is "desperately preoccupied with sexiness and so blinded to real sexuality."

LASAGNA, LOUIS: *The VD Epidemic*, Temple University Press, Philadelphia, 1975. Discusses symptoms, diagnosis, treatment, incidence, history of gonorrhea and syphilis in nontechnical language. What can be done about the current epidemic. Symptomless cases.

LINDEMANN, CONSTANCE: *Birth Control and Unmarried Young Women*, Springer Publishing Company, New York, 1974. Based on research. Reasons for failure to use contraception. Misinformation and lack of information concerning pregnancy and contraception. Abortion.

MAZUR, RONALD MICHAEL: *Commonsense Sex*, Beacon Press, Boston, 1968. "This book is dedicated to the proposition that sexual relations can and should be positive, rewarding collaborations—not accidental and often destructive confrontations." The author leaves it up to readers to ask, "Does this make sense to me?" and to determine their own answers within their own frame of reference. The author is a Unitarian Universalist minister.

PACKARD, VANCE: *The Sexual Wilderness*, David McKay Company, Inc., New York, 1968. (Paperback.) A study of sexual attitudes and behavior. Contains numerous references to other studies and quotes numerous investigators, writers, and commentators.

PANNOR, REUBEN, FRED MASSARIK, AND BYRON EVANS: *The Unmarried Father*, Springer Publishing Company, New York, 1971. (Paperback.) Report of a "comprehensive study that focused on the unmarried father and his impact upon the unmarried mother and the decision-making about the baby."

PIERCE, RUTH I.: *Single and Pregnant*, Beacon Press, Boston, 1970. (Paperback.) The alternatives available to a single, pregnant woman. Persons and agencies she may turn to for help. Medical, legal, financial aspects.

POMEROY, W. B.: *Dr. Kinsey and the Institute for Sex Research*, Harper & Row, Publishers, New York, 1972. The story of Kinsey and the Institute, related by one of his colleagues.

REISS, IRA L.: *Premarital Sexual Standards in America*, The Free Press, New York, 1960. Analysis of sexual standards rather than a statistical analysis of sexual practices. What the future trend will be.

——: *The Social Context of Premarital Sexual Permissiveness*, Holt, Rinehart and Winston, Inc., New York, 1967. A study of the sex attitudes of almost 3,000 persons, about half of whom were students.

ROBERTS, ROBERT W. (ed.): *The Unwed Mother*, Harper & Row, Publishers, New York, 1966. A book of readings covering a theoretical overview; an assessment of research findings; alternatives open to unwed mothers and reasons for choosing them; sociological and cross-cultural perspectives.

SORENSEN, R. C.: *Adolescent Sexuality in Contemporary America*, World, New York, 1973. The report of a study of a national random sample of both male and female teen-agers.

VINCENT, CLARK E.: *Unmarried Mothers*, The Free Press, New York, 1961. A study of unmarried mothers; their personal characteristics, family backgrounds, and attitudes toward their pregnancies; what they did with their babies.

YOUNG, LEONTINE: *Out of Wedlock*, rev. ed., McGraw-Hill Book Company, New York, 1963. A study of the problem of premarital pregnancy based on the author's experience as a social worker with 350 unmarried mothers.

ZUBIN, J., AND J. MONEY (eds.): *Contemporary Sexual Behavior: Critical Issues in the 1970's*, The Johns Hopkins University Press, Baltimore, 1973. Readings in current topics in the area of human sexuality.

Chapter 6

Preparation through Choice

Choosing a marriage partner is a complex process, but one which is fascinating to study. In the ancient Hebrew family, marriage typically was arranged by the fathers of the young persons involved. The man's family paid the woman's family a *bride price* to compensate them for the loss of her services. Girls were permitted to marry at age 12 and males at age 13. The Baganda peoples of Uganda, in Central Africa, also place a great deal of importance on the bride price. Girls marry at 13 or 14, boys at 15 or 16 if they have accumulated sufficient property. Although wives may be inherited as gifts or captured in war, they are usually purchased. The girl's brother and her paternal uncle act as go-betweens for the boy and the girl's father. In China, before the revolution, marriages were arranged for their children by the heads of families. Although romantic love before marriage was known to exist, it was considered dangerous and contrary to the children's primary roles of respectful son and subservient daughter-in-law. Matchmakers played central roles in mate selection. Couples rarely saw each other before the wedding, and a *dowry*, a gift provided by the girl's parents to the man's family, was given, since a daughter was considered an economic burden to the family (Queen and Habenstein, 1974).

These three examples illustrate the diversity of methods of mate selection which may exist from one culture to the next and in different time periods. Contrast these methods with the customs of contemporary America, and we can see that the love-based, partner-centered type of mate selection we experience is certainly not universal. The method of mate selection which prevails in a given society is likely to be determined by which individuals have the greatest stake in the marriage that is to be formed. In some societies, it may be the parents or families of the young persons involved, whereas in other societies, like ours, it may be the young persons themselves. Although there appears to be a worldwide movement toward mate choice by the marriage partners themselves (Goode, 1970), no society leaves the process of falling in love and choosing a marriage partner solely in the hands of the young persons themselves. And as we shall see later, American parents can exert a great deal of pressure on their offspring which may influence their choice of a marriage partner.

PRINCIPLES GOVERNING MATE SELECTION

There are two basic principles which govern mate selection in all societies (Winch, 1971). The first, *the principle of incest avoidance*, is based on the fact that every known society has a rule preventing certain closely related persons from marrying each other. Marriage is generally forbidden between mother and son, father and daughter, and brother and sister. In some cultures, the prohibition against incest includes relatives of more remote degrees of kinship. There are many explanations as to why this principle developed. One plausible reason is that it was necessary to prevent jealousy, social conflict, and family breakup from occurring. Other reasons such as potential hereditary complications are mentioned today, but the former reason must certainly have been a dominant one in more primitive societies.

The second principle may be termed *the principle of ethnocentric preference*. This principle follows from the observation that in every culture studied there appears to be a tendency for young people to marry persons from their own locality and/or segment of society. In short, young persons tend to marry those who are similar to themselves in social characteristics. The principle may, in primitive societies, prevent people from marrying outside the village or outside a particular social class. The disapproval of interracial and cross-national marriages that exists in most societies is an example of the principle of ethnocentric preference (Winch, 1971).

These two principles state that some persons are ineligible for marriage with each other, while others are not only eligible but preferred. The term *field of eligibles* refers to those individuals who realistically could be considered possible marriage partners. It is within the field of eligibles that marriage choices are usually made. Dozens of studies have observed that in American society, individuals tend to marry those who are *similar* to themselves in social characteristics (Lewis and Spanier, 1978). This norm is called *homogamy*, marriage between persons of similar characteristics. In the next chapter we shall see how the norm of homogamy works by considering similarities and differences in factors such as age, nationality, race, family background, education, previous marital status, and religion.

In contrast to that of many other cultures, then, our process of mate selection centers upon young persons making a choice. From childhood through adolescence through early adulthood, the typical American man and woman learn about persons of the opposite gender, narrow their field of eligibles, develop preferences, date, and eventually make the choice of a partner. This choice is based on a multitude of factors, some of which the participants may control and some of which they may be unable to control. In this chapter, we shall consider some of the personal and interpersonal factors which may enter into the mate selection and marriage preparation process.

CHOOSING A MARRIAGE PARTNER

Of all the choices an individual is called upon to make, the choice (or lack of choice) of a marriage partner can go as far as any, and farther than most, toward determining the quality of one's life. It is safer and easier to choose well than to attempt to alter personalities after the wedding. Change may occur through experience, self-effort, or the influence of one's spouse; but it can take place only on the foundation of personality traits present before marriage began.

Personality traits are characteristics or behaviors that determine an individual's adjustment to his or her environment. They are abstractions deduced from observation of concrete, overt acts. Changing those traits is not a simple process. It is, rather, a process of change in behavior, which entails the development of new habit patterns. As a rule people do not like to be changed, especially when the suggested alteration implies inferiority, and they are made the subject of a reform program concocted by someone else.

Each of a person's traits is relative to all others and is manifested against the background of his or her total personality. None ever stands alone, isolated from the rest of the individual. Each is also relative to the attitude of every individual who makes a judgment of it. Besides, traits are not always constant. A person may exhibit a given trait under one set of circumstances but not under another. He or she may, for example, be honest when trusted but dishonest when subjected to suspicion. Temper may be controlled at home but lost on the golf course.

The same trait may appear in a different light as circumstances vary. If a person has fought his or her way to the top in business, we might expect that individual to be aggressive. Aggression, however, is more acceptable at a meeting of the board of directors than at the family dinner table. Absorption in work may be commendable; but if the individual cannot escape it long enough to spend some time with his or her spouse, it becomes an annoyance rather than a virtue. An individual cannot be two personalities simultaneously—one with family, another with other persons. If the person seems to be so dually constituted, it is because the traits of personality appear different under different circumstances.

Qualities of a Marriage Partner

It would be an interesting and perhaps provocative exercise to attempt to list all the qualities desirable in a marriage partner. The end result would probably be an inventory of all the virtues and some of the vices, depending upon one's point of view, of which the human race is capable. Our difficulty in presenting such a list would be that we should be attempting to catalog the desirable traits to be found in marriage partners in general. Actually, there is no such thing as a generalized husband or wife; there is only some particular woman's husband, some particular man's wife. It is useless to talk about the qualities of a spouse until we answer the question, "Whose spouse?" The qualities held to be desirable are variable and depend upon the personality and expectations of the individual making the choice. Qualities are not absolutely desirable or undesirable. They are relatively so and are weighted according to the attitudes of the maker of the list.

In choosing a marriage partner further considerations are also important, such as the following: (1) The type of person one wants. This person may be either a reflection of an ideal or the individual to whom one has already developed an emotional attachment. (2) The type of person one needs—that is, the person one can best get along with, who will complement one's own personality, who will afford emotional and economic security, to whose life one can make a contribution, and with whom one can maintain a desirable standard of living and life-style. (3) The type of person one is likely to be able to get. In this connection we are making no implication of superiority or inferiority but only of difference, and we do not mean that one's standards should be low. Individuals who fall in love with married or engaged persons, who in hero-worshiping fashion fill their daydreams with visions of movie stars or other celebrities to the exclusion of more available contacts, who seek to attract persons who are obviously not interested in them, who refuse to consider any but a very wealthy person—these and numerous others are thinking only in terms of what they want and are overlooking the important question of what they are probably able to get. One person cannot choose another unless that other person is available. Availability is determined not only by existence, proximity, and acquaintance but also by interest in and inclination toward the individual hoping to make the choice. There must be reciprocal attraction, which in its turn increases attractiveness. One cannot make a choice without simultaneously being a choice.

A good choice is the beginning, not the end, of marital adjustment. The situation is not dissimilar to that found in choosing an occupation. No matter how wise one may be in making an occupational choice, no matter how well one is adapted or prepared, there still remain many adjustments to be made and much work to be done before success in that occupation is achieved.

Choice involves not only the personality of the other person but also things associated with that person, the circumstances under which the couple will live, the demands of the husband's or wife's occupation, the place of residence, and the type of in-laws. This is in some ways more true of a woman's choice of husband than of a man's choice of wife, because, in the majority of cases still today, the nature of the husband's occupation reaches further into their family life and plays a large part in determining the wife's role. The husband's and wife's occupations also play a large part in determining the couple's place of residence and status in the community.

There is almost sure to be antagonism if a man wants his wife to be very domestic but marries a woman who neglects homemaking because of her career interests, if a woman wants a husband interested in participating in shared family recreation but marries a man who prefers strictly masculine pastimes "with the boys," or if a woman expects a husband to participate in housekeeping and marries a man who shuns "woman's work." Conflict in marriage is normal. In some marriages, of course, there is more than in others. Some conflicts are at least hypothetically resolvable. For example, a couple might resolve conflict over money by earning more, spending less, or making alterations in the handling of funds. On the other hand, conflict growing out of a difference in religious faith, moral standards, age, or cultural background may prove to be unyielding. When an individual chooses a marriage partner, to a considerable degree he or she chooses some of the conflict that the marriage will entail.

Background Factors

Undoubtedly, factors in an individual's background play a significant part in marriage preparation. Whether one comes from a happy or an unhappy home; one's relationship to parents and their treatment of him or her as a child; whether one developed relative independence or emotional overattachment to parents; the degree of socialization, sibling relationships, and what one learned in the early years regarding human sexuality—factors such as these affect the development of personality, and this is related in turn to the individual's behavior in marriage. Each such factor needs to be understood and evaluated in each individual. Broad generalizations are of little help except in calling attention to the importance of such factors. Research studies are, of necessity, based upon groups (samples). Their findings give a picture of a group but may not apply with equal vigor to each individual in the group. Caution in interpretation is therefore indicated.

If, for example, we studied a thousand persons who came from very happy home backgrounds, and another thousand who came from very unhappy home backgrounds, we should find more unsuccessful marriages among the second group than among the first group. But we should also find some unsuccessful marriages among persons coming from happy backgrounds and some successful ones among persons coming from very unhappy backgrounds. Whether a given individual being considered as a marriage partner falls into the majority or the minority of either group can be ascertained only by understanding that individual. Hence, background factors may be given attention but need not be considered deterministic in making a final choice.

Sexual Attraction

Sexual attraction is naturally important in choosing a marriage partner. Nevertheless, sexual attraction is very obtrusive, overshadowing other considerations more often than being overshadowed by them. In choosing a marriage partner, one cannot depend upon sex appeal alone or too much or for too long. There are so many aspects of marriage besides the sexual, and it is important that perspective not be lost. When many college students, particularly males, are asked to think ahead to marriage, one of the first things that often comes to mind is the unlimited access to a sexual partner and the satisfaction which such opportunity in a relationship can provide for the couple. Couples interviewed after marriage, however, state that their sexual relationship is only a part of their marital relationship, and a small part for most of them. Only a tiny portion of one's time is spent in sexual relations.

Physical Health

Health is an important consideration. Most of us have physical examinations from time to time, and females who have begun having sexual intercourse are advised to begin to have regular gynecological checkups, including "Pap smears" (clinical tests to detect possible cervical cancer). Nevertheless, the couple may want to have a premarital medical examination in which the physician would give special attention to any factors which might be relevant to the couple's relationship. There are five functions of such an examination: (1) to ascertain the state of general health and to point out, if necessary, any symptoms that might affect the couple's decision to continue their future conjugal relationship; (2) to discover details of anatomy that might affect the couple's sexual adjustment; (3) to discover, if possible, any anatomical characteristics that would make it inadvisable for the woman to become pregnant; (4) to test for the presence or absence of the Rh factor in the couple's blood; (5) to permit the couple to get advice, if they have not already, on some method of controlling conception.

The purpose of the premarital medical examination is not to ascertain whether the couple can have children. The physician may make observations that suggest possible relative infertility, but many of the conditions contributing to infertility are not taken into account in a premarital medical examination at all. Its chief purpose is to assist the marriage in getting a better start and to enable couples to make the best possible adjustment.

Hereditary Traits

In mate selection, one chooses not only an individual and his or her relatives but also, in a sense, more distant ancestors insofar as the individual exhibits hereditary traits or carries the determiners of them with the possibility of passing them on to children. Consequently, the question of heredity is important. This matter not infrequently comes to the attention of the counselor via the worries of some person who is concerned about the advisability of marriage or parenthood, because of either his or her own hereditary constitution or that of the other person.

Reliable data on human heredity are not so plentiful as one might wish. Those that are most uncontestable apply to such traits as eye color, skin color, supernumerary fingers or toes. Some persons, however, want to know about the inheritance of such things as insanity, cancer, tuberculosis, diabetes, sickle-cell anemia, mental retardation, or birth defects. Sometimes the data are conclusive, sometimes inconclusive. There are frequent apparent exceptions. The whole matter of human heredity is more complex and less well understood than the arithmetic ratios of coat type in guinea pigs or color in peas, often employed to illustrate Mendelian laws to the beginning student. Human traits result from multiple hereditary determinants acting together, and most traits are profoundly influenced by the social environment. The problem is so complicated and ramifies in so many directions that in this book we can do no more than touch upon a few broad generalizations and then make a suggestion.

Although some investigators are reopening the question of the inheritance of acquired traits, for our purpose we may assume that such traits are not inherited. In order to be inheritable a trait must be carried in the genes. If an external influence affects the genes of a given individual, mutations may be produced and the traits of the offspring affected. External influences that affect only the body tissues of an individual do not affect inheritable traits.

Hereditary traits and congenital traits are often confused. Hereditary traits are those produced by factors carried in the genes. Congenital traits are those present at, or immediately following, birth, whether or not they are inherited. "Hereditary" refers to causation. "Congenital" refers to time. This distinction is important because it is sometimes assumed that, because a trait is present at birth, or occurs soon after birth, it must be inherited. For example a student is worried because his fiancée's brother is mentally retarded. Inquiry reveals that the retardation is due to a birth injury and is, therefore, not inheritable.

Hereditary traits are passed down to us not only from our immediate ancestors but from all our ancestors. Many of us would probably find abnormalities on our family trees if we examined them carefully and traced back far enough. The purpose in saying this is not to minimize the importance of heredity or to pass lightly over those cases in which it is a serious consideration with regard to a given marriage. Our purpose is rather to remove some of the unnecessary fears with which persons looking forward to marriage are sometimes plagued.

Marriage decisions are rarely based on the hereditary characteristics of the partners. Furthermore, a distinction may be drawn between the advisability of marrying and the advisability of having children. If the individual does not manifest the defect but there is reason to believe that he or she carries it in the genes and may pass it on to children, then marriage may occur, with the possibility of taking adequate steps to prevent conception. Adoption allows a couple to have children when it is ill-advised for them to bear their own.

In any case, the solution to the problem lies in knowledge and intelligent planning, not in worry. Worry over the inheritance of defects sometimes causes more damage than the defects themselves. Worry that a defect will be exhibited by one's children often leads to expecting that it will occur and to such continual "reading into" the child's behavior that the stage is set for his or her developing the trait one hoped the child would avoid.

If there is reason to believe that one party has in his or her family line a questionable hereditary trait that might make marriage or parenthood inadvisable, there are four things to be done before a final decision is made. (1) Gather all available information about the individual's background. (2) Submit the data to the best authority available, telling the whole truth insofar as this is possible. Students are especially fortunate in this connection because they may consult with a professor of genetics or a physician, that is, with someone who is likely either to know the answer or to know where it can be found if it is known at all. In some cases, such as with certain types of mental deficiency, our knowledge is such that the couple may be assured that the likelihood of their children's inheriting the trait is no greater than that of children in general. In other cases a less favorable answer would have to be given, but it could be given with reassurance. In still other cases, the possibilities are not so clear-cut, so it would be advisable to get the judgment of more than one expert. (3) Draw a careful distinction between traits that would make marriage inadvisable and those that would make parenthood inadvisable. (4) When the judgment of the experts has been communicated to the couple and accepted by them, the couple should consider it carefully, to be sure that they understand it and all its possible implications and ramifications, then draw their own conclusion, make a plan for the future, and adhere to it.

Common Interests

In one sense the term *common interests* connotes such things as hobbies, interest in sports, and taste in music, art, and drama. It is important that the couple have some such interests in common. It is also important that they have individual interests. In addition, each person needs to have understanding of, tolerance of, and appreciation for the other person's interests, that is, "an interest in the other's interests." It is desirable that each one's interests be compatible with and acceptable to the other. When such interests are not mutually acceptable, they may wedge a couple apart instead of drawing them together. A hobby may be an intruder instead of a binder.

The term *common interests* also connotes common purposes and sense of purpose, common goals, similar ideas concerning the couple's activities, similar expectations concerning the role of each, similar interpretations of life in general and of their own life-style, and similar attitudes toward children, home, religion, values, sex, people, money, and property. It is apparent without explanation how significant such common interests are in marriage. Yet many young people assume that recreational interests are the only common interests they need.

The more enduring common interests are, the more important they are likely to be in marriage. Pursuit of them must also be sincere and well founded. Sometimes, in order to advance the courtship process, one individual will superficially take up the interests of the other, only to drop them again after the wedding and thereby dissolve what the other person had assumed would be a bond between them. This temporary pursuit of an interest is not always insincere, as the individual may confuse interest in the other person with interest in what that person does. One of the best tests of supposedly common interests is to compare them in retrospect—that is, before the two individuals met, as well as after. Common dislikes as well as common likes may draw a couple together, but dislikes are too negative to take the place of common interests in marriage.

Standards of Behavior

It is important to consider a disparity in standards of behavior because it indicates a difference in attitude toward something that at least one of the couple considers a value. Difference in attitude is often accompanied by difference in behavior, and this may be fertile soil in which to grow the seeds of friction.

In contemplating a marriage in which there is a difference in standards of conduct, an individual might well answer one important question to his or her own satisfaction: What does this difference mean to me? If judgment becomes clouded by romance, an individual may make an unwise choice that will not stand the test of time. If he or she rests the decision on a verbal promise to reform made in response to a request to change or an expression of disapproval, when the other person's intent is merely to remove a barrier to getting married, the decision may be precarious indeed. If he or she depends upon reforming the other person after marriage, the person is falling into the trap of wishful thinking. It often happens that the person with the lower standard pulls the other down rather than that the person with the higher standard raises the other.

Economic Elements in Selection of a Partner

At no known period in history, among no known people, has marriage succeeded without some degree of cooperation, through division of labor, in the maintenance of a way of life. In the present-day United States this involves occupation and earning, and home management and other activities. Such division of labor has traditionally been along gender lines, but this is changing in America. But between earning and the maintenance of a way of life there is the intermediate step of spending. This involves a complex of attitudes, objectives, knowledge, choices, and activities that do not come naturally to a young couple when they fall in love and contemplate marriage. The effective handling of this intermediate step requires the development and focusing of skills and processes on objectives that have been mutually agreed upon. Hence it would seem appropriate for two individuals considering each other as possible marriage partners to begin to explore this intermediate zone together.

Such exploration might include a consideration of such questions as the following: At the time of marriage will the couple's income be sufficient to maintain a home and provide for the arrival of a possible child? If not, how will their income be supplemented? Will they receive any money from their parents? How important do the couple consider homemaking? How do the two persons use their present incomes? For what does each spend beyond necessities? Do they manage to save anything? Is either wasteful? Do they budget their money and stay within the budget? Do they spend without plan until their money is exhausted and then borrow, go into debt, or appeal to their parents? Do they exhibit similar degrees of generosity? What is their attitude toward home ownership? Toward cars? Toward insurance? Toward installment buying? Do they agree on how and by whom the family income will be handled? Do they know how to shop wisely? If they have had ample allowances from parents, would they be prepared to take a possible step down in their standard of living when they marry? Have they worked out trial budgets based on realistically projected family income and a realistic understanding of the cost of living? If in attempting to do so they ran into snags, did this motivate them to get further information or to sidestep the problem and say, "We'll find a way. We'll cross that bridge when we come to it"?

"Likes" and "Opposites"

Proverbially, "Likes repel, opposites attract," as if human beings were the poles of a magnet and their behavior were governed by relatively simple forces. Such a broad generalization might easily be carried to ridiculous extremes. If opposites attract, then the intelligent should marry morons, large persons should marry small ones, and college students should marry illiterates. If likes repel, similar interests, values, temperaments, or backgrounds would produce discord rather than harmony. Husband and wife should have complementary rather than clashing characteristics, enough similarity to be mutually agreeable and enough dissimilarity to be mutually stimulating. Even this is a broad generalization. In the last analysis all depends upon the two personalities involved. In some cases "likes" and in others "unlikes" have happy marriages.

There are combinations of traits, however, that may cause conflict. We may mention several by way of illustration. A meticulously neat individual and one who carelessly leaves clothes and other things lying about; a person who is punctual and one who disregards time; two individuals whose tempo of life is different; a person who pays particular attention to manners and one whose manners are crude; a person who is affectionate and one who does not like to touch or be touched; a person who is interested in acquiring possessions and one who would like to sacrifice possessions for travel; an individual whose rhythm of life makes him or her nocturnal and one whose rhythm makes him or her diurnal; one who is gregarious and one who does not like to be with groups of people; a very modest individual and one who is uninhibited; a person with a sense of humor and one lacking it; a conventional individual and one inclined to be conspicuously unconventional; an individual who has enthusiasm for living and one who is bored with life; an optimistic person and a cynic; an individual who functions more effectively under pressure and one who "goes to pieces" under stress; a sexually "warm" and responsive person and one who is sexually "cold" and unresponsive—such combinations can, of course, be successful when the differences are accepted or are offset by other traits and circumstances, but such combinations can also contribute to perennial conflict, especially when the differences crystallize as focal points of irritation.

One of the most controversial theories in the study of marriage formation has been the theory of complementary needs in mate selection (Winch, Ktsanes, and Ktsanes, 1954;

Winch, 1958; 1967). This theory proposes that "in mate selection each individual seeks within his or her field of eligibles that person who gives the greatest promise of providing him or her with maximum need gratification" (Winch, 1974b). This theory proposes that the principle of homogamy applies with regard to social characteristics, but that with regard to interpersonal characteristics, complementarity applies.

Winch and his colleagues outlined two types of complementarity:

Type I: The same need is gratified in both person A and person B but at very different levels of intensity. For example, if one spouse is highly dominant, the other will be very low on that need.

Type II: Different needs are gratified in A and B. For example, if one spouse is highly nurturant, the other will be found to be high on the succorant (or receptive) need.

The original test of the theory found some support for the notion that we tend to select as marriage partners those who are best able to complement our needs. Several other studies have been conducted during the past twenty years to test the theory. Without reviewing these studies in detail, it is possible to say that we really do not know whether this theory holds true or not. Most studies have been unable to verify Winch's findings, although these subsequent researchers used different methods to do follow-up studies. Still other studies, although they are in the minority, lend additional support for the theory. It is best to conclude at the present time that we really do not know yet whether individuals choose persons with complementary needs or with the same needs.

With human nature so variable and so complex and with the final judgment to be made by the reader anyway, we might never strike upon exactly the combination of traits that is in one's mind as he or she thinks of a possible union with some particular person.

We cannot even go so far as to say that it is always essential that the husband be masculine and the wife feminine, although this is the most commonly accepted and expected type of "opposites" that attract. It is better to suggest that the reader make his or her own careful analysis than to give the impression that a short list of generalizations will pigeonhole his or her particular problem and yield a ready-made judgment. Furthermore, it is not only the difference or similarity in one or a few particular traits that counts but all the traits of each person, the constellation of traits which constitutes one's total personality. A sense of humor may offset a quick temper; a lovable disposition may counteract the impracticality of the dreamer.

Choosing a Partner Like One's Parent

Not uncommon is a tendency to seek a marriage partner like one's father or mother, as the case may be, the parent of opposite gender having been an adolescent ideal. It may be well to desire that a husband or a wife possess some of the admirable qualities of one's parent, and the parent's qualities may form a good basis upon which to found an ideal that will grow as time goes on. But to set up one's parent as an ideal and to insist that one's spouse conform is to establish an impossible expectation and to set an unattainable goal, for several reasons. There are no two persons exactly alike. Parents and future spouse were born in different cultural eras. Typically, the former are also some twenty to thirty years ahead in their development. Twenty-five years from now one's husband or wife may be more like one's father or mother, but at the moment it is impossible to eradicate the age difference. Furthermore, an individual does not know firsthand what his or her parent was like when the parent was the age of the future spouse. Because parents love one another and have a happy marriage does not prove that the child could duplicate their experience with one of them. In order to live with one of the parents as the other does, the child would have to be that parent rather than himself or herself. In many cases, it is not the actual qualities of the real person that are set up as the standard but rather the idealized image of the parent. Actually, not even the individual completely attains this unreal standard. Naturally, then, no other person could be expected to attain it.

If a child's relationship with the parent of opposite gender has been unpleasant, he or she may seek a marriage partner having quite different qualities. This is understandable and not unreasonable, as long as the child allows for difference of degree in various personality traits and realizes that traits may be exhibited differently under varying circumstances, judges by the whole individual, and knows at least in part which of the parent's traits were present at the time of marriage and which developed because of the marital situation.

Length of Acquaintance

How long should two people know each other before they marry? There is a relationship between length of acquaintance and success in marriage, longer periods of association being related to more successful marital adjustment (Spanier, 1976b). There is a qualitative as well as a quantitative aspect of this matter, however. It is not only how long but how well a couple have known each other.

When two individuals marry after a relatively brief acquaintance, they learn things about each other after the wedding that they might better have learned before. They learn them in a new atmosphere with a different "freedom" of choice. There is greater pressure toward either acceptance or conflict. They may be called upon to revise their expectations regarding one another, especially with respect to each person's role in marriage. Inability to revise such expectations and to accept the other person as he or she is rather than as he or she was thought to be is one of the factors commonly contributing to marital failure. Putting it another way, they marry before they know each other well enough to reject each other as marriage partners.

Although no one can say with reasonable certainty precisely how long acquaintance should be, of some cases it may safely be said that the period is too brief. In student groups, instances of whirlwind romances continually come to light. The following cases illustrate this point. A couple had a "blind date" on June 9. On June 16 the man proposed marriage; on June 22 the woman talked with a counselor, wondering whether she should marry immediately. In another instance a woman's parents arranged to have her meet a man of whom they strongly approved. With some reluctance she had a date with him. She found that she liked him better than she had anticipated. On their fourth date he gave her a ring. The wedding followed shortly thereafter.

Occasionally, one of these abbreviated acquaintances prefaces successful marriage because the two persons are highly compatible and their relationship expands and deepens after the wedding. But the chance element is greatly increased, and they are successful in spite of, not because of, the brief acquaintance. Their rare experience is a very precarious basis upon which to rationalize one's own desire for haste.

Let us perform an imaginary experiment. We shall choose at random 1,000 college men and 1,000 college women, none of whom is married. We shall blindfold these 2,000 individuals and let them mill about in a large enclosure. At a given signal they will stand still and take off their blindfolds. Then each man will marry the woman standing nearest his right hand. It is highly probable that in this group of a thousand marriages there would be some successful, just by chance. There would be persons who married without ever having seen each other before but who, nevertheless, would have fallen in love and married if they had met. By chance some individuals would make a good "choice" of marriage partner. How many people, however, would want to acquire a spouse by such a process? They would argue that the chances were against a good choice and that it was a mistake to give too much weight to the exceptions. Yet when similar exceptions occur in day-to-day life, some persons use them as a basis for broad generalizations, unfounded assumptions, and wishful thinking.

A variation of this type of acquaintance is the one in which the couple are separated most of the time and see each other only during brief vacation periods, when there is a holiday atmosphere. Each puts his or her "best foot forward," problem "solving" is limited to discussion, and the objective is to have as good a time as possible in the few days available. In one case, for example, the couple were together for a total of only forty to fifty days in four years, never more than three days at one time. Yet they planned to marry soon.

Another type, deceiving because it gives a superficial appearance of sufficient length, is that which begins relatively early in life. For example, a student says, "I have known her for five years and gone with her for three. That ought to be long enough." But they are both 18 years old. Thus, they became acquainted when they were 13 and started dating each other when they were 15. Certainly this five-year period should not be given the same weight as the period, say, from age 18 to age 23.

Some Developmental Theories about Marital Choice

Psychologists and sociologists have given considerable attention to the process of mate choice. Several theories have been developed and at least partially supported by research studies (Lewis, 1973; Murstein, 1970; Kerckhoff and Davis, 1962; Bolton, 1961; Coombs, 1961; Winch, 1958). Let us briefly examine some of these ideas about how two individuals eventually come to choose each other as mates.

Once a relationship has begun, it may develop a momentum that carries a couple toward marriage. Bolton (1961) calls the components of this momentum "*escalators.*" There are five escalators that move us toward marriage:

1 The *involvement escalator* "comes into operation as the individual finds that his education and career plans, his religious and moral identity, his daily schedule of going to and fro, and so on, become involved in the relation with a particular person."

2 The *commitment escalator* "operates mainly through the sequence of formal, publicly announced commitments, but also through the fact that an informal or even implicit commitment is not only a pledge to another but a commitment to a definition of self and of one's broader situation. The commitment escalator is not only binding but propellent, for one commitment contains the seeds of propulsion to another—for example, a commitment to love in our culture implies one is thinking about a commitment to marry."

3 The *addiction escalator* "seeks to perpetuate a relationship in order to avoid the psychological withdrawal symptoms accompanying cessation of sexual, affectional, or prestigeful relations."

4 The *fantasy escalator* "provides a compulsive propulsion to maintain the relation as a symbol of some fantasy, whether the institutionally provided romantic fantasy or some more individual one."

5 The *idealization* escalator "comes into play as a result of the involvement of the individual's self-esteem in his indications to others of his choice of mate, creating in some cases a tendency to idealize the image of the partner in order to maintain self-esteem."

The theory of escalators suggests that mate selection is a developmental process. Lewis (1973) also developed a developmental theory suggesting six stages of the mate selection process. Individuals first perceive *similarities* in each other. They may then go on to develop *rapport* with each other. If they are successful at this stage, it is likely that they will engage in *self-disclosure*. The process of *role taking* follows, where the couple learn mentally to put themselves in the position of the other person. If the couple get along well and the partners complement each other nicely, they can be said to have achieved *role fit*. Finally, the couple who continue as a pair will have achieved *dyadic crystallization*. This means that they identify themselves and others identify them as a couple, they are committed to each other, and they function as a dyad (pair) in numerous ways.

The filter theory of mate selection (Kerckhoff and Davis, 1962) suggests that the various stages are really filters that we pass through. Exhibit 6-1 shows that there are six filters. Beginning with all possible dating partners, we are immediately limited in our dating choices since only persons accessible to us could actually be considered. This is the propinquity (or nearness) filter. The attractiveness filter works by eliminating from consideration those persons who do not appeal to us and would therefore not be dating or marriage partners. Couples who are attracted to one another pass through a social background filter. This means that the principle of homogamy operates here to encourage the formation of relationships among those with similar social backgrounds while discouraging relationships among those with different social backgrounds. These couples must pass through a consensus filter, which eliminates those who do not agree on matters important to their relationship. The theory suggests that the remaining couples pass through a complementarity filter, with couples remain-

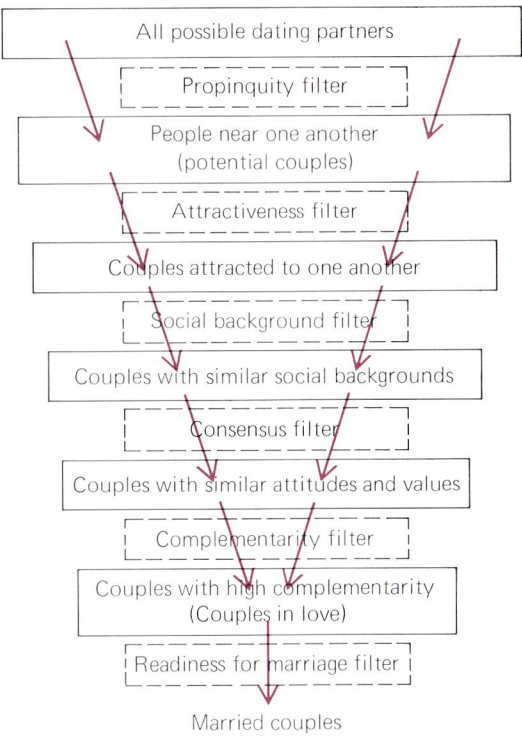

Exhibit 6-1 A filter theory of mate selection. (*Source*: Kerckhoff and Davis, 1962.)

ing together if they complement each other's needs. Finally couples with high complementarity who are in love will marry if they are ready and the circumstances are appropriate. The last filter, then, eliminates those not ready for marriage.

These theories of mate selection have in common the principle that we go through a series of stages in coming to a decision to marry. Although there are different ideas about what the stages are, how they are ordered, and why they operate the way they do, we can see that once a relationship begins, there are forces which encourage its continuation as well as forces which may encourage its termination. The weight of these opposing forces will vary depending on the individuals involved as well as factors over which they may have little control, such as a necessary separation, lack of financial resources for marriage, or legal problems which may prevent them from marrying at a given time.

Reasons for Poor Choice of Marriage Partner

Some of the factors making for poor choice of marriage partner have already been implied. Confusing infatuation with love; hoping to reform the other party; judging by too few qualities; marrying before tastes and attitudes are well understood; overemphasizing money; acting under the stimulus of rebound, spite, habit, pity, and similar attitudes these obviously contribute to errors in judgment. Among other factors are those that follow.

Some persons make a poor choice of partner because they marry in haste. Less care and intelligence may be exhibited in choosing a husband or wife than in choosing an occupation, registering for courses, or even selecting new garments. Marrying the first person who is willing, without waiting for experience broad enough to give ground for comparison and contrast, sometimes makes for poor choice. This does not mean that the first person is invariably a poor choice. It suggests only that one should exercise caution and judgment and should not assume that if the first person is not accepted, there will be no other.

There are individuals who are not sufficiently conversant with the requirements of marriage. They do not understand what marriage involves and do not realize that it is a most intimate relationship with responsibilities as well as pleasures. Some go so far as to think only up to, rather than beyond, the wedding or even to think of marriage as if it were a lifelong date. Some persons gloss over problems or irritating personality traits because they do not recognize that the time element in dating is different from that involved in marriage. A personality trait that is annoying may be like a pebble in one's shoe. If you walk across the room with a pebble in your shoe, you will notice it, but it will not be excessively painful or injurious. If, however, you walk twenty miles with the same pebble in the same shoe, at the end of your trip you will have either an open wound or a callus. Dating is like walking across the room. Marriage is like taking a twenty-mile hike.

Marrying to please one's family rather than oneself is risky, since the individual rather than the family has to live with the person chosen. In some cultures where more emphasis is put upon institutional factors in marriage, such as support, protection, and reproduction, and less upon personal factors, such as companionship and love, families may make better choices than individuals, since what is sought is stability rather than personal satisfaction. In our culture, where the personal factors are held in such incomparable esteem, only the individual can make the final choice, although he or she may, of course, give weight to his or her family's opinions.

In one sense, everyone who marries does so to escape something as well as to achieve something. One wants to escape various unpalatable elements in his or her unmarried state. But to marry in order to escape circumstances that are unusually unpleasant, such as an unhappy home situation, the irksomeness of earning one's own living, or the demands of a school program that is not to one's liking, when the factor of escape carries more weight than the relationship with the other person, is a precarious basis upon which to make a choice of marriage partner. One case will serve to clarify the point. The parents of the woman in this case were divorced when she was an infant. When she was 10 years old, her mother married an alcoholic. The daughter never got along with him. There were frequent quarrels, especially when he had been drinking, and there were perpetual ill feelings. The woman had for some time felt a desire to leave home. At the age of 17 she became engaged to two men and accepted a ring from each. Because she could not make up her mind which she loved more, she wavered between them. Usually she was partial to the one who was present. Her decision was made for her when one of the men left town. Soon afterward, she married the other. An impersonal observer could recognize almost immediately that the woman was deeply infatuated with both men and not ready to marry either. Her desire to escape from home was so great that she could not resist and blindly made her choice. Two years later she obtained a divorce.

Parental Objections

Parents' objections to their son's or daughter's marriage can pose a threat to the success of the marriage. When there is parental disapproval, it is essential to ascertain first the nature of the objection. Do the parents insist upon lifelong celibacy, or do they object to the child's marrying immediately or in the near future? They may later approve of a marriage to which they now object because of the age factor. Or is opposition due to the fact that they do not approve of the individual chosen, or his or her religion?

If the parents object to their child's marrying immediately or soon, it may be feasible to wait a bit longer, especially if the child is of student age. It can mean enough to a young couple to have their parents' approval that a brief wait may prove a good investment in future happiness.

If the objections are not directed against marriage as such or the time of marriage but apply only to a particular individual chosen, they should not be disregarded until one is certain that he or she understands the reasons behind them. If the objections grow out of prejudice or incomplete knowledge, they may be given little weight if the parents remain immovable. Perhaps the objections may be softened by arranging contacts between the parents and the individual in question, so that they may see the potential partner in a different light.

When parental disapprobation is directed toward a specific individual, the situation becomes even more difficult. The objections may have an effect opposite to that intended; instead of making the love object seem less attractive, they make him or her seem more so. The young person may confuse attitudes toward the other individual with the reaction against his or her parents. Since many an ill-advised choice is made for this reason, it might have been included among the reasons for poor choice listed above. In some cases, parents will continue to object to the marriage for reasons which their son or daughter cannot accept. A great many people no longer see or communicate with their parents because they married against the latter's wishes. It is difficult to say whether such situations could have been avoided by anything short of canceling the wedding. Individuals intending to marry sometimes find they have no choice but to marry and accept the consequences of parental disapproval.

ENGAGEMENT

Engagement affords added security during the period prior to the wedding and provides the couple with an opportunity to make final plans to announce their intention to marry. It affords opportunity for the first, or perhaps for further, steps in the assimilation of each person into the in-group that constitutes the family of the other person. It is the beginning of a shift from the family of orientation to the family of procreation. Virtually all marriages have been preceded by an engagement of some duration, but not all engagements end in marriage. Whereas a broken engagement was considered a serious breach of one's intention to marry in previous eras, it is now considered unfortunate but sensible, if warranted, since relationships that do not survive engagement would not be likely to have survived marriage.

Some societies have created premarriage rituals for the purpose of adding strength and importance to the subsequent marriage ceremony. This function may still be a latent part of American engagements, but we now consider this period to be more related to compatibility testing, planning for marriage, and making wedding plans. Engagement is a more or less public statement of an intention to marry. As a result the couple identify themselves, and others also identify them, as committed to each other and to marriage. This labeling process undoubtedly influences the couple's concept of themselves and their relationship. The period of being "an engaged couple" is more than just a time to wait for marriage. It may ultimately be very instructive for the couples, since in this new status they may learn something about each other that was not evident when they were just going together or dating casually.

How Long Should Engagement Be?

This question is a reasonable one but difficult to answer. Engagements range from nonexistent to several years long. The data show that there is a positive correlation between length of engagement and the quality of the marital relationship (Spanier, 1971; Locke, 1951). The longer the engagement, the more likely it is that the couple will have a healthy marriage. Of course, there is the possibility of an engagement which is too long. Couples who are engaged for several years should ask themselves why they have remained in this state without marrying or terminating the relationship. In some cases there may be good reasons for an engagement of three or four years, but in other cases it might be an indication that there is sufficient fear of marriage on the part of one or both partners to suggest that marriage is not advisable.

Engagements which are too brief are much more common. Short engagements are often associated with premarital pregnancy, which itself is strongly related to poor adjustment in marriage (Lewis and Spanier, 1978). Whether or not a pregnancy is involved, short engagements may be indicative of haste in the decision to marry, and research shows that they are associated with poor marital adjustment (Spanier, 1971). Data collected during several different studies indicate that the average American engagement lasts six to seven months (Spanier, 1971; Spanier, Lewis, and Cole, 1975; Spanier, 1976b). There is, however, considerable variation, and much depends on the personalities, proximity, the wedding plans, how often the couple see each other, whether they date other people while engaged, and other similar factors.

Engagement As Transition

In modern American society, engagement is probably a more critical transition for females than it is for males. We say this because the activities of the engagement period and the wedding itself seem to be more focused on the female than the male. Most young couples marrying for the first time appear to follow the custom of putting the female's picture in the paper. Why is the male's picture not put in the paper? Traditionally, marriage was considered to be of primary significance to the female, and the tradition of putting her picture in the paper with a statement that "Mr. and Mrs. John

Jones announce the engagement of their daughter . . ." is still with us. More couples are putting a joint picture in the paper, but the authors have never seen the male only. The female's family tends to bear most of the wedding costs. Wedding showers tend to be for women only, although more and more "couple" showers are occurring. And only females wear engagement rings.

Thus, from a symbolic point of view, females are more closely identified with the engagement and marriage rituals and customs. But perhaps more important is the social-psychological dimension of the couple's adjustment. Females more often give up their jobs after marriage, they more often stay home after the birth of a child, they are more likely to have to move as a result of a husband's job acquisition or transfer, and studies show that their initial sexual adjustment in marriage may be more difficult than is the case for males (Christensen and Gagnon, 1965).

By pointing to the more critical transition for females, we do not intend to imply that engagement is taken lightly by males. Engagement for them is also likely to be an important period of transition. Although they are more likely than females to continue whatever occupational or educational activities they were involved in before the engagement, they are not immune from the planning which accompanies engagement or the anxiety about marriage that most individuals experience. Of course, these tendencies are only that—tendencies. Changes are occurring with regard to male-female differences during this transitional period. Couples often plan to delay having children for several years or do not plan to have children at all. Women increasingly desire careers and intend to complete their education. Women may be as likely as males to find employment after graduation from school; and a small number of couples expect that the female will be the primary breadwinner and the male the primary homemaker.

Rings, Pins, and Other "Ornaments"

An engagement ring has a meaning which is generally agreed upon. Sometimes, however, partners may have different ideas about the meaning of a ring. This applies even more to the meaning of pins and other ornaments such as drops, lavaliers, pearls, or friendship rings. Because of this lack of a clear, commonly accepted and understood definition, a pin or other piece of jewelry may vary in significance from group to group or individual to individual. A man who gives someone a ring or pin may give it a meaning different from that given to it by the woman who accepts it. There may be agreement about the meaning when it changes hands, but as time goes on the meaning may become altered for one person while it remains constant for the other. It is easier to exchange rings, pins, or other symbols of love, commitment, or interest, than to return them or have them returned.

Questions to Be Discussed during Engagement

When a couple are contemplating marriage, there are several questions which they might well consider during the engagement at the very latest—preferably before. (1) Are they going to plan to have children? If so, when, and about how many? What is each person's attitude toward control of conception and abortion? (2) Where will they live after the wedding? (3) What type of wedding will they have? When will it take place? Whom will they invite? (4) Will they have a honeymoon? If so, where will they go? How long will it be, and how much will they let it cost? (5) What are their attitudes toward the sexual side of marriage? (6) What will be their source of income? How will money be managed? (7) How will they work out any differences in religious commitment which may exist? (8) Will their marriage require any shifts in career or educational plans? (9) How will household tasks be allocated between them? (10) How will they divide their time with and attention to parents and in-laws?

The reader may think that such questions are too trite to be mentioned, that every couple naturally discuss such topics and reach mutually acceptable answers before the wedding. By and large this is probably true; but it is not universally true. In counseling, the writers have had persons come to them with marital problems emerging from a failure to answer one or another of these questions.

Telling about Oneself

How much of one's past should be revealed to one's fiancé? No universally applicable answer to this question is possible. It depends upon a number of factors which vary in individual cases: the other person and his or her attitude toward oneself and one's behavior; what he or she volunteers about himself or herself; what the incidents are that cause the question to be raised; how long ago they occurred; how much possibility of continuation or repetition there is; one's own present attitude toward the past; what has happened between the incidents and the engagement; how much danger of discovery there is or how much risk of information reaching the fiancé through indirect channels; how much each wishes to know about the other; the reason for which the individual feels he or she should tell. Of course openness and honesty during engagement are desirable. Anything that may readily be learned through a third party is better told in advance. Whatever is revealed is better told before the wedding. It is important to avoid overstressing the facts for the sake of feeling that one has made a confession. Because of the hypersensitivity of both persons during engagement, it is easy to exaggerate either the revelation or its interpretation. What is told should be told as information that will further the marital adjustment of the couple. It should not be told only to obtain emotional release, important as this release may be. The effects on the other party, as well as the effects on oneself, should be taken into consideration.

Many young people struggle painfully with this question of revealing the past. They feel guilty when they think of keeping some fact secret. They are fearful when they think of making it known. They are torn by conflict and indecision. Such persons may find help in discussing the problem in confidence with a counselor, either to bring a plan to a focus or to confirm a plan already determined.

Broken Engagements

Engagements entered with best intentions and sincerest motives are sometimes broken. Those entered without careful thought and after very brief acquaintance are especially ephemeral. The younger the couple are at the time of engagement, the more likely they are to change their attitudes toward one another, and, consequently, the greater the probability that the engagement will not endure.

Many an engagement is broken because a couple "put the cart before the horse" and expect the engagement to do something it cannot accomplish. They are insecure in their relationship and fear they will lose each other. They become engaged in order to create the security they desire. But an engagement cannot produce security. It can only express security that already exists.

In an early study of 1,000 engaged couples, at least a third of the men and about half the women had had one or more broken engagements (Burgess and Wallin, 1953). In a study of 8,000 women who had been married, more than one-fourth (26.8 percent) had been engaged at least once before becoming engaged to the men they married; about 10 percent (included in the 26.8 percent) had been engaged twice before (Bowman, 1950).

Some of the more common problems that couples may experience while engaged that they may not encounter before engagement are:

- How to deal with future in-laws and parents
- Allegiances to previously acquired friends
- Economics (spending money and financial planning)
- Public appearance as a committed couple

Once a commitment to marriage has been made, parents and in-laws are likely to take a more active role in the couple's relationship. Many young persons experience difficulty with this parental intervention. The problems can be especially difficult when there is a difference is religious, racial, or ethnic background which troubles the parents. Each partner may have developed his or her own set of friends over the years, and with engagement and the couple's identity as a committed dyad, they may experience difficulties in how to allocate their time with friends. Do they bring the two sets of friends together, do they deal with each set of friends as a couple, or does each partner maintain his or her own friends without involving the fiancé(e)? With marriage in sight, every decision to spend money while engaged will reflect on the resources ultimately available to the couple after marriage. Spending habits may therefore be different during engagement from what they were during dating. Couples may have conflict over the excessive spending of one of the partners. Finally, since the couple have become publicly committed, the behavior of each person may reflect on the other. Conflict may sometimes develop over the way in which one person may act around others.

The early Burgess and Wallin (1953) study asked persons why their engagements had been broken. In order of frequency mentioned, from greatest to least, couples gave the following reasons:

1 Slight emotional attachment
2 Separation
3 Parental opposition
4 Cultural divergences
5 Personality problems

It is reasonable to expect that the greatest reason for broken engagements is that the couple no longer get along well with each other. They may learn that they are not suited for marriage to each other, and the love that they initially experienced may disappear. Conflict over issues ranging from trivial to important may have developed and interfered with their relationship. Sometimes the attachment to one person is lost because one of the partners develops a relationship with another person.

Separation has always been a major reason for the termination of relationships, both before and during engagement. A bond is difficult to maintain over distance, and the individuals may grow apart in their interests. They may want to meet and date other persons, or they may both change in such a way that when they return to the same environment, they find that they do not share the interest and affection that they once thought they did. It is not uncommon for a man to join one of the armed forces and to return two or three years later to hear statements like, "The service sure changed you," or "You seem different now than you did before." Of course he is different. But we fail to realize that we all change over time. Males and females who are separated both change, but they do not change together. Couples who can share experiences on a daily basis and thus change together do not face the same problem that separation can produce. Nevertheless, despite a separation many relationships continue, remain strong, and end in a successful marriage. This attests to the dedication and commitment of the parties involved.

Parental opposition has already been mentioned as potentially troublesome. Many parents feel they have a responsibility, if not a right, to pass judgment on the persons their children date and marry. Most young persons hope that their mate choice is satisfactory to their parents, but they are reluctant to give up someone they love because of parental objections. Nevertheless, parental objections can be so overwhelming and cause enough of a problem for the couple that the relationship deteriorates. Other engagements end because the couple find that their social backgrounds are too different or that their beliefs, values, priorities, or plans for the future are sufficiently different that marriage is ill-advised. Personality problems may threaten a relationship by producing conflict or tension which forces the engagement to end. And of course, more than one of the reasons stated could be present at the same time.

A broken engagement is distressing, to say the least, but it is not so painful as a broken marriage. It is better for the couple to learn before their wedding that they are incompatible than to marry blindly and discover this later. The purpose of the engagement is to enable them to make the final adjustments before the wedding. It is inevitable that some of these attempts at adjustment will fail.

As a rule, the time to break an engagement is as soon as either party wishes to break it. This does not mean that it is to be broken and remade each time they have a quarrel and then patch up their differences. When either one, after careful thought, decides that he or she cannot go on with the wedding plans, the other person should be told. Once a couple have become enmeshed in a relationship as permeating as an engagement, it is usually impossible for one to get out without hurting the other, unless they both desire release. The longer the break is postponed, the greater the hurt is likely to be, and during the delay the one who is going to make the break must "put up a false front" and misrepresent himself or herself to the other party. To marry a person against one's better judgment is only to increase the injury. It is neither a favor nor a charity to marry a person against one's will. Neither pride, the opinions of family or friends, the fact that wedding plans are under way, nor the embarrassment of facing the other person is sufficient reason to postpone the effecting of one's decision.

Another not infrequent deterrent to making one's decision known is the fear that the disappointed individual will commit some rash act as a result of the break. Consider such cases as the following.

After a brief acquaintance, and on the basis of what later proved to be infatuation, a college woman became engaged to a man who soon afterward joined the Army. When the woman discovered that she was not in love and did not want to marry him, the man threatened to desert the Army and do something desperate. His mother tried to prevail upon the woman to marry her son, insisting that a broken engagement would result in the ruination of his future. The woman was confused and did not know what to do.

Another couple had been going together for several years. The man was sure he loved the woman and was very persistent about their marrying. For some time she had felt that she was no longer in love with him and was convinced that she would never marry him. She had repeatedly tried to explain her attitude, but he refused to listen. The man had periods of depression and moodiness. Once, after she had told him she could not marry him, he became very depressed. He went for a walk and met a friend, and the two men decided to go hunting. When the man in question took his gun from its rack, it went off, and the bullet penetrated his chest just over his heart. At the time it was reported as an accident, and the woman accepted that explanation. Later, however, when they had talked of marriage again and once more she had told him she could not marry him, he told her that what had passed as an accident had been an attempt at suicide. After that she was afraid that if she persisted in her refusal he would make another attempt to take his own life.

What should an individual do under circumstances such as these? There is only one feasible plan of action: Break the engagement as painlessly as possible, take a firm stand, and tenaciously adhere to the decision. If the engagement was seriously entered and the break is founded upon a sincere change of heart, what the other person does, even if it be self-destruction, is not the fault of the one making the break. This may seem like a heartless statement; but it is not so heartless as it would be to suggest that the future happiness of two persons be jeopardized by plunging them into a loveless, incompatible union. Again, a counselor may be able to help the individual work out a plan.

In the great majority of instances, suicide threats in this sort of circumstance never get any further than the self-pity stage. If an individual seeks alcoholic escape from problems or threatens suicide, he or she exhibits an instability of personality which in itself might be ample reason for breaking the engagement, even if love had not died or reason had not intervened. An individual threatening vengeance demonstrates a type of immaturity that would be highly undesirable in a marriage partner. Most couples recover from the shock of a broken engagement more readily than they imagine possible at the time of the break. In a state of emotional upset it is easy to exaggerate possible consequences, most of which never occur.

Some individuals recover slowly. A few never recover. But such cases do not constitute sufficient reason for entering an undesired marriage, though they do constitute a weighty argument for avoiding insincerity, shortsightedness, and premature commitment in becoming engaged.

It is to be expected that both parties, and especially the unwilling participant, in a broken engagement will be temporarily upset and disillusioned. It is not easy for one who is hurt to avoid permanent bitterness and frustration, but as far as possible he or she has to face the facts and, after allowing for a period of adjustment, start over.

TERMS TO BE LEARNED

bride price
complementary needs (complementarity)
conflict
consensus
developmental theory
dowry
dyad (dyadic)

dyadic crystallization
engagement
escalators
field of eligibles
filter theory
gynecology (gynecological)
homogamy
incest

Pap smear
principle of ethnocentric preference
principle of incest avoidance
propinquity
reciprocal attraction
role fit
role taking

SELECTED READINGS

HUSTON, T. L. (ed.): *Foundations of Interpersonal Attraction*, Academic Press, New York, 1974. Presents a wide-ranging analysis of how affectional bonds between persons develop, the nature of these bonds, and the relationship of attraction to social interaction.

MONTAGU, M. F. ASHLEY: *Human Heredity*, 2d ed., The World Publishing Company, Cleveland, 1963. Discussion of heredity with special emphasis on human heredity. Included is a "census of inherited disorders which should enable the reader to look up any condition in which he is interested."

SCHEINFELD, AMRAM: *Heredity in Humans*, J. B. Lippincott Company, Philadelphia, 1972. Nontechnical. Genetic risks of drugs, chromosome abnormalities, racial differences, inheritance of certain diseases, genetic engineering, genetic codes governing male and female. Answers many questions.

WINCH, R.: *Mate-Selection: A Study of Complementary Needs*, Harper & Row, Publishers, Incorporated, New York, 1958. One of the classic works dealing with mate selection, this book examines various theories and research, focusing particularly on the theory of complementary needs.

Chapter 7

Partner Selection and Mixed Marriages

The tendency for persons to marry others who are similar to themselves in social characteristics—homogamy—is the norm in mate selection. There is a great deal of evidence to suggest that Americans prefer as mates persons who are similar to rather than different from themselves with regard to age, nationality, race, family background, education, intelligence, previous marital status, and religion (Burgess and Wallin, 1953; Hollingshead, 1950; Burgess and Locke, 1953; Jacobson and Matheny, 1962; Kirkpatrick, 1963; Winch, 1971; Lewis and Spanier, 1978; Leslie, 1973; Clayton, 1975). Preferences aside, there are a multitude of social forces which encourage homogamy. Many of these forces are subtle. For example, many couples meet while attending high school or college. As a result, educational homogamy operates without much consideration on our part. Other forces are not so subtle. For example, parents may make the point over and over again to their children that they would oppose a marriage to someone of a particular religion. Despite the tendency to homogamy, there are, of course, many marriages among persons who are dissimilar in one or more social characteristics. These variations should be expected in a society such as ours where individuals continually interact with persons from diverse social backgrounds. In most high schools, colleges, universities, urban areas, and employment settings there are likely to be persons from a variety of backgrounds with diverse social characteristics. Let us define a *mixed marriage* as one in which there is considerable or significant difference between the spouses in one or more relevant characteristics.

MIXED MARRIAGE

In all marriages there are some differences. Many of these, if accentuated, might be sufficient to classify the marriage as mixed. Sometimes in a mixed marriage there is more than one element of mixture. The elements of difference in a mixed marriage usually do not change after the wedding. The couple must, in the typical case, adjust to the differences in order to make the marriage successful. Many young persons contemplating marriage assume that it is easier to change the elements of difference than it actually is. Theoretically there is no type of marriage that contains within itself the germs of its own inevitable failure. Any marriage can be successful if the couple face and solve the special problems involved. There probably are a few marriages which are hopelessly doomed from the beginning, but these marriages are not common. We shall see in later chapters that there are many factors associated with marital failure, and when marriages do fail it is usually because of a combination of influences, rarely a single one. But no set of variables is known to be universally associated with marital failure, and many marriages succeed in spite of overwhelming pressures which would encourage their dissolution.

There is no single element that is always present in successful relationships and always absent in unsuccessful ones, or vice versa. Success or failure depends upon one whole personality reacting with another whole personality and both reacting to the whole marital situation. In mixed marriage, too, success or failure depends upon total adjustment rather than merely upon the elements of difference. For example, in an interfaith marriage, success or failure depends not only upon the religious difference as such but also upon the husband's attitude toward the wife's religion and her attitude toward his; upon their personal qualities; and upon the extent of conflict that might exist in such areas as in-laws, sex, money, children, or recreation.

Although the success of mixed marriage depends upon the total situation and the two personalities involved, rather than upon only the elements of mixture, those elements sometimes become the focal point for conflict or are blamed for conflict which is due to other causes. Suppose, for instance, that there is conflict between a husband and wife because their personalities are incompatible. Suppose that to this situation there is added a disparity in religion. Unconsciously the couple seek an explanation of their poor adjustment. From their point of view the most obvious explanation is the religious difference. Consequently, they fasten upon that. They feel that if they could resolve the conflict over religion, their problems would be solved. As a matter of fact, the religious difference is only one among many contributing factors playing a part in their marital disharmony. In almost every case, disharmony, discord, and failure in marriage are the result of multiple causation. There is seldom only one single cause, although there are cases—such as that in which one partner is a psychopathic personality—which are so one-sided that they cannot be worked out by the other partner, no matter what he or she does to solve the problem.

THE MARRIAGE RATE

The marriage rate (the number per 1,000 population who marry in a given year) fluctuates. It decreased during the Great Depression, for instance, and increased at the beginning and end of World War II. More than a year before the United States entered World War II, when selective service was under consideration, the marriage rate rose (see Exhibit 7-1). After Pearl Harbor the rate reached another peak. Then, while millions of men of marriageable age were in military service, many of them abroad, the rate decreased. It rose again after the surrender of Germany and Japan, reaching an all-time high in 1946. After that it declined for a while, only to rise again as the young people of the "baby boom" of the 1945–1957 period reached marriageable age (U.S. Department of Health, Education, and Welfare, *Monthly Vital Statistics Report*, 1971). In 1972–1973 the rate reached 10.9, the highest postwar point reached since the early 1950s (U.S. Bureau of the Census, *Statistical Abstract*, 1975). Currently the rate is declining. In 1976 it was 10.0, the lowest since August 1968 (U.S. Department of Health, Education, and Welfare, *Monthly Vital Statistics Report*, 1977).

The *number* of marriages has also declined. In 1975, there were estimated to be 2,126,000, or about 104,000 fewer than in 1974 and 158,000 fewer than in 1973. This decline occurred even though there were about 2,000,000 more single, widowed, and divorced persons of marriageable age (U.S. Department of Health, Education, and Welfare, *Monthly Vital Statistics Report*, 1975, 1976). As suggested above, statistics such as these fluctuate from year to year. In spite of varying rates, most people do marry, some more than once. So it cannot be assumed that

Exhibit 7-1 Marriage rate per 1,000 population: United States, 1925–1975. (Adapted from U.S. Department of Health, Education, and Welfare, *Monthly Vital Statistics Report*, May 5, 1976.)

these figures indicate that marriage in this country is becoming passé.

Let us examine several types of social factors in mate selection and attempt to ascertain the special problems that each may contribute to marital adjustment.

PROPINQUITY

Propinquity, or nearness, is an important factor in mate selection. It is such an obvious one that we tend to take it for granted and not even think of it as a social factor. But residential propinquity in mate selection has important implications for marital choice. A number of studies have demonstrated that within eligible groups, the probability of marriage varies directly with the probability of interaction (Katz and Hill, 1958). The probability of interaction in turn is related to the distance and segregation of racial, religious, economic, and other groups.

Even in this time of automobiles and other forms of transportation, we still find individuals marrying within the same neighborhoods, the same communities, and the same college campuses. "It appears that when all is said and done, the 'one and only' may have a better than 50-50 chance of living within walking distance!" (Kephart, 1972)

AGE

Age at First Marriage

When the ages at first marriage for all persons who marry in the United States are arranged in order from lowest to highest, the middle, or median, age is about 23 for males and 21 for females. In other words, half the males who marry do so at about age 23 or younger, and half the females who marry do so at about age 21 or younger. As indicated in Exhibit 7-2, the median age at first marriage has shown an overall decline since 1890, but there has been a slight increase since 1955. It appears that in recent years individuals have begun to marry somewhat later than was customary before (Glick, 1975). This increase in age at marriage could be attributed to several factors. The increase in sexual freedom experienced by the current generation of young persons contributes to a later age at marriage, since access to a partner for sexual intercourse may no longer be a powerful motivating reason to marry while young. The rapidly spreading existence of cohabitation outside of marriage provides some young persons with an opportunity to live together, share intimacies, and provide many of the same functions for each other that marriage does. Thus, many couples who will eventually

Exhibit 7-2 Median Age at First Marriage

Year	Male	Female
1975	23.5	21.1
1974	23.1	21.1
1973	23.2	21.0
1972	23.3	20.9
1971	23.1	20.9
1970	23.2	20.8
1965	22.8	20.6
1960	22.8	20.3
1955	22.6	20.2
1950	22.8	20.3
1940	24.3	21.5
1930	24.3	21.3
1920	24.6	21.2
1910	25.1	21.6
1900	25.9	21.9
1890	26.1	22.0

Source: U.S. Bureau of the Census, *Current Population Reports,* March 1975.

marry live together for a period of time beforehand, and this decision delays the time of marriage. Whereas many cohabiting couples state that they have no intention of marrying their partner or at least have not yet made a marriage decision, others do intend to marry but are waiting until circumstances for marriage are more convenient or appropriate than they may seem at the present time.

Age at first marriage is correlated with educational attainment. In other words, the higher the educational level, the later the age at marriage. Thus, college students tend to marry later than those who have not attended college. The recent increase in marriage age, however, applies to all educational levels, and is especially pronounced among the noncollege population.

Despite these recent increases in age at marriage, the overall trend in the twentieth century has been downward. There are several social trends which are conducive to early marriage (K. Davis, 1972). A century ago, agriculture was the dominant way in which a male earned his living in the United States. He was expected to be self-supporting before he was permitted to take a bride. This often took several years. Consequently, males in 1890 married at age 26, on the average. Females were not tied to the role of breadwinner and thus married earlier, at 22 on the average. But whereas in 1890 about 95 percent of men farmed, today the figure is less than 5 percent. As we have moved away from agriculture as a means of subsistence, so has marriage become more removed from the ability of the male to establish financial independence. Now a male and female can both begin working the moment they finish school and can have incomes sufficient to support them. They need not wait for the same reasons that couples did a century ago. The declining necessity of male earning power is therefore a factor conducive to early marriages.

The spread of contraceptive practice is another change conducive to early marriage, since marriage can now be better separated from childbearing and parenthood. Whereas many years ago it was assumed, and indeed followed, that couples would have children soon after their marriage, this is no longer customary. Couples today increasingly plan their families, and postponement of the first child is more common than not. By delaying the birth of a child, the couple can also delay the expenses associated with a child and can therefore marry earlier.

Perhaps another factor associated with early marriage is the rapid increase in divorce rates. With well over one-third of our marriages ending in divorce, we have, as a society, come to accept the notion that marriage is not always "until death do us part." Although individuals rarely enter a given marriage expecting it to fail, some may, in the back of their minds, realize that there is a way out if it doesn't work, and this realization may contribute to earlier (and more hasty) marriage. Other factors such as liberal support of military dependents; educational and housing benefits for veterans; federal subsidization of home ownership; increased governmental assumption of educational, medical, and other costs of children; food stamps; college housing services for married students; unemployment compensation; and parental willingness to continue supporting offspring after they are married may all contribute to early marriage (K. Davis, 1972).

Age and Marital Stability

Studies show that the younger people are when they marry, the greater the likelihood of both poor adjustment in marriage and a subsequent divorce (Bumpass and Sweet, 1972; Landis, 1963; Inselberg, 1962). Persons who marry when they are relatively young (in the teens for women and under 22 for men) are about twice as likely to obtain a divorce as persons who marry when they are older (U.S. Bureau of the Census, *Current Population*

Reports, 1971). Almost one-fifth of all men and almost one-half of all women who were divorced in one recent year had married while in their teens, and an additional 40 percent of men and 30 percent of women had married in their early twenties (Plateris, 1973). Age is related to social and emotional maturity, and thus individuals marrying at especially early ages may find it difficult to cope with the adjustments of early marriage (Burchinal, 1959; Eshleman, 1965; Martinson, 1955, 1959; Moss and Gingles, 1959).

Persons who marry young are more likely than those marrying later to be confronted with the responsibilities of parenthood early in the marriage. Their educational attainment at the time of marriage is not likely to be as great, and consequently their occupational status and income may not be as high. These factors may collectively result in a poor economic situation for the couple, making marital adjustment more difficult. While many youthful marriages succeed, they appear to have some special challenges which predispose the couple to a greater likelihood of divorce.

Age Difference

From time to time newspapers carry reports of marriages in which the spouses differ in age by many years. Situations such as an 82-year-old man marrying a 21-year-old woman, a woman of 62 seeking a divorce from her 30-year-old husband, or a man of 19 marrying a woman of 65 are not very common, but they do exist. Women marry men who are about two years older than they are, on the average. The age discrepancy is somewhat greater for women who marry in their teens, where their husbands average three years older, and after the early twenties the gap between the ages of husbands and wives begins to increase (Hetzel and Cappetta, 1971). The age range between men and women is relatively narrow when both partners are marrying for the first time, but it becomes greater when one or both partners are remarrying after divorce or widowhood (Hetzel and Cappetta, 1971).

To summarize, men tend to marry women who are somewhat younger than they are, although there is considerable variation. Most persons who marry do so during a relatively short span of time ranging from the late teens to mid-twenties. The forces that encourage marriage appear to be quite vigorous during the periods surrounding high school graduation, college, and college graduation. Age differences are greater than average when women marry in their teens and for couples who are somewhat older than average when they marry. The lack of research on the relationship between age differences and marital adjustment does not allow us to state definitively what sorts of complications may exist in a marriage with significant age difference. There are data, however, which indicate that divorce is no more or less likely when such differences exist (Bumpass and Sweet, 1972).

When there is a particularly dramatic difference in age, four questions are significant: (1) Why does the younger person want to marry the older one? (2) Why does the older one want to marry the younger one? (3) What special problems may they face? (4) Will this kind of marriage meet their individual needs better than one with less age difference?

Either person may have failed to meet an eligible mate of an age more nearly comparable with his or her own. A young woman may be flattered by the attentions of an older man because she assumes that he has chosen her from among many alluring women whose hearts he might easily have captured. Either may be motivated by a desire to dominate. The younger may accomplish this because of the elder spouse's gratitude for having a young person marry him or her. The older individual may accomplish it because of his or her age and experience. Such a person may have a parental attitude toward the youthful spouse. There is sometimes a desire to regain lost youth. This desire may be the rationalization of emotional regression. In the case of an older man and a younger woman, there may be a special sexual element involved. Some older men find younger women physically more attractive than they do women of their own age.

NATIONALITY

Nationality differences imply variations in customs, standards, and points of view. The greater the contrast in the backgrounds of the two spouses, the greater the possibility of there being special problems of adjustment. If there is also a language difference, the situation is rendered even more complicated.

In some ways difference as to nationality and difference as to family background are similar; but the latter is a difference that occurs in a single matrix of custom, while the former involves the more basic ways of life. Every people believes its accepted way of life to be superior and right. In their dealings with each other, people set out with preconceived ideas and prejudices. When an individual reflects the attitudes of the group, these may have a direct bearing on the marital relationship.

One of the most pertinent differences between this country and some others, as far as marriage is concerned, is the dissimilarity in attitude toward women—in relation to their status, their role, the degree of restriction placed by custom upon their behavior, and their attitude toward their own position and toward men. Attitudes toward such things as authority in the home, the organization of the family with respect to relatives and in-laws, or morality and esthetics may vary. Such differences may make a contribution to marriage. On the other hand, they may make adjustment difficult, depending upon which spouse is American and where the couple live.

The problem of deciding whether or not to marry a person of another nationality is not uncommon among students who are in a position to meet men and women from other countries. If an American meets a foreign student who is taking college work in this country, knows the language, is partly assimilated through his or her school experience, and plans to live here permanently, the problem of adjustment in marriage is one thing. But for the American who plans to marry a foreign student and reside permanently in the latter's homeland without first having experience in that country, it may be quite another. Let us remember, however, that the potential problem is relative to the degree of difference between the two nationalities. One would scarcely consider the marriage of a citizen of this country and an English-speaking Canadian to be "mixed."

It is exciting and romantic to fall in love with someone whose foreign extraction casts a halo and stimulates the imagination. If residence abroad is contemplated, the thrill of travel is added. In some cases that have come to light in conferences with college students, the thrill, excitement, and glamor have often tended to becloud judgment and discourage the individual from looking further ahead than the wedding.

There are few data available which indicate the extent of cross-national marriages and their probability of success. One study was made of Western wives who lived in their husbands' joint families in India (Cottrell, 1975). Some Western wives who have had experience in a joint family like the arrangement, make the necessary adjustments, and get along with and love the members.

On the other hand, in this study wives collectively reported the following problems: (1) The size and complexity of the joint family were confusing. Types of relationships were difficult to learn. The family was considered more important than the individual. There was a feeling of being overwhelmed by the family. (2) The absence of privacy and of personal property was difficult to accept. (3) Role restrictions were irksome. The wife was accorded inferior status, and the family had authority over the wife. (4) Relations among siblings were determined by birth order. (5) Segregation of males and females both at home and at social functions was difficult to accept. (6) The wife felt she lacked emotional support from the husband. His ties to his parents took precedence over his ties to her. He was expected to be superior to his wife. Husband and wife were not to show affection. (7) Children were considered to belong to the husband's family. It was difficult for the wife to discipline her own children.

This is one of relatively few studies focusing on the problems of an American wife in another culture. This study in India is only an illustration of the points mentioned above, since each culture would present its own special problems. Nothing said in this section is meant to imply that marriages of persons of different nationality cannot succeed. The point is that problems *may* be complex, and not everyone is equipped to solve them. Indeed, cultural differences may be negligible in many cases; and even where they are considerable, the couple may be willing and prepared to deal with the complexities of the situation. In either case, the difference in nationality is one factor to be considered among many.

RACE

The norms which encourage homogamy are perhaps strongest with regard to race. No form of mixed marriage seems to generate as much interest or elicit such strong disapproval as racial intermarriage. There has been little research on interracial marriages, but an analysis of United States census data provides some information on the extent and stability of black-white marriages (Heer, 1974).

▶ Just under 1 percent of black males and females were interracially married in the United States in 1970: black males, 1.2 percent; black females, 0.7 percent.

▶ Less than 0.1 percent of whites were interracially married in the United States in 1970.

▶ During the decade from 1960 to 1970 there was an overall substantial increase in the prevalence of such marriages.

▶ There was a very large rise in marriages involving a black husband and a white wife and a small decline in those with a white husband and a black wife.

▶ There was a very sharp increase in interracial marriages in the North and West and a substantial decline in the South between 1960 and 1970.

▶ The stability over the decade of black-white marriages is shown to have been less than that of racially homogeneous marriages. Of marriages involving a white husband and a black wife contracted in the ten years prior to the 1960 census, only 47 percent were still in existence in 1970; and of those involving a black husband and a white wife, only 63 percent were still in existence (compared to 78 percent for marriages with black husbands and black wives and 90 percent for marriages with white husbands and white wives).

Interracial marriages appear to occur mostly among persons who are more likely to interact with individuals of different racial groups. Thus, we are more likely to find interracial marriage in cities, among university students, and among professional people. Rates of interracial and interethnic marriage are highest in the United States, for example, in Hawaii, where there is a great deal of interaction between members of different racial and ethnic groups (Leon, 1975; Parkman and Sawyer, 1967). Couples marrying interracially tend to be older than other marrying couples and are more likely to have been previously married (Barnett, 1963).

Many states have had laws prohibiting interracial marriage, but these were declared unconstitutional in 1967. Although it is now possible for whites and nonwhites to intermarry freely, it is unlikely that the incidence of such marriages will increase significantly. The greatest barrier to interracial marriage lies in the mores, the established customs of the group that are deemed essential for societal welfare, together with the attitudes and prejudices to which such mores give rise. But mores and attitudes are subject to change. There is no natural, inborn, instinctive, biological aversion to interracial marriage, as some persons assume. This is shown, for example, by the acceptance of interracial marriage in some countries. It is also suggested by the fact that, if there were a natural aversion to it, legal and social efforts to prevent it would be unnecessary.

Although not so clear-cut and rigorously prescribed as in some cultures, our mores do sustain a degree of exogamy and endogamy. *Exogamy* defines the group outside which an individual is expected to marry. *Endogamy* defines the group within which an individual is expected to marry. We are, for example, exogamous relative to family (at least within certain degrees of consanguinity). We tend to be endogamous relative to race. We do not penalize people for crossing endogamous lines as severely as some cultures do. But there is an underlying attitude—and although this attitude is now changing, it is still more or less uncritically accepted—that people should "marry their own kind." There are many cases in which the husband is white and the wife nonwhite, in part because of the fact that many men in military service during World War II married Oriental women (U.S. Department of Health, Education, and Welfare, 1968; Carter and Glick, 1970). More black-white marriages, however, involve black males and white females than vice versa.

Factors contributing to the increase in interracial marriage are urbanization, with its attendant indifference relative to individual behavior so long as such behavior does not encroach directly upon the freedom and welfare of others; the influx of foreign students and other visitors; the extension of American business and political interests throughout the world; the increased intermingling of peoples; greater racial integration; and a growing feeling that people should be free to make their own choices. A black-white marriage, like any other marriage, should be entered because two people want to marry and to make a free choice, regardless of their race.

A gradual increase in interracial marriage of various types is possible. But numerical increase would not automatically remove possible problems and make success easier to achieve. During the period in which the reader of this book will make his or her choice of marriage partner, and for some time thereafter, interracial marriage will entail problems with which many mixed couples will be ill prepared to cope and which only some will be able to solve successfully (Pavela, 1964). Sociologists examine social change objectively and describe their observations impersonally. But a young couple contemplating marriage must work out a highly personalized relationship within the undercurrents and crosscurrents of a social milieu. They are not called upon to use their marriage as a contribution to the solution of a complex social problem.

In many communities a racially mixed couple have difficulty in finding friends who are sufficiently unprejudiced to accept both spouses without hesitation or discrimination. Many families are not prepared to accept a child-in-law of another race (Washington, 1970). The spouses may find themselves the target of prejudice and discrimination directed by segments of society toward them. Families of both partners usually object to the

An interracial marriage is a union of two persons, not two races. Nevertheless, the couple may experience some social stigma. (United Press International)

union. The situation is, of course, changing. But we are discussing the reality of the immediate future, not a hypothetical, more distant future in which contemporary problems will have disappeared.

What of the child born to interracially mixed parents? The child's associates are inclined to relegate him to the status of one of the two racial groups he or she represents, according to the child's physical appearance. Often the child is torn by conflicting loyalties.

Racial difference per se is not the basic problem in interracial marriage. The basic problem is one of degree of acceptance or rejection of each other on the part of the two races involved and hence the degree of acceptance or rejection of the interracial marriage in a given community. For example, in one part of this country a marriage between a white and an American Indian may be fully accepted, even glamorized. In another part of the country such a marriage may be considered unthinkable and the couple ostracized.

There are instances of marriage which, strictly speaking, are not interracial. Yet, by the general public in some communities, they are treated to some degree as if they were. In some parts of the country where there is a large Latin-American population, a marriage of a Latin-American and an Anglo-American may be put into such a quasi-racial category. The false assumption underlying such classification is that all persons of darker skin belong to non-Caucasian races. Actually skin color is only one criterion of racial classification, and a not-too-accurate one at that.

FAMILY BACKGROUND AND SOCIAL CLASS

As everyone knows, there are superior individuals who have sprung from seemingly poor family backgrounds and inferior persons who have derived from apparently good ones. The basic question in this connection is not only the nature of the family background of the person with whom marriage is contemplated, but also how much it has affected him or her. Not all persons are affected to the same degree by similar circumstances; but in many cases environment leaves its mark, and an individual's family experience is carried into his or her marriage.

Difference in family background may seem relatively innocuous to college students who are temporarily isolated from such background and are in circumstances where judgments of other people may not take into consideration family circumstances and extraction. But difference in background may imply dissimilarity in any number of things taken for granted as part of an acceptable and appropriate way of life by one or the other spouse—for example, food tastes and levels of quality in cookery; degrees of neatness and cleanliness; table manners; English usage; types of recreation; definitions of husband and wife roles; attitudes toward arguing, quarreling, or spouses striking each other; standards relative to the use of alcohol, tobacco, or even coffee; scales of values; the celebration of holidays; definitions of authority within the family; and prejudices and biases of one sort or another.

Consider an example. The wife was an only child in whose family birthdays and holidays had always been days of special celebration and gifts. The husband was one of eight children in a family that was too poor to give special attention to any holiday except Christmas. On the couple's first wedding anniversary, the wife surprised the husband with an attractive, expensive gift. The husband gave the day no thought and bought nothing for her. His reaction to her disappointment was, "I felt so small that I could have left the room through the keyhole."

In some cases a problem arises because one of the pair "bends over backward" in an effort to get as far as possible from his or her family background. For example, a husband whose mother was a careless housekeeper demands that his wife be meticulous, or a wife whose parents used poor English continually badgers her husband because of his careless speech.

Another pertinent reason for taking background into consideration is that, whether we like it or not, the wedding delivers to each spouse free of charge a complete set of in-laws. These in-laws will visit and be visited, will make demands of one sort or another, and in many cases will try to hold the child to their own pattern of life, even though he or she has departed from it. Much depends upon proximity of residence; but geography does not always eradicate family bonds or extricate a child from the cultural pattern that has been woven around him or her.

Individuals tend to marry at their same social class level (Scanzoni, 1968). Social class is usually determined by considering one's education, income, occupation, and family background. It is not surprising, then, that the family background factors discussed above largely stem from traditions or customs common to the family's social class. Social-class homogamy is easily explained, since we tend to grow up, attend school, and take jobs with persons who are similar to ourselves in social class. Hence, we are more likely to meet, date, and subsequently marry persons who are similar to rather than different from ourselves in social class background.

In some social class groups the opportunity to date and marry persons from similar backgrounds is formalized. For example, upper-class families have a tradition known as the debutante ball. A young woman is "presented" to all eligible males (those of the same age or a few years older) in the community (other upper-class families) when she is about 19 years of age. A lavish party is customarily held, the expectation being that she is now eligible to be married by any of the males in the group. The tradition still exists but is declining, since some of the young women find their mates while attending college, where there is less parental control. Others reject the traditional function of the debutante ball altogether, and others object to the lavish expenditures for just one evening and instead choose to attend a ball with other young women to raise money for charity. But class homogamy is still encouraged and usually results in any case, since most upper-class women will attend exclusive prep schools and colleges where they are likely to find many other persons with similar social backgrounds.

In one research study (Pearlin, 1975) it

was found that, when two persons of different family background marry, it is not difference in social status per se that matters but rather the meaning and importance attached to status. If an individual marries "down" while striving to move "up," that is, marries a partner of lower status while valuing status advancement, there may be dissatisfaction and a sense of loss. "When a sense of loss does occur, there is also a good chance that stress will occur, too." Communication and exchange of affection may be affected. "Vital elements of marital exchange are influenced by whether one must, as he regards his mate's origin, cast his gaze upwards or downwards."

Social Class and Marital Stability

Generally speaking, the lower the social class, the less stable the marriage (Goode, 1956; Udry, 1966, 1967). Persons from upper-class backgrounds are more likely to have marriages which are better adjusted and less prone to divorce. It is likely that income is an important factor here (Cutright, 1971). Lack of financial resources can be a great burden for a family and can add sufficient strain to a marriage relationship to cause marital breakdown.

While the data clearly indicate the positive relationship between social class and marital stability, the data are not as clear with regard to social class *differences* between the spouses. Whereas an early study indicates that social class differences do not influence marital adjustment (Roth and Peck, 1951), a later study indicates that differences in status are associated with marital instability (Scanzoni, 1968). We can speculate that slight differences in status may not be particularly troublesome for the couple, but significant differences may pose problems, especially when the male, as the primary breadwinner, is of a lower social class than the woman, forcing her to accept a standard of living she finds difficult.

EDUCATION

The question of whether to marry anyone of considerably different educational experience is not uncommon, in the public at large or among college students. The latter may be away from the home town, where the fiancé(e), who is not planning to attend college, has remained after graduation from high school. The answer is not simple, because there is a distinction to be made between real and formal education. Usually these two types overlap, but they are not necessarily identical. There are many self-educated persons who have never attended college, and there are many poorly educated men and women who have been awarded degrees.

A distinction must also be made between technical, specialized, occupational, or professional training and education for living. A person with a bachelor of arts degree has three or four years less formal schooling than a person with a medical, engineering, or law degree; but so far as education for living is concerned, they may have approximately equal amounts. Two high school graduates may have about the same amount of education for living, even though one of them goes on after graduation and takes several years of specialized business training.

Individuals tend to marry at their own educational level (Rockwell, 1976). College graduates are most likely to marry other college graduates, high school graduates are most likely to marry other high school graduates, and so on. When there are differences, it is slightly more likely that the male will marry a female of lower educational attainment (Rockwell, 1976), but this finding may be partially due to greater likelihood that males will graduate from college or go on to graduate school.

Education and Marital Stability

The higher the educational level, the greater the marital adjustment and stability. Educated persons are less likely to divorce and more likely to report that their marriages are going well. Greater education is also correlated with a later age at marriage and high income, and research shows that when age at marriage is taken into account, the relationship between education and marital stability is diminished, particularly for females (Bumpass and Sweet, 1972). Other research shows that while the inverse relationship between education and divorce generally holds, there is an exception to the rule. Women with some graduate work are significantly more likely to divorce (Houseknecht and Spanier, 1976). We can speculate that these women are more independent, may be more threatening to their spouses, are more likely to have careers that would conflict with their husband's career and the marriage, or may have personality profiles that make successful marriage more challenging for them. Regardless of the reason, which will need to be determined by additional research, we know that these very highly educated women are more likely to divorce than women with bachelor's degrees. Apart from this exception, all educational groups of males and all other educational groups of females are described by the *inverse* relationship between education and divorce.

Even though educated persons, on the whole, divorce less, they are more likely to seek a divorce when the marriage falters (Landis, 1963). In other words, the higher the educational level, the more likely that the individual will select divorce as a remedy for an unhappy marriage.

With regard to differences between spouses in educational level, homogamy is again associated with better marital adjustment (Blood and Wolfe, 1960). Education differences appear to influence marital stability most negatively when the wife has a higher educational level than the husband (Bumpass and Sweet, 1972). When differences are slight or when the husband has a higher educational level, the influence on marital stability is of less significance.

INTELLIGENCE

Difference in intelligence and difference in education are not necessarily concomitant. Some individuals, by good fortune, devious means, or misplaced charity, are able to zigzag through the maze of hurdles that better students jump, escaping academic elimination and receiving degrees that are no proof of either ability or achievement. On the other hand, there are persons of high intelligence whose interest is not stimulated by a college program and who drop out.

In uncommon cases, couples of noticeably different intelligence get along well in marriage because, as we have said, success is in part relative to expectations. A genius and a dullard may make a mutually satisfactory adjustment if the former is not unhappy in intellectual isolation, enjoys a pleasant home, and has his or her emotional needs satisfied, and if the latter finds it agreeable to serve the superior spouse and bask in reflected brilliance with hero-worshiping admiration. Still, such marriages of genius and dullard are not common enough to furnish the basis for generalization.

In more ordinary unions in which there exists a difference in intelligence between the spouses, there is danger that the two may grow apart (Lewis and Spanier, 1978). Intellectual isolation may prove irksome and unsatisfying to the superior individual. They may both discover that in marriage mental stimulation is as important as emotional satisfaction, that exchange of ideas and contact of minds are as essential as exchange of caresses and contact of bodies. Intellectual isolation may result on the one hand in withdrawal, so that the superior spouse becomes less and less a part of the total marital situation, or on the other hand in looking elsewhere for the stimulation and intellectual contacts that the other spouse cannot supply. Either condition may produce a loneliness that makes marriage disappointing.

The less intelligent spouse, if keen enough to sense the real situation, may develop a feeling of inferiority. If he or she is not so perceptive, the difficulty may be aggravated by apathy and blindness. If the former occurs and he or she does grow to feel inferior, that too may produce loneliness that will eventuate in withdrawal or the seeking of companionship upon a more acceptable level. A feeling of inferiority may produce unhappiness, insecurity, and frustration. The inferior spouse aspires to keep pace with the superior partner but comes to realize that his or her "mental legs" are not long enough to maintain the stride. A satisfactory adjustment may be achieved, however, if the husband and wife find areas in their relationship which represent common ground and put them on a more nearly equal footing, or if each spouse is encouraged to use his or her special abilities, or if they both recognize and accept their differences.

MATE SELECTION DIFFERENTIALS

Why is it that the typical man marries a woman who is smaller, shorter, lighter, and younger? And why, if there is a marriage across educational or social class levels, is the male slightly more likely to have the higher status and education that the female (Rockwell, 1976)? The tendency for men to date and marry at the same level or downward and for females to date and marry at the same level or upward has some interesting implications for mate selection and marriage.

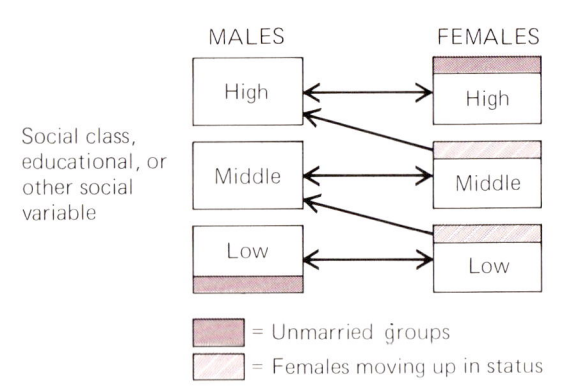

Exhibit 7-3 Mate selection differentials.

Exhibit 7-3 shows what happens when males marry females at the same or lower educational or social class level. A residual group of females are left at the top, with a group of men left at the bottom. In America, we generally assume that a female takes on the social standing of her husband. Thus if an upper-class male marries a middle-class female, as a couple they will likely be regarded as upper-class. Females, however, are not as likely to marry downward, since it is against the social norm and since a female may lose status if, as a couple, they are identified through the husband. Consequently, we find many women of high social class status or education who are unmarried. These high-status women customarily engage in lifelong careers. The marriage rate is lower among female Ph.D.s, for example, than among women with bachelor's degrees.

This phenomenon can be illustrated by considering Jacqueline Kennedy Onassis. As a woman from an upper-class family, her field of eligibles was quite restricted to begin with. She initially married another member of the upper class, the late President John

Kennedy. After his death, her field of eligibles was again very restricted. Custom would have it that if she was to marry again, it would have to be an upper-class male of greater wealth than she—and older. Indeed, Aristotle Onassis, one of the world's richest men, was such a person. It is unlikely that Jacqueline Kennedy would have considered marriage to anyone other than a wealthy upper-class person, for her own social status might then have been severely affected.

Women at the highest educational and social class levels have a small field of eligibles to begin with, are competing for these males with middle-class or lesser-educated women as well, and thus may have difficulty marrying. On the other side are lower-class or poorly educated males, who have a narrower field of eligibles since some lower-class or poorly educated women have married middle-class men.

There is one class of exceptions to this tendency. Among blacks, the tendency is reversed for females at the higher educational levels; they are more likely to marry down in educational level than are whites. Since mortality rates are higher for blacks than for whites at all ages, the sex ratio decreases more rapidly for blacks than for whites. Among blacks in their twenties, where there are only 85 males for every 100 females, the field of eligibles for the females is especially limited. Since black women tend to be more educated than black men, a very high proportion of black females marry black males of lower educational status (U.S. Bureau of the Census, 1970).

PREVIOUS MARITAL STATUS

Although the divorce rate is higher in marriages in which one spouse has been married before than it is in those which represent first marriage for both persons, these marriages are often happier. Marrying a widowed or a divorced person is not the same as marrying one who has always been single, no matter how similar the external conditions may seem to be. When such a union is contemplated, answers to a number of important questions might well be ascertained to the satisfaction of the person to whom marriage will be a new experience.

Whether the previously married person was widowed or divorced, there is the question of rebound. Is the individual marrying in an attempt to fill a void in his or her emotional life and doing so before becoming sufficiently readjusted to make a wise choice based upon sound judgment? How much time has elapsed since the divorce or bereavement?

What is his or her attitude toward the first spouse? Is there any possibility of that person coming between you, either actually or in the imagination of one or both of you? Are you continually being compared with the other person? Is the comparison favorable or unfavorable? How do you react to this comparison? Could you tolerate it over a long period in the close contacts of wedded life? Does he or she continue to display reminders of past experience, and if so, might they become barriers between you or make you self-conscious in your new relationship?

Will you, when you marry this person, step into a home already furnished and established by the previous spouse? Or will the two of you begin a new home together? Could you make an adjustment if the former were the case?

After the wedding, where will you stand in the estimation of his or her friends and relatives, especially those of the former who were friends of both husband and wife? This problem becomes more than usually complicated if the friends and relatives feel that remarriage occurred too soon.

There are further special questions applying to marriage with a divorced person. One of the most important considerations is the real situation out of which the divorce grew. It is essential to know whether your partner has readjusted after the divorce crisis. The concept of successful divorce is provocative in this connection. Was your partner at odds with the former spouse, with marriage, or with life in general? If the first is true, then marriage to another person may prove successful. If the second is the case, previous maladjustments may again develop, or on the other hand a new start may make for better adjustment because the first marriage and its termination, though painful, were instructive. If the individual was and is at odds with life, of which marriage is only one maladjusted part, a second marriage will in all probability turn out like the first, unless those personality traits or circumstances that set him or her at odds with life are readjusted. This is not a simple, quick process. A divorced person may also develop an attitude of self-protection inconsistent with freely outgoing love for a second spouse, so that the capacity to love another person wholeheartedly is impaired.

For obvious reasons, in marriage to a divorced person the possibility of the former spouse's becoming a disrupting factor is greater than in widowhood. There is not only a possible emotional bond but the very real possibility of appearance or communication. The former spouse may be met at a social gathering. News of him or her is spread through common friends. The person may be in trouble and ask for assistance, as in one case in which the husband did not hear from his former wife until several years after his second marriage, when she wrote for money. There may even be an attempt to win back the divorced spouse who has remarried. Whether or not a marriage can withstand the pressure of such circumstances depends upon the personalities of the two spouses.

If a divorced man pays alimony or child support to his former wife, this fact may serve either to maintain the tie with the earlier marriage or to keep alive bitterness and disappointment. In either case, the economic problem of living on a reduced income may be irksome, especially since it is easy to project the blame for it onto the recipient of the alimony.

If the divorced individual had children by the first spouse, they may serve as a tie to the past, even though they live with the other person. A marriage may be so unhappy that divorce is a release and the two persons are gladly rid of each other. But one can scarcely be divorced from his or her children. Parental attachment is usually too strong to be severed by court decree. If there are children through the new marriage too, the whole situation becomes complicated, as the relationships between the two sets of offspring become tangled, equivocal, and sometimes hypersensitive.

Nearly one-fourth of all marriages involve at least one spouse who has been married at least once before. This figure includes a significant percentage of marriages where both spouses have been married once before. Nevertheless, 17 percent of marriages involving previously widowed persons are with single persons, and 36 percent of marriages involving previously divorced persons are with single persons (Williams and Kuhn, 1973). As we can see from these data, marriage to a divorced or widowed person is common and will likely become more common since divorce rates have risen in recent years.

RELIGION

Religion is more important in marriage than some persons in love are inclined to think. It may be a uniting force or a disrupting influence. It may be the prop that supports a couple during a crisis, or it may precipitate a crisis. It may make for peace and happiness or for dissension and ill will. It may serve as a means of dissipating potential conflict or as a focal point upon which incipient conflict may crystallize. It may be a common interest orienting husband and wife in the same direction, or it may produce a divergence of interests, drawing husband and wife toward opposite poles. It may make possible a profound sharing or it may militate against sharing.

Younger persons sometimes fail to realize the potential importance of religion in mate selection and marriage. This can easily occur since the majority of Americans, including college students, are inactive with respect to religion. Many persons become inactive during college and continue this inactivity permanently. However, many college students abandon religion and the church temporarily, only to return to them later in life. When this occurs, early training often reasserts itself. If the religious backgrounds of husband and wife are basically different, that difference may again come to the fore, especially in time of crisis, even though in earlier years it was somewhat overshadowed by romance. Religion often plays relatively little part in dating. The result is that young people may become emotionally involved with each other before questions of religious difference arise, since such questions assume importance in their thinking only when marriage is contemplated. People in love often fail to realize, too, that it is not only religion as such that is important but also what is done in connection with it. If religion involved only faith, entirely separate from life activities, religiously mixed marriage would present few problems. But differences in faith entail differences in practice, in verbal expression, and in attitudes toward children, foods, holidays, and numerous other things. They also involve families and other people with divergent attitudes and patterns of behavior. These can result in pressures and conflicts as each family attempts to hold one member of a couple to the pattern which the family has set.

Trends in Interfaith Marriage

After race, religion appears to be the most important social factor in mate selection (Moss et al., 1971). There have traditionally been strong customs encouraging marriage between persons of the same religious faith. Consequently, Americans tend to marry persons within their own broad religious groups—Jewish, Roman Catholic, Protestant (Glick, 1960). Sociologists have had a great interest in religious intermarriage, and much research has been done on this topic. However, since no national census data are collected on religion and interfaith marriage, we do not know precisely how many such marriages exist. Some limited evidence allows us to make a few speculations, however (Barron, 1972; Mueller, 1971; Besanceney, 1970; Gordon, 1964; Sklare, 1964; Bumpass, 1970):

▶ Interfaith marriage is increasing in the United States. One study has indicated that it has doubled in the last generation (Bumpass, 1970).

▶ There is greater tolerance now of interfaith marriage than there has ever been before.

▶ Interfaith marriage will probably continue to increase.

▶ Interfaith marriage may be related to or a reflection of the declining importance of organized religion in America.

Research has shown that rates of interfaith marriage will vary in a given community depending on the likelihood that persons of different faiths meet and interact with each other. The greater the possibility of meeting a person of a different religion, the greater the likelihood of interfaith marriage (Udry, 1974). In other words, the higher the proportion of a given religious group in a community, the lower the intermarriage rate for that group. Furthermore, the more cohesive a religious or ethnic group is, the lower their rate of intermarriage. Interfaith marriage is more likely for persons who are remarrying (Rosenthal, 1970), persons who are especially young or significantly older than other individuals when they marry, and persons from lower socioeconomic groups (Burchinal and Chancellor, 1962).

Despite the widespread tendency to marry within one's own religion, there is now greater acceptance of interfaith marriage. It is rarely the deterrent to marriage that it once was, even though some couples experience parental or other pressures which result in the termination of their relationship. Few college students object to dating persons of different religions. Since religion is rarely ascertained at the beginning of dating relations (unless, of course, the couple meet at a place of worship or a religious student center), many couples begin a courtship without having considered religion as a factor. Religion, then, is rarely a basis for beginning a relationship, but it sometimes becomes a factor in its termination. The diversity of religious groups in universities and urban areas has undoubtedly contributed to the increase in occurrence and tolerance of interfaith dating and marriage.

What Are the Options?

When an interfaith marriage has occurred, the couple in general have five options:

1 Each partner remains affiliated with his or her own religious group.

2 The couple choose a compromise religion.

3 The couple alternate worship between religious groups.

4 One mate converts to the religion of the other.

5 The couple do not practice religion at all.

Since only a minority of Americans practice their religion with any regularity at all, the fifth option is the most common one in all marriages. Thus, if we state that the fifth option is most common when there has been an interfaith marriage, it should not be concluded that a married couple of different faiths will necessarily cease their participation in religious activities. This is the most common alternative in interfaith marriages, but it is also quite characteristic of other couples as well. Of the remaining options, the fourth is probably the most common—one mate converts to the religion of the other. The first three options, and other creative solutions not mentioned, are undoubtedly employed by a smaller number of couples, perhaps because they involve conflicting, divided, or new religious loyalties or affiliations. When marriage to anyone of different religious background and affiliation is being contemplated, there are several questions to be answered. How much does religion mean to you? Is it something of little importance, in which your interest is superficial, or is it something so vital that you could not conceive of living without it? Do you believe that your particular faith is the only right one, or are you tolerant and broad-minded? Do you have a driving zeal to convert others to your belief, or are you willing to let each adhere to the belief of his or her choice?

How great is the religious difference between you and the other person? Is it a Catholic–Protestant difference, Jewish–non-Jewish, Christian–non-Christian (such as Buddhist or Moslem), fundamentalist-liberal, religious-nonreligious, denominational (such as Baptist-Methodist)? Or is it a matter of degree, one of you being more religious than the other but both adhering in general to the same faith? How tolerant and broad-minded is the other person? Would either or both of you make religion a bone of contention? How did you deduce your answer to this question?

Have you ever discussed religion together? Do you argue about it and find yourselves emotionally overwrought and unable to find any common basis for agreement? Do you contemplate avoiding an interfaith marriage by having one person convert to the faith of the other? Are you expected to change your religion, or did you offer to do so? Would you expect your spouse to change, or did he or she suggest it? Has either of these alternatives been discussed? If so, when you discussed them, did you mean change in religion or change in church affiliation? It is easy to talk glibly about the latter when romance casts a rosy hue upon problems. But is the former really, at least readily, possible? If one changed, would it be because of conviction or to remove a barrier to marriage? Is your plan for the eradication of the religious difference the choice of a compromise affiliation which both persons will join? For two persons who belong to somewhat similar Christian denominations this may not be too difficult. But for the Catholic–non-Catholic, Jewish–non-Jewish, or Christian–non-Christian couple a mutual compromise is another matter. There is no church "between" Roman Catholic and non-Catholic, for example. Each church is either one or the other or neither. The other types mentioned are similar. Hence in some cases what is suggested as a compromise is actually a somewhat one-sided concession. Have you planned that each will retain his or her own faith and affiliation? If so, have you carefully thought through the problems that this might involve in later life, when there are children to be reared?

Children can scarcely adhere to two divergent faiths; some choice must be made. To plan to let the child make the choice when he or she reaches the age of discretion is more easily said than done. Children must either be subjected to some religious influence in early life and thus have their choice colored, or they must be allowed to grow to the age of discretion without having any religious influence exerted upon them, and thus be expected to make a choice with a minimal foundation upon which to make it. Frequently the husband and wife who are tolerant of each other's religion find themselves unable to agree upon the training of offspring. The child may be pulled simultaneously in two directions; if, then, the child goes the way of one parent, the other may feel resentful. A satisfactory solution can be difficult, but the problem can be solved.

This is a discussion of marriage, not of theology. We are interested in the role of religion in mate selection and marital adjustment, especially in the part that religious difference may play and in the problems that such difference may create or accentuate. Our discussion is not to be interpreted as a criticism of any religious group. In this discussion all faiths are considered of equal merit and are on an equal footing.

In the United States today there are almost 300 Christian denominations and sects, three branches of Judaism, and miscellaneous other groups, plus a great body of unaffiliated believers and nonbelievers. Within such heterogeneity, differences range from one extreme to the other relative to the authority of the clergy, theology, ritual, demands upon members, attitudes toward life, and day-by-day behavior. Even within a given group differences may be noted; for example, Missouri Synod Lutherans differ from other Lutherans, Southern Baptists are not identical with American Baptists, and Episcopalians exhibit considerable variation. It is therefore a mistake, except within very broad limits, to lump subgroups together as if they were alike—for example, to compare Christians with Jews as if all Christians and all Jews were alike, to compare Roman Catholics with Protestants as if there were no range of variation within these groups.

It is a mistake, too, to overlook the fact

that every group is composed of individuals who also exhibit a range of variation. Some are more devout, some less. Some are liberal in their point of view, some conservative. Some attend religious services regularly, some are like "Christmas-Easter Christians." Some claim to believe but do not participate in the activities of a religious organization, while others participate but are not sure what they believe. Some are tolerant, some intolerant. And so it goes.

People seldom have friction over true religion, but they may be at odds over all sorts of dogmas and practices. Some churches frown on such commonly accepted things as movies, instrumental music, and drinking coffee. A couple may easily run their marriage aground in the shallows of denominational difference.

Persons of different faith may have a minimum common orientation in that they are both religious and have some appreciation of the importance of religious values, although they disagree on particular items of belief and practice. But a religious and a nonreligious person do not have this common orientation, and so their marriage may provide fertile soil for conflict. On the other hand, two tolerant individuals who are willing and able to give each other freedom of both thought and action may well work out a faith–no-faith marriage.

The point here is to suggest that "interfaith marriage" is not a simple uniform entity and therefore subject to the same arguments pro and con as if all such marriages were alike and generalization were easy. In contemplating interfaith marriage, the broad overall differences between the two faiths in question, plus the differences represented by the subgroups to which the two parties belong, plus the particular personalities and points of view of the two individuals, are all worthy of serious consideration. In short, then, Catholic–non-Catholic marriage, Jewish–non-Jewish marriage, even Protestant-Protestant marriage must be particularized. "Interfaith marriage" is only a term.

Catholic–non-Catholic Marriage

No one book would have space to discuss all the possible forms that "interfaith marriage" might take. There is one form, however, that is common and involves considerations often overlooked or not understood, namely, Roman Catholic–non-Catholic marriage. Certain points should be understood before a particularized judgment can be reached in a given situation, partly because the Roman Catholic Church establishes a framework for its members within which a valid marriage with a non-Catholic may be contracted. In so doing, the Church does not take individual differences into account in all respects. "There are 'good practicing Catholics' and some careless ones. But in canon law what counts is whether or not one belongs to the Catholic Church" (*A New Catechism*, 1967).

The Roman Catholic Church is a worldwide organization with different levels of authority. Ultimately authority is vested in the College of Bishops, among whom the Pope, the "Vicar of Christ," is considered the "first among equals." The bishops, with the Pope as their head, constitute the Magisterium, the teaching authority, of the Church. Under certain well-defined circumstances, and then only in matters dealing chiefly with doctrines of faith, the Pope is considered capable of making infallible pronouncements binding on all Catholics. Thus far, only one such pronouncement has been made in this century. But even when pronouncing a dogma infallible, the Pope must consult the bishops and the faithful. Not all religious decrees have the same binding force so far as obedience is concerned. Not even all the clergy agree with the bishops on everything. Nor do Catholic laymen always agree with the clergy. Many individuals, both lay and clerical, make their disagreement known (Noonan, 1966). Roman Catholic laymen exhibit a range of belief and behavior, but within certain limits, since to remain Catholic they must accept some things in common.

The Catholic Church has always been subject to change. In recent years, partly in response to scientific discovery, new thinking, and evolving life conditions, a number of changes have occurred in a relatively brief time, and more are being demanded by both clergy and laymen. Let us look briefly at the Catholic Church's liberalization of marriage rites in interfaith marriages over the last quarter century. In 1955, it was determined that interfaith marriages could take place in church, but not at the altar. Before that time an interfaith marriage involving a Catholic could not even occur in the church. In 1960 interfaith marriages could be performed at the altar. In 1963, Mass could be said at an interfaith marriage for the first time. Before then, Mass was allowed only in Catholic–Catholic marriages. In 1969, it was decided that a Catholic–non-Catholic marriage would be recognized by the Church if it took place in a Protestant church. Before then, such a marriage would not have been allowed. In short, the Church has considerably liberalized its approach to interfaith marriage. It should be noted, however, that not all priests have accepted these changes, and in some jurisdictions, some of the older policies may still be in operation.

Another major change has been the discontinuation of the written "Ante-nuptial Contract and Promises" to be signed by both the Catholic and the non-Catholic party, a document which until recently was a "thorn in the flesh," especially for non-Catholics. The Catholic party now promises, either orally or in writing, to "do all in my power to share the faith I have received with our children by having them baptized and reared as Catholics." Before the wedding, "the non-Catholic must be informed of the promises and of the responsibility of the Catholic.... No formal statement of the non-Catholic is required" (Foy, 1976). To promise that children "will be" reared as Catholics and to promise to "do all in my power" to have them reared as Catholics do not seem to carry the same weight of obligation. "Parents ... have the right to determine, in accordance with their own religious beliefs, the kind of religious education that their children are to receive." But the child's faith is "the source of a serious obligation in conscience on the part of the Catholic, whose conscience in this regard must be respected" (Foy, 1976).

Students sometimes express the belief that the Catholic Church approves of the couple's rearing boys in the faith of the father and girls in the faith of the mother. Such a belief is erroneous. One of the chief reasons for which the Catholic Church disapproves of interfaith marriage is the danger that the children will be lost to the faith and to the Church. The influence of the non-Catholic parent may prove a hindrance to the child's acceptance of Catholic doctrine and his or her devotion to Catholic ideals, unless this influence is counteracted by the Catholic parent, the Church, and the parochial school. Another reason is that the faith of the Catholic and/or the non-Catholic party may be compromised.

"Where there are serious difficulties in observing the Catholic canonical form in a mixed marriage"—for example, when there is a special need to preserve family harmony or prevent family alienation, when it is necessary in order to obtain parental consent, when there is a special friendship with a non-Catholic clergyman, or when there is a desire that the wedding occur in a church that has special importance to the non-Catholic—permission may be obtained to have a non-Catholic wedding in a non-Catholic church. In exceptional cases, for example, in certain Catholic-Jewish marriages, permission may be obtained to have a civil ceremony. The Catholic Church does not permit two religious ceremonies, or a single ceremony in which both Catholic and non-Catholic rituals are used jointly or successively. With permission, a non-Catholic clergyman may participate in a Catholic ceremony or a priest may participate in a non-Catholic ceremony by giving additional prayers, blessings, or words of greeting or exhortation or by reading a lesson or preaching—provided the wedding is not part of the Eucharist, that is, communion or Lord's Supper (Foy, 1975).

The Catholic Church does not approve divorce in the case of a valid, sacramental, and consummated marriage. In case of a marriage declared null and void by the Church from the beginning, divorce for civil reasons—to satisfy state law—is acceptable and is considered a "civil ratification of the fact that the marriage bond really does not exist" (Foy, 1976). Under certain circumstances the Church permits the "innocent or aggrieved party," with permission from Catholic authority, to obtain a civil divorce "for the purpose of acquiring title and right to custody of children," but such divorce does not "break the bond of a valid marriage" (Foy, 1976). Excommunication is automatic if a Catholic attempts to remarry after a divorce from a valid marriage (Foy, 1976).

In July 1968, Pope Paul VI issued an encyclical, *Humanae vitae*, in which he emphatically and unequivocally reiterated and upheld the Church's traditional position on contraception and other practices related to reproduction. There was an immediate storm of protest, and the Church was thrown into a state of turmoil so apparent that shortly after issuing the encyclical Pope Paul published a plea to Catholics for understanding, acceptance, and obedience. These two pronouncements not only sharpened the controversy in the Church relative to contraception but also complicated the issue of papal authority and caused a new dilemma for some of the clergy—that is, for priests who do not agree with the Pope's point of view but are nonetheless expected to obey his injunction in giving counsel to married couples both inside and outside the confessional. Whether change will be brought about during the lifetime of the present Pope remains to be seen.

Data from national samples of women indicate that the Pope's encyclical is essentially ignored in practice by American women, since most Catholic women use contraceptive methods other than rhythm (Westoff, 1976). In a study of currently married white Catholic women living with their husbands, data from surveys made in 1955, 1960, 1965, and 1970 were compared. It was found that women of childbearing age who used contraceptive methods other than rhythm increased from 30 percent in 1955 to 68 percent in 1970, with the greatest change occurring between 1965 and 1970, namely, from 51 percent to 68 percent. Women aged 20 to 24 showed the greatest increase in nonconformity, namely, 30 percent to 78 percent. Say the researchers, "It does not seem at all unlikely that by the end of the decade Catholics and non-Catholics will be virtually indistinguishable in their birth control practices" (Westoff and Bumpass, 1973).

In spite of its emphasis upon the importance of reproduction, the Catholic Church condemns artificial insemination, whether the donor of the seminal fluid is the woman's husband or an anonymous male chosen by a physician, or both. The reasons given for such disapproval are that children should be the product of a loving relationship between husband and wife rather than the result of a laboratory procedure; that artifical insemination involves the perversion of a natural faculty, since sexual intercourse is naturally a cooperative act; and that such insemination typically involves the collection of the seminal fluid either through the use of a contraceptive device or through masturbation, which is considered to be grievously sinful (Good and Kelly, 1951; Pope Pius XII, 1951). The Catholic Church is not alone in disapproving artificial insemination. Many non-Catholics assume it to be a matter of personal decision. But some Protestant clergymen have vigorously expressed objections to artificial insemination involving a donor other than the husband on the ground that such a procedure savors of adultery. Some courts have raised questions regarding the legitimacy of a child fathered in this way. The question of whether the woman's husband should be required to adopt the child in order to make it his legal heir has still not been answered to everyone's satisfaction.

As we pointed out at the beginning of this section, a group such as the Catholic Church is composed of individuals who exhibit a range of variation. Hence, we must not be surprised when some Catholics do things not approved, or at least not encouraged, by their Church, especially since not all Catholic clergy agree on certain issues. On one major issue, contraception, Pope Paul VI has made a pronouncement strongly questioned by many clergy. "Abstract polemics concerning Catholic teachings," say two Catholic scientists (Duffy and Wallace, 1969), "cannot always be directly translated into uniform behavior patterns among Catholics throughout the world. The individual conscience is more meaningful to people who value individual responsibilities and the respect for the rights of others."

An increase in interfaith marriages in which one party is Catholic may be anticipated. "The trend toward more mixed marriages will undoubtedly continue to gain momentum, propelled by the ecumenical spirit and the relaxation of Church regulations. It is predicted that before long one out of two valid Catholic marriages will be mixed. The number of invalid mixed marriages, also on the rise, will increase the figures even more" (Wakin and Scheuer, 1966).

Preparing for Catholic–non-Catholic Marriage

If Catholic–non-Catholic marriage is seriously contemplated, there are two things to be done. These are the *sine qua non* of common sense and successful adjustment. (1) As much as possible should be learned about the other person's religion. This may be done through reading, church attendance, and conference with both the non-Catholic clergyman and the priest. (2) The couple should agree upon a practical, workable plan, which should be more than an easily entered and equally easily broken compromise. This plan should be discussed with both clergymen and, if possible, with both sets of parents. We are assuming, of course, that both parties are the type who will adhere to agreements once made.

Jewish–non-Jewish Marriage

Among the problems to be confronted in Jewish–non-Jewish marriage are many of those met in the Catholic–non-Catholic type, and we shall not elaborate upon these again. There is, however, no well-organized, centrally controlled worldwide church hierarchy to bring pressure to bear upon the individual Jew and to mold his or her thinking, as there is in the case of a Catholic. This leaves the Jew freer and also permits a wider range of variation among Jews than among Catholics. Officially, the latter tend to be perhaps more nearly uniform, and those who do deviate from the commonly accepted tenets of the Church do so without the Church's sanction. With Jews there is a variety of points of view, each represented in one or more organizations, ranging from the strictly orthodox group, who adhere closely to ancient Hebrew belief and custom, through the conservative, to the most liberal or reform Jews, who dispense with much ancient ritual and more freely reinterpret the Scriptures. As a group, Jews hold marriage and family life in very high esteem. Their attitude toward contraception is liberal, similar to that found among Protestants. Among Jews there is no celibate priest class. Rabbis may marry, as Protestant clergymen do. Among some Jews, most notably the orthodox, Jewish–non-Jewish marriage is prohibited. Some rabbis will not officiate at a Jewish–non-Jewish wedding but, nevertheless, do recognize the marriage as valid.

Prejudice does form one of the important elements in the background against which Jewish–non-Jewish marriage takes place. This problem is not one-sided, however. Jews are often prejudiced against non-Jews, the same as the other way round (Gordon, 1964). Prejudice, no matter who exhibits it, is unfortunate enough. But prejudice on the part of the majority group against members of the minority contains the seeds of great hurt. Try as one may to prevent it, and sincere as one may be, the non-Jew in a mixed marriage does in some cases find himself or herself subjected to anti-Semitic prejudice because of a Jewish spouse, and in other cases he or she is put on the defensive.

In some of the more orthodox Jewish families a non-Jewish child-in-law is not readily accepted. Prejudice and discrimination are painful to Jews. But somehow through the centuries they have learned to live with them and even to survive persecution. Hence, when the mixed child of a Jewish–non-Jewish marriage is the victim of prejudice and discrimination, the Jewish parent is not surprised. The non-Jewish parent, on the other hand, never having had to learn to live with this sort of social pressure, may be ill prepared to meet the situation when his or her child is the target of such hurt. This parent, being a member of the majority group, may take his or her privileges for granted. Often the individual assumes that the child will have the same privileges. When the child is classified as a member of a minority group and is treated accordingly, the non-Jewish parent may be at least nonplussed and at most deeply hurt.

Religion and Marital Stability

Marriages between persons of different faiths are less stable than marriages between persons of the same faith, but the extent of such difference has probably been exaggerated over the years. Research clearly indicates that interfaith marriages are slightly more prone to divorce than religiously homogamous marriages (Burchinal and Chancellor, 1963; Christensen and Barber, 1967; Bumpass and Sweet, 1972; Spanier, 1976b), but much writing on this topic misrepresents the research findings. Perhaps because of the great interest in interfaith marriages, especially on the part of church organizations, it is understandable that the data on this topic would be presented in a manner that is sometimes misleading. Statistics can be used to make almost any point a person wishes. For example, if divorce happened to 10 percent of one group and 5 percent of another, one could conclude that the difference (5 percent) was only *slight*. On the other hand, one could say that divorce was *twice* as likely (10 percent to 5 percent) for one group. Very different messages would be given depending on the use of the same statistics.

Using data from a national study of marital stability (Bumpass and Sweet, 1972), it can be shown that interfaith marriages are less stable than intrafaith marriages, but the differences are not as great as some might assume. Among intrafaith marriages, Jews have the most stability and Protestants the least, with Catholics intermediate (Bumpass and Sweet, 1972; Burchinal and Chancellor, 1963; Christensen and Barber, 1967). Catholic-Protestant marriages are less stable than unmixed religious marriages of either faith. To these findings can be added another important one—Protestant interdenominational marriages (e.g., Methodist-Lutheran, Baptist-Presbyterian, Episcopalian-Methodist, etc.) do *not* have a higher level of instability than intradenominational marriages. In other words, Protestants do not increase their chances of divorce by marrying other Protestants of different denominations (Bumpass and Sweet, 1972).

The lower than average divorce rate among Catholics may give a misleading impression about the quality of Catholic-Catholic marriages generally, since the strong antidivorce position of the Roman Catholic Church undoubtedly prevents some couples who might otherwise divorce from doing so. It is interesting to note the lower divorce rate among couples in the "other" category (see Exhibit 7-4). Another relevant finding is that, given the same level of unhappiness, less devout couples are more likely to end an unhappy marriage by divorce than religiously devout couples, who are more likely to stay together when unhappy (Landis, 1963).

CONCLUSION

As was said at the beginning of this chapter, theoretically *any* type of marriage can be made to succeed *if* the special problems involved are faced and solved. We have attained some insight into the possible magnitude of this "if," and we should have reached the conclusion that in real life the problems are more obtrusive than a brief written exposition might seem to indicate. In many cases

Exhibit 7-4 The Stability of Intrafaith and Interfaith Marriages*

Religion of Husband	Religion of Wife	Percent of Unstable Marriages
Protestant	Protestant	14.7
Catholic	Catholic	8.9
Jewish	Jewish	4.0
Protestant	Catholic	20.2
Catholic	Protestant	19.5
Protestant	Other†	22.2
Other	Protestant	27.7
Catholic	Other	17.8
Other	Catholic	13.4
Other	Other	12.0

*Percent of first marriages which ended in divorce or separation by the time of the study for married women under the age of 45.

†Refers to persons who are neither Protestant, Catholic, nor Jewish.

Source: Bumpass and Sweet, 1972.

mixed marriages turn out to be happy and successful. But readers should be sure that they have taken a careful inventory of their own and the other person's personal qualities before blithely assuming that they will fall into the category of the favored.

Mixed marriage may be approached in one of two ways. Looking at it from the point of view of the sociologist, it is apparent that whenever groups of people are brought into contact over a long period of time, there will be intermingling and, in many instances, intermarriage among them. If they are groups within a highly mobile population, such as that in the United States, this process will be accelerated. But the process itself appears to be inevitable (Gordon, 1964).

On the other hand, mixed marriage may be approached from the point of view of the couple contemplating such marriage within a given social milieu, with its attendant pressures, expectations, customs, attitudes, and prejudices. The couple are concerned about the success or failure of one marriage, not about a sociological process. They have no obligation to contribute to social change. Therefore, what the sociologist assumes is inevitable a given couple may decide is for them unwise.

TERMS TO BE LEARNED

alimony
antenuptial contract
artificial insemination
civil (ceremony, divorce)
consanguinity
denomination
divorce
divorce prone
dogma
emotional regression
encyclical
endogamy
excommunication
exogamy
focal point (for conflict)

grounds for divorce
homogamy
inverse relationship
interethnic marriage
interfaith marriage
interracial marriage
Jew (Jewish)
joint family
Judaism
marital stability (instability)
marriage rate
mate selection differential
median age for marriage
mixed marriage
mores

nationality
null and void
propinquity
Protestant
psychopathic personality
quasi-racial
race (racial mixture)
Roman Catholic
sect
sine qua non
social class
social milieu
social status
societal matrix

SELECTED READINGS

BAER, JEAN: *The Second Wife: How to Live Happily with a Man Who Has Been Married Before*, Doubleday & Company, Inc., Garden City, N.Y., 1972. Discusses many aspects of second marriage. Based on 220 interviews plus personal experience.

BARRON, MILTON L. (ed.): *The Blending American: Patterns of Intermarriage*, Quadrangle Books, Inc., Chicago, 1972. (Paperback.) A collection of writings on various types of intermarriage—religious, racial, ethnic. Includes research studies. Discusses problems, husband-wife relationships, impact on children.

BERMAN, LEWIS A.: *Jews and Intermarriage*, Thomas Yoseloff, Publishers, Cranbury, N.J., 1968. Discusses the attitudes toward and the reasons for intermarriage and resistance to it; discusses married couples, their children, and their relationship with in-laws; characteristics of persons who intermarry; Jewish traits and sexual attitudes and behavior; many case histories. Author is a psychologist, teacher, and counselor.

BESANCENEY, PAUL H.: *Interfaith Marriages: Who and Why*, College and University Press Services, Inc., New Haven, Conn., 1970. (Paperback.) A Catholic sociologist discusses reasons for various types of interfaith marriages, their frequency, and the people involved. Also includes discussion of interethnic marriage.

CUBER, JOHN F.: "May-September Marriages," *Sexual Behavior*, vol. 1, no. 2, pp. 9–17, May 1971. A sociologist discusses the pros and cons of marriages in which there is marked age difference, especially the older man–younger woman marriage.

FURLONG, WILLIAM BARRY: "Interracial Marriage Is a Sometime Thing," in William J. Goode (ed.), *The Contemporary American Family*, Quadrangle Books, Inc., Chicago, 1971, pp. 136–151. (Paperback.) Discusses some of the problems of interracial marriage and presents specific cases.

GORDON, ALBERT I.: *Intermarriage*, Beacon Press, Boston, 1964. (Paperback, 1966.) Discussion of interfaith and interracial marriage. Includes statistical material not readily available elsewhere, summary of opinions of some 5,000 college students, and seventeen recorded interviews with the intermarried. Author is a rabbi.

HALSELL, GRACE: *Black/White Sex*, Fawcett Publications, Inc., Greenwich, Conn., 1972. (Paperback.) The author, a white woman, who through medication darkened her skin and lived as a black in preparation for another book, presents an analysis of black-white sex and marriage based on numerous interviews and observations.

HATHORN, RABAN, WILLIAM H. GENNÉ, AND MORDECAI BRILL (eds.): *Marriage, An Interfaith Guide for All Couples*, Association Press, New York, 1970. The editors are a Catholic priest, a Protestant minister, and a rabbi. They say, "This book is *not* directed to those who unite two different faiths in a religiously mixed marriage. Rather it is a compendium of insights from our three traditions which we believe will enrich any couple. . . . We have tried not to gloss over our differences."

KELLEHER, STEPHEN J.: *Divorce and Remarriage for Catholics?* Doubleday & Company, Inc., Garden City, N.Y., 1973. Critical analysis of the Catholic Church's stand on divorce and remarriage and a recommendation that both be accepted. Author is a priest who served for many years on Church marriage tribunals.

KREYKAMP, A. M. J., L. SCHELLEVIS, L. G. A. VAN NOORT, AND R. KAPSTEIN: *Protestant-Catholic Marriages: Interpreted by Pastors and Priests*, translated by Isaac C. Rottenberg, The Westminster Press, Philadelphia, 1967. (Paperback.) A constructive, cooperative effort by Protestant and Catholic clergy to help couples in mixed marriages understand the meaning of marriage and each other's faith.

LARSSON, CLOTYE M. (ed.): *Marriage across the Color Line*, Lancer Books, Inc., New York, 1965. (Paperback.) Discussion of interracial marriage presenting both favorable and unfavorable reactions to such marriage and including statements by persons who have such marriages. Also includes a discussion of the history of racial intermixture in the United States and of persons who have "crossed the color line."

LEWIS, R. A., AND G. B. SPANIER: "Theorizing About the Quality and Stability of Marriage," in W. Burr, R. Hill, I. Reiss, and I. Nye (eds.): *Contemporary Theories About the Family*, The Free Press, Glencoe, Ill., 1978. The factors affecting marital quality and stability are outlined in this summary and integration of research studies.

PYLE, LEO (ed.): *Pope and Pill*, Helicon Press, Inc., Baltimore, 1969. (Paperback.) Presents reactions pro and con to *Humanae vitae*. Discusses need for change in Catholic Church. Includes Catholic statements on sex, marriage, and contraception both before and after *Humanae vitae* and the majority and minority reports of the papal commission on birth control.

ROCK, JOHN: *The Time Has Come*, Alfred A. Knopf, Inc., New York, 1963. The author is a Catholic gynecologist who, through his research on infertility, contributed to the development of oral contraceptives. He makes proposals for ending the controversy over birth control and considers the possibility of reconciling oral contraceptives with the Catholic point of view.

SICKELS, ROBERT J.: *Race, Marriage, and the Law*, University of New Mexico Press, Albuquerque, 1972. History of the legal status of interracial marriage in America. Problems of interracial marriages. Trends and public opinion. Analysis of the *Loving versus Virginia* case, as a result of which the U.S. Supreme Court declared state laws prohibiting interracial marriage unconstitutional.

SIMON, PAUL, AND JEANNE SIMON: *Protestant-Catholic Marriage Can Succeed*, Association Press, New York, 1967. A Protestant husband and a Catholic wife discuss how they solved various problems in their marriage.

STUART, IRVING R., AND LAWRENCE E. ABT (eds.): *Interracial Marriage: Expectations and Realities*, Grossman Publishers, New York, 1973. Discusses reasons for interracial marriage, incidence, expectations, values, problems, conflicts, children, transracial adoption, interracial dating. What interracial marriages mean to the persons in them. The contributors to this volume have had personal and/or professional experiences with racial relationships.

WASHINGTON, JOSEPH R., JR.: *Marriage in Black and White*, Beacon Press, Boston, 1970. Author feels black-white marriage must become a matter of free choice with support for either choice.

"Marriage in black and white is . . . the ultimate criterion of an open society." Discusses the children of black-white marriages.

WRENN, LAWRENCE G. (ed.): *Divorce and Remarriage in the Catholic Church*, Newman Press, New York, 1973. A collection of articles on the Church's stand on divorce and remarriage. Catholic interpretation of New Testament teachings on divorce. Authors feel that many people believe the Church's stand is "needlessly stringent, excessively legal, and insensitive to contemporary sociological and theological insights."

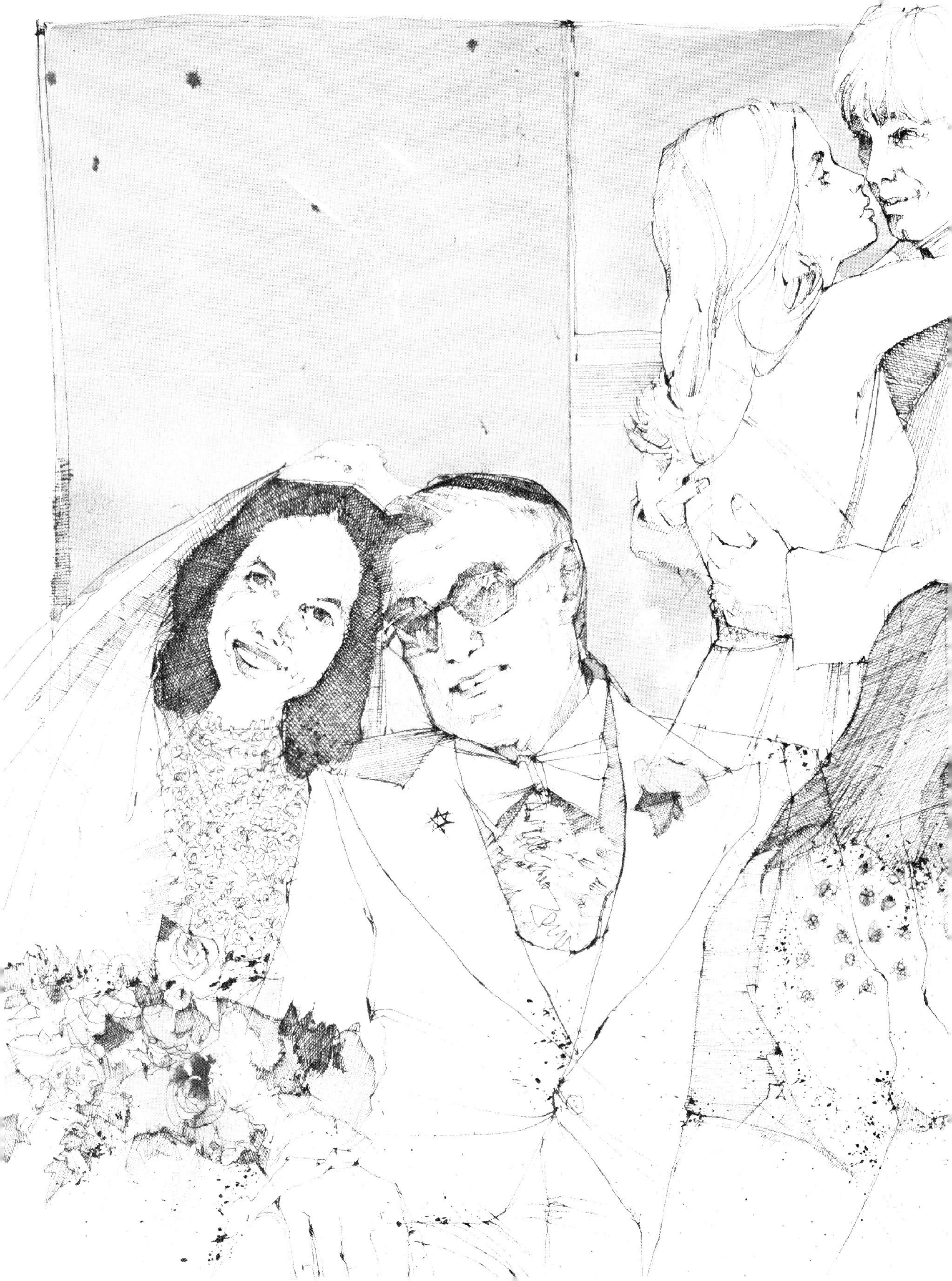

Part III
Marriage in Process

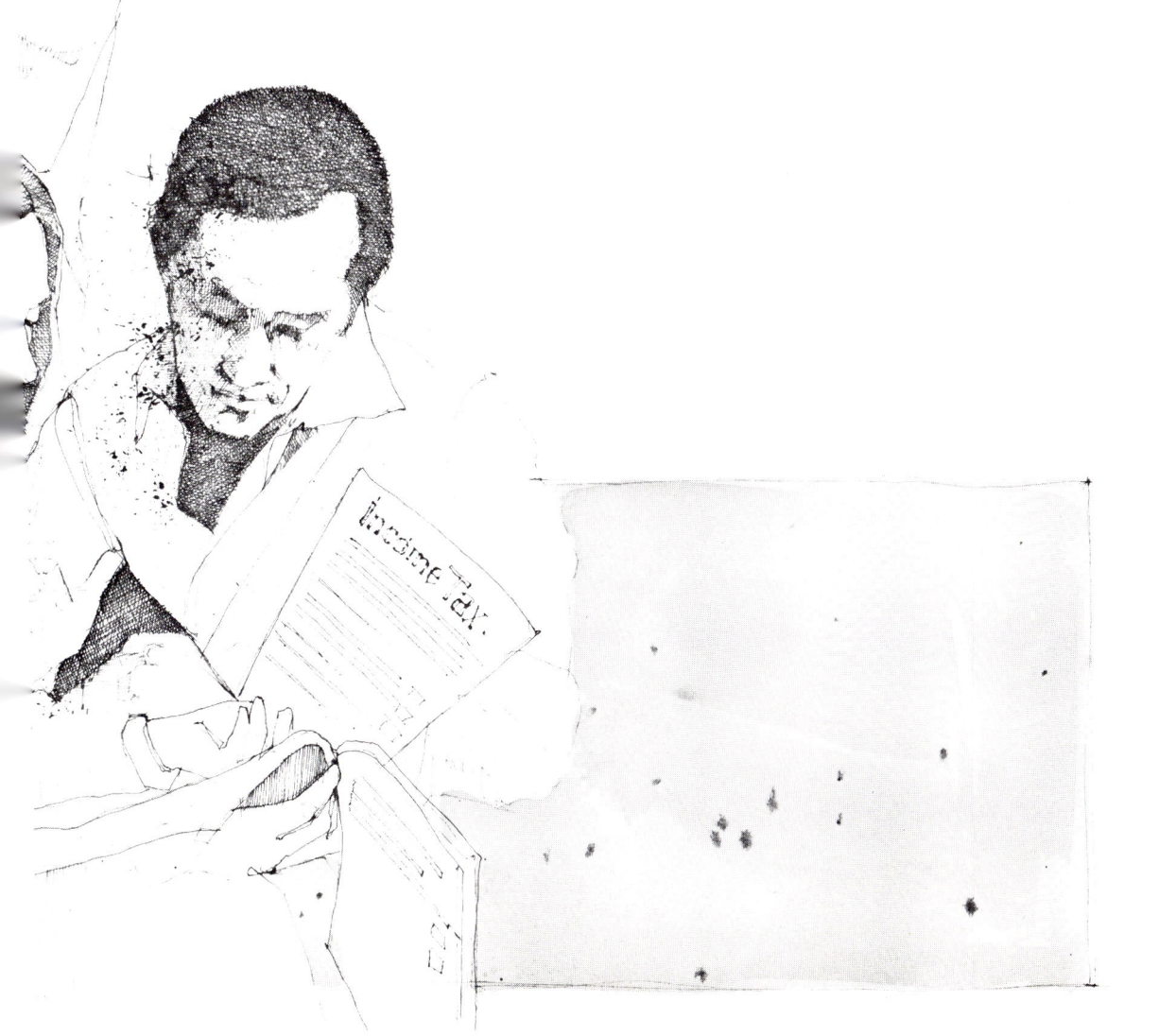

Chapter 8

Launching Marriage

To understand how marriages are launched in present-day America we will not only consider what a couple do to begin their marriage but also the circumstances under which they do it. Ordinarily what they do includes a wedding, a honeymoon, and a series of transitions from singleness to the married state. The circumstances under which they do these things vary somewhat from couple to couple, and we cannot discuss all the possibilities. There is one set of circumstances, however, under which a very large number of couples are launching their marriages, namely, the combination of marriage and higher education. Because these circumstances have arisen only in relatively recent years in appreciable numbers of cases, there are still aspects of such marriages that call for special understanding. In these cases "launching" has something of a double meaning. It implies a two-stage beginning, involving a transitional state (the first stage) from which a couple will eventually emerge into marriage that more nearly fits the customary pattern (the second stage). Hence, we shall discuss marriage during college as one of the elements in the background within which present-day marriages are being launched.

LAW

Marriage had its origin in human prehistory; and the mores and folkways of a particular culture constitute the backdrop against which present-day marriage occurs. But in a narrower, more specific sense, marriage occurs within the framework of the law. The law defines limits placed on individual choice. It reflects the mores. It constitutes a "launch pad," so to speak—a societal starting point, since marriage affects persons other than the couple directly involved. Because we live in groups, not as isolated hermits, certain limitations on individual behavior are widely and commonly accepted.

It is important for those who marry to be protected against exploitation and misrepresentation, and for society to have some minimum assurance relative to property ownership, the validity of marriage, the legitimacy of children, and the responsibility for children. In the United States, laws concerning marriage are determined by the state legislatures. Therefore, every state and the District of Columbia has its own laws concerning marriage. There are many similarities from state to state, but also some differences. It should also be noted that in some cases individual judges in local jurisdictions have the authority to make their own interpretations and judgments concerning the implementation of a given marriage law, and consequently there may even be some variation within a given state. The various American laws concerning marriage and divorce are summarized in the appendix.

We cannot discuss all aspects of the laws pertaining to marriage, and we must generalize; but we may mention a few aspects as follows.

The Capacity to Marry

All states set forth some general conditions that must be met before a couple can be married. In most cases the couple must have a valid marriage license, be of proper age, demonstrate that they are free of syphilis, and otherwise comply with the statutory formalities which apply in their jurisdiction. In many states special permission must be obtained from a judge if one of the potential spouses is insane or mentally deficient or has been in a mental institution.

Every state has laws stating that marriages between blood relatives, termed *consanguineous relationships*, are prohibited. In most states one is not allowed to marry one's mother, father, brother, sister, grandparent, uncle, aunt, nephew, niece, or first cousin. The law also generally covers stepparent–stepchild, step grandparent–step grandchild, and parent-in-law–child-in-law relationships. Relationships by adoption are also generally included.

Age

In all fifty-one jurisdictions the law specifies a minimum age at which an individual may marry. The objective is to prevent the marriage of persons too immature to assume marital responsibilities. Ages specified in the law fall into several categories (different in different jurisdictions): (1) the age at which a male and female may marry without consent of parent or guardian; (2) the age at which a male or female may marry with consent of parent or guardian; (3) the age below which an individual may not marry at all. The ages are sometimes lower for females than they are for males. This difference has traditionally been based on the assumption that the female matures earlier than the male. It is also a carry-over of the assumption that the female is prepared for homemaking and motherhood earlier than the male is prepared for economic independence. Some states have done away with these age differentials in recent years. There is not, and has not been, any legal restriction on the marriage of a couple of widely different ages providing the younger one met the legal requirement of minimum age.

Void and Voidable Marriages

If a marriage violates the requirements of the law, it may be *null and void*. In some instances, the marriage is void without any court action—for example, if one of the persons is already married, or if the two persons are too closely related by "blood" (prohibited degree of consanguinity). In other cases, the marriage is *voidable* through court action (annulment) upon the complaint of one of the parties. For example, marriage may be annulled if fraudulent claims were made premaritally by one of the parties; force was exerted to get one of the parties to agree to the marriage; one of the parties is "insane," but this fact was not revealed before the wedding. The difference between void and voidable marriage, then, is that a void marriage never existed. A voidable marriage can either be declared void by a judge or can be declared valid by the judge. It is not automatically void without a judge's declaration. The grounds for declaring a marriage null and void are almost as numerous and varied as the grounds for divorce. A marriage which is annulled is assumed never to have existed, and the parties are still single since they have not been legally married. A divorce, in contrast, is the severing of legal ties and terminates an existing marriage. After divorce the parties become ex-husband and ex-wife. (Actually, in the above statement the words "marriage" and "premaritally" should be used in quotation marks since they are applied to a relationship which was assumed to have been established but was invalid and not legally established.)

One hears of marriages annulled by the Roman Catholic Church. The Church cannot annul a marriage legally; it can only annul a marriage declared invalid according to Catholic doctrine. After such a Church annulment, the couple must get a legal annulment or, in some cases, even a divorce, to satisfy the requirements of the law. The Catholic Church may then accept such a divorce because it is considered only a procedure to satisfy the law, and the couple were not considered to have a valid marriage by the church in the first place.

In all jurisdictions, "bigamy" (having more than one "spouse" at a time) is not only a ground for voiding marriage but is a criminal offense. Actually, the term is a legal one and to the layman may be misleading. No one is permitted to have more than one husband or one wife at a time; an individual may only attempt to do so by having an invalid second marriage while a valid first marriage already exists. "Bigamy" is not synonymous with "polygamy," which means actually having more than one legal spouse at one time.

Waiting Period

Most states require a variously stated time period to elapse between application for a marriage license and the date at which the license becomes valid and the wedding may occur. Such a waiting period gives a hasty couple time to reconsider their decision. It also permits bringing fraud or force to light or allows individuals to object to the marriage for other reasons.

Health Certificate

All but a very few states require applicants for a marriage license to present a laboratory report or a physician's affidavit certifying that the applicants are free of venereal disease, specifically syphilis. The reason for this requirement is the seriousness of this disease and the fact that a child can be born with syphilis if the mother has the disease. (This is congenital, not inherited, syphilis; syphilis cannot be inherited.) The requirement is probably a carry-over of an attitude of the past regarding venereal diseases as "loathsome" or "immoral"; the assumption was that the disease is contracted through "immoral" sexual relations, and therefore a person about to marry has a right to know whether the other party is free of the disease. The blood test given before marriage (called a "VDRL") is commonly thought to check for all venereal diseases. This is incorrect. Most state laws check only for syphilis. Thus, an individual who has gonorrhea or some other venereal disease will probably not have this detected by the test.

License

With the exception of common-law marriage in the states in which it is still legal, persons seeking to be married must get a license, usually obtained from the county courthouse. Such a license indicates that the couple has met the requirements of the law and is a means by which the marriage may be entered in public records.

Officiant

After a license is issued, a couple are expected to have their marriage solemnized (to have a wedding performed) by an officiant authorized by the state. If the officiant is unauthorized and the couple did not know this at the time of the wedding and married in good faith, their marriage is usually considered valid, and the unauthorized officiant is subject to penalty.

Marriages are typically solemnized in one of four ways (Pennsylvania Bar Institute, 1976):

1 By authorized civil authority, such as state and federal judges and local civic officials.

2 By authorized religious authorities, such as ministers, priests, and rabbis of any regularly established church or congregation. Bishops are also authorized.

3 By a religious society, institution, or organization in which at least one spouse is a member.

4 By the parties themselves in a religious ceremony. This method is not to be confused with a common-law marriage. Certificates are required either from the clerk of the orphans' court or from the parties themselves.

Witnesses are always required to verify that the agreement to marry was carried out.

Even an authorized officiant does not "marry" the couple as we customarily think. In the last analysis, the couple marry themselves through consensus, that is, through a statement of agreement to be married made in the presence of an officiant and witnesses, that is, their "I do's" or the equivalent. The wedding ceremony itself may take any form the couple desire, and they may write it themselves, as discussed below, so long as it contains an expression of consensus. When an officiant says, "I now pronounce them husband and wife," or something similar, he or she is not marrying the couple at that point; he or she is acknowledging the fact that they have married themselves through consensus. It may be compared to a physician's saying, "I pronounce the patient dead." The physician does not kill the patient; he or she declares a state of being.

Residency

States generally require that marriages be performed in the state in which the license is issued. Generally speaking, a couple may marry in any state they wish, so long as they meet the marriage requirements of that state. They need not, however, be residents of that state. It is widely known that states with particularly lenient marriage laws, such as Nevada (where there is no waiting period of any kind and no blood test required), have more than their share of marriages.

Change in Status

Within the law, a couple's status changes when they are married. Many states still have laws which are discriminatory in that they imply the husband's dominance over the wife, but these are gradually being struck down by the courts or being changed by state legislatures. Thus, it would be too cumbersome to review here the intricacies of the financial obligations spouses have to each other or the rights they have to property and material possessions in the event of divorce, separation, or death of a spouse.

There are some other changes in status that are likely to remain with us. In most cases husbands and wives cannot be required to testify against each other in criminal court proceedings. Of course, females generally take on the last name of their husband following the wedding, although this shift is not mandatory under the law and some women choose to keep their last name. When changes in name are made, however, it is important for a woman to change her voter's registration, driver's license, passport, social security registration, and any other important documents.

Proxy, Shipboard, and Alien Marriages

There are three kinds of marriages which are somewhat unusual but which are nevertheless allowed in some states. A proxy marriage (where a substitute "stands in" for the real spouse-to-be) is valid in some states where the resident of that state freely consented beforehand to such a ceremony. The ceremony is then valid where performed. Shipboard marriages are recognized in many states. The law of the flag of the vessel is the governing law in the typical case. Since there is no federal marriage law, marriages on a United States ship may pose problems. Therefore, one of three approaches may be used to determine proper jurisdiction for registering the marriage: the domicile of the ship owner, the domicile of the parties involved, or the port of registry of the ship. There are adequate precedents for all three ways of establishing residency.

States vary in how they deal with marriages to aliens. In Pennsylvania, for example, where a couple agree to marry only to permit the alien spouse to enter or to remain in the United States and they do not intend to live together, a valid marriage results nevertheless. The alien spouse may enter as a non-quota immigrant. A fiancé(e) may enter if marriage is performed within ninety days after entry. The only requirement is that the alien be "of good moral character" and in good health. The normal five-year residency requirement before an alien may file for citizenship is shortened to three years for an alien spouse.

Premarital Pregnancy

A valid marriage legitimates a child born after the wedding, even though the pregnancy started before the wedding and the birth of the child occurs as early as the day of the wedding. Unless someone else is admitted to be the father, and when there has been no court action regarding paternity, the woman's husband is presumed to be the father of the child. If he does not know about the pregnancy at the time of the wedding and learns about it later, either from the woman or otherwise, and he can establish to a court's satisfaction that he is not the father of the child, this circumstance is typically ground for annulment if he wishes to use it; but the marriage is not automatically void—it is voidable.

Interracial Marriage

Until 1967 a number of states had laws prohibiting marriage between persons of different race. In that year the United States Supreme Court declared such statutes unconstitutional, in violation of the Fourteenth Amendment (Sickels, 1972).

Remarriage after Divorce

In some states the law stipulates a given time period that must elapse after a divorce before the parties may remarry. In other states they may marry on the day of the decree.

Reciprocity

By and large, each jurisdiction accepts as valid a marriage considered valid in another jurisdiction. That is, if a couple married in, say, New York, their marriage would be accepted in all other states. On occasion an exception to this generalization has occurred when a couple were considered still legally married in one state but divorced in another. This situation used to arise not infrequently when couples procured "quickie" divorces in Mexico.

Antenuptial Contracts

Some couples write and sign contracts before the wedding. Such contracts include a wide range of provisions extending from the disposal of property in case of divorce to inheritance in the event of death. Antenuptial contracts are valid in most states if they are fair to both parties and have been properly made. Antenuptial contracts which are legally binding should not be confused with "marriage contracts" that many young persons write up concerning their roles and duties in marriage. Formal antenuptial contracts are most common in second marriages and in cases where one spouse is very wealthy. They may specify how money or property may be divided when someone dies. They usually take into consideration an individual's financial status, the spouse's status, gift taxes, estate taxes, and inheritance taxes.

"Marriage Contracts"

"Marriage contracts," such as those two young persons may write defining roles, duties, expectations, and behavior in marriage, have a different legal status from formal antenuptial agreements. Any couple may agree on a division of labor in household tasks, set ground rules for their sexual interaction, specify who will have responsibility for child rearing, or agree how money will be spent. Indeed, most marriage and family counselors encourage discussion of such issues. A written agreement about these matters, however, has no legal force. The law of the state will almost always take precedence over marriage relationships, and unless very special legal steps are taken, a "marriage contract" will not be sufficient to overturn the normal procedure for making decisions about divorce, separation, property settlements, child custody, and other matters which surface when relationships terminate. Furthermore, it is unlikely that a judge would intervene in an intact marriage relationship solely because a condition of a "marriage contract" was being violated by one of the parties involved.

Despite these legal limitations to such agreements, there are many counselors and instructors of marriage relationships who encourage such agreements to foster communication and understanding between the couple.

MARRIAGE READINESS

Many persons have had the experience of meeting the right person at the wrong time. In other words, many have had relationships which—had circumstances been different—might have ended in marriage. For example, perhaps geographical separation resulted in the termination of a very successful high school dating relationship. Perhaps a couple in love decide they are too young to marry, knowing that it is unlikely that they will ever marry each other if they date others. Some couples take jobs in different locations, knowing that this may influence the continuance of their relationship. Other conditions which might terminate what is otherwise a very successful relationship might be strong parental opposition, a decision that circumstances of one sort of another are not conducive to marriage at the present time, or, in the extreme case, death of the potential spouse. These situations may be called *circumstantial factors* which set limits on readiness for marriage. We do not marry simply because we are in love and want to marry, but also because circumstances are conducive to marriage at the present time.

Other criteria which are important in establishing marriage readiness are *socioemotional factors*. For example, individuals must consider whether they have the emotional and social maturity to enter into marriage and accept the responsibilities that come with it. One particularly important question concerns whether the individuals have had a full quota of premarital experiences. Counselors can cite countless cases of married persons who complain that they were pressured into marriage too early by their spouse. With many couples, one person wishes to wait longer than the other before marriage. *It is important that the less eager partner be ready*, since this person may have more regrets after the wedding. Many married persons wish that they had dated more before marriage, that they had gotten to know their spouse better, that they had traveled more, or that they had finished their schooling first—in short, they did not have what *they* considered to be a full quota of premarital experiences. It can be said that the things you do not have are often more important than the things you do have.

The couple must consider whether they are prepared to make the transition to marriage. Are they able to handle the shift in roles that oftentimes occurs? Finally, they must consider whether they have the ability to stabilize after a quarrel. *Virtually all couples quarrel*. No marriage is without its differences of opinion, quarrels, or outright fights. This is also the case for most engaged couples. Fighting in and of itself is not a sign of a doomed relationship. Rather, what is important is the couple's *ability to stabilize after a quarrel*. Does one hold grudges for several days? Does one try to hurt or "get back at" the spouse? What has been accomplished by the fight? A couple that can demonstrate after a fight that they have benefited from it, that they are still friends and lovers, and that they have now returned to a state of equilibrium are much better candidates for marriage than couples who are brought deeper into turmoil by every fight.

Finally, couples often overlook the importance of *financial factors*. That "two can live as cheaply as one" is an unfortunate myth with many victims. Two who are married may be able to live more cheaply than two who are single, but they *cannot live* as cheaply as one. A wedding can be a significant financial commitment for some couples, but the more important financial factors may be applicable only after the wedding. Couples will need to establish their own health and auto insurance policies. After marriage, they will no longer be eligible for coverage under their parents' policies. They will need to consider whether they want life insurance. They may purchase a home or rent an apartment. If the birth of a child follows shortly after marriage, the financial burden will be even greater. There are, then, many important factors which should be considered prior to marriage.

THE WEDDING

The wedding does not have as its purpose the creation of personality traits that are not found in the two persons before the ceremony. It contains no magic. There is no administering of a love potion, no laying on of hands to remove evil spirits. No oracle speaks on the wedding day to communicate to the bride and groom the divine will or to teach them how to "live happily ever after." Whatever happiness they achieve is the result of intelligence, knowledge, love, effort, and commitment.

The wedding creates status, rights, and opportunity. It gives the couple the opportunity to achieve a new degree of mutuality; it does not provide the wherewithal to make that achievement. It does play a part in crystallizing and focusing the meaning of the couple's relationship. The wedding is a major vehicle for the couple's expression of mutual commitment. Therefore, it has a personal as well as a social function.

The Wedding Ceremony

The wedding ceremony may vary from the barest minimum, with a brief statement before a civil official, to an elaborate church affair. There is a great variety of forms, hence a couple planning a religious ceremony might well discuss meaning as well as procedure with the clergyman involved. A couple may write their own ceremony, which introduces the possibility of almost infinite variability.

During a religious wedding ceremony a couple utter some of the most profound intentions and acknowledge some of the most far-reaching responsibilities of which human life is capable. Yet circumstances are often such that their attention is directed toward what is happening rather than toward the meaning of what is said.

"Dearly beloved, we are gathered together here in the sight of God" is a commonly used opening statement in the Protestant ceremony. In the exhortation before marriage, the Catholic priest says, "You are about to enter into a union which is most sacred and most serious, a union which was established by God himself." At the beginning of the Jewish ceremony there is this invocation: "Blessed may you be who come in the name of the Lord; we bless you out of the house of the Lord. May He who is mighty, blessed and great above all, may He send His abounding blessings to the bridegroom and the bride." Such statements affirm the religious nature of marriage and serve to remind the couple of the fundamental orientation of their new life together.

The phrase "and in the face of this company" usually follows the statement mentioned above in the Protestant ceremony. This is more than a courteous nod in the direction of the assembled guests. It is more than a speaker's beginning with "Mr. Chairman, friends." It is a reference to the importance of marriage as a basic social institution. Because society has always been deeply interested in and concerned with marriage, it is taken for granted that representatives of society will witness a wedding. All three cere-

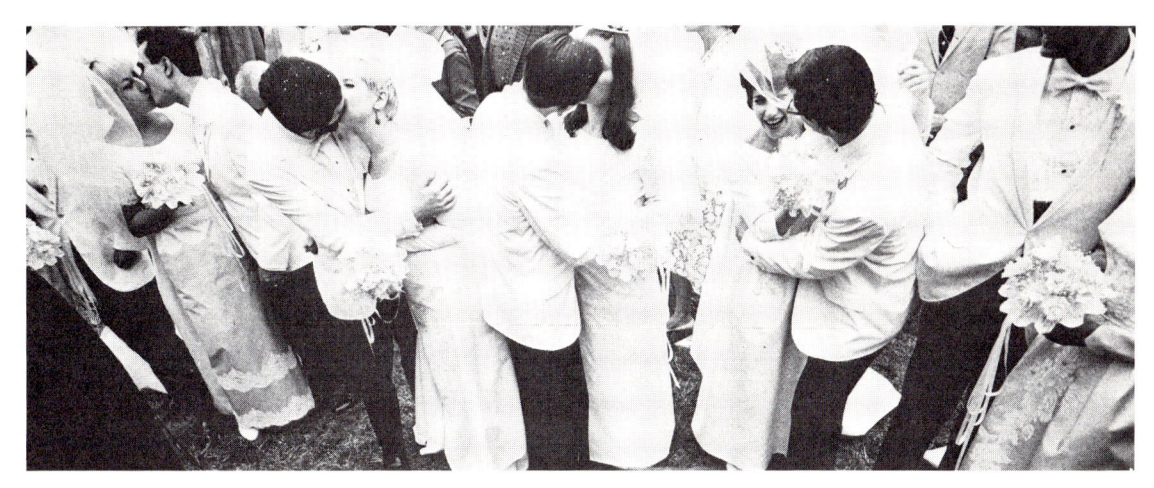

Wedding ceremonies can range from the traditional to the unthinkable. These couples are among sixteen couples who chose to marry in an unusual group ceremony. (Ann Douglas, Photo Researchers)

monies include such witnesses, and in the Jewish ceremony they are to be unrelated to the bride and groom. This same societal interest in marriage is also implied in a later statement in many Protestant ceremonies, "If any man can show just cause why they may not lawfully be joined together, let him now speak, or else hereafter forever hold his peace." Such interest is indicated, too, in the publication of the banns before certain religious weddings.

Just what a particular couple will include in their wedding ceremony, under what circumstances the wedding will take place, what preparation for the ceremony they will make, and what expressions of commitment they will include depends upon the attitudes, idealism, imagination, and beliefs of the couple themselves. Some couples include a religious element. For others a more humanistic flavor seems more acceptable. Some make the promises of the conventional ceremony—"till death do us part," "forsaking all others," "for better for worse, for richer for poorer, in sickness and in health." Others include "so long as love lasts," or something equally conditional. The ceremony may take place in a church or under the trees in a favorite woodland spot. The bride may wear an elaborate gown or a cotton print, the groom a tuxedo or blue jeans. There may be a reception with catered food, or the refreshments may consist of Cokes and hot dogs.

Perhaps the central point of emphasis and significance is that, regardless of social changes which have occurred in recent years, increased sexual permissiveness, unconventional living arrangements, and the inclination of some young people to discard tradition and the trappings of traditional ways, many of those young people, in their own way, seek to express publicly their love and commitment. This need for a public expression of commitment upon which an enduring relationship may be founded seems to be personally and culturally persistent, suggesting that it must involve deep meaning and value.

Marital Adjustment Implied

In the commitments which a couple declare, there are statements that both implicitly and explicitly suggest the nature of marriage adjustment. Examples from the three major religions follow.

Protestant: "Wilt thou love her (or him), in sickness and in health; and, forsaking all others, keep thee only unto her (or him), so long as ye both shall live?" and "To have and to hold from this day forward, for better for worse, for richer for poorer, in sickness and in health, to love and to cherish, till death do us part." Catholic: "I, (Name), take you, (Name), for my lawful wife (or husband), to have and to hold, from this day forward, for better, for worse, for richer for poorer, in sickness and in health, until death do us part." Jewish (Reform): "Do you (Name) take (Name) to be your wife (husband), promising to cherish and protect her (him), whether in good fortune or in adversity, and to seek together with her (him) a life hallowed by the faith of Israel?"

These statements suggest (1) that the couple will accept one another as they are; (2) that they will both love and respect each other in spite of possible shortcomings; (3) that they will exert continued effort to make the marriage succeed; (4) that they may well anticipate problems; (5) that marriage is an exclusive relationship; (6) that they commit themselves to it.

Following the statement of commitment, there is an exchange of a ring or rings. We shall discuss rings and their meaning later in this chapter. Suffice it to say here that in the modern wedding ceremony the ring is a token, a symbol of the pledge made and of the hope that the marriage will be permanent.

Is Marriage Dissoluble?

In one form or another, the Christian ceremony typically contains the following statement made by Jesus: "Those whom God hath joined together let no man put asunder." This statement, plus the phrases "so long as ye both shall live" and "till death do us part," raises a basic issue. Is marriage dissoluble? Is divorce ever justified? We know, of course, that divorce is possible within the law. We know, too, that the great majority of Americans regret the occurrence of divorce but, nevertheless, accept it. But how does divorce harmonize with religious teachings? Here, again, we find far from universal agreement. Divorce is possible within the Jewish faith. The Roman Catholic Church holds that valid marriage once established and consummated is indissoluble because it is under the jurisdiction of God and not within the jurisdiction of any human agency. By and large, Protestant churches permit divorce.

WEDDING CUSTOMS

Many contemporary wedding customs are so old that their origins are lost in antiquity. In numerous cases we can only speculate as to how they started. Such customs are survivals; that is, they have maintained their form but have lost their original meaning and endured beyond the time when they had a function in connection with the ceremony. They might be called social fossils or be compared to vestigial parts of the body, such as the appendix.

When we know nothing of the origin of one of these survivals, or when the original function, though known, is no longer acceptable, we rationalize the custom and convince ourselves that we carry it out for good luck. When doing something for luck savors too much of the superstitious, we are inclined to continue to do it "for fun." In most cases we carry it out because it is traditional and we accept tradition uncritically.

The term "wedding" itself is a carry-over from ancient times. Originally the "wed" was the money or goods that the prospective groom gave to the father of the girl to secure or pledge the purchase of the bride.

The throwing of rice is common in this country. According to one theory, the rice constitutes a symbol of fertility. Throwing the rice is an expression of a wish that the new couple will have many children, or it is an offering to the spirits with this end in view. It is apparent that this custom has lost its original meaning, since having many children is not an immediate objective sought by most newlyweds. According to another theory, the rice was originally an offering to appease evil spirits bent on doing harm to the bride and groom. Or the throwing of the rice may be an outgrowth of the ceremonial eating of it.

The bride often wears "something old, something new, something borrowed, and something blue." The origin of this custom is not known. Part of it may be attributed to the ancient Israelites, who were bidden to wear blue upon the borders of their garments, blue signifying purity, love, and fidelity.

The bride may wear a veil, or part of her costume may be what might be considered a remnant of a veil. It seems strange that on her wedding day, when she should be proud of her appearance, the bride should wear what is ordinarily a face covering. The veil may originally have been a means of indicating difference in status between an unmarried and a married woman. Typically peoples in some way indicate this difference. It may be a carry-over of the canopy held over the bridal couple during the ceremony among the ancient Hebrews and sometimes still used in the Jewish wedding. Or it may have originated as a means of disguise from evil spirits. All our remote ancestors believed in such spirits. On her wedding day a girl was considered especially vulnerable to their influence, and in many parts of the world today a bride is disguised as a means of protection. Originally the veil may have indicated the woman's submission to her husband or her change of identity (Brasch, 1965).

The use of a ring as a token or pledge is ancient. After Joseph had interpreted Pharaoh's dreams to the latter's satisfaction, the ruler said to Joseph, "'See, I have set thee over all the land of Egypt.' And Pharaoh took off his ring from his hand, and put it upon Joseph's hand" (*Genesis* 41:41–42). Other early peoples used rings in a similar manner. Eichler (1925) says that the ancient Egyptians were the first to use the ring in connection with marriage vows. In hieroglyphics a circle represents eternity, and the ring probably symbolized the eternal nature of marriage ties. Among the early Anglo-Saxons a ring was included in the wed mentioned above. The ring was worn on the bride's right hand until the time of the wedding ceremony, when it was transferred to her left hand. Wedding rings were employed by the Christians as early as A.D. 860.

There are several theories as to why the ring is worn on the fourth finger of the left hand. It is said that in early times the right hand signified power and authority, while the left signified subjection and submission. The ancient Greeks believed that there was a vein extending directly from the ring finger to the heart, the seat of love. It may be that the ring is worn on this particular finger merely because it is the least used of all fingers and ornaments worn upon it cause no inconvenience (Brasch, 1965).

In many wedding ceremonies, both bride and groom have attendants. With the possible exception of the best man, these attendants no longer have any save a decorative function. This custom may have its origin in the ten witnesses required in ancient Rome, the witnesses usually being friends of the bride's family. Or the custom may be a carry-over of marriage by capture. It is thought that in very early days wives were stolen or captured

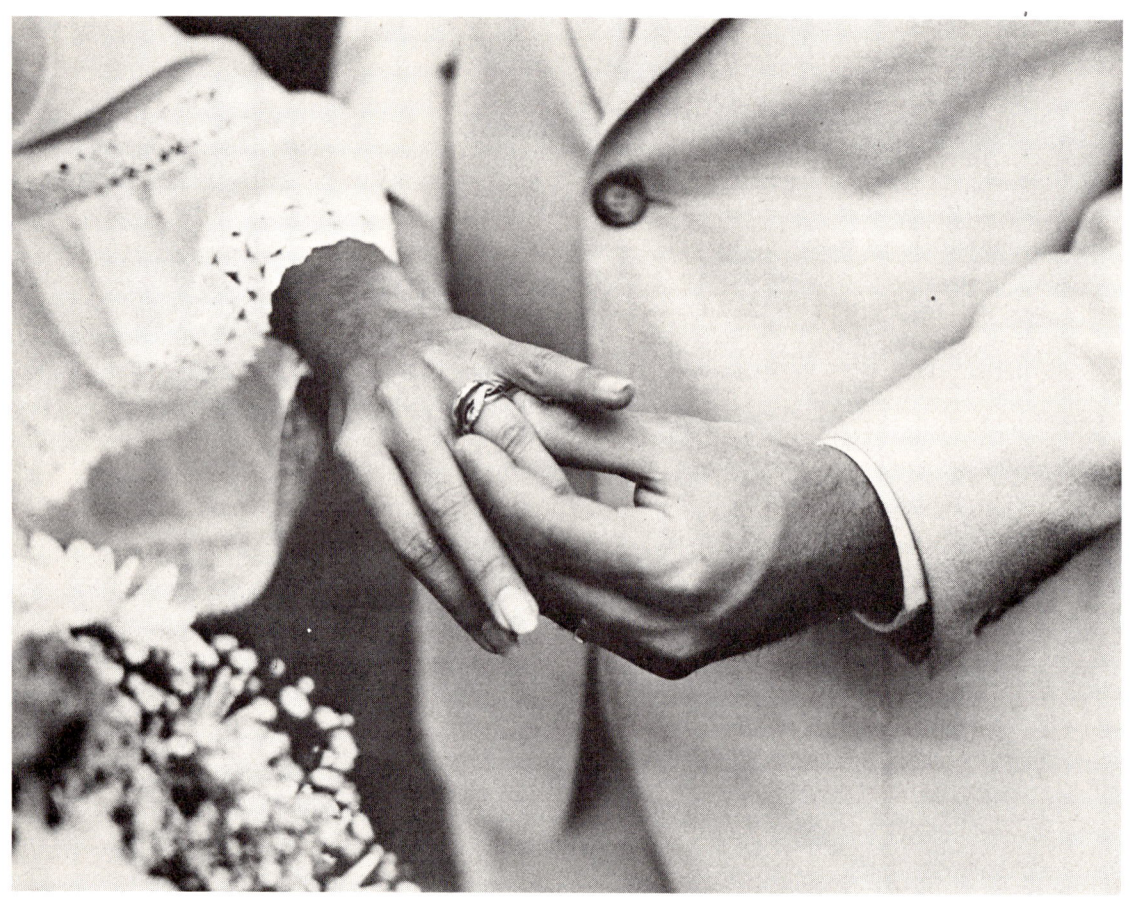

Wedding rings have been used as meaningful symbols for centuries. Weddings are surrounded with traditions and symbolism. (Ken Heyman)

and that parties of friends and relatives to protect the woman or assist the prospective husband gave rise to the custom of having attendants. Among some peoples there is still mock capture at the wedding ceremony (Sumner and Keller, 1927).

Until recently the bride promised to "love, honor, and obey." Nowadays obey is commonly omitted. The status of women has changed, and the relationship of husband and wife has been considerably altered. Hence, there is no use in including superfluous words in the ceremony. It is significant, however, that the word "obey" was until recently commonly employed and is still sometimes used and also that at no time did the groom promise to obey; he promised to "love, honor, and cherish," or something similar.

The custom of the bride throwing her bouquet to the young unmarried women after the ceremony is still not uncommon, although bouquets are now sometimes composed of numerous sections wired together and ready for convenient distribution. When the bride does throw her bouquet, the belief is that the girl who catches it will be the next to marry. It is said that in the early fourteenth century in France it was considered good luck to procure one of the bride's garters after the ceremony—a custom rather inconvenient for the bride. From this grew the custom of throwing a stocking, a practice that was common during the fifteenth century. This, too, was inconvenient and gave way to throwing the bouquet (Eichler, 1925).

It is believed to bring ill luck if the groom sees the bride in her wedding dress or sees her at all before the ceremony on the wedding day. The origin of this custom is uncertain. It may be that it began when parents feared elopement and consequently being cheated out of the bride price. It may have originated in the belief that the groom could direct evil spirits or the evil eye to the ever-vulnerable bride.

In many cases noisemakers are used before or after a wedding. A bell is rung, tin cans are tied to the couple's vehicle, or other cars follow the bridal car with horns sounding. We accept the wedding bell without question, and the other two types of noisemaking are rationalized as "fun." But one wonders what the origin of this custom was. It may have begun with the belief that noise frightens evil spirits, as many peoples still hold. It may be only a means of publicity.

It is not unusual for the groom to carry the bride over the threshold of their new home. In ancient Rome the threshold was considered sacred to Vesta, the goddess of virgins, and it was thought to be an ill omen if the bride stumbled over it. To prevent her stumbling, the young husband carried her into the house. What happens if he stumbles with her is not clear.

THE TRANSITION FROM SINGLENESS TO MARRIAGE

In spite of what has already been mentioned regarding couples who cohabit before the wedding and the number of persons who have had premarital sexual intercourse, most couples must make many important adjustments following the wedding, and all couples make transitions from singleness to the married state.

Originally the term *honeymoon* referred to the period immediately following the wedding during which the couple's affection was thought to wane like the moon. Nowadays, the term usually refers to a post-wedding trip. Not every couple have such a trip, of course, and there is no reason to assume that married life cannot have an auspicious beginning without one. If, however, a couple do have a honeymoon, a post-wedding trip, it is reasonable to plan such a trip with the objective of facilitating the transition to marriage. This can hardly be achieved if the honeymoon is so expensive that the couple spend money that would more appropriately be saved for home furnishings, if one of the parties becomes so involved in individual interests that the other party is excluded, if it involves dashing from one tourist attraction to another as if the couple felt they had to see every monument and witness every spectacle in order to get their money's worth, or if the trip is so long and so exhausting that fatigue sets in and increases irritability.

Actually, of course, the honeymoon represents only part of the transition from singleness to marriage. The total transition begins with the couple's premarital relationship and extends through the honeymoon period into marriage itself (see Lopata, 1971). To make marriage succeed a couple must pass through a number of transitions, some more applicable to a given couple than others. Some of these are as follows:

From independence to interdependence; from independence to a "team" relationship. This "team" relationship is, in a sense, unique because it involves two persons of opposite gender. When two complementary equals are united in common purpose, a new oneness, a new entity, is created. Their relationship extends not to a part of life but to a fundamental way of life. Such a transition entails concessions on either side. It requires a new perspective in that the relationship is in some ways considered more important than the individuals in it. Obviously, a person who cannot make this transition and who as a result continues to think, act, make demands, and set expectations as if still single is an impediment to the success of the "team."

From a premarital sexual pattern to a marital sexual pattern. For many persons, especially but not exclusively women, this involves a transition from premarital chastity or infrequent, often incomplete, sexual relations to unrestrained marital sexual experience. For some women this expected about-face is not easy, and the full transition takes time. But certainly it is appropriate to expect a woman who marries to redefine her sexual objective and shift it from premarital self-protection and reluctance to marital acceptance and enthusiastic sharing.

Depending upon his premarital experience or lack of it, the man may be called upon to make a transition from giving first consideration to his own sexual satisfaction to giving first consideration to the satisfaction of his wife, through which his own satisfaction is increased. He is called upon to think of sex as a mutual rather than only as a self-oriented experience. The couple are called upon to make a transition from thinking of sexual intercourse as being subject to premarital limitations, or from the woman's reluctant acceptance for the sake of the man's pleasure, to integrating it into the totality of their common life.

From a focus on romance to the responsibilities associated with establishing and maintaining a marriage. For this transition many people are not well prepared. The man may fail to understand that homemaking and family living today put demands upon him other than in his role as breadwinner. He may expect his wife to continue to wait upon him as his mother did or to perform without reciprocation on his part the personal services for which in his premarital days he was accustomed to pay and for which, therefore, he felt no call to express appreciation. The woman may be unprepared to carry out housekeeping duties with efficiency and dispatch. Her attitude toward gainful employment may lead her to resist or even to reject the role of homemaker, to which, she feels, there is attributed too little prestige.

From single purchasing to family purchasing. With some exceptions, college students usually do the bulk of their purchasing in a small number of stores of relatively limited type adjacent to the campus. Family purchasing presents a somewhat different problem because of the greater variety of items to be purchased and because of the resulting greater complexity of the budget. With the exception of gifts, student purchasing involves largely items for oneself. Family purchasing requires knowledge of buying items for a home, for a member of the opposite gender, and perhaps children.

From a single-person spending pattern to a "double-person" spending pattern. In some cases the man continues to think in terms of "my money," a portion of which he reluctantly doles out to his wife when her need is clearly apparent or her pleas are sufficiently convincing. Cases are known in which such an attitude is so ingrained in a man that he even thinks of her income as "my money." In one case, in which the wife was working to put her husband through school, he would accompany her to the bank when she deposited her paycheck and then give her a small allowance from her salary. The woman, in some cases, continues to spend family income as if she were still single and receiving an allowance from her parents and as if her own desires were the only ones to be considered.

From premarital identity to marital identity. This transition is more conspicuous for the woman than for the man, since in most cases she assumes her husband's surname preceded by "Mrs." A few women combine their maiden name with the husband's surname into a hyphenated "married name," and some women use "Ms." rather than "Mrs." Nonetheless, many women come to be thought of and, perhaps more importantly, come to think of themselves as the wife of so-and-so. This shift in identity is difficult, even traumatic, for women who fear a loss of individuality. Other women accept it as part of getting married and are not threatened by it.

Men, too, change their identity at marriage but not to the degree that women do. Married couples come to be thought of as pairs. Unless a man is dishonest about it, he comes to be thought of as the husband of so-and-so. The wearing of wedding bands is an outward indication of this shift in identity, and men are increasingly accepting rings.

From being a child of one's parents to being husband or wife. This raises the question, "Who will be put first in one's scale of values, spouse or parents?" The individual who cannot put spouse first is not ready to be married. Couples for the first time are confronted with questions such as: Where will we spend Christmas? Thanksgiving? How will we celebrate holidays? Traditions developed in two families of orientation need to be merged into one family of procreation. For example, will Christmas presents be opened on Christmas Eve, Christmas morning, or in the afternoon? Every family has different customs for holidays, and these have to be integrated.

From being a child of one's parents to being a child-in-law of the other person's parents. This transition takes time, and calls for understanding and effort on the part of all concerned. Individuals often find it difficult to choose a suitable form of address to use with their new in-laws.

From marriage to the family, that is, from having no child to having a child. Not all couples have children. Among those who do, the arrival of the first child is most critical so far as this transition is concerned. "A marital relationship undergoes irreversible change with the arrival of the first baby" (Ehrlich, 1972). A question arises as to the spouse's and the child's relative position in one's scale of values. In a successful family there is an integration of such a nature that spouse and child are not thrown into competition for the attention of the other parent. In some families, however, the arrival of the first child means that husband or wife, more frequently the latter, allows attention to the child, in a sense, to squeeze the other party out of the marriage relationship. In other words, the woman becomes so much a mother that she is correspondingly less a wife. In occasional cases the situation is the other way round. For example, in one case the couple got along apparently happily until the birth of the first baby. Then the husband refused to go out with his wife in the evening because he would not leave the child with a baby-sitter. He objected to his wife's shopping, visiting friends, or attending church for the same reason. He would not go out or let her go out and take the child along, because he feared it would contract some contagious disease. The wife felt that she was virtually a prisoner in her own home because of her baby.

From one's own habits to a merging of habits. We spend our entire lives developing habits that may or may not be shared by our future spouse. For example, there are "day people" and there are "night people." What happens when a day person (someone who likes to go to bed early and get up early and works well during the day) marries a night person (someone who likes to go to bed late and sleep late and works well during the night)? If they intend to work together and spend leisure time with each other, or if they develop preferences for sexual intercourse at certain times of the day when the other person is not available, tensions can develop. A day person who is sound asleep at 2 A.M. may not appreciate being awakened by the night person who comes to bed wanting to share some affection in the middle of the night.

Other changes in habits may involve meal times. Single persons often develop their own peculiar eating habits. They may not eat certain meals, may snack all the time, or may eat three regular meals each day. Couples often need to adapt to eating habits which are different from those they are accustomed to.

COLLEGE MARRIAGES

Number and Composition of Student Population

In 1975, there were 9,697,000 students enrolled in institutions of higher learning. Of these, 45 percent were women. But the number of women is increasing more rapidly than the number of men. Also, about one-third of college students are aged 25 or older, and this number is increasing more rapidly than the number of younger students (late teens and early twenties). A "large majority" of the older students were attending on a part-time basis (U.S. Bureau of the Census, *Current Population Reports*, 1976). In 1974, of students aged 14 to 24, 11.2 percent of the males and 12.5 percent of the females were married, with spouse present. This figure does not, therefore, include students who were married but whose spouses were absent—for example, for occupational, military, or similar reasons. Of married male students, 61.6 percent were enrolled full time and 38.6 percent part time, while of the females 50.8 percent were enrolled full time and 49.2 percent part time (U.S. Bureau of the Census, 1975). These figures suggest that one of the "costs" of marriage while in college is the longer time it takes married students to get a degree.

Since present-day college education is so closely tied in with occupational training for many students, males and females are subjected to somewhat different social pressure toward getting degrees. There are males who drop out of college because they cannot handle satisfactorily the combined task of marriage, study, and earning. On the other hand, there are males whose motivation toward completing a degree is increased with marriage. Generalizing, this increased motivation is more likely to be seen in the male than in the female because the male is subject to the social expectations associated with family support and standard of living.

In contrast, after their weddings, many non–career-oriented women lose their motivation for getting a degree. Such a woman may see a less apparent connection between her college work and her new role as a wife-homemaker than her husband sees between his studying and his occupational objective. She may become absorbed in her new responsibilities. She may feel that her husband's burden would be lightened if she got a job. She may find it inconvenient to get to classes at times when she would prefer to be doing something domestic. Since she is under less social and occupational pressure to get ahead in the sense in which her husband is expected to get ahead, she may fail to see the importance of continuing her education. She may feel that when she married, she "arrived." Overlooking the relationship between education and satisfaction in living, she may feel that it is pointless to continue to work for a degree when she is already where she wants to be. Her motivation gradually slips away, and she drops out.

Dropping out is sometimes followed by projection of blame in later life. For example, suppose a woman drops out in order to get a job so that her husband may graduate. In later life, when she has forgotten how eager she was to leave school but now feels different from the wives of her husband's professional associates because she has no degree, she may project the blame onto him. Or suppose a male student drops out because his wife becomes pregnant and must give up her job, and there is no way for the family to be supported except through his efforts. He gets a blind-alley job whose only advantage is that it pays well immediately. As the years go on, the men who would have been his professional associates move ahead in the field in which he would prefer to be working. He begins to feel like a "might-have-been." It would not be difficult for him unintentionally to project blame for his failure onto the wife and child. The accusation "if it hadn't been for you" can be devastating for a person to live with.

There is an increasing awareness of such problems among both men and women. Increasing numbers of men are willing to make short-term sacrifices in their education or careers for the sake of their wife's advancement. And many couples who marry while in school make an agreement right from the beginning that neither should be expected to give up his or her educational advancement at any cost. Such a decision can be carried out if there is parental or some other means of support. In other cases, it may be difficult to live up to it. Nevertheless, this kind of thinking reflects an increasing concern for the careers and education of women.

Let us examine some considerations in connection with college marriages.

Status

An individual's or a couple's place in the college scheme is an important consideration so far as marriage is concerned. Contrast these two cases with respect to the advisability of marrying. One case involves two seniors who plan to marry in March and who graduate in June. The other case involves a seventeen-year-old first-year woman and an eighteen-year-old sophomore man who plans to go through medical school. They met in September and plan to marry during the Christmas vacation. Both of these would be considered college marriages.

Grades

When the increase in college marriages began, grade studies made in certain schools suggested that, as a group, married students earned higher grades than unmarried students (Riemer, 1947; Busselen, Jr. and Busselen, 1975). In evaluating such studies one might well wonder whether sufficient weight was given to two factors, namely, the ages of the students studied and the fact that grade studies must of necessity be made on students who are in school rather than on ex-students, who for one reason or another dropped out of school, or on persons who might have become students had there been nothing in their situations to prevent them from doing so. There are cases in which marriage has provided a student or a couple with a sense of security, motivation toward study, and time free from pressures of dating; thus it has contributed to the improvement of grades (Schroder, 1963). On the other hand, there are students whose grades suffer because of marriage. The research data are not conclusive (Samenfink and Milliken, 1961). Certainly no one would seriously suggest marriage as a way to raise one's grades.

Spouse's Mobility

In some occupational fields a beginner, even with a professional degree, is expected to be able to move about from one location to another. It is a method used by large companies to find the proper niche for promising young men and women and to train them in the intricacies of the organization. In some instances an unmarried person may be moved about more readily than a married person, and the former is more amenable to such mobility. A married individual may give more weight to income, housing, schools, and similar items than to the opportunity presented when moving is suggested. In some cases wives particularly object to moving, for example because they want to remain near parents, because they just get one apartment arranged to their liking when they are called upon to leave it and start over on another, or because they do not like the prospect of living in the community in which the spouse's new job would be located. Hence, an individual contemplating a college marriage might well give serious consideration to the question of whether he or she would help or hinder a spouse in the crucial early days of a career.

Attitude of Parents

Parental approval and good will are assets to be preserved, if possible, in any marriage. College marriage is no exception. In many cases parents disapprove of a marriage when one or both of the couple are students, whereas these same parents would be more likely to approve if the young couple were not students. No matter how this may be explained—as cultural lag, failure to understand present-day trends, conservatism, fear of dropping out, insight, concern, love—it is part of the reality of the situation within which college marriage occurs. This is not meant to imply that, no matter how old or how mature the young couple may be, the judgment of their parents must be the final determining factor in whether or not they marry. It is meant to imply that parental judgment is not to be lightly disregarded as if it had no bearing on the marriage.

Finances

In a college marriage there is not only the problem of sufficient income per se but a correlative, and sometimes more sensitive, problem of who depends upon whom for what and for how long. In any discussion of the financial problems of marriage while in college, the question of parental subsidy is certain to be raised. Should or should not parents contribute to the support of married students? Should they be expected to do so?

Parents who willingly subsidize a son or daughter as a single student may refuse to continue such subsidy after the student marries. Others equally willingly continue subsidy after the wedding. Some increase it. In a few cases the two sets of parents and the student couple work out a cooperative plan.

In those cases in which parents refuse to contribute to a child's support after the latter marries, one wonders whether there is merely bias expressed or a principle involved. They draw the line of support very sharply at the wedding—"When you marry, don't expect any more help from us."

Parental subsidy does not necessarily mean a regular allowance. It may take the form of special gifts, aid in time of financial stress, such as at the birth of a child, or payment of special costs, such as insurance premiums. It must also be noted that in any case of parental subsidy, no matter what form it takes, the gain is not worth the cost if the subsidy is given grudgingly, is accompanied by parental interference in the young marriage, if the subsidy is so generous and can be anticipated for so long in the future that the young couple grow to depend upon it and therefore lose their ambition, or if the young couple cannot accept the subsidy without a feeling of resentment or inadequacy yet the parents insist upon continuing it.

Whether parental subsidy of college marriage is desirable or undesirable is still an open question. No universal generalization can answer the question. In some cases it has worked out well; in others, poorly. In many cases it has not been tried. Whether it is good or bad, whether it should be more common or less common, the fact remains that at present not all parents favor it. The young persons contemplating marriage while in college must face the reality of the present as well as the hopes of the future. Unless they are sure of their parents' willingness and ability to subsidize a contemplated marriage, they would be buying a grab bag if they married and depended upon the continuation of allowances for support.

Reversal of Role

In many college marriages the wife is the primary, sometimes the only, breadwinner. In some cases the husband resents this reversal of role and is uneasy under it. He may feel guilty. He could accept support from his wife if he were incapacitated, for such support would be socially approved. But he is able-bodied; and commitment to getting a degree does not carry the traditional weight carried by physical need. Under the circumstances it might appear logical for him to give a good deal of time to housework, but this he is not necessarily able or willing to do. His wife resents this because she has to carry a double load. There are also cases in which conflict arises because of the wife's resentment of the fact that the husband is not earning enough. Being less appreciative than he of the importance of his degree, she would like him to leave school and get a job so that she may stop working. This he will not do. In short, role reversal may be a problem for either or both spouses (see Hepker and Cloyd, 1974).

Wife's Responsibilities

Many a student wife carries an unusually heavy load of responsibility. She may be a student herself, have employment, do housekeeping, and take care of one or more children. Even when she herself is not a student, her load may be heavy. In some cases this one-sidedness stems from lack of cooperation on the part of the husband, but in others it is not entirely his fault. If he is a poor or average student and has to struggle to maintain his grades but is determined to get a degree, he may literally not be able to help his wife as much as either of them would like. It is difficult for some wives to understand this and to accept a heavy load of responsibilities, with so little in the way of material goods and comforts to show for it. In some cases the total load is more than one person can carry successfully. If, in such a case, the husband criticizes the wife for neglecting part of the load, say certain aspects of housework, her resentment may be bitter indeed.

Academic Pressures

There are pressures involved in breadwinning, but they have been recognized and accepted since time immemorial. Family life is adapted to them. For example, the meal schedule, recreation plans, vacation trips, place of residence, and similar things are determined in part by the requirements of a man's and/or a woman's job. The pressures imposed by academic work, when compared with those above, are both atypical and irregular. They are not universally understood and accepted. As a result, there are husbands or wives, who are themselves not students, who are irritated by and resent the spouse's attention to study. If the couple have no children and one spouse is gainfully employed, he or she may want to leave the home for social contacts and recreation in the evening, which is the only time the other spouse has for study. When final examinations, bar examinations, and similar pressures enter the picture, the working spouse may fail to understand the other's increased preoccupation, tension, irritability, and fatigue, and interpret this behavior as an indication of lack of interest in him or her.

There are women who have as great determination to complete their education as their husbands have. Yet some husbands fail to understand this. If the husband also depreciates the importance of a woman's education, thinking of it as something casual which she can readily give up without regret, the stage is set for his misunderstanding the effect of academic pressures upon her.

In cases where the husband is a student and is employed, and the wife is also a student and perhaps also employed, their schedules involving times of arising and retiring, time of greatest busyness and preoccupation, and leisure time may coincide so infrequently that they seldom talk together at length without a feeling of pressure or without distraction. Communication suffers. Sometimes even their sexual adjustment is affected.

Making College Marriage Successful

Assuming maturity, an adequate period of acquaintance, a wise choice of marriage partner, and similar items that play a part in the success of any type of marriage, the first step in making marriage in college successful is to recognize it for what it is. This implies that the couple understand that there is a discrepancy between the stereotype of young marriage and college marriage. There is a difference between common expectations and actual reality.

The next step is to accept the fact that marriage as students involves special "pressure points" and to plan and act accordingly. This may be more easily said than done in some cases, but it is possible to achieve. One of the most helpful factors is an understanding of the relative temporariness of many of the special problems involved. In appraising their marriage and each other, the couple may differentiate between the permanent and the temporary in their situation and by the same token decide which aspects of their marriage call for permanent decisions and which for tentative ones. If they can hold on until education is completed, then they may emerge into a type of marriage in which roles are more to their liking, their expectations are more nearly within reach, and their temporarily thwarted hopes may more readily be realized.

A good plan is one which (1) is realistic and includes a critical appraisal of the couple's assets and liabilities; (2) takes into account the total job to be done and includes a mutually agreeable means for doing the job; (3) is flexible enough to be adapted to changing circumstances but sufficiently rigid and strongly enough motivated to withstand the ups and downs of day-to-day trials and errors; (4) is not so critically vulnerable at one point that the success of the entire plan rests upon the achievement of one part of it; (5) gives the couple some assurance of getting what they want; (6) at least to a reasonable degree eliminates conflict among their objectives so that these objectives are not set in opposition to each other in a way which permits one to be jeopardized by another.

TERMS TO BE LEARNED

alien
annulment
antenuptial contract
circumstantial
consanguineous
consensus
dissoluble (dissolubility)
dowry
elopement
exploitive

honeymoon
identity (premarital, marital)
jurisdiction
mobility
null (and void)
officiant
ordinance
proxy
reciprocity
residency

role reversal
socioemotional
survival
"two-stage launching"
VDRL
void
voidable
waiting period
wed

SELECTED READINGS

ARISIAN, KHOREN: *The New Wedding: Creating Your Own Marriage Ceremony*, Vintage Books, New York, 1973. (Paperback.) Presents a number of wedding ceremonies written by the author and in some cases supplemented by the couple. Author feels that traditional wedding ceremonies do not meet the needs of many modern couples.

CENTER FOR A WOMAN'S OWN NAME: *Booklet for Women Who Wish to Determine Their Own Names after Marriage*, Barrington, Ill., 1974. Provides information for women who want to retain their own names after marriage. Includes explanations of common law, court procedures, recent court decisions, and legal opinions.

DONNELLY, C.: "Wedding Bills, and How to Peel Them," *Money*, vol. 4, pp. 46–54, May 1975. Helpful tips on how to cut the cost of assorted wedding "necessities"—food, flowers, invitations, photographs.

GOLDEN, BORIS A.: "Honeymoon Sexual Problems," *Medical Aspects of Human Sexuality*, vol. 5, no. 5, pp. 139–152, May 1971. The Niagara Falls area attracts some 35,000 honeymoon couples annually. Dr. Golden has practiced in this area for twenty-three years. He interviewed twenty-one other physicians in preparing this report on honeymoon sexual problems.

KIRSCHENBAUM, HOWARD, AND ROCKWELL STENSRUD: *The Wedding Book: Alternative Ways to Celebrate Marriage*, The Seabury Press, New York, 1974. (Paperback.) Describes alternative weddings that are "personal and creative. . . . Gives practical guidelines for planning any phase of a wedding." Includes a discussion of wedding customs and rituals.

LEACH, WILLIAM H. (ed.): *The Cokesbury Marriage Manual*, rev. ed., Abingdon Press, Nashville, Tenn., 1961. Descriptions of several Protestant wedding ceremonies with comments about marriage.

MACE, DAVID R.: *Getting Ready for Marriage*, Abingdon Press, Nashville, Tenn., 1972. Author is optimistic about marriage. Discusses what each person brings to marriage, goals and plans, "how to live with sex," and how to locate a marriage counselor. Author is one of the pioneers and an outstanding world leader in the development of marriage counseling.

The Mass on the Day of the Marriage according to the text in the *Collectio Rituum* 1964 by the National Catholic Welfare Conference, revised in accordance with the directive of May 4, 1967, Sacred Congregation of Rites, Leaflet Missal Company, St. Paul, Minn., 1968. A Roman Catholic wedding ceremony.

NEWMAN, C.: *Your Wedding, Your Way: A Guide to Contemporary Wedding Options*, Doubleday and Company, Inc., Garden City, N.Y., 1975. A practical guide for planning and implementing a wedding.

ROUTTENBERG, LILLY S., AND RUTH R. SELDIN: *The Jewish Wedding Book*, Schocken Books, Inc., New York, 1968. Description and discussion of a Jewish wedding ceremony.

SELIGSON, MARCIA: *The Eternal Bliss Machine*, William Morrow & Company, Inc., New York, 1973. (Paperback.) An examination of American weddings from "new weddings" taking place outdoors, weddings for which the couple write their own ceremony, homosexual weddings, traditional ceremonies, ceremonies on skates and under water, to extravaganzas costing tens of thousands of dollars. Includes discussion of "honeymoon havens."

Chapter 9

Marriage and the Social Climate

In earlier times in this country the family exhibited more prominently than it does today what are termed its *institutional aspects.* Such elements as the support of the family by the husband-father, the maintenance of the home and the bearing and care of children by the wife-mother, mutual protection, and the production of goods were considered important criteria for evaluating the success or failure of marriage and family life. The man was accepted as the head of the family. He had considerable authority over both his wife and their children. This authority was supported by the mores and to some extent by the law. There was a clear-cut division of labor by gender both in the home and in the occupational world outside the home. One could accurately speak of "men's work" and "women's work."

There were couples who developed deep conjugal love

and devotion. But love, especially love with a romantic coloring, was not considered the *sine qua non* which it appears to be today (Gordon and Bernstein, 1970). The sexual aspect of marriage was tolerated by women as essential to childbearing and as unavoidable in fulfilling the function of wife. We may safely assume that fewer women than at present either achieved or were aware of the possibility of achieving satisfaction in their sexual relations. We may be sure that fewer women expressed such interest and awareness and that still fewer demanded such satisfaction as an essential criterion for the evaluation of marriage.

In their activites leading up to the wedding, young people had, of course, to get acquainted. But their contacts were restricted both by the mores and folkways and by the common practice and probably universal acceptance of chaperonage. There were restrictions not only on the topics a young couple might discuss but also upon the content and extent of their discussion. Undoubtedly young people made some appraisals of each other in terms of personal attractiveness and had romantic inclinations toward each other. There was a place for romantic love, but it was not allowed to overshadow other considerations.

Under such circumstances, the answer to the question "What are the qualities of a good husband or a good wife?" would reflect the emphasis upon the institutional aspects of family life. One might well imagine that many an American woman in the early days set up criteria rather like those expressed by a Boer woman who lived on the African frontier. Said she, "I am sick of all this talk of choosing and choosing.... If a man is healthy and does not drink, and has a good little handful of stock, and a good temper, and is a good Christian, what great difference can it make to a woman which man she takes? There is not so much difference between one man and another" (Leyburn, 1935). Such an attitude makes choice of marriage partner relatively easy because the criteria of choice are readily observable and do not depend largely on personal taste. It therefore permits both more help in making the choice and more control of the choice on the part of the young couple's families.

In those early days many a couple considered their marriage to be successful in the absence of love. Because of this, and also because of the widespread opposition to divorce and the division of labor which made husband and wife economically necessary to each other, the divorce rate remained low. In a sense, in earlier times the marriage was considered more important than the persons in it. The couple were expected by society to perform duties, make sacrifices, and accept circumstances, unless extreme, for the good of the marriage. Now the marriage is considered to be less important than the persons in it (and to be dissolvable when it ceases to meet their personal expectations). Such an appraisal is the outgrowth of individual judgment and voluntary perspective rather than the result of law and custom.

In the past, education, religious worship, recreation, and manufacturing were to a considerable extent carried on in or through the family. Because communities were small and travel to and communication with the outside were both slow and difficult, the pressure of primary group control was great. That is, the same group lived together, worked together, traded with one another, worshiped together, played together, and banded together for mutual aid in time of crisis. Hence each family was an integral unit in a face-to-face society. Therefore, whatever the conditions and relationships within a marriage, the marriage was held together in part by forces exerted from the outside.

CHANGES IN AMERICAN MARRIAGE

Present-day American marriage still entails an ample economic element, and the institutional factors in family living are far from absent. Division of labor by gender, support, protection, mutual aid, childbearing, and child rearing still exist. Manufacturing activities, education of children, recreational pursuits, and religious worship are still carried on in the home or through the family. But the picture is changing. Many of these activities, at least to a considerable degree, increasingly center on nonfamily agencies, as shown in Exhibit 9-1. The increase in urban and suburban living has broken down the primary face-to-face groups, thus removing some of the societal support from marriage, not in the sense of reducing societal approval of marriage but rather in the sense of there being fewer external, societal, and institutional forces acting to keep marriages structurally intact. There is increased emphasis upon how persons of opposite gender feel about one another and what kind of interrelationships they establish. In short, in present-day America there is much less emphasis upon the institutional aspects and much more upon the interpersonal aspects of marriage and family life. This change is manifested in numerous ways. It is important to note, however, that at no known period in history, among no known people, has marriage succeeded on the basis of emotion alone. There is always found some degree of cooperation, through division of labor, in the maintenance of a way of life. American marriage is no exception.

In the activities and events preceding the wedding, young persons have a degree of freedom not so great as that found in some cultures but conspicuously greater than that which existed in this country in earlier days. Some degree of physical contact between individuals is widely and casually accepted. Discussion is almost, but not quite, unrestrained. Young persons of college and even high school age discuss topics such as sex and reproduction more freely and with less embarrassment with dating partners than married couples of yesteryear discussed such topics with each other after the birth of their first baby.

In marriage and in mate selection, that element given greatest prominence is love. "Marrying for love" implies a primary emphasis upon emotion, upon how two individuals feel about one another, and upon personal satisfaction, and a corresponding reduction in emphasis upon the institutional aspects of marriage. Hence, new criteria of success in marriage are established. New qualities desirable in a husband or wife are highlighted. New opportunities are presented for richness of living and completeness of sharing in marriage. But along with those opportunities go new problems, for when people do not find in marriage the personal satisfaction that they anticipated, they feel justified in seeking escape. Other social changes have made such escape easier than it used to be. One of the side effects of "marrying for love" is an increase in marital instability and hence in divorce. This is not meant to imply that more marriages are unhappy today than in earlier times, for there is no known way of making such a comparison. "Unhappy" and "unstable" are not synonymous, and happiness is relative to expectation.

When marriage is based upon love and when personal satisfaction is given more weight than institutional factors, the responsibility for wise choice of marriage partner rests upon the shoulders of the individuals making the choice. Today they can and do get little help from their families. Often the help that is volunteered is rejected. In a way this makes choice of marriage partners more difficult than it used to be because the elements upon which it is based are less readily observ-

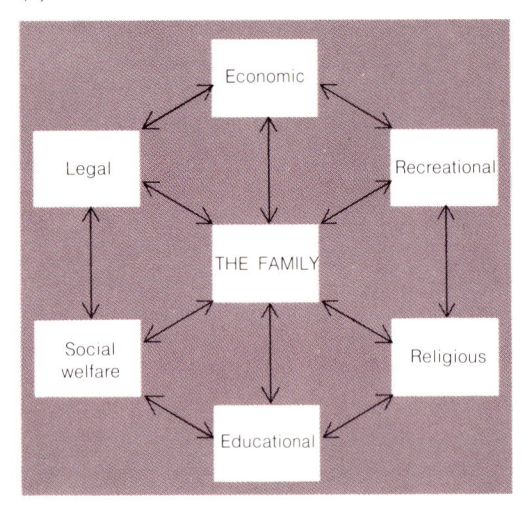

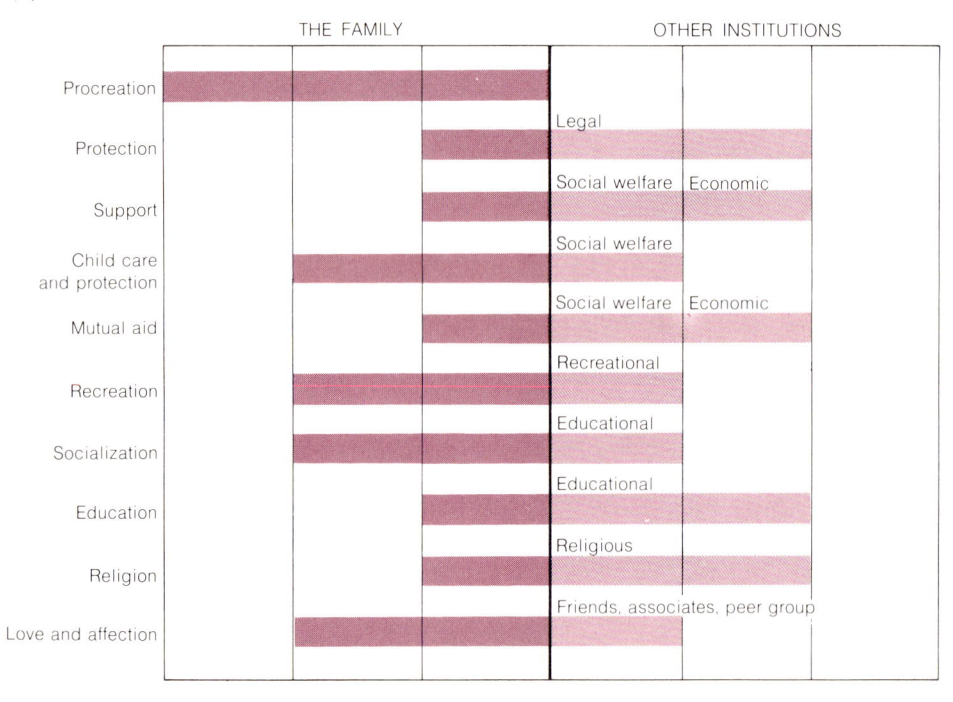

Exhibit 9-1 The interrelatedness of social institutions: (a) the family as an integral part of the social structure; (b) the way in which nonfamily agencies have taken over family functions (the proportions indicated are not intended to be exact). One problem of the present-day American family is to develop personality functions to replace those lost to institutions.

able, depend upon personal taste rather than a cultural standard, rest upon an appraisal of another personality largely extracted from that individual's background, and are so variable that each individual who makes such a choice assumes it to be unique. One can hardly imagine a young American college student of today saying anything even remotely approximating the statement of the Boer woman quoted earlier.

As contrasted with marriage of the past, present-day American marriage presents both men and women with a changed and expanded concept of the roles expected of husband and wife. Put another way, each gender is expected to play a greater multiplicity of roles, to do a wider variety of things.

The Role of the Husband

American society gives evidence of moving toward an equalitarian type of family life (Goode, 1963). But not all groups and subgroups are moving toward this end at the same rate. There are differences among the various segments of society; and within groups families are not necessarily uniform. The result is that, while many men are assuming the new husband-father role as described below, there are other men whose roles are more nearly traditional and whose wives, with themselves, accept a patriarchal (husband dominant) type of family life. Hence, the generalizations below are not universally applicable. They do, however, represent a trend.

The male is still expected to be the primary provider for the family. In some states his wife may sue for divorce on the ground of nonsupport should he fail to do so. However, he is not necessarily the only provider. There is an increasing number of families in which that role is shared by both spouses and a small but slowly growing number in which the wife is the provider.

In his role as father, the present-day male is more than a biological parent, a provider, and a disciplinarian. Many a man shares the lives of his children, understands them and openly shows affection for them, plays a part in their rearing, and participates in infant care. He may attend classes for prospective fathers, read books on child psychology, participate in the PTA, and force his growing bulk, softening muscles, and queasy stomach through the "survival test" of a Boy Scout or Girl Scout hike and cookout in order to be a pal to his son or daughter. He not only does not expect his children to be "seen but not heard" but is more likely to resign himself to being the one who is neither seen nor heard when his children reach adolescence and begin to date. He is often unashamed to be seen carrying a baby or hanging out a baby's laundry which he himself has done. If his children attend college, he may willingly continue their financial support beyond the point at which they have become emotionally and socially independent of him and resistant to whatever remnant of paternal authority he has sought to retain. In some cases such financial support continues after the wedding. In earlier times financial independence and personal independence were more likely to occur simultaneously, thus drawing a sharper line of demarcation representing the termination of parental control. Nowadays that line of demarcation is often ragged, and the parent-child relationship is equivocal, making for problems with which neither side is well prepared to cope.

There is a growing feeling that the home is no longer only a place of comfort and refuge for the male; it is becoming an area of participation. This means that there is not only sharing of family life on the part of the husband-father but also more participation in the tasks of housekeeping. Clear-cut division

For the modern male the home has become an area of participation as well as a refuge. (Ken Heyman)

of labor by gender within the home is breaking down. We can no longer speak of "men's work" and "women's work" with the simple accuracy of earlier days. The shift is far from complete, of course. There are still many males who resist housekeeping and participate reluctantly, if at all, or participate only in emergencies. Their resistance is often most apparent when the task in question is symbolic, and doing it regularly might seem to indicate acquiescence in a change in masculine status or authority. For example, preparing breakfast is for many a man such a symbolic task. In earlier times when a man did predawn chores on the farm, he could well expect his wife to have a substantial breakfast ready for him when he returned to the house. Nowadays breakfast tends to precede work rather than follow a part of it, and is often light, requiring little or no preparation. Yet, not because of inability to do it or because of time or energy limitations but rather because a carry-over of attitude has made breakfast symbolic, many a man insists that it be prepared by his wife. In his estimation, "getting up to fix my breakfast" is an indication of wifely commitment and effectiveness. There are some women who do not want their husbands to take part in housekeeping. On the other hand, however, there is an increasing number of husbands who willingly do household tasks.

Exactly how much housekeeping a particular man or woman will do is determined by a number of factors: the time available to each spouse; how much of the total housekeeping job must be done after regular work hours; how the job may best be done, given the skills and interests of the husband and wife; the attitude of each person toward his or her own role and toward the other person and that person's role; what kind of marriage the couple expect to achieve; and how much they appreciate leisure time together. Too broad generalizations as to what responsibility a modern husband should assume are likely to be less than helpful. What is needed is not generalization but rather particularization. The question is, "What is the best arrangement for this couple with their personalities and abilities and their specific situation?" A problem arises when an attempt is made to impose in advance a traditional pattern of family living without taking into account emerging and shifting variables.

In the last analysis, the final appraisal of a man's success or failure as a husband is made primarily by one person, his wife. This appraisal essentially rests on what kind of person he is and what her feelings about him are. It is at its core a personal appraisal, one which largely strips the husband of cultural props and the protective coloration of overt conformity to cultural norms and relative success in meeting the criteria which reflect the institutional aspects of marriage. A man may be admirable in the eyes of his friends or even of his wife, have prestige in his occupation, supply his family with all that is necessary to maintain a more than adequate standard of living, be moral and law-abiding, be a good father; yet if his wife no longer loves him and they do not get along happily together, the assumption is made that he has failed as a husband. The converse may also be true.

This suggests that the expected role of husband or wife is defined only in part by society at large. It is also defined in part by the tastes, attitudes, hopes, expectations, assumptions, and biases of one other person, the marriage partner.

The Role of the Wife

A woman's choice of role is complicated today by the fact that she is caught between the pressures of several forces. On the one hand, there is the weight of tradition pushing her in the direction of homemaking and motherhood. On the other hand is the open door of opportunity in the world of gainful employment. Her choice is complicated by the fact that the four elements—marriage, homemaking, childbearing and child rearing, and employment—may be considered separable, so that with one exception a woman may have any element or combination of elements with social approval. She may marry without becoming a homemaker. Control of conception makes it possible for her to marry but have no children, whether or not she becomes a homemaker. She may have a home of her own without marrying. Employment may be combined with the other three elements in a variety of ways. The only element she cannot have with complete social approval is motherhood without marriage, although a few unmarried women adopt children, and, in spite of a public opinion still largely unfavorable to nonmarital childbearing, some women keep the babies they bear out of wedlock.

As a result of this separability of the four elements mentioned, women face a greater number of alternatives than formerly, and their choice is therefore more complex. In one respect, however, it is easier because the choice is made among more alternatives, with the result that there is less compulsion exerted by any one of them; in earlier times there was more inclination to squeeze all women into the same mold. In those earlier days, though there were the same four elements involved, three of them—marriage, homemaking, and childbearing—were combined and accepted as a constellation, much as a man accepts the combination of marriage and breadwinning today, so that actually a woman's choice was limited to two alternatives. Most women chose to marry, and social expectations supported their single-mindedness. Relatively few married women were gainfully employed.

It may be that the other side of this coin is coming into view. As equal economic opportunity becomes more widespread and more and more women enter the professions, rise to upper executive levels in business, hold political office, or become independent entrepreneurs, some will have more prestigious, more remunerative, and more influential occupations than their husbands. Of course, some, but not a great many, women already fall into this category. But it would be safe to guess that such situations will multiply. If so, there will be increasing need for husbands to be prepared to accept a seemingly inferior economic status without too great threat to their egos. In some cases, the couple may find that full-time employment by the wife and full-time homemaking and child care by the husband constitute for them the most workable plan. But many, perhaps most, present-day men are not prepared by experience, culture, or ideology to accept such a role as women have had (often reluctantly, to be sure) in the past. In a way, men will be called upon to accept a status that some women have sought to escape and one that is sharply criticized by feminists.

Whereas in earlier times the wife was expected to be able to produce many of the goods used by the family, her role has now shifted from that of producer to that of consumer. She is expected nowadays to be skilled in the art of purchasing. By economical and careful expenditure she "stretches" the purchasing power of income. The shift in role is not complete, however. Many wives make clothing or raise and preserve garden produce, and the traditional attitude toward "good home cooking" still prevails in our cultural climate.

In other ways, too, the wife's role is somewhat mixed. She has more independence, is given less direction and supervision, and has more freedom of choice than formerly. At the same time, through both law and public opinion, she is accorded more protection and in some circumstances may make demands upon her husband which a man very seldom makes upon a wife, such as suing him for divorce on the ground of nonsupport, making him responsible for her debts, or having the right to be awarded alimony.

In the last analysis the wife's role, too, as we said was true of the husband's, is in part at least a matter of his definition of her role and his appraisal of the degree of success or failure she exhibits in fulfilling it. She, too, may seem to meet all the cultural criteria and norms of a "good wife." But if her husband is disappointed in her and does not love her and they do not get along happily together, she is assumed to have failed as a wife.

GAINFULLY EMPLOYED MARRIED WOMEN

A phenomenon which simultaneously reflects the wife's changing role and contributes to it, and which is also affecting the role of the husband, is the rapid increase in married women's gainful employment in recent years.

The actual number of married women who are gainfully employed is increasing. Also, the proportion of married women among the employed is increasing. In 1900, 5.5 percent of married women were gainfully employed, and 15 percent of all employed women were married (Breckinridge, 1933). In 1975, 45.0 percent of married women were employed, and 62.2 percent of employed women were married (U.S. Bureau of the Census, *Statistical Abstract*, 1975). The dramatic increase in the number and proportion of women in the labor force cannot be attributed primarily to any one group of women. A common assumption is that the increase can be associated mainly with women who have reentered the labor force following the youngest child's entrance to school. This is not the case, however. The increase in working wives and mothers is characteristic of women of all ages. In the early years of this century very few women with children under 18 were employed. By 1940 the percentage was only 9, but by 1975 the percentage had risen to 34.3 (U.S. Bureau of the Census, *Statistical Abstract*, 1975). In 1975, of women with children under 6 years of age, 36.6 percent were employed, and of women with children 6 to 17 years of age, 52.4 percent were employed (U.S. Bureau of the Census, *Statistical Abstract*, 1975). Regardless, however, of the presence of children, married women are more likely than unmarried women to work part time.

Figures such as those above raise serious questions regarding the common assertions that married women are confined to the home and chained to the dreary, monotonous tasks of housekeeping and child care. Such an attitude appears to be outmoded. Nowadays, if a woman wants to escape from the home, the door of employment is open. If she chooses to remain in the home as a full-time homemaker, she has chosen the disadvantages as well as the advantages of homemaking, just as she would choose the disadvantages as well as the advantages of employment.

There has been an increase in the number and proportion of couples where both spouses are employed. In 1950, 22 percent of all married couples were employed (U.S. Department of Labor, *1969 Handbook on Women Workers*). By 1970, almost 40 percent of all married couples were employed (*Statistical Bulletin*, 1970). The percentage of wives in the labor force when the husband is not employed has always been higher than the percentage of those with employed husbands. In recent years, however, the difference between the percentages has become very slight. Women with employed husbands have been entering and remaining in the labor market more frequently than those with unemployed husbands. "It appears, then, that the trend is for wives to be in the labor force whether or not the husband is employed. Formerly . . . it appeared to make a difference, but at present . . . the husband's employment has little effect on the wife's labor force status" (Ferriss, 1971).

As might be expected, most women begin working or continue to work following marriage and until the birth of a child. There is a

A working wife and mother leaves for the day as her husband stays home with the baby. (Photo Researchers)

dropoff in the number of employed women following the birth of the first child. Many women return to work after a leave of absence. Some return to the labor force after the last child has entered school. Some women prefer to return to the labor force only after their children are adolescents or adults, and some women never return to wage-earning or career pursuits.

Problems Growing out of Married Women's Gainful Employment

Arguments against the gainful employment of married women, as so often propounded in the recent past, sometimes with considerable emotional coloring, are today as outmoded as arguments against women's suffrage. The employment of married women is here to stay. Widespread, though not universal, acceptance does not necessarily result in the elimination of all problems. There are no formulas for the solution of such problems.

Insofar as a given family is concerned, however, it is not a question of whether married women should be employed. It is a question of whether a particular married woman, with her particular skills, personality, opportunities, interests, and tastes, with her particular husband and home situation, should be employed in a particular occupation. The effects of her employment on herself, her husband, her children, and her home will depend upon many factors—such as time, fatigue, type of work, and income—which no one but she and her husband can fully evaluate.

Children of employed mothers Although many women cease gainful employment, at least temporarily, when their children are young, many do not. Often, the wife cannot afford to stop except, perhaps, for a very brief time after the birth of each child. The result is the significant problem of providing daytime care for small children outside the home by persons other than parents. Opinions differ about whether such care is beneficial or harmful, but it is often necessary.

Not all the facts are known, but research indicates that it is not the mother's employment per se that is detrimental to children (Ferriss, 1971). The critical considerations are the type of person that she is, the quality of the relationship that she establishes with her children, the quality of care which the children receive, and whether or not the woman enjoys her work (Hoffman and Nye, 1974). In a study of some 13,000 high school students, it was found that students whose mothers were better educated and employed were aware of no more problems of adjustment than children of similarly educated, nonemployed mothers (Ramsey, Smith, and Moore, 1963). Another consideration is whether the mother's employment affords her children an opportunity for cooperation and learning in the home or prematurely imposes upon them too heavy adult responsibilities. If we condemn wholesale the gainful employment of mothers, as some persons do, we indict unjustly those women whose circumstances give them no alternative to employment. Many widowed or divorced women, and women whose husbands do not earn enough to meet family needs, must be gainfully employed. Yet they do an excellent job of child rearing. The presence of the mother in the home does not guarantee the quality of her relationship with her family. As Iscoe says (Ramsey, Smith, and Moore, 1963), "the mere passage of time with a child does not constitute 'good motherhood.'" If the woman has a strong desire to be employed and feels that her children keep her from it, her relationship with her children may be adversely affected.

Breakdown of division of labor outside the home This has not been the result exclusively of married women's employment

Gender-related stereotypes are changing. There is no longer "men's work" and "women's work"—just work. (United Press International)

but rather of the great influx of women in general into remunerative occupations, many of which had previously been monopolized by men. But married women have contributed abundantly to this influx. There has been infiltration from both sides; in recent years men have entered occupations previously assumed to be restricted to women, and vice versa. Today one is hard put to find an occupation exclusively reserved for one gender.

As the division of labor has broken down, the old concept of "men's work" and "women's work" as distinct entities has begun to disappear. In earlier times, when occupational lines were clearly drawn, males and females did not compete. Nowadays they seek the same jobs and at times accept different rates of pay for those jobs, thus sharpening the edge of competition.

Breakdown of division of labor within the home The traditional clear-cut line of demarcation between "women's work" and "men's work" within the home has not disappeared, but it is gradually growing less clear. This has come about through many factors, one of which is employment of married women. The question, "How much should a husband be expected to participate in housework?" does not arise only because of wives' employment. But such employment sharpens the issue. It constitutes an additional push toward overcoming the inertia of tradition and increasing the momentum of social change.

In the present-day family, especially that in which the wife is employed, there is no accurate way of determining in advance and on the basis of tried and known traditional practice what portion of the total homemaking responsibility each spouse will accept. A problem arises when one spouse assumes that this can be done, while the other expects to have the housekeeping tasks apportioned on a functional or opportunistic basis rather than a traditional one.

The problem is not only one of the amount of work a given spouse does in the home, but also one of attitude. For example, some wives complain that their husbands do not help enough with housekeeping and child care. Other wives, however, are not so much concerned with how much the husband does as they are with the reasons he gives for not doing more. If her husband does little because he rests his case on tradition and therefore resists doing "woman's work," the wife may be angered. Conversely, the husband may face a similar problem of attitude in his wife's success or failure in her role as homemaker as he defines it. From his point of view it may be one thing for her to "let the house go" because of time and energy limitations involved in the twofold task of homemaking and employment. It may be quite another thing for her to neglect housework because of lack of interest or slovenly habits.

Comparative prestige In earlier days a woman's prestige depended upon her doing "woman's work." There was no problem for her in choosing that channel of activity which in her judgment would lead to greatest prestige. Today she may choose, and there has arisen the problem of the prestige accorded homemaking compared with the prestige accorded gainful employment. Many women choose the latter. Many other women accept the former reluctantly. Women often complain that men do not give enough prestige to woman's role as homemaker. That may be true. But many women make the same mistake they attribute to men in that they underrate their own importance as homemakers and accord homemaking too little prestige. Some women have no problem in this connection. They appreciate the importance of their homemaking role, and for prestige which comes from the "outside" they substitute conviction which comes from the "inside."

People who insist that every individual has the right of freedom of choice in determining his or her life-style often assume that freedom of choice means choice of one alternative, in this case, employment. They seem to forget that freedom of choice may also mean choice of the other alternative, namely, homemaking. A woman should have freedom to choose either, without judgment or criticism and with equal prestige, recognition, and appreciation (Lopata, 1971).

It must also be pointed out that the services performed for a family by a homemaker, whether male or female, represent great social and economic value to the family, even if the person is not compensated in dollars and cents. How does one put a price tag on a homemaker's work? One recent study (Gage, 1975) determined that the total value of a wife's household production for her entire economic productive life is approximately $252,000 for a woman with two children. The figure is $285,000 for a woman with four or more children. Allowing for inflation since the time these estimates were made, the figures would be between $300,000 and $400,000 in 1978 dollars.

The Social Security Administration prepared estimates of the yearly economic value of housewives at different ages by assessing the cost of replacing services such as babysitting, cooking, and housework. Exhibit 9-2 presents these figures, increased by an inflation adjustment of 6 percent per year through 1978. The study found that the American homemaker's average economic value in 1972 was $4,705. Allowing for inflation, this would put a value of approximately $6,674 on her services for 1978. Such figures would, of course, vary widely from one family to the next, but they do illustrate the value of a homemaker's services to a family.

Consistency Some women, to be sure, are subject to the economic necessity of employment to support themselves, children, parents, or husbands who are incapacitated or to supplement their husbands' income. Other women whose husbands have adequate income are free to choose or not to choose gainful employment.

If married women's employment is one important factor in both the reflection and the causation of social and family change, there arises the problem of achieving a reasonable degree of consistency in expectations and demands which marital partners set up for one another. For example, can a husband expect his wife to finance his education, bear babies, keep house, be an enthusiastic sexual

Marriage and the Social Climate

Exhibit 9-2 Average Economic Value of Homemakers in 1978 Dollars*

Age Group	Average Economic Value of Woman Keeping House
15–19	$7,644
20–24	8,598
25–29	9,103
30–34	9,101
35–39	8,358
40–44	8,381
45–49	7,408
50–54	7,408
55–59	5,132
60–64	4,173
65–69	3,192
70–74	2,272
75–79	1,546
80–84	899
85–89	509

*Based on 1972 figures increased by an inflation factor of 6 percent per year.

Source: Social Security Administration, 1972.

partner, and be an interested and stimulating companion at the same time? Can the wife expect the husband simultaneously to provide for her, agree to her freedom to have employment outside the home, participate in housekeeping, be a sexual partner, be a companion, be a father to her children, and accept traditional legal protection for her while she demands new rights?

Effect of Working Wives on Marriage Relationships

What changes develop in marriage relationships when wives work outside the home? Although research is far from conclusive, there have been a number of studies giving some insight into this question. Research has shown that a wife's marital power tends to increase when she enters the labor force. Stated differently, she gains more influence in decision making, family finances and other marriage and family matters. Husbands correspondingly give up some of their power or influence. When women work, there is greater equality in decision making (Bahr, 1974). There is also a shift in the division of labor, as mentioned earlier. Men tend to take a greater role in child care and household tasks. Women take a lesser role when the wife works; however, she still tends to take the primary role for child care and household tasks.

The research data also show that the full-time employment of mothers contributes slightly to more conflict, more tensions, and less marital happiness, although these factors are influenced by a number of other forces as well. The most recent studies suggest that this increase in conflict and tension may be disappearing in middle-class marriages but still exists in lower-class marriages (Nye, 1974). With regard to the impact of working mothers on marital happiness, Nye concludes: "The consequences are a little more likely to be positive if the number of children is small, the job she takes is one she enjoys, the husband's attitude is positive, and the husband and wife have advanced education" (Nye, 1974).

If there is an economic necessity for the wife to work, she may ease the family financial burden by working, and this may in turn enhance marital adjustment. If there is no need for the money and the husband or children resent her absence from the home, conflict may be enhanced. When a wife works, leisure time is decreased, and less time is available for housekeeping and other activities. These factors must be weighed against the rewards to the woman and to the family from her employment. It should be noted that just as with parenthood, it may not be the amount of time spent with a spouse that is critical, but the quality of the interaction during the time spent together. Many women report that part-time employment was a solution to a number of problems associated with employment-family conflicts.

Effect of Working Mothers on Children

Many readers may be concerned about the impact of mothers' employment on their children. The research is not entirely clear on this question. Nye and Berardo (1973) state two relevant questions: (1) Does the performance differ between children of employed mothers and those of nonemployed mothers? Specifically, do the children of employed mothers achieve less in school competition, do more of them become juvenile delinquents, and do they have more mental health problems? (2) Do the employed mothers and their children interact less, do the children perform more household tasks, and do children confide less in working mothers?

School performance generally does not differ significantly between the two groups. One study found, however, that this conclusion does not apply in the *lower classes*. Indeed, lower-class children of working mothers did perform less adequately than middle-class children of working mothers (Hoffman and Nye, 1974). Rates of delinquency do not differ significantly, and there appears to be little effect on mental health of children when mothers work. The quality of interaction, the nature and adequacy of child care provided, and the general relationship with the children are undoubtedly more important than the amount of time spent in the presence of the child. Often overlooked is the extent of the father's participation in child care. Children of working mothers tend to participate more in household tasks.

A mother who works may be enhancing the emotional climate of her family if her job provides her with an outlet or "safety valve" for frustration which might otherwise surface in the home (Nye and Berardo, 1973). Mothers who work may provide a more positive concept of the female role for daughters, since the young girl develops a concept of the female role which includes a wider range of possibilities, a more clearly formed self-concept, and a less traditional feminine personality. Such daughters are more "work-oriented" and are more likely to have part-time jobs outside the home (Hoffman and Nye, 1974).

Particularly among college-educated females, employed mothers get more satisfaction out of their work than full-time homemakers. Data indicate that employed mothers who enjoy working use milder discipline. In small families, employed mothers report getting more pleasure from their children than nonemployed mothers, although they also more often report doubts and feelings of inadequacy as parents. In sum, it is probably safe to say that there are negligible effects, if any, on children solely because the mother does or does not work. It is considerably more important to examine other aspects of the marital, family, and parent-child relationships to determine what the effects are likely to be.

THE POSITION OF WOMEN IN MODERN AMERICA

The following appeared in the *Journal of the American Medical Association* on June 22, 1895: "Man has his place in the world, so has woman, and nature has drawn the line. . . . The modern false emancipation of woman . . . is a perversion of nature. . . . [The laws of nature] stand forever as a barrier to the attainment by women of that equality so much desired by the agitation of the present generation" (*JAMA*, 1970). That such a statement appeared in a journal as prestigious as that of the American Medical Association less than a hundred years ago suggests how much progress has been made since that time.

It is not difficult to say that woman's

social position has changed and still is changing. More and more women are gainfully employed both before and during marriage. As we have seen, this affects their relative position by giving them a type of independence that they did not have formerly. Technically, at least, a large proportion of the nation's wealth is "in the wife's name." Men are often still expected to contribute to the support of their wives after the marriage tie is broken by divorce, but in many quarters there is a growing opposition to alimony.

Women have achieved suffrage. They have educational opportunities essentially equal to those of men. As a group they have made intelligent use of those opportunities. Mothers have been somewhat emancipated from their children and are gradually being freed from bearing a greater number than they desire or can care for adequately. In earlier times, when less was known about, and there was not such widespread use of, contraceptives, to an appreciable degree the number of pregnancies a woman had depended upon her husband's interest in sexual intercourse and the exercise of his legal right to such intercourse, regardless of her interest. More recently contraceptives have permitted control of conception regardless of frequency of intercourse. Now, for the first time in history, with the development of oral contraceptives and IUDs a wife can prevent conception even without her husband's knowledge.

With the development of modern warfare women have lost some of the inviolability in war which they formerly had. Men are still the chief participators in warfare, both as fighters and as victims, but women are playing a more extensive role, especially as victims. The number of women in various branches of the military service is increasing, but women are not yet allowed to participate in combat. However, as war becomes more and more mechanized and less dependent upon individual strength, women's participation has been suggested in order to achieve equality (Brown, Emerson, Falk, and Freedman, 1971).

Women's social influence is increasing. As Exhibit 9-3 illustrates, women are making progress in the professions but have not yet achieved professional status equal to men's. They are also making progress in other occupations, but there is still a tendency for them to be given subsidiary jobs with lower salaries. Women still receive more protection than do men, on the one hand, but on the other hand they are more subject to some kinds of discrimination. Such discrimination is designed to be remedied by the Equal Rights Amendment to the United States Constitution, but as of this writing the amendment has not yet been ratified.

For centuries, there has been an inclination for men to treat women as if they were a minority group, a subject class (see Millett, 1970; Hacker, 1951). Jensen (1971) refers to women as the "majority minority." Women have been the victims of groundless generalizations; uncritical stereotypes; implications of inferiority; personal, social, political, and economic discrimination; legal and social restrictions; superstitious fear; occupational stratification; moral inconsistency; exploitation; and lack of understanding and appreciation in much the same way as minority peoples. So long as women "kept their place," men, in their idealistic moments, were willing to "put them on a pedestal" and gloss over their inferior status with a code of chivalry. The present trend is toward thinking of men and women as integral parts of the same group on a more nearly equal footing. Men's attitude toward women and treatment of them are changing. Today women are thought of as individuals more than they were formerly. There are still men who treat their wives as if those wives were minors under the guardianship of the husband, but the trend is toward equalitarian marriage.

Exhibit 9-3 Changes in the proportion of women in selected professions. (*Source: Monthly Labor Review*, U.S. Department of Labor, Bureau of Labor Statistics, 1974.)

[1] Similar trend lines, omitted because of space limitations, are indicated for social workers and clerics; photographers; designers and illustrators; pharmacists; and dentists.

[2] Similar trend lines, omitted because of space limitations, are indicated for musicians and music teachers; teachers, not elsewhere classified; actors, dancers, and entertainers; and accountants and auditors.

Perhaps the most important change that has occurred—the one that in a way epitomizes the others—is increased freedom of choice. Women have more freedom of choice than ever before—in educational, social and occupational matters; in choosing a husband; in getting married; in escaping an unhappy marriage; in bearing children. They are coming to play a larger part in determining their own destinies. But there is still a long way to go before there is complete equality, and that is the underlying reason for the women's liberation movement.

The Women's Liberation Movement

Early stirrings of the demand for women's rights and equality between men and women began to appear in print about two hundred years ago. Momentum was gained during the nineteenth century as women became involved in the antislavery issue, and later in the first part of the twentieth century as they campaigned for suffrage. Then the movement slowed somewhat. In recent years it has been revitalized by what some women's liberationists refer to as the "second wave."

Now, however, though neither the significance nor the impact of the women's liberation movement has been diminished, some of the early vehemence is receding. Extremists on both sides (both for and against liberation) are less vociferous. Stereotyping is fading somewhat, and demands are being put into perspective. But by no means have all problems been solved nor have all objectives been reached.

The women's liberation movement, like other social movements, involves a variety of women (and some men). Most participants have the same overall objective: freedom and equality for women through the elimination of the "double standard" in the broadest sense of the term. But within this general context stated objectives vary. The most commonly stated objectives of the women's movement are complete freedom of self-determination and equality of the genders, including sexual freedom equivalent to that of men. Equal pay for equal work is another, as is equal occupational opportunity. Some feminists advocate the release of women from excessive pressures of homemaking, childbearing, and child rearing, with provision for day care for children when needed. Ready availability of both birth control information and contraceptives is widely sought. The elimination of male dominance and men's traditional power over women is also an objective. Men's holding women in low esteem, sometimes in contempt (referred to as *male chauvinism*), and discriminating against them are particularly galling to most women, and the eradication of contempt and discrimination is demanded.

It is not difficult for concerned persons of either gender to subscribe to objectives such as these. But there are other objectives on which there is far from universal agreement.

Many feminists, as well as other women and men, for example, have promoted legalized abortion as an adjunct to contraception and to establish the right of women to make unhampered judgments relative to their own bodies and the continuation or interruption of a pregnancy. Abortion is a major issue in present-day America. There is far from universal agreement on it, and the issue has yet to be solved to everyone's satisfaction.

Like any social movement, the women's movement has its supporters and its detractors. Many black women, for example, while in sympathy with the basic goals of the women's movement, have chosen not to become active advocates. Many feel they were liberated long ago, and many consider racism a more relevant social concern. Undoubtedly the women's movement is making an impact on American culture, law, the status of women, and the relationships between men and women.

There are a number of things that the individual modern woman must do if she is to adjust to new and evolving life circumstances. She must in most instances prepare for gainful employment. In earlier days she passed directly from her parental home to that of her husband. What she learned about homemaking she learned chiefly from her mother. Now she usually prepares for at least temporary employment before marriage. In increasing numbers she is continuing to work after the wedding. If she does not marry, she has greater occupational freedom of choice than women have ever had before. If her husband dies, she usually must earn her own living.

If she marries, she must prepare for a new type of marriage relationship involving new attitudes of husband and wife toward each other with new expectations and new demands—but a relationship in which roles are no longer so clearly defined as formerly. Lack of clear-cut cultural definitions makes necessary greater insight, a higher degree of adaptability, and more carefully focused motivation if she is to contribute to the success of her marriage.

THE POSITION OF MEN IN MODERN AMERICA

In recent years so much attention has been given to the question of the status of women that almost none has been given to that of the status of men. There are even some persons who assume that there can be no problem concerning men's position. Actually men, like women, can have a problem of definition of status, of determination of position, when and as social changes occur that upset traditional roles and expectations and make new definitions necessary. Helen Mayer Hacker (1957) writes of the "new burdens of masculinity." Bednarik (1970) discusses "the male in crisis."

One of the problems men face today is that there seems to be a widely accepted, clear-cut conception of what it means to be a "real he-man" in terms of the highly individualistic, frontier, sexually bisected society of the past, but there has not as yet been formulated a universally accepted concept of what it means to be a "real he-man" in the competitive, industrialized, urbanized, sexually blended society of the present. The individual man is expected to meet simultaneously both the traditional and the contemporary criteria of masculinity. How can a man satisfy his needs in this country today if there is lack of agreement on what a man is supposed to be, and if he is expected to be at the same time more than one kind of person? For example, a man is expected to be simultaneously "red-blooded and two-fisted" on the one hand, gentlemanly and peace-seeking on the other. He is under one type of pressure to "get ahead," under another type of pressure to avoid giving too much weight to material success. He is supposed to feel sorrow and sympathy but not give way to crying. He is expected to cooperate with women as equals at the same time that tradition tells him that at times, especially in times of crisis, he must "take charge" and under no circumstances ever let a woman dominate him or "get the best" of him. And so it goes.

There cannot be such penetrating changes as those which have swept over the female world without correlative changes in the male world. The point is that the worlds of both men and women are in transition. There is no immediate prospect of a crystallization of these worlds into a *status quo*. There is no way of knowing what the ultimate outcome will be. In the meantime there will remain an active issue concerning the position of men.

The Men's Liberation Movement

Recently there has begun to emerge a men's liberation movement. It is not, as yet, a full-fledged movement—there are only initial stirrings. Perhaps it is more like a demand for a movement rather than a movement itself. At any rate, many men, as well as women, have seen the need for, and suggested the possibility of, liberating the male. Some men's liberation groups have already been formed. There have been national conferences, and several books on the topic have appeared in bookstores.

From what does the male need to be liberated? Primarily from a cultural pattern that restrains the male emotionally, sentimentally, and socially as effectively as a straitjacket restrains arm movements. As mentioned earlier, the male is put under cultural pressure to suppress certain emotions, to be a "real man," to live up to a traditional standard of manliness, to succeed in whatever he undertakes or is expected to undertake, to consider women inferior to men, to fear and resist competition with and domination by females. Until such shackles are broken, the male cannot be free to express and utilize his fullest potentialities. He is as much a puppet dancing on cultural strings manipulated by unseen hands as women have been. But while both men and women are reacting against the cultural pattern, men do not seem to focus on women as the cause of their plight to the extent that women focus their cause on men. Part of the explanation for this, of course, is the fact that women have historical reasons for assuming that men are the cause of their problems in a way that men do not have relative to women.

Some persons say that instead of discussing women's liberation or men's liberation, we should think in terms of human liberation. There is much to be said for such a point of view. It emphasizes the fact that there are problems and needs on both sides and coincides with the present-day emphasis on human beings as persons rather than as males or females.

No doubt there are women who find the idea of men's liberation ludicrous, annoying, sexist, or chauvinistic—just as there are men who criticize and depreciate women's liberation and laugh at or are threatened by women's liberationists. But the stirrings of a men's liberation movement are already audible. Where these stirrings will lead remains to be seen.

Men need to adjust to the unalterable fact that a new type of competition has arisen in a way previously unknown. They cannot afford to let the attitudes of their early male ancestors so color their thinking and so determine their course of action that they find themselves either in the position of a man standing on the shore trying to stop the tide by shouting at it, or in the position of a player who seeks to win a game by haranguing his opponent or refusing to let him play.

Men need to introduce consistency into their treatment of women. A man who strikes a woman violates a code of chivalry and is branded a coward and a cad. But a man who uses a woman for selfish purposes, who exploits her sexually, is assumed to be merely "sowing his wild oats."

Men need also to change their attitude toward homemaking and to improve their preparation for participation in it. The day is past in which homemaking was solely a wife's responsibility, with the husband in the role of permanent guest who assumed he was head of the family because he supported it financially. As we have seen, the trend today is for the family to have no head or two heads, and homemaking is becoming a joint responsibility of husband and wife. This does not mean necessarily that they divide equally between them all aspects of housekeeping, family feeding, purchasing, and child rearing. It does mean that a man has a new role to play in the home and that he can no longer assume that domestic illiteracy is the only preparation he needs for it. It means also that a man should recognize that homemaking represents a total job to be done. How the various aspects of it are apportioned between husband and wife may change as time goes on or even from day to day. But a problem arises when a man assumes that this apportionment can be arbitrarily determined in advance and permanently fixed solely on the basis of tradition.

OTHER FACTORS IN THE SOCIAL SITUATION

Legislation

We speak of American marriage as if it were something uniform throughout the country. Actually it is not exactly the same under any two jurisdictions. The variation in state laws not only reflects a lack of standards but contributes to confusion and to the inclination to seek the most convenient legislation. If a couple want to marry and cannot conveniently do so in their own state because restrictions are irksome, they may go to another where the law is more lenient. In some states, for example, a couple must wait five days after applying for a license before the wedding may be performed; in others, three days; in others, not at all. In one county in Wisconsin it was found that in a nine-year period 235 couples applied for marriage licenses and did not return to claim them. "Those deflected from marriage by legal requirements seem to be poor risks for satisfactory marriage" (Shipman and Tien, 1965). Such laws are often influenced by financial considerations. In 1961, for example, Iowa raised the minimum age for marriage and instituted a three-day waiting period. As a result many Minnesotans who formerly might have been married in Iowa were married in North Dakota, which had no waiting period. In 1962 marriages taking place in Iowa dropped almost one-fourth below the number for 1960 (*Statistical Bulletin*, 1963). A similar situation exists relative to seeking lenient divorce legislation.

In many states there is little check on the couple at the time they apply for a license. They may swear to false ages. In one study of applicants for marriage licenses, it was found that in the case of 22.3 percent of the persons involved there was some discrepancy between age stated on the application and age shown in the birth record (Christensen, Andrews, and Freiser, 1953). The couple may give false addresses. Unless one of them later complains, there is no attempt to ascertain the truth.

Marriage laws are an illustration of cultural lag. Modern social conditions are so different from those under which our marriage laws developed that new legislation is needed. But law tends to lag behind the need for change. Many marriage laws are not adapted to the present-day social scene, although progress is occurring.

Lack of Preparation for Marriage

Society does not demand or even expect preparation for marriage. Anyone may marry, provided that he or she seems to fulfill the meager requirements of the law. It is easier to obtain a marriage license than a driver's license. At least we take an exam before we can drive. One may know practically nothing about marriage or its responsibilities. Success in marriage is assumed to come "naturally."

Preparation in the form of marriage education is gradually increasing in quality and extent and in the consciousness of certain portions of society. The process still has far to go before it can be said that America prepares its youth for marriage. Anyone who, in any sort of counseling capacity, has contact with young unmarried people or with married couples knows that among them can be found tragedy after tragedy, many of which would have been preventable through adequate preparation.

Obscurantism

Until recently there has been a veil of obscurantism (a tendency to prevent enlightenment) cast about marriage and sex. This veil has now begun to lift. Substantial remnants of it are, however, to be observed on every hand. Even in these presumably sophisticated times instances come to light in which a high school administration has the chapter on human reproduction literally cut out of a new biology textbook. In one recent case coming to our attention, the administration even had the section on childbirth deleted from a syllabus on sex education. In one sense this obscurantism is part of society's lack of demand for preparation for marriage. In another sense it is more than simply a negative, a lack; it is a definite, positive impediment to preparation. In spite of all our supposed open discussion of sex and marriage, there is still an ample element of taboo.

Anyone who is at all familiar with the behavior of young people knows that they discuss sex and other marriage-related topics. Then the question to be answered is this: Is it better for young people to discuss such topics with sound information or with poor information, under good auspices or under poor auspices, with competent guidance or without such guidance? Thoughtful persons dare give only one set of answers, and these spell education.

When society realizes that to lift the veil of obscurantism on marriage does not mean to tear back the curtain that shields the intimacies of life from wanton public gaze, but rather to substitute knowledge for ignorance, planning for drifting, effort for chance, idealism for superstition, and education for an agglomeration of misinformation, then preparation for marriage will be immeasurably advanced. If we believe in education, and Americans do, we must believe that education can make a contribution to the improvement of marriage and family life.

Premarital Romance and Sex

There is an overemphasis on premarital romance and sex and an underemphasis on marital success, as if the former guaranteed the latter. In movies, television, magazines, some books, many plays, and the public's attitude, the boy-meets-girl situation tends to take precedence over the situation of the happy marriage.

There is also in America a glorification of the youthful body. On billboards, in magazine advertisements, on television, in motion pictures—everywhere we turn—the youthful body is brought to our attention. From automobiles to citrus fruit, feminine beauty runs the entire gamut, associating more attention-getting qualities with supposedly less interesting events and objects.

Success in marriage depends upon something more than youthful beauty, sex, and the intensity of premarital romance. Putting the emphasis on these aspects gives a false impression of the factors making for long-time success. In a subtle way and without either party's being aware of it, many a husband or wife, especially the latter, is in competition with the more or less standardized youthful beauty that is so widely publicized.

Lack of Serious Attitude

In many quarters there is a lack of serious attitude toward marriage. Many people are more familiar with the caricature of marriage than with real instances of happy, successful married life. There are many jokes about marriage and the people involved in it. It is a well-worn subject for television comedians and situation comedies. It is held up to ridicule. Unpalatable expressions, such as "getting hooked" and "putting one's head in the noose," lightly describe marriage in terms of its worst actualities rather than of its greatest possibilities.

Stereotypes

There are two ways to erect a house. One is the process of adding brick to brick and board to board at the site of building until the structure is completed. The other is to fasten together large sections of prefabricated materials constructed in advance to fit a prearranged plan and delivered ready for use at the site of building. In our working out of a point of view relative to life in the society in which we live, we use, figuratively speaking, a combination of these two methods. We do put together experience with experience, idea with idea, and fact with fact to contribute to the erection of a "structure" partly of our own making. We also build, in part, with large sections constructed by society and fitted, with few alterations, into the pattern of our thought. These large blocks of concept, attitude, and definition are stereotypes.

Stereotypes are seldom valid. They seldom even roughly fit the facts. They are ready and easy, but lazy, ways of arriving at judgments of other people and of various phases of social life. They standardize the thinking of the uncritical and color the thinking of many Americans. College professors are absent-minded, disheveled, and impractical. Farmers are "hayseed" types. Redheads are hot-tempered. Fat persons are jolly and good-natured. Businesspeople are interested only in profits and are insensitive to human welfare. Politicians are open to suspicion. Men are brave, strong, impersonal, and independent; women are easily frightened, weak, personal, and dependent. Our frequent and uncritical use of the term *typical* shows to what degree these stereotypes have come to be taken for granted.

There are similar stereotypes relative to home, marriage, family, husband, and wife. People are assumed to date, fall in love, marry, set up a home, bear and rear children, divide labor between husband and wife, and accept traditional roles, all according to stereotypes. When these stereotypes continue to affect our thinking at the same time that they have become less well adapted to modern conditions, when they define the shape of the hole into which both round and square pegs are expected to fit, when they play a part in determining the criteria by which success and failure in marriage are measured, when they become substitutes for insight, understanding, information, and a desire to plumb more deeply into the possibilities of marriage and family living, then they in turn also become factors which play a part in producing failure.

Publicizing of Failure

Marital failure is played up in the press, and marital success is taken for granted. Failure is more spectacular, and apparently the public is more interested in it. Successful marriage is not news. When one sees headlines announcing the divorce of a well-known public figure, one feels as if something of importance has been learned. It is a subject to talk about. Just the thought of picking up a newspaper and reading headlines to the effect that millions of Americans are happily married seems ridiculous, so far have we taken success for granted and overstressed the significance of failure. Relatively little mention is made of marriages that endure.

TERMS TO BE LEARNED

ambisexual
bisexual
chauvinism (chauvinistic)
comparative prestige
economy (money economy)
equalitarian marriage
institutional aspects
  of family
marital adjustment
masculine ideology

matriarchal (matriarchy)
mobility (horizontal, vertical)
men's liberation movement
obscurantism
patriarchal
personality functions
power structure
primary group
role conflict
secondary group

sexually bisected society
sexually blended society
social institutions
socioeconomic
standard of living
status
stereotype
struggle for existence
symbolic task
women's liberation
  movement

SELECTED READINGS

ALBERT, ETHEL M.: "The Roles of Women: Question of Values," in Seymour M. Farber and Roger H. L. Wilson (eds.): *The Potential of Woman*, McGraw-Hill Book Company, New York, 1963, pp. 105–115. (Paperback.) Similarities and differences between the genders; sex roles. "Who is qualified to make an objective investigation of women?"

ALEXANDER, SHANA: *State-by-State Guide to Women's Legal Rights*, Wollstonecraft, Incorporated, Los Angeles, 1975. (Paperback.) State laws pertaining to marriage, divorce, children, abortion, widowhood, employment, rape, etc. Includes comments by the author.

ALTBACH, EDITH HOSHINO (ed.): *From Feminism to Liberation*, Schenkman Publishing Company, Inc., Cambridge, Mass., 1971. (Paperback.) This book aims "to further critical analysis of the Women's Liberation Movement and its revolutionary potential."

AMUNDSEN, KIRSTEN: *The Silenced Majority: Woman and American Democracy*, Prentice-Hall, Inc., Englewood Cliffs, N.J., 1971. (Paperback.) The author feels that to change the image of woman, women will have to gain control of the media, educational institutions, and decision making on a governmental level and push through legislation necessary to free women.

ANDREAS, CAROL: *Sex and Caste in America*, Prentice-Hall, Inc., Englewood Cliffs, N.J., 1971. (Paperback.) "For those who feel either overwhelmed or impressed by the rapid growth of the movement for the liberation of women, those who would like to know where it is coming from and where it is going, this book will offer some clarity...."

BEDNARIK, KARL: *The Male in Crisis*, trans. by Helen Sebba, Alfred A. Knopf, Inc., New York, 1970. The effect of the increasing organization of modern society on the male; as power becomes more centralized, male aggressiveness is repressed with the result that masculine authority and erotic capacity are weakened; it is not woman that is a threat to man.

BERNARD, JESSIE: *Women and the Public Interest*, Aldine-Atherton, Inc., Chicago, 1971. (Paperback.) "An attempt to bring into focus . . . some of the issues that policy makers are going to have to wrestle with in relation to the functions of women in modern society."

BIRD, CAROLINE, WITH SARA WELLES BRILLER: *Born Female: The High Cost of Keeping Women Down*, rev. ed., Pocket Books, a division of Simon and Schuster, Inc., New York, 1971. (Paperback.) Discusses discrimination against women, women as an oppressed and underprivileged group, and the women's liberation movement.

BOSMAJIAN, HAMIDA, AND HAIG BOSMAJIAN (eds.): *The Great Argument: The Rights of Women*, Addison-Wesley Publishing Company, Reading, Mass., 1972. (Paperback.) Includes statements by historical as well as present-day writers; report of Senate hearings and House debates on equal rights; recommendations of the President's Commission and Task Force on Women's Rights; women's liberation.

BRENTON, MYRON: *The American Male*, Fawcett Publications, Inc., Greenwich, Conn., 1967. (Paperback.) "The fundamental purpose of this book is . . . to encourage men to be men." Discusses problems of masculine identity, men's involvement in the family, relationship of men and women, "myths" about sex differences, men and the sexual revolution.

CADE, TONI (ed.): *The Black Woman*, New American Library, New York, 1970. (Paperback.) A collection of essays, speeches, discussions, poems, stories by black women on their position in contemporary American society; the relation of black women to the women's liberation movement; the relations of black women and black men.

CARDEN, MAREN LOCKWOOD: *The New Feminist Movement*, Russell Sage Foundation, New York, 1974. An objective analysis of achievements and shortcomings. Structure, membership, and development of organizations. What women want and where they are headed. Includes extensive bibliography and list of organizations.

COTTON, DOROTHY WHYTE: *The Case for the Working Mother*, Tower Publications, Inc., New York, 1965. (Paperback.) A book addressed to women. Discusses a woman's relationship to husband and children; day care and help with housework; advantages and costs of employment; going back to school after marriage and work; going back to work after time out to have children; suggestions for employed mothers.

CUDLIPP, EDYTHE: *Understanding Women's Liberation*, Coronet Publications, Inc., New York, 1971. (Paperback.) Discusses the development of the women's liberation movement and some of the persons and groups involved; also gives reasons why the author believes the movement has failed women and is not yet a "real movement."

DAVID, DEBORAH S., AND ROBERT BRANNON (eds.): *The Forty-Nine Percent Majority: The Male Sex Role*, Addison-Wesley Publishing Company, Reading, Mass., 1976. (Paperback.) A collection of readings on the male sex role, how the role is learned, how it is changing, what the future is likely to be. Problems males face. Male liberation.

DE BEAUVOIR, SIMONE: *The Second Sex*, trans. and ed. by H. M. Parshley, Alfred A. Knopf, Inc., New York, 1953. (Paperback.) Discusses biological data, historical aspects, myths about women, woman's development and roles, women's liberation. The central thesis is that women have been forced to occupy a secondary place in the world, not by nature but by men.

DECROW, KAREN: *The Young Woman's Guide to Liberation: Alternatives to the Half-life While the Choice Is Still Yours*, Bobbs-Merrill Company, Inc., New York, 1971. (Paperback.) The subtitle indicates the tone of the book. The author describes the book as a "cry to revolution." Discusses what girls learn about being women; women's lack of power.

DECTER, MIDGE: *The New Chastity and Other Arguments against Women's Liberation*, Coward, McCann & Geoghegan, Inc., New York, 1972. A critical analysis of women's liberation, its shortcomings and weaknesses, and the "impassioned, not always accurate, rhetoric of its prophetesses." The author contends that women's real difficulties are not with the denial of freedom but with unprecedented freedom that gives them a wide range of choices from which the movement is advocating retreat.

DENMARK, FLORENCE (ed.): *Who Discriminates against Women?*, Sage Publications, Inc., Beverly Hills, Calif., 1974. (Paperback.) A collection of articles, some based on research, discussing discrimination against women. The point is made that women as well as men discriminate against women.

DIZARD, JAN: *Social Change in the Family*, Community and Family Study Center, University of Chicago, 1968. (Paperback.) The report of a follow-up of 400 married couples originally included in a study of 1,000 engaged couples (by Ernest W. Burgess and Paul Wallin) in an effort to predict adjustment in marriage.

ELLIS, JULIE: *Revolt of the Second Sex*, Lancer Books, Inc., New York, 1970. (Paperback.) Discusses a number of women's liberation organizations and women who have "crashed barriers" or are active in the "new revolt." Has a chapter on women's liberation on the campus and one on abortion laws.

EPSTEIN, CYNTHIA FUCHS: *Woman's Place*, University of California Press, Berkeley, 1971. (Paperback.) How and why society "wastes" its best women and how and why they "waste" themselves. "Our best women . . . underperform, underachieve, and underproduce."

——— **AND WILLIAM J. GOODE** (eds.): *The Other Half: Roads to Women's Equality*, Prentice-Hall, Inc., Englewood Cliffs, N.J., 1971. (Paperback.) A symposium. Discusses status of women, social and civil rights, women and the professions, "sexual politics," women's liberation.

FARRELL, WARREN: *The Liberated Man: Beyond Masculinity: Freeing Men and Their Relationships with Women*, Random House, Inc., New York, 1974. Based on research and author's experience in consciousness-raising groups. Author maintains that men are confined and limited by concepts of masculinity and need to be liberated. Describes means by which this can be accomplished.

FILENE, PAUL GABRIEL: *Him/Her/Self: Sex Roles in Modern America*, Harcourt Brace Jovanovich, Inc., New York, 1974. What historically has it meant to be a man or a woman? What does it mean today? The meaning and need for male as well as female liberation.

FIRESTONE, SHULAMITH: *The Dialectic of Sex: The Case for Feminist Revolution*, William Morrow & Company, Inc., New York, 1970. (Paperback.) The author accepts the biological inequality of the sexes but says that to survive in our time traditional sex roles must be politically broken down.

FOLKMAN, JEROME D., AND NANCY M. K. CLATWORTHY: *Marriage Has Many Faces*, Charles E. Merrill Publishing Co., Columbus, Ohio, 1970, pp. 261–277. Problems and adjustments in the marriages of clergymen, lawyers, physicians, businessmen, military men, theatrical people.

FRIEDAN, BETTY: *The Feminine Mystique*, W. W. Norton & Company, Inc., New York, 1963. (Paperback.) One of the leaders of women's liberation discusses the modern woman's confusion and conflict of roles.

GAGER, NANCY (ed.): *Women's Rights Almanac*, Harper & Row, Publishers, New York, 1975. (Paperback.) A source book of information about women and women's issues, such as laws, organizations, employment, politics, and marriage and divorce. Includes a state-by-state directory and analysis.

GOLDBERG, LUCIANNE, AND JEANNIE SAKOL: *Purr, Baby, Purr*, Hawthorn Books, Inc., New York, 1971. A rebuttal of the claims and arguments of the women's liberation movement. Authors favor equal opportunity for women but oppose "all schemes to masculinize or neuter the basic female nature." They celebrate the differences between the genders and maintain that in many ways women are more privileged than men. The reader is cautioned not to be misled by the title and jaunty style. This is a serious and critical analysis.

GOODE, WILLIAM J. (ed.): *The Contemporary American Family*, Quadrangle Books, Inc., Chicago, 1971. (Paperback.) Nature, functions, and problems of the family, how it is changing and may change in the future. Also includes material on the women's liberation movement.

GORNICK, VIVIAN, AND BARBARA K. MORAN (eds.): *Woman in Sexist Society: Studies in Power and Powerlessness*, Basic Books, Inc., New York, 1971. (Paperback.) "Here some thirty scholars and writers—all of them women—move beyond manifestos and personal reminiscence to lay the scholarly and critical foundations for a new field of research and study—Women's Studies." Discusses numerous issues, including women as a deprived and subjugated class.

GREER, GERMAINE: *The Female Eunuch*, McGraw-Hill Book Company, New York, 1971. (Paperback.) Author's objective is to advocate the emancipation of women rather than to promote any organization. Women are "the most oppressed class" for whom "slaves is not too melodramatic a description." "If women are to effect a significant amelioration in their condition . . . they must refuse to marry." "Women have very little idea of how much men hate them."

HOBBS, LISA: *Love and Liberation: Up Front with the Feminists*, McGraw-Hill Book Company, New York, 1970. Author is critical of many common assumptions as well as some assumptions of feminists. Believes in importance of love and "warns that the feminist movement runs the risk of being bogged down in hatred." Says the sexes are complementary and believes marriage will endure because it is needed.

HOFFMAN, L. W., AND F. I. NYE: *Working Mothers*, Jossey-Bass, San Francisco, 1974. A comprehensive review of research done on factors influencing maternal employment, and its effects on women and families.

JANEWAY, ELIZABETH: *Between Myth and Morning (Women Awakening)*, William Morrow & Company, Inc., New York, 1974. Contains considerable history of and background to the women's liberation movement but is directed mainly to "practical problems and potentials of women here and now."

———: *Man's World, Woman's Place: A Study in Social Mythology*, William Morrow & Company, Inc., New York, 1971. A discussion of the "myths" that have been built around the differences between the sexes and the forces that influence the roles and status of women and that have produced the "current drive for women's rights."

JENSEN, OLIVER: *The Revolt of American Women*, rev. ed., Harcourt Brace Jovanovich, Inc., New York, 1971. (Paperback.) A history of the women's movement including more than 540 photographs, some taken during the nineteenth century. Since the original edition was published in 1952, the book shows what happened before that date and gives a basis for evaluating what has and has not happened since then.

KOMISAR, LUCY: *The New Feminism*, Warner Paperback Library, New York, 1972. An introduction to the women's liberation movement for the younger woman "who wants to know where she stands."

KORDA, MICHAEL: *Male Chauvinism: How It Works and How to Get Free of It*, Berkeley Publishing Corporation, New York, 1974. (Paperback.) How men "keep women in their place." "At the heart of male chauvinism is a false concept about modern man." "Until men have freed themselves from fixed attitudes toward women, we are never going to be free as men."

KRADITOR, AILEEN S. (ed.): *Up from the Pedestal*, Quadrangle Books, Inc., Chicago, 1968. (Paperback.) A collection of writings in the history of American feminism from 1642 to the present. Some antifeminist writings are included.

LIFTON, ROBERT JAY (ed.): *The Woman in America*, Beacon Press, Boston, 1965. (Paperback.) Discusses woman's nature, image of women in literature, comparisons between two generations of women, changing place of women in America, and related issues.

LOPATA, HELENA ZNANIECKI: *Occupation: Housewife*, Oxford University Press, New York, 1971. (Paperback.) Report of a study of 1,000 urban housewives, all of them with young children. What housewives think of their role. The diversified roles of the wife. Can satisfaction still be found in the role of homemaker?

MARINE, GENE: *A Male Guide to Women's Liberation*, Avon Books, New York, 1974. (Paperback.) Author's objective is to help men understand the women's liberation movement, to show how women think and feel about men, and to present what men need to understand about their own attitudes and behavior.

MILL, JOHN STUART: *The Subjection of Women*, with an introduction by Wendell Robert Carr, The M.I.T. Press, Cambridge, Mass., 1970. (Paperback.) The original edition of this book was published in 1869. This is "unquestionably the most eloquent, the most ambitious, and . . . among the most heartfelt pleas . . . for the equality of the sexes." "The present-day Women's Liberation Movement is not soon likely to surpass it."

MILLETT, KATE: *Sexual Politics*, Doubleday & Company, Inc., Garden City, N.Y., 1970. (Paperback.) A critical analysis of the "sexual revolution" (using the term in a broader sense than just sexual freedom), especially the effect of the patriarchal system on the relationships of the sexes.

MORGAN, ROBIN (ed.): *Sisterhood Is Powerful*, Random House, Inc., New York, 1970. (Paperback.) A variety of writers cover a wide range of topics to provide an introduction to the women's liberation movement "in our own words, not those of the distorting mass media."

NICHOLS, JACK: *Men's Liberation: A New Definition of Masculinity*, Penguin Books, Inc., New York, 1975. (Paperback.) What men's liberation means. It will include "new modes of mental awareness once thought 'womanly.'" Men's sexual fears, striving for success, status. Author says that men's relationships with women are becoming increasingly difficult.

O'NEILL, WILLIAM L.: *Everyone Was Brave*, Quadrangle Books, Inc., Chicago, 1969. (Paperback.) The history of feminism in America; "an inquiry into the failure of feminism"; "how the feminists contributed to their own downfall."

PERNTZ, K.: *Liberated Marriage*, Pyramid Books, New York, 1972. More than "the case against marriage," the author revives old arguments and presents different suggestions for reform.

PERRUCCI, CAROLYN C., AND DENA B. TARG (eds.): *Marriage and the Family*, David McKay Co., Inc., New York, 1974. (Paperback.) A collection of articles to "acquaint the reader with feminist critiques of and alternatives to various aspects of marriage and the family and do so in such a way as to reveal the suffering of women as underdogs in our society and their active opposition to barriers to sex equality."

REED, EVELYN: *Problems of Women's Liberation*, new ed., Pathfinder Press, New York, 1970. (Paperback.) "How women lost control of their destiny and how they can regain it." The myth of women's inferiority; the women's liberation movement.

REEVES, NANCY: *Womankind: Beyond the Stereotypes*, Aldine-Atherton, Inc., Chicago, 1971. (Paperback.) "There are two Americas, the male and the female, separated by a psychological gulf scarcely bridged by the culture's devices for keeping them coupled." Suggests a "moratorium on marriage."

SAFILIOS-ROTHSCHILD, C. (ed.): *Toward a*

Sociology of Women, Xerox College Publishing, Lexington, Mass., 1972. Articles dealing with "women's options and their effects on the lives of women and men."

SHORTER, EDWARD: *The Making of the Modern Family*, Basic Books, Inc., New York, 1975. A study of marriage, family, sexual behavior, sex roles, etc., and of changes occurring in the United States and Europe. Puts present situation in historical perspective. Presents insights not always found in studies of these topics.

STASSINOPOULOS, ARIANNA: *The Female Woman*, Random House, Inc., New York, 1973. A very critical analysis of the women's liberation movement, its philosophy, assumptions, objectives, and the women associated with it, especially Kate Millett and Germaine Greer. Author says, "The frenetic extremism of Women's Lib seeks not to emancipate women but to destroy society." She says that the leaders have sought to "question and destroy the whole concept of woman."

STEINMANN, ANNE, AND DAVID J. FOX: *The Male Dilemma: How to Survive the Sexual Revolution*, Jason Aronson, New York, 1974. Men's and women's confusion regarding their roles. Women's problem is to adjust to expanding freedom, while men's problem is to adjust to diminished status and loss of power. The sexual revolution "has posed a more severe problem for the man than for the woman."

STEMBLER, SOOKIE (ed.): *Women's Liberation: Blueprint for the Future*, Charter Communications, Inc., New York, 1970. (Paperback.) Includes "articles by outstanding advocates of an ever-growing Social Revolution," articles on men by women, on women by women.

THOMPSON, MARY LOU (ed.): *Voices of the New Feminism*, Beacon Press, Boston, 1970. Includes a discussion of remedies for injustices to women, of women's revolt as a revolution in human relationships that involves the emancipation of men as well as women. Includes an extensive annotated bibliography.

WARE, CELLESTINE: *Woman Power: The Movement for Women's Liberation*, Tower Publications, Inc., New York, 1970. (Paperback.) "Radical feminism is working for the eradication of domination and elitism in all human relationships. This would make self-determination the ultimate good and require the downfall of society as we know it today." ". . . The oppression of women begins in the family."

Chapter 10

Making Marriage Meaningful: Marital Adjustment and Interaction

In this chapter we shall discuss some of the factors which play a part in making marriage succeed or fail. We cannot hope to discuss all such factors since many are beyond the scope of this book. Therefore, we shall discuss those about which the reader may do something either through self-examination on a conscious level, through putting them into effect, or through avoiding them. This is not equivalent to an oversimplified "do-it-yourself" manual, for such advice is not easily given or received. The reader is addressed as a person concerned about marriage and therefore presumably motivated to do whatever can be done to contribute to its success. Any discussion such as that which follows is unavoidably generalized. In working out an individual marriage there is ample room for ingenuity, imagination, and the infusion of reflections of many facets of individual personalities. The cultural framework within which marriages occur exerts some pressure toward similarity of structure. But within that structure a couple have almost limitless flexibility of interrelationship and function.

MARITAL QUALITY AND MARITAL STABILITY

What makes one marriage succeed and another fail? This is a complex question which social scientists have been struggling with for about fifty years. After hundreds of studies we know something about marriage and the factors that contribute to its success or failure, but there is still much to be learned. This is particularly true in contemporary America, where life-styles are changing and marriage is having to adapt to many of the social changes which we have already discussed in this book.

Let us begin our examination of marital adjustment and interaction with some definitions. *Marital stability* refers to whether or not a marriage remains intact. Strictly speaking, a stable marriage is one which is terminated only by the natural death of one spouse. An unstable marriage can be terminated by divorce, separation, or desertion. More marriages are terminated by the death of one spouse than any other way. Divorce as a cause of termination is a not-too-distant second, however. Marital stability, then, tells us only about the state of a marriage—it tells us nothing about what is happening within the marriage relationship.

Marital quality is a general term referring to a wide range of characteristics about the dynamics of a couple's relationship. High marital quality indicates good adjustment, adequate communication, a high level of happiness with the marriage, and a high degree of satisfaction with the relationship (Lewis and Spanier, 1978). *Marital adjustment* is a more specific term which has traditionally

What contributes to good marital adjustment? One element might be a couple's interest in spending time with each other, such as working together on a project. (Richard Frieman, Photo Researchers.)

been used to indicate how well a couple are getting along with each other. Couples with high adjustment are usually described as having little conflict, little disagreement on matters of importance to them, little tension in the relationship, and a fair amount of cohesion or togetherness.

Part of our discussion of the quality and adjustment of marriages in this chapter and of divorce in Chapter 15 will be related to the diagram presented in Exhibit 10-1. This figure suggests that there are a multitude of factors which ultimately influence the stability of a marital relationship. "All marriages have unique histories which begin long before the marriage ceremony and which follow a complex course, finally resulting in dissolution by death of one spouse, divorce, separation, annulment or desertion" (Lewis and Spanier, 1978). Exhibit 10-1 shows that marital quality is a dynamic rather than a static concept. Marriages are always changing, and like most human events they have a history. As we discussed in Chapters 5 through 7, there are a number of premarital factors which influence the quality and stability of marriage: personality factors, attitudes and values, social factors, circumstantial factors, marital expectations, and social maturity level. The day-to-day interactions between the spouses and the multitude of social factors acting on the marriage during the period of its existence are certainly important. Thus, all marriages are influenced by the history of the relationship which preceded the wedding, the circumstances surrounding the marriage, the daily interaction between spouses, and many social forces that act on the relationship from outside the household.

Marriages with the greatest adjustment and quality are, of course, the ones with the greatest stability. In other words, marriages which end in divorce or separation tend to be those which are of poor quality and adjustment. This is an obvious conclusion. But the

Exhibit 10-1 Factors influencing marital stability. (*Source*: Lewis and Spanier, 1978.)

PREMARITAL PREDISPOSITIONS	MARRIAGE	THRESHOLD	POSTMARRIAGE
Personality factors		Marital expectations	
Attitudes and values		Commitment and obligations	
Social factors	Marital quality →	Tolerance	
Circumstantial factors		Religious doctrine	Separation → Divorce
Marital expectations		External pressures and social stigma	
Social maturity level		Divorce law and legal aid	
		Real and perceived alternatives	

Adjustment
Satisfaction
Happiness
Conflict and role strain
Communication
Integration
Etc.

correlation between marital quality or adjustment and marital stability is not a perfect one. In fact, many marriages with low quality and adjustment remain intact, and a few marriages which appear to some individuals to be quite well adjusted end in divorce nevertheless. What, then, determines whether a couple with a given level of adjustment will remain married or dissolve their marriage through divorce or separation? Exhibit 10-1 illustrates several "threshold" variables which may influence this decision.

Whether a couple at a given level of marital quality will remain married depends on what expectations they had about marriage in the first place. If their expectations were very high and they find that they cannot live up to them, they more readily divorce. If, however, they had realistic expectations about marriage and find that they are meeting those expectations, they may be more likely to judge their marriage as satisfactory and remain married.

Their commitment to the marriage is important. Stated differently, how committed are they to keep the marriage going, to work out problems that present themselves, and to seek help when the relationship is faltering? Couples with a low tolerance for conflict and disharmony are more likely candidates for marital failure than are couples who realize that conflict is normal and that a certain amount of it must be tolerated.

Religious doctrine is influential. If an individual is a devout member of a religious denomination which prohibits divorce, this will certainly influence a decision to keep the marriage intact. Thus, in the case of two couples with equally unhappy marriages, we might find that one will divorce and the other will not if one has a particularly strong identification with a religion which does not allow divorce.

External pressures from in-laws, within the community, and from work associates may be considered a threshold factor. Some couples are reluctant to divorce for fear of social stigma. Others feel it would damage their standing in a corporation, in the community, or in a political office, for example.

Divorce laws have an influence. States that have a history of laws which make divorce difficult for its residents have lower rates of divorce than states that have liberal laws. This does not mean that the liberal laws encouraged divorce, for oftentimes couples who were reluctant to divorce when the laws were strict either separated, resorted to desertion, or crossed state lines to obtain a divorce. Nevertheless, divorce laws play some part in a couple's willingness to end a marriage. The availability of legal aid to low-income couples may make it easier for them to terminate an unhappy marriage.

Some couples will divorce and others will not depending on what they see as their alternatives after the divorce. The alternatives may be real ones or simply perceived ones—what they *think* it will be like after divorce. Again, we can look at two unhappy couples, one divorcing and the other staying together. In one relationship, one or both spouses may value the alternatives to the unhappy marriage more highly than the individuals in the other unhappy marriage. The alternative attractions might include such factors as a third person with whom one spouse is in love, freedom from the responsibility of marriage, a new feeling of independence, or the attraction of a new life-style. For some persons, however, the alternatives may not be attractive. For example, a woman who has been financially supported by her husband for twenty years and has no career skills may find herself in a position of financial hardship if she becomes divorced, especially if she must be responsible for the care of children. A man who has come to depend on the household services of his wife may similarly be reluctant to divorce even when the marriage has gone sour. Finally, it should be noted, as Exhibit 10-1 indicates, that divorce is almost always preceded by separation. In most cases the separation is an informal one, as opposed to a court-ordered one.

The threshold variables presented in Exhibit 10-1, then, may influence whether or not a couple stay married or divorce. Some persons who are unhappy find the barriers insurmountable and remain married. Others cross over and find that divorce is their preferred way to end an unhappy relationship. Only a small number of couples have what would be considered happy marriages which result in divorce, although such an occurrence is a possibility. Finally, there are the couples who are happily married and whose marriages remain intact. This is the American ideal for marriage. We shall now consider a number of factors which may give us some insight into these types of marriages.

CONFLICT IS NORMAL

Some conflict in marriage is normal and to be expected. Two personalities could not live in such intimate union without it, unless both of them were completely apathetic, accepting the relationship with bovine placidity. Men and women being as they are, each having to take account of the existence of the other, there is a pull away from as well as an attraction toward each other. Sumner and Keller (1927) term the association *antagonistic cooperation*. There is much to be said for such a description. Conflict is not always overtly manifest; it may be covert. It does not always mean quarreling, nor does it necessarily mean failure. A couple need not give up their marriage as lost the first time there is conflict, tension, or a difference between them. A husband and wife need not agree upon everything or even like each other's every trait. It is not only disagreement but the manner in which it is expressed that causes difficulty. It is important, however, to agree upon basic goals, or at least to reach a workable compromise concerning them.

As we have previously indicated, conflict and quarreling does not signify a maladjusted couple. What is important in distinguishing a poorly adjusted marriage from a well-adjusted one is the couple's ability to return to a state of equilibrium after the fight. Couples who hold grudges, attempt to hurt the other spouse through the fighting, and use the quarrel as a platform for escalating the conflict can be said to lack adjustment more so than couples who quarrel but then use that fight as a basis for behavioral change or mutual understanding. Many times couples are simply tired, frustrated, irritated, or in a bad mood. If, after the quarrel, they calm down, let the problem subside, and attempt to put it in a proper perspective, it can be said that they have returned to a state of equilibrium. A couple who can wake up the following morning and not be angry about what happened the night before, who can forgive each other for a mistake, or who can simply acknowledge that they disagreed and will continue honestly to do so without malice, are likely to have a healthy relationship.

Conflict Resolution

When a couple do have a particularly troublesome issue to deal with, there are several steps they can follow to achieve conflict resolution (Blood, 1969):

- Identifying the issue
- Proposing solutions
- Evaluating the alternatives
- Selecting the best alternative
- Carrying out the decision
- Reviewing the decision in operation

Many couples know there is a problem but have difficulty defining it. They may be angry about one thing but end up arguing about another. Some couples who are quarreling bring up issues and fights that are days or even years old. Many times a couple can identify the issue but have difficulty sticking to it. It is preferable, of course, for them to identify the relevant issue and stick to it. They may then propose solutions to the problems. Sometimes the solutions are few, sometimes many; sometimes they are obvious, sometimes elusive. The alternatives must be evaluated in light of the needs of both partners. After the best alternative is selected, the couple must make a commitment to carry out the decision. A great many couples make decisions about an issue, but one (or both) of them never follows through, thus continuing the conflict or allowing it to resurface. Finally, it is critical to review the decision in operation, since no decision is irrevocable—nor should it be. A couple may decide that an alternative plan should be introduced or that the original plan must be modified.

MARITAL ADJUSTMENT OVER THE FAMILY LIFE CYCLE

How does the quality of a marriage change over time? Most marriages start out in an atmosphere of celebration, good will, happiness, and great expectations. After all, the couple are in love, they are likely to have a great interest in their sexual relationship, they have much to look forward to, and there is an aura of romanticism which may help them over some of the rough spots in early adjustment. But what happens when some of the romance wears off and the couple settle down to the day-to-day business of being married to each other twenty-four hours per day and living in the same household? A large number of studies show that marital adjustment begins to decline for the typical couple during the first few years of the marriage (Spanier, Lewis, and Cole, 1975). In fact, there has never been a study which has found anything other than a consistent decline in marital adjustment over the first several years of marriage. Studies are not clear, however, about what happens during the later stages of the life cycle.

This finding of decline may scare some individuals. However, it is a phenomenon which is not surprising to social scientists. Most individuals have a highly romanticized idea of marriage, and it is possible that this romanticism leads individuals to have expectations about marriage which can never fully be met (Spanier, 1972). It is unlikely that many couples could maintain throughout their marriage the level of happiness that they experienced at first. This is not to imply, however, that maintaining such a level of adjustment is impossible. Indeed, this may be an important and realistic goal for some individuals. However, the most important point we can make in this regard is that in the normal course of events, research conclusively demonstrates that marital adjustment will decline in the early years of marriage.

This decline typically begins during the first year of marriage and appears to be further related to or accelerated by the birth of the first child. The intensity of the decline in adjustment begins to lessen several years after marriage. There is some disagreement about how marital adjustment changes in the later years of marriage. Some researchers claim that adjustment actually begins to increase as retirement approaches, but the studies which found this to be true have significant weaknesses. Other researchers believe that the adjustment stabilizes after many years of marriage and does not change very much. Still others claim that the downward trend in adjustment that characterizes the early years of marriage continues through the later years, although the rate of decline is not as great. Exhibit 10-2 illustrates these three different ideas about what happens to marital adjustment over the life cycle. Future research may demonstrate which explanation is most appropriate.

The early decline in adjustment need not trouble most persons if they have a realistic perspective regarding its occurrence. Marriage hurls two individuals into an interdependent and complex situation which brings a multitude of pressures, conflicts, and difficulties in addition to its many satisfactions. Many persons claim that their spouses begin to "take them for granted" following marriage. This is to be expected to some extent, since each will find it difficult to maintain the same level of attention to the spouse that was characteristic of their days of courtship. But couples can avert this feeling if they wish to by doing the little "extra" things that they know their spouse will appreciate.

Individuals may legitimately ask if adjustment *must* decline. Furthermore, it is reasonable to wonder what can be done to keep the marriage at a high level of adjustment. First, let us state that although most marriages decline in adjustment and many end in divorce, this is not a universal phenomenon for all couples, nor is it a predetermined, required, or expected event. A couple who are willing to make the effort to maintain their marriage at a high level of adjustment stand a good chance of doing so. It must be emphatically stated, however, that *marriage requires hard work in order to succeed at a continuously high level of adjustment.* Too many individuals have a glamorized view of marriage which leads them to believe that the normal course of events is for a couple to "live happily ever after." Romance stories portrayed in the cinema and mass media often give us this impression. Research has shown that marriage is prone to disenchantment, disengagement, and a multitude of forces which would encourage its disruption

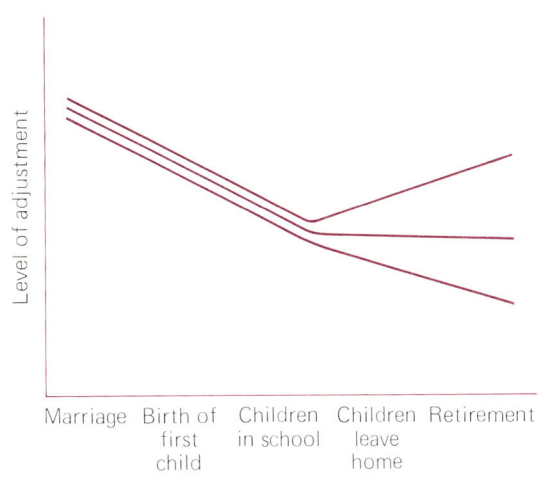

Exhibit 10-2 Three possible courses of marital adjustment over the life cycle. (*Source:* Spanier, 1976.)

and dissolution. In order to contend with these influences, a couple committed to their marriage must be aware of these influences and *actively* work at maintaining their marriage at a high level of adjustment. This is not an awesome or cumbersome task—it is rather one which requires moderate amounts of insight, commitment, and interpersonal skill. Our discussion in this chapter assumes that most couples are capable of achieving good marital adjustment if both spouses so desire and are willing to work at it.

Measuring Marital Adjustment

How do social scientists go about assessing the quality of a marital relationship? This has been a question debated for years among professionals. Most of the measures of marital adjustment which have actually been used are paper and pencil measures in which couples respond to several questions about their marriage. Most of the questions focus on the extent of conflict in the couple's relationship, the extent of agreement or disagreement on matters of importance, how satisfied they are with their marriage, and the amount of cohesion or togetherness between the spouses. Other questions assess characteristics such as a couple's commitment to the marriage, how they manage difficulties that crop up on a day-to-day basis, and how similar or different they are in areas which might influence their ability to get along with each other. An example of one type of marital adjustment scale is shown in Exhibit 10-3 (Spanier, 1976b). It should be noted that there are no cutoff points which indicate success or failure. Research using this scale has shown that couples with unusually low scores (below 75) are particularly prone to divorce, and couples with high scores are more likely to have marriages which succeed; but no absolute interpretations can be made about a given score. The proper coding for the scale is indicated on each line, and the numbers earned on each of the thirty-two items may be added for a total score. It is interesting to point out that women tend to report higher scores than men do. The scale can also be used to some extent by engaged or committed couples as a starting point for discussion about agreements and disagreements. The scale is presented to illustrate the kinds of measurements researchers sometimes use and should be used only for discussion purposes by readers of this book, never as an absolute guide to decision making.

AN UNDERSTANDING OF PERSONALITY AND BEHAVIOR

Personality may be thought of as the sum total of the individual—habits, thought patterns, emotional responses, moods, attitudes, reactions to people and situations, hopes, fears, aspirations, and countless other things that make the individual a person, things that taken together distinguish the individual from all other persons. Personality is not quantitative. No one has any more than anyone else. Personalities vary as to type but not as to amount.

Strictly speaking, personality is not inborn, although some of its "ingredients" are. An individual's body structure, the way a person functions, temperament, and aptitudes constitute equipment with which the newborn child meets and begins to adjust to his or her environment. Personality, then, becomes a product of the interaction between equipment and environment. Part of an individual's environment is other people. Reactions to them and their reactions to the individual play a significant part in molding personality. The reactions of others begin even before an individual is born. Parents, for example, may want a boy or a girl, as the case may be, and may begin to think of the unborn child accordingly. They may choose a name, and they notice growth and prenatal movements. So the stage is set for personality development even before birth.

A personality may be compared to an iceberg, only a small portion of which is visible above the surface of the water. This small portion, however, and the much larger portion hidden from sight below the surface are integral parts of the same mass. An individual's observable, overt behavior represents only a relatively small proportion of total personality. The rest is there, nonetheless, some portions permanently hidden from view or appearing above the surface only now and then as the waves of circumstance cause the berg to rise and fall in the experiences of life.

Most of us exhibit traits and types of behavior that are not readily changed through our own efforts. What is true of ourselves is also true of our wives, husbands, or fiancé(e)s. They, too, are not readily changed. On the other hand, there are some traits that may be altered through self-evaluation and effort. Fuller understanding of human reactions may contribute significantly to the improvement of mutual adjustment. If we understand why a person is as he or she is, that very understanding tends to make relationships more agreeable even though change does not occur. We may not be able to alter an individual's behavior, but we may alter the interpretation of that behavior. Fuller knowledge also enables us to play a more effective role in directing our own development. Although a person may not be able to change all undesirable traits, knowledge and understanding may permit making the most of limitations and prevent making undesirable traits worse, more obvious, or more obtrusive.

All Behavior Has Causes

Perhaps, to be more nearly accurate, we should say that all behavior has antecedents or is the outgrowth of contributing factors. To think in terms of causes as such often leads to oversimplification. At any rate, the behavior which an individual exhibits always has roots. These may arise in relatively recent circumstances or may extend to remote childhood. They may go back to important experiences or to relatively insignificant incidents. Physiological processes also are not without their effect. The individual is the product of inborn characteristics plus experience. This concept, however, should not be oversimplified. Experience is not to be thought of only in terms of large segments, such as crises, shocks, family life, or college career. It may also be considered in terms of a continuum of change in environment, moods, physiology, contacts, ideas, emotions, and events, extending through more than 85,000 seconds per day and through every day of life. None of this experience is lost.

Since we live in only the instantaneous present, the roots of behavior must of necessity be in the past, except in so far as current physiological processes may affect behavior. Naturally, the past itself cannot be changed. But an individual can build new patterns of behavior, with past experience serving as a matrix in which change occurs. Such change occurs through new experience, so that ultimately each person is the product of his or her total biography.

Some Aspects of Behavior

Without going into detail, we may mention some considerations relative to behavior that have a bearing on marital adjustment. Behavior is affected by physiological processes. Fatigue, hunger, illness, moods, worry, and the menstrual cycle, for example, may all leave their mark. Individuals differ in the degree to which their behavior shows the effects of such items and in the degree to which they voluntarily control them.

People are inclined to become angry or irritated when they are thwarted. Such irritation may be reduced either by decreasing the irritant or by increasing resistance to it. Each individual seeks to maintain what is considered a satisfactory position in his or her own estimation and in the eyes of others. If this position cannot be maintained through actual achievements, self-defense may lead to an attempt to maintain it through other means, such as projection of blame, rationalization, aggression, alcoholic escape, hypochondria, withdrawal, or psychosomatic illness.

Observable "surface" phenomena often represent only the symptoms rather than the cause of an individual's behavior. On the other hand, "surface" phenomena are not necessarily a reflection of an individual's underlying attitudes. An expression of anger, for example, may be only an instance of habitual response on the part of a person with a quick temper. It does not necessarily indicate a lack of love. How surface phenomena are to be evaluated can be determined only on the basis of insight into a given personality.

An individual cannot be expected to change behavior unless the situation is provided in which change can occur.

EXHIBIT 10-3 Dyadic Adjustment Scale

Most persons have disagreements in their relationships. Please indicate below the approximate extent of agreement or disagreement between you and your partner for each item on the following list.

	Always Agree	Almost Always Agree	Occasionally Disagree	Frequently Disagree	Almost Always Disagree	Always Disagree
1 Handling family finances	5	4	3	2	1	0
2 Matters of recreation	5	4	3	2	1	0
3 Religious matters	5	4	3	2	1	0
4 Demonstrations of affection	5	4	3	2	1	0
5 Friends	5	4	3	2	1	0
6 Sex relations	5	4	3	2	1	0
7 Conventionality (correct or proper behavior)	5	4	3	2	1	0
8 Philosophy of life	5	4	3	2	1	0
9 Ways of dealing with parents or in-laws	5	4	3	2	1	0
10 Aims, goals, and things believed important	5	4	3	2	1	0
11 Amount of time spent together	5	4	3	2	1	0
12 Making major decisions	5	4	3	2	1	0
13 Household tasks	5	4	3	2	1	0
14 Leisure time interests and activities	5	4	3	2	1	0
15 Career decisions	5	4	3	2	1	0

Making Marriage Meaningful: Marital Adjustment and Interaction

	All the time	Most of the time	More often than not	Occa- sionally	Rarely	Never
16. How often do you discuss or have you considered divorce, separation, or terminating your relationship?	0	1	2	3	4	5
17. How often do you or your mate leave the house after a fight?	0	1	2	3	4	5
18. In general, how often do you think that things between you and your partner are going well?	5	4	3	2	1	0
19. Do you confide in your mate?	5	4	3	2	1	0
20. Do you ever regret that you married? (or *lived together*)	0	1	2	3	4	5
21. How often do you and your partner quarrel?	0	1	2	3	4	5
22. How often do you and your mate "get on each other's nerves?"	0	1	2	3	4	5

	Every Day	Almost Every Day	Occa- sionally	Rarely	Never
23. Do you kiss your mate?	4	3	2	1	0

	All of them	Most of them	Some of them	Very few of them	None of them
24. Do you and your mate engage in outside interests together?	4	3	2	1	0

EXHIBIT 10-3 Continued

How often would you say the following events occur between you and your mate?

	Never	Less than once a month	Once or twice a month	Once or twice a week	Once a day	More often
25 Have a stimulating exchange of ideas	0	1	2	3	4	5
26 Laugh together	0	1	2	3	4	5
27 Calmly discuss something	0	1	2	3	4	5
28 Work together on a project	0	1	2	3	4	5

There are some things about which couples sometimes agree and sometime disagree. Indicate if either item below caused differences of opinions or were problems in your relationship during the past few weeks. (Check yes or no)

Yes	No	
29 0	1	Being too tired for sex.
30 0	1	Not showing love.

31 The dots on the following line represent different degrees of happiness in your relationship. The middle point, "happy," represents the degree of happiness of most relationships. Please circle the dot which best describes the degree of happiness, all things considered, of your relationship.

0	1	2	3	4	5	6
Extremely Unhappy	Fairly Unhappy	A Little Unhappy	Happy	Very Happy	Extremely Happy	Perfect

32 Which of the following statements best describes how you feel about the future of your relationship?

5   I want desperately for my relationship to succeed, and *would go to almost any length* to see that it does.
4   I want very much for my relationship to succeed, and *will do all I can* to see that it does.
3   I want very much for my relationship to succeed, and *will do my fair share* to see that it does.
2   It would be nice if my relationship succeeded, but *I can't do much more than I am doing now* to help it succeed.
1   It would be nice if it succeeded, but *I refuse to do any more than I am doing now* to keep the relationship going.
0   My relationship can never succeed, and *there is no more that I can do* to keep the relationship going.

(*Source:* Spanier, 1976b)

People are often most easily offended by those closest to them in affection and esteem. The more a personal relationship is idealized, the smaller the pinprick necessary to deflate it.

If you agree with a person on little things, you may more effectively disagree over more important matters. If you regularly disagree with someone over little things, you have already lost part of the battle when it comes to a more important issue, because the latter is merely another in a series of items upon which to disagree.

No one is entirely introvert or extrovert. But different persons may lean to one side or the other of the introvert-extrovert fence. In so doing, they exhibit both different behavior and different needs. One type of individual cannot suddenly be made into the other, no matter how much a spouse may desire such a change.

Whenever possible, it is better to be positive rather than negative—the word "positive" being used in the sense of constructive and complimentary, not in the sense of dogmatic and overconfident, and "negative" in the sense of censorious and depreciatory, not in the sense of a negative reply to a question. An ounce of appreciation, it is said, is worth a pound of criticism. Reward is more effective than punishment. Praise accomplishes more than blame. Noting an individual's successes is preferable to noting his or her failures. The old saying, "If you can't say something good about a person, don't say anything," may be trite, but it has values as well as limitations. One need not be a Pollyanna, but certainly many unfavorable remarks result in no gain and are better left unsaid. They may be made about inconsequentials, but the remarks themselves are not inconsequential.

Criticism, censure, and blame have their place; but it is only a rare person who can accept them impersonally and objectively without resentment. This is due in part to the double-barreled nature of criticism; an individual reacts to both the fact of criticism and the content of criticism. Constructive criticism is more effective than destructive criticism. When one must use the latter, it is usually more readily accepted if prefaced with something favorable. Suppose, for example, you have two things to tell a person, one favorable, the other unfavorable. If you begin with the latter, a barrier is immediately erected between you. By the time you have reached the favorable comment, the resentment, hurt feelings, and defenses of the other person have already become part of the situation. If, however, you begin with the favorable comment, the way is paved for the unfavorable one, and the criticism is put into a new perspective. The other person feels supported rather than attacked, so to speak, and is more likely to accept the criticism with grace.

To make criticism effective, the other person's goals and motivations must be taken into account. If the criticism seems like a means of helping to achieve those goals, instead of a means by which desires are thwarted, it will more readily be acted upon.

Nagging is so much more likely to be an expression of feeling on the part of the nagger, rather than an insightful attempt to influence the motivations and behavior of the person nagged, that it seldom accomplishes what it is presumably intended to accomplish. Instead, it may make the other individual more determined to do or not to do what the nagging is about. The person nagged may fight back or may seek other outlets for emotions. Nagging may make emotions accumulate, only to explode eventually. Continuous nagging may make the one nagged give up in desperation, become completely defeated, or become immune to everything the spouse says. There may be a carry-over from one instance of nagging to the next. Separate instances of nagging are not entirely discrete phenomena. After each instance of nagging both the nagger and the recipient of the nagging carry over a mood, sustain a hypersensitivity, so that there is a residue of emotion giving the next instance of nagging a head start. After the separate instances of nagging, the couple do not return to the zero line of emotion. Each instance sensitizes them further in preparation for the next. The recipient, then, tends to think of the nagging almost as a continuous process.

None of these responses can produce better human relationships or more satisfactory marriage. One cannot change the "inside" of a person by continual hammering upon the "outside." Nagging also reveals the points at which the nagger is vulnerable. It calls attention to the items concerning which the individual may readily be hurt or irritated.

People more readily accept criticism directed at what they do or say than criticism directed at them as persons. Criticism which amounts to classification is especially likely to be resisted. For example, "What you did was careless" is directed toward an act; "Only a careless person would do what you did" is directed toward a person and amounts to classification. "You spoiled the party by your behavior" is criticism; "You always spoil parties by your behavior" approaches classification. The use of supercharged words, such as "stupid," "lazy," and "selfish," may seem to the person criticized like classification. For example, an individual might react more strongly against being told that a mistake was stupid than to being told that it was unfortunate.

Some persons do improve themselves through criticism. Others respond more readily to encouragement. Criticism makes them self-conscious. They then have difficulty in improving, especially if their efforts are witnessed by the person who did the criticizing, and even more especially if that person depreciates their efforts at improvement with further criticism or reminds them of the former criticism as the reason for their efforts.

Suggestions are most effective when given at the so-called "psychological moment," even if that moment has to be waited for or created. It is useless to expect a person to give full attention and consideration to a suggestion if the person is absorbed in something else. The individual will listen more closely if the suggestion has been asked for, and in many cases such a point may be reached.

Advice is a type of suggestion. Usually advice that is given when not sought is worse than useless. There is no more fruitless activity than the wholesale distribution of advice as if it were advertising handbills. One of the most pointless types of advice is that prefaced by the phrase "If I were you." Obviously I am not you and therefore cannot look at a situation through your eyes. There is no validity in assuming that what I think would be good for me in your situation would also be good for you. Advice, too, is only advice. It is to be taken or not taken as the other person sees fit. It is not command. The adviser has performed the proper function when the advice has been given. There is no obligation to insist upon its acceptance and no need to feel a personal affront if the advice is not acted upon.

Perspective

If you hold a penny very near one eye and shut the other, you can blot out a roomful of people or the whole panorama of nature. This does not happen because the penny is more important than the people or the landscape, but because something near your eye blinds you to more important objects farther away. You lack perspective. If you toss the penny away from you, it becomes an insignificant speck in your field of vision.

In marriage, perspective may be absent.

Something close may blind one to something more important. One element in a situation may be fixed upon and magnified to the detriment of the whole.

If an individual fails to see the whole marital situation with its parts in their proper relationships; if there is failure to discriminate between essentials and nonessentials, between the temporary and the permanent, between those things that do and those that do not bear a relationship to the more important elements in the marriage, between those which can damage the marriage and those which are only irritating; if the person cannot see the forest for the trees, perspective is lacking. As time goes on, many couples grow to realize that something which upset them at first actually did not affect their marriage. Looking back, they see that their relationship has been unimpaired. If at first they had discriminated between things of lesser and things of greater significance, their initial concern would have been unnecessary.

In the early days of marriage, adjustments have to be made to relatively minor circumstances; some couples fail to anticipate these, and therefore they get them out of perspective and find them disturbing. For example, a couple may have a problem sleeping in a double bed or using the same bathroom, with her cosmetics and his shaving materials in evidence. They may be annoyed by each other's appearance at breakfast, with the husband still unshaved and the wife still wearing her hairstyling equipment.

Accuracy is sometimes gotten out of perspective. Under certain circumstances accuracy is important. But it is not equally important under all circumstances, as some couples seem to assume. Some husbands and wives constantly correct one another, even in the presence of other persons, in a way that amounts practically to nagging. The least inaccuracy calls forth a correction, although it may have no bearing on the point of a story or the interpretation of a report of personal events.

Overemphasis upon sex in marriage is a symptom of distorted perspective. Sex is not all of marriage, any more than the room in the penny experiment is all copper. The more unsuccessful their sexual adjustment is, the more prominent sex is likely to be in a couple's thinking.

If an individual fails to see self in relation to the total situation and to the spouse—if, for example, personal desire, selfish whims, and hurt feelings are given precedence over the success of the marriage—perspective is lacking. If the marriage is more important than part of it, what difference does it make who takes the initiative in patching up a quarrel during which perspective has been momentarily lost? In this latter statement, however, the implication is that after patching up the quarrel the couple's relationship will be a happy one and the marriage successful. It is conceivable, too, that the relationship as it is or as it would have to be reestablished would not be more valuable than the feelings of one of the parties if the latter were seriously affected. When we suggest that it makes no difference who takes the initiative in patching up a quarrel, we are referring to the ups and downs of normal marriage rather than to the steady trends of alienation which, in some cases, have already led the couple to the brink of disaster.

Failure to think of successful marriage as a goal worth striving for is a symptom of lack of perspective. Unawareness that success requires effort, understanding, and idealism and is not incidental and automatic is a symptom. Unwillingness to go more than halfway to achieve success is another.

Working out a successful marriage may be compared to writing a theme. If the theme does not seem perfect after the first attempt, the writer does not tear it up and start anew with an entirely new subject and then repeat this process again and again until a perfect finished product is achieved without revision. Rather, a topic is chosen, then worked and reworked; words are changed here and there, sentences and paragraphs are written and rewritten, new ideas are injected and irrelevant ones deleted, and so on until the final product is what the writer wants it to be and is as well done as capacities permit.

If successful marriage is a goal worth striving for, it may be set up as a definite objective. Instead of following the path of least resistance, the couple may work toward that objective. Suppose that you are going on an automobile trip. Someone asks you where you are going, and you say, "I don't know; I'll tell you when I get there." You step into your car and drive down every well-paved road merely because it is well-paved. You may arrive somewhere; you may not. That would not be your plan. First, you would decide upon a destination. Next you would work out an itinerary. Then you would take the roads leading to your destination, even though some of them were rough, the driving was sometimes hard, and you had to make some detours. You would not turn back at the first detour or stretch of poor pavement. It is sensible to lay out the best possible itinerary, but that is not the same as following the path of least resistance.

Generalizing on too few instances is an indication of lack of perspective. When an individual makes *once* become *always* or *never*, the whole is not seen because of the part. "You never remember a thing I tell you," says the irate wife whose husband has forgotten a single instruction. "You're always spending too much money," says the husband whose wife's latest shopping venture has been expensive. The person who concludes that the inevitable little mistakes of the first years of marriage represent permanent maladjustments lacks perspective.

A philosophy of life enabling a couple to meet a crisis is a factor contributing to successful adjustment; its absence is a factor contributing to failure. A mature person knows that sooner or later in everyone's life crises come. Friends and relatives die. Illness occurs. Children are born. Disappointments of one sort or another impose themselves upon existence. The inability to make the best of an unchangeable situation or to tolerate a situation until there is time or opportunity for change may lead to poor adjustment. At times people must learn to live with insoluble problems. Someone has said, "It takes internal props to withstand external pressure." Someone else has said, "Not all the water in the seven seas can sink a ship unless that water gets inside." A philosophy of life to meet a crisis supplies those internal props and acts as the agency for keeping the water from getting inside.

Tremendous Trifles

Loss of perspective is also apparent when a couple get to the point where anything that happens in the marriage in a way represents the entire marriage, and conflict over a relatively inconsequential incident can be almost as bitter as if the whole marriage were threatened. In one case, for example, the wife went to the refrigerator to get a drink of cold water. On a shelf she found a can of fruit opened but uncovered. She called her husband and said, "Why do you leave a can of fruit in the refrigerator like this?" He retorted, "Why should I cover it when I'm soon going to eat it?" An argument ensued. Out of the argument grew an evening-long quarrel which the couple considered serious enough to discuss with a counselor the next day.

A *tremendous trifle* is something which may be considered a tremendous irritant to one spouse but a mere trifle to the other. Examples of tremendous trifles are leaving dirty clothes lying around the floor, leaving hair in the bathroom sink, not rinsing off dirty dishes at the time they are used, allowing catchup to accumulate around the top of the bottle, leaving newspapers around the house (or throwing them away too soon), leaving a wet shower mat down, forgetting to take money or other objects out of pockets before clothes are washed, always running "a few minutes late," always "missing" the wastebasket when throwing tissues away, and drinking directly out of bottles from the refrigerator. The list is endless.

It can be observed that it is the tremendous trifles that couples mostly quarrel about in their marriages. Rarely do a couple sit down and have a major argument about their political or religious beliefs, for example. But they may quarrel once a week about allowing the house to turn into a terrible mess. Marital breakdown is rarely caused by just one circumstance or one issue. It is much more often a result of a multitude of factors—and tremendous trifles play their part.

Thus, "little things" often contribute to failure in marriage. The term *little things* may be defined only from a specific point of view. They may be "little" to a casual observer, but not to the couple themselves. Much depends upon the relative significance assigned to them, upon perspective. When perspective is lacking, "little things" may damage a marriage. Deriving the suggestion from a hunting situation, someone has said, "If you spend all your time swatting mosquitoes, you will never shoot your deer." Some couples give so much attention to "tremendous trifles" that they miss the essential meaning of marriage.

One tremendous trifle which illustrates this point and about which there are many jokes, perhaps because it actually is a problem in many a marriage, is toothpaste. Individuals who leave the cap off or squeeze the tube in the middle are often a source of irritation to those who put the cap back on or squeeze the tube from the end, assuming that their way is naturally the only right way and failing to see that their perfectionism and criticism may be a source of annoyance for the individual whose approach to toothpaste is less meticulous and more casual. Some couples start each day with conflict over toothpaste, sacrificing for a trifle the good spirit that might otherwise begin another day of their marriage. One student reported that her parents had had such conflict over toothpaste during their entire marriage. Her mother was a "middle-squeezer" and her father an "end-squeezer." On their twentieth wedding anniversary they discussed the problem, and each bought the other a tube of toothpaste, thus ending two decades of conflict by a very simple means that might have been thought of years before.

This matter of tremendous trifles is two-sided, however. It is partly a question of whose perspective is involved. It is granted that "I" should have perspective on the little things that "you" do. But if "you" permit an accumulation of little things which annoy "me" because "you" do not have perspective on "me" and the marriage, if your self-concern outweighs your other-concern, you cannot expect "me" to live in oblivious complacency.

Focal Points

If there is tension in a marital situation, anything may become a focal point for conflict. The focal point may be relatively unimportant and may not be the true cause or even closely connected with it. With a couple, as with an individual, the obvious cause of behavior is not always the real one. Conflict in marriage is very obtrusive to the couple who experience it. If it becomes serious and permeating enough to produce failure, that failure, impending or actual, is extremely important to both husband and wife. Failure in marriage is a "big" thing. Therefore, the couple, oversimplifying, reason that it must have a "big" cause, and they seek for one. Among the most obvious, most tangible, possible "big" causes are such things as children, sex, money, in-laws, religion, and use of leisure time. Sometimes one of these is the true cause of conflict. At other times it is only the hook on which the conflict is hung; and the true causes are numerous subtle influences less obvious and hence less readily analyzed. Failure is usually the result of numerous contributing factors rather than the result of a single, simple cause, no matter how important this one cause may seem.

Depending upon personalities and circumstances, the same things that serve to bind some couples closer together serve to wedge others apart. Children, in-laws, property, money, religion, sex, and numerous other factors may serve either as adhesive or as repellent, depending upon the way the couple react to them. None of these factors can produce conflict unless the couple have attitudes and personality traits that permit conflict to arise. Some marriages succeed while containing elements that contribute to the failure of others. Maladjustment is largely a subjective process, a result of whole personalities reacting to a total situation. The situation alone cannot produce maladjustment.

Focal points may also be considered in a positive sense. A couple may further their marital adjustment by centering their marriage on meaningful points of interest. This does not imply permanent crystallization. It implies only the employment of a kind of emotional centripetal force that draws them together. For example, a child or their home may be a focal point. So may participation in a common activity such as a hobby. A regular ritual of some sort, such as a traditional manner of celebrating a special occasion, for example, a holiday or birthday, may serve periodically to bring attitudes, memories, and aspirations to a focus. A couple with imagination and ingenuity may set up such focal points most meaningful to themselves.

IMPORTANT ASPECTS OF MARITAL FUNCTIONING

Use of Money

The use of money may serve as a binding factor for a couple, affording common interests and establishing common goals. It may also be a focal point for, or a cause of, conflict. One couple may find happiness on an income identical to that of another couple who are suing for divorce because of it.

Amount of income and its relation to happiness are also relative to expectations. If both husband and wife are accustomed to a modest standard of living, or if they are committed to an occupational field in which monetary returns are typically low, they may never hope for a large income. If, however, their expectations run higher than their possible income, the amount of the latter may be a thorn in their flesh.

So far as marital happiness is concerned, the actual method of handling income is not so important as the means by which the couple arrive at the employment of that method. If the method is agreeable to both partners, almost any method can be made to work successfully. If, on the other hand, the method represents an imposition upon one partner by the other, through either insistence or irresponsibility, and it is therefore reluctantly tolerated rather than willingly accepted, any method can give rise to conflict.

There is no standard budget, no distribution of income that will automatically fit every couple's needs. Published materials help, but they alone cannot solve a couple's problem. To expect them to do so would be the same as to expect every one to wear the same size mail-order clothes.

A budget need not be considered absolutely inflexible. As unpredictable needs or opportunities arise, it may be adjusted to them. Furthermore, the couple must expect to make mistakes. The budget is a tool, a means to an end. It is not an end in itself and should not become master rather than servant. It need not be so much in evidence at all times that it becomes a source of irritation, thus defeating its own purpose. It can become a bone of contention, a cause of friction, a source of conflict. But so can a hand-to-mouth handling of income.

Both husband and wife are consumers, and modern economic conditions are putting an ever-increasing responsibility upon the consumer. This is especially true of the wife, since ordinarily so much of the family purchasing is done by her. One of the modern couple's chief functions has become their role as specialists in consumption. By careful buying to lower expenses, they may raise the relative family income.

Use of Leisure Time

Leisure time may be defined as time that is free from economic pursuits, including homemaking. It is time in which the individual has greater freedom of choice as to how it shall be employed. Modern social conditions have increased the amount available to both men and women. They have also created new opportunities and new problems.

Young couples frequently are not aware of the importance of the use of leisure or of the fact that its use may constitute a problem in marriage. An opinion often expressed by students is that a person who has leisure will know what to do with it and there is no use talking about it. Experience proves that many do not know what to do with leisure time. They pass time instead of using it. They spend it instead of investing it. The expression "kill time" is indicative of a not uncommon attitude. The use of time is important in marriage because it is usually in their nonworking hours that husband and wife are most closely associated. Their leisure-time pursuits contribute, for good or ill, to the development of their relationship. Those pursuits may become focal points in either a positive or a negative sense. They may serve as common interests or as points of departure for conflict. They may increase tension or dissipate it. They may preserve romance or allow it to atrophy. It is not essential that all these pursuits should represent common interests. In marriage it is important that there be individual interests as well as those held by both partners.

A husband's schedule is often more rigid than a wife's because of the difference in occupational pressure, unless, of course, she too is employed. Both members of the couple may budget their time so that they will have leisure together. If they do the "unpostponables" first, they can adjust schedules so that leisure-time pursuits may be included. If, on the other hand, they have an inclination to do postponables first, they may find that there are things they must do when their spouse is free.

One source of conflict in marriage is boredom. When two people are bored, they may magnify little things in their relationship because their perspective is distorted. Little things occurring in a setting of interesting activities and imaginative, enthusiastic approaches to life are more likely to remain little things. But the same little things occurring in a setting where there is little to contrast them with or to draw attention from them may loom out of proportion to their importance. Also, open conflict over them may break the monotony. It is difficult to understand how intelligent, educated people with all their faculties can be bored in present-day America, where all about them are opportunities for interesting pursuits. Yet the fact remains that some of them are bored, and their marriages often suffer because of their boredom. One place where a start can be made in making life and marriage more interesting is in the imaginative, creative use of leisure time.

Motivation

One of the most important factors in making marriage succeed is motivation, commitment, the will to succeed. This suggests setting up marriage as a goal toward which the couple will strive, taking care that other goals, perhaps worthy in themselves—such as occupational ambition or child rearing—do not divert the couple's efforts from achieving success in the marriage itself and lead them to relegate marriage to a position subordinate to that of their other objectives.

Such commitment involves work, not in the sense of employment, but rather in the sense of the expenditure of time and effort for marital success. Such effort entails ego surrender, that is, a conviction that the success of the relationship is more important than the feelings of the persons in it; self-discipline in channeling one's own behavior; and the application of patience and perseverance to problem solving. It entails ingenuity in providing new experience in marriage so that there is no "letdown." This does not imply that there must be as much romanticizing in marriage as there is before the wedding. But it does imply that marriage does not inevitably have to involve a loss of enthusiasm and adventure.

The demands of family living make some routine in marriage necessary. But routine may be servant, not master. It may be a means to an end rather than an end in itself. Some husbands and wives grow to take each other for granted. Each one becomes a sort of habit to the other. "Marriage," said Balzac, "must continually vanquish a monster that devours everything: the monster of habit." Habit may destroy spontaneity. It may make husband and wife as unstimulating and as predictable as a perpetual-motion machine. Constant rubbing in one spot may wear the garments of romance so thin that the original cloth is no longer seen because of the patches.

Why should two complex personalities lack variety in their relationship? Monogamy and monotony are not synonymous. Seeking variety in the sense of discovering new facets of the other spouse's personality, looking for new things that can be done together or old ones that may be revived—this makes for sustained interest and prevents the marriage from falling into a rut of habit. It is possible to have variety in a marriage relationship, rather than a variety of partners where there is only a partially complete relationship with each one.

Habit is not an unadulterated evil, however. Many of its aspects may enrich a marriage. For example, habits of courtesy make any relationship smoother. It is puzzling to know why some people seem to assume that a wedding ceremony creates the privilege of being rude, that it is a signal for discontinuing toward husband or wife the courtesies that are exhibited toward less meaningful persons.

Acceptance

By the fact of voluntary participation and consensus a wedding implies each person's acceptance of the other as that person is. This does not preclude expectation of growth. It does raise a serious question about the advisability of attempted reform. To accept another person as that person is does not mean that there is never any conflict or irritation in marriage. It does mean that conflict and irritation are kept in perspective. Ideally, this acceptance should be complete and unqualified.

In day-by-day living, however, with more or less ordinary personalities, there may be limits to acceptance. The threshold of intolerance is lower in some persons, higher in others. For example, what if there is found a considerable discrepancy between role expected and role played? A man expects his wife to be highly domestic and maternal but finds himself married to a woman who rejects the wife-mother role in favor of employment. A woman expects her husband to be an interested, attentive, affectionate companion but marries a man who is "all business" and is no more romantic than the proverbial "bump on a log." How far can a person be expected to go in accepting such things as impotence, frigidity, infidelity, mental illness, homosexuality, brutality, or what is defined as immorality?

Some couples, even with a problem less serious than any of those mentioned, find themselves at what seems like a crossroads in their marriage; they reach a low point two or three years after the wedding. It appears to them that their marriage has deteriorated to the point where they have almost given up. Yet they still cling to the marriage in the hope that something can be made of it. Their problem is basically a discrepancy between what their marriage is and what they hoped it would be. If they go on as they have been going, the marriage may terminate in failure. On the other hand, they may, if they will, take a new inventory. They may reevaluate the marriage and each other in terms of actual present assets and liabilities rather than in terms of their dreams at the time of the wedding. Often, at this point, if they can accept one another and the marriage as each is, they can work out a good marriage, even though it may not coincide exactly with their earlier, perhaps less realistic, expectations.

This process of reevaluation plus new acceptance, combined with more realistic expectations based on greater insight into what each spouse is and what each has to contribute to the marriage, is not infrequently called for in a young marriage. This is especially true if the couple knew each other only a relatively brief period and therefore not too well before the wedding. They married with romantic enthusiasm at a high pitch and a great deal of momentum generated by physical appeal. They are carried along for a while but ultimately reach the point where their marriage, if it is to endure, must be put on a more realistic footing. Like opening a Christmas gift in fancy wrapping, they need to strip the unreality from their expectations and look inside to see what they actually have to work with. Klemer (1965) refers to unrealistic expectations as a major cause of what he terms "marriage disease."

Communication

Communication is important in marriage, although it cannot be perfect and complete. An awareness of this inevitable incompleteness, however, is itself a contribution to marital adjustment. Unawareness, on the other hand, may create an impasse.

One often hears it said that when a couple have a marital problem, they should talk it over. So far as it goes and to the extent to which this implies getting the problem out into the open instead of "bottling it up," this is good. But because of the inevitable incompleteness of communication, discussion is not an automatic solution to all problems. There can be discussion without communication.

How may communication in marriage be improved? There is no formula, no shortcut, no "quick and easy way." But a few suggestions may be made. Both the individual who has something to say and the individual who is expected to listen must be motivated to try to improve their mutual communication.

Communication is not a one-sided process. There is a difference between talking and communicating.

There is also a difference between listening and hearing. *Hearing* connotes merely the perception of sound. *Listening* connotes attention to sound in an effort to derive meaning. Granted functioning auditory apparatus, sound may be thrust upon an individual in a way that makes hearing unavoidable. Or the sound may not be perceived because the hearer's mind is "closed" to it. Listening would involve the hearer's mind being "open" through attention, interest, and concern. A couple are having an angry quarrel. They are shouting at each other. They cannot avoid hearing the sound. Neither pays attention to what the other loudly says, and the exchange goes on as if each were reciting a monolog. Another couple discuss a topic of mutual concern. They are eager to reach an understanding. Each lets the other know that what is being said is being "received" and considered. The first couple are talking. The second couple are communicating.

The content of communication may be resisted because of the tone of voice or attitude of the speaker; a listener reacts not only to what is said but also to the manner in which it is said.

Listening is an active, rather than a passive, art. One person can facilitate another's speaking or make it more difficult by the way listening is done. If attention is diverted or haphazard, if the listener does something like read the paper or drum on the table with fingers, the speaker's problem is increased. Conversely, the speaker cannot expect full attention if the listener is addressed in such a way that it is practically impossible; for example, a husband talks to his wife as she puts dinner on the table or bathes the baby, and she talks to him when he is sleepy or tense from business worries.

Luce (1970) points out that people "walk to different drumbeats." There is individuality in tempo and rhythm. "Individual variation in time structure appears to be quite as pronounced as is variation in athletic talent, height, and temperament." One's ability to think, discriminate, solve problems, and do tasks, as well as one's feelings, alertness, and sensitivity, all change within the twenty-four-hour cycle. "We are different persons at 10 A.M. than at 10 P.M." If husband and wife seek to improve their mutual communication, attention needs to be given to the point in each individual's time structure at which communication is attempted.

There are what may be termed *selective attention* and *selective inattention*. What the listener wants to hear is heard; what the listener does not want to hear is "tuned out." Selective inattention may occur when a worried husband hears nothing of what a wife says except a reference to the money she spent in shopping, or a tired wife "tunes out" all of a husband's report of his day at work except his mention of his business partner's going on a weekend trip with his family. Selective inattention, as suggested earlier, is also one of the reasons for the ineffectiveness of nagging.

Not even commonly used words necessarily have the same meaning for both persons. Hence it becomes important for each person to seek to learn the other's vocabulary, not only the colloquialisms and special words used but also the shades of meaning and emotional tones of words. For some persons certain words are emotionally supercharged, in the sense of being especially unacceptable, because they are reacted to against a backdrop of highly individualized personal experience and point of view.

A speaker ordinarily assumes that the meaning of a word used will evoke the same meaning for the listener. But, because of experience, the listener may interpret the word differently or give it no meaning at all.

Use of a word does not by itself create understanding of it. Communication may be improved by ascertaining the meaning of words, especially key words. This may seem too obvious to mention. Yet people continue to talk without knowing whether the person listening knows what they are talking about. Harper (1958), a marriage counselor of long experience, says, "One of the most common sources of communication difficulty in a marriage relationship is that situation where one spouse *assumes* he knows what the other means."

Looking at this problem another way, we may say that a word fits more or less well or not at all into a listener's frame of reference. If it fits reasonably well, speaker and listener communicate. If it does not fit, no communication occurs. Speaker and listener may have frames of reference sufficiently similar in some respects to permit the word to fit even though their total frames of reference are different. In Exhibit 10-4, the shaded circle represents a given word, as used by speaker A. The word fits into the frame of reference of listener B, but not into the frame of reference of listener C. Hence A can communicate with B but not with C.

Communication is furthered to the degree that each person is aware of special sensitivities, fears, values, biases, and points of resistance of the other person so that no unnecessary barriers to communication are introduced. Communication is also furthered to the degree that each individual is confident that there will be understanding and acceptance, not judgment and rejection. Hence, there is freedom to divulge thoughts and feelings, worries and concerns, failures and mistakes. Masters and Johnson (1970) recommend that couples learn to communicate and "exchange vulnerabilities."

Insight into the other person's handling of facts and ideas facilitates communication. Are facts used with accuracy, or with distortion and exaggeration? Are new facts welcomed or resisted? The placard which reads, "Don't bother me with facts; my mind's made up" is intended to be humorous, but it is descriptive of a large proportion of the population, especially regarding the nonmaterial aspects of life and human relations. An understanding of the topic under discussion also facilitates communication. Two people can hardly communicate effectively unless they are talking about the same thing.

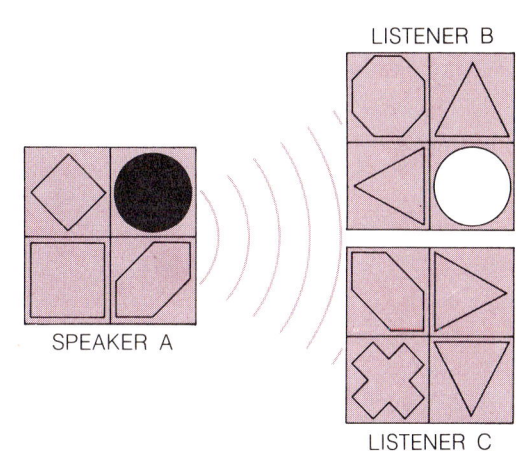

Exhibit 10-4 The relationship of a word to frames of reference.

Fear

Various sorts of fear may play a part in marital adjustment. Fear of submerging one's own personality in that of the spouse, fear of losing one's liberty, fear of one's own abilities (or rather of their lack or inadequacy) may elicit reactions that are unfavorable to adjustment.

Fear of losing the affection and fidelity of the other person is common. This is *jealousy*. Jealousy is a fear reaction. There are two shades of meaning for the term. If an individual has an intense desire to preserve something meaningful and would defend it against any attempt to destroy it, but in fighting for it is confident of winning, the person may be said to be jealous. If, on the other hand, an individual seeks to preserve something meaningful but *fears* losing it, the person also may be said to be jealous. Grold (1972) refers to jealousy as "the rage at being dispensed with or betrayed." The first type of jealousy may be illustrated by a couple's efforts to preserve their home against the attack of some relative seeking to destroy their happiness. The second type is that exhibited by the husband who sees another man manifesting interest in his wife and fears that he will be unable to retain her affection and fidelity against the onslaught of a seemingly more attractive person. The husband may not analyze his fear to this extent; but it is present, nevertheless. His reaction may be anger or hate, as far as he is aware of it; but at bottom it is due to insecurity.

Jealousy may be divided into two types upon another basis, namely, (1) justifiable jealousy, that based upon observation of the behavior of the spouse; and (2) unjustifiable jealousy, that based not upon fact but only upon the insecurity, inferiority feeling, or suspicion of the jealous person. In the first type, the wife may know that her husband is interested in another woman and may feel helpless to hold him. In the second type, the husband has exhibited no suspicious behavior; but because the wife feels insecure, she becomes jealous when he no more than talks with a woman business associate or converses with the woman who sits next to him at dinner.

For several reasons jealousy is self-defeating. (1) Love and fidelity cannot be forced through suspicion and surveillance. The only love worth having is that which is given freely and voluntarily. (2) The other person resents the lack of trust. (3) Even when justifiable, jealousy is not addressed to the true causes of the infidelity. Therefore, effort which might be directed to the solution of the problem is dissipated without gain. (4) A jealous person is likely to be hard to live with and, therefore, is likely to become unattractive. This may make the spouse lose interest and do exactly what it was feared would be done, thus furthering the end the jealousy was intended to prevent. (5) Jealousy tends to be a symptom of immaturity and is often part of an immature pattern of behavior not conducive to happy marriage. (6) Jealousy often involves projection of blame. The jealous person does not say, "I am jealous because I am fearful and insecure," but rather "I am jealous because of what you are doing."

It is not the fact of jealousy alone, but also its expression, that affects a marriage. Expression of it entails criticism, suspicion, questioning, nagging, demands for explanation, displays of temper, moodiness, loss of respect, attempted domination, restriction of freedom, or any of a number of other irritating and irksome attributes and experiences. Sometimes the jealous spouse refuses to believe the truth. The more the other person tries to explain that there is no cause for jealousy, the more jealous the first one becomes, insisting that the explanation is only an attempt to "cover up." Thus the couple sink deeper and deeper into the quicksand of alienation.

Jealousy, however, may have one mitigating quality that compensates in a minor way for its unpleasantness and may make the bitter pill easier to swallow. The fact that an individual manifests it may be an indication of not wishing to lose the other person and wanting to preserve their relationship. This thought is worth the consideration of anyone who has a jealous spouse.

Domination

The results of actual or attempted domination are relative and depend upon the personalities involved. By and large, however, domination is unhealthful. Some marriages become what might be termed "battles for prestige." The question to which the couple seek the answer is not "How may we work best together?" but "Who will give in?" (Knopf, 1932). An individual who makes marriage a power struggle because he insists upon exercising masculine authority or because she has a personality need to dominate is seeking to get his or her own way rather than to contribute to the adjustment of the marriage.

Some individuals resort to "illness" in order to dominate a spouse. Some marry persons who are physically disabled; behind a pretense of pity and sympathy may be a wish to dominate. One not uncommon type of attempted domination is a demand for gratitude. "If it were not for me, you wouldn't be where you are today"; "I've put up with a lot for you"; "Think what you were before I married you." When gratitude is voluntary and spontaneous, it is good for both concerned. When it is demanded, it is likely to become resentment. It throws new light upon the thing done and upon the person who makes the demand.

When the demand for gratitude takes the form of supposed martyrdom, playing up sacrifices and flaunting them in the face of the other person, it becomes especially insidious. "A sacrifice labeled as such is like a gift with the price tag deliberately left on; it is more of an insult than a compliment" (Wile and Winn, 1929).

Overdependence

Marriage is for mature persons; the overdependent, parasitic, clinging-vine type of individual does not fall into that category. Some dependence of one spouse on the other is natural and desirable. When it reaches the point of evasion of responsibility, failure to make a contribution to the success of the marriage, or inability to carry out one's part of the bargain, it is detrimental.

Overdependence may also be a symptom of immaturity in that it may result partly from narcissism, that is, self-love. A wife, for example, may identify herself with her husband and by inference praise her wise choice of spouse by continually calling attention to his virtues. She subordinates herself to him, bowing, scraping, yes-yesing, taking his slightest wish as a command. To the husband this may become tiresome. If he actually believes that he is all she seems to think he is, this type of behavior may affect his personality.

What sometimes passes for overdependence may actually be domination. By submission and yielding, by manifesting an apparent need for help and guidance, and by expecting another to make one's decisions and assume one's responsibilities, one person may in part control the other's behavior.

"Homeopathic Remedies"

Years ago there was a school of medical thought one of whose tenets was: To cure a disease there should be administered a drug which in a healthy person would produce symptoms similar to those of the illness. For example, to cure a fever, the physician would administer a drug that would raise the patient's temperature. This was homeopathic medicine, "homeopathic" being derived from two Greek words meaning "like" and "suffering."

In medical practice homeopathic remedies are outmoded. In marriage they should be, but unfortunately they are not. Such remedies in marriage take the form of retaliation in kind. An attempt is made to remedy a maladjustment by deliberately doing what the other person has done, when that proved annoying, instead of seeking and remedying the real cause of the maladjustment. In other words, there is a duplication of the undesirable behavior of the spouse. A wife is hurt by something the husband does. To remedy the injury and prevent his doing it again, she intentionally hurts him. A wife is sarcastic; the husband responds with sarcasm. Criticism is countered with criticism. One attempts to dilute one's own offense or error by pointing out that the other does the same thing or something equally bad. A husband is extravagant. To cure him of his weakness for spending money and to show him the difficulties caused by an extravagant spouse, the wife becomes extravagant. This is supposed to balance the budget and also to change the husband's behavior. "Homeopathic remedies" balance neither the financial nor the marital ledger. Two minuses do not make a plus, nor two wrongs a right. Such behavior not only fails to alleviate the condition toward which it is directed, but it has a tendency to multiply irritations, since the number of offensive stimuli as well as the sensitivity of both persons is increased. Each one reacts to the other's action plus the other's attitude.

Tension

Tension may be defined as a physiological, emotional, or mental state tending to give rise to activity. The activity is not necessarily directed toward removing the cause of the tension. The tension tends to spread from one area of life to others, to be cumulative, and to explode as a result of a slight stimulus which may have little or no relation to the cause of the tension. For example, a man has been harried all day by complaining, cantankerous clients. His emotions have been frequently aroused, and fatigue has gradually increased. For professional reasons he has had to maintain an appearance of patience, good nature, and self-control. At the end of the day he goes home. One of the children does some trivial thing to disturb him, and he explodes in a fit of anger. The gun is loaded, and the child pulls the trigger. The explosion is not directed toward removing the cause of the tension, and the stimulus has little relation to the cause.

Some couples are skilled at reading the signs of each other's tension. Others are not. It would not be unthinkable to utilize special signals as a means of letting each other know that unusual tension exists and of appealing to the other for patience and consideration. Such signals may seem silly and juvenile, but they are not so silly as a pointless quarrel growing out of tension and precipitated by something inconsequential. Also, the use of such simple signals indicates that each spouse is aware of his or her own tension and hypersensitivity; this is the first step toward an effective handling of the situation.

Tension may be dissipated so that the cumulative effect is prevented and relief is afforded. Every married couple and every individual need what might be termed *tension relievers*. Often a little ingenuity, like a little oil, is all that is needed to smooth troubled water or prevent friction from wearing down a relationship. A couple may develop techniques for letting off steam as it accumulates, instead of waiting until it blows up their marriage. It is difficult to say just what these tension relievers may be for a given couple because each case is individual. Each couple may through observation, experiment, and the exercise of imagination determine them and put them into effect.

Sometimes, in spite of all efforts at prevention, tension gives rise to quarreling. It is somewhat risky either to recommend or deliberately to plan upon quarreling as a means of reducing tension. Only a rare couple are equipped to handle it in that way. There is no way of guaranteeing that both persons will react to it in the same manner. There is too great a possibility of its producing more tension than it was intended to relieve. When and if, however, a couple do quarrel, there are several things which they might try to keep in mind. We might term these "rules" for quarreling. (1) Unless cumulative experience suggests the contrary, each may assume that what the other says and does during the quarrel is the product of the tension involved and is not always a true reflection of that individual's personality. (2) Whatever judgments are made during the quarrel should be reevaluated at a time of less tension. The judgments upon which actions are based are better formed at a time when the individual is relatively calm and has regained perspective. (3) Both may try to keep the quarrel within bounds. It need not be allowed to spread to aspects of their relationship, their situation, or their personalities that had nothing to do with its origin. The couple need not shift from attacking the problem to attacking each other. (4) A quarrel may be kept private. It need not be allowed to occur in the presence of others. (5) A quarrel may further a couple's adjustment if, instead of letting it generate ill will and insecurity, the couple forget it when it is over, let bygones be bygones, carry no grudges, and take a step forward in the clarified atmosphere following the storm. (6) Since the marriage is more important than the feelings of either party and in most cases much more important than the difference which precipitated the quarrel, it is important that each be willing to go more than halfway to effect a reconciliation. Sometimes the first step in this direction is easier for the person less at fault because pride is not so great an obstacle to an apology. (7) The sooner after the quarrel the couple return to the pattern of affection and conversation which characterizes their marriage, the easier it will be; the longer they delay such a return, the more difficult it is likely to be.

In spite of the fact that we pride ourselves on living in a scientific age, most of us do not approach life scientifically. Actually we live in an age in which science is given a great deal of attention and in which science and scientists contribute to a technology that is widely enjoyed. But the "average person's" world view and his or her attitude toward, and relationships with, other people are highly colored by assumptions, impressions, tradition, folklore, emotions, and wishful thinking. These make fertile soil in which to germinate tension, argument, and quarreling because they are more likely to befog the need for facts than to lead to an elucidation of them. When two people argue, each one is convinced that truth is being defended. If each could see that it is not necessarily truth, but in all probability an unsubstantiated point of view, less tension would be generated.

In-laws

It is a stereotypic notion that in-laws are selfish, scheming, short-sighted, prying, interfering, demanding, or malicious. There are, to be sure, those who have not kept pace with the development of their children and fail to realize that the latter have grown up and become independent. There are others, however, who are unselfish, generous, farsighted, and considerate. Some of them grow to be closer to the child-in-law than natural parents have been. Some in-laws make a real contribution to the success of a marriage and help a couple over rough spots in their adjustment. More is said about the first type, and there is a tendency to generalize upon them.

Whenever there is an in-law problem, the young couple as well as their parents are in the midst of it. But no person can have in-laws without being an in-law. Not all the friction is precipitated by the older generation. So much has been said about in-laws, so many jokes have been made about mothers-in-law, that they have acquired a regrettable reputation. As a result, young couples often enter marriage on the defensive, with a chip on the shoulder, so to speak, almost daring their in-laws to knock it off. If ever inadvertently or intentionally it is knocked off, the trouble begins.

In-law problems are not uncommon. The authors have had dozens of married couples in counseling who do not speak to their parents, who intentionally avoid them, who have been disowned, or who have in one way or another severed relations solely because the parents objected to their child's choice of a marriage partner or the circumstances surrounding the marriage. Most persons, of course, enjoy some degree of cordial relations with their parents and in-laws. When problems do exist, they seem to center on such topics as religion, celebration of holidays, amount of time spent with parents and in-laws, interference in decision making and child rearing, financial commitments, and care of the aged.

If there is a bona fide in-law problem, the young couple need first of all to be certain of their perspective. Is the success of their marriage to be put above everything else, even above attachment to parents? Husband and wife usually decide that the marriage comes first. The situation then calls for all the tact, diplomacy, and consideration the couple can command, but it calls for firmness and intelligence as well.

Understanding the problem faced by the couple's in-laws may help to facilitate adjustment. A family is an in-group; it exhibits cohesion. Even when the members are in conflict with each other, there is an inclination to stand united against external pressure and against members of the out-group. A child-in-law is a member of the out-group. It takes time and requires some readjustment fully to accept such a person as a member of the in-group. The individual is an outsider, and there are some things one does not ordinarily do with an outsider. One does not tell the outsider family secrets. One does not express affection for such a person without reserve. One does not appear in the individual's presence in a state of undress.

Parents acquire their natural child when it has no opinions to express, no prejudices, resentments, habits, tastes, or ideas of its own. The child is gradually assimilated into the family and molded by the parents to fit their pattern of life. The child-in-law is precipitated into the family, sometimes unexpectedly, sometimes against the family's will, and always with ideas, tastes, habits, and personality already developed. The mutual assimilation and adjustment of in-laws is not always easy. Anything that can serve to further the process is worth trying. What hinders the process is worth avoiding.

Law of Diminishing Returns

The law of diminishing returns is ordinarily mentioned in the field of economics. Freely interpreted, it may be applied to marriage. In economics this law suggests that as a series of units of a given economic good are acquired or consumed, each successive item in the series, though similar to the one preceding it, is less attractive or less valuable to the collector or consumer. For example, if a man is acquiring real estate, the tenth piece will be less important to him than the first or second piece, and the hundredth piece would be less important still. A similar thing would be true of cars, money in the bank, or clothes. Suppose a person is very hungry when sitting down to dinner. A first helping is consumed with great relish. A second helping is eaten enthusiastically, but not quite as enthusiastically as the first. A third, fourth, fifth helping, and so on, decrease in attractiveness until, if the person were put under pressure to eat more and still more, eventually the food would seem repulsive rather than attractive. Yet each helping of food is approximately like the ones before it.

The law of diminishing returns is applicable to a number of aspects of marriage. Perhaps its most important application is in connection with the couple's sexual experience. When sex is combined with love and integrated into a growing, expanding marital relationship, the sexual element itself is enriched. True, the couple may note a decrease in frequency of intercourse as time goes on, but this does not necessarily imply a decrease in interest, responsiveness, or meaning.

Principle of Least Interest

This principle, which we discussed in conjunction with dating in Chapter 4, also is applicable to marital relationships. According to this principle, when two persons are emotionally involved in a relationship, the conditions of the association will be dictated by and the relationship will be controlled by the person who has the lesser interest in it. The less involved individual can afford to make the greater demands because he or she has less at stake. The more involved individual is impelled to make more concessions because the discontinuance of the relationship would be more serious for him or her.

A similar and related but not identical principle is this: If a husband and wife have a pronounced difference in their degree of insight into the marital relationship and in their awareness of each other's needs and of the nature of marriage, the person with the greater insight and awareness often has to make the greater adjustment in order to assure the continuance of the relationship (Waller, 1951). This may seem at first glance to be unfair. But looking at it realistically, there may be no alternative.

If a relationship is dominated by the person with less interest in it and/or less insight into it, it is clear that in cases where the demands are excessive they may contribute to failure. In other cases, where the more interested, more insightful person can manage the relationship satisfactorily or can make the required adjustments, there can be success. In any case, however, there is likely to be loss of mutuality.

In some couples, one spouse continually attempts to put himself or herself into the "less interested" position by threatening divorce. This tactic often succeeds, since the other spouse may be so fearful of this threat that he or she gives in to the demands of the threatening spouse. In other cases, however, the tension produced by continual threats of this kind leads the spouse to agree to a divorce or even to initiate the action. Thus, continual efforts to put oneself in the position of "less interested" in order to gain concessions from a spouse may eventually become intolerable to that spouse.

TERMS TO BE LEARNED

acceptance	"homeopathic remedies"	perspective
alienation	in-group	predisposition
antagonistic cooperation	law of diminishing returns	principle of least interest
communication	marital adjustment	selective attention
conditioning	marital quality	selective inattention
conflict resolution	marital stability	surface phenomenon
contributing factor	motivation	tension
counseling	nagging	tension reliever
dyadic	out-group	threshold
ego surrender	personality	"tremendous trifle"

SELECTED READINGS

BACH, GEORGE R., AND PETER WYDEN: *The Intimate Enemy: How to Fight Fair in Love and Marriage*, William Morrow & Company, Inc., New York, 1968. (Paperback.) This book is based on experience with several hundred couples who were trained in "a system for programming individual aggression through ... constructive fighting" and whose marriage adjustment improved. Includes many case studies.

BAILARD, T. E., D. L. BIEHL, AND R. W. KAISER: *Personal Money Management*, Science Research Associates, Inc., Chicago, 1973. A family finance textbook that doubles as a valuable resource for anyone seeking basic information on financial topics.

BERNARD, JESSIE: "The Adjustments of Married Mates," in Harold T. Christensen (ed.): *Handbook of Marriage and the Family*, Rand McNally & Company, Chicago, 1964, chap. 17. The inevitability of conflict; concept of adjustment and maladjustment; adjustment as functional change; models of adjustment. Refers to many research studies.

BERNE, E.: *Games People Play*, Grove Press, New York, 1964. Transactional game analysis used to explain 120 of the games which people "jump, fall or get pushed into."

BIRD, JOSEPH, AND LOIS BIRD: *Marriage Is for Grownups: A Mature Approach to Problems in Marriage*, Image Books, Doubleday & Company, Inc., Garden City, N.Y., 1971. (Paperback.) A husband-wife team of marriage counselors discuss some of the problem areas in marriage, including communication, sex, use of alcohol, infidelity, and in-laws.

CROMWELL, R. E., AND D. H. OLSON (eds.): *Power in Families*, John Wiley and Sons, Inc., New York, 1975. Collection of articles covering theoretical, methodological, and substantive issues in family power.

FISHER, ESTHER OSHIVER: *Help for Today's Troubled Marriages*, Hawthorn Books, Inc., New York, 1968. An experienced marriage counselor discusses the genders and their roles, problems of marital adjustment including sex, children, in-laws, alcoholism, etc., and what marriage counseling can do to help. Includes many case histories.

GROSS, M. I., E. W. CRANDALL, AND M. W. KNOLL: *Management for Modern Families*, New York, 1973. An important text in the area of family management; see especially chap. 6, "Decision-making."

LOBSENZ, NORMAN M., AND CLARK W. BLACKBURN: *How to Stay Married*, Cowles Book Company, Inc., New York, 1968. Based on the experience of the Family Service Association of America, a counseling organization with more than 300 agencies and 3,000 social work counselors, which in 1968 alone served more than 2 million persons in over 400,000 families. Discusses various aspects of adjustment in marriage. Includes many case studies and a list of FSAA member agencies.

MACE, DAVID R., AND VERA MACE: *We Can Have Better Marriages If We Really Want Them*, Abingdon Press, Nashville, Tenn., 1974. Authors maintain that, rather than denouncing modern marriage as a failure and seeking alternatives to it, we should work to improve it. They make suggestions to this end. Authors have devoted their professional lives to this objective and are internationally renowned for their contributions.

McGINNIS, TOM: *Your First Year of Marriage*, Doubleday & Company, Garden City, N.Y., 1967. A book for the newly married and about-to-be-married. Discusses a variety of topics. The author tells the couple to "accept their uniqueness ... and to believe that what is mutually agreeable to them, and strengthens their unity, is good and right for them." Includes case histories. The author is a psychotherapist and marriage counselor.

MUDD, EMILY H., HOWARD E. MITCHELL, AND SARA B. TAUBIN: *Success in Family Living*, Association Press, New York, 1965. Successful families: what makes them so. Based on research on 100 "normal" families especially chosen because of their level of success.

PORTER, SYLVIA: *Sylvia Porter's Money Book*, Doubleday and Company, Inc., Garden City, N.Y., 1975. A noted columnist assembles financial management information, advice, and tips on a variety of topics relevant to every family.

SCANZONI, J.: *Sexual Beginning: Power Politics in the American Marriage*, Prentice-Hall, Inc., Englewood Cliffs, N.J., 1972. Discusses marital power as well as other aspects of the husband-wife relationship.

STEINMETZ, S. K., AND M. A. STRAUS (eds.): *Violence in the Family*, Dodd, Mead, and Co., New York, 1974. Readings in family dysfunction, specifically violence within the family.

TROELSTRUP, ARCH W.: *The Consumer in American Society: Personal and Family Finance*, 4th ed., McGraw-Hill Book Company, New York, 1970. Discussion of various aspects of money management and purchasing.

WAHLROOS, SVEN: *Family Communication: A Guide to Emotional Health*, The Macmillan Company, New York, 1974. "A practical and useful description of what it is that interferes with the communication between one person and another, together with specific suggestions and rules concerning how to counteract such interference." "A common-sense guide to better communication in the family." Author is a clinical psychologist of many years experience in counseling.

Chapter 11

Sex in Marriage

The reader may wonder why this text contains a chapter on sex in *marriage* when, as indicated earlier, a large proportion of females and an even larger proportion of males have already had sexual intercourse before the wedding. The reasons are several: (1) Regardless of the fact that many men and women have had premarital intercourse, the fact remains that not everyone has, and there is not agreement, through research or otherwise, on the percentage who have. There are many sexually inexperienced individuals who marry. This text contains discussions of other topics, such as choice of marriage partner, divorce and remarriage, abortion, and childbirth, even though some readers may not have had and may never have experience in these areas. So it is with a discussion of premarital and marital sexual behavior. (2) Many of the persons who have had premarital intercourse have had casual, infrequent, "hit-and-run" experiences which have not permitted sufficient time for an adequate sexual relationship to develop. (3) If it is true, as counseling experience reveals, that many married couples do not know what they need to know about sex, it must be even more true that many unmarried couples have not learned all that they need to learn. (4) Disillusioning early marital experiences brought to counselors' attention suggest that many people enter marriage unprepared for the sexual aspect of it. (5) Only a minority of Americans plan to remain permanently unmarried or to make marriage a temporary relationship. Regardless of their premarital experience, most Americans expect (at least hope) some day to make a commitment to a relationship they expect will be permanent. This may call for a reevaluation of their sexual attitudes and behavior and the degree of their understanding. (6) Discussing sex in the context of marriage throws more light on sex in any relationship than discussing it in a nonmarital context throws light on sex in marriage.

Of course, some individuals do know a good deal about sex whether or not they are married. But even for such persons a review of the topic is not entirely inappropriate, since no one knows all that there is to be known, and anyone who thinks he or she does is in great need of a critical evaluation of his or her own point of view. Every discussion of sex—including this one and those that claim to tell you "everything you've always wanted to know"—has limitations. So there is always room for further understanding and insight.

SEX AND MARRIAGE

Would there be marriage if there were no sex? Perhaps not. It is the sexual and reproductive element that makes marriage different from other enduring human relationships. Sex is by no means the whole of marriage, but it is important. At times it is underemphasized, at other times overemphasized. Satisfactory adjustment sexually and in other ways (if they may be separated for purposes of discussion) go hand in hand, reacting one upon the other. Where there is failure, it may be cause or effect, depending upon circumstances. If the couple's adjustment in general is unsatisfactory, there may be a sexual element at the root of the difficulty. On the other hand, unsatisfactory sexual adjustment may be the result of nonsexual factors. Success in either increases the probability of success in the other, but neither guarantees the other (Clark and Wallin, 1965). More women in very happy marriages reach orgasm most of the time, but some women in very unhappy marriages also reach orgasm most of the time (Gebhard, 1970a). A research study of 2,372 women (Bell and Bell, 1972) revealed that 63 percent of the women who rated their marriage "good" or "very good" experienced orgasm every or almost every time they had intercourse, but 41 percent of the women who rated their marriage "fair," "poor," or "very poor" also experienced orgasm every or almost every time they had intercourse. Often sexual maladjustment is blamed for marital failure when it may be only one among several causes or the result of the factors that are working together to make the marriage fail. Under such circumstances sex may become a focal point, the hook on which the couple hang their marital wraps, so to speak.

Sexual adjustment and personality adjustment are aspects of a single process. There is not one problem of adjusting personalities in marriage and another separate one of sex. Sex in marriage is not a simply physical act, distinct in itself. It is one component of a complex whole, ramifying through other elements, which in their turn ramify through it.

THE NATURE OF SEX

As has been said before, the physical aspects of sex are important, but sexual experience is more than physical. Sex in a meaningful relationship contains emotional, other-than-physical elements which in a way are more important than the physical elements as such. In sexual union there is not only the contact of bodily organs but also the contact of personalities. "Sexual response represents interaction between people.... Sex removed from the positive influence of the total personality can become boring, unstimulating, and possibly immaterial" (Masters and Johnson, 1970). Unless a man and a woman share interests and values outside the bedroom and are linked by emotional bonds separated from a purely physical relationship, "sexual functioning is not sufficient in itself to establish enduring friendships" (Masters and Johnson, 1975).

However, it is incorrect to think of sex as being only psychic or emotional. The physical element can be neither avoided nor denied. It is the matrix out of which the psychic elements grow and is simultaneously one of their most potent means of expressions. Allan Fromme (1965) refers to sexual intercourse as "bodily conversation." It is a form of communication, just as a kiss or a handshake is a form of communication. In humans the sexual relationship goes beyond procreation. It is creative as well as procreative.

In lower animals the function of the sex act is reproduction. Animal mating is a transitory, fleeting experience often limited to one or more brief periods during the year. In humans, sexual experience is not limited either to the act itself or to a specific time. It is part of an extensive process of growth and discovery. In its broadest sense it is one of the most fruitful sources for some of the deepest, richest satisfactions known. Assuming that sex is for reproduction alone is like assuming that since we depend upon eyesight to move about and to make a living, seeing is for practical purposes only, and there should be created no beauty beyond the line, form, and color necessary for self-maintenance. It relegates humans to the level of the lower animal and denies persons the ability to take the raw materials of nature and out of them fashion a work of art.

We may think of the sexual urge as "instinctive," that is, as the product of inborn behavior patterns. We cannot, however, leave sexual adjustment in marriage to "instinct" because the biological urge is overlaid with tradition, habits, and attitudes, all of which make it more complex than the mating instinct of lower animals and, at the same time, more subject to inhibition, repression, and distortion. Instead of the sexual act being a simple, automatic, biological reaction for which little or no training is necessary and which training could not improve, in its most highly developed form in humans it becomes a complex type of behavior which depends not only upon physical desire and its satisfaction but also upon ideas, ideals, the influence of custom, past experience, and the attitude of husband and wife toward each other. It is as different from the mating of lower animals as the building of a home is different from the construction of a nest, as the composition of a symphony is different from the warbling of a bird.

AN UNDERSTANDING ATTITUDE TOWARD REACTIONS

Mutuality

The most nearly complete complementary relationship is sexual intercourse. It cannot be said that male and female derive identical satisfaction from such intercourse, because their experiences are not completely comparable. It can be said, however, that the experiences of males and females in intercourse are potentially equally intense and satisfying. Stating that sexual intercourse is the most nearly complete complementary relationship for a man and woman is obviously equivalent to saying that it is a shared experience. It is mutual. Women have natural sexual desire, just as men do, although it may take a somewhat different form and be aroused by different stimuli. When a woman does not experience such desire, there are two probable explanations. (1) It has been trained out of her. It has been so overlaid with inhibitions and/or fears that it cannot find expression. She has built up, or has had built up for her, a wall about herself so effectively corralling natural impulses that they have ceased to demand exercise. (2) There has been nothing in her experience up to date to arouse her desire. Some women remain so until their experiences with loving partners bring out an urge that they were not aware could exist. There are women who have a sexual urge but do not recognize it as such. Some refuse to admit what they feel. But there are relatively few women who for some underlying physiological cause are completely devoid of sexual interest. Unfortunately, our cultural tradition has all too frequently taught that women should be neuter, that sex is not "ladylike," and that sexual union is a masculine prerogative for masculine satisfaction to which a woman is bound to submit. There could be nothing further from the truth.

This is not equivalent to saying that all women have an equally ardent interest in sexual experience or an equal responsiveness to sexual stimuli. The sexual urge, like all things natural, falls on the normal curve of variability. Some women, like some men, are more passionate; some are less so. There is the possibility for all gradations from greatest to least. It is difficult to say that a woman who seems sexually cold is therefore unable to respond, even though we think in terms of inhibitions rather than physiology. All that may safely be said is that under a given set of circumstances she seems unresponsive. Under other circumstances she might be different. Furthermore, sexual unresponsiveness is the result of multiple causation. There is not one thing, no one condition, that will invariably produce it.

Let us go back for a moment to a point mentioned above. Young men and women are sometimes worried about their sexual adequacy. In their reading or in discussions they have learned that women experience a sexual urge, just as men do. Some women, however, have never experienced anything that they identified as sexual desire. Often they are not averse to a controlled amount of affection and fondling on the part of men, and they like to date. But they have come to feel that they are "undersexed" or that they will be unable to respond in the way they vaguely realize that women can. The probability is that after they fall in love, and perhaps marry, such women will eventually find themselves as responsive as any, allowing, of course, for individual variations. When they marry, however, such women need not insist upon maintaining their former attitude. They may permit themselves to move on to new experiences. In several cases, a woman who had been unresponsive before marriage found herself very responsive with her husband. Yet one woman seen in counseling cried for two years after the wedding each time she had intercourse and orgasm (climax) because early in life she had been taught that only "bad" women were passionate, and she continued to have feelings of guilt.

In the last analysis, sex cannot be shut out. Whether it finds natural expression or not, no matter where it is put, from one extreme of manifestation to the other, it will play a part in affecting the individual's life. If it is repressed or avoided, it is still not without its effect.

Male-Female Differences in Reaction

Although there is great variation, a woman's sexual arousal tends to be less spontaneous than a man's and depends to a greater extent upon her partner, his expression of affection, his own desire, and his insight, understanding, and skill as her lover. This is not meant to imply that she can leave her arousal entirely up to him. No matter what his skills, he cannot "give" her an orgasm. She has a responsibility for her own sexuality and can hinder or help in this arousal process by her attitudes, her "letting herself go," and her active participation in intercourse.

Typically the male is readily aroused sexually, although there are males who are not, and there are some who are less interested in intercourse than their wives. Here again there is a wide range of individual variation. There are also differences between men and women in the "need" for sex. As we discussed in Chapter 2, sex drive has a physiological basis but is largely controlled and considerably influenced by social and cultural forces. There are important differences between men and women in this regard. Men have a biological need for sexual release which will invariably occur from time to time either through nocturnal emissions, masturbation, petting to orgasm, or sexual intercourse. Beyond this biological requirement, which lasts throughout most of a man's life following puberty, much of his sexual drive is socially and culturally influenced. Women, however, have sexual needs which are much more fully determined by social and cultural influences. Freedman (1967) says "I have been impressed in the course of my research by the capacity of young women to carry on very well without any physical sexual activity whatsoever—including masturbation."

Women as well as men can reach a climax in intercourse. In earlier years this fact tended to be obscured, and we might guess that many women were not aware of it. In recent years woman's sexual nature has been at least partially elucidated, and woman's capacity for orgasm has been both clarified and accepted. But such orgasm has been so overstressed that a misplaced emphasis on sexual performance has entered the picture.

In men there is a dual reaction, namely, orgasm, which is a neuromuscular response, and ejaculation, which is the discharge of seminal fluid. Actually the two reactions occur so nearly simultaneously that they are thought of as one. In women there is nothing equivalent to ejaculation. There are vaginal lubricating secretions, but they do not involve special sensations, as does ejaculation. A woman may be aware of the moisture but she does not feel the process of secretion as a man feels ejaculation. Woman's orgasm has no relationship to the production of egg cells, which are secreted at the rate of, roughly, one per month, irrespective of intercourse. Nor is there any established relationship between orgasm and conception, as sometimes assumed. Some women believe that if they do not have orgasm, they cannot become pregnant. Conception can occur with or without orgasm. The female orgasm is sometimes referred to as a "nervous explosion," an "explosive physiological entity" (Masters and Johnson, 1966). It is important that the reader realize that "explosion" and "explosive" are used here figuratively. During orgasm accumulated tension is released, and there are muscular contractions and relaxations and sensations of touch, all of which prove physically pleasurable and satisfying.

The intensity of orgasm varies from woman to woman and from time to time in the same woman. It is a mistake to assume that all women should respond in the same way. It is an even worse mistake to assume that women should respond exactly as men do. It is important for each woman to be herself and to respond in her own way.

Some women never achieve orgasm. This does not prove that they are unhappy in their marriage. Nor does it indicate an absence of love. Nor does absence of orgasm or infrequent orgasm indicate that a woman does not enjoy sexual intercourse. A considerable proportion of wives report that they enjoy intercourse yet seldom or never reach orgasm (Wallin and Clark, 1963; McGuire and Steinhilber, 1970; Raboch, 1970).

A woman may find a peculiarly feminine satisfaction in intercourse when her partner reaches a climax, and this fact makes her "feel like a woman." She may also experience another peculiarly feminine satisfaction, namely, being held, that is, cuddled, as an end in itself, as part of foreplay before intercourse, and after intercourse during the "afterglow" (Hollender, 1971; Golden, 1971). In one study of 2,372 married women who filled in questionnaires, in answers to the question: "Of all aspects of sexual activity, what do you like best?", 22 percent said, "Closeness or feeling of oneness with partner." This percentage was higher than that for orgasm (21 percent), intercourse (20 percent), or foreplay (19 percent) (Bell and Bell, 1972). A man may also derive a special satisfaction in a feeling of closeness during foreplay. He may deprive himself of some of the richness of the experience if he thinks only of hurrying both himself and his partner to orgasm.

A small number of women never achieve any satisfaction in their sexual life. Such women not only miss the pleasure that their relationship with their husbands might produce but often must endure what to them is uninteresting or repugnant. They may be psychologically virgin, though not so anatomically. They tolerate sex; they do not really experience it. Others become physically and emotionally aroused but fail to reach orgasm. Instead of their finding pleasure and release, their experience ends in nervous tension, restlessness, disappointment, or irritation.

No woman need conclude that occasional failure will be harmful. Either type of woman—the one who is indifferent, inhibited, repressed, unresponsive, or the one who is responsive but whose experience tends habitually to be incomplete, unsatisfying, and productive of tension rather than relief of tension—may often be assisted in making a more adequate adjustment if she, and her husband, will consult a marriage counselor.

Rights and Duties

Sexual intercourse is sometimes considered a masculine right and feminine duty. This attitude was more common in the past, but it has not yet disappeared. It is still reflected in the laws of some states, where a man may demand that his wife submit to intercourse and may divorce her if she refuses. This duty–right attitude is cold, one-sided, and unchallenging compared with the attitude that sex is a mutual experience, entailing mutual satisfaction and the expression of affection, trust, and desire by both parties rather than the imposition of rights and the unwilling performance of duty.

In a sense, a right is established at the wedding, but only in the sociological and legal sense. It is better to think of the situation as presenting opportunities for both persons rather than to think of it as a trap for the woman or a bargain by which she agrees to submit to masculine demands in return for which she gains status and security. Any man who enters marriage with the intention of demanding his rights shows plainly the shallowness of his attitude toward his wife. He is more than old-fashioned; he is medieval.

Success and Failure

As already explained, the achievement of the deepest, most lasting satisfaction in sexual intercourse is not "natural" in the sense of being "instinctive." It is an art. An art requires time, patience, thoughtfulness, perseverance, and understanding for its fullest development. Interest and urge are "instinctive," but human beings have worked out means of expression that are more than automatic and that transcend the "natural." Sex has been raised to the plane of creative achievement.

Since this is true, a couple need not be discouraged if success is limited or absent at first. Few couples reach the greatest possible success immediately. The sexual relationship of husband and wife is not merely a series of isolated, unrelated incidents. It is a growing relationship which becomes deeper and richer as time goes on. There is no reason to assume that the achievement of the first success is the end and goal and that there is nothing to look forward to. As they grow older, the couple may grow closer to each other in this as well as in other ways.

It takes time to develop a full sexual adjustment. One cannot learn all there is to know about sex in a fleeting, abbreviated episode. "Many young couples expect to experience the sexual equivalent of the San Francisco earthquake the first time they have coitus. If, as is usual, the experience is a shade milder, many head for the nearest technical manual to see what they are doing wrong; Mark Twain noted that, on the typical honeymoon, 'The second biggest disappointment is Niagara Falls'" (AMA Committee on Human Sexuality, 1972).

They need not be disappointed if they never reach perfection in their sexual life. Human beings never reach perfection in anything; at best, they merely approach it. They may strive for it but never actually expect to attain it. If the couple are successful a good proportion of the time, that is about all that can be expected. If in rare instances a couple approach more closely the perfect ideal, so much the better. Most couples, even though very happily married, fall short. This is not the equivalent of being content with mediocrity, but there is a danger in setting an impossible, unattainable goal, such as, for example, the expectation of the wife's having orgasm every time intercourse occurs or the couple's having simultaneous orgasm every time intercourse occurs.

In developing a new skill or new art, the novice makes many errors. In learning to walk, skate, play tennis, swim, drive a golf ball, or bid a bridge hand we perpetrate so many mistakes that after mastering the necessary technique we look back in embarrassment at the immensity of our previous ignorance and the magnitude of our original awkwardness. We do not let our mistakes defeat us; nor do we stop with them. We overcome them. We correct them. A newly married couple in many instances are novices confronted with the problem of learning a new art and acquiring a new skill. They are almost certain to make mistakes at first. They may feel that their ignorance is stupendous and their clumsiness colossal. They need not leap to conclusions and defeat themselves. They may learn by their mistakes. With patience, understanding, intelligence, self-analysis, an ample amount of love, and a liberal sprinkling of a sense of humor, errors may be corrected. Each successful act of intercourse plays a part in conditioning both husband and wife so that success in the future becomes easier. Hence care, patience, perspective, and a will to success pay large dividends.

In almost all cases where there are difficulties that prevent adequate sexual adjustment, those difficulties are matters of attitude and habit rather than of anatomy. There are relatively few cases of structural defects that prevent sexual harmony, and most of these may be discovered in a medical examination and remedied by medical treatment. A couple who have unusual handicaps or hindrances need not conclude that these are irremediable until every resource, including professional counseling, has been drawn upon.

The majority of couples have no difficulties at all, except perhaps the normal readjustments involved in making any transition such as that from single life to marriage. These require only time, patience, and intelligence. We do not mean to imply that a couple direct their attention toward nothing but possible difficulties. Quite the opposite is true. Nevertheless, if there are difficulties, these may be faced frankly and objectively.

In working out a satisfactory sexual adjustment, husband and wife may help each other considerably. Each may help the other understand reactions and attitudes. The wife may explain to the husband what pleases and what displeases her. Reticence or secrecy based upon false modesty, conceit, or ignorance is one of the most effective obstacles to success.

Understanding Each Other

Though a man's sexual experience may appear to be largely of a physical nature, it also includes a considerable degree of emotional involvement. A man is likely to derive some pleasure from sexual intercourse whether or not his wife is responsive. But his experience is intensified if she responds because he knows he has contributed to her pleasure. If, over a long period, she is unresponsive and he grows to feel that he is imposing himself on his wife, especially if she lets him know that she feels it is an imposition, he may eventually come to avoid intercourse or even become impotent and be unable to perform the sexual act. Assuming that a husband has any sensitivity at all, he wants to feel enthusiastically accepted by his wife both as a man and as her sexual partner. If she rejects him as the latter, she can defeat him. "The susceptibility of the human male to the power of suggestion with reference to his sexual prowess is almost unbelievable" (Masters and Johnson, 1970).

In our sex-oriented culture, it is customarily assumed that men are sexual beings who are always ready to perform. We should note that many men are sensitive persons who take sex seriously and for whom sexual intercourse is an experience reserved for the most special relationships. Men may have the same anxieties and inhibitions as women. In fact, a great number of men find that they are unable to achieve an erection the first time they attempt sexual intercourse, even though they are able to have very fulfilling and responsive sex lives once the relationship is under way. Men and women should both be prepared for some anxiety and awkwardness the first time coitus takes place. Should there be a failure to carry the act to completion, an understanding and thoughtful couple will realize that this is a natural occurrence characteristic of many initial sexual relationships. If the problem persists for some time, a counselor may then be consulted.

Even if a couple had premarital sexual experience, this does not guarantee that they will both be responsive, passionate, interested in intercourse, and devoid of inhibition and fear. A man may have premarital intercourse and still not learn what he needs to know regarding a wife and their relationship in marriage. In some cases the wife scarcely knows what to expect in marriage. She may be ignorant of some of the most elementary facts. There are educated women who are ignorant of male anatomy and do not fully understand the anatomy and functions of their own bodily organs. Many women do not know how men react. Many are unaware that women as well as men may derive satisfaction from sex. If the wife has gathered any general knowledge from reading or discussion, she needs to apply this to the individual situation. She may have good intentions and be anxious to do the right thing and to please her husband, but she may not understand fully what is involved. She needs to be given time to learn.

If the wife is a woman who before marriage was conscious of no desire that she identified as sexual, that desire will not be created by the wedding. Some men act as if the ceremony were all that is necessary to change an unawakened woman into a passionate wife. They fail to understand that this transformation depends upon the husband, not upon the ceremony.

A husband needs to realize that his wife is more inclined than he to have inhibitions and fears centering on sex and its expression. Sometimes her fear is vague. At other times it is more specific, and sexual intercourse recalls a fear situation that occurred early in her life. In recalling the situation, she may again experience emotions similar to those that she felt at the time.

Sexual maladjustment may make marital adjustment difficult, especially if in the early days of marriage something occurs that the woman does not understand and that seems to bring her fears to a focus. But attitudes are acquired, and they may be changed. Behind each one there is an underlying cause, some experience or educative process out of which the attitude grew. Discovering the underlying factors and looking at them from the vantage point of greater maturity and fuller information usually leads to dispelling what otherwise might become a cloud hanging over a marriage. This is especially true if the woman herself realizes the need for change and takes the initiative in talking with someone who can help her.

In addition to the attitudes mentioned above, many women, and some men, have inhibitions in connection with the exposure of their own bodies or feel embarrassed at witnessing the bodies of others. Some women, about to be married, express more uneasiness at the prospect of seeing the husband unclothed than at the prospect of being seen unclothed themselves. These inhibitions, too, are the result of conditioning or training, and the latter is highly colored both by the need for self-protection and by convention. Convention still prohibits complete exposure of the body under many conditions. But marriage alters circumstances. What is forbidden among the unmarried is not only acceptable but expected between husband and wife. There is no conventional restriction on their bodily exposure. If one spouse carries into the marriage relationship inhibitions that originate in the premarital standard, he or she is like someone who insists upon swimming fully clothed because a bathing suit is not appropriate apparel for a shopping trip or a formal reception. Students sometimes wonder how anybody these days can be embarrassed at bodily exposure. With bikini swimsuits, low-cut gowns, "skinny dipping," and X-rated movies, how can this be? But not everyone approves of bodily exposure even though it may be generally approved. Modesty, as mentioned earlier, is a matter of attitude, not a matter of yardage.

If a husband understands that his bride may be concerned over the bodily exposure of both persons, he will approach such exposure with tact, patience, and consideration. If he becomes impatient and blurts out something like, "What are you acting like that for? We're married, aren't we?", he may set deeper the inhibitions he ought to help her to remove. If a bride understands not only that her husband is likely to take bodily exposure for granted but also that he is "visual-minded" and that his is not the wanton gaze of "men" but rather the observation of the man whose love for her and idealization of her make her attractive in his sight, she may anticipate bodily exposure with more insight and less apprehension.

SEXUAL ADJUSTMENT
Fear of Pain

A woman's first sexual intercourse sometimes involves pain. This may be partly due to the fact that the opening of her genital tract, or more specifically the external aperture of the vagina, is partially closed by a membrane called the *hymen*. With the widespread use of tampons long before females begin having sexual intercourse, however, the hymen may have already been stretched, and consequently this is not likely to be a major deterrent to successful coitus at the beginning of a sexual relationship. If the hymen is intact, however, there may be a few drops of blood present when it ruptures. If the lining of the vagina is dry because of a paucity of lubricating secretions which accompany responsiveness, this fact may contribute to the woman's discomfort.

In a study of 1,000 marriages that were still unconsummated (that is, the couple had not yet had sexual intercourse) after periods of one to twenty-one years, Blazer (1964) found that in one-fifth of the sample the reason given for the nonconsummation was fear of pain in initial intercourse. It cannot be emphasized too strongly that such a fear is unnecessary. Granted, a partner who is a savage may inflict pain. But in most cases there is little discomfort or none whatsoever. What discomfort does exist will for most women disappear when they become more accustomed to having sexual intercourse with their partners.

In rare instances a wife's fear reacts upon the muscles near her genital organs, causing them to contract so vigorously that the very pain she is afraid of is increased. She then finds herself in a vicious circle; the more she fears the experience, the greater is the pain, and the greater the pain, the more she fears it. If she can be brought to accept the experience without resistance, the cause of discomfort will be removed. In only rare instances does some anatomical defect prevent intercourse. In any case in which there seems to be unusual difficulty, in which the pain is experienced more than a few times, a physician should be consulted. Practically all such difficulties can be remedied. Even in unusual and extreme instances there is no cause for alarm.

There is considerable variation among females as to the extent, toughness, and elasticity of the hymen. Allowing for generalization and oversimplification, the diagrams in Exhibit 11-1 depict five possible conditions of the virginal hymen. In life, since the tissues are soft, the labia (see Exhibit 13-4) touch or almost touch (except as they may separate during tumescence, as mentioned below), and the vagina is a collapsed tube, like a toy balloon with no air in it. Sometimes the vagina is referred to as a "potential cavity." Obviously, if it can stretch to accommodate the passage of a baby in childbirth, it can stretch enough to accommodate the erect penis in intercourse. In some women the hymen is so slight as to be almost nonexistent (Exhibit 11-1*a*). In most women there is an irregular opening amply large for menstrual discharge, and perhaps tampons, but not large enough for intercourse without the hymen's being stretched (*b*). In a diagram, of course, only the shape and size of the opening can be depicted. There is no way of indicating the thickness or elasticity of the hymen. In some cases there are two or more openings (*c*), and in some a number of small openings (*d*), permitting menstrual discharge, but not large enough for the insertion of a tampon or intercourse. In a rare case, there is no opening; the hymen forms a "drum-head" closure (*e*). In such case, a woman may menstruate for some time but the menstrual discharge is dammed up behind the imperforate hymen. Eventually the discharge becomes dehydrated and forms a tarry mass which causes discomfort and makes necessary an incision to create an opening.

A condition sometimes mistaken for imperforate hymen is one in which the hymen has an opening so tiny that it is difficult to visualize it. This condition is termed *micro-*

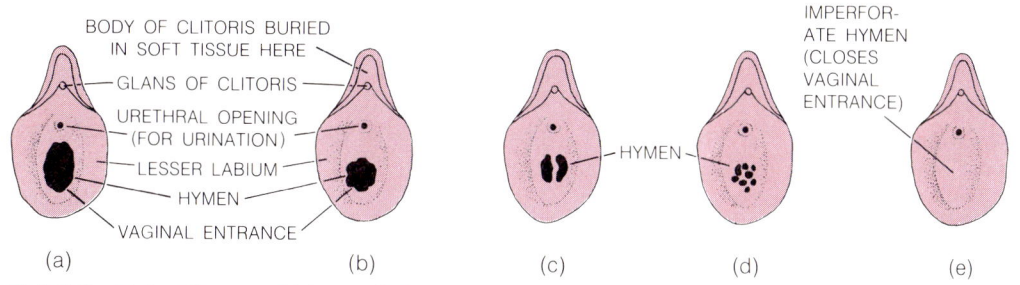

Exhibit 11-1 Five conditions of the virginal hymen. The dark areas represent openings into the vagina.

perforate hymen (Capraro, Dillon, and Gallego, 1974), and although there is not a damming up of the menstrual flow to the extent found in imperforate hymen, the two conditions require similar treatment and, so far as sexual intercourse is concerned, would present similar problems.

Assuming tumescence and/or the use of lubricating jelly, as mentioned below, in first intercourse a woman with hymen (*a*) would have no problem. A woman with hymen (*b*) would have the problem of stretching, as discussed above. If the hymen is unusually tough and inelastic or the opening is unusually small, first intercourse for such a woman is facilitated by medical assistance. A woman with hymen (*c*) or (*d*) would have pain and bleeding at first intercourse. The possibility of a woman's having hymen (*c*) or (*d*) is one of the strongest arguments for a pelvic examination. If a woman has successfully used menstrual tampons, she has evidence that she does not have hymen (*c*) or (*d*). Hymen (*e*) would present a woman with a serious problem in her first intercourse. But a woman with such a hymen is likely to seek medical aid before marriage.

In some cases the hymen is stretched by accident, by masturbation, by sports activities, by the use of the tampon type of menstrual protection, during a medical examination, or manually or mechanically at a physician's suggestion. Consequently, the condition of the hymen is no certain, never-failing indication of the virginity or nonvirginity of a woman presumably virgin at the time of marriage. A husband who hastily concludes that his bride has had previous intercourse because she has neither pain nor bleeding as a result of their first sexual intercourse betrays his ignorance of anatomical variations and reflects an outmoded attitude. So does a responsive woman who fears, or the husband of such a woman who concludes, that if she exhibits responsiveness the first time they have intercourse, it seems to indicate that she has had previous sexual experience and is not virgin.

When a woman is sexually aroused, her labia become tumescent, that is, somewhat swollen because of the increased blood supply, and this tumescence causes them to move apart and turn outward slightly so that the entrance to the vagina is enlarged and made more "funnel-shaped." Accompanying this tumescence there is a transudation, a "sweating," of fluid from the wall of the vagina, lubricating both the vagina and the labia (Masters and Johnson, 1966). This transudation is not a glandular secretion, as often assumed, since there are no glands in this area of the vaginal lining. It is, rather, a direct passage of fluid from the blood vessels surrounding the vagina through the vaginal lining (Debrovner, 1975). Both tumescence and lubrication facilitate the penetration of the vagina by the erect penis. As mentioned earlier, a woman may feel the presence of this lubricating fluid as moisture, but she does not feel the process of its transudation as a man feels the process of ejaculation. In the absence of tumescence and lubrication, penetration of the vagina by the erect penis may be uncomfortable or painful, especially for the female but in some cases as well for the male (Debrovner, 1975). A solution to this problem may be found in the use of a vaginal jelly which melts at body temperature and is a substitute for natural lubrication. Such lubricating jelly may be purchased at a drugstore without a prescription.

Pelvic Examinations and Premarital Counseling

Partly because of the possibility of discomfort experienced by some women in their first intercourse and partly because of the relatively remote possibility of there being some unusual anatomic condition, some women prefer to have the hymen stretched mechanically by a physician or according to his or her directions, in which case the woman herself stretches it manually. In some cases the hymen needs to be cut. This requires only a local anesthetic. To ascertain the condition of the hymen the physician does a pelvic examination. In any case, the process is associated with the impersonal atmosphere of the physician's office rather than with a sexual partner.

It is recommended that a couple who plan to marry both have a medical examination. They may go to the same physician at different times or to different physicians. They may also wish to consider premarital counseling. In either case, they should try to choose professionals who understand human sexuality, are aware of new developments in this field, and are interested in these types of examinations. The physician or counselor should be willing to take time to talk with the couple and answer their questions. If the couple go to different physicians, they may visit specialists, the man going to a urologist, or internal medicine specialist, the woman to a gynecologist or obstetrician. A woman who contemplates such an examination with embarrassment may realize that the physician is unlikely to be presented with anything new or anything not observed many times before. Similarly, there is virtually nothing one could say to an experienced counselor which he or she has not heard before.

Several hundred years ago, when the practice of midwifery in Europe was taken over by men, these first obstetricians were known as "male midwives." At that time there was so high a premium upon feminine modesty, especially in the upper class, that women insisted that during delivery they be completely draped in sheets and the obstetrician deliver the baby only by his sense of touch without ever seeing any part of the woman's genital anatomy (Findley, 1933). Nowadays a woman who insisted upon such a procedure during delivery would not be able to find an obstetrician to accede to her wishes, and she would be considered eccentric, to say the least. It is taken for granted that an obstetrician will examine a woman's anatomy both before and during delivery. There is need for similar acceptance and objectivity relative to the pelvic examination. Unfortunately, however, there are some women whose attitude still reflects the modesty of the distant past.

Even if a woman does find it difficult to have a pelvic examination, she may well ask herself this question: "Which is better, to have such an examination in spite of hesitation and embarrassment, or possibly at the time of first intercourse confront an anatomical problem which neither I nor my partner can solve?"

Scheduling the examination far enough

in advance of the first intercourse will make it possible to carry out the physician's recommendations without excessive haste, to read what he or she suggests, and to return for further discussion. If they choose their physician carefully, a couple may feel free to ask about anything that they do not understand in connection with sex and reproduction. No matter what they may have read or gathered from other sources, it is often advisable for a couple to talk through with a physician or marriage counselor the matter of sexual adjustment. They should not consider the matter closed until they have had answered all the questions that they feel the need for asking. In most cases one of these will pertain to control of conception, and on this the physician may make recommendations. Such discussion may also facilitate their own communication relative to sex later. Similarly counselors may be helpful in leading a couple to make a healthy and satisfactory transition to sex in marriage.

The Husband's Responsibility

By the exercise of gentleness and patience, by the sacrifice of his own immediate pleasure, if necessary, the husband may carefully lay a foundation for a satisfactory relationship for the future. Roughness, haste, selfishness, and thoughtlessness in the early days of sexual adjustment may produce severe psychological trauma, leaving permanent scars upon a marriage and an unbridgeable gulf in the husband-wife relationship. Referring to honeymoon husbands, Golden (1971) says, "They usually probe, push, and are quickly satisfied, leaving the female with mixed feelings about this sexual act. This is often a rude awakening during the honeymoon which may set in motion a train of emotional traumas which extend throughout married life." Kaplan (1974) mentions couples who "have intercourse as soon as the husband has an erection without considering where his partner is in the sexual response sequence." With their attitude toward sex and their ignorance of a woman's reactions and of what successful adjustment in marriage requires, some men are in the position of a person who is employed for a job but fails to inquire what the job involves. With pick and shovel on his shoulder, he reports for work, thinking of the contractive power of his biceps, only to find that he is to do watchmaking and that the requirements are patience, finesse, delicacy of operation, and lightness of touch. Fortunately, not all men—not even most—are like this.

The demonstration of masculine virility is nothing for a husband to be proud of, nor is unnatural reserve or false modesty on the part of a wife. It is no more womanly to be inhibited and emotionally undeveloped than it is manly to be bestial and inconsiderate.

SEXUAL RESPONSE

There are two general physiological responses which govern sexual response and orgasm in both males and females, *vasocongestion* and *myotonia*. Vasocongestion refers to congestion of the blood vessels. It is the primary physiologic response to sexual stimulation (Masters and Johnson, 1966). When sexual excitement occurs, blood engorges the sexual organs in both males and females. In the male, an erection is the most obvious example. In the female, the clitoris and labia become enlarged. In both males and females there are changes in the coloring of the sexual organs to a more reddish state. Following orgasm, the blood leaves the excited sexual organs and they return to their pre-excitement state. Orgasm, then, is partially a response to a state of vasocongestion.

Myotonia refers to increased muscular tension. It is a secondary physiologic response to sexual stimulation. Males and females alike increase their muscular tension. A number of bodily changes demonstrate this occurrence. During male orgasm, there are rhythmic contractions associated with ejaculation and a heightened, pleasurable sensation. Female orgasm involves heightened, pleasurable sensations without ejaculation. Thus, orgasm is also a response to myotonia. A male's response tends to be more localized in his genital organs, whereas a female's tends to be more diffused, involving the entire body.

Similarities and Differences

There are more similarities than differences in male-female sexual response. Both men and women experience and respond to vasocongestion and myotonia. Both have similar phases of sexual response, to be described later. And both are capable of intensely satisfying orgasmic reactions. There are, of course, important differences, many of which are associated with their differing anatomies. The female's vagina, for example, is not as sensitive to pain or sexual stimulation as is commonly assumed. However, she has muscles (especially the pubococcygeus muscle) surrounding the vagina which are sensitive to stimuli (Kegel, 1952). These muscles may play a part in her sexual response. The labia at the entrance to the vagina are sensitive, however, and the most sensitive organ of all is the clitoris, buried in soft tissue just above and forward of the entrance to the vagina.

Many women are unaware of the presence of the clitoris as an organ, although they may be aware of its location as an area of stimulation and response in sexual intercourse or masturbation. The clitoris is stimulated by bodily contact and movement during intercourse. It may also be stimulated by manual or other rubbing of the area of its location by either the woman or her male partner. But direct manual stimulation of the glans of the clitoris is uncomfortable for many women (Masters and Johnson, 1966).

Structurally the clitoris is like a rudimentary penis. It is to the penis what the rudimentary breast of the male is to the developed breast of the female. The rudimentary breast and the clitoris in the male and female, respectively, constitute a clear-cut instance of overlap, or blending, of sexual characteristics due to common embryological development, as discussed in an earlier chapter. In structure the clitoris is homologous to the penis (that is, derived from the same source and similar to, but not identical with it). It has a glans, a spongelike interior, and a similar nerve and blood supply. Unlike the penis, however, it has no passage through it and therefore has no function in either secretion or excretion.

In response to sexual stimulation the clitoris becomes tumescent, that is, enlarged, because of an increased blood supply in the "spongy" internal tissue. Research indicates that the clitoris is slower to respond than the penis (Winokur, 1963). The specific terminology to be applied to the reaction of the clitoris is not so important for our purpose as the fact that the clitoris does respond to sexual stimulation in a way not dissimilar to that of the penis, and that the clitoris is a major seat of sexual response in the female. Kistner (1964) refers to it as the "nerve center" for intercourse. While orgasm may be brought about by stimulating the clitoris after the surgical removal of the vagina if a woman has been conditioned to sexual stimulation and response, the opposite is also true, namely that after conditioning a woman may have orgasm following removal of the clitoris (Masters and Johnson, 1970, 1966; Jones, Jr., and Scott, 1971; Capraro, 1974; Beach, 1965; Verkauf, 1975).

There has been a "debate" for years on whether there is a difference between clitoral orgasm and vaginal orgasm. Some say that there is a difference and that the difference is important. Others say there is no difference and the "debate" centers on a false issue.

Statements such as the following are not uncommon: "Attainment of orgasm during intravaginal intercourse is usually more deeply satisfying than that reached solely through clitoral or other stimulation" (Harper and Stokes, 1971). "Women's vaginal orgasm is pure fiction" (Ejlersen, 1969). "The old idea that the clitoris is entirely the site of erotic sensation in the woman must be modified" (Jones, Jr., and Scott, 1971). "If the vaginal orgasm is widely believed to be a myth it is because it *is* a myth for all but a few women" (Hobbs, 1970). Millett (1970) says, "While there is no 'vaginal orgasm' per se, there is of course, orgasm in vaginal coitus (and probably one of a different experiential character than that produced by exclusively clitoral stimulation) just as on any occasion when the clitoris is stimulated." Koedt (1971) says: "A false distinction is made between the vaginal and the clitoral orgasm." She goes on to say that while there are many areas of sexual arousal, there is only one area of orgasmic response, namely, the clitoris. "All orgasms are extensions of sensation from this area.... They are all clitoral orgasms.... Vaginal orgasm ... does not exist."

Women reading such conflicting statements may be confused or even become concerned that their own sexual response is abnormal. Or a husband reading such statements may approach his wife in a way that prevents orgasm instead of promoting it. For example, if he reads that orgasm is clitoral, he may attempt to stimulate the glans of his wife's clitoris directly, a procedure which can produce discomfort, even pain (Masters and Johnson, 1966, 1970), as mentioned above.

During masturbation and during the foreplay preceding intercourse there is likely to be considerable clitoral stimulation. During intercourse there is considerable vaginal stimulation. A woman is already on the way to response psychologically before she voluntarily begins the act of masturbation. This fact undoubtedly contributes to the intensity of her response. During intercourse a woman may or may not be aroused. Intercourse may occur without her complete arousal. Hence her response may be less intense. On the other hand, during intercourse the relationship with her male partner is part of the total situation, and her response is not exclusively physical. Whatever fantasies she may have during masturbation are not equivalent to the relationship with an actual partner during intercourse. Also, during masturbation the woman herself regulates the stimulation, while stimulation in intercourse is regulated largely, but not entirely, by the male partner (Gebhard, 1970b).

Perhaps the point of view most likely to lead to understanding is one that considers a woman a totality rather than a cluster of somewhat disconnected parts—one that thinks of her as responding as a total person rather than only in some particular part of her body. "Are clitoral and vaginal orgasms truly separate anatomic entities? From a biologic point of view, the answer to this question is an unequivocal No.... From an anatomic point of view, there is absolutely no difference in the responses of the pelvic viscera to effective stimulation.... Clitoral and vaginal orgasms are not separate biologic entities" (Masters and Johnson, 1966). Sherfey (1972) says that "it is a physical impossibility to separate the clitoral from the vaginal orgasm" and that "one must think and talk in terms of a clitorally produced or a vaginally produced orgasm (or both, or a breast-produced, a thought-produced, or a whatever-produced orgasm). Physiologically all orgasms are the same" (see also McGuire and Steinhilber, 1970; Fisher, 1973). Ramey (1974) says, "There *is* erotic sensation in the *entire* female genital area, and therefore the entire area as a whole must be taken into consideration, not just the clitoris or the vagina.... The female orgasm is an example of the physiological phenomenon called space summation, for it is a summation of sensory impulses from the entire genital area." Kaplan (1974) mentions "the incredibly stupid controversy surrounding female orgasm."

After interviews with more than 250 women concerning their sexual experience, McDermott (1970) says that in her opinion the distinction between clitoral and vaginal orgasm "is relevant only to medical science at present." She believes that "once a woman has discovered the best means of realizing sexual satisfaction, has conveyed this to her partner and is happy with the result, she should turn a deaf ear to all the various theories." She goes on to say that, if a woman is worried because she does not seem to have vaginal orgasms, she should "forget it and enjoy what she has got. . . . When some women say that they cannot have a vaginal orgasm, what they really mean is that they cannot have an orgasm through intercourse but only through manual or oral stimulation." Furthermore, there is no reason to assume that orgasm is the same for all women or the same for any particular woman at different times. Based on an examination of all evidence available to date, it is probably safest to say that the clitoris is the focal point of sexual response for the female and is potentially her most sensitive sexual organ. When orgasm occurs, however, it may be precipitated through stimulation of the vagina alone, the clitoris alone, the two in combination, or even other parts of the body alone or in combination. Furthermore, when orgasm occurs, the response is likely to involve the vagina as well as the clitoris and many other parts of her anatomy.

For a woman sexual intercourse is more likely to be part of a larger experience in which ideal elements play an important role. This is not to say that a man's experience is limited to the physical, for his, too, may be more comprehensive. But in his reactions the physical is more clear-cut and specific. In men sexual desire is aroused by both internal and external stimuli, whereas in women it is more subject to external influences, though internal ones play a part. Both genders respond to such stimuli as sight of each other, expressions of affection, and physical contact. Both have memory and imagination. Such factors affect a man more readily and more quickly than they affect a woman. In addition, a man is subject to an internal stimulus, namely, the accumulation of seminal fluid in the seminal vesicles (Mahan and Broderick, 1969; Guyton, 1971) and possibly to some extent in the prostate gland, which secretes part of it. If one could divide the sex drive into segments, one might say that part of it in a man is the desire for relief from this accumulation of fluid. There is nothing in a woman's experience quite analogous to this. She may be subject to nervous or muscular tension, but no more so than a man.

Because of the accumulation of fluid, the ease with which it is evacuated, and the pleasure derived from that process under almost all circumstances, a man tends to be less dependent upon his partner than she is upon him. As a result, he may be dominated by his own reactions, forgetting her and her dependence upon him. Masters and Johnson (1970) mention that, because of "the fact of women's physical necessity for an effectively functioning male partner," the female is in a "relatively untenable position from the point of view of equality of sexual response."

By and large, keeping in mind the overlap of sexual characteristics mentioned in an earlier chapter, women are slower than men to reach orgasm and also to "subside" afterward. Sometimes this latter period is referred to as the "afterglow." The metaphor is taken from a sunset—the sun has gone down, but the sky is still red. A woman may "experience profound and prolonged sensuous pleasure" during this stage (Kaplan, 1974). "The postorgasmic female has a subconscious need to relate, to remain *in touch* with her partner. The male does not need to relate physically to the degree that the female evidences" (Masters and Johnson, 1975).

A man's reactions are more likely to be very quick and to end more or less abruptly. Shortly after orgasm he may be subject to almost overwhelming sleepiness. If he yields to this sleepiness, from her point of view deserting his partner when she wants attention, an expression of love, and affection beyond the momentary culmination or orgasm, ecstasy may be followed by devastating disappointment (Goldman and Milman, 1969). When this happens repeatedly, some women conclude that they are being "used" because the man seems interested only in his own satisfaction.

Masters and Johnson (1966) describe four phases of sexual response for both men and women: *excitement, plateau, orgasm*, and *resolution*. While males and females both go through the same stages when orgasm is reached, they may do so with different speed and intensity. Furthermore, for a given female there may be great variability from one time to the next, whereas for a male the experience is much more nearly equivalent from time to time. Exhibit 11-2 illustrates these phases separately for males (11-2a) and for females (11-2b).

1 *Excitement.* Variation in the male is usually in terms of duration rather than intensity. Thus, only one diagram is presented. In the male, excitement is rapid, and little stimulation is usually required to produce its most visible sign, an erection. For the female, excitement may occur rapidly, as with the male, or it may require more stimulation, perhaps in the form of foreplay. Three patterns of sexual response are illustrated for females to indicate the diversity in their responses.

2 *Plateau.* Individuals enter the plateau stage if effective stimulation is continued. Males will not advance to this point if there is no indication that it is possible for an orgasm to occur. Once a male reaches the plateau phase, there is usually a strong desire to continue the excitement through orgasm. A female, once having reached the plateau phase, may continue at that point for some time or may seek to advance toward orgasm. Some females have difficulty advancing beyond the plateau phase, but others advance readily.

3 *Orgasm.* The orgasmic phase is limited to a few seconds. Vasocongestion and myotonia are released at this time. In the male, orgasm is charac-

Exhibit 11-2 Sexual response cycles. (*Source*: Masters and Johnson, 1966.)

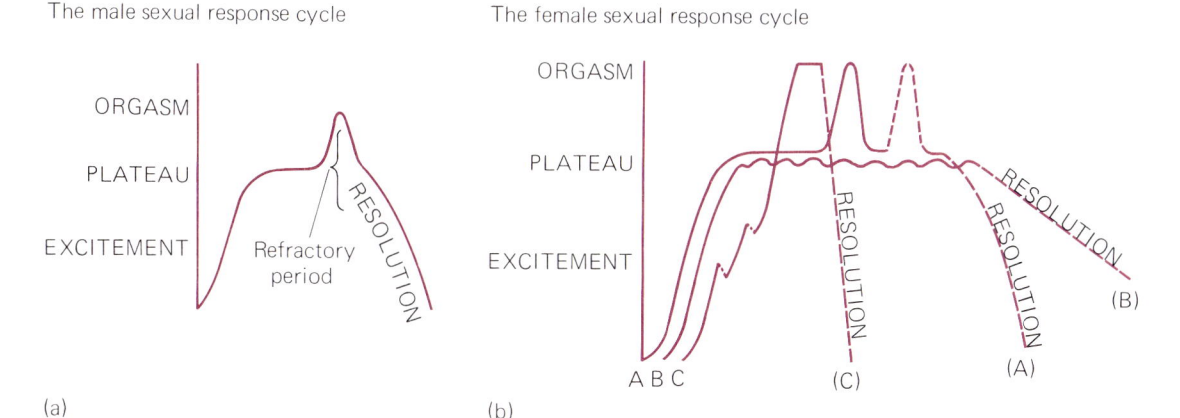

The male sexual response cycle

The female sexual response cycle

(a)   (b)

terized by rhythmic contractions of the penis, ejaculation of seminal fluid, increased heartbeat, faster respiration (breathing), higher blood pressure, involuntary sweating, change in skin tone (called sex flush), and other changes. Females also have a range of responses, including rhythmic contractions around the outer one-third of the vagina, which vary in intensity from woman to woman. There may also be rhythmic contractions in other nearby organs, such as the uterus and rectal sphincter. Some women will not notice vaginal contractions, others will. Some will be intense and others will be mild. Exhibit 11-2b illustrates many possible variations. Nipple erection is visible following orgasm, as well as sex flush, rapid heartbeat, faster breathing, and higher blood pressure.

4   *Resolution.* The resolution phase is a return to the sexually unexcited state. Males reach this stage quickly. Females vary in how fast they go through the resolution stage. Females are different from males in that they are capable of being restimulated to another orgasm before reaching the termination of the resolution stage, although this is characteristic of only a portion of females. Kinsey and his associates (1953) found that 14 percent of their respondents regularly experienced multiple orgasm. Males, however, are typically incapable of restimulation during the refractory period, the first part of the resolution phase. Having reached a lower level of excitement they may be restimulated, but this takes longer than it does for females. Females who have mild orgasms or none at all will generally take longer to reach the unexcited state than those who have more intense orgasms. Such females (Exhibit 11-2b, pattern B) may be left with a partial feeling of physical frustration from the left-over vasocongestion.

Some writers set up simultaneous orgasm as the ideal; but such an ideal is probably reached by only a small proportion of couples and then not every time intercourse occurs. For a couple to expect simultaneous orgasm every time intercourse occurs is unrealistic. Kaplan (1974) mentions the "myth of the mutual orgasm" and adds that it has probably "destroyed many relationships." She goes on to say that "the compulsive striving for simultaneous orgasm can exert a highly destructive effect on a couple's sex life." In many cases, it is acceptable and satisfactory for the woman's orgasm to occur first. If the man's orgasm occurs first, he needs to stimulate the woman either by continued intercourse, if he can sustain his erection, or by manual or oral means if her orgasm is to follow. In some cases the wife may resort to masturbation if orgasm is desired. As mentioned earlier, for most couples it is not essential that a woman reach orgasm each time intercourse takes place.

Typically, a woman needs preparation for intercourse—some women more, some less. This preparation, which is commonly referred to as foreplay, is not a mechanical thing. It is an outgrowth of frequent expression of affection and trust intensified periodically as a direct preface to a culmination in intercourse. In this process, especially in its final stages, there need be no barrier, physical or otherwise, between husband and wife. No parts of the body need be considered subject to taboo so far as tactile contact is concerned. Any act or expression that furthers the process is acceptable and desirable, provided that (1) it does not cause pain or disgust to either party; (2) it does not indicate or produce a fixation at a low level of adjustment; (3) it does not make either person feel guilty; (4) it is safe. An occasional case is reported in which a wife was stimulated sexually by her husband's blowing air into her vagina to inflate it. Aronson and Nelson (1967) mention seven such cases. Air under pressure has been known to enter the bloodstream of the uterus, causing an air embolism which proved fatal. Such an embolism is more likely to occur if the woman is pregnant, has just recently had a baby, is menstruating, or has just stopped menstruating (Aronson, 1969; Freeman, 1970; Herzig, 1972; Mace, 1972b). Long, rough, dirty fingernails can be a special hazard, since the membranes of the labia, vagina, or clitoral area may be scratched during manual stimulation of the female by the male.

In mentioning their sexual behavior couples often say something to this effect: "We do thus and so. Is this right? Is it good?" In the last analysis, whatever the husband and wife do together—*anything*—provided it is mutually agreed upon and not imposed by one upon the other, provided that it is safe, and provided that it does not become a problem to other people, is right and good. There are no rules, no standards but their standards.

In preparing for sexual intercourse, frequently it is assumed that some mechanical process is all that is needed or that such a process supersedes and replaces love, affection, trust, and other similar qualities. In one case, both husband and wife were frustrated to the point of complete impasse. He had been trying to stimulate her to orgasm by the use of a small, soft paintbrush. The more he tried, the farther from orgasm she seemed to be, and the more desperate they both became.

The use of a hand-held electric vibrator to stimulate the wife is sometimes recommended. There are women who respond to such stimulation, especially in masturbation, but many couples expect intercourse to be part of a highly personalized relationship rather than a depersonalized manipulation. Some current books, even best sellers, recommend practices so bizarre that the reader may well doubt the author's seriousness in suggesting them and may certainly doubt the author's understanding of the sexual relationship. There are of course some interesting, accurate, and helpful popular books. But if one were to take some books on this subject at their apparent face value, one might assume that, overnight, any man could become a great lover and sweep any woman, whether she loved him or not, to supreme and incomparable heights of ecstasy by the mastery of some sleight of hand. Nothing could be more misleading. Technique is important, but not all-important. When a couple's relationship is successful, technique is only one of the factors to which credit is due. When it is unsuccessful, only part of the blame may be put upon this aspect. To be complete, the sexual act must involve meaning as well as sensation. Meaning has a permanence about it that sensation lacks, and meaning cannot be produced by technique. "Technique alone can never produce satisfying sexual response just as giving a man a dictionary does not make him a poet" (AMA Committee on Human Sexuality, 1972).

Far too much is sometimes made of so-called "positions in intercourse" or "coital postures." Some writers list, describe, divide, subdivide, classify, diagram, name, number, or present photographs or drawings of dozens, even hundreds of positions. Some of these more nearly resemble acrobatics than expressions of love. A newlywed couple relying on such books would have to take a research assistant on their honeymoon to help them make choices from such extensive catalogs. To many persons, such cataloging makes intercourse seem like an engineering problem, whereas it should be a spontaneous expression of love, affection, and desire with the emphasis on abandonment and oneness, not on posture. A variety of positions in intercourse is possible, and any position which a couple enjoys is likely to enhance their sexual relationship. A particular couple may discover which ones are best for them through experimentation or reading, but their main concern should be what they prefer. Sex is a natural, normal, desirable aspect of life in which both male and female participate without fear, guilt, or inhibition and from which both derive satisfaction.

It is true that much may be gained from reading and discussion, and some of the prerequisites for sexual harmony are readily learned. There is, however, no standard technique, no universal formula. Individual differences, attitudes, background, fears, relative intelligence, depth of affection, irritating circumstances, personality traits, understanding of anatomy and similar items need to be taken into account. A couple need to work out what to them is an acceptable relationship, not only on the basis of stock information and injunction, but also by exploration, experimentation, variation, ingenuity, and discovery. This latter process is in itself one means toward successful adjustment.

Other Considerations

Several miscellaneous considerations bearing upon sexual adjustment may be mentioned briefly.

▶ Both husband and wife need some knowledge of the anatomy and physiological reactions of both self and the other person. In the study of 1,000 unconsummated marriages already referred to (Blazer, 1964), two main reasons given for nonconsummation were ignorance regarding the exact location of the sex organs and the avoidance of an attempt at intercourse to prevent embarrassment and mistakes. A third frequent reason for wives remaining virgin is "plain ignorance on the part of one or both partners about how to proceed" (Harper and Stokes, 1971). Although "it seems inconceivable that such lack of knowledge of sexuality should exist," Dubin (1972) mentions two couples who "didn't know that they never actually had intercourse." There are no statistics to show how common such ignorance is in the general population. That such ignorance should be found at all in these presumably enlightened times is interesting. It is reflected in the queries of college students who ask such questions as the following, reported verbatim: "What is circumcision?" "Can a girl become pregnant without reaching a climax?" "When does a woman achieve orgasm—before or during the act of sexual intercourse?" "Is it possible to become pregnant as a result of mouth-genital contact if the semen is swallowed?" "In intercourse, how far does the penien (*sic*) penetrate the vagina, or does it; what happens?" "Is intercourse possible after a hysterectomy?" "What is a douche?" "What is oral intercourse, is it kissing or otherwise? (P.S. I have to know before the weekend.)" "During childbirth where does the baby come out of the mother's body?" "Do boys menstruate?" (See Werner, 1975, for a report on similar questions asked of a physician in the health center of a large university.)

▶ In their sexual life there need be no mechanical regularity as to time, place, or frequency. Spontaneity furthers responsiveness; mechanism destroys it. Usually sexual intercourse should be mutually desired, allowing for the difference in degree of preparation needed by husband and wife. Sexual intercourse may be considered mutually desirable at times even though one spouse may not be interested, but if this is always the case adjustment is bound to be affected. Young persons often wonder about the danger of too frequent intercourse. There is no such danger as long as the experience is mutually desirable and as long as it is followed by a sense of well-being, relaxation, and oneness rather than a sense of regret, repugnance, guilt, or excessive fatigue.

▶ In the female, the urethra (the tube that leads from the bladder to the exterior) is relatively short, and its opening is near the opening of the vagina (see Exhibit 13-4). Typically, there is a variety of organisms found in this area. Hence, it is not uncommon for bacteria to be forced into the urethra and bladder during intercourse. When this occurs, a *urinary tract infection*, such as *urethritis* (in the urethra) and/or *cystitis* (in the bladder), may result. Such infection may occur in any woman (Marshall, 1974). But women in their early years of sexual experience seem to be especially susceptible, probably because they have not had time to develop an immunity. The term *honeymoon cystitis* is sometimes used to refer to the condition in newly married women. Some women become panicked at the onset of symptoms, such as pain, a burning sensation, and a feeling of urgency in urination. Some fear they have a venereal disease. Cystitis is not a condition calling for panic, but it is a condition calling for immediate medical attention for accurate differential diagnosis and treatment (Linton, 1971; Golden, 1971).

▶ An attitude of leisure is important. Haste, like sexual "mechanics," can be defeating. A couple should not consider intercourse something to be hurried through because there are other things waiting to be done. Nor should either party be put under pressure to achieve. "The male partner must be careful not to inject any personal demand for sexual performance into his female partner's pattern of response. The husband must not set goals for his wife. He must not try to force responsivity. . . . Sexual response can neither be programmed nor made to happen" (Masters and Johnson, 1970).

▶ Physical cleanliness is important, since sexual contact is so intimate.

▶ A young couple should be able to have privacy when they want it. Inquisitive neighbors, obtrusive relatives, a feeling of general uneasiness because of the possibility of intrusion or because of thin apartment walls—all make adjustment difficult.

▶ Fatigue often hinders adjustment. It cannot always be avoided in daily life, but the relation between fatigue and sexual adjustment should be understood and kept in mind. Johnson and Masters (1964) consider fatigue and preoccupation to be major deterrents to sexual responsiveness.

▶ Because of the esthetic element involved, there are probably many couples who do not have intercourse during the wife's menstrual period. But intercourse at that time is not dangerous and can be enjoyed by couples then the same as during other times (Martin and Long, 1969; Lane, 1974).

▶ Whether intercourse is advisable or inadvisable during all or part of a woman's pregnancy is a decision to be made by the woman and her obstetrician on the basis of knowledge of her particular condition. Medical opinions differ about the advisability of such intercourse in late pregnancy. Data derived from a study of 200 pregnant women suggest that orgasm, but not intercourse per se, may be a factor in initiating premature labor (Goodlin, Keller, and Raffin, 1971). Greenhill (1965a) believes we should ". . . urge deemphasizing abstinence during the final weeks of pregnancy," since intercourse at this time seems to be of little obstetrical significance if the woman is comfortable while it occurs. Hyams (1972) says, "While there is no proof that coitus in the second or third trimester induces premature labor, it is undoubtedly safest to abstain from intercourse in the last four weeks of gestation." Mann and Cunningham (1972) say that "in the average, normally progressing pregnancy there is no reason to interdict intercourse." Gorbach (1972) makes this statement: "If sexual intercourse in pregnancy caused miscarriages, the human race probably would have petered out many millions of years ago." In the light of divergence of opinion, the wisest course of action for a couple is to discuss the matter with their obstetrician and follow his or her suggestions. Except for the hypothetical possibility of inducing premature labor, there is no evidence that intercourse endangers the fetus.

Periodicity

Many women manifest *periodicity of sexual desire*. Both genders exhibit variations in intensity of interest and desire, not only from individual to individual but in the same person at different times. These latter variations depend upon fatigue, other interests and concerns, bodily functions, proximity of husband and wife, and frequency and recency of intercourse. Superimposed upon this irregular series of changes in the individual, there is in many women a more nearly regular cyclical or rhythmic change, which bears a relation to the menstrual cycle. Some women are conscious of no such periodicity. Others experience a heightened desire just before menstruation, just after menstruation, before and after, midway between periods, or at some other time relative to the menstrual cycle. In some the periodicity is regular and recurs each month; in others it is irregular. Whether this variation in interest is physiologically, psychologically, or otherwise conditioned is irrelevant here. If it exists, it is important in marriage.

A summary of the studies of seventeen investigators indicates that they all report periodicity before menstruation, after menstruation, or in mid-cycle, or a combination of two or three of these times in various numbers of women (Cavanagh, 1969). Ascertaining the exact number of women who are conscious of this cyclical change in their sexual interests is not so important as recognizing that a considerable proportion of women do experience it. A given husband is confronted with the problem of understanding one wife, not with a problem in statistics. Both husband and wife may learn how to detect and recognize each other's needs and desires, as well as feel free to make their own desires known. This need not always be done by direct statement. There are other more indirect and subtle means available.

It is interesting to note in passing that, in women who are aware of the periodicity of sexual desire, heightened interest does not always coincide with that phase of the menstrual cycle when the ovum is released and conception is possible.

Premenstrual Syndrome

For some women there is a brief period during the menstrual cycle, usually just prior to the onset of menstruation but sometimes earlier and at times persisting for a day or two after menstruation begins, when they exhibit one or more of a cluster of symptoms. These symptoms together are termed the *premenstrual syndrome*, sometimes referred to as *premenstrual tension*, although tension is only one of the possible symptoms. Some prefer the term "perimenstrual tension syndrome," "peri" meaning "around" (Kaplan, 1974), since the symptoms do not always cease abruptly at the onset of menstruation. Fluhmann (1956) says that though estimates of the number of women who exhibit the premenstrual syndrome vary, a reasonable estimate would be 60 percent; Israel (1967) estimates about two-thirds. Sutherland and Stewart (1965) found 39 percent in a study of 150 women. In discussing the premenstrual syndrome, writers (Gill, 1943; Novak, 1944; Hoffman, 1944; Hamblen, 1945; Lamb, Ulett, Masters, and Robinson, 1953; Kroger and Freed, 1956; Bowes, 1956; Fluhmann, 1956; Kessel and Coppen, 1963; Dalton, 1964; Lloyd, 1964c; Janowsky and Gorney, 1966; Greenhill, 1961, 1966; Israel, 1967; Paschkis, Rakoff, Cantarow, and Rupp, 1967; Ivey and Bardwick, 1968; Novak, Jones, and Jones, Jr., 1970; Daly, 1974) mention headache, anxiety, inability to concentrate, depression, emotional outbursts, crying spells, hypersensitivity, unexplainable fears, imperative ideas, insomnia, contrariness, exaggeration of trifles, loss of inhibitions, cruelty, and a host of other symptoms. One of these is "going on food binges," which Melody (1961) found in 80 percent of 200 women studied. In a sense, such symptoms are uncontrollable by the woman herself. At least the feelings are uncontrollable; their expression may be controlled. Certainly a woman need not take undue advantage of the situation because she gets the impression that statistics justify any type of behavior and that she is the victim of something beyond her control. (See Neu and DiMascio, 1974 for a summary of research studies.)

During the period immediately preceding menstruation many apparently normal women have a slight increase in body weight (Lloyd, 1964c; Southam and Gonzoga, 1965; Reeves, Garvin, and McElin, 1971). This increase in weight is manifested in generalized swelling, in swelling of the hands and feet, in puffiness of the face and eyelids. Some women complain of feeling bloated. They are aware of a noticeable increase in girth, and their clothes feel tight. This swelling is due to water retention in the body tissues, not in the bladder (Dalton, 1964); it is considered by some to be at least one of the factors contributing to the premenstrual syndrome, but there is not universal agreement on this point (Bruce and Russell, 1962). Symptoms such as water retention and its resultant weight gain may be relieved by limiting fluid intake, eating a salt-free diet, and taking a diuretic, that is, a drug which causes an increase in urination (Fluhmann, 1956; Bowes, 1956). But there is disagreement as to whether this relieves other symptoms (Page, Villee, and Villee, 1972). It is also suggested that the administration of progesterone may be helpful (Dalton, 1964). Treatment should, of course, be prescribed by a physician.

MARITAL SEXUALITY

Frequency

The changes in our society which have been responsible for increases in premarital sexual behavior appear also to have had their influence on marital sexual behavior. Data from national samples of women interviewed in 1965 and 1970 (Westoff, 1974) indicate an increase in marital coital frequency over this five-year period. Exhibit 11-3 shows that in 1965 the median monthly coital frequency was 5.8, whereas in 1970 it was 7.5. This trend is probably due to a combination of factors including availability of better contraception, better use of contraception, greater acceptance of sex, and changes in women's roles. The study found that women who work have higher coital frequencies, for example, and a greater number of women were in the work force at the end of this period than at the beginning. Coital frequency increases as educational level increases. In other words, more highly educated women have sexual intercourse more often. Women using effective methods of contraception, such as the pill, have coitus more often. Finally, increase was characteristic of all age groups, thus making invalid the argument that only youthful couples are responsible for the increase.

It should not be surprising that the frequency of sexual intercourse decreases with age and with length of marriage (Westoff and Westoff, 1971). Whereas couples who are married less than a year have coitus 11.2 times per month on the average, couples married between one and four years have a mean monthly coital frequency of only 7.5. Thus, there is a considerable decline in the amount of sexual activity for most couples. Studies have demonstrated that this is a nearly universal phenomenon, one which most couples ought to expect. As the newness of any sexual relationship wears off, the amount of interest, excitement, and eroticism generated by that relationship is likely to decrease. This does not mean that the couple's love or commitment to marriage is changed. It only suggests that the intensity of their

Exhibit 11-3 *Distribution of Coital Frequency in Four Weeks Prior to Interview, 1965 and 1970**

Coital Frequency	Percent 1965	1970
0	7.0	6.1
1-2	12.8	9.9
3-4	20.9	17.0
5-6	15.6	14.6
7-8	16.6	15.2
9-10	9.3	10.4
11-14	9.8	11.4
15-18	4.4	7.2
19 or more	3.8	8.1
Median	5.8	7.5
Mean	6.8	8.2

*Based on interviews with 4,603 women in 1965 and 5,432 women in 1970.

Source: (Westoff 1974).

Exhibit 11-4 Mean Monthly Coital Frequency, by Age and Duration of Marriage, in a National Sample of Married Females Age 15 to 44.

Characteristic	Mean
Age:	
Under 20	10.3
20–24	8.1
25–29	7.3
30–34	6.7
35–39	5.9
40–44	5.1
Marriage Duration:	
Less than 1 year	11.2
1–4	7.5
5–9	7.4
10–14	6.7
15–19	6.0
20–24	5.2
25 years or more	4.7

Source: (Westoff and Westoff 1971).

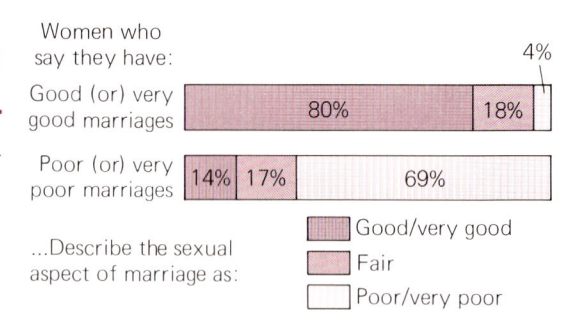

Exhibit 11-5 How satisfaction with marriage varies in relation to sexual satisfaction. (*Source: Levin and Levin, 1975.*)

Women who say they have good (or) very good marriages describe the sexual aspect of marriage as: Good/very good 80%, Fair 18%, Poor/very poor 4%.

Women who say they have poor (or) very poor marriages describe the sexual aspect of marriage as: Good/very good 14%, Fair 17%, Poor/very poor 69%.

sexual relationship may diminish. The extent of the change varies from couple to couple, of course. Some couples maintain a relatively high frequency of coitus throughout their married life, and others have little or no sexual intercourse at any period.

Marital Adjustment and Sexual Adjustment

Numerous studies have shown that there is a relationship between marital adjustment and sexual adjustment (Lewis and Spanier, 1978). This correlation is illustrated in Exhibit 11-5. The direction of causation between the two variables has been difficult to determine, however. Does a happy marriage lead to better sexual adjustment, or does good sexual adjustment lead to a happier marriage? Some researchers have concluded that the direction of causation is different for men and women. For a man, sexual adjustment influences his marital adjustment, while for a woman, marital adjustment influences sexual adjustment (Clark and Wallin, 1965). This finding is an interesting, but tentative, one which must be substantiated by further research. If such a difference does exist today, we might expect that it would be diminished in future years, with both males and females alike finding that their overall marital adjustment influences their sexual adjustment rather than vice versa. Since sex is just one component in marital adjustment, it will become increasingly unlikely that a problem in this particular area would be so overwhelming that it could cause a marriage to break down. More likely is the possibility that the symptoms of a troubled marriage will appear in the form of sexual problems. Most couples list their sexual relationship as a very important part of their overall adjustment (Spanier, 1976*b*), but they also usually recognize that problems in sexual adjustment may be rooted in poor marital adjustment.

EXTRAMARITAL SEX

Extramarital sex, also referred to as adultery, is no doubt as ancient as marriage itself. It is difficult to get accurate statistics, but apparently such relations are common. In American society adultery has been condemned on moral or religious grounds by the majority of the population—even by some who have engaged in it. At the same time there has been a "closed-eyes" policy in some quarters. Adultery is a ground for divorce in most states, even in some which do not specify grounds in the law. Most Americans enter marriage with the expectation of sexual exclusiveness, and the discovery of adultery on the part of one spouse may be deeply traumatic to the other.

In recent years, however, an attitude that may not be new but is newly articulated and publicized theorizes that, since monogamous marriage no longer meets the needs of its participants, extramarital sexual relations are desirable. Such relations are recommended as a means of giving husband and wife freedom, providing sexual variety, being a test of love because they remove all restrictions on love, meeting a human need to love more than one person at one time, and having a bolstering and therapeutic effect on a marriage which has lost its zest or "gone stale." Terms such as *beneficial experience* and *healthy adultery* are used.

Although most individuals still believe that extramarital sexual relations are wrong, data indicate that large numbers of Americans have engaged in them at one time or another. In Kinsey's studies in the 1930s and 1940s, 50 percent of the men and 26 percent of the women had engaged in extramarital intercourse by the time they had reached 40 years of age. More recent data suggest that there has been perhaps a small increase among men, but a rather dramatic increase among young women and working women (Bell and Peltz, 1974; Hunt, 1974; Levin and Levin, 1975). In short, the younger generation of married women seems to be catching up with men. The greater incidence of extramarital sex among young women is undoubtedly related to changes in attitudes toward sexuality, greater freedom for females, and the increase in the number of working women. As women go outside the home more and are put into settings where they are likely to meet, become friendly with, and develop close personal relationships with men other than their husbands, it is reasonable to expect that—as has been true of men in the past—some of these relationships will come to involve sexual intercourse.

As we did in discussing premarital sexual behavior, we must point out that there is a difference between active incidence and cumulative incidence. Although perhaps a majority of married persons will have extramarital sexual relations sometime during their marriage, the number who are doing so at any given time is likely to be small. Many of these relationships are temporary or transitory and have little emotional involvement. Many persons have a sexual relationship with someone whom they will never see again. This appears to be particularly characteristic of men. Of course, some extramarital relationships do have significant emotional impact on the participants, are not temporary, and may come to compete with the marital relationship.

Couples vary in their reactions to a partner's extramarital relations. Some spouses are insanely jealous if their partner even has lunch or goes for a walk with a member of the opposite gender. In this case, an adulterous sexual relationship may cause irrevocable damage to the marriage. Other couples have an understanding that extramarital sexual relationships are acceptable so long as they are transient and do not interfere with the marriage. This may be difficult to control, however. Other couples are very open about extramarital sex, perhaps even encouraging it. The great majority of sexual relationships outside of marriages are clandestine, or secretive. Most persons do not tell their spouses, since they know that they would receive a negative reaction.

One recent study found that 25 percent of married females aged 20 to 25 had already had extramarital coitus, while 38 percent of those in the 35 to 40 age group had. Among working women in this 35 to 40 age category, the cumulative incidence was 48 percent. It is also interesting to note that 12 percent of the women who had been married less than one year stated that they had already been involved (Levin and Levin, 1975). These data are from the *Redbook* study of 100,000 females who volunteered information and may not be representative of the entire population. Extramarital sex does not always involve intercourse. One study found that 10 percent of the respondents reported extramarital petting but no coitus (Hunt, 1974).

Although accurate data are hard to come by, there is no doubt that extramarital sexual relations involve a great number of persons in the United States. Despite widespread norms against such behavior, an increasing number of individuals choose to participate. We might speculate that the trend will continue into the future. Cross-cultural data give us some insight into possible trends. It has been observed (K. Davis, 1971) that a sexual custom is accepted to the degree that it is perceived as supporting the marriage and family institutions. If extramarital sexual behavior is, in the future, defined as enhancing marital relationships, or at least not interfering with them, perhaps it will be more readily accepted. Murdock's (1949) examination of other cultures found that 20 percent of them normatively allowed extramarital coitus, although about two-thirds allowed it if the partner was a future mate (as could be possible in a polygamous marriage). Thus, the norm prohibiting sex outside marriage that has been stated for our culture is not a universal one.

Of course, every couple must decide for themselves whether extramarital sexual relationships will be permitted. Men tend to have the greater interest in such affairs, and thus it is likely that many couples will be unable to reach agreement on this question. This lack of agreement may partially account for the great number of clandestine relationships. Some marriages are able to tolerate extramarital affairs without much stress. Other marriages are severely strained by the outside sexual activities of one of the partners.

How is adultery related to marital adjustment and stability? A great deal of research shows a very high correlation between adultery and marital failure. But we must be careful about generalizing here. Many adulterous relationships commence only after a marriage has failed or the couple have separated. Thus while adultery is commonly acknowledged by divorcing couples, in many cases it did not contribute to the marital discord which led to divorce. Some state divorce laws in America attempt to prevent a "third party" from disrupting a marriage by making it illegal for a person divorced on grounds of adultery to marry the "paramour" after the divorce. This is the case in Pennsylvania, for example. However, thirty case studies of divorced persons conducted by one of the authors of this text in 1974 revealed that whereas twenty-one of these persons had been sexually involved outside the marriage, in not a single one of the cases did the spouse go on to marry the "third person." Thus, adultery often appears to be associated with poor marital adjustment, but the cause-effect sequence is not fully understood. Whether extramarital sexual relations will influence the quality of a given marriage will depend more on the spouses involved than on anything else. It cannot be said, in light of the high incidence of extramarital sex, that it necessarily predisposes a couple to divorce. For some couples, it may not influence their adjustment at all. It is clear, however, that for many couples it may put special strain on the marriage and contribute to marital discord.

Swinging

"Swinging," or "mate swapping," is one form of extramarital sexual relationship which has received a great deal of attention in recent years. Mate swapping refers to the sexual exchange of partners among two or more married couples. Other terms such as comarital mate sharing, wife swapping, and group sex have all been used by various authors to refer to the phenomenon. The term "group sex" is misleading because most swinging encounters do not involve group sexual activities. "Wife swapping" is a sexually biased term which participants reject, and concepts like "comarital sexual mate sharing" are used mainly by social scientists. Books about mate swapping began appearing over a decade ago, but it was not until about 1970 that professionals became fully aware of the phenomenon. A multitude of swingers' magazines became available, swinging received attention in the mass media, and a book was published entitled *Group Sex* (Bartell, 1971), based on an anthropologist's participant observation study of swinging.

In a 1971 study conducted in a midwestern community of 40,000, 1.7 percent of the community were found to have participated in mate swapping on at least one occasion (Spanier and Cole, 1973). Almost 7 percent of the respondents, however, indicated they would consider participating if the opportunity presented itself. Over half of the respondents in the sample said they had heard about mate swapping, and over 10 percent claimed to have first-hand knowledge about mate swapping in the community. Of course, what was found in one community may not be a sound basis for generalizing about other communities, but our data suggest that mate swapping does exist among a small portion of the population and is known to a considerably larger portion of the community.

During the past several years there have been over a dozen studies of various aspects of the swinging phenomenon. Although national data are not available, a fairly detailed picture of swinging activity has emerged. Data are available primarily from the many participant observation studies which have been conducted. Perhaps of greatest significance is that swinging is characterized by great variability. Although it is most common in urban areas, it exists in rural areas as well. Although it involves persons primarily in their thirties and forties, studies have had respondents from the teens to the mid-seventies. And although it is most common among middle- and upper-middle-class persons, it can be found among all social class groups, involving persons with diverse backgrounds, occupations, and interests. The most consistent picture of mate swappers that emerges is of the middle-class, middle-aged American couple, with children, who have been married ten to twenty years, live in an urban or suburban area, and are in most aspects of their life-style, political activity, and behavior conservative, stable, and conventional. The suggestion that mate swappers are sexual freaks, political radicals, or nonconformists in life-style does not find any support in the research literature.

There appear to be five primary ways in which swingers are recruited (Denfeld and Gordon, 1970):

1 *Swinging magazines*. There are several magazines that serve the primary function of presenting advertisements to which interested couples may respond. The ads usually include basic information about the couple, although the woman is usually featured, with details about what kinds of social and sexual activities interest the advertising couple. Contacts are made by phone or letter, an arrangement for a social meeting is planned, and a potential mate swapping exchange develops. Some couples travel great distances to meet other swingers.

2 *Swingers' organizations*. A number of mate swapping organizations have developed around the country. They exist in many urban areas. Members are personally recruited or solicited through magazines. These organizations hold social activities at which couples can meet other swingers and make arrangements for mate swapping at some time after the party. Meetings are sometimes held at

resorts to facilitate such exchange during the gathering.

3 *Swingers' bars.* Most major cities have bars which are known to swingers. Some bars are not exclusively for swingers, but may cater to them, especially during certain nights of the week. Other bars are patronized mainly by swingers. Couples frequent the bars to meet other couples, and arrangements are usually made for a more private get-together involving the two couples.

4 *Personal recruitment.* Swingers often "feel out" other couples, sometimes over a long period of time, to determine whether they might be interested in mate swapping. A mate-swapping couple may interest friends or casual acquaintances in trying swinging.

5 *Swingers' parties.* In some communities, mate-swapping couples may throw a party to which swingers and potential swingers are invited. Couples (but especially the males) engage in a recruitment process, which may result in a swinging encounter at the party or sometime afterward.

Most mate swappers claim that the reason they began swinging was to alleviate boredom, both sexual and nonsexual, which developed in their marriages. Their ultimate objective is to improve their general marital and sexual relationship. The husband is usually the first one to suggest swinging, and he engages in a long process, often extending over several months, in which he convinces his wife that swinging would be good for the marital relationship, would bring them closer together, and would revitalize their sex lives. Although the wife is often a reluctant participant initially, swingers report that the attention she receives and the realization that she is desirable to many men may subsequently enhance her evaluation of swinging.

Mate swappers claim that swinging is preferable to adulterous relationships because it is more honest, involves both partners, is in the open, and is designed to prevent the development of emotional attachment and jealousy. Thus, swingers claim that mate swapping is the least threatening form of extramarital sex. The equalitarianism suggested by mate swapping is more theoretical than real. Jealousy and other problems do exist. Of interest, however, is the observation that middle-aged mate swappers, who were socialized before women's liberation, still tend to retain conventional sex-role stereotypes. Mate swapping, then, is dominated by men. Researchers report that when the husband wants to initiate a contact, go home, or drop out entirely, the wife usually consents. Arrangements are typically in the hands of the men, and the social interaction at mate-swapping parties is most often male-dominated.

The sexual activities of swingers are as varied as their backgrounds and methods of participation. Most typically, swinging involves two couples who have met through a party, bar, organization, or advertisement. They meet in the home of one of the couples and spend the evening in much the same way nonswingers would. At the end of the evening, however, the couples will exchange partners and have coitus. Most swinging is "closed," in that each sexual encounter involves one couple in the privacy of a bedroom. Among some swingers, however, sex may be "open," may involve more than two persons, or may involve homosexual activities. Single persons usually are not part of the swinging scene, although couples consisting of two singles may participate in some cases. Single females are welcome at some swingers' parties, but in other social settings the single female is considered threatening to the married females.

Perhaps the best way to gain insight into the problems and pitfalls of mate swapping is to consider the persons who have dropped out of swinging activities (Denfeld, 1974). The reasons swingers give for dropping out are jealousy, guilt, development of outside emotional attachments, boredom and loss of interest, disappointment, divorce or separation, wife's inability to "take it," and fear of discovery. Some couples report that swinging improved their marriage, and they cite the following reasons: excitement, sexual freedom, greater appreciation of mate, learning of new sex techniques, sexual variety, and better communication and openness between partners.

We must conclude that swinging may be problematic for some couples but may enhance the marital relationship for others. Apparently the swingers' norms designed to prevent jealousy, threats to the marriage, and emotional attachments do not work for many couples. For others, it is possible that swinging may help change their relationship in positive directions. Despite the reinforcement women usually receive from their husband and the attention they receive from other men, the majority of couples who drop out do so at the insistence of the wife.

Our speculation is that mate swapping will continue to exist among a small portion of Americans. It will increasingly be tried on an experimental or temporary basis, but it is not likely to become very widespread.

SEXUAL DYSFUNCTIONS

Sexual dysfunctions are impaired or faulty sexual functions. They may appear in any sexual relationship, and Masters and Johnson (1970) estimate that as many as half of all married couples experience some form of sexual dysfunction during their lives. Sometimes sexual dysfunction occurs temporarily and disappears without treatment after a short period of time. Other cases persist and require the attention of a trained sex therapist or a marriage and family counselor who has had training in the treatment of sexual dysfunction. The success rate for therapy involving sexual dysfunctions is very high compared with other forms of therapy, and individuals or couples can be optimistic about having a sexual dsyfunction successfully treated if they are motivated to remedy the problem. Of necessity, our discussion will be oversimplified. For a full discussion of sexual dysfunctions and their treatment see Masters and Johnson (1970) or Kaplan (1974).

Sexual Dysfunctions in the Male

Impotence Impotence refers to a man's inability to maintain an erection sufficient to permit successful sexual intercourse. In *primary impotence*, the male has never been able to achieve and maintain an erection sufficient to permit sexual intercourse, although in some cases he has been able to masturbate and has erections at other times. *Secondary impotence* exists when the male has been able to achieve an erection and have successful intercourse previously, but is now unable to do so. Secondary impotence is the more common of the two types.

There are numerous possible causes of impotence, and in some cases more than one operate simultaneously. Most of the causes of impotence center on fears, anxieties, and tension surrounding the sex act, the relationship with the partner, or the circumstances under which intercourse is taking place. Although most cases of impotence involve psychogenic, or emotional, factors, there may be an organic or functional cause. Organic causes of impotence are rare. They involve anatomical defects in the reproductive or central nervous systems. Functional causes involve nervous disorders, hormonal functioning, or physical exhaustion. Drugs may also cause a temporary, or in rare cases permanent, condition of impotence. Diseases such as diabetes may impair potency. For these reasons, physical causes should not always be ruled out in impotence.

Nevertheless, in the majority of cases, the cause of impotence is not a physical one. Social-psychological factors, such as insecurity and anxiety regarding sexual performance or fear of failure, are more prevalent. Fear of failure may contribute to actual failure. The wife's attitude and criticism may contribute to impotence if she lets him know that she feels intercourse is an imposition upon her. If she makes demands on him for successful performance and makes the husband entirely responsible for her orgasm, if she repeatedly criticizes his approach, or if she rejects the husband as a sexual partner, his confidence may be undermined and impotence may result. Men and women should both communicate with their sexual partners, but hostility and excessive criticism can be harmful.

Other factors which may contribute to impotence are religious taboos on sex; a belief that sex is immoral or unclean; incestuous encounters in the early years, especially mother-son sexual encounters; homosexuality; failure in premarital sexual encounters with prostitutes; parental dominance destroying the male's confidence in his masculinity; marital discord; depression, stress, or fatigue; use of addictive drugs; excessive use of alcohol; castration; hormone imbalance; surgery on the prostate gland or inflammation of the organ; and infections and other diseases.

Most men experience a bout of impotence sometime in their lives, for example, after a hard, tiring day. A couple need not be alarmed if from time to time one type of sexual dysfunction presents itself. When a man is ill, worried, under the influence of drugs or alcohol, or especially fatigued, it is not uncommon for him to be unable to attain an erection. Counseling should be sought, however, when there is concern or when the problem persists.

Premature ejaculation Premature ejaculation refers to the male's inability to control the ejaculation of seminal fluid either before the penis actually enters the vagina or for a sufficient period after entry to permit the wife to achieve sexual satisfaction. Such control of ejaculation is not always possible, of course. Once the male has reached a level of stimulation that represents a "point of no return," ejaculation becomes inevitable. But before this point is reached, some control is usually possible, and a male may voluntarily condition himself to increase it. The male with premature ejaculation reaches this "point of no return" too soon.

Premature ejaculation is also likely to have its roots in psychological or emotional adjustments. Many of the causes of impotence are also causes of premature ejaculation. Fears, tension, anxiety, and concern about performance may be the cause of premature ejaculation in some males. Other causes are the male's inexperience; a high degree of sexual stimulation and tension compared with his partner's; disregard of the female partner's need for stimulation through foreplay; and an unusually high degree of sensitivity to stimulation. If premature ejaculation becomes an habitual pattern, it can lead to impotence. In any case, it is likely to produce dissatisfaction and tension in the female partner and embarrassment and possibly humiliation in the male.

Since many women do not always have orgasm in sexual intercourse, it would be unreasonable to define premature ejaculation as a condition in which a man ejaculates before his partner reaches orgasm. Furthermore, many couples prefer that the male or female have their orgasm first and then satisfy the other partner afterwards. Thus, the definition of premature ejaculation is a relative one. If the male ejaculates too soon *for that couple* to achieve sexual satisfaction, we may then consider premature ejaculation to exist. Regardless of the point at which a couple considers the timing a problem, treatment programs have been successful in dealing with this form of dysfunction.

Retarded ejaculation This is the opposite of premature ejaculation and is sometimes referred to as "ejaculatory incompetence." A male with retarded ejaculation can achieve and maintain an erection long enough to have intercourse and perhaps satisfy his partner, but he is unable to ejaculate during intercourse. This is the rarest of the three forms of male sexual dysfunction. Among possible causes are rejection by the wife; dislike for or enmity toward the wife; desire not to have children coupled with the wife's refusal to use contraception; emotional trauma; homosexuality; religious beliefs that consider sex immoral or unclean; and an obsession with the need for a partner's sexual satisfaction.

Sexual Dysfunctions in the Female

Orgasmic dysfunction "Frigidity" is the common term for this dysfunction, but some prefer the term "orgasmic dysfunction" since the term "frigid," when applied to the female, has been misused and abused. A woman with orgasmic dysfunction may be devoid of sexual feelings, or she may have sexual feelings but fail to achieve orgasm. Orgasmic dysfunction is not the female equivalent of impotence. A woman may be able to have intercourse but be unable to respond. In contrast, an impotent male is unable to have intercourse because he is unable to achieve an erection. Orgasmic dysfunction may be *primary*, in which case the woman has never responded, or it may be *secondary*, in which case she has been able to respond at least once with a given partner but is unresponsive in a specific situation or with a specific male.

Among possible causes of orgasmic dysfunction are: the cultural expectation that women be disinterested in sex and the depreciation of female sexuality; religious teaching that sex is immoral or unclean; guilt or shame produced by early training; the woman considering sex frightening or disgusting and thinking of intercourse as an imposition, an ordeal, an obligation, or a duty to be performed reluctantly; an underlying sexual conflict in the woman, denying her sexuality either consciously or subconsciously; ignorance of sex; fear of pain in intercourse; lesbian (homosexual) inclination or preference; illness, fatigue; use of addictive drugs; and sexual trauma, for example, rape or incestuous sexual relations with her father in her youth. As with male sexual dysfunctions, orgasmic dysfunction in females is primarily related to emotional and psychological dispositions.

The husband may be involved in her dysfunction for one of several reasons—the woman's lack of identification with him; her disapproval or nonacceptance of him; his failure to meet her expectations; his demand for performance on her part; his mechanical, unenlightened, or hurried approach to sex and the resulting inadequate stimulation of her before or during intercourse; something he does or says which causes discomfort or disgust, such as his insisting on postures in intercourse which seem to her animallike; his habitual direct approach to intercourse without any accompanying or preceding expression of love and affection.

Circumstances surrounding the sexual relationship may cause dysfunction, since a woman is more sensitive than a man to the circumstances under which intercourse occurs. For example, orgasmic dysfunction may develop if the couple cannot have privacy and there is the continual possibility of intrusion by another person; if intercourse occurs in unattractive, unappealing surroundings; or if there is distraction such as noise in a neighboring apartment or the crying of a baby.

Many young women who have just begun to have sexual intercourse have sought counseling stating that they were experiencing sexual dysfunction. The authors have counseled many who, because they have not yet had an orgasm, feel that they are sexually abnormal. It should be stated that "orgasmic dysfunction" is not a term which adequately describes these young females. Many counselors and researchers prefer to call such young women "preorgasmic." This distinction is not simply a euphemism. It is intended to convey the idea that they do not necessarily have a serious problem. Attainment of orgasm is difficult for some young women, but it is likely to come in time through practice and experience. Kinsey and his colleagues (1953) found, for example, that 36 percent of married females had never experienced orgasm from any source (including masturbation) prior to marriage. In the first year of marriage, only 63 percent of coitus resulted in orgasm, and 25 percent of the females never experienced orgasm even once. Yet after fifteen years of marriage, 90 percent of married women experienced orgasm at least some of the time. Thus, a preorgasmic female may well be frustrated, but she should not conclude that she has a serious problem. Lack of orgasmic response is a common characteristic of adjustment to an early sexual relationship. If the condition persists or is of great concern, however, the female and her partner should not hesitate to see a counselor.

Dyspareunia Dyspareunia is difficult or painful intercourse. It may occur in either males or females, but it occurs more often in females and is usually considered a female sexual dysfunction. Since pain is subjective, it is often difficult, or even impossible, to pinpoint the cause of dyspareunia. Some women claim dyspareunia in order to avoid intercourse which is distasteful to them. In others there are anatomical or physiological causes of pain. As with the other forms of sexual dysfunction already mentioned, the most common causes of dyspareunia are pain, fear, and tension surrounding the sexual relationship. A great deal of fear and anxiety can, for example, prevent adequate vaginal lubrication, which may be painful for the female. Add to this condition the woman's subjective feeling that sexual intercourse is distasteful and painful, and a typical condition of dyspareunia may develop. Among other possible causes are infection or inflammation in or injury to the vagina; irritation of or injury to the clitoris; adhesions following surgery; remnants of the hymen bruised during first intercourse or by accident; allergic reaction to chemicals used in douching or for contraception; and conditions in the ligaments surrounding the vagina. Among possible causes of pain in males are irritation to the external surface of the penis; injury to the penis; allergic reaction to chemicals used by the female for douching or contraception; infection or inflammation in the urethra, seminal vesicles, prostate gland, or bladder; and gonorrhea and its after-effects.

Vaginismus This is a condition in which muscles surrounding the vaginal entrance contract involuntarily and this spasm or contraction prevents penetration by the penis, hence preventing intercourse. Emotional causes are almost always involved in vaginismus, mainly the female's fear of sexual intercourse, her nervousness with her partner, or anxiety. Specific causes associated with vaginismus are religious teaching or early training that depicts sex as immoral or unclean; a woman's belief that intercourse is for reproduction only, and she is not ready to have children; or fear of intercourse because of dyspareunia or a previous sexual trauma, such as rape.

Many females experience mild cases of vaginismus on given occasions, just as a man may be impotent on a given occasion. If this happens on only rare occasions, it is probably no cause for alarm. However, if the condition persists or if it causes concern, a counselor should be consulted. While there are stories of couples who have had to be carried in each other's arms to an emergency room to be separated after a sudden onset of vaginismus, there are no cases whatsoever of this kind on record.

Treatment of Sexual Dysfunction

We have already mentioned that success rates in the treatment of sexual dysfunction are high compared with other forms of therapy (Masters and Johnson, 1970; Kaplan, 1974). Like other forms of treatment and counseling, sexual therapy has many variations, techniques, and objectives depending on the therapist or counselor and the problem and circumstances of the counselee. In recent years, a behaviorally oriented form of treatment has been adopted by many therapists with great success. A *behavioral treatment program* is one directed primarily at relieving the specific symptoms of the sexual dysfunction and, therefore, the dysfunction itself. For example, the primary goal in the treatment of impotence is to get the male to achieve an erection, to have sexual intercourse, and to be able to continue to have a successful sexual relationship well beyond the period of the therapy. The treatment goal of orgasmic dysfunction would be to get the female to become more sexually responsive, achieve orgasm, and continue to be responsive beyond the period of the therapy. Other therapists use a behavioral form of therapy combined with more traditional psychotherapy or marriage and family counseling. In such cases, other problems are dealt with before or concurrently with the sexual dysfunction.

Since many sexual problems are a result of or happen in conjunction with marital discord, it is often very important to have marriage counseling as a part of the sexual therapy. Other therapists prefer to bypass the marital discord when symptoms of sexual dysfunction exist and direct attention to the sexual aspect of the relationship. Although the two areas cannot be readily separated in reality, different therapists have different goals for the couples they see depending on the treatment program used, the couple's situation, and other factors. Couples often arrive at the counselor's office stating that a sexual problem exists, but upon probing further the counselor realizes that the sexual problem is rooted in other, more basic marital problems. Each counselor or therapist will make a decision about the most appropriate form of treatment for a given couple.

Most sex therapists depart from traditional counseling techniques by employing prescribed sexual experiences as a part of the treatment. Stated differently, counselors and therapists will usually instruct the couple carefully as to what course their sexual behavior should take during the treatment. They may ask couples to try exercises such as "pleasuring" masturbation, genital touching, back rubs, or manual manipulation, and they usually set ground rules to be followed in the sexual relationship. This structure and the exercises which are prescribed have been found to result in successful treatment for many couples.

Treatment formats and programs vary. Sometimes a team approach is used, involving one male and one female therapist. In other cases, only one counselor is present. Some therapy involves physical examinations, while other types do not. Most counselors will make a referral for a physical examination if they suspect that a physical cause may be involved in the sexual dysfunction. In most cases, the husband and wife are seen jointly. The use of *surrogates* (substitute partners) for persons who want individual counseling for sexual dysfunction has been controversial but is endorsed by many respected persons and is still used in some treatment programs. Some programs are intensive, involving full-time, daily treatment over a period as long as two weeks. Most treatment programs involve therapy over several weeks, with the sessions occurring only once or twice a week.

As in any profession, there are quacks who profess to be sex therapists. Persons who are concerned about the legitimacy of a sex therapist or counselor should ascertain whether that person has a license or is certified for this type of counseling. Persons seeking treatment should not hesitate to ask the counselor about his or her credentials. The American Association of Sex Educators and Counselors certifies therapists. Many persons licensed by the American Association of Marriage and Family Counselors are also competent sex therapists. We shall treat the subject of marriage and family counseling more fully in Chapter 16.

Conclusion

It is important that the reader understand that we have been discussing conditions which may possibly occur and which, when they do occur, are found in a wide variety of persons and couples. No one person or couple exhibits all of them. It is like reading a medical textbook; no one person has all the diseases discussed.

A couple or an individual having a sexual problem will do well to discuss it with a counselor. Since some problems are the outgrowth of a total situation involving two persons plus circumstances, it cannot be emphasized too strongly that both persons should consult the counselor. Treatment of sexual dysfunction can be helpfully recommended only after diagnosis of the cause. In most instances there is little to be gained by talking the problem over with friends or other lay persons. The probability is that they know no more than the couple. Reliance on advertisement, gadgets, and drugs such as aphrodisiacs erroneously believed to increase sexual interest and responsiveness may not only do more harm than good, but at best is unlikely to get at the basic cause of the dysfunction.

TERMS TO BE LEARNED

adultery
afterglow
climax
clitoris
coital postures
coitus
conception
cystitis
diuretic
dyspareunia
erection
extramarital sex
foreplay
frigid (frigidity)
homologous
honeymoon cystitis
hymen (hymenal)
imperforate hymen

impotent (impotency)
labium (labia)
lesbian (lesbianism)
mate swapping
microperforate hymen
mutuality
myotonia
normal curve
orgasm
orgasmic dysfunction
pelvic examination
periodicity
plateau
positions in intercourse
premarital counseling
premarital medical
   examination
premature ejaculation

premenstrual syndrome
premenstrual tension
pubococcygeus muscle
refractory period
resolution
retarded ejaculation
rudimentary
surrogates
swinging
technique
transudation
tumescence (tumescent)
urethra (urethral)
urethritis
urinary tract
vagina (vaginal)
vaginismus
vasocongestion

SELECTED READINGS

BARTELL, GILBERT D.: *Group Sex: A Scientist's Eyewitness Report on the American Way of Swinging*, Peter H. Wyden, Inc., New York, 1971. (Paperback.) A study of swinging and the people who swing.

BELLIVEAU, FRED, AND LIN RICHTER: *Understanding Human Sexual Inadequacy*, Bantam Books, Inc., New York, 1970. (Paperback.) A nontechnical discussion of the research findings presented in Masters and Johnson's *Human Sexual Inadequacy*. Also includes personality sketches of Masters and Johnson, tells how their work started, and how it was first received.

BIRD, LOIS: *How to Be a Happily Married Mistress*, Doubleday & Company, Inc., Garden City, N.Y., 1970. The author is happy to be a woman and wants wives to be sexual companions rather than "just housewives." "This is a book on the fun of loving a husband. . . ." Hence the use of the word "mistress" in the title. Makes suggestions on understanding a husband, improving communication, and how a wife may contribute to the couple's sexual relationship.

CUBER, J., AND P. B. HARROFF: *The Significant Americans: A Study of Sexual Behavior Among the Affluent*, Appleton-Century-Crofts, Inc., New York, 1965. An examination of the marriages and sexual activity of people in the upper income brackets.

FISHER, SEYMOUR: *The Female Orgasm*, Basic Books, Inc., New York, 1973. The report of a five-year study of the sexual life of 300 middle-class wives. The author's "objective was to ascertain the relationship between personality and sexual responsiveness . . . with special attention to personality traits which are correlated with orgasm capacity."

GITTELSON, NATALIE: *The Erotic Life of the American Wife*, Delacorte Press, New York, 1972. Discussion and analysis of the attitudes and behavior primarily of women relative to men, sex, and marriage (but also of some men relative to women, sex, and marriage) based on interviews with more than 600 persons.

HASTINGS, DONALD W.: *A Doctor Speaks on Sexual Expression in Marriage*, Little, Brown and Company, Boston, 1966. Discusses the honeymoon, sexual intercourse, impotence, frigidity, masturbation, menopause, sexual development, and children's curiosity about sex.

JOHNSON, RALPH E.: "Attitudes toward Extramarital Relationships," *Medical Aspects of Human Sexuality*, vol. 6, no. 4, pp. 168–191, April 1972. Analysis of both old and new points of view.

KATCHADOURIAN, HERANT A., AND DONALD T. LUNDE: *Fundamentals of Human Sexuality*, 2d ed., Holt, Rinehart and Winston, Inc., New York, 1975. This book grew out of a course on human sexuality at Stanford University. The authors are psychiatrists. Discusses many aspects of human sexuality, including variations and deviations in sexual behavior; the erotic in art, literature, and films; sex and the law; current trends.

LEHRMAN, NAT: *Masters and Johnson Explained*, Playboy Press, Chicago, 1970. (Paperback.) Analysis in nontechnical language of both the Masters and Johnson reports. Includes reports of interviews with Masters and Johnson.

MCCARY, JAMES LESLIE: *Human Sexuality*, 2d ed., D. Van Nostrand Company, Inc., New York, 1973. A discussion of many aspects of human sexuality, including sexual disorders, variant behavior, aphrodisiacs, myths, and fallacies.

———: *Sexual Myths and Fallacies*, Van Nostrand Reinhold Company, New York, 1971. Myths and fallacies concerning sexual behavior.

MCDERMOTT, SANDRA: *Female Sexuality: Its Nature and Conflicts*, Simon and Schuster, Inc., New York, 1970. A report on interviews with more than 250 British women on their premarital, marital, heterosexual, and lesbian activities and attitudes. Includes many quotations from the women and fourteen taped interviews.

MACE, DAVID R.: *Sexual Difficulties in Marriage*, Fortress Press, Philadelphia, 1972. (Paperback.) Addressed to readers who have sexual difficulties in marriage. Discusses role of sex in marriage, sexual problems, what can be done about them, and how professional counseling may help.

MASTERS, WILLIAM H., AND VIRGINIA E. JOHNSON: *Human Sexual Response*, Little, Brown and Company, Boston, 1966 and *Human Sexual Inadequacy*, Little, Brown and Company, Boston, 1970. Important technical contributions by well-known sex experts; their research and findings and the implications of these findings.

———AND———(in association with Robert J. Levin): *The Pleasure Bond (A New Look at Sexual-*

ity and Commitment), Little, Brown and Company, Boston, 1975. (Paperback.) The authors have distilled extensive research in sexual behavior and dysfunction into a nontechnical discussion of some of the things they have learned and some of the convictions they have formed. They discuss young marriages, women's liberation, extramarital sex, swinging, commitment, and second marriages and report on discussions of such topics with groups of persons representing each of them.

MORNELL, PIERRE: *The LoveBook: What Works in a Lasting Sexual Relationship*, Harper & Row, Publishers, New York, 1974. The author, a psychiatrist, says: "I have attempted to present an optimistic view of lasting intimacy . . . the 'what does work' side of living together." Nontechnical, with many references to cases.

NEUBECK, GERHARD (ed.): *Extramarital Relations*, Prentice-Hall, Inc., Englewood Cliffs, N.J., 1969. (Paperback.) A symposium presenting various points of view.

PIERSON, ELAINE C., AND WILLIAM V. D'ANTONIO: *Female and Male: Dimensions of Human Sexuality*, J. B. Lippincott Company, Philadelphia, 1974. (Paperback.) A female physician and male sociologist discuss various aspects of human sexuality.

REISS, I. L.: *Heterosexual Relationships: Inside and Outside of Marriage*, General Learning Press, Morristown, N.J., October 1973. The author explains his research and findings and develops the implications for heterosexual relationships within and outside marriage.

SCHAEFER, LEAH CAHAN: *Women and Sex: Sexual Experiences and Reactions of a Group of Thirty Women as Told to a Female Psychotherapist*, Pantheon Books, New York, 1973. Based on in-depth interviews. Discusses early sexual experiences, reactions to menarche, early sex education, masturbation, premarital intercourse, orgasm.

SEAMAN, BARBARA: *Free and Female*, Coward, McCann & Geoghegan, Inc., New York, 1972. "The first book to report on women's sexual needs and capacities from a feminist point of view. . . . Gives the facts, untainted by male prejudice." Discusses clitoral versus vaginal orgasm, what women like in men, women's criticisms of men's sexual techniques, malpractice among gynecologists, venereal disease, a criticism of the pill, and children of liberated women.

SINGER, IRVING: *The Goals of Human Sexuality*, W. W. Norton & Company, Inc., New York, 1973. "This book argues for a pluralistic approach to human sexuality." The author holds that sexual response in both sexes is characterized by variation rather than similarity. He examines critically the work of Masters and Johnson and others. Includes a discussion of the controversy over clitoral versus vaginal organism.

SMITH, JAMES R., AND LYNN G. SMITH: *Beyond Monogamy: Recent Studies of Sexual Alternatives to Marriage*, The John Hopkins Press, Baltimore, 1974. (Paperback.) A collection of articles and research reports on extramarital sex, group marriage, communes, swinging, and sexual freedom as alternatives to conventional monogamy.

STONE, HANNAH M., AND ABRAHAM STONE: *A Marriage Manual*, rev. by Gloria Stone Aitkin and Aquiles J. Sobrero, Simon and Schuster, Inc., New York, 1970. Written by a husband and wife, both physicians, in question-and-answer form, as if a couple were talking with their doctor. Discusses various aspects of sex and reproduction.

SYMONDS, CAROLYN: "Sexual Mate-Swapping: Violations of Norms and Reconciliation of Guilt," in James M. Henslin (ed.): *Studies in the Sociology of Sex*, Appleton-Century-Crofts, New York, 1971, pp. 81–109. A study of swinging in Southern California.

TRAINER, JOSEPH B.: *Psychologic Foundations of Marriage Counseling*, The C. V. Mosby Company, St. Louis, 1965. The author is a physician. Chapters on male and female sexual response; hormones; sex in marriage; the premarital examination.

WHITEHURST, ROBERT N.: "Violence Potential in Extramarital Sexual Response," *Journal of Marriage and the Family*, vol. 33, no. 4, pp. 683–691, November 1971. Analysis of extramarital relationships and of ways in which they are and might be handled.

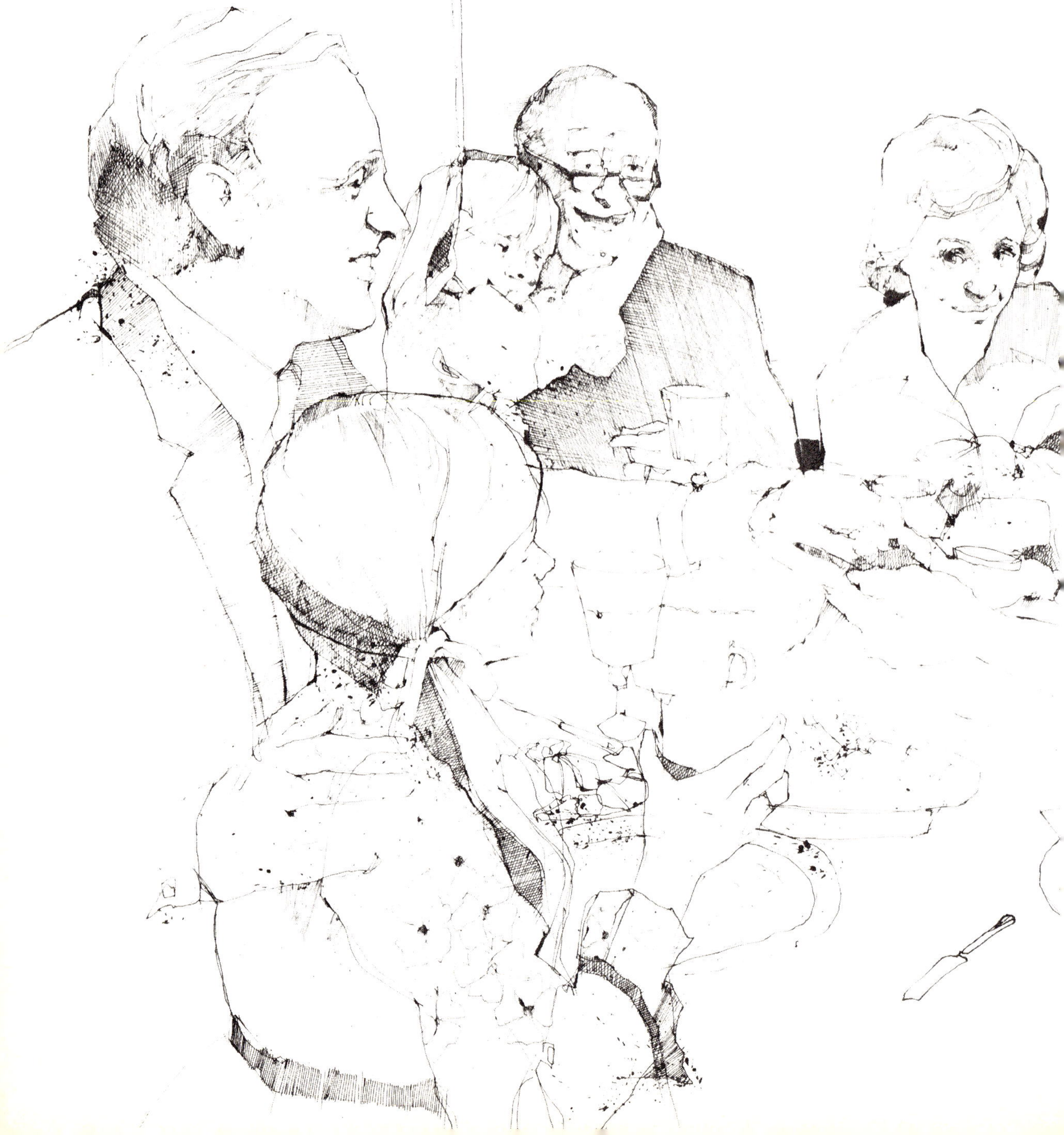

Part IV

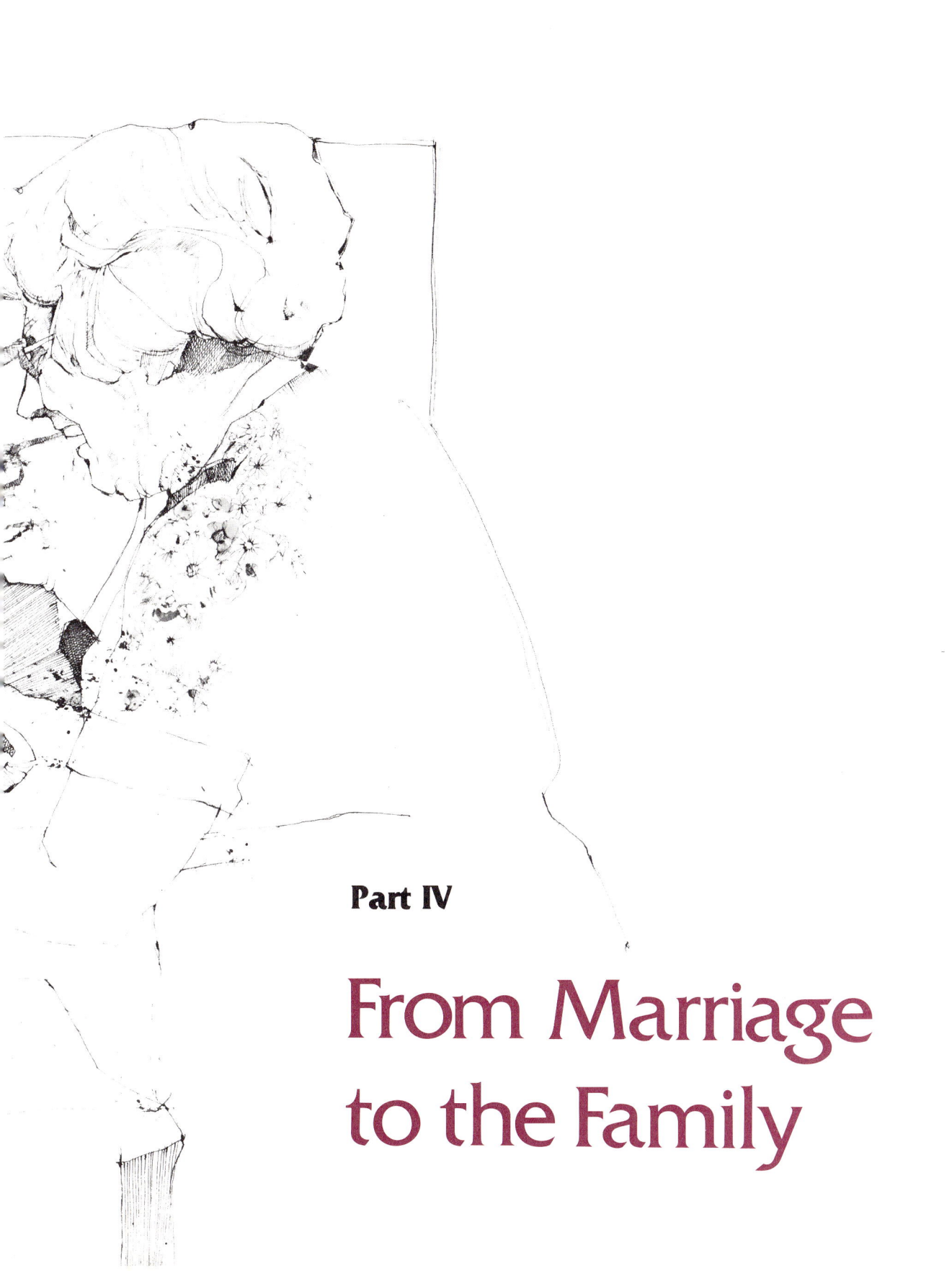

From Marriage to the Family

Chapter 12

Birth Control and Fertility

Every couple having sexual intercourse must make a decision whether they wish to have children. Most unmarried persons having sexual relations prefer to avoid pregnancy, although many do not avoid it. Among married couples, there is a small, but increasing number who wish to remain childless throughout their marriage (DeJong and Sell, 1975). Among the great majority of married persons who do wish to have children at one time or another, there is an increasing desire to limit family size, plan the spacing of children, and postpone the birth of the first child following marriage. When children are not wanted, pregnancy and childbirth can be an unfortunate experience. For the above reasons, family planning and conception control are discussed in this chapter. However, when children are wanted, pregnancy and childbirth can be an exhilarating, fascinating, and satisfying experience for a happily married pair. Since reproduction ordinarily requires the participation of both husband and wife and literally a part of each is necessary for fertilization to occur, pregnancy and childbirth can be an important shared experience that can add meaning and fulfillment to a marraige, and these experiences are discussed in the next chapter.

Strictly speaking, *birth control* refers to one's ability to prevent a birth from occurring. *Family planning* is a more general term which refers to a couple's ability to have the number of children that they want when they want them, when they are ready for them, and at sufficient intervals to permit the wife to maintain good health and to give birth to healthy babies. Both birth control and family planning imply parenthood by choice rather than parenthood by chance.

There is not unanimous opinion about the exact meaning of conception and pregnancy relative to fertilization and implantation (nidation). In some quarters fertilization (the union of sperm and ovum) and conception are assumed to be synonymous, and pregnancy is assumed to begin when either occurs. This is the traditional point of view and probably that of the majority of the general public. In other quarters fertilization and conception are assumed to be different, while conception and pregnancy are assumed to be synonymous; conception (pregnancy) begins, not at fertilization, but at nidation (when the zygote implants itself in the wall of the uterus). According to the first point of view, *conception control* implies any means of preventing fertilization; and the destruction of the zygote, even before implantation, is considered to be induced abortion. According to the second point of view, conception control includes not only the prevention of fertilization but also the prevention of implantation; and induced abortion would be limited to any means employed to destroy the zygote (or embryo or fetus) after implantation. To aid in clarifying the distinction, the term "interception" has been suggested for the prevention of implantation (Morris and van Wagenen, 1973).

We shall include in the following discussion of birth control mechanical and chemical contraceptives which either prevent fertilization or prevent implantation. We shall also include the rhythm method and sterilization. We shall discuss induced abortion as a process which interrupts pregnancy after nidation, recognizing that while this is a means of birth control, it is not a means of conception control.

REQUIREMENTS FOR MEANS OF BIRTH CONTROL

Whatever may be the means of birth control that a couple employ, it should fulfill the following requirements: (1) It should be relatively effective, that is, as effective as modern medical science can make it. No method is entirely foolproof. The methods most commonly recommended by informed physicians and reliable clinics, when used with intelligence and care, are close to 100 percent reliable, making possible the removal of fear of unwanted pregnancy. (2) It should be relatively easy to use, simple, and readily understood. (3) It should be readily available and relatively inexpensive. (4) It should be esthetically acceptable to both parties and distasteful to neither. (5) It should permit satisfactory sexual intercourse. (6) It should be relatively safe. (7) It should be temporary, in the sense that its use may be terminated at will, unless for some special reason the couple desire sterilization.

Calderone (1964) states three "contraceptive axioms": "1. Any method . . . is more effective than no method. 2. The most effective method is the one the couple will use with the greatest consistency. 3. Acceptability is the most critical factor in the effectiveness of a contraceptive method."

Birth control should be adapted to the individual couple by a family planning clinic or a competent, well-informed physician upon the basis of his or her knowledge of the couple's needs. It should not be used upon the recommendation of friends, drugstore clerks, advertisements, or oversimplified publications.

UNDERSTANDING BIRTH CONTROL

In order to understand how birth control functions, we must understand how ova and sperms are produced and how fertilization takes place. We must also understand the nature of the menstrual cycle.

Menstrual Cycle

Let us assume that ovulation occurs but that fertilization does not follow. The *Graafian follicle* (described more fully in the next chapter) secretes a hormone (estrogen) which causes certain changes in the uterus. After the ovum has been discharged from the follicle, the cells of the latter undergo change, forming the *corpus luteum* (yellow body). The corpus luteum secretes another hormone (progesterone) which, together with the estrogen, causes further changes in the uterus and prepares this organ for the reception of the zygote. One of the changes occurs in the blood vessels in such a way that small "lakes" of blood (lacunae) are formed within the wall of the uterus. This process of preparation requires about two weeks. If fertilization does not occur, after about ten days the corpus luteum degenerates and ceases to function (see Exhibit 12-1). The hormones (estrogen and progesterone) which it secreted and which sustained the uterus in its receptive, prepregnant state are withdrawn. This causes the lining of the uterus (endometrium) to break down and loosen itself from the uterine wall. The lining and some of the blood from the lacunae and blood vessels are discharged. This is menstruation. Getting rid of the preparation for pregnancy requires several days, and then the cycle begins over again. Thus we see that it is not ovulation that causes men-

Exhibit 12-1 The menstrual cycle.

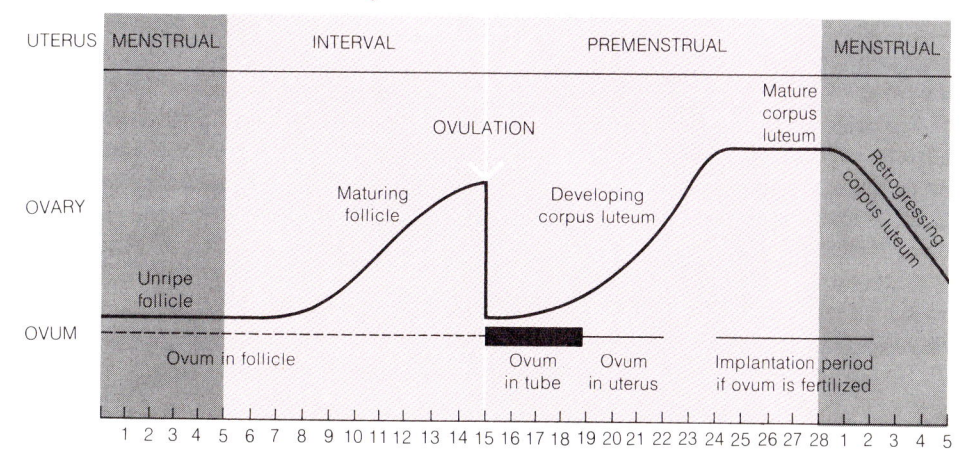

struation. Menstruation is caused by the withdrawal of the hormones (estrogen and progesterone) secreted by the corpus luteum, which in the event of fertilization would continue to be produced for a while until the placenta began to secrete a hormone with a similar function.

In some cases a type of menstruation occurs without there having been ovulation and the formation of a corpus luteum. Such menstruation, termed anovulatory, is the result of estrogen withdrawal and the Graafian follicle forming and being absorbed without bursting to release the ovum. The difference between the two types of menstruation is shown in summary form in Exhibit 12-2.

The length of the menstrual cycle varies in different women. Often for some time after puberty the cycle is irregular. Then, as the girl matures, a rhythm is established. When women are considered as a group, the length of this rhythm falls on the normal curve of variability. Twenty-eight days, the ordinarily assumed cycle, is the one that falls near the middle of the curve. In one study it was found that about 10 percent of the women had cycles ranging in length from 6 to 23 days; about 10 percent ranged from 35 to 409 days; and the great majority (about 80 percent) ranged from 24 to 34 days (Greenhill, 1957).

In the individual woman the length of the cycle may vary from time to time for different reasons. Most women are regularly irregular, if we may so express it for emphasis. The majority of women have cycles which vary by a few days from month to month. Hartman (1962) refers to a "regular" cycle as one varying no more than six days and states that about 75 percent of women have such cycles; the other 25 percent have cycles even more irregular. One early investigator, Fraenkel (Hartman, 1962), made a statement which has now become classic relative to the study of the menstrual cycle: "The only regular feature of the menstrual cycle is its lack of regularity." Another investigator, Holt (Hartman, 1962), has said, "Not the slightest evidence pointing toward perfect regularity has so far produced even a single exceptional individual." He goes on to say that if such a perfectly regular individual is ever found, "she will constitute a true medical curiosity." Still another investigator (Beer, 1970) has said, "Complete temporal regularity of menstruation throughout the life span in any individual is a myth." Pincus (1965) refers to "a completely normal woman" as "primarily a statistic."

When we think only in terms of time sequence, we see that ovulation and menstru-

Exhibit 12-2 Steps in menstrual cycle

Ovum matures.
Follicle forms.
Follicle secretes estrogen.
Estrogen changes uterus.

OVULATORY
Follicle bursts (ovulation).
Corpus luteum forms.
Corpus luteum secretes progesterone and estrogen.
Progesterone and estrogen change uterus.
Corpus luteum degenerates.
Progesterone and estrogen withdrawn.
Menstruation.

ANOVULATORY
Follicle does not burst (no ovulation).
Follicle absorbed.
Estrogen withdrawn.
Menstruation.

ation alternate (assuming ovulatory cycles). But when we think in terms of cause and effect, we must think of menstruation as following ovulation, not of ovulation as following menstruation. Yet, in seeking to predict the time of ovulation, a woman may erroneously think of menstruation-ovulation, since she knows the dates of her last menstrual period but not the date of ovulation. This error is made easier to commit by the fact that in numbering the days of the menstrual cycle, the day on which menstruation begins is considered the first day of the cycle as well as the first day of the period.

Ordinarily menstruation begins about two weeks after ovulation, no matter how long the cycle. In other words, the preovulatory phase of the cycle (the period between menstruation and ovulation) is much more variable than the postovulatory, or premenstrual, phase of the cycle (the period between ovulation and menstruation). Here again, however, there is both wide variation among women and variation in the cycles of any given woman. The two-week period mentioned above represents a generalization based upon averages. Hartman (1962) cites studies based on different methods of ascertaining the date of ovulation which indicate that (1) ovulation may occur on any day of the menstrual cycle from the fourth onward and (2) the preovulatory phase may vary from a few days to several months and the postovulatory phase from less than a week to almost a month. Young (1961a) points to evidence suggesting that ovulation may even occur during menstruation.

Various attempts have been made to pinpoint the time of ovulation. Among them are measurement of the hormones in women's blood or urine, microscopic study of the corpus luteum, study of changes in cells from the vagina, examination of uterine tissue and activity, correlation of artificial insemination and conception, studies of the pregnancies of the wives of military personnel home on short leaves, records of pain which may possibly be associated with ovulation, studies of intermenstrual bleeding, and the correlation of ovulation and basal body temperature.

Some women experience pain in the region of the ovaries at about that time of the menstrual cycle when ovulation occurs. Some of these women state that the pain alternates from side to side in alternate months. This is referred to as intermenstrual pain, or *Mittelschmerz*. Since the opening of the follicle to release the ovum requires only a few moments, intermenstrual pain can hardly be produced only by the actual momentary bursting of the follicle. But data do suggest that it is associated with the overall process of ovulation. It may be caused by a slight hemorrhage following ovulation (Lloyd, 1964c).

Some women experience intermenstrual bleeding—that is, vaginal bleeding—at about the time ovulation might be presumed to occur. Such bleeding, sometimes called "midmonth stain," leads some women to the erroneous conclusion that they menstruate twice a month. It is caused by the fact that there is an increased blood supply in the woman's ovaries and uterus at the time that the follicle ripens. This blood supply produces congestion in the wall of the uterus, resulting in the leakage of a small amount of blood into the uterus through the lining of that organ, but without any break in that lining.

There is a correlation between ovulation and a woman's basal body temperature (BBT). BBT is the temperature taken immediately upon waking in the morning, before the woman gets out of bed or has anything to eat or drink. As soon as she begins to move about, her temperature rises slightly. The temperature must be taken by a special or clinical thermometer and read to within tenths of a degree. Differences between the lowest and highest temperature in a given menstrual cycle must be at least 0.4°F to be considered significant (Hartman, 1962).

Presumably the estrogen secreted by the growing follicle is a temperature depressant and causes the woman's BBT to fall as ovulation is approached. Her BBT reaches its lowest point at about the time of ovulation. Then the progesterone secreted by the corpus luteum causes the BBT to rise. This is termed the thermal shift. The BBT remains at the higher level until about the time of menstruation (Hartman, 1962). If pregnancy occurs, the BBT remains at a relatively high level (see Exhibit 12-3).

BBT records are difficult to interpret because they are not so clear and regular as an oversimplified explanation seems to suggest. There is much variation among women and in a given woman during a series of cycles. BBT and ovulation do not always coincide (Greenhill, 1954; Farris, 1956). Conception has been recorded in a case where intercourse occurred ten days prior to the thermal shift and in other cases where isolated intercourse took place more than forty-eight hours before the shift (Garcia, 1967). There are many factors, other than those involved in the menstrual cycle, which can cause a change in body temperature.

Menstruation is a natural, normal function and produces varying degrees of discomfort among women. It may also be accompanied by a brief period of depression, fatigue, or irritability. Painful menstruation (dysmenorrhea) may be the result of hypersensitivity of the lining of the uterus, too tightly closed cervix, unusual flexion of the uterus backward or forward, atrophy of the uterus, tumors, inflammation of organs adjacent to the uterus, infection, congestion due to constant standing, disorders of the endocrine glands, allergies, constipation, and other similar contributing factors. It may also be due to subtle psychological factors, for example, resistance to the fact of being a woman. Many cases of dysmenorrhea may be relieved by adequate medical treatment. A woman subject to painful periods should see her physician. She should not depend upon patent medicines purchased on the recommendation of advertisements or clerks in drugstores.

Menstruation is not only natural and normal but, if we may personify Nature for a moment, is given special attention as a somewhat exceptional phenomenon. It is limited to human beings and some of the primates. In all other instances, bleeding is an indication of trouble. Menstrual discharge, which is a combination of blood and other secretions, is an indication of good health. In other instances, the blood clots to stop the bleeding. Menstrual blood does not clot in the usual way, thus permitting the bleeding to continue. Occasional small clots are within normal limits. Actually, menstrual blood does clot, but the clots tend to liquefy before the blood leaves the uterus (Novak, Jones, and Jones, Jr., 1970).

METHODS OF CONTRACEPTION

Oral Contraceptive Pills

Ovulation occurs as the result of the combined action of two hormones (FSH, follicle-stimulating hormone, and LH, luteinizing hormone) produced by the pituitary gland in response to signals from the hypothalamus, a part of the brain. Estrogen, produced by the follicle, and estrogen and progesterone, produced by the corpus luteum, bring about changes in the uterus in preparation for pregnancy. If pregnancy does not occur, the corpus luteum degenerates, estrogen and progesterone are withdrawn, and menstruation takes place. If pregnancy does occur, the corpus luteum continues to secrete estrogen and progesterone until the placenta produces a hormone with a similar function. This placental hormone thus sustains the pregnancy and,

Exhibit 12-3 Typical oral basal body temperature curves in (a) a normal cycle, (b) an anovulatory cycle, and (c) early pregnancy. (From Ernest W. Page, Claude A. Villee, and Dorothy B. Villee, *Human Reproduction*, W. B. Saunders Company, Philadelphia, 1972; used with permission of author and publisher.)

through hormonal influence on the pituitary gland, inhibits the secretion of FSH and LH and prevents ovulation during the pregnancy.

The type of contraceptive pill which is the most widely used—the "Combination" birth control pill—contains a combination of synthetic estrogen and synthetic progesterone (progestin). Oral contraceptive pills regulate the hormonal balance in a woman so that ovulation does not occur. They are extremely effective since, without ovulation, conception is not possible.

Pills are taken according to one of two regimens. Counting the first day of menstruation as day 1, some brands of pills advise that the woman take the first of twenty-one pills on day 5, whether or not she has stopped menstruating. She takes one pill each day for twenty-one days. Other brands recommend that the woman begin taking the pill on a given day of the week (for example, Sunday) and then continue taking the pill for twenty-one days. Within two or three days after taking the twenty-first pill, she will begin to menstruate. Then seven days after she took the last pill she begins another series of twenty-one pills. Thus, most brands of pills require that the woman is on a "three weeks on, one week off" calendar. The woman is then able to always start each series of pills on the same day of the week. Some brands of pills come in containers which are designed to prevent forgetfulness. The woman takes a pill every day—twenty-one pills containing hormones followed by seven placebos (pills containing inactive ingredients) of a different color (DiSaia, Davis, and Taber, 1968). Women are usually advised to use an additional method of contraception during their first month on the pill since, with some regimens, a woman may not be fully protected during the first cycle.

Since they are a combination of estrogen and progestin, the pills act in two ways: They bring about changes in the uterus, then after the twenty-first pill has been taken, the equivalent of estrogen-progesterone withdrawal occurs, as in the natural menstrual cycle, and menstruation begins. While the twenty-one pills are being taken, a condition equivalent to the secretion of hormones by the corpus luteum during pregnancy is established, and ovulation is inhibited. In a sense, then, the pills set up a "pseudopregnancy." But there may also be other factors at work. One possibility is that the mucous secretion of the cervix is reduced in quantity and its viscosity increased, thus tending to prevent penetration of it by sperms (Peel and Potts, 1969; Garcia, 1970; Beacham and Beacham, 1972). Implantation and ovum transport may also be influenced by oral contraceptives (Hatcher et al., 1976).

The pill is now used by 80 to 100 million women throughout the world, including some 10 to 15 million women in the United States (Hatcher et al., 1976). It has become the most popular method of contraception in the United States. Oral contraceptives are essentially 100 percent effective when used correctly. As with all methods of contraception there are two types of failure—failure due to the method and failure due to the user. With oral contraceptives, virtually all known failures are a result of incorrect use of the pills, missing pills, or not using them at all following prescription. Oral contraceptives were first marketed in 1960. When they were first developed, researchers were not sure how great a dosage of the estrogen and progestin was necessary to prevent pregnancy. Consequently, the early pills contained relatively high dosages of the hormones used, and side effects were more likely. Over the years, it was learned that considerably reduced dosages of hormones could be used and pregnancy prevented. Thus, today the most widely used oral contraceptives contain only 50 microcentigrams (mcg) of the estrogen (either mestranol or ethinyl estradiol) and varying dosages of the progestin. Generally speaking, women should take a pill with the lowest dosage of estrogen which will keep them contraceptively protected. Over 90 percent of women can use a low-dosage pill, that is, 50 mcg or less (Hatcher et al., 1976). Some women, depending on a number of factors, may need to take a higher-dosage pill. There are more than twenty brands of oral contraceptives on the market. Although the estrogen content does not vary much from one pill to the next, the many different types and dosages of progestins used, in combination with the estrogens, produce considerable variation in the possible effect of each pill. Each woman should be evaluated by the physician to determine what type of pill is more appropriate for her.

Until 1975, a second type of oral contraceptive, the *sequential pill*, was prescribed for some women. Sequential pills contained estrogen alone for the first fourteen to fifteen days followed by a progestin and estrogen combination for the next five to seven days of the cycle. The effectiveness of the sequential pills was not as great, and complications led to their demise. Sequential pills are no longer prescribed for routine oral contraception.

It is very important that the recommended regimen be adhered to meticulously. A pill should be taken at approximately the same time each day, for example at bedtime. Otherwise what appears to be calendar regularity may amount practically to missing a pill. For example, if a woman took a pill at breakfast time at 7:00 A.M. yesterday and does not take her next one until bedtime at 11:00 P.M. today, she has taken a pill "each day" but with an interval of forty hours, almost two days. For each pill missed, the possibility of ovulation, and hence the risk of pregnancy, increases. If a woman misses one pill, she should take that pill as soon as she realizes it. She should then take her next pill at the usual time. She probably will not get pregnant. If she misses two pills, she should take two pills as soon as she remembers and two the next day. There may be spotting, and she should use an additional means of contraception during the remainder of that period. If she misses three or more pills, ovulation may occur. Thus, she should begin using another method of contraception immediately. She should call her physician or family planning clinic for instructions about how to proceed. She will usually be advised to begin a new set of pills soon, while using an additional method of contraception for the first two weeks of the next cycle (Hatcher et al., 1976).

When used correctly, the combination pills constitute practically a 100 percent effective contraceptive. "The oral contraceptive tablets are the most effective means known for the control of fertility for family planning purposes" (Drill, 1966). Pregnancies do occur in women "taking" pills, but the indications are that such pregnancies are due to human failure rather than to method failure.

Effective as they are, however, contraceptive pills are not perfect. Some women cannot (or at least should not) take them. For example, pills are contraindicated (that is, conditions in the woman make the use of the pills inadvisable) for women who have undiagnosed vaginal bleeding, a history of circulatory disease or blood clotting, malignant tumors (cancers) of the breast or genital tract, fibroid (benign) tumors of the uterus, or liver disease. Some women with kidney disease, asthma, epilepsy, diabetes, sickle-cell anemia, migraine headaches, and other selected conditions may use them, but only with caution and under a physician's careful supervision. Pregnancy should be ruled out before a woman starts using pills. Since the pills may inhibit lactation and thus reduce the secretion of milk, they are contraindicated for nursing mothers. In one study (Gambrell, 1970) it was found that twice as many women who started taking oral contraceptives immediately after childbirth, compared with women who did not take them, stopped breast feeding by the end of six weeks because of decreased milk secretion.

It is because of considerations such as those mentioned above that it is so important for a woman to have a medical examination, including a vaginal examination and a "Pap smear," before beginning to use the pills. The Pap test, so called because it was introduced by Dr. George N. Papanicolaou, involves a technique for the detection of possible cancer through the microscopic examination of cells taken from the cervix.

It is inadvisable for women to procure pills in some manner other than through responsible medical channels (for example, from other women). How could such women know whether it was safe for them to take the pills? How could they know which pills were best for them? In light of the attitudes toward sex and oral contraceptives that have developed in the past few years, there is no excuse for a woman who wants to use the pill in premarital intercourse to do so without competent medical advice. Unfortunately, some physicians are indiscriminate in prescribing the pill, merely granting a woman's request for it without medical precautions. This, too, is contraindicated. On the other hand, some physicians refuse to prescribe the pill for unmarried women because of their own attitudes toward premarital intercourse. It is not the physician's role to judge how a woman will use the pill but only whether she can use it safely. In addition to a medical examination before she begins using pills, a woman should have a periodic checkup (at least yearly) while she is using them. Oral contraceptives are composed of powerful ingredients. A woman takes the pill to avoid pregnancy. It would be only sensible for her to do everything necessary to prevent any possible unfavorable side effects.

Side Effects

Oral contraceptives do cause side effects in some women. Among these are nausea, dizziness, fatigue, nervousness, depression, irritability, headache, intermenstrual bleeding (break-through bleeding or spotting), increased susceptibility to vaginal and urinary tract infections, breast soreness, acne, weight gain, and melasma (or chloasma). The last condition is a "blotchiness" or brownish patches on the skin, particularly on the face and forehead. Ordinarily side effects, if they occur at all, are mild and temporary. Occasionally side effects are so severe or of such long duration that a woman has to shift to another brand of oral contraceptive or discontinue the use of pills altogether.

Available data reject a causal relationship between oral contraceptives and cancer of the breast or genital organs (Drill, 1966; Goldzieher and Rice-Wray, 1966; Peel and Potts, 1969; Kistner, 1969a; Garcia, 1970; Vessey, Doll, and Sutton, 1972; Connell, 1975). In fact, the opposite has been suggested, namely, that oral contraceptives may inhibit cancer (Ayre, Reyner, Fagundes, and LeGuerrier, 1969; Connell, 1975). It is known that oral contraceptives will cause a more rapid growth of already-existing fibroid (nonmalignant) tumors. Hence, as a precautionary measure, pills are contraindicated in cases of detectable existing malignancies. The fact that the pill has been available for contraception since 1960 and is now used by millions of women throughout the world with as yet no conclusive evidence linking it to the cause of cancer will no doubt lead to its continued acceptance.

Research data do not suggest either an increase or a decrease in fertility following the discontinuation of oral contraception, although a woman's body may need several weeks following pill discontinuation to begin ovulating again. Following this adjustment period, pill use does not alter chances of fertility. There is no rebound effect of hyperfertility, as is sometimes assumed. Nor is there any unfavorable effect on subsequent babies (Wallach, 1968; Peterson, 1969; Mears, 1968; Garcia, 1970; Robinson, 1971).

The effect of oral contraceptives on the female libido (sex drive) is uncertain, and, in fact, there may be none. Some women report an increase, others a decrease, and still others no change in sex drive (Goldzieher and Rice-Wray, 1966; Bakker and Dightman, 1966; Garcia, 1968; Loraine and Bell, 1968).

It is sometimes difficult to distinguish

between physiological causes and psychological causes of the side effects of oral contraceptives. Since they are powerful chemical agents to which women react differently, they undoubtedly produce side effects in some women. But there is also evidence that in some women side effects are produced by the knowledge—or by the assumption—that they are taking the pill (Kroger, 1968; Lidz, 1969). In one study of 398 women, some were given placebos (pills containing inactive ingredients) while the others were given oral contraceptives, and the incidence of nervousness, depression, and weight gain was similar in the two groups (Goldzieher, Moses, Averkin, Scheel, and Taber, 1971). In another study 167 women whose fertility had been proved by pregnancy and who were interested in becoming pregnant again were given a daily placebo tablet but were told that they were taking oral contraceptives. The women reported a great variety of side effects, including decreased libido, increased libido, headache, abdominal pain, dizziness, dysmenorrhea, nervousness, nausea, sleeplessness, increased appetite, decreased appetite, weight gain, and "cured" dysmenorrhea, as if they had actually been taking oral contraceptives (Aznar-Ramos, 1969).

Pills may be obtained only with a prescription. A woman who is seeing a physician for treatment of a medical problem should advise the doctor that she is taking birth control pills. A woman should specifically seek medical attention if she has severe pain or swelling in the legs, severe headache, blurred vision, abdominal pain, chest pain, or shortness of breath. These may be signs of complications related to pill use.

How long should a woman stay on the pill? There is no agreement on this question in the medical community. Many physicians recommend to their patients that they go off the pill for a while every two or three years in order to let the body return to its non-pill-influenced state. Others, however, state that the female should stay on the pill if she wants to avoid pregnancy, since she increases her risk of pregnancy if she goes off and since she is putting her body through another change. A recent review of hundreds of studies of oral contraceptives (Connell, 1975) concludes:

A practice of many physicians is to advise women to stop using the pill for a month or two each year. The major consequence of such therapy is unwanted pregnancy. There is no evidence that this practice in any way affects the ultimate side effects of oral contraceptives. In fact, since many of the side effects are related to a change in the hormonal status of the patient, there is compelling evidence to suggest that this practice is not only *not* advantageous, but may actually be *detrimental* to her health.

Considering the lack of agreement about long-term use of the pill, a female is best advised to discuss the matter with her physician and reach some agreement about long-term pill use. There is agreement, however, that women over 40 should discontinue pill use, since complications are more likely in this age category.

Even assuming, however, that as the years go on, cases of unfavorable long-term effects are observed, this fact will have to be evaluated in the light of the widespread beneficial effects the pills have had for countless women, just as the unfavorable side effects now known are evaluated in terms of benefits. This is done with all types of medical procedures. Any medication, even one widely used and considered an "old standby," produces ill effects in a few persons who are especially sensitive to it or take it in excessive dosage. For example, aspirin produces mild side effects in many persons and severe side effects in some. Some individuals cannot tolerate penicillin. And so it goes. The disadvantage to a few must be weighed against the advantage to the many, and acceptance of oral contraceptives is no exception.

Objections are sometimes raised to comparing oral contraceptives to medication for disease, because pregnancy is not a disease and therefore does not present the same type of urgency. But in the mind of the woman who wants to prevent conception, pregnancy is equivalent to a disease, involving discomfort, inconvenience, and risk, just as disease does. If a woman has an unwanted pregnancy, she may even have an abortion to remedy it. Hence, she looks upon oral contraceptives as drugs to prevent a threatening condition.

Oral Contraceptives and Thromboembolic Disease

Reports of some side effects of oral contraceptives are based on women's subjective judgment relative to their own symptoms. For example, who but the woman herself knows whether her sex drive has increased or decreased? Reports of other side effects are based on medical diagnosis, for example, coagulation of blood and growth of benign tumors. Among the latter type of side effects, namely those based on medical diagnosis in which a woman's subjective judgment plays no part, one of the most serious is thromboembolic disease (thrombophlebitis). A thrombus is a blood clot that is stationary, and an embolus is a blood clot that moves from its site of origin. In the type of thrombophlebitis of concern in connection with oral contraceptives, a blood clot (or clots) forms in a deep vein (or veins) of the leg. Such a clot may move, for example, to a lung, thus producing a pulmonary embolism.

Does the pill cause thrombophlebitis? In 1967 the Medical Research Council of Great Britain reported that "there can be no reasonable doubt that some types of thromboembolic disorder are associated with the use of oral contraceptives.... We conclude ... that the oral contraceptives are themselves a factor in the production of the disease." The report stated further that "the attributable risk of death from these diseases may . . . be of the order of 3 per 100,000 users per year." This is the report that triggered the furor regarding the safety of oral contraceptives and led some women to discontinue using the pill. A more recent study (Vessey et al., 1976) of 17,000 women during a period of seven years confirmed the increased risk of thrombophlebitis among oral contraceptive users.

The risk, however, is relatively small, and the risk of dying from pulmonary embolism resulting from thromboembolic disease is small indeed. A woman's choice is not between risk and no risk; her choice is between various degrees and types of risk. If a woman uses no contraceptive or a contraceptive with a failure rate higher than that of the pill, she runs the risk of pregnancy, and with pregnancy goes the risk of developing conditions—including thromboembolic disease—which may prove serious, even fatal. The "risk of thromboembolic disease is much greater in pregnant women than in subjects receiving oral contraceptives" (Loraine and Bell, 1968). There are many life activities which involve risk but which are accepted because the risk/benefit ratio is considered favorable. All modes of travel involve risk. Smoking has been shown to be a cause of lung cancer, yet millions of Americans continue to smoke. In fact, "for normal healthy women the danger of oral contraception has been calculated to be less than that of smoking one cigarette a day" (MacDonald, 1971a). Such comparisons must, of course, be interpreted with caution.

Suggesting that a woman assume that there is a possible risk involved in using oral contraceptives is an indirect way of emphasizing again the importance of a preliminary examination before starting to take the pill, of follow-up examinations while the pill is being taken, and of giving attention to and reporting to the physician any warning symptoms so that more serious symptoms may be prevented. A writer in the *British Medical Journal* warns that "while there is no cause for panic about the possible consequences of widespread use of the present types of oral contraceptives, neither is there room for complacency" (*BMJ*, 1968). In "What You Should Know About 'the Pill,'" the pamphlet prepared by the American Medical Association (1970), appears the following: "Oral contraceptives, when taken as directed, are drugs of extraordinary effectiveness. As with other medicine, side effects are possible. The most serious side effect is abnormal blood clotting. The fact is that serious problems are relatively rare, and the majority of women who would like to use the pill can do so safely and effectively."

Other Benefits of Oral Contraceptives

Not all the side effects of oral contraceptives are unfavorable. In some women the pill relieves symptoms of the premenstrual syndrome (Barber, Graber, and O'Rourke, 1969), reduces the discomfort of menstrual cramps (dysmenorrhea), and/or shortens the menstrual period and decreases the quantity of menstrual discharge (Pincus, 1965; Hatcher et al., 1976). Available evidence does not support the assumption that oral contraceptives postpone the onset of the menopause (Goldfarb, 1964; Böving, 1965; Goldzieher and Rice-Wray, 1966). Some persons have expressed fear that women who take the pill may bear children in their fifties or later. Such fears are without foundation it fact.

Pills decrease the likelihood of iron-deficiency anemia. Acne is often improved in women on oral contraceptives. Anxiety or depression is reduced in some women. Some women have an increased sex desire (although this may largely result from the loss of fear of pregnancy). Some women are prescribed a particular brand of pill to facilitate weight gain. Some women are pleased to note an increase in breast size while on pills. Menstrual periods may be moved to or away from weekends, although this should be done only after consulting a physician or family planning clinic. Pills have been used in the treatment of medical conditions such as endometriosis, gonadal dysgenesis, and idiopathic thrombocytopenic purpura, and to eliminate the pain of *Mittelschmerz*. There is also a decreased incidence of functional ovarian cysts, fibrocystic breast disease, and fibroadenomas of the breast, and other medical conditions (Hatcher et al., 1976).

The Mini-Pill and Progestins

Although they are not very widely used, *mini-pills* or *progestin only pills* have been marketed in the United States since 1973. Mini-pills contain the same progestins available in combined oral contraceptives, but they are used without estrogen. Mini-pills are less effective than combined oral contraceptives but are nevertheless extremely effective. A female may be advised to switch to a mini-pill if she has one of the many estrogen-related side effects of combination oral contraceptives. Since most of the side effects of combined oral contraceptives are estrogen-related, there are fewer side effects from mini-pills.

Mini-pills are taken on the first day of the woman's period and then taken continuously. In other words, they are taken each and every day, even when the woman is having her period. In addition to the slightly lower effectiveness rate, mini-pills are characterized by a greater incidence of irregular menses, increased or decreased duration and amount of menstrual flow, spotting, and amenorrhea (Hatcher et al., 1976).

Long-acting progesterone injections are currently marketed in sixty-four countries and are used by over one million women throughout the world (Hatcher et al., 1976).

These injections (also known as "the shot" or referred to by the name of one of the drugs used, Depo Provera) are shown to be highly effective in early studies—almost as effective as combined oral contraceptives. "The shot" is given every three months and provides contraceptive protection during the entire time. Other progestin contraceptives involve subdermal silastic capsules which are implanted under the skin. This technique is still in the experimental stages.

Intrauterine Contraceptive Device (IUD or IUCD)

The IUD is a small device which is placed in the uterus by means of a special inserter. IUDs are usually plastic, although the newest types are plastic with a tiny band of copper wrapped around a part of the plastic. The IUD inserter is usually a tube resembling a thin straw which is narrow enough to pass through the cervix. The uterus is "sounded," a simple procedure of measuring the uterus and identifying its precise position. The IUD is retracted into the inserter. The inserter is then placed into the vagina and the IUD is pushed into the uterus. IUDs are often inserted during menstruation or shortly after termination of pregnancy, because at such times there is certainty that the woman is not pregnant. Also, during menstruation she is bleeding, and the cervix is open. Hence, the IUD causes little, if any, additional discomfort. An IUD may, however, be inserted at any time. After insertion the device assumes its original shape and adapts itself to the inside contour of the uterus. The insertion must be done by medical personnel; it cannot be done by the woman herself. Once inserted, the device may be left in place indefinitely, providing there are no side effects necessitating its removal. The copper IUDs need to be replaced periodically, however, because the copper disintegrates. The IUD does not interfere with menstruation, ovulation, or sexual intercourse. IUDs are made in various shapes and sizes, not all equally effective. Commonly used forms are shown in Exhibit 12-4. Other forms are being developed and tested. Which device is to be chosen depends upon a particular woman's condition and tolerance, her physician's preference, and whether she previously has been pregnant.

How the IUD prevents conception is not fully understood. According to one theory, by increasing tubal peristalsis it hastens passage of the ovum through the fallopian tube so that the egg is not sufficiently prepared or "capacitated" for fertilization (Willson, 1965), but other investigators say this has not been demonstrated (Davis and Lesinski, 1970). There is no evidence that the device causes the zygote to be expelled from the uterus, as is sometimes believed (H. Davis, 1972). Another theory, for which evidence is accumulating, suggests that since the IUD is a foreign body, it produces a biochemical response in the endometrium (lining of the uterus). This response includes an increase in the number of cells that are naturally present and that play a part in reducing the number of sperms in their passage through the female genital tract. The result is destruction of sperms before they can reach the ovum for fertilization, and thus no implantation occurs (Moyer and Mishell, 1971; Tatum, 1972; H. Davis, 1972, 1971).

Probably more than size and shape, there are at least two other factors that play a part in determining the effectiveness of IUDs. One is the extent of contact between the device and the inside surface area of the uterus: the greater the extent of contact, the greater the degree of effectiveness (Davis and Lesinski, 1970; H. Davis, 1972, 1971). Another factor is the chemical composition of the device. For example, it has been found that very fine copper wire wound around the stem of the Tatum T device increases its effectiveness

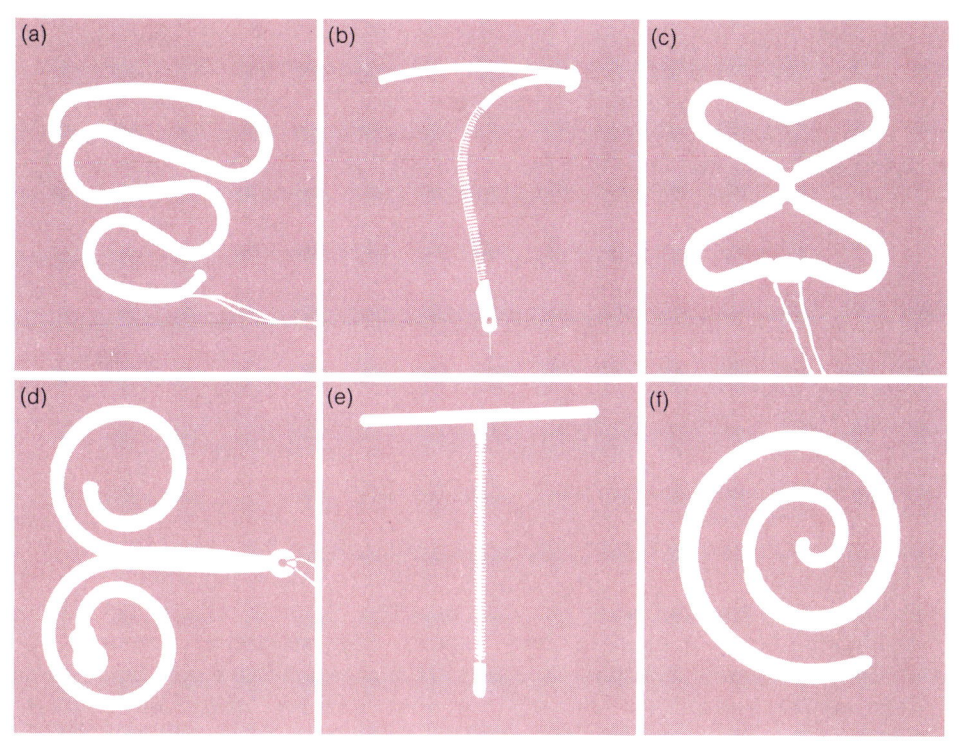

Exhibit 12-4 Common forms of IUDs. Top row, left to right: Lippes loop, Copper 7, Birnberg bow. Bottom row, left to right: double coil, Tatum T, Margulies spiral.

(Tatum, 1973, 1974; Timonen, Toivonen, and Luukkainen, 1974; Cooper, Millen, and Mishell, Jr., 1976). A modification of the Copper T is the Copper 7 (Newton, Elias, McEwan, and Mann, 1974). The means by which copper exerts a contraceptive action is not fully known. It is probably partly, at least, through inhibiting sperm motility and thus decreasing the sperms' penetration of the mucus in the cervix (Zielske, Koch, Badura, and Ladeburg, 1974). Another T-shaped device contains progesterone which is slowly released into the uterus (Brenner, Cooper, and Mishell, Jr., 1975; Scommegna, Avila, Luna, Rao, and Dmowski, 1974).

Some women, particularly those who have not yet been pregnant, expel the IUD, often during menstruation and sometimes without being aware that expulsion has occurred. For this reason most of the devices have "tails" which are left protruding from the cervix when the device is inserted. The woman may feel the "tail" with a finger and thus be sure that the device is still in place. It is difficult to generalize with accuracy on the rate of expulsion because rates vary for different devices and statistics in studies of expulsion vary. But, to make a broad generalization, we may say that the IUD is expelled by about 10 to 20 percent of women who use it. Southam (1965) refers to expulsion as "one of the most troublesome problems," and Margulies (1964), the inventor of the spiral, refers to it as the "major unresolved problem."

The IUD has a high success rate, but failures do occur. In some cases, women become pregnant with the device in place. But the story of a baby born grasping its mother's IUD in its little hand is fiction, not fact. In other cases, the cause of failure is the woman's unawareness that the device has been expelled. Again, generalization is difficult for the reasons mentioned above. Failures are reported for all forms of IUDs. To assume a failure of 2 to 10 percent would be a generalization not out of keeping with the facts that are presently known (Hall, 1967, 1966; Tietze, 1967, 1966; McCammon, 1967; Loraine and Bell, 1968; Peel and Potts, 1969; H. Davis, 1971). However, with newer IUDs, both the failure rate and the expulsion rate are declining (H. Davis, 1972).

In a few cases IUDs have been found in the body cavity outside the uterus. One possible explanation of this phenomenon is that the device worked its way through the wall of the uterus. A more probable explanation is that at the time of insertion, the inserter perforated the wall of the uterus, and the IUD was placed in the body cavity. The plastic material of which most IUDs are made is relatively inert chemically. Hence, usually, but not always, an IUD in the body cavity is "clinically silent" (Davis, 1966), that is, it causes no symptoms. Perforations occur with an overall frequency of perhaps 1 in 1,000 insertions (Davis, 1966) and with a frequency of perhaps 1 in 5,000 when the insertions occur ten or more weeks after termination of pregnancy (H. Davis, 1971). Serious consequences are rare, and fatal infection occurs in perhaps one case in 500,000 (Scott, 1968; H. Davis, 1971).

In some women the IUD causes side effects other than those mentioned. Pain, bleeding, inflammation, ectopic pregnancy, or increased blood loss during menstruation sometimes occur and in some cases result in the removal of the device for medical reasons. The IUD can be inserted in women who have never been pregnant "provided the device is compatible with the smaller range of uterine cavities and has good retention qualities" (H. Davis, 1971). Recent evidence suggests that the use of the Copper 7 device with such women has proved successful (Roy, Cooper, and Mishell, Jr., 1974; Mishell, Jr., Israel, and Freid, 1973). However, women who have never been pregnant have a high incidence of side effects, and for this reason some physicians do not fit them with IUDs (Hall, 1970). There is no evidence that the IUD causes cancer or infertility (H. Davis, 1972).

Women should regularly check to make sure that their IUD has not been expelled. If they discover that it has, they should use another form of contraception until a new one can be inserted. Women beginning IUD use may expect some discomfort, cramping, or spotting. If such a condition persists, however, they should return to the physician or clinic. Women with IUDs should have yearly pelvic examinations.

If a pregnancy occurs with an IUD in place, it should be removed because of the danger of infections. Chances are about 25 percent that removal will cause an abortion, and 50 percent the spontaneous abortion will occur if the IUD is left in place (Hatcher et al., 1976).

One of the newest contraceptive developments is the first hormone-releasing IUD, the Progestasert, approved in 1976 by the Food and Drug Administration. The Progestasert is a T-shaped device which releases a small (65 mcg a day), steady amount of progesterone into the uterus. The device must be replaced after each twelve months of use, which is shorter than the two- to four-year period recommended for some of the other IUDs. The hormone appears to enhance the effectiveness of the IUD (*Family Planning Perspectives*, May/June, 1976).

IUDs are convenient for women who can

tolerate them because they do not interfere with sexual intercourse, side effects are slight, the effectiveness rate is high, and nothing needs to be done each day in order to be contraceptively protected. Chances of pregnancy following IUD use are the same as before.

Diaphragm

This is a shallow, cuplike device made of soft rubber with a springy outer edge. It fits snugly against the wall of the vagina and covers the cervix. The diaphragm should be used with a jelly or cream which is put into the diaphragm and around the edge before the device is inserted into the vagina. The jelly or cream both seals the contact between diaphragm and vaginal wall and also is spermicidal (kills sperms). The diaphragm forms a relatively effective barrier to sperms' entering the uterus. It causes no side effects. It is made in a variety of sizes and must, therefore, be fitted by a physician. The diaphragm should be inserted by the woman shortly before intercourse (using her fingers or a plastic inserter—see Exhibit 12-5). After intercourse it should be left in place for at least six hours—perhaps until the next morning—and then removed for cleansing and drying.

Diaphragms were in widespread use among women before the advent of oral contraceptives and the acceptance of IUDs. Although only a small portion of women now use diaphragms in comparison with some of the other methods, it appears there has been an increase in use of the diaphragm in the last few years, particularly among younger women who prefer to avoid the use of oral contraceptives. Diaphragms are very effective if used correctly and faithfully. Diaphragms which sit in dresser drawers contribute to much of the method's failure rate.

Diaphragm users should have yearly examinations in which they are remeasured to ensure that their diaphragm is still fitting properly. Women who have had a child or experience a weight gain or loss of more than

Exhibit 12-5 The diaphragm and its use: (a) the diaphragm; (b) application of spermicidal jelly; (c) compressing the diaphragm before manual insertion; (d) plastic introducer; (e) checking for correct insertion.

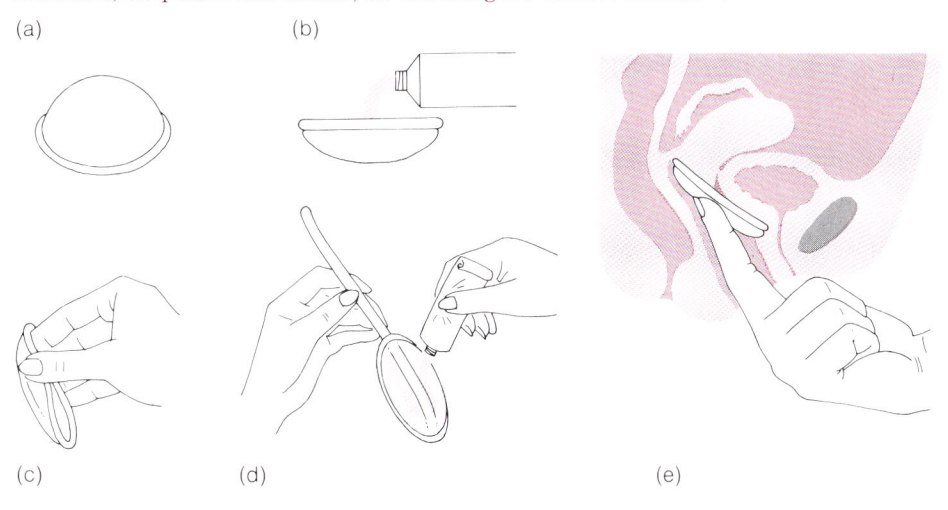

a few pounds should be refitted. Women should ask their physicians or family planning clinic about which cream or jelly to use since some are more highly recommended than others.

If the diaphragm has been inserted more than two hours before intercourse, an applicator should be used to insert more cream or jelly, since the original application may have lost its effectiveness. If the couple is having intercourse for a second time, the woman should leave the diaphragm in and insert a new application of cream or jelly.

Condoms

The condom (rubber, prophylactic, safe) is a thin rubber sheath which fits over the erect penis. It is put on the penis shortly before intercourse. At ejaculation, the seminal fluid is retained in the condom and does not enter the vagina. Condoms come in a variety of forms—in single packages, or in packages of several dozen; in colors; lubricated or unlubricated; with a little pouch at the end to catch the seminal fluid, or with no pouch. A condom should always be worn so that a little space is left at the end for the seminal fluid to accumulate following ejaculation.

The condom is a readily available and widely used means of contraception. It is the most common form of contraception worldwide. It is common on college campuses in America, although it is not the method of choice for large numbers of married couples in the United States. Some men claim that condoms reduce sensitivity, and some dislike them because putting them on may interfere with lovemaking.

Standards of manufacture are regulated by the Food and Drug Administration (FDA), and the production of condoms in recent years has been such that an individual need not test each condom that he wears. Couples should avoid tearing the condom and must remember to have the male withdraw his penis before he loses his erection, since seminal fluid can escape from the condom if this happens. The male should hold the condom on the penis while withdrawing so that it does not slip off. Condoms should be used only once, then discarded.

The condom is an effective method of contraception if used correctly and conscientiously. It should be put on before intercourse begins, since there may be ejaculation or secretion of the preejaculate before the condom is in place. Many couples use condoms in conjunction with vaginal foam. This is permissible and recommended, since any two methods of contraception are better than one and may considerably reduce chances of failure. Condoms may be purchased without prescription in drugstores. They are the one method of contraception which helps prevent the spread of venereal disease, since direct contact between the genitals is minimized.

Spermicides

Vaginal foam, creams, jellies, foaming tablets, suppositories, and similar chemical contraceptives are widely available in drugstores. They act by killing sperm on contact. Their failure rates when used alone, however, are considerably higher than the methods of contraception mentioned so far. They can be of considerable value when other methods of contraception are unavailable, when used to supplement other methods, or in emergencies. They should be inserted shortly before intercourse, since they lose their effectiveness after a time. Generally speaking, two hours should be considered the maximum time they will remain effective. Some types may lose their effectiveness even earlier. Foams, creams, and jellies can be inserted with an applicator which is readily purchased along with the spermicides. Some brands of spermicides are prepackaged with an individual inserter for each application of foam or cream.

The "Safe Period" or "Rhythm"

In constructing a diagram, Exhibit 12-6, to represent the fertile period and the infertile or "safe" period in a woman's menstrual cycle, broad generalization and oversimplification are unavoidable. In this figure, *m* indicates the menstrual period (as distinguished from menstrual cycle), which lasts about five days. The menstrual period begins about fourteen days after ovulation, *o*. The ovum is thought to be fertilizable for a maximum of twenty-four hours. But even though the day of ovulation might be ascertained, the moment of this occurrence cannot be pinpointed. There may also be variation in the effective life of ova. Also, chronologically the difference between, say, one day and two days may be just a couple of minutes—11:59 P.M. to 12:01 A.M.—and we are discussing "safe period." Hence two days have been allowed as the period during which the ovum might possibly be fertilized. This two-day period is designated as *oy*. Sperms deposited in the woman's genital tract are thought to have an effective life of forty-eight to seventy-two hours. Sperms deposited during the three-day period *xo* may live long enough to fertilize an ovum released at *o*. Sperms deposited during the two-day period *oy* would be present at the same time the ovum is present. The period *xy*, then, represents the fertile period, and the period *yx* represents the "safe period," since there is no ovum to be fertilized then.

Theoretically, then, every woman has a "safe period." The problem is to know when it occurs. There are so many variables involved that determination is impossible with completely constant accuracy and in all women. The "safe period," which depends upon avoidance of intercourse just before and just after ovulation, would be further negated if ovulation ever occurred at an unusual time during the menstrual cycle.

At the present stage of knowledge, all means of ascertaining the time of ovulation have limitations. Furthermore, they are more useful in indicating that ovulation has occurred than in predicting when it will occur, and they are therefore more helpful to couples who want to determine the *fertile* period in order to have a child than to those who want to determine the *infertile* period in order to avoid having one. For these two types of couples failure has different consequences. The former may simply try again to carry out their plan. But the latter may be called upon to abandon one plan and adopt another. What is needed to make the "safe period" safe is an accurate means of predicting the time of ovulation. The two most common methods of

Exhibit 12-6 Phases of the menstrual cycle to show the "safe period." Abbreviations: *m*, the menstrual period (5 days); from first day of menstrual period to last day before next period, 28 days; *o*, ovulation; *xo*, period during which sperms deposited might live long enough to fertilize ovum released at *o*; *oy*, period during which fertilizable ovum is possible; *xy*, fertile period; *y*, point after which no fertilizable ovum is present; *yx*, "safe period."

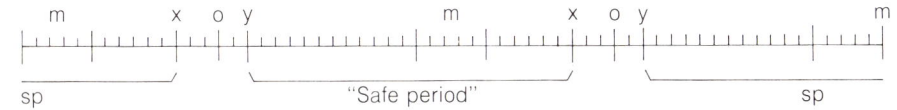

estimating the time of ovulation when using the rhythm method consist of keeping track of the longest and shortest menstrual cycles during the past year (the calendar method), using these extremes to calculate the days during which ovulation is most likely (see Exhibit 12-7), and taking the basal body temperature before rising each morning to estimate when ovulation has occurred. Both methods have great disadvantages, of course, since what has happened during the past year is no guarantee of what will happen next month, and since an increase in body temperature following ovulation will not tell the couple when to abstain *before* ovulation, only after.

The menstrual cycle, including the time of ovulation, may vary from month to month in a given woman. Even though she may keep a record for several months and may seem to be regular, there is no way for her to know that she will be regular in the future. The irregularity of the menstrual cycles of women as a group has already been discussed.

It is impossible to ascertain precisely how long it takes sperms to make their way to the ovum, since this may vary from time to time and depends in part upon anatomy and conditions within the female genital tract (such as the mucous plug in the cervix) and the vitality of the sperms. The "safe period" is useless during the interval between delivery of a baby and the reestablishment of menstruation, since ovulation precedes menstruation. This interval may be of several months' duration.

Because of the variables involved, the "safe period" is not entirely safe. A significantly higher failure rate is reported by couples who employ the rhythm method than by couples who employ the most effective methods of contraception (Freedman, Whelpton, and Campbell, 1959; Hartman, 1962). We cannot, however, dismiss it arbitrarily. Further research may make dependence upon it more reliable. For couples whose religious convictions forbid the use of chemical or mechanical contraceptives, rhythm is the next best thing. If they choose to rely upon it, they need to keep careful records of the woman's menstrual periods and discuss the problem with an informed counselor, rather than depend upon oversimplified printed tables or guidebooks.

In addition to the uncertainty of the method, there is another argument against relying upon the rhythm method to prevent conception. With this method the couple's sexual life is regulated by the probability and avoidance of conception—that is, by the calendar—rather than by their mutual love and desire. If a couple are especially anxious to prevent pregnancy, they may allow more than five days for the fertile period. Couples have been known to allow fifteen days. This results in what might be termed semicontinence.

Incomplete Intercourse (Withdrawal)

Coitus interruptus is a form of incomplete intercourse sometimes referred to as withdrawal. In coitus interruptus the penis is withdrawn from the vagina just before ejaculation, and the seminal fluid is discharged outside the woman's body. This is an ancient and widely known method of conception control. It is the type mentioned in the Old Testament (*Genesis* 38:8–10). It is unreliable because it requires precise timing and a very high degree of self-control on the part of the male. When the point of orgasm-ejaculation is reached, muscular contractions occur that are not subject to voluntary control. Masters and Johnson (1970) refer to "ejaculatory inevitability." Also, before the ejaculation of the seminal fluid, there is a discharge of a small amount of glandular secretion (the preejaculate) of which the man is unaware and the function of which is apparently lubrication

Exhibit 12-7 How to Calculate the Interval of Fertility Using the Calendar Method

If Your Shortest Period Has Been (no. of days)	Your First Fertile (Unsafe) Day Is	If Your Longest Period Has Been (no. of days)	Your Last Fertile (Unsafe) Day Is
21	3rd day	21	10th day
22	4th	22	11th
23	5th	23	12th
24	6th	24	13th
25	7th	25	14th
26	8th	26	15th
27	9th	27	16th
28	10th	28	17th
29	11th	29	18th
30	12th	30	19th
31	13th	31	20th
32	14th	32	21st
33	15th	33	22nd
34	16th	34	23rd
35	17th	35	24th

Source: Adapted from Hatcher et al. (1976).

and/or acid neutralization. The preejaculate may also contain sperms (Masters and Johnson, 1966; Sjövall, 1970). Ordinarily the number of sperms in the preejaculate is not large enough to effect fertilization, but fertilization by this means is possible. Coitus interruptus is likely to be less satisfactory to both men and women than is complete intercourse.

Coitus reservatus is another form of incomplete intercourse in which ejaculation is intentionally suppressed so that the point of "ejaculatory inevitability" is not reached. The exact mechanism of such suppression is difficult to explain. Perhaps a parallel familiar to both genders is the intentional "holding back" of urination under stress. Coitus reservatus entails the same shortcomings as coitus interruptus.

Douching

Strictly speaking, douching is not a method of birth control, since its effectiveness in this regard is minimal. Sperms may enter the uterus seconds after ejaculation, well before douching is complete. It is, however, better than nothing. Some women douche with dangerous or irritating substances. If a woman feels that she must douche, she may use just warm water, which is as effective as strong chemical solutions in killing sperms.

Modern women need not douche regularly, if at all. Douching is necessary only when a physician recommends it for a particular medical condition, in which case he or she may recommend a particular douching compound. Douching is unnecessary for cleanliness. Internal areas need no cleansing. External areas may be cleansed with soap and water. Douching washes away "protective levels of residual acidity in the vagina" and makes that organ more vulnerable to infection. It is not necessary after intercourse. "External washing with soap and water is all that is necessary to maintain security from postejaculatory drainage and to avoid any suggestion of postcoital odor" (Masters and Johnson, 1970).

The Morning-after Pill (DES)

DES (diethylstilbestrol) received approval from the Food and Drug Administration in 1976 as a postcoital contraceptive agent for women who have had unprotected sexual intercourse in midcycle. DES should be used as an emergency measure only. It should never be considered a substitute for other forms of contraceptive protection. DES is an estrogen which is prescribed as a morning-after treatment in massive doses. If taken as directed, the woman stands a good chance of preventing a pregnancy from developing. Failures have been observed, however, so the method should not be considered foolproof. DES is often used when a woman has been the victim of rape or for other emergencies.

DES must be taken within seventy-two hours after intercourse. A medical history should be taken, since there are several conditions that the massive dose of DES could accentuate. Two pills are usually taken each day for five days. Side effects are common, with nausea and vomiting being experienced by approximately half of all women. Other estrogens such as ethinyl estradiol and premarin are sometimes used in place of DES. Some physicians advise their patients to wait and see if a pregnancy occurs and then consider abortion. Others prefer a "menstrual extraction," or very early abortion, since there may be greater complications with the DES treatment.

Other Forms of Contraception

Research continues on other forms of contraception. One approach involves the prevention of sperm formation. Contraceptive pills will prevent sperm formation, but their feminizing effect and their depressing action on the male's sex drive has ruled them out in the past as antifertility drugs in men (Garcia-Bunuel, 1966). A drug which has no feminizing effect and which can induce infertility in the male for periods up to 140 days per injection is being studied (Garcia-Bunuel, 1966). Substances acting directly on the testes provide another possible method of preventing sperm formation. Attempts have been made to immunize males in such a way as to prevent sperm formation, but so far these attempts have had little success (Garcia, 1968). There have also been attempts to immunize women against sperms, but again they have had little success (Garcia-Bunuel, 1966). However, immunological techniques do hold promise (Meyer, 1967). A drug which may prevent pregnancy by rendering the cervical mucus hostile to sperms has been reported (Connell, 1966).

The IVD (intravaginal device—not to be confused with the IUD, intrauterine device) consists of a plastic ring which contains a progesterone-like hormone. The ring is inserted into the vagina, and the hormone is slowly absorbed and inhibits ovulation. After the initial fitting by a physician, the woman herself removes the ring for menstruation and for sexual intercourse and then reinserts it. Although it is being studied further, this device has not proved as successful as was at first hoped (Mishell, Jr., Lumkin, and Stone, 1972; Zañartu and Guerrero, 1973). All these approaches to contraception are still experimental. None, as yet, replaces the methods explained earlier.

Sterilization

Sterilization, although not a form of contraception, is a means of conception control. It may be voluntary or involuntary. There are numerous ways by which it may occur. Examples include overexposure to x-rays; castration; removal of the ovaries (ovariectomy or oophorectomy); cryptorchidism (undescended testes); and disease, such as mumps, gonorrhea, or tuberculosis. The methods commonly employed in effecting voluntary sterilization are vasectomy in the male and salpingectomy (tubal ligation) in the female. These operations are usually, but not always, successful. Hence voluntary sterilization, like other forms of conception control, has a failure rate—low, to be sure, but nonetheless real. Because of its high success rate, however, voluntary sterilization is becoming increasingly common in this country. The latest authoritative estimates suggest that almost 5 million living Americans, about half men and half women, have obtained voluntary sterilization. Among blacks, however, more than nine out of ten sterilization procedures are performed on females. Among all age groups, races, and both genders, sterilization as a method of birth control is increasing. By 1973, 28.5 percent of contracepting couples in which the wife was 25 years of age or older relied on sterilization. Among couples in which the wife was between 30 and 44 years of age, sterilization was relied on by 33.7 percent of women (Westoff, 1976). A trend toward more sterilizations being performed on men has developed in recent years.

Vasectomy involves tying and cutting or cutting and electrically cauterizing (fulgurating) the vasa deferentia, the tubes through which the sperms pass from the epididymis. The vasa deferentia are near the surface of the scrotum. They are readily accessible to the physician through a small, superficial incision. This incision is made under local anesthesia, and the tube on either side is tied and cut or cut and cauterized. This provides a barrier, a "roadblock," to the passage of sperms. The sperms, which continue to be produced in the testes and are prevented by the "roadblock" from passing through the tubes, are absorbed by the body. Since the interstitial cells which secrete the masculinizing hormone in the testes remain undisturbed, vasectomy produces no change in the man's physique, secretion and discharge of seminal fluid, sexual drive, or capacity to have intercourse. The only change is the absence of sperms in the seminal fluid, but several ejaculations must occur for this to be accomplished, since there may be sperms beyond the vasa deferentia at the time of the operation. The absence of sperms can be ascertained by semen analysis. Since vasectomy does not affect masculinity, vasectomy and castration are radically different and are not to be confused.

Hypothetically, vasectomy may be reversed by rejoining the cut ends of the tubes and assuring that the internal passageway is unobstructed. The method for attempting this is to put a nylon thread or some other chemically inert substance in each tube when the ends are sewn together, leave it there until the tubal tissue heals around it, and then to remove it. But reversal of the vasectomy cannot be accomplished in the majority of cases, partly because of the difficulty of reestablishing the passageway through the tube and partly, perhaps, because after vasectomy a man may produce antibodies against his own sperms (*JAMA*, 1971). Thus, a vasectomy should not be performed unless the man anticipates that it will be a permanent, irreversible procedure.

Because of the possibility that a man might want a vasectomy reversed, and because of the difficulty of reversing it, techniques for achieving the same effect as surgical vasectomy without actually cutting and tying or cauterizing the vas are being studied. One of these involves obstructing the vas by injecting a substance through the skin of the scrotum (Coffey and Freeman, 1975). Another technique involves inserting into the vas a valve that can be turned on and off (Brueschke and Zaneveld, 1975). All of these techniques are still experimental.

Salpingectomy (tubal ligation) involves tying and cutting or cutting and electrically cauterizing the fallopian tubes (oviducts), or using clips to close them (Haskins, 1972). The tubes are accessible to the physician through an incision in the abdominal wall or an incision in the posterior wall of the vagina (Smith and Symmonds, 1971). In recent years a new technique (laparoscopy) has been widely used. While the patient is under anesthesia, a tubular instrument is introduced through the abdominal wall into the abdominal cavity. Through this instrument others are inserted, and in this way the physician can cut each fallopian tube and electrically cauterize the open ends. It has proved as successful as other methods. The woman may leave the hospital the day of the operation or the following morning. There is a reduction in the size of the scar. "Not only is the cosmetic factor important here, but there is a psychologic factor that appears to be important in some cases, since there is no visible scar to remind the patient of her sterility" (Barton, 1972).

Salpingectomy provides a barrier, a "roadblock," to the passage of the ovum and sperms through the tube and prevents them from meeting. Since the ovaries remain undisturbed, it produces no change in the woman's physique, sexual interest, or sexual capacity. In fact, her interest in sexual intercourse may be increased if it was previously colored by fear of unwanted pregnancy. Ova prevented from passing through the tube are absorbed. As in the case of vasectomy, hypothetically salpingectomy may be reversed, but this is not readily accomplished. It involves a second operation and is less likely to be requested than in the case of vasectomy, because so large a proportion of sterilizing operations on either partner are sought because of some condition in the wife or in her pregnancies which makes conception inadvisable and which is not likely to change after the salpingectomy.

In spite of the fact that salpingectomy is a more complicated procedure than vasectomy, in some cases in which a couple seek sterilization the husband insists that his wife rather than he have the necessary operation. He confuses sterility with lack of masculinity or mistakenly assumes that if he has a vasectomy, his sexual capacity will be altered.

Ignorance of the effects of sterilization is found even among educated persons. A questionnaire regarding attitudes toward sterilization submitted at Cornell University drew 1,059 respondents, 75 percent of whom were male. They represented the physical and biological sciences, the humanities, and the social sciences. There were 294 faculty members, 174 graduate students, 264 upperclassmen, and 327 freshmen. Almost half (49 percent) of the respondents expressed ignorance or uncertainty about whether vasectomy would prevent ejaculation, and 37 percent were certain, or thought it probable, that salpingectomy would interfere with the menstrual cycle (Eisner, Van Tienhoven, and Rosenblatt, 1970).

It should also be noted that among every 100 women in the United States who are of reproductive age having sexual intercourse regularly, but not using contraception of any kind, approximately 20 will not become pregnant. About half of these women are naturally sterile (infertile). The other half are marginally sterile (or marginally infertile), meaning they will need more than a year to become pregnant, and/or they will require fertility treatment. There is a common misconception that if a couple are unable to have a child, it is always the wife's "fault." A woman *or* a man may be sterile, or the couple together may be unable to have a child. Infertility will be discussed shortly.

The Effectiveness of Conception Control

In summarizing and in generalizing on the effectiveness of means of birth control, it is important to remember that pregnancy rates

Exhibit 12-8 Number of Pregnancies During the First Year of Use of Selected Methods of Contraception Per 100 Nonsterile Women

Method	When Used Correctly and Consistently	Average U. S. Experience Among 100 Women Who Want No More Children
Tubal ligation	0.04	0.04
Vasectomy	0.15	0.15
Combined oral contraceptives	0.34	4–10
Condom + spermicidal agent	Less than 1.0	5
Low-dose oral progestin (mini-pill)	1–1.5	5–10
IUD	1–3	5
Condom	3	10
Diaphragm (with spermicide)	3	17
Spermicidal foam	3	22
Coitus interruptus (withdrawal)	9	20–25
Rhythm (safe period)	13	21
Chance (sexually active)*	90	90
Douche	?	40

*This figure is higher in younger couples having intercourse frequently, lower in women over 35 having intercourse infrequently.

Source: Adapted from Hatcher et al. (1976).

---

are the result of both method failure and human failure. It is also important to keep in mind that no one method is best for all couples or necessarily best for a given couple at all times. Research data vary, and we can only generalize broadly. We might divide methods of conception control into categories (Pincus, 1965; Drill, 1966), not including abstention from intercourse, which is guaranteed to be 100 percent effective. These are only categories of relative effectiveness, disregarding side effects. Hence they are not categories of desirability.

▶ Most effective: sterilization, oral contraceptives. The pill is virtually 100 percent effective when used properly. The overall failure rate is very low. In evaluating the pill we must keep in mind that there is a difference between effectiveness of use (some women forget pills and use them incorrectly) and effectiveness of the method.

▶ Low failure rate: IUDs, diaphragms, condoms. These devices have the lowest failure rate after oral contraceptives and sterilization. Some investigators would put IUDs into the first category. The failure rate of diaphragms is decreased when used with cream or jelly, and the failure rate of condoms is decreased when used with foam.

▶ Considerable failure rate: jellies, creams, foams, suppositories used alone.

▶ Highest failure rate: "safe period" (rhythm), incomplete intercourse, douche.

In short, the perfect means of conception control has not yet been developed. There are contraceptives other than the pill with a high rate of effectiveness. If a woman cannot use or prefers not to use the pill, she or her husband, or both, may use a form of conception control which cannot fully guarantee prevention of pregnancy but can give reasonable assurance of such prevention; alternatively they may seek voluntary sterilization, an alternative being sought by increasing numbers of Americans, as suggested earlier.

Trends in Contraceptive Practice

Data from a national study of women in the reproductive years (ages 15 to 44) indicated that by 1973 seven in ten married couples were using contraception, and as many as nine out of ten of them were using relatively effective methods. Most of the couples who were not using contraception were trying to have children or were sterile or subfecund (marginally sterile). All evidence indicates that the trend toward more widespread use of contraception and use of more effective methods will continue to increase (Westoff, 1976).

The most significant trend in the last few years, as mentioned earlier, is the increased reliance on sterilization (23.5 percent of all married couples). The use of oral contraceptives also continues to increase. By 1973, 36 percent of all married contraceptive users were using the pill. It is still the most common method among young women, among whom nearly two out of three use oral contraceptives. Among older women, pill use has been replaced by sterilization as the most widely used method.

Ten percent of married women use the IUD. The diaphragm, which had been declining steadily in popularity, was used by only 3.4 percent of all married women and just 1.6 percent of women aged 15 to 24. However, there is reason to believe that diaphragm use might increase slightly in coming years, primarily due to the adverse publicity about oral contraceptives. Condom use is declining slightly. Condoms are used by 13.5 percent of married contraceptive users. Five percent of the couples rely on foam.

The rhythm method, which has been on the decline during the past decade, attracts less than 2 percent of all contraceptive users, and it appears to be continuing to decline. Withdrawal is still practiced by only 2 percent of married couples. By 1973, the douche had almost disappeared as a contraceptive method (Westoff, 1976). Westoff concludes: "It seems highly probable that by the end of the 1970s, almost all married couples at risk of unintended pregnancy in the United States will be using contraception, and almost all contraceptors will be protected by the most effective medical methods."

INFERTILITY

There is confusion with regard to the terminology employed to describe childlessness. Some persons use "fecundity" to indicate the capacity to have children, "subfecundity" thus meaning reduced capacity, and "fertility" to indicate actually having children, "infertility" thus meaning childlessness. Others employ the terms with the definitions reversed: "fertility" is used to refer to the capacity to have children, with "relative infertility" meaning reduced capacity, and "fecundity" used to indicate children born. In either case, "sterility" indicates zero capacity, hence no children. We shall use "fertility" and "infertility" as meaning capacity and "childlessness" as meaning the absence of children. Childlessness may be voluntary or involuntary.

Involuntary childlessness is commonly referred to as "sterility." Actually, only part of the cases are due to this cause, if the term is used in the strict sense. It is better to speak of relative fertility and relative infertility. The population is not divided into two distinct groups of which one is fertile and can produce offspring and the other is sterile and cannot do so. The ability to produce offspring falls on the normal curve of variability, as do all human traits, and consequently ranges from very high fertility on the one hand to absolute sterility on the other.

Among the factors contributing to infertility are chance, age, general health, certain infectious diseases, tumors, overexposure to x-ray or radium, removal of the genital organs, relatively low fertility in both spouses, genetic incompatibility (a condition in which the genes contain lethal, that is, death-producing, factors which kill the zygote), excessive acidity in the female genital tract, hormone deficiency, infantile genital organs, abnormal position of the uterus, too tightly closed cervix, closed or defective fallopian tubes, varicocele (abnormally swollen veins of the spermatic cord in the scrotum), or too few or defective sperms. When there are fewer than 20 million sperms per cubic centimeter of seminal fluid, relative infertility may result. A lower sperm count does not render conception impossible but does make it less likely. Cases have been found in which pregnancy occurred when the husband's sperm count was between 1 million and 10 million. The situation is similar when the man produces a high percentage of defective sperms.

Another factor contributing to infertility in women is anovulatory menstrual cycles. This kind of menstruation can occur without ovulation. Some women have more such cycles than do others. There is evidence to suggest that the average fertile woman ovulates normally only about 85 percent of the time, and a healthy woman may have three or four anovulatory cycles per year (Young, 1961). It would be safe to assume, then, that some women have an even higher incidence of anovulatory cycles. Some women do not menstruate at all.

Clomiphene, a drug commercially called Clomid, has been found to induce ovulation in nonovulating women in some cases when used in conjunction with certain hormones. Pregnancies have occurred following such induced ovulation. Compared with pregnancies in general, an increased proportion of such pregnancies terminate in spontaneous abortion or in multiple births (Kistner, 1966; Goldfarb, 1967; Loraine and Bell, 1968). In one study of 160 pregnancies it was found that there was a 10.8 percent spontaneous abortion rate and a 12.3 percent multiple pregnancy rate (compared with about 1 percent for pregnancies in general). There were eighteen pairs of twins, one set of triplets, and one set of quadruplets (Goldfarb, Morales, Rakoff, and Protos, 1968). In another series of 300 clomiphene-related pregnancies, there were twenty-two pairs of twins, two sets of triplets, and one set of quadruplets (Kistner, 1965). Clomiphene has also been found effective in increasing the production of sperms and in improving their quality (Palti, 1970). Another drug, menotropins, commercially called Pergonal, is a purified preparation of gonadotropins extracted from the urine of postmenopausal women. It contains primarily the follicle-stimulating hormones (FSH) and some luteinizing hormones (LH). When administered for nine to twelve days and followed by the administration of human chorionic gonadotropin (HCG), it effects ovulation in certain cases of infertility in women. As with Clomid, an increased proportion of pregnancies following the administration of Pergonal terminate in spontaneous abortion or in multiple births. Multiple births have accounted for 20 percent of all Pergonal-related births. Three-fourths of these multiple births were twins; one-fourth produced three or more babies (Cutter Laboratories). In one series of forty-three pregnancies, there were twenty singletons, fourteen sets of twins, and nine sets of triplets. In another series of fourteen pregnancies, six resulted in multiple births and included one set of quadruplets (Shearman, 1969). In a series of 1,450 pregnancies, 129 were multiple: 113 sets of twins, eight sets of triplets, six sets of quadruplets, and two sets of quintuplets (Shearman, 1969).

Clomid and Pergonal are both useful in

the treatment of infertility, but they are limited to only certain types of cases, and both drugs sometimes produce side effects in addition to excessive ovulation.

During the menopause, a woman's fertility decreases, When the menopause is complete, she is infertile. During the menopause, a woman may have anovulatory menstrual cycles. On the other hand, she may possibly continue to ovulate occasionally without the follicle and corpus luteum producing enough hormones to bring about menstruation when they are withdrawn. Some women cease menstruating rather abruptly at the onset of the menopause. In others the menstrual discharge gradually diminishes in quantity. In still others the menstrual periods become farther and farther apart until they cease altogether. Because of this last possibility, which might mislead a woman into concluding that the menopause was complete when it was not, and because of the possibility that a woman may continue to ovulate without menstruating, thus concluding that the menopause was complete, some women dispense with conception control and have unexpected pregnancies late in life—sometimes twenty or more years after the birth of the last previous child.

If a woman has her ovaries removed (ovariectomy, oophorectomy) for medical reasons, she will have the equivalent of abrupt, immediate menopause. Her physician may give her hormone therapy to assist her body in making the necessary transition. When her ovaries are removed, a woman does not necessarily lose her sex drive and responsiveness; they may be maintained by hormones secreted by the adrenal glands, especially if she has been conditioned to a pattern of satisfactory sexual response (Winokur, 1963; Oliven, 1965; Kane, Lipton, and Ewing, 1969). In popular parlance, surgical removal of the uterus, tubes, and ovaries is referred to as a "complete hysterectomy." Strictly speaking, however, "hysterectomy" refers to the removal of only the uterus.

In males a cause of infertility is cryptorchidism. The testes develop within the body cavity. During the seventh and eighth prenatal month they descend into the scrotum, where the temperature is low enough to permit the formation of sperms. If the testes do not descend normally by the time puberty is completed and nothing is done medically or surgically to effect their descent, the male may be sterilized by his own body heat. Also, a high percentage of undescended testes are abnormal; that is, they are undescended because they are abnormal, not abnormal because they are undescended (Scott, 1961).

It is estimated that one-third of infertile marriages are due primarily to the husband, one-third to the wife, and one-third to impaired fertility in both (Lloyd, 1964b). The exact proportion is not so important as the fact that husbands are more frequently at "fault" than some of them have known or have been willing to admit.

Through careful diagnosis by a medical specialist the contributing factors in infertility may in many instances be discovered. Once these factors are discovered, remedy is possible in a large percentage of cases. The first step for the couple who want a baby and have been unsuccessful is to visit a specialist, explain their situation and marital history, and follow his or her advice. If they are serious about wanting a child, the physician will suggest that they submit to a series of examinations and tests. The process may be long and perhaps expensive, depending upon the readiness with which causal factors are discovered and corrected. Complete cooperation of the couple—both of them—is essential.

Some husbands are offended when it is suggested that they may be at fault. Some even object to examination and testing. Such behavior is unwarranted since there is no necessary relationship between masculinity and fertility, and a man cannot increase his fertility by refusing to measure it.

Some physicians suggest that the husband be tested first. The tests for him are easier to administer than those for the wife. If there are found in him factors that may contribute toward the couple's infertility, the physician may begin to remedy these and thus possibly save the couple much time and expense. The tests for the wife are more extensive and require more time. To start with her might involve following a long and expensive procedure, only to find at last that the husband was responsible anyway.

There is a not uncommonly held theory to the effect that some cases of relative infertility are "cured" by adoption. The assumption is that the infertility is caused by a combination of delicately balanced factors (Grant, 1969). As the couple try unsuccessfully to have a child, the increasing tension tips the balance in the direction of infertility. Then, at long last, they adopt a child. This turns their attention away from their infertility and concern. Thus tension is reduced, and the balance is tipped in the direction of fertility. Soon after adopting a child, the wife becomes pregnant. In one study made some years ago (Perkins, 1936), it was found that in 273 cases of adoption, 200 of the adoptive mothers who had never been pregnant before had a child within an average of thirty-nine months after the adoption and within ten years after the wedding. But does this prove that fertility was increased by the adoption? Or would they have become pregnant anyway in a period that long? Undoubtedly some women become pregnant soon after adopting a child. But recent evidence does not support the view that there is a cause-and-effect relationship between adoption and conception. There may be exceptions. The percentage of previously childless women who become pregnant after adoption is not greatly different from the percentage of such women whose infertility is ended spontaneously without adoption (Greenhill, 1961, 1962b; Weinstein, 1962; Aronson and Glienke, 1963; Rock, Tietz, and McLaughlin, 1965). In one study of 533 infertile couples (Arronet, Bergquist, and Parekh, 1974), 133 couples (25 percent) adopted a child while 400 couples (75 percent) did not. The pregnancy rate was higher among the 400 non-adopting couples than among the 133 adopting couples. Over a third of women who have fertility tests administered also become pregnant—without ever knowing why they were infertile (Grant, 1969).

ARTIFICIAL INSEMINATION

Artificial insemination is the process of transferring seminal fluid from the male to the female by mechanical means rather than by sexual intercourse. The seminal fluid is ejaculated during masturbation or incomplete intercourse into a glass container. This fact has given rise to the term "test-tube baby." Currently, "test-tube baby" is sometimes used to refer to a child that is the result of *in vitro* fertilization, that is, largely hypothetical and speculative fertilization which occurs outside a woman's body when sperms and ovum are brought together in a glass container and the zygote is then transferred to the uterus of either the woman who provided the ovum or some other woman who carries the pregnancy to term. It is important that the two meanings of the expression not be confused. In artificial insemination, the fluid is then redeposited in the vagina at the entrance to the cervix, or sometimes directly into the uterus, by means of a syringelike device. It is done at the request of the couple in cases in which the husband has low fertility, in which there is some anatomical condition making natural insemination difficult, or in which there is some eugenic consideration, such as the husband's carrying an undesirable hereditary trait, or for some similar reason. There is no way of ascertaining with accuracy how frequently it occurs, since physicians' records are not made public. One "guess" is 20,000 times per year (Finegold, 1964). Artificial insemination is of two types. In one type, referred to as AIH (artificial insemination—husband), the woman's husband provides the seminal fluid. This type might be used, for example, if some anatomical condition made natural insemination unusually difficult; if the woman had to maintain an unusual posture so that the seminal fluid could remain at the cervix long enough for sperms to enter the uterus; or if the husband's sperm count was low and, by combining the sperms from several samples of seminal fluid, a higher concentration of sperms was achieved. In the other type an anonymous donor, to whom the couple are also anonymous, is chosen by the physician and provides the seminal fluid for remuneration (Novak, Jones, and Jones, Jr., 1970). This type is referred to as AID (artificial insemination—donor). Some physicians mix a small quantity of the husband's seminal fluid with that of the donor. Then, if the woman conceives, there is no way of proving which man is the father of the child. Such a procedure, it is claimed, facilitates the husband's acceptance of the child and eliminates legal problems that might arise relative to the child being the husband's heir. Other physicians feel that AID should be performed only with carefully chosen, mature couples and that with such couples subterfuge is unnecessary. In cases of AID, legal complications may be avoided by the husband's adoption of the child. But adoption involves court procedure and a degree of publicity which many couples want to avoid. Hence, they simply keep the fact of artifical insemination secret and present the child to relatives and friends as their natural offspring. Courts have ruled that a child born to a married couple is legally the husband's if the couple have regular intercourse and if the husband accepts the child as his own (Karow, Gentry, and Payne, 1969).

In recent years seminal fluid has been frozen and stored, then thawed and used in artificial insemination. In such freezing, liquid nitrogen or some similar substance is used to lower the temperature rapidly, sometimes to as much as about 350°F below zero. In such a process the sperms are not killed, as they would be in ordinary freezing. Artificial insemination with frozen sperms is not always successful, but successes have occurred and normal children have resulted (Sherman, 1964; Freund and Wiederman, 1966; Behrman and Sawada, 1966; Bunge, 1970; Ersek, 1972). The first such baby was born in 1953 and at latest report, some nineteen years later, was in good health. Between 1953 and 1972 some 300 healthy babies were conceived in this manner (Ersek, 1972). In one study (Steinberger and Smith, 1973) 107 attempts at artificial insemination were made with 74 women. There were 35 women who became pregnant with the use of fresh seminal fluid, 36 with frozen seminal fluid. The longest recorded time that frozen human sperms were stored and then used successfully in artificial insemination is about ten years (Ersek, 1972). But such a length of time is unusual.

The freezing of sperms makes it possible to maintain sperm banks (sometimes called "cryobanking"), just as there are blood banks and organ banks, and several depositories are already in operation. This permits a further extension of methods employed to assist childless couples by means of artificial insemination. If further research reveals methods of storing seminal fluid successfully for longer periods, a man might have his seminal fluid frozen and stored to be used if he changed his mind about fathering additional children after having a vasectomy; if he became widowed or divorced and remarried; if he were in an occupation, such as working with radioactive material, that might endanger his fertility; or if he married a woman much younger than himself who might want more children during his old age or even after his death.

Many persons resist the idea of sperm banks. Such banks provide an extension of artificial insemination, not a substitute for natural fruitful insemination where it is possible. Only yesterday the idea of blood banks and organ banks was resisted, and although they have not yet been universally accepted, all such depositories represent a beneficial adjunct to modern medicine.

ABORTION

Abortion is usually defined by state laws as the expulsion or removal of the fetus (or embryo or zygote) from the woman's body before it is viable, that is, before it can survive outside her body. It is defined by the medical profession as expulsion or removal of the fetus (or embryo or zygote) before the end of the twentieth prenatal week (*Stedman's Medical Dictionary*, 22d ed., 1972).

Types of Abortion

Spontaneous This type of abortion occurs because of some condition in the woman or the fetus (or embryo or zygote)—in other words, in the pregnancy—and without deliberate interference. Spontaneous abortion is commonly termed miscarriage.

Many factors may play a part in causing spontaneous abortion. One of them is a defective fetus. Thus, such an abortion is not always an unmixed tragedy. In one study, 48 percent of spontaneously aborted fetuses were found to be abnormal. In another study, 46 percent were abnormal. In still another, it was found that 80 percent of the fetuses aborted at the end of the first month were defective, and half of those aborted in the second month were defective. In the third and fourth months, only about 12 percent were abnormal (Greenhill, 1944). In another study (Brotherton and Craft, 1972), 60 percent of the fetuses were abnormal. In one study of spontaneous abortion, chromosome complications were found in almost one-fourth of the cases (Carr, 1965). Broadly speaking, about one-third of the fetuses in spontaneous abortions are defective (Greenhill, 1948). Greenhill (1945) estimates that there are at least five times as many deformed fetuses among those aborted as there are deformed babies among those born at full term. The proportion may be even higher than this, since by no means all aborted fetuses are subjected to examination.

Potter (1962) concludes from her studies that there are "probably well over a million spontaneous abortions" each year in this country, that "most of them result from abnormal development of the embryo or villi," and that if those that occur so early that the woman is unaware or uncertain that she is pregnant are included, the number would be "in the neighborhood of four to five million." Some occur so early that the woman is not even aware that she has been pregnant and assumes that she has had an unusual menstrual period. Such very early abortions are sometimes referred to as silent abortions.

Therapeutic This is a legal abortion induced by a physician in cases where (1) continuation of the pregnancy would endanger the life or jeopardize the health (physical or mental) of the woman, or (2) serious fetal deformity is suspected. Actually, with modern antibiotics and chemotherapy there are relatively few cases in which therapeutic abortion is indicated literally to save the life of the woman. Therapeutic abortions for medical reasons have become less common and those for nonmedical reasons more common in recent years. Today therapeutic abortions are performed for psychiatric, eugenic (fetus may be defective), humanitarian (cases of rape), or socioeconomic reasons. In the light of the U.S. Supreme Court decision discussed below, such reasons, or at least some of them, may be expected to continue, especially relative to abortion in the last three months of pregnancy. Thus, even if abortion on request during the first six months of pregnancy continues to be accepted, the concept of therapeutic abortion will not become passé.

Abortion on request This is legalized abortion for the reason that the woman desires to terminate the pregnancy. Whether abortion should be controlled by law is one question. Whether it *can* be is another. Experience has shown that abortion cannot be legally controlled, and the only feasible and realistic alternative is to put the responsibility for the decision where it belongs, namely, upon the woman and her physician. In a democracy laws are enforceable to the degree to which they are supported by the mores, by public opinion. American society learned this during the days of Prohibition. There is far from universal support for antiabortion laws, and penalties for infractions of such laws in the past have proved infeasible.

The issue of abortion, especially since the U.S. Supreme Court decision of 1973, has demonstrated tremendous potential for generating discussion (both rational and irrational), emotion, bitter debate and recrimination, moral judgments, polarization into proabortion and antiabortion ("pro-life") camps, and much confusion. There are several factors underlying such reactions. One, of course, is the existence of deep and sincere convictions in persons on either side of the issue, convictions often grounded in religious faith. Another factor is the difficulty of reaching consensus on issues not resting on scientific data and proof and therefore depending on value judgments, for example, the nature of the fetus (to be discussed later). Still another, and this is a very important one, is the common tendency to treat abortion as a "one-pronged" issue when in actual fact it is a "two-pronged" issue.

One prong of the issue concerns the nature and consequences of abortion: Should women have abortions? Do they have a right to have them? Is abortion moral or immoral? What is destroyed in abortion? Is the fetus human? What are the safest methods of inducing abortion? The other prong of the issue is the legal one: Should abortion be prohibited by law?

It is possible to live together in disagreement regarding the first prong of the issue without one group's attempting to impose its will on others by means of law. Parallels to this situation readily come to mind. The question of the advisability and morality of the use of alcoholic beverages has not been resolved to everyone's satisfaction. But, without consensus, Americans have found that they can live together in disagreement without legal restriction, as in the case of Prohibition. Until recently some states had laws prohibiting the use of contraceptives. Most of those laws have been rescinded in spite of the fact that there is not universal agreement on the morality, or even the advisability, of using contraceptives. There is certainly widespread disagreement regarding premarital and extramarital sexual relations. But would it be feasible to attempt to prohibit such relations by law? Abortion presents another case in point. So long as the advisability of having abortions and the legal prohibition of abortion are treated as one issue instead of two, there will continue to be dissension without resolution of the issues. So long as the question remains: Should women have abortions? there can be limitless discussion with differences of opinion tolerated. But when the question becomes: Should women be *allowed by law* to have (or more accurately, be *prohibited by law* from having) abortions? confrontation is inevitable because both sides seek mutually exclusive action. There can be pro and con attitudes simultaneously, but there cannot be pro and con laws simultaneously; a choice must be made.

Sometimes abortion on request is referred to as "voluntary abortion," "elective abortion," or "abortion on demand." The latter term can be taken to imply that the physician has no choice in the matter, whereas "abortion on request" implies freedom of choice by both woman and physician. Advocates of abortion on request sometimes forget that the physician may have scruples against it or may refuse to perform the operation because of the risk involved in a particular case. We take for granted that in any type of case a physician will make a judgment relative to medical risk and that there is no obligation to become a party to a risk deemed too great. In abortion on request the final decision is made by the woman and her physician with no legal restrictions except those relating to safety, the age of the fetus, and the qualifications of the physician. The term "voluntary abortion" does not specifically distinguish between "voluntary" and "request." A woman has a therapeutic abortion voluntarily in the sense that she agrees to it; it is not forced upon her, except perhaps in some rare or hypothetical case in which a woman's condition prevents her giving consent, so that her husband or her physician makes the decision. "Request" implies that there is nothing to which a woman agrees; she simply wants the abortion. In a similar way, the term "legal abortion," as sometimes used to include both therapeutic abortion and abortion on request, makes no distinction between the differences in motivation in the two types. A woman may not want an abortion but may feel it is necessary.

Early in 1973, in a 7-to-2 decision, the U.S. Supreme Court (*Roe v. Wade*, no. 70-18) declared restrictive abortion laws unconstitutional because they represent an invasion of a woman's privacy, to which she has a constitutional right, determined by Court interpretation, since "the Constitution does not explicitly mention any right of privacy." The Court stated that a decision regarding abortion during the first three months of pregnancy rests with the woman and her physician (see also *Doe v. Bolton*, no. 70-40), because during this period abortion is relatively safe for the woman. During the second three months of pregnancy, state law may regulate conditions and procedures pertaining to the woman's safety, for example, the qualifications of the physician performing the abortion and the medical facility in which the abortion occurs. Thus, during the second three months of pregnancy the state may begin to intrude on the woman's privacy.

The Court held that at some time during the last three months of pregnancy the fetus becomes viable, that is, able to live outside the woman's body. At this point the state's interest in "potential life" outweighs the woman's individual rights, and the state may prohibit abortion except when necessary to protect the health or preserve the life of the woman. The Court refers to the fetus as "potential life" in the later months of pregnancy but not in the earlier months. In the later months the state may also prohibit abortion because "the risk to the woman increases as her pregnancy continues." This Court decision, in effect, established abortion on request, at least during the first six months of pregnancy, on a nationwide basis.

The number of legally reported abortions performed in the United States during 1973 and 1974 totaled approximately 1,650,000 (Weinstock, Tietz, Jaffe, and Dryfoos, 1975). The total number of abortions may actually be higher, since not all abortions are reported. It would not be unreasonable to estimate that there are at least one million abortions performed in the United States each year. Approximately one-third of all abortions are performed on teenagers, about one-third on women between 20 and 24, and about one-third on unmarried women (Center for Disease Control, 1976).

The total number of women who died from abortions in the United States declined from 88 in 1972 to 56 in 1973 to 48 in 1974. Almost all of the decline can be accounted for by a shift from illegal to legal abortions (Cates and Rochat, 1976). There are 3.3 maternal deaths for every 100,000 legal abortions performed (Center for Disease Control, 1976). The maternal death rate due to complications of pregnancy and childbirth is 10.8. At first glance it appears that abortion is more than three times as safe as pregnancy and childbirth. But such a comparison must be made with caution. Deaths resulting from pregnancy and childbirth are more likely to be reported than abortion-associated deaths. Furthermore, pregnancy and childbirth typically involve a nine-month period, while a large proportion of abortions occur in the first three months of pregnancy. Nevertheless, the fact remains that legal abortion, especially when performed during the first three months of pregnancy, does not entail either the risk of illegal abortion or the degree of risk often stressed by antiabortionists. However, this is by no means equivalent to saying that abortion involves no risk. "Speakers and writers who . . . promote the concept that abortions are simple, easy, and innocuous . . . are doing women a grave disservice" (Pakter, Harris, and Nelson, 1971). As new techniques for abortion are developed and as practitioners become more experienced in the use of these techniques, undoubtedly the risks involved in legal abortion will be further reduced.

The Nature of the Fetus

One of the unresolved, and perhaps unresolvable, issues relative to abortion is the nature of the fetus (or embryo or zygote). What is it? Is it merely tissue, a mass of cells? Is it a human being, a human life, a human organism, a human person, or a human individual? When does human life begin—at fertilization; at implantation; at a given point in prenatal development; at quickening (which represents the woman's perception of fetal movement rather than such movement itself, which begins long before the woman becomes aware of it); when the fetus becomes viable; or at birth? Empirical data cannot provide the answers. The answers depend upon value judgments, and, as implied earlier, these value judgments are subjective and individual and involve emotional, ethical, moral, philosophical, religious, biological, psychological, and sociological considerations. The Supreme Court did not attempt to define the nature of the fetus. "We need not resolve the difficult question of when life begins. When those trained in the respective disciplines of medicine, philosophy, and theology are unable to arrive at a consensus, the judiciary, at this point in the development of man's knowledge, is not in a position to speculate as to the answer" (*Roe v. Wade*, no. 70-18). It stated further, "The Constitution does not define 'person' in so many words." Its use of the word "person" is such that it has application only postnatally and does not indicate "with any assurance, that it has any possible pre-natal application. . . . The word 'person,' as used in the Fourteenth Amendment, does not include the unborn" (*Roe v. Wade*, no. 70-18). Therefore, the fetus's right to life is not guaranteed by the Fourteenth Amendment.

On the one hand, abortion on request is supported, in part, because of the assumption that the fetus is not human. On the other hand, there is a growing science of fetology, and efforts are being made medically to save fetal life, for example, through intrauterine transfusion and even transfusion of the fetus temporarily removed from the uterus. A case occurred in which the court ordered an intrauterine transfusion in spite of the fact that the parents' religious conviction led them to refuse consent. In the conflict between the fetus's right to life and the parents' religious freedom, the court decided in favor of the fetus (Noonan, 1970). "All states . . . now allow recovery for prenatal injuries, sometimes those occurring as early as the first month of pregnancy" (Granfield, 1970). Once a child is born alive, legal action in its name may be brought against anyone who caused it injury before birth.

The Rights of the Man

In the U.S. Supreme Court decision of 1973 discussed above, the rights of the husband of a woman who seeks abortion on request are not mentioned except in a footnote which reads, "Neither . . . do we discuss the father's rights, if any exist in the constitutional context, in the abortion decision. . . . We are aware that some statutes recognize the father under certain circumstances" (*Roe v. Wade*, no 70-18). To be noted is the Court's reference to the man with whom the woman had the intercourse that initiated the pregnancy as "father." At that time, in the voluminous publications regarding abortion on request, little was said about the rights of the man. This led one writer (Rovinsky, 1971) to say, "The legal question . . . of a husband's proprietary rights to wife and/or fetus (is) unresolved, and (is) generating much heat but little light in academic legal circles."

The issue of the husband's rights was finally faced by the Supreme Court in 1976 (nos. 74-1151 and 74-1419). Again, the Court was divided. The majority opinion was that state legislation requiring the consent of the husband to his wife's procuring an abortion is unconstitutional. Said the majority, referring to the decision in which the Court declared restrictive abortion laws unconstitutional, "We cannot hold that the State has the constitutional authority to give the spouse unilaterally the ability to prohibit the wife from terminating her pregnancy, when the State itself lacks that right." The majority said further, "We recognize, of course, that when a woman, with the approval of her physician but without the approval of her husband, decides to terminate her pregnancy, it could be said that she is acting unilaterally. The obvious fact is that when the wife and husband disagree on this decision, the view of only one of the two marriage partners can prevail. Since it is the woman who physically bears the child and who is more directly and immediately affected by the pregnancy, as between the two, the balance weighs in her favor."

The majority decision established, at least for the time being, the unconstitutionality of a legal requirement of a husband's consent to a woman getting an abortion. The decision also further polarized proabortion and antiabortion groups, the former enthusiastically hailing it as a milestone of progress, the latter sharply criticizing it as a step backward.

Other Effects of Liberalized Abortion

There is no universal agreement on the possible harmful psychological effect of abortion. Studies seem to indicate that such consequences are uncommon and, when they occur, are not serious (Walter, 1970; Pasnau, 1972). These studies seem to show that, in general, women who have abortions accept them. Perhaps this is to be expected, since they make a free choice in most cases. The abortion situation is a selective one. Some advocates of abortion emphasize the absence of psychiatric symptoms among women who have had abortions, but not all possible psychological consequences can be measured by such symptoms. It is difficult to ascertain whether women feel guilt, because an investigator has only the woman's word and her subjective reactions to judge by.

Methods of Inducing Abortion

It is sometimes assumed that safe abortion may be brought about by self-administered abortifacient drugs. Such is not the case. "There is no safe, reliable drug available at this time which will cause termination of pregnancy in human beings" (Nathanson, 1970). This statement applies to self-administered abortifacient drugs; prostaglandins will be discussed later. Many of the drugs used are not only ineffective, but also dangerous. Some may cause injury or death.

Sometimes women attempt self-induced abortions by introducing sharp objects into the uterus or by douching with poisonous or caustic solutions. Needless to say, such procedures are extremely dangerous. Of all the douching solutions used in attempts to induce abortions, "perhaps the most common, as well as the most lethal, are soap solutions" (Schwarz, 1968). A soapsuds douche may result in an air embolism (air in the circulatory system) or in kidney failure due to the chemical in the soap (Deep and Jacobson, 1965; Hibbard, 1969), either of which may prove fatal.

Women sometimes resort to violent procedures such as rolling downhill or driving over rough roads in an attempt to bring about an abortion. Such procedures are scarcely to be recommended. Often, in spite of the violence, no abortion is produced. The woman finds that a healthy pregnancy is difficult to dislodge.

Medical methods employed to induce abortion will now be described. They are not of equal merit in all circumstances. Which one will be employed for a particular woman is something to be decided by her physician on the basis of her condition, the duration of her pregnancy, the hospital facilities available, and similar considerations. None is without risk.

Menstrual extraction (also referred to as menstrual induction, menstrual regulation, endometrial aspiration, uterine evacuation, preemptive abortion, mini-abortion, mini-suction, lunch-hour abortion, and other terms) This is removal of the contents of the uterus by suction, as in vacuum aspiration (mentioned below). Whether or not it is actually abortion depends upon the condition of the woman. In other words, menstrual extraction may be performed if there is a possibility that a woman is pregnant but before pregnancy can be accurately ascertained by means of a pregnancy test, that is, less than about fourteen days after a missed menstrual period. Various studies have shown that from 15 to 50 percent of women having menstrual extraction were not pregnant. Menstrual extraction is an outpatient procedure, performed under local anesthesia, with an instrument similar to but smaller than the one used in vacuum aspiration. It is not always successful, and cases have been known in which pregnancy continued in spite of the extraction. It is of no use in a case of tubal pregnancy (outside the uterus). Complications are few but do occur. "The invasion and evacuation of the uterus is not a harmless, innocuous procedure. This surgical procedure should not be delegated to paramedical personnel, nor should it be performed routinely or haphazardly without definite indication" (Hodgson, 1975). Some physicians feel that any such procedure performed without accurate diagnosis constitutes poor patient care, and that nothing is lost by the woman's waiting just a short time longer until a pregnancy test is positive and vacuum aspiration is performed. On the other hand, many physicians favor menstrual extraction because it relieves the woman's worry about the possibility of pregnancy. Long-term effects are not known.

Dilatation and curettage This method, referred to as "D & C," involves a physician's dilating (stretching) the cervix and scraping away the contents of the uterus (fetus, placenta, and amniotic sac) with a sharp instrument (curette). The operation is done under anesthesia. It is used for abortion through the twelfth week of pregnancy.

Vacuum aspiration This operation, now the most widespread form of abortion, involves removal of the contents of the uterus by suction. It is used for abortion through the twelfth week of pregnancy. Vacuum aspiration is a relatively new procedure. It has several advantages over D & C; for example, it can be done with or without cervical dilation, it takes less time than a D & C, and it causes less bleeding. Because of the size of the instruments a vacuum aspiration can be performed with no anesthesia or with local or general anesthesia. It can be done on an outpatient basis requiring no hospital stay. Reports suggest that this method is relatively safe and produces few complications (Strausz and Schulman, 1971; Goldsmith and Margolis, 1971; Loung, Buckle, and Anderson, 1971; Ingraham and Longood, 1971; Nathanson, 1971). In one study of 10,453 abortions by vacuum aspiration, there were few complications and no maternal deaths (Hodgson and Portmann, 1974).

Saline injection (amnioinfusion) This technique, sometimes referred to as "salting out," is used after sixteen weeks of pregnancy. It involves the insertion of a hypodermic needle-like instrument through the abdominal wall—under local anesthesia—and into the amniotic sac. A small amount of amniotic fluid is withdrawn and replaced with a 20 percent salt solution. Within a few hours the woman will usually go into labor and deliver fetus and placenta. This, of course, should occur in a hospital. Usually a woman may leave the hospital within a few hours after the expulsion of the contents of the uterus. Complications can occur (Mackenzie, Roufa, and Tovell, 1971; Ingraham and Longood, 1971; Ballard and Ballard, 1972). The earlier in pregnancy that abortion is performed the safer it is. Hence, partly because saline injection is used during the second trimester (second three months), and partly because of the technique itself, the risk is much greater than with vacuum aspiration, which is used during the first trimester. Studies show that this method carries "an increased risk of maternal mortality . . ." (Bolognese and Corson, 1975). However, in one series of saline injections performed under carefully controlled conditions and techniques, although there were some complications, there were no maternal deaths (Kerenyi, Mandelman, and Sherman, 1973).

Use of prostaglandins Prostaglandins are complex chemicals produced by the human body. The first prostaglandin was discovered over fifty years ago. It was misnamed, because it was believed to be produced by the prostate gland. Since that time, a number of prostaglandins have been identified, and they have been found in menstrual fluid, the endometrium, amniotic fluid, the umbilical cord, blood during labor, placental blood vessels, the thyroid gland, the lungs, and other tissues in both male and female (Moghissi, 1972). The richest source is seminal fluid; thirteen separate prostaglandins are found in it alone (Moghissi, 1972). These prostaglandins are thought to be produced by the seminal vesicles (Anderson and Speroff, 1971; Moghissi, 1972; Karim, 1972).

Prostaglandins are known to stimulate smooth muscles to contract. Therefore, they have been used recently in experiments to bring about contractions of the uterus. Several investigators have used prostaglandins to bring about labor at term (Karim, 1972). They have also been used in induced abortion but have the disadvantage of side effects (Horton, 1972; Moghissi, 1972). Because of these side effects, some investigators feel the method has "limited clinical usefulness" (Csapo, Sauvage, and Wiest, 1971; Gillett,

Kinch, Wolfe, and Pace-Asciak, 1972) and "offers little advantage over classical means of inducing abortions" (Cantor, Jewelewicz, Warren, Dyrenfurth, Patner, and Vande Wiele, 1972). Some investigators (Karim, 1972; Kirshen, Naftolin, and Ryan, 1972; Anderson, 1974) feel that the use of prostaglandins for abortion does not compare favorably with suction in the first three months but does compare favorably with other methods during the second three months.

The use of prostaglandins is not the same as the use of the abortifacient drugs mentioned earlier. Research continues on various prostaglandins and different methods of administration. They hold some promise as a means of inducing abortion, especially in the early months of pregnancy (Moghissi, 1972). Whether this promise is fulfilled depends upon the results of further research.

Hysterotomy This method (not to be confused with hysterectomy, the removal of the uterus) involves a surgical opening of the uterus through abdominal incision, as in cesarean section. It is used when other methods cannot be employed, or when a woman wants to combine a sterilizing operation (salpingectomy) with the abortive operation. This method involves considerably more risk than any of the methods mentioned above (Bolognese and Corson, 1975).

The Future of Abortion

In the last analysis, as the U.S. Supreme Court has indicated, whether a woman has an abortion is not a matter to be regulated by law, but a decision to be made by herself and her physician. Liberalized legislation should not lead us to consider abortion lightly or casually. Liberalizing laws and making judicial declarations are not equivalent to recommending that women have abortions. They are only means by which women may be allowed legally to decide whether they will have abortions. All reasonable help should be provided so that women can understand what abortion involves and understand the importance of having an abortion as early as possible after pregnancy is diagnosed. The later an abortion is performed, the greater the risk, and the risk increases drastically after the first trimester. It is important that women be educated in techniques of contraception, that they know where and how to procure contraceptives, and that they be motivated to use contraception so that they may more fully take responsibility for their own sexual behavior.

ADOPTION

In recent years, there have been fewer babies available for adoption. Declining birth rates, better contraceptive use, and the increased availability of legal abortion have contributed to this situation. Virtually all couples who wish to adopt may still do so, however, although in some locations they may not be able to adopt "preferred" babies (healthy, white infants are in greatest demand). Adoption is no longer considered an act of charity through which a homeless child is given maintenance. It is deemed a privilege for the adoptive parents as well as for the child. The future welfare of all concerned is taken into consideration. Not only is the child chosen; the adoptive home and parents also are chosen. Actually, in recent years the concept of "adoptability" has changed. Formerly the emphasis was upon finding a child for a family, but now it is upon finding a family for a child. The staffs in the better agencies insist upon meeting the prospective adoptive parents, investigating their social and economic position, and sending a special investigator to see the home and talk with friends. In this way adults and child are "fitted" to each other.

Race, religion, intelligence, nationality, education, and cultural background of natural and of adoptive parents are often matched insofar as this is possible. Many couples desire the similarity. On the other hand, as the world situation has changed owing to war and other catastrophes, an increasing number of couples are adopting children of other races and nationalities. Some couples combine sterilization with this sort of adoption as their contribution to zero population growth, seeking to care for children already born rather than adding new ones to an already overpopulated world. There is also a beginning trend which will result in more adoptions by single persons, although this phenomenon is still rare.

Usually the agency collects all available facts pertaining to the child's background. These are kept on file. Some agencies reveal as much as the adoptive parents wish to know. Others hold that the less the new parents know the better off both the child and they will be, since knowing the child's background may lead them to "read into" its behavior something that is there only in their own imagination. In general, trusting the staff of a reliable agency is a better safeguard than knowing the necessarily incomplete data on the child's origin. The identity of natural parents is usually not revealed to adoptive parents, and vice versa. Hence there is very little chance of the former's appearing at an inopportune time to upset the child's adjustment. At the time the baby is left with the agency, or shortly after, depending on state law, all claim to it is relinquished.

No child with known physical or mental defects is offered for adoption without the prospective adoptive parents' being apprised of the defects. They are not obliged to accept the baby if they do not want it. Some agencies place children in a temporary home for observation, medical attention, and testing for a brief period before being placed.

When the child is taken by the prospective adoptive parents, it is on probation, so to speak, for a time. In some states, this probationary period is mandated by law. If, during this period before the final papers have been signed, it develops any defects not observable in infancy, it may be returned to the agency. The original parents may reclaim the child during this time in some states, although the laws vary. Similarly, the agency may reclaim the child during this probationary period if there is a good reason for doing so (such as neglect on the part of the adoptive parents).

Experience proves that adopted children love and are loved as much as natural ones. The biological parents, if anything is known about them, are strangers; if nothing is known of them, they are merely words and a source of mild curiosity. Occasionally cases come to light in which an individual adopted as a child and now grown to adulthood becomes sufficiently curious to seek out the identity of the parents and arrange for a meeting. Sometimes such a meeting is a happy one; at other times it is disappointing.

In the rearing of the child, its adoption should be made a natural part of its life, something taken for granted. The child should be told of it as soon as this can be understood. The adoption should continue to be discussed with the child as he or she gets older, but the child should not be reminded of it in a disparaging way. No gratitude should be demanded, and shortcomings should never be blamed on the fact of adoption. Some adoptive parents speak of their "adopted child" or "chosen child." In this way the child grows up with the idea of adoption accepted casually. Cases are known in which a child has boasted to playmates, "I was chosen because my parents loved me, but yours had to take you." In one case in which a couple had adopted several children, two of them were overheard discussing a new friend, who was the natural child of her parents. "Let's not tell her that we're adopted," they agreed, "it might make her feel bad."

Not all adoptions are arranged through agencies. Adoptions may be "direct," indicating that the adoption was arranged through a physician or lawyer and the child placed directly in the home. Many couples prefer this method of adoption, since they may bypass the scrutiny of an agency. There are disadvantages, however, in that some of the safeguards and tested procedures provided by agencies are not available. Any couple interested in adopting a child should determine what would be most suitable for them. They might start by learning about how most adoptions are arranged in their community. They may want to discuss the matter with a state- or county-related agency or with an adoption agency affiliated with a religious organization. If a couple decides on a direct adoption, it is mandatory that they consult an attorney so that proper legal arrangements may be made. Even couples who adopt through an agency may want to consult an attorney to check on the legality of the adoption arrangements. Nothing could be more tragic than for a couple to think a child is legally theirs, raise it for a few months or longer, and then learn that due to a legal problem they must give the child up. "Black market" adoptions refer to babies bought for sums of money. Couples who adopt directly should be charged for no more than the actual medical and/or legal fees involved in the delivery, medical care, or legal work. Any additional fees are illegal and represent black market adoption.

It is standard practice, according to state laws, that once an adoption has been finalized, a new birth certificate is issued to the new parents. This new birth certificate is exactly like the first except that it has the names of the new parents. The original birth certificate is impounded by the state and can never be obtained or viewed except by a court order.

TERMS TO BE LEARNED

abortion (spontaneous, induced, therapeutic, on request)
abortifacient
adoption
adrenal gland
amnioinfusion
anovulatory menstruation
antibody
artificial insemination (AIH, AID)
basal body temperature (BBT)
Birnberg bow
birth control
cervix
chloasma
Clomid
clomiphene
coitus-induced ovulation

coitus interruptus
coitus reservatus
conception
conception control
condom
Copper 7
corpus luteum
cryobanking
cryptorchidism
diaphragm
dilatation and curettage (D & C)
douche (douching)
dysmenorrhea
ejaculatory inevitability
embolus (embolism)
empirical data
endometrial regulation
endometrium

estrogen
fecundity
fertile period
fertility
fetology
follicle
follicle-stimulating hormone (FSH)
hyperfertility
hysterectomy
hysterotomy
infertility
interception (interceptive)
intermenstrual bleeding
intermenstrual pain
intrauterine contraceptive device (IUD, IUCD)
intrauterine transfusion

333
Birth Control and Fertility

intravaginal device (IVD)
in vitro
lacunae
laparoscopy
libido
Lippes loop
luteinizing hormone (LH)
Margulies spiral
melasma
menopause
menotropins
menstrual cycle
menstrual extraction
mid-month stain
mini-pills
miscarriage
Mittelschmerz
morning-after pill
mucous (adj.)
mucus (n.)
oral contraceptive
ovulatory menstruation
Pergonal
peristalsis
pituitary gland
placebo
preejaculate
progesterone
progestin
prostaglandin
pseudropregnancy
rebound effect
reflex ovulation
rhythm
risk benefit ratio
safe period
saline injection (salting out)
salpingectomy
scrotum
semicontinence
sperm bank
spermicide (spermicidal)
sterility
sterilization
Tatum T
test-tube baby
thermal shift
thromboembolic disease
thrombophlebitis
thrombus
tubal ligation
vacuum aspiration (suction)
varicocele
vas deferens (vasa deferentia)
vasectomy
viable (viability)
withdrawal

SELECTED READINGS

Abortion, Part 1: Hearings before the Subcommittee on Constitutional Amendments of the Committee on the Judiciary, United States Senate, Ninety-third Congress, on S.J. Res. 119 and S.J. Res. 130, Government Printing Office, 1974. (Paperback.) Contains a great many opinions and points of view regarding abortion, the nature and rights of the fetus, the rights of the woman, etc.

(THE) BOSTON WOMEN'S HEALTH BOOK COLLECTIVE: *Our Bodies, Our Selves: A Book By and For Women*, 2d ed., Simon and Schuster, New York, 1976. Women's health care explained by women for women; case histories included.

CALDERONE, MARY STEICHEN (ed.): *Manual of Family Planning and Contraceptive Practice*, 2d ed., The Williams & Wilkins Company, Baltimore, 1970. Compilation of materials prepared by some sixty persons relative to contraceptive methods, effectiveness, legal aspects, research, and sterilization, and organizations involved in family planning.

Family Planning Perspectives, Planned Parenthood Federation of America, The Alan Guttmacher Institute, 515 Madison Ave., New York, N.Y. 10022. Journal of research and program development in the area of family planning and population control.

FINEGOLD, WILFRED J.: *Artificial Insemination*, Charles C Thomas, Publisher, Springfield, Ill., 1964. Nontechnical discussion of medical, legal, emotional, and religious aspects. Includes case histories and anecdotes.

GILLETTE, PAUL J.: *Vasectomy: The Male Sterilization Operation*, Paperbook Library, New York, 1972. What the operation is and its effects and legal aspects, what religious leaders say about it, and what men who have had it say about it. Includes a list of vasectomy clinics and a list of organizations and agencies that assist financially.

HARDIN, GARRETT: *Mandatory Motherhood: The True Meaning of "Right to Life,"* Beacon Press, Boston, 1974. (Paperback.) Author advocates acceptance of abortion and presents arguments against the right-to-life movement. Discusses nature of fetus and question of when human life begins.

HATCHER, R. A., G. K. STEWART, F. GUEST, R. FINKELSTEIN, AND C. GODWIN: *Contraceptive Technology*, 1976–1977, Irvington Publishers, Inc., New York, 1976. Comprehensive technical resource for doctors and laymen on methods of contraception.

HILGERS, THOMAS W., AND DENNIS J. HORAN (eds.): *Abortion and Social Justice*, Sheed & Ward, Inc., New York, 1972. (Paperback.) It is the objective of this book "to present to the still open-minded, and concerned, the full range of argumentation against abortion." The arguments are not religious. Includes discussion of the Supreme Court decision.

KASIRSKY, GILBERT: *Vasectomy, Manhood, and Sex*, Springer Publishing Company, Inc., New York, 1972. Answers to commonly asked questions; frozen sperm banks; techniques; reversibility; clinics where vasectomy is available. One chapter on vasectomy from a woman's point of view written by the author's wife.

LADER, LAWRENCE: *Abortion II: Making the Revolution*, Beacon Press, Boston, 1973. The author "brings the history of the abortion movement up-to-date." This is "an insider's story . . . bristling with the excitement of a truly momentous social revolution." Includes portraits of important leaders in the struggle for abortion law reform.

——— (ed.): *Foolproof Birth Control: Male and Female Sterilization*, Beacon Press, Boston, 1972. Discusses voluntary sterilization for both sexes, newer techniques, frozen sperm banks, medical insurance for voluntary sterilization, effects on marital adjustment, how to select a physician or clinic. Includes list of clinics.

LUKER, KRISTIN: *Taking Chances: Abortion and the Decision Not to Contracept*, University of California Press, Berkeley, 1975. Based on a study of 500 women who sought abortion. Discusses reasons for which women do not use contraceptives. Concludes that women make conscious decisions to engage in risk-taking behavior.

MACE, DAVID R.: *Abortion: The Agonizing Decision*, Abingdon Press, Nashville, Tenn., 1972. (Paperback.) Written for the pregnant woman who wants information to help her reach a decision regarding abortion in accordance with her value system.

NATIONAL ACADEMY OF SCIENCES, INSTITUTE OF MEDICINE: *Study on Legalized Abortion and the Public Health*, IOM Publication 75-02, National Academy of Sciences, Washington, D.C., May, 1975. The Institute of Medicine Committee reviews the evidence on the relationship between legalized abortion and the health of the public.

PLANNED PARENTHOOD OF NEW YORK CITY, INC.: *Abortion: A Woman's Guide*, Pocket Books, New York, 1973. A guide to various methods of abortion and options open to women.

RAMSEY, PAUL: *The Ethics of Fetal Research*, Yale University Press, New Haven, Conn., 1975. (Paperback.) A discussion of the pros and cons of research on live fetuses in the light of the permissibility of destroying the fetus in abortion.

REINING, P., AND I. TINKER: *Population: Dynamics, Ethics, and Policy*, American Association for the Advancement of Science, Washington, D.C., 1975. Readings from *Science Magazine* on family planning, population, growth, birth order, family size, etc.

SARVIS, BETTY, AND HYMAN RODMAN: *The Abortion Controversy*, 2d ed., Columbia University Press, New York, 1974. (Paperback.) Discusses the moral, social, legal, and medical aspects of abortion, the Supreme Court decision, risks and after-effects, the activities of proabortionists and antiabortionists. An objective presentation of both sides of the issue.

WOOD, H. CURTIS, WITH WILLIAM S. RUBIN: *Sex without Babies*, Lancer Books, Inc., New York, 1971. (Paperback.) The author is a former president of the Association for Voluntary Sterilization. Discusses sterilization for both sexes; laws; costs; medical attitudes; contraceptive methods and abortion techniques.

WYLIE, EVAN MCLEOD: *The New Birth Control*, Grosset & Dunlap, Inc., New York, 1972. Nontechnical discussion of tubal ligation and vasectomy, voluntary sterilization and health insurance, sperm banks, doctors, hospitals, and the Church. Includes list of vasectomy clinics and of clinics and hospitals where female sterilization is performed by laparoscopy and culdoscopy. Also contains a list of sperm banks.

Chapter 13

Pregnancy and Childbirth

If one were asked to choose that thing in the universe which has the greatest relative potential, one could advance reasonable arguments for choosing the fertilized human egg (*zygote*)—that almost microscopic bit of protoplasm that constitutes the beginning of the new human individual and is smaller than the period at the end of this sentence. Here is a potential that dwarfs the awesome release of nuclear energy, that makes the explosion of a supernova seem like pointless force. For perhaps a billion years Nature has been working to perfect the organism that arises from that fertilized egg and the determiners of hereditary traits which that egg contains—determiners passed to it in unbroken succession from countless generations of ancestors and to be passed on to countless generations of descendants.

Contained within the zygote are also the regulators of a pattern of growth that is complex beyond comprehension. Two hundred billion times the egg multiplies itself between fertilization and birth, trillions of times between fertilization and adulthood, by a process involving not only increase in numbers but also specialization of form and function and a continuous series of interrelated changes, a chain reaction, extending from fertilization to death. It is a pattern that produces multiplicity and diversity but also unity, as the multicelled body behaves as an entity and says, "This is I."

Start with an almost microscopic zygote. "Add" nothing but food, water, salts, oxygen, and other nonliving materials. Give it a few years in a favorable environment, and we find it falling in love, establishing enduring relationships, creating beauty, contemplating values, seeking truth, and asking, "Who am I? Where did I come from? Why am I here? Where am I going?" All the art, literature, government, science, ethics, philosophy, and religion that we know spring from that zygote. All the reaching and searching that characterizes the human mind is, in a sense, contained within it. For the first nine months it lives and grows in complete darkness, continuously submerged in fluid, and, during the latter part of the period, upside down a good part of the time. This it can never do again. From the moment of fertilization it is a separate organism, living within its mother, to be sure, but never part of its mother. In a sense, the zygote controls the mother's body more than it is controlled by her body. It is her body that changes to adapt itself to the zygote, while the zygote takes advantage of the adaptations. When we take into account the difference in size, it is not surprising that the means by which the zygote communicates to the mother's body that fertilization has taken place is not completely understood. When at last the baby emerges from the mother's body, ordinarily by forces that she neither voluntarily initiates nor can willfully control, it is already a highly complex and well-developed individual, endowed with a unique ability to learn and a unique capacity to grow.

DETERMINERS OF HEREDITY

Chromosomes and Genes

The nucleus of each cell in the body contains *chromosomes*, in which are located *genes*. The genes are complex molecules and are the determiners of hereditary traits. For each such trait exhibited by the organism, with some exceptions, there are two genes or sets of genes, one received from each parent. In the *somatic* (body) *cells* there are forty-six chromosomes (twenty-three pairs), while in the *gametes* (sex cells—*ova* and *spermatozoa*) there are only twenty-three chromosomes, one member of each pair. Thus in order to recreate the twenty-three pairs found in each body cell, two gametes must unite.

Cells increase in number through a process of division (*mitosis*); that is, each cell divides to form two cells, these two to form four, and so on. Each chromosome is longitudinally double. When the cell divides, each chromosome splits lengthwise and each half goes to a new cell, where it duplicates itself. Thus each new cell has the same chromosomal content, the same genetic constitution, as the original cell. This process is shown schematically in Exhibit 13-1, where the number of chromosomes is kept to one pair to make the illustration simpler.

After division each "half chromosome" develops into a whole one, which has the same relative genetic content (genes) as the half. Each new cell is, therefore, like the original cell as far as chromosomal content is concerned. Since all body cells have a common origin in a single cell, all have the same chromosomal content.

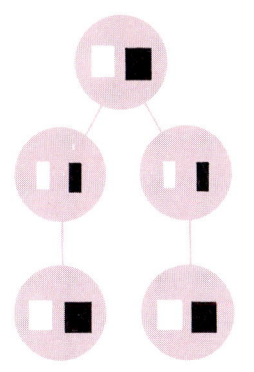

Exhibit 13-1 Schematic representation of mitotic cell division.

In the formation of the gametes, however, the chromosomes, instead of splitting into halves, act as units. One whole chromosome of each pair goes to one new cell. The other whole chromosome goes to the other new cell. The number of chromosomes in each new cell is reduced to half, and the process is termed *meiosis* or *reduction division*. When two cells unite in fertilization, the original number of chromosomes is restored. This process is shown schematically in Exhibit 13-2.

For each hereditary trait exhibited by the organism there are, with some exceptions as mentioned above, at least one pair of genes. Since chromosomes act as units in the formation of the gametes, only one of the genes for a given trait is carried by a gamete. The chromosomes may be "shuffled" and "dealt" to the gametes as playing cards are shuffled and dealt to players. The statistical probability of two gametes having identical genetic content may be compared to the probability of a player's receiving two identical hands after two separate shufflings and deals, assuming that on each deal he received half of the fifty-two cards. His chance would be expressed in figures of astronomical magnitude. Since this same enormous number of possible combinations of genes is found in the gametes of each parent and the number of gametes also is colossal, one may readily see why, even with the billions of people in the world, there are no two exactly alike. (One-egg twins have the same genetic constitution and in this sense are alike.) It has been estimated that the odds against two identical individuals (other than one-egg twins) being born are 1 followed by more than 9,000 zeros. Such a number does not even have a name.

The Gametes

An *ovum* (plural, *ova*), or female gamete, commonly called *egg*, is globular and about $1/200$ inch in diameter. It is just visible to the naked eye. All the ova needed to produce the population of the world—about 4 billion—could be contained within the shell of a hen's egg (Hartman, 1962). At that, ova are the largest cells in the body and are 60,000 times the volume of sperms. A clump of 60,000 sperms would be just visible to the naked eye (Hartman, 1962). In an egg such as a hen's, the ovum itself constitutes only an infinitesimal fraction of the whole; the rest is food material for the developing embryo. There is no correlation between the size of the ovum and body size. The ova of rabbits, whales,

Exhibit 13-2 Schematic representation of reduction division and fertilization.

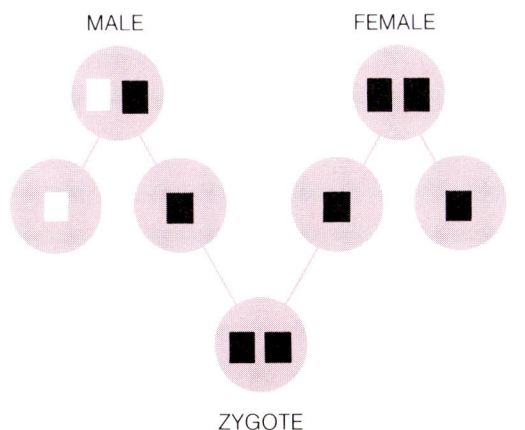

MALE FEMALE

ZYGOTE

dogs, gorillas, pigs, and cows, for example, all have approximately the same dimensions.

Sperms (*spermatozoa*), or male gametes, are minute and shaped roughly like tadpoles. There is an oval head approximately $1/5000$ inch long, a middle piece, and a comparatively long tail, making the total length about $1/500$ inch. The 4 billion sperms needed to produce the population of the world could be accommodated in a container about the size of an aspirin tablet.

Ova are nonmotile; that is, they cannot move by their own power. Sperms, however, propel themselves by lashing their tails in much the same way as a tadpole swims. Relative to their size, they get about fairly well, moving approximately $1/7$ inch per minute. Since each sperm is about $1/500$ inch long, this means that it swims 500 times its length in 7 minutes. A human being walking at an average pace covers about 500 times his or her height, or approximately $1/2$ mile, in 7 minutes. Relative to their size, sperms swim about as fast as we walk.

ORGANS AND PROCESSES IN REPRODUCTION

The Production of Sperms

Sperms form in minute tubes within the *testes* (*testicles*), which are two oval-shaped organs suspended in the *scrotum*. (See Exhibit 13-3 for a diagrammatic representation of male genital anatomy.) These tubes are coiled and would total several hundred feet in length if straightened out. Among the tubes lie the *interstitial cells* that produce the male hormone, *testosterone*, which plays a part in masculinization. The temperature within the scrotum is 2.5 to 4.5° F lower than body temperature. Were it the same, sperm formation could not take place. This is why it is a biological necessity for the scrotum and testicles to be outside of the male's body. The scrotum has the ability to expand and contract on its own as the temperature changes in order to move the testicles closer to or further away from the man's body. This built-in temperature regulation allows sperm production to continue without interruption. While the sperms are still immature, they pass, by ciliary action, from the tubules in each testis into the corresponding epididymis (a tightly coiled tube about twenty feet long). Here, and to some extent in the lower portion of each *vas deferens* (plural, *vasa deferentia*), they are stored (Bishop, 1961; Oliven, 1974; Odell and Moyer, 1971). During their sojourn in the epididymis (Bishop, 1961) the sperms acquire the capacity for motility, but they remain in a quiescent state.

The *seminal fluid (semen)* is a whitish, viscous mixture composed principally of the secretions of the *prostate gland* and the seminal vesicles (Mitsuya, Asai, Suyama, Ushida, and Hosoe, 1960; Price and Williams-Ashman, 1961). During sexual excitation the "spongy" interior of the penis becomes engorged with blood, causing the organ to increase in both size and rigidity and enabling it to enter the vagina. During ejaculation, the sperms are moved up through the vasa deferentia by *peristalsis* (waves of muscular contraction) and/or by a contraction-shortening process in the vasa deferentia, and enter the *urethra*. At this point, through a delicately timed mechanism, they are mixed with the seminal fluid which is being ejaculated. At this time the sperms become active (Odell and Moyer, 1971) owing to the acid-neutralizing effect of the prostatic secretion (Guyton, 1971).

Seminal fluid is ejaculated during sexual intercourse. It may also be discharged during masturbation and periodically is discharged spontaneously during sleep, as mentioned in an earlier chapter.

Sperms are produced in prodigious numbers. It has been estimated that during his lifetime an average human male produces about a trillion sperms (Hartman, 1962).

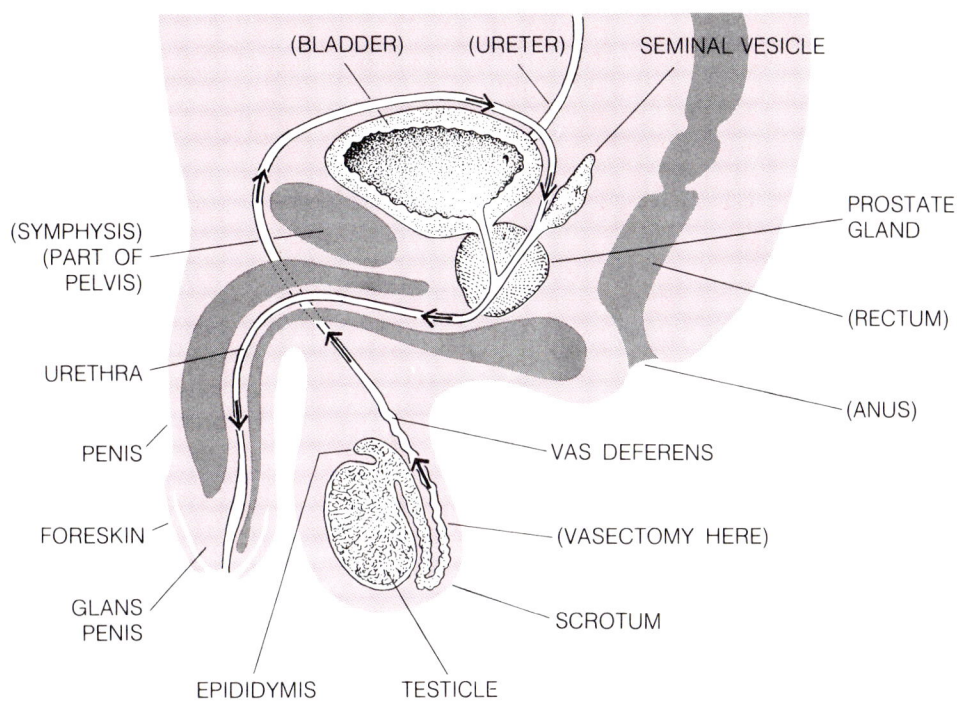

Exhibit 13-3 Male genital organs. Names in parentheses indicate other than genital organs. Note the arrows showing the path of sperms.

Such an estimate is of necessity a broad and only loosely accurate generalization. But it does serve to dramatize the number of sperms. Counting at the rate of five per second and continuously with no break at all, it would take more than 5,000 years to count the sperms produced by one man. In a single ejaculation of seminal fluid (about a teaspoonful) there may be between 150 and 600 million sperms. Yet, compressed together, they would occupy a space equivalent in size only to the head of a pin. In a single ejaculation, then, there are often more than enough sperms, if every one were used, to produce a population larger than that of the United States.

Once discharged, the sperms move in all directions and diffuse through the vagina. Unless they are prevented from doing so by contraceptives, some sperms may pass into the uterus and subsequently move into the fallopian tubes (see below). It is not yet fully known what encourages sperms to move into the uterus. In the acidic environment of the vagina, however, sperms die in a few hours. How long sperms live after leaving the vagina is not certain. Assuming that there are no unusual conditions, estimates as to the life of the sperms within the uterus or fallopian tubes vary. The period during which they remain effective is probably not more than forty-eight to seventy-two hours.

The Production of Ova

Ova are produced in the *ovaries*, two oval-shaped organs 1 to 1½ inches long situated on either side of the *uterus*. (See Exhibit 13-4

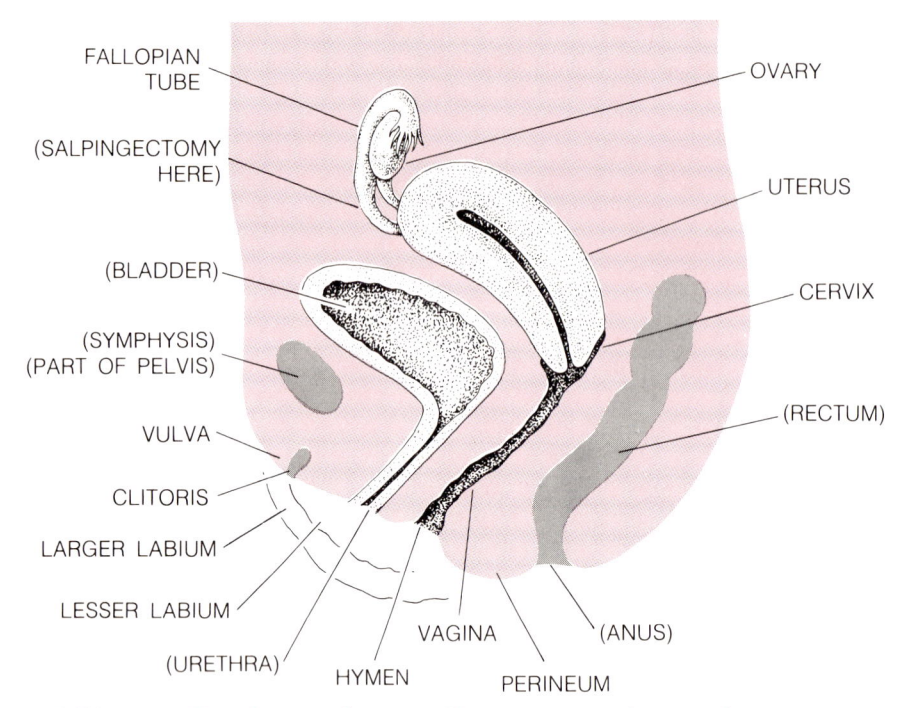

Exhibit 13-4 Female genital organs. Names in parentheses indicate other than genital organs.

for a diagrammatic representation of female genital anatomy.) Formation of ova occurs only in prenatal life. Before birth most of them degenerate, and the total number is very much reduced. It has been estimated that there are about a half million immature ova in the ovaries of a newborn female infant. By puberty this number has been greatly reduced. Fewer than 400 are ovulated during a typical woman's reproductive life. There is no evidence that new ova are formed after birth, as is sometimes assumed (Baker, 1964; Arrata and Iffy, 1971).

Ordinarily, ova mature and are released from the ovary one at a time in response to hormones produced by the pituitary gland. The *follicle-stimulating hormone (FSH)* causes the formation of the *Graafian follicle*, a blisterlike prominence about ¾ inch in diameter which is filled with fluid and eventually bulges out the surface tissue of the ovary. The follicle secretes a hormone (*estrogen*) which brings about preliminary changes in the uterus in the process of that organ's preparation for the reception of a zygote. At length, in response to FSH plus the *luteinizing hormone (LH)*, also produced by the pituitary gland, the follicle bursts and the ovum is discharged. This release of the ovum is termed *ovulation*, and on the average it occurs once in twenty-eight days.

After ovulation, the lining cells of the follicle undergo change and form the *corpus luteum* (yellow body), which secretes another hormone (*progesterone*) which, together with the estrogen, carries still further the preparation of the uterus for pregnancy. If pregnancy occurs, the progesterone and estrogen secreted by the corpus luteum hold the uterus in a condition favorable to sustaining it until this function can be taken over by a hormone secreted by the placenta. Eventually the corpus luteum degenerates, leaving a small scar on the surface of the ovary. This also occurs in the menstrual cycle, which will be discussed later.

After the ovum leaves the ovary, its effective life, the period during which it may be fertilized, is not more than twelve to twenty-four hours. The ends of the tubes in close conjunction with, but not directly connected to, the ovaries divide into fringelike projections (*fimbriae*) which, at the time of ovulation, are activated to come into even closer contact than usual with the ovary. There is also evidence to suggest that the muscles in the wall of the tube may contract and relax, developing suction similar to that in a bellows, and that by this suction the ovum is drawn into the tube (Engle, 1952). Both the fimbriae and the interior surface of the tubes are lined with tiny hairlike protuberances (*cilia*) which move more vigorously toward the uterus than toward the ovaries on the return stroke. Thus a current is set up. The ovum, which has been released from the ovary, typically is drawn into the tube near which it has been released and starts its migration toward the uterus. The passage through the tube has a diameter only about as large as a broom straw, but that is ample for the movement of the egg. (See exhibit 13-5).

The ovum is moved along also by tubal peristalsis, that is, waves of muscular contraction in the tube (Greenhill, 1960; Kistner, 1964). One may envisage the process of tubal peristalsis by imagining a marble in a rubber hose. By pressing the walls of the hose with one's fingers at the back of the marble and sliding the fingers along, one may move the marble. The entire journey from ovary to uterus requires a period of about six to seven

Exhibit 13-5 The journey of the ovum (enlarged for illustration) from ovulation to implantation.

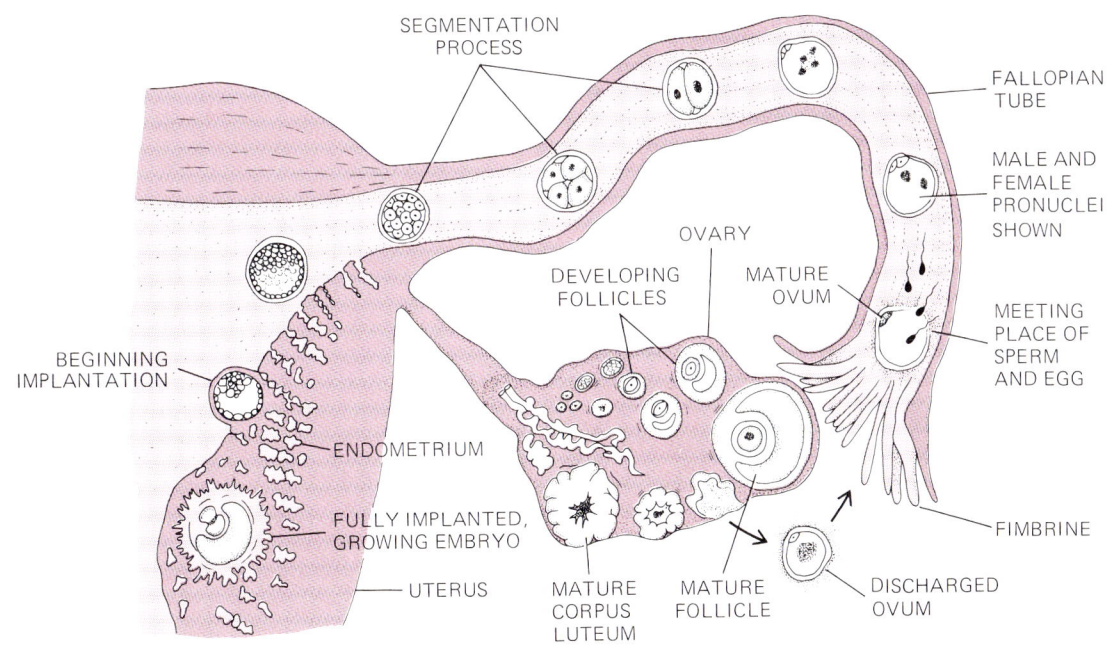

days. Unless it has been fertilized, the effective life of the ovum will have ceased before it has reached its destination.

Fertilization

Fertilization is the union of sperm and ovum. It ordinarily takes place in one of the fallopian tubes. Sperms are usually deposited in the vagina near the relatively small entrance to the uterus (external *os* in the *cervix*, that is, the small end of the uterus). They immediately begin to swim in all directions in the vagina. Some pass into the uterus and into the tubes, but, as mentioned earlier, by what specific means this is brought about is not fully known. Of all the sperms in one deposit of seminal fluid, even though there may be several hundred million, most will never enter the uterus. Of those that do, many will enter the wrong tube, since ovulation takes place in one tube or the other, and an ovum may be released from either ovary in a given month. Many sperms are likely to be defective, to die shortly after being deposited, or for some other reason to make little or no progress in the direction of the ovum. Only relatively few will actually reach the egg. It has been estimated that, of the millions of sperms deposited in the vagina, only a few will reach the site of fertilization, a reduction of 99.99 percent (Odell and Moyer, 1971). Hence, typically, a large number of sperms must be deposited for fertilization to occur.

When a sperm meets the ovum, its head penetrates the ovum's outer wall, and its nucleus fuses with the nucleus of the egg, reestablishing the twenty-three pairs of chromosomes. After one sperm has penetrated the ovum, ordinarily other sperms are prevented from doing so. Since the life span of both the sperms and the ovum is relatively brief, it is obvious that, for fertilization to occur, the sperms must be deposited very near the time of ovulation. Whether the new individual will be a male or female is determined at the time of fertilization. Hereditary traits are also determined at this time. After fertilization the zygote continues its journey through the tube to the uterus, in the wall of which it implants itself. *Implantation* is also referred to as *nidation*.

Conception occurs through *insemination* (entrance of sperms into the female genital tract). Insemination may be by natural means or by artificial (mechanical) methods in those instances where natural means fail or there is need for special control.

Parthenogenesis

This is the process by which an ovum develops without fertilization. It is known to occur naturally among some lower animals and has been brought about experimentally with some such animals. There is no authenticated instance of human parthenogenesis. How, then, may reports of "parthenogenesis" be explained? For example, a newspaper headline reads, "VIRGIN BIRTH" REPORT "CONFIRMED" IN ENGLAND.

Parthenogenesis might be erroneously presumed in a case of pregnancy following incomplete intercourse and due to sperms in the preejaculate, a secretion preceding ejaculation. There is also another possibility of erroneous assumption. If conditions of moisture, temperature, acidity-alkalinity, location of the ovum in the tube, and number and vigor of sperms contained in seminal fluid deposited at the external entrance of the vagina (for example, in "heavy petting" which was just short of intercourse) all happened to be exactly right, some of the sperms might swim through the vagina and uterus, and into the tube. Or sperms might be propelled into the vagina by the force of ejaculation. Under such circumstances fertilization could occur in a woman still technically virgin because the penis had never penetrated the vagina in sexual intercourse (Friedman, 1962; Masters and Johnson, 1966; Neubardt, 1967; Kistner, 1969a; Sjövall, 1970; Glass and Kase, 1970; Oliven, 1974; Crist, 1973; Huffman, 1975). In one case reported to one of the authors by the attending obstetrician, a woman having an intact hymen with two small openings (as in Exhibit 11-1), neither large enough for intercourse to have occurred, had to have the hymen cut before she could be delivered of a full-term baby. Occasionally a case is reported in which a physician is convinced, but of course cannot prove, not only that the above occurred but also that the sperms passed through the fabric of underclothing. Such a case is reported by Golden (1971). The woman was on her honeymoon when pregnancy was diagnosed. On examination the hymen was found to be thick and intact with a very small opening. She admitted having done some "heavy petting" before marriage but insisted that she had never removed her panties. She had felt moisture at times but did not understand where it came from. In fact, though a college graduate, she admitted that she did not even understand sexual intercourse. This case was "substantiated by surgical photographs." All such examples are, of course, extremely rare. Unless there is clear evidence to the contrary, it should always be assumed that conception was the result of sexual intercourse.

Development of the Fetus

After fertilization, the zygote continues its migration through the tube to the uterus, a journey requiring six to seven days. By the time it reaches the uterus, it has already divided and redivided to form a cluster of cells. When it reaches the uterus, it remains free for a period. Then, after several days, it embeds itself in the wall of the uterus, which, through hormone action, has been prepared for its arrival. This process of implantation is accomplished through corrosive action, the zygote dissolving the tissues of the uterine wall and burying itself. In this process the zygote literally digests some of its mother's tissue as food.

As the cells of the zygote continue to multiply, some become specialized to form the *placenta*, the roots, so to speak, through which the fetus receives its food and oxygen. These will be described later. Other cells form the *umbilical cord*, the *amnion*, and the *fetus* proper. Many students have difficulty in visualizing this process because they think of the placenta and the cord (also the amnion) as being part of the mother. Fetus, cord, and placenta make up one unit (see Exhibit 13-9). They develop from the zygote in much the same manner as the leaves and branches, trunk and roots of a plant develop from a seed, though, strictly speaking, there are important differences between a zygote and a seed.

Let us carry further the comparison of the zygote to a seed, a comparison which must be made with caution. The most favorable place for a seed to grow is in a specially prepared garden plot. But a seed can grow, at least for a while, anywhere that its roots can find nutriment—the lawn next to the garden plot, a crack in a walk, or a pile of debris. Similarly, the most favorable place for the zygote to grow is in the uterus. But it can grow, at least for a while, anywhere that its "roots" can find food, water, and oxygen. The most common nonuterine location of growth is in one of the fallopian tubes. A tubal pregnancy is one form of *ectopic* pregnancy, a pregnancy which occurs outside of the uterus. Rare cases of tubal pregnancy which occurred after total hysterectomy (removal of the uterus) have been reported (Niebyl, 1974; *British Medical Journal*, Dec. 21, 1974). In occasional cases the ovum is fertilized before it reaches the tube (Berlind, 1960), even before it leaves the ovary (Kistner, 1964; Greenhill, 1965a;

Pratt-Thomas, White, and Messer, 1974; Fernandez and Barbosa, 1976; Mofid, Rhee, and Lankerani, 1976). There are cases in which a tubal pregnancy ruptures but the embryo does not die and continues to develop outside the uterus in the abdominal cavity. In such cases, the placenta may be attached to the ovary, the outside of the uterus, ligaments, or other abdominal organs. "Abdominal" pregnancies rarely continue to full term, but instances have been known. In these, of course, the child must be delivered by cesarean section. The purpose of this discussion is not to emphasize ectopic pregnancy. But often the unusual highlights the usual, and these infrequent cases of extrauterine pregnancy highlight the fact that fetus, placenta, and cord constitute a unit and are all part of the prenatal baby.

Prenatal development extends through approximately nine calendar months. During this period the following changes occur. Figures and stages mentioned represent averages. Allowance must be made for variation in individual cases. (See Exhibit 13-6 for early stages of development.)

End of the first month By the end of the first month the embryo is about $1/4$ inch long. It weighs only a small fraction of an ounce. Many organs have begun to form, but the embryo does not look human. At this early stage, only an expert could distinguish a human embryo from that of a lower animal. Blood has begun to form. What will develop into the heart has already begun to pulsate.

End of second month The embryo is now about $1 1/4$ inches long. It weighs about $1/14$ ounce. The organs have continued their development, and some have assumed their permanent functions. Budlike projections that will form the limbs are noticeable, but fingers and toes are not yet completely formed. The tail has shrunk and will soon disappear, except for a few bones at the lower end of the spine (*coccyx*), which are embedded in other tissue. The face begins to look more nearly human. The embryo may move, but this movement is not detectable by the mother or her obstetrician. Genital organs have appeared, and if the embryo is aborted and carefully examined, the gender may be ascertained. After the second month the new individual is termed a *fetus* rather than an embryo.

Exhibit 13-6 Early development of embryo and fetus.

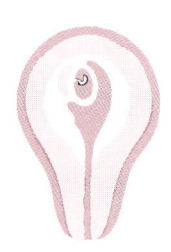

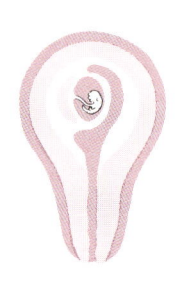

1. Four weeks
2. Six weeks
3. Seven weeks
4. Two and one-half months
5. Three and one-half months

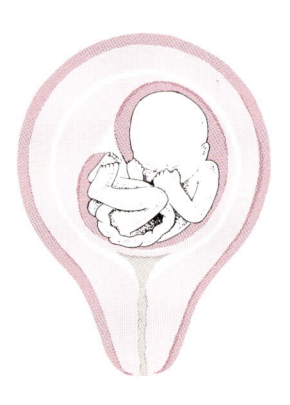

End of third month The fetus now weighs about an ounce and is approximately 3 inches long. Arms, legs, hands, fingers, toes, and ears are formed. Nails have begun to form. The fetus appears definitely human, but the head is very large in proportion to the rest of the body. Teeth have begun to develop in sockets in the jawbones. Vocal cords are formed.

End of fourth month The weight is now 5 to 6 ounces, and the length is 6 to 8 inches. This latter represents about one-third the height at birth. The head is still disproportionately large. The heartbeat is audible through a stethoscope. Limb movements may sometimes be felt by the mother. The body of the fetus is covered with a downlike coat (*lanugo*), which in most cases disappears during the eighth or ninth month. Eyebrows and eyelashes have appeared. The skin is somewhat transparent. The skin ridges, which in later life will make fingerprints possible, have already formed.

End of fifth month The fetus now weighs about 1 pound and is 10 to 12 inches long. Nails are well formed. Head hair has appeared. A mixture of fatty secretion and dead skin cells forms a cheesy covering (*vernix caseosa*) on the surface of the body. Fetal movements may be clearly felt by the mother. If born at this time, the fetus is unlikely to survive.

End of sixth month The weight is about 2 pounds and the length about 14 inches. The child may live for a few hours if born at this time but has only an extremely slight chance of survival.

End of seventh month The weight has increased to about 3 pounds and the length to about 16 inches. A child born at this time has a fair chance of survival.

Eighth and ninth months The weight increases by this time to about 7 or 8 pounds and the length to about 20 inches. The lanugo disappears. Body organs have assumed their permanent functions in most cases. The skin of white babies is reddish and the eyes are bluish in color, but their final tone cannot be predicted. Fatty tissue has formed under the skin, so that the fetus looks less wrinkled than in earlier months. The vernix caseosa may persist even until birth at full term.

It may be seen by reviewing what has been said above that the fetus gains about 80 percent of its weight after the fifth month and about 50 percent during the last two months. A child born at the end of the eighth month has a good chance of survival, much better than at the end of the seventh month. The closer to full term (nine months) the birth occurs, the better the chances of survival.

During a good part of prenatal life the fetus goes through processes similar to those it will perform after birth. It moves its limbs. It swallows amniotic fluid, about a pint per day near term (Pritchard, 1965), which is then absorbed through the walls of the digestive tract much as food and water will be later. The fetus takes shallow "breaths," drawing small amounts of amniotic fluid into, and then expelling it from, the lungs (Duenhoelter and Pritchard, 1973). It excretes small amounts of urine. In one research study, where observers used a "fetoscope" (an instrument which permits the visualization of the fetus), an eighteen-week-old fetus was seen to defecate and a seventeen-week-old fetus appeared to be sucking its thumb (Benzie and Doran, 1975). A remarkable photograph by Lennart Nilsson (Tanner and Taylor, 1965; *Life*, April 30, 1965) shows a 4½-month fetus apparently sucking its thumb. The fetus has alternate periods of activity and rest and may even wake and sleep as it does after birth. It responds to sound (Ferreira, 1969) and to pressure, for example, on the mother's abdomen. A husband applying gentle pressure to his wife's abdomen during the latter part of pregnancy may feel the fetus move and thus begin the process of becoming acquainted with the child before it is born.

Duration of Pregnancy

Pregnancy usually lasts 266 to 270 days (about 39 to 40 weeks, or 9 calendar months). Conception cannot occur unless there is an ovum to be fertilized. Thus conception usually occurs somewhere in the middle of the menstrual cycle. It is impossible to ascertain the exact date of fertilization, even though the exact date of insemination may be known. A variation of a few days in the length of pregnancy is neither unusual nor abnormal. It is, therefore, difficult to forecast the exact date of the child's birth.

A physician who promises delivery on a predetermined date because he or she plans to go on vacation or because the couple want the child born on a holiday, or for some similar reason, is either misleading the couple or planning to resort to induced labor. The latter is not considered by some physicians to be the best obstetrical practice when there is no acceptable medical indication for it (Greenhill, 1965a, 1966; Taylor, 1969; Hatch, 1969).

The nine-month period is considered full term. Delivery of a viable child before term or weighing less than $5^{1}/_{2}$ pounds is considered premature. An abortion may be induced at any time before normal delivery, but abortions are performed after five or six months only for special medical problems. The term *miscarriage* is commonly applied to spontaneous abortion.

Not uncommonly there are reports of unusually long pregnancies. A pregnancy can continue for a relatively brief period beyond the typical 266 to 270 days. But this overtime period cannot ordinarily be extended for very long, because the placenta begins to degenerate (Greenhill, 1961). Reports of unusually long pregnancies are subject to errors of calculation. For example, a woman has a baby eleven months after her last menstrual period. She assumes an eleven-month pregnancy. Actually she had a normal nine-month pregnancy preceded by two months of amenorrhea.

Fetal Protection and Food and Oxygen Supply

As the fetus grows, the uterus enlarges to accommodate it, growing and expanding from a small, pear-shaped organ about 3 inches long and weighing about 2 ounces to an oval organ about 15 inches long and weighing about 2 pounds. Fitting snugly against the inside surface there develop several membranes. The one that will concern us is the *amnion*, which, like the placenta and umbilical cord, arises from the zygote and is thus part of the fetus rather than part of the mother. What is left of the amnion after delivery is expelled with the placenta and cord as afterbirth. Inside the amnion are 1 to 4 pints of amniotic fluid. In this fluid the fetus is suspended. At first it floats about, anchored by the placenta and cord. As it increases in size it fits more snugly inside the uterus (see Exhibit 13-7).

Earlier in this chapter it was stated that when the zygote implants itself in the wall of the uterus, it continues to divide, and some of the cells form "roots," so to speak. These "roots" multiply, eventually forming the placenta, a disk-shaped organ which when fully developed is 7 to 9 inches in diameter, is about 1 inch thick in the middle, and weighs about 1 pound. Strictly speaking there is a maternal as well as a fetal portion to the placenta, namely, the changed tissue of the uterus at the site of attachment (*decidua basalis*). But for our purpose we shall consid-

Pregnancy and Childbirth

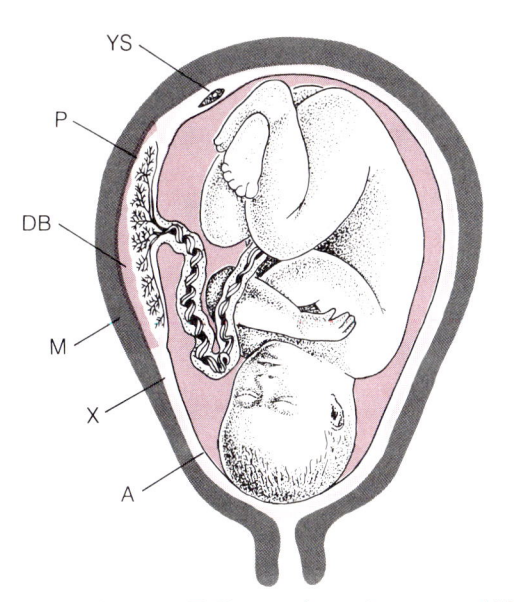

Exhibit 13-7 Full-term fetus in uterus. Abbreviations: YS, yolk sac; P, placenta; DB, decidua basalis (the portion of the endometrium—that is, the lining of the uterus—to which the placenta is attached); X, decidua vera (the remaining portion of the endometrium); M, muscular wall of the uterus; A, amnion.

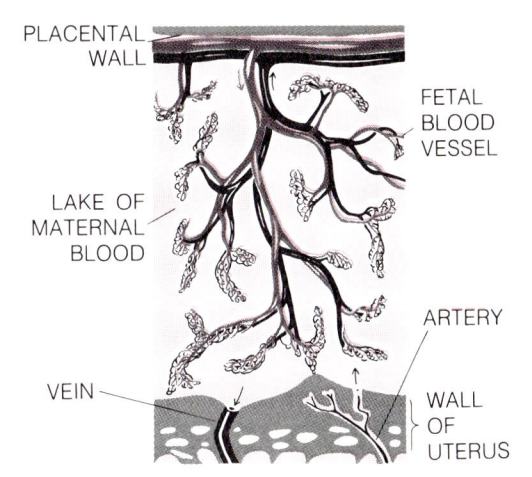

Exhibit 13-8 Highly magnified, diagrammatic representation of placental villi.

er the placenta only as being part of the fetus. On the side in contact with the uterine wall, the placenta is covered with thousands of rootlike projections (*villi*), which branch out in all directions and ramify through the tissue of the uterus (see Exhibit 13-8). The area of a smooth disk 9 inches in diameter is approximately 64 square inches. The branching and rebranching of the villi increase the area of the uterine side of the placenta to some 70 square feet, about four times the skin area of an adult, a fact that is important when we consider that this means 70 square feet of absorption surface for food, water, and oxygen.

The villi are loops of blood vessels. These converge to form several large vessels (two arteries and one vein), which extend through the umbilical cord to the fetus. The cord is about 2 feet long and ½ inch in diameter. It is twisted into a spiral by the uneven growth of the blood vessels and the movements of the fetus.

There is no direct connection between the bloodstream of the mother and that of the fetus. The fetus manufactures all its own blood; it gets none from its mother. Its circulatory system is a "closed circuit." The villi protrude into the *lacunae* ("lakes" of blood in the wall of the uterus). All food material that reaches the fetus must pass through the membranes of the villi. The process may be compared to the absorption of water through the roots of a plant in an ivy bowl (see Exhibit 13-9). Waste products pass in the opposite direction and enter the mother's bloodstream through the membranes of the villi. The actual process of food passing through the membranes is not difficult to understand when one stops to realize that all food passing into one's own bloodstream must be in solution and pass through the membranes of one's intestinal tract and blood vessels, since there is no direct, open-ended connection between blood

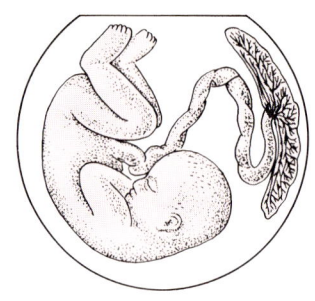

Exhibit 13-9 Fetus, cord, and placenta compared to a plant. (Adapted from a sculptured birth series by Dickinson and Belskie in "Birth Atlas," Maternity Center Association, New York.)

vessels and intestines. Oxygen is absorbed from the mother's blood as food is. One writer (Barron, 1960) refers to the placenta as the "fetal lung." Thus the fetus can live without breathing, that is, without breathing air.

The fetus lives in a controlled environment, and relatively little that occurs in the outside world seriously affects it. Temperature is controlled by the mother's body temperature. Food and water are filtered through the membranes of the villi. The amniotic fluid distributes pressure evenly over the body of the fetus and, in so doing, acts as a shock absorber and renders the fetus virtually "weightless." The fluid also acts as lubrication between the fetus and the membranes of the uterus, assuring the fetus unimpeded motility (Ostergard, 1970). Most disease germs are filtered out by the membranes of the villi. Only relatively few bacteria can pass from mother to child, and these not in every case. The organisms producing syphilis and tuberculosis do sometimes penetrate the defenses.

Viruses can pass from mother to fetus through the placenta (Hardy, 1973). In a study of 1,915 cases of mumps, measles, polio, and other viral diseases, Kaye and Reaney (1962) found abnormalities in the babies in 86 cases (4.5 percent) and spontaneous abortion in 115 cases (6 percent). In a study of 94 cases of mumps, Hyatt (1961) found that 15 percent of the babies were aborted or stillborn and that 16 percent had congenital defects. The virus causing smallpox can affect the fetus (Villee, 1960). The fetus is much more vulnerable to such diseases during the first trimester (three months) of pregnancy. After that the disease is unlikely to cause damage unless, of course, it precipitates spontaneous abortion or premature delivery.

In recent years *rubella* ("German measles"), a viral infection, has come into prominence as a cause of fetal abnormalities. If the mother has rubella during the first trimester of pregnancy, there is a chance that her baby will be affected. If she has it during the first two months, the chance is greatly increased. If she has it after the third month, the chance is markedly decreased. The most common consequences of rubella are fetal death, deafness, cataracts, heart conditions, and mental deficiency caused by damage to the central nervous system (Mayes, 1963). Because of shortcomings in the method of investigating this problem, earlier reports suggested that the chances that the child would be defective were about nine in ten. As a result, many physicians advised therapeutic abortion. Now it appears that a woman's chances of bearing a normal baby are about nine in ten. In other words, generalizing broadly and keeping in mind the increased risk if rubella is contracted during the first two months of pregnancy, the situation is the reverse of what it was originally assumed to be. As a result, some physicians are now reluctant to recommend therapeutic abortion, unless there is good reason to assume that the fetus has been affected.

A vaccine for the prevention of rubella became commercially available early in 1969. Since that time millions of people have been vaccinated, especially children between the age of one year and puberty. Women of childbearing age may safely be given the vaccine, but it is very important to avoid administering it shortly before or during pregnancy, since the vaccine may be hazardous to the fetus (Meyer and Parkman, 1971; Chin, Ebbin, Wilson, and Linnette, 1971; Maeck and Phillips, 1972; Fleet, Benz, Karzon, Lefkowitz, and Herrmann, 1974; Wyll and Herrmann, 1973; Brandling-Bennett, Modlin, and Herrmann, 1974). "The main hope for the future lies in the active immunization of non-immune adolescent girls with the rubella vaccine" (Smithells, 1971).

In rare cases fetuses have been affected when the mother was vaccinated for smallpox during pregnancy (Bourke and Whitty, 1964), especially if the woman was previously unvaccinated (Moloshok, 1966). There is evidence to indicate that a female fetus may be masculinized by hormones administered to the mother during pregnancy (Greenhill, 1960). Too much anesthesia during childbirth may cause the reactions of the fetus to be depressed to the point where breathing is affected. Narcotic drugs may pass through the placenta to the fetus. A large proportion of the babies of narcotic-addict mothers, estimated by some to be approximately 85 percent (Perlmutter, 1974), are born addicted and experience withdrawal symptoms; their birth weight is low and their death rate high (Stone, Solerno, Green, and Zelson, 1971; Zelson, Rubio, and Wasserman, 1971). Thalidomide, a synthetic drug once used as a sedative, tranquilizer, and sleeping medication, caused several thousand cases of severe malformation (*phocomelia*, a condition in which arms or legs or both are malformed or absent) before it was discovered to be the causative agent and was subjected to control (Greenhill, 1962a; Taussig, 1962).

There is a growing body of evidence to the effect that babies of mothers who smoke during pregnancy have a lower birth weight—and are therefore a higher risk and have a higher death rate—than the babies of nonsmoking mothers (Savel and Roth, 1962; Gillespie, 1964; Donnelly, 1964; McDonald and Lanford, 1965; Peterson, Morese, and Kaltreider, 1965; Illsley, 1967; Underwood, Kesler, O'Lane, and Callagan, 1967; Murphy and Mulcahy, 1971; Comstock, Shah, Meyer, and Abbey, 1971; Ochsner, 1971; Surgeon General, 1972, 1971; Butler, Goldstein, and Ross, 1972; Rush and Kass, 1972; Williams and Meyer, 1973; Rush, 1974; Forfar, 1974).

Alcoholic beverages used in moderation appear to have no effect on the fetus. Alcohol used in excess, however, may have an effect unfavorable to the fetus's functioning after birth (*Medical News*, October 29, 1973, July 1, 1974; Green, 1974), including mental deficiency (Hanson, Jones, and Smith, 1976).

If the maternal blood does not afford the fetus the food materials it requires, being a "parasite" it will draw upon her tissues for its own growth. A woman should regulate her diet so that the child is supplied with the food, salts, calcium, and other substances that it needs. There is a relationship between the quality of a woman's diet and the health of her baby. The relationship between the amount of food she eats and the size of her baby is not so clear, although there is evidence that there is a positive association between the mother's weight gain and the baby's birth weight.

There is also a positive association between the mother's pre-pregnancy height and weight and the baby's size. According to the Committee on Maternal Health, Food and Nutrition Board (1970), "taller, heavier mothers have larger babies than smaller, lighter mothers." If a woman overeats because she believes she must "eat for two," the excess is likely to be stored as fat in her own body rather than simply transferred to the baby. On the other hand, she cannot keep the weight of the baby down, presumably to make delivery easier, merely by reducing the quantity of food consumed—unless she reduces it to the point of starvation (Bourne and Williams, 1953; Committee on Maternal Health, Food and Nutrition Board, 1970). Generalizing, we may say that the size of the baby is determined by heredity, duration of pregnancy, possibly to some extent by the mother's food intake (Page, Villee, and Villee, 1972), and perhaps by the development of the placenta (Abdul-Karim and Beydoun, 1974), although this last item is being increasingly questioned. There may be other factors involved, such as the biochemistry and circulation of the mother's blood.

One may readily understand why a woman gains weight during pregnancy. There is a tendency for fat to be deposited. The breasts enlarge, preparatory to supplying the baby with food. Her blood volume increases by 20 to 40 percent, adding about 2 to 3 pounds, and there is some retention of water in body tissues (Ferreira, 1969; Hytten and Thomson, 1970). The fully developed placenta weighs 1 to 2 pounds, the enlarged uterus about 2, the amniotic fluid 1 to 4, and the child itself, when it has reached full term, 7 to 8. Most experts recommend that women gain between 20 and 25 pounds during their pregnancy. A weight gain of less than 20 pounds may be dangerous for the fetus, and a weight gain of more than 25 pounds may contribute primarily to an excess weight gain for the woman, which she will have to struggle with after delivery (Guttmacher, 1962; Newton, 1972).

Maternal Impressions

Can the baby be affected by what the mother does, sees, or thinks during pregnancy? There is a common but erroneous belief that it can. The following "instance" of a maternal impression is typical. As is common during pregnancy, a woman developed a craving for a particular food, in this case, cherries. At the market she found that cherries were unavailable (they were out of season), and therefore she could not buy any. When the baby was born, it had a growth "just like a cherry" on its arm.

What happens in cases of "observed" maternal impressions and birthmarks is probably this: A child is born with some particular trait. The mother wonders about the trait and seeks an explanation. During her nine-month pregnancy she is almost certain to have had some experience into which she can read what she thinks should be there. Then by turning the situation around she has an "explanation" of the trait. If the child has no birthmark, no explanation is required, and so the woman's experiences during pregnancy are not recalled.

There are some investigators, however, who interpret research data as indicating that a woman's emotional state during pregnancy can affect the development of the fetus and its behavior after birth (Ferreira, 1969). Other investigators are not convinced. At best it is difficult to separate the effect of the woman's experiences from the effect of hereditary factors and immediate postnatal factors; that is, a woman with a given physiological and psychological makeup has both the experiences and the baby.

Gender Determination

The gender of the fetus is determined by the combination of chromosomes in the zygote. Other factors may play a role in some cases, as discussed in an earlier chapter, in causing the individual to shift from one side of the fence to the other or to fall into an equivocal position somewhere between maleness and femaleness. Nevertheless, at the moment of fertilization the pattern is usually set.

With regard to the chromosomes of gender determination, all ova are alike; they all bear an X chromosome. Sperms bear either an X or a Y chromosome. When in the process of fertilization an XX combination is produced, the individual develops into a female. An XY combination produces a male. On the X and Y chromosomes there are genes other than those determining gender. The Y chromosome, however, is smaller than the X and contains fewer of these than the corresponding X chromosome. Therefore, in the male certain traits are the result of the action of one gene alone, while in the female these traits are the result of two genes acting together. Hence, some traits tend to be gender-linked and occur much more frequently in males than in females.

Guttmacher (1933) mentions a number of supposed "tests" used by some to determine gender. According to these "tests," if the baby kicks on the mother's right side, it will be a boy; if it kicks on her left side, it will be a girl. A boy is "carried high"; a girl is "carried low." Loss of hair by the mother indicates a girl; more profuse hair growth, a boy. A boy is more active than a girl. If the mother develops a preference for sweet foods, the baby will be a girl; a preference for sour foods indicates a boy. Boys are believed to cause more nausea. As Guttmacher points out, all such "tests" are without foundation in fact.

It is interesting to note how such "tests" reflect traditional attitudes toward males and females, as do standards of behavior mentioned earlier. A male baby presumably kicks on the right side and is carried high (superior status), is more active and causes the mother to have more nausea and a taste for sour foods (aggressive and troublesome). A female baby, on the other hand, presumably kicks on the left side and is carried low (inferior status), is less active and causes the mother to have less nausea and a taste for sweet foods (submissive and agreeable).

Until recently there was no accurate means of ascertaining the gender of the fetus in the uterus. The difference between male and female heartbeat is not reliable, since there is so much overlapping. This is true also of fetal size. If the fetus is aborted after the first six or seven weeks of pregnancy, gender may be ascertained, but such a fetus, of course, dies. Before six or seven weeks of pregnancy have passed, the cells that will form the gonads (testes or ovaries) are undifferentiated, and the genital organs exhibit the same development in both genders; hence the gender of the fetus cannot be ascertained by examining these organs.

It is now known that in the somatic cells of the female there is usually a dark mass (*sex chromatin* or *Barr body*) that is usually not present in the cells of the male. The presence or absence of this mass may be established through microscopic examination by the end of the second week of embryonic life. But, of course, no such examination could be made at this early stage unless the fetus were aborted. During prenatal development, fetal skin cells flake off and remain in the amniotic fluid. By midpregnancy such cells may be examined by withdrawing a small quantity of amniotic fluid from the uterus by means of a hypodermic needlelike instrument which is introduced into the uterus through the abdominal wall. This procedure is termed *amniocentesis*. It is relatively safe, but not completely without risk, and is not always successful (Hutchinson, 1967; Papp, Gardo, Herpay, and Arvay, 1970). Another method of ascertaining the gender of the fetus, also dependent upon amniocentesis, is the examination of cells taken from the amniotic fluid, stained, and examined microscopically under ultraviolet light. Y chromosomes appear fluorescent; X chromosomes do not (Cervenka, Gorlin, and Bendel, 1971; Khudr and Benirschke, 1971; Valenti, Lin, Baum, Massobrio, and Carbonara, 1972). There are sometimes medical reasons for which it is important to ascertain the gender or other characteristics of the fetus. The procedure is rarely performed just to satisfy parental curiosity, and the end rarely justifies the means.

Means for controlling the gender of the child are as fantastic as some of the "tests." Popular books and technical articles (Shettles, 1972) have advanced various ways in which parents can influence gender, and such discussions have made their way into textbooks on sexuality and reproduction (McCary, 1973). Most of these methods suggest douching techniques to change the acidity of the vagina, deep or shallow penile penetration during intercourse, need for the female to have or to avoid an orgasm, and time of intercourse relative to ovulation. Such techniques have not been adequately researched and are questionable. At the present stage of scientific knowledge there is no practical means by which the gender of the child may be controlled.

SIGNS OF PREGNANCY

When a woman has reason to believe that she may be pregnant, she wants to know the facts as soon as possible so that she may plan accordingly. There are several types of symptoms that may aid in diagnosing her condition. These are termed *presumptive* and *positive* signs. Disregarding for the moment the conditions that make tests for pregnancy possible, the relationship between mother and baby may be dramatized by pointing out that the presumptive signs of pregnancy are exhibited by the mother, while positive signs are exhibited by the fetus.

There are cases of "false pregnancy" (*pseudocyesis*) in which emotional factors, such as a great desire for a baby or a deep fear of having one (McDonald, 1968), cause a woman to exhibit signs of pregnancy when she is not pregnant at all (Fried, Rakoff, Schopbach, and Kaplan, 1951; Greenhill, 1965a; Israel, 1967). Such signs may include menstrual disturbances, abdominal enlargement, breast changes, softening of the cervix, nausea, weight gain, and "movements of the fetus" as "felt" by the woman (Brown and Barglow, 1971). In an unusual case, a thirty-three-year-old male with developing schizophrenia and messianic yearnings was convinced that he was pregnant and showed signs of pregnancy, namely, distention of the abdomen, morning nausea, and "felt" movements of the fetus. Examination uncovered no physiological illness or medically pathological condition. His symptoms disappeared after psychiatric treatment (Knight, 1971). Several primitive cultures, such as the Siriono of Eastern Bolivia (Holmberg, 1950) have a phenomenon known as *couvade*, in which the husband mimics many of the same symptoms as the wife, although he does not actually have the symptoms. Such reactions are psychological or cultural in origin, of course, and are entirely different from the physical responses to pregnancy that females experience.

If a woman can exhibit signs of pregnancy when she is not pregnant, can the reverse also be true: Can she be pregnant and not know it? Of course, no woman can know that she is pregnant immediately after the pregnancy begins. Apparently there have been women who go to term and are not aware that they are pregnant until labor starts. In such cases, of course, the only evidence of the woman's unawareness is her own statement. If, however, a woman were subject to long periods of amenorrhea, if she were very obese so that abdominal enlargement would not show or would appear to be "more of the same," if for neurotic reasons she would "shut out" the signs of pregnancy, if she were unusually imperceptive or ignorant, or if some other similar condition existed, she could be pregnant and not know it. Cases do come to one's attention through newspaper reports, personal experience, or case histories from counseling. For example, in one case coming to our attention, after becoming parents a university coed and her husband both insisted that they had not known she was pregnant. She visited the university health center because of abdominal cramps and was astounded and disbelieving when the physician informed her that she was in labor. On the way to her room in the hospital she remonstrated with the nurse, saying, "This is ridiculous." But she soon had about six pounds of proof that the physician's diagnosis was correct.

Presumptive Signs

Temporary cessation of menstruation This is one of the first noticeable signs, but it is not reliable, since factors other than pregnancy (for example, illness, tumors, nervous shock, experience highly colored with emotion, change of climate, even minor emotional stress) may interrupt the menstrual cycle. Worry about possible pregnancy may cause menstruation to be delayed or cause a period or two to be missed. The authors have counseled several women who were so fearful that they were pregnant that they stopped menstruating. This physical reaction further convinced them they were pregnant and worried them more. Following a negative pregnancy test, they all had menstrual periods. Some women are so irregular that an occasional rather long delay is not unusual.

If for some reason implantation is delayed, or the ovary continues to function, or some other unusual condition occurs, a woman may have what appears to be menstruation after fertilization takes place (Arrata and Iffy, 1971). When this occurs, the flow is usually scanty. In some instances bleeding due to other factors is mistaken for menstruation.

Morning sickness About half of pregnant women have some degree of nausea in the morning. In most of these cases the symptoms are mild; in a few they may be severe. Morning sickness may be relieved by medication and usually disappears by the end of the third month. Some cases are due to physiological changes, but there is reason to believe that others are the result of suggestion or emotional disturbance. If a woman has heard that illness accompanies pregnancy, she may expect it and have her expectations fulfilled through the machinations of her mind. If she fears or resists pregnancy, that too may contribute to her illness.

Increased frequency of urination This is due to congestion in certain blood vessels.

Increased vaginal secretion This is especially noticeable in women who have previously had considerable vaginal discharge.

Changes in the breasts Slight tenderness, a sense of fullness, increased size of nipples, increased pigmentation around the nipples, secretion of a fluid termed *colostrum*, increased size of breasts, prickling or tingling sensations, increased blood supply so that blood vessels may be seen under the skin are all symptoms accompanying pregnancy but are not positive proof that conception has occurred.

Changes in the vaginal lining The lining becomes congested and more bluish in color.

Enlargement of the abdomen This occurs rather late for diagnosis in ordinary cases and may be due to some factor other than pregnancy, for example, a tumor.

Softening of the cervix In the nonpregnant state, the cervix is firm.

Changes in the form, size, and position of the uterus As pregnancy progresses, the uterus becomes larger, less pear-shaped and more nearly globular, and at first tends to slope forward more than ordinarily.

Intermittent uterine contractions At about the end of the second month the uterus begins to contract at irregular intervals (Braxton-Hicks contractions). These contractions may be detected by the obstetrician but are not felt by the mother. Since no dilation of the cervix accompanies these contractions, they do not constitute true labor.

Ballottement, or repercussion The fetus is at first too small, and late in pregnancy too large, for this sign to be used, but between the sixteenth and the thirty-second week the physician may, during an examination of the woman, push the fetus gently and feel it rebound against the wall of the uterus (Greenhill, 1965a).

Basal body temperature The basal body temperature is the body temperature of an individual upon waking in the morning. It tends to be maintained at a relatively high level during pregnancy. A level of 98.8 to 99.9°F, maintained for more than sixteen days, is highly suggestive of pregnancy. Diagnosis of pregnancy based on body temperature is accurate in 97 percent of cases (Greenhill, 1965a). In order to use this method, records of temperatures must be kept both before and after conception, and other possible causes of elevated temperature must be ruled out.

Positive Signs

The positive signs of pregnancy are certain evidence of its occurrence, since these signs can be produced by no factors other than a fetus.

Movement of the fetus in the uterus This movement is noticeable for the first time usually during the fourth or the fifth month, that is, about halfway through the pregnancy. The fetal movements are often vigorous and may be distinctly felt by the mother. In advanced pregnancy they may be seen or felt by an observer.

Fetal heartbeat This is audible to the physician by means of a stethoscope, usually at about the fourth month. By means of an ultrasonic instrument (ultrasound) the heartbeat of the fetus can be detected as early as the twelfth week, sometimes even the tenth week, after the last menstrual period (Johnson, Stegall, Lein, and Rushmer, 1965). The fetal rate varies from 120 to 160 beats per minute, which is about twice the mother's rate under normal conditions. Thus the two beats may be distinguished.

The shape of the fetus This may be felt through the abdominal wall.

The appearance of the fetus in an x-ray photograph This method of diagnosis is possible only late in pregnancy after other signs have appeared. Therefore, it is usually unnecessary. X-ray studies are sometimes made before delivery, however, to determine the size of the fetal head relative to the opening in the mother's pelvis or to assist in the diagnosis of multiple pregnancy. Such studies should supplement, not replace, careful clinical observation. X-rays are taken only when absolutely necessary. Exposure to x-rays for photographic purposes is not to be confused with exposure for therapy.

TESTS FOR PREGNANCY

The positive signs are observable only when pregnancy is well advanced. The presumptive signs are not conclusive, and few of these are observable during the very early stages of pregnancy. The importance of some means of diagnosing pregnancy shortly after it begins is apparent. This means has been provided by pregnancy tests.

The placenta produces several hormones, one of which is termed *human chorionic gonadotropin* (HCG). Through the processes of metabolism and excretion, HCG passes into the urine of the pregnant woman, where it is detectable within a few days after implantation. Since HCG is produced by the placenta, it is found only during pregnancy. Also, since it is produced by the placenta rather than the fetus, its presence indicates only live placental tissue, not a live fetus (Hon, 1961). Placental tissue may live after the death of the fetus, but the death of the fetus follows promptly upon the death of the placenta. In some cases a test may be positive after childbirth or abortion, since enough HCG remains in the woman's blood to pass into the urine.

Biologic tests for pregnancy, in which urine from a presumably pregnant woman is introduced into test animals (in female rabbits, mice, or rats HCG causes ovulatory changes in the ovaries; in frogs or toads HCG causes the release of eggs in females and sperms in males), have a high degree of accuracy along with the disadvantage of having to keep the animals on hand. Biologic tests have largely been replaced by immunologic (chemical) tests that have the advantages of (1) giving results both early in pregnancy and soon after the test is made and (2) being easy to administer even in the physician's office. One test, utilizing latex particles coated with HCG and requiring only one drop of urine, can be used as early as ten to fourteen days following the first missed menstrual period, can be completed in only three minutes, and is reported to have a reasonably high degree of accuracy (Yahia and Taymor, 1964; Jacobson and Davis, 1965). In another test, previously preserved red blood cells and an antibody in a special disposable container are mixed with one drop of urine and one drop of water. The mixture is allowed to settle for forty-five minutes. This test requires minimum equipment and is 96 percent accurate (Lav, 1971). In another test, serum instead of urine is used. In still another, a hormone is administered orally or hypodermically. Since the dosage is limited, a condition of hormone withdrawal is produced. If the woman has vaginal bleeding following this procedure, she is assumed not to be pregnant. If she has no vaginal bleeding, she is assumed to be pregnant.

The perfect test for pregnancy has not yet been devised. All known tests involve a margin of error. Some are contraindicated (not advisable) in a few cases. If a test is administered very early in a presumed pregnancy and is negative, it should be repeated later. At the present stage of knowledge, accuracy of diagnosis is increased by supplementing a test with a vaginal examination. Even then there is a margin of possible error.

CHILDBIRTH

Some two weeks before the onset of labor, the fetus shifts its position so that it is lower in the pelvis and has started to enter the birth canal. This process is termed *lightening*. Sometimes women refer to it as "settling" or "dropping." In some cases, at about this time there are nonprogressive contractions of the uterus continuing for perhaps a few hours and termed *false labor*. When the fetus has reached full term, that is, when it has reached its full prenatal development, complicated factors not fully understood cause the uterus to contract, and labor begins. Recent research suggests that the fetus itself may be at least one factor in initiating and sustaining labor through the release of substances causing uterine contractions (Chard, Hudson, Edwards, and Boyd, 1971; Turnbull and Anderson, 1971). During pregnancy the uterine muscle cells increase, not only in number but also in size, to prepare the organ for its role in expelling the fetus. As the uterus contracts from the top downward, pushing the child against the cervix, the cervix dilates until it is practically effaced for the time. Changes in the uterus and the progress of the child during labor are shown in Exhibits 13-10 to 13-17.

Labor may be divided into three stages: first stage—from the beginning of contractions (not of dilation, since in many cases dilation is under way before labor starts) to the complete dilation (opening) of the cervix; second stage—from this point to the birth of the child; third stage—from the birth of the child to the expulsion of the afterbirth and the final contraction of the uterus. At the beginning of the first stage the pains accompanying contractions are slight and rather far apart (twenty minutes or more). As labor progresses, they occur closer together in an increasingly rapid rhythm. As contractions proceed, one side of the amniotic sac ("bag of waters") is forced by pressure to protrude through the opening in the cervix. At length the sac bursts and some of the amniotic fluid is discharged. In some cases this discharge is the announcement of the onset of labor. If the membrane ruptures prematurely (*dry birth*), the cervix may be dilated too rapidly. In some cases the onset of labor is announced by a somewhat bloody vaginal discharge caused by the loosening of the mucous plug which is normally found in the cervix; but such discharge may occur before or after the onset of labor and is, therefore, not a reliable indication of its onset.

The average (mean) duration of labor in

Exhibit 13-10 Fetus at term before beginning of labor.

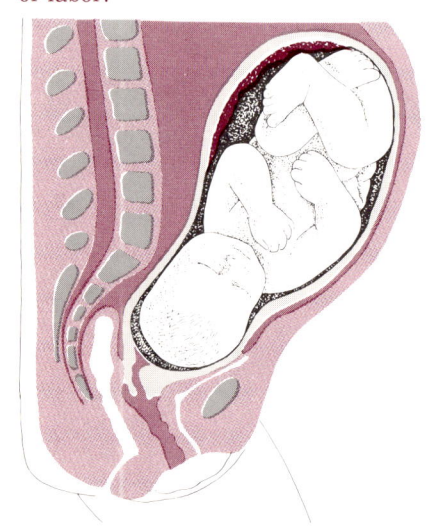

Exhibit 13-11 Labor: cervix dilating.

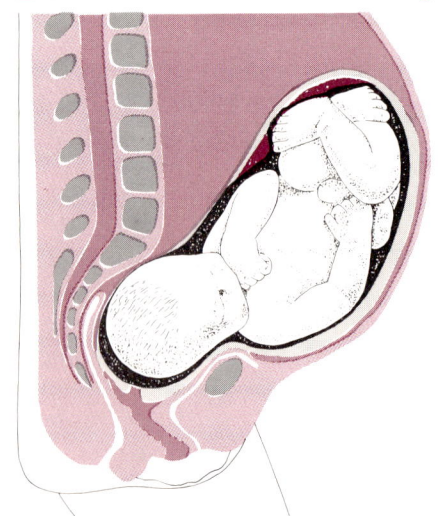

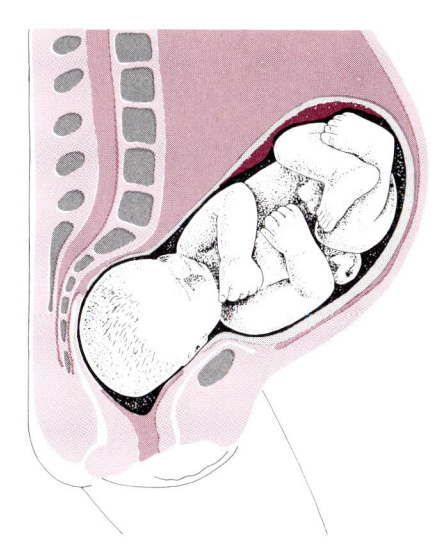

Exhibit 13-12 Labor: cervix completely dilated. Note the amniotic sac.

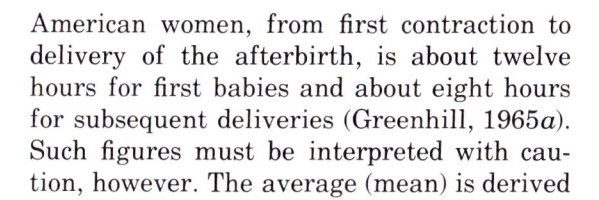

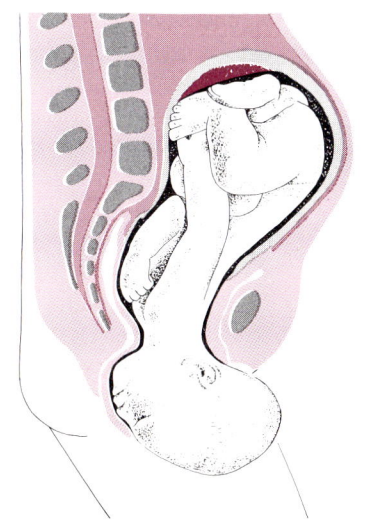

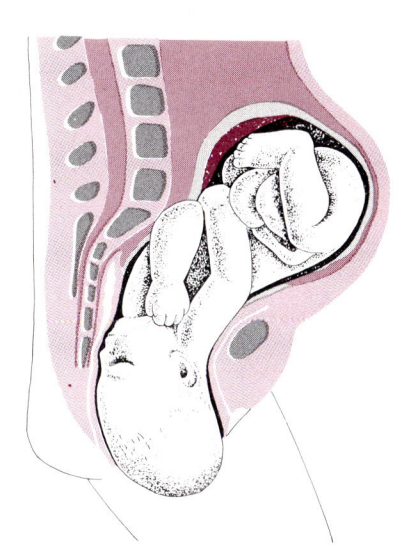

Exhibit 13-13 Labor: head begins to appear. Note the rotation of the head.

American women, from first contraction to delivery of the afterbirth, is about twelve hours for first babies and about eight hours for subsequent deliveries (Greenhill, 1965a). Such figures must be interpreted with caution, however. The average (mean) is derived by including all labors, those that are longer than average as well as those that are shorter. It may, therefore, be misleading. The modal duration of labor—that is, the length that occurs most frequently—is about half the mean.

Exhibit 13-14 Labor: head turns upward.

Exhibit 13-15 Labor: birth of shoulders.

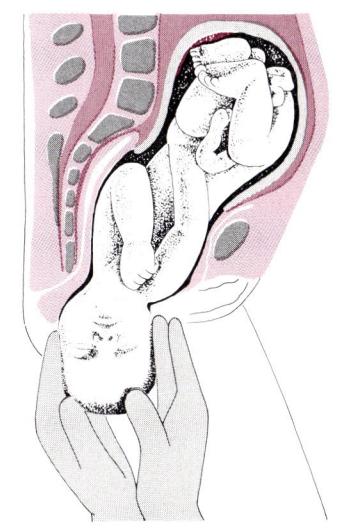

From Marriage to the Family

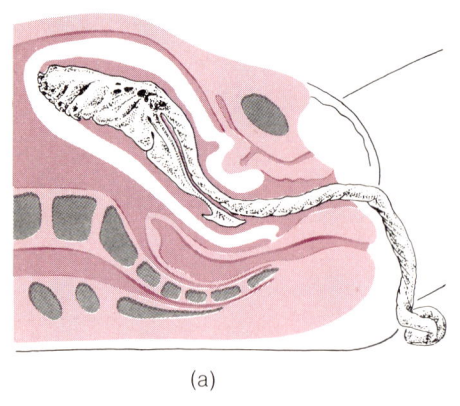

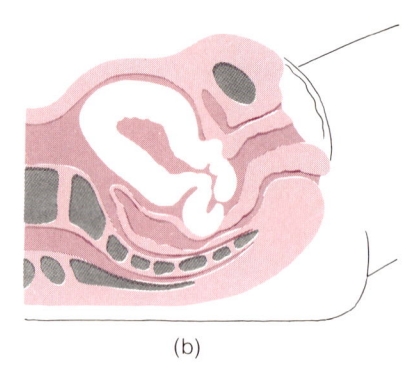

Exhibit 13-16 Labor: uterus after birth of the baby. (a) Placenta almost separated from the uterus; (b) uterus after expulsion of the placenta.

Women who have never borne a child are sometimes disturbed by descriptions such as the above because they do not visualize the situation accurately. They imagine themselves lying on the delivery table with their knees drawn up and their feet in supports throughout labor. Such an imaginary picture is inaccurate. Ordinarily when a woman goes to the hospital for delivery, labor is already well advanced, a good part of it having occurred at home. The woman is put to bed in a labor room where her husband may usually visit her and where she will remain until it is almost time for the baby to be born. Then she is taken to the delivery room where she will be for a relatively brief time, in some cases only a few minutes.

During the early part of the first stage of labor the discomfort is relatively mild. It increases in intensity as labor progresses and the contractions of the uterus become stronger and closer together (every two to three minutes). The discomfort increases during the second stage of labor, which lasts an hour or so for first babies and about twenty minutes for subsequent ones (Greenhill, 1965a),

Exhibit 13-17 Uterus after delivery: (a) fifth day after delivery; (b) fourteenth day after delivery.

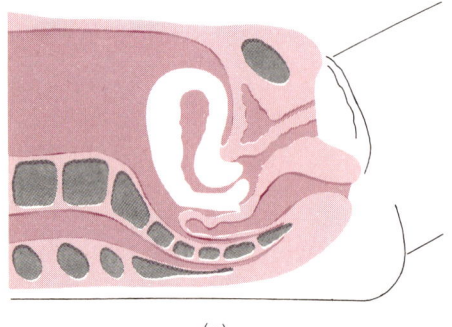

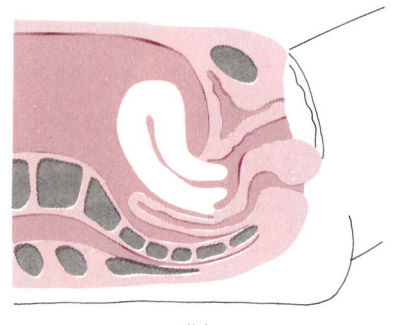

though there is, of course, considerable variation among women. Put differently, a woman in a normal delivery with her first child may be expected to pass through the second stage in no more than twenty or thirty contractions, and in some cases less than twenty. The number may be expected to be reduced in subsequent deliveries. The pain or discomfort of labor reaches its crest during the last two centimeters of cervical dilation. This is just before the baby's head begins to pass through the birth canal (Bradley, 1974). The discomfort of the third stage of labor is usually not severe. Ordinarily this stage is relatively brief, usually lasting just a few minutes.

As labor progresses from first through second stage, the child moves slowly through the birth canal, pushed along by the contractions of the uterus. Progress is not continuous, however. When the uterus contracts, the child is moved forward. When it relaxes, the child slips back, but not so far back as it was moved forward. Progress is made, therefore, by alternate forward and backward movements in increasingly rapid rhythm, until at the very end it is predominantly forward. The tissue of that portion of the uterus that is normally the cervix, but is now more or less indistinguishable from the rest of the organ except for the opening, moves past the child's head. In about 95 percent of cases the baby enters the birth canal head first. In the other 5 percent it enters feet first, buttocks first (breech presentation), or in some other manner. One of the problems in such deliveries is that the umbilical cord, instead of passing from the child's abdomen past the feet to the placenta, passes between the child's head and the wall of the birth canal. Hence it may be subjected to so much pressure that the circulation of blood through the cord ceases and the child's oxygen supply is cut off. In some instances in which there is not a head presentation the obstetrician may turn the child in the uterus. This process is termed *version* and may be done by external manipulations, as one would turn a baby under a blanket, or by the doctor's working through the vagina, grasping the baby with one hand while assisting externally with the other.

The child's head is almost as broad as its shoulders. Owing to the relatively large proportion of cartilage and small proportion of bone in its skeleton, its body is somewhat flexible. The head is more rigid than most parts, but even the head yields somewhat to pressure. At times a child's head is pressed out of shape during the birth process (*molding*). This is often a matter of concern to couples who have just had their first baby. They conclude that it is abnormal, not knowing that Nature takes care of this situation and that, unless there has been some complication, the head will soon reshape itself.

The child's head must pass through the opening in the mother's pelvis, and the fit is close. For this reason it is most important for the mother to have the obstetrician measure her pelvis as soon as she becomes pregnant, if not before. When the obstetrician knows what to expect, preparation may be made for it. Any opening through which the head will pass will accommodate the rest of the body. Hence, after the head is born the rest is relatively easy, and the body is rapidly expelled.

There is evidence to show that during pregnancy, especially in young women, owing to a softening of the cartilage, there is a degree of relaxation in the pubic joint (the place at which the pelvic bones meet in the fore part of the body) and that this relaxation permits a slight increase in the gap between the bones. This process prepares the pelvis for childbirth. Opinions differ, however, as to the extent to which this condition influences the course of labor. The probability is that in most cases the influence upon labor is relatively minor. We can be sure that the pelvic bones do not open in the manner of a double door to permit the baby to pass through without resistance.

In addition to the resistance afforded by the snug fit of the birth canal, during childbirth the child's head meets three points of resistance, namely, the cervix, the mother's pelvis, and the muscles surrounding the external opening of the vagina. If these muscles are unyielding, and if in pressing against them the child's head is subjected to too great pressure for too long, the blood supply to the brain may be reduced to the point of damage to brain tissue due to oxygen deprivation. There may also be damage to the mother. The obstetrician may facilitate the child's progress and relieve the pressure on its head by one or both of two procedures. He may use obstetrical forceps (see Exhibit 13-18), whose function is as much to protect the child's head as to facilitate its movement through the muscular ring. The other procedure involves an incision in the muscle tissue below the entrance to the vagina. Such an incision is usually made under local anesthesia and is termed an *episiotomy*. Its function is to increase the size of the vaginal opening and permit the ready passage of the child through it. It is safe and constitutes a small price in maternal discomfort for the welfare of the baby. Many physicians and women prefer not to have an episiotomy performed, although the practice is customary.

In extreme cases, when the passage of the baby through the mother's bony pelvic opening is impossible or would entail too great risk, when the uterus does not contract properly and is ineffective, or when the physician determines that the time of delivery must be advanced and executed immediately (due to problems with the survival of the fetus or mother), cesarean section may be used. A cesarean section is an abdominal operation in which the uterus is opened surgically and the child is removed from the mother without passing through the birth canal. Ordinarily, by measuring the baby's head by means of x-ray or ultrasound (Willocks, McDonald, Duggan, and Day, 1964), the obstetrician can predict whether such an operation will be necessary, and plans may be made accordingly. Sometimes, however, the obstetrician elects to let the mother go through trial labor to see whether the baby can be delivered normally. If not, a cesarean section is then performed. Childbirth is a natural process. Cesarean section is not, and it involves risk, as any major operation does. In skilled hands the outcome is usually favorable, especially when the operation is planned, and it is also usually fraught with less risk than an extraordinarily difficult delivery. Cesarean section is not, however, as some persons suppose, a simple means of avoiding vaginal delivery. Cesarean section also involves risk to the baby. Ordinarily, once a woman has a child by cesarean section, all subsequent births must occur in this manner. There are exceptions, however. Babies born by means of cesarean section have a higher mortality rate than babies born by the natural vaginal route. A woman may have several cesarean sections without any unfavorable consequences. "We are no longer afraid to perform four and more cesarean sections on a patient. . . . Today we encounter women who have had six and more cesarean sections, apparently without any harm" (Greenhill, 1964). One report mentions a woman who had thirteen cesarean sections over an eighteen-year period, resulting in

Exhibit 13-18 Obstetrical forceps.

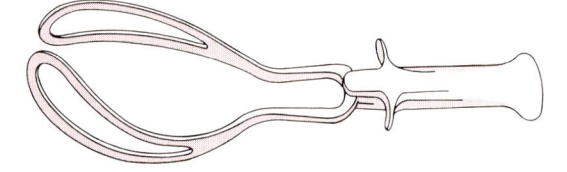

thirteen healthy babies (*Ob. Gyn. News*, October 15, 1967). Some physicians used to recommend that, if a woman had two living children delivered by cesarean section, she be sterilized during her third such operation. But "the clinical evidence no longer supports such a practice" (Piver and Johnston, 1969), attitudes on this matter are changing, and today fewer physicians are inclined to make such a recommendation. Certainly it should not be made routinely.

Normally the child cries and begins breathing as soon as it is born; in some cases, as soon as the head is born. In rare cases the child cries while it is still in the uterus. This cry fills the lungs with air. If the child does not cry spontaneously, oxygen is introduced into its respiratory tract. This method usually resuscitates the infant. Violent manipulations, such as swinging by the feet, immersion into hot and cold water alternately, and pulling on the tongue, belong to a past era and have no place in modern obstetrics.

Immediately after it is born, the baby is identified. This is accomplished by placing an identification band on the baby, recording its palm prints, recording its footprints (which are easier to obtain with a newborn infant than are palm prints), or a combination of methods.

After the baby emerges from the mother's body, the umbilical cord is bound or clamped near the baby's abdomen. This is not done until the cord has stopped pulsating, however, showing that circulation of blood through the placenta has ceased. If it is done too soon, more blood than the baby can afford to lose may still be in the placenta and cord. The cord is then severed. The mother feels no pain when this is done because the cord is part of the baby. The baby feels no pain because there are no nerves in the cord. The stub of cord attached to the child's body eventually drops off, leaving a small scar, the navel or umbilicus. To prevent infection that might cause blindness, an antiseptic substance is put into the infant's eyes.

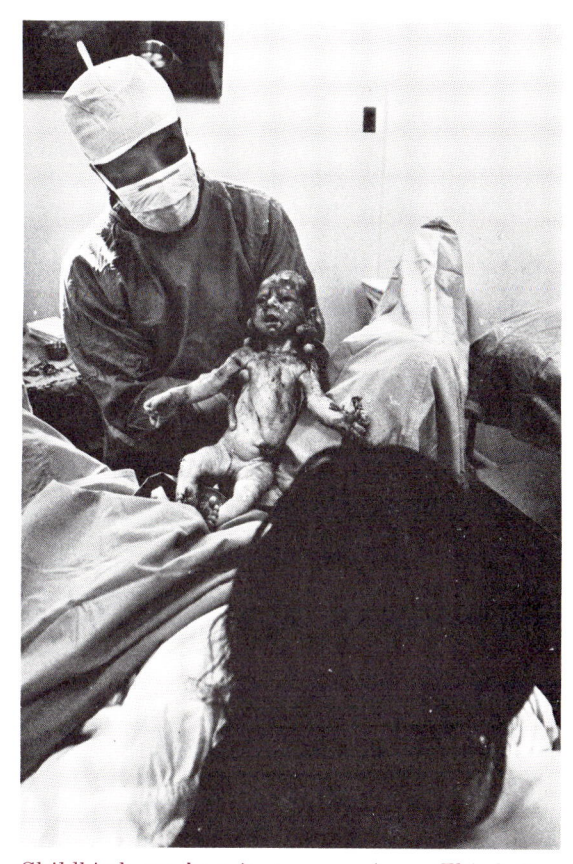

Childbirth can be a joyous experience. This baby girl is being introduced to her mother. (*Gary Freedman*)

Shortly after the birth of the child the contractions of the uterus separate the placenta from the uterine wall, and the placenta, with what is left of the cord and amnion, is expelled. This is the afterbirth. It has served its purpose and is now waste material, though the placenta is carefully examined to make sure that no portion of tissue has remained in the uterus to serve as the seat of infection or to cause hemorrhage. When the afterbirth has been expelled, hormones cause the uterus to contract, squeezing the ends of the blood vessels together and preventing bleeding. If an episiotomy was performed, the physician will sew up the incision, which will heal completely within a few weeks and which will leave hardly any trace of a scar.

From this point on for about four to six weeks, the mother goes through a period of recuperation, during which the genital organs gradually assume approximately their original size and shape. Recovery is usually rapid and proceeds without mishap if the woman follows the physician's instructions. Women vary in their preference for and physicians vary in their advice about sexual intercourse in the days and weeks before delivery. There is no rule about abstaining from coitus before childbirth. The main consideration should be the woman's own comfort. It is usually recommended, however, that she abstain for a few weeks after delivery until she is fully healed.

A competent obstetrician will do what can be done with safety to make a woman comfortable during labor and delivery, but complete absence of pain cannot be guaranteed. At the present stage of knowledge there is no drug, combination of drugs, or nonchemical technique that can eliminate all the discomfort of labor with complete safety in all cases (Flowers, Jr., 1967; 1970). Excessive anesthesia may damage the child. "In his response to drugs, the newborn infant is qualitatively and quantitatively different from the mother.... The newborn shows marked susceptibility to the depressant effects of drugs used in labor" (Flowers, Jr., 1970). Therefore no woman should make impossible demands of her obstetrician, and no obstetrician should make promises that cannot safely be fulfilled.

Generalizing, there are four types of drugs used for obstetrical pain relief: *tranquilizers*, the mildest form of medication; *anesthetics*, which produce insensitivity to pain and sometimes unconsciousness; *analgesics*, which produce insensitivity to pain without affecting other sensibilities; *amnesic agents*, which produce forgetfulness. Generalizing again, these drugs are administered in one of the following ways (Flowers, Jr., 1967; Guttmacher, 1962):

1 Oral administration of tranquilizers, which tends to relax tension and produce drowsiness. These can be administered in tablet form. Librium, Valium, and Miltown are examples.

2 Hypodermic injection.

3 Paracervical block, in which an injection is made into the tissue on either side of the cervix.

4 Pudendal block, in which injections are made to block the nerves supplying the lower part of the vagina and the surrounding area.

5 Inhalation of a gaseous substance, often associated with general anesthesia.

6 Spinal anesthesia, in which the anesthetic drug is introduced into the space between the spinal cord and the bony structure of the spinal column. *Saddle block* is one type of spinal anesthesia in which the part of the body that would touch a saddle is numbed.

7 Continuous conduction anesthesia, in which a flexible needle or a small plastic tube is introduced into the space within the bony structure of the lower part of the spinal column and taped into position, permitting the introduction of the anesthetic solution a little at a time.

8 General anesthesia, in which the woman is unconscious and consequently feels nothing.

Exactly what drugs, if any, are to be used and how they are to be administered is a decision that must be made by the obstetrician and/or anesthesiologist in consultation with the woman in each case. Generalization is impossible. The decision will depend upon the woman's preference, the physician's preference and special skills, the woman's condition and reaction to certain drugs, the hospital staff and equipment available, and other similar considerations. All known methods of pain relief have advantages and disadvantages. None is perfect.

Much has been written in recent years about anesthesia in obstetrics. Some of the controversy has centered on whether anesthesia should be used at all, and some of the controversy has centered on particular techniques. Varieties of spinal and conduction anesthesia have been given special publicity because of their dramatic effects. When conduction anesthesia is successful, it is very good. However, it cannot be used in all cases. Some women cannot tolerate the drugs employed. Its administration requires special skill. There is an element of risk involved in all types of medication, but much less risk than there was many years ago. In obstetrical anesthesia and analgesia encouraging steps forward have been taken, but the final answer has not yet been found. This is, however, no reason for a woman to fear childbirth; as we shall see, for a woman in good health having a baby is one of the safest things she can do. Her answer to the questions about anesthesia is to choose a competent obstetrician.

"Natural childbirth" implies labor and delivery without anesthesia or analgesia or with a minimum of either, as advocated originally by Grantly Dick-Read. Other physicians such as Fernand Lamaze have since developed programs in natural or "psychoprophylactic" (mind prevention) approaches to childbirth. The basic principle involved in natural childbirth is that most of the "pain" associated with childbirth can be prevented or controlled through proper education about the childbirth process, through exercises, relaxation, proper breathing techniques in labor and delivery, improved general health and diet, acceptance of childbirth, and the elimination of tension and fear. Millions of women have had natural childbirth with great success. Nonmedicated childbirth, of course, was the only kind of childbirth before modern medicine and is still normative in some societies, such as Sweden and the Netherlands. The advocates of natural childbirth have performed a valuable service in calling attention to the importance of physiological and mental preparation for childbirth and have established educational programs in communities and hospitals throughout the country.

But natural childbirth is not for everyone. We must beware of thinking of any method as *the* method and must think in terms of what is best for a particular woman under particular circumstances. Otherwise, what might be a helpful addition to the art and science of obstetrics becomes a cult that may do more harm than good. Natural childbirth has gained great popularity in the United States today. However, many physicians are reluctant to participate in a natural childbirth. Many advocates of and participants in natural childbirth prefer to include the husband in childbirth preparation classes, labor management, and the actual delivery. It should be pointed out, however, that the medical community is divided about whether a husband should be permitted in the delivery room. Couples who wish to have the husband in the delivery room should discuss this with the obstetrician. This might be one consideration in choosing an obstetrician.

Most women are able to have successful natural childbirth and find the experience a rewarding one. Others prefer to be medicated. Generally speaking, the more medication, the greater the effect on the mother and infant. But there are a number of medical, as well as social and psychological, considerations which must enter into each decision. Furthermore, a woman who anticipates a natural childbirth should understand that, in some instances, medical complications may indicate that this approach be abandoned for a particular delivery. Thus, physicians must be

Preparation for natural childbirth involves a partner. This father-to-be times exercises which will help his wife prepare for the contractions of labor. (Erika, Photo Researchers)

prepared to administer anesthesia should the need arise.

Some physicians have experimented with an approach to childbirth developed by a French physician, Frederick LeBoyer. This approach involves creating an atmosphere in the delivery room as close as possible to the atmosphere in the uterus. Lights are low, people speak in hushed voices, the baby is not subjected to any abrupt or harsh movements or slaps, and the baby is put immediately into a lukewarm bath, much like the amniotic fluid. Some physicians have reported much success with this technique. Selected reports indicate that the babies respond well and may even be better adjusted than other children during early infancy. There are no available data on the success of such a technique yet, however, and we must wait to learn whether the technique will gain acceptance and will prove to make a difference in the development of the child.

Even in cases where no anesthetic or analgesic is employed and the birth occurs with none of the benefits of modern medical science, the discomfort of childbirth is soon forgotten. It is difficult to remember any pain. A woman may remember her reactions to the pain, but to recall the actual experience is quite another matter. In the fascinating experience of seeing the newborn offspring, nursing it, caring for it, and planning for its future, the mother quickly forgets the inconvenience of pregnancy and the difficulty of labor. Many women plan for a second child before leaving the hospital with the first one.

The discomforts of childbirth should not be approached in the light of old wives' tales or in the light of an individual woman who happened to have difficult labor or did not want to have a baby. It should be approached in the light of modern science and put into correct perspective. Pain may be the most immediately obvious aspect of childbirth while the process is going on, but it is not the most important aspect. Furthermore, pain and risk are not necessarily correlated. The more the woman dissociates them in her thinking the more readily she can accept the process.

Childbirth without fear is possible for every woman who is willing to face the facts intelligently, maturely, and squarely for the very simple reason that there is no longer anything to fear. Many of the unfavorable attitudes that some women hold toward childbirth have their roots in the past, when having a baby was a "descent into the valley of the shadow." But those days are gone forever. If she is in good health at the time she becomes pregnant, if she has adequate prenatal care, and if she is attended by a competent obstetrician, having a baby is now one of the safest things a woman can do. Childbirth without risk has been all but completely achieved.

When we include all the women who have babies in and out of hospitals, all those who have inadequate as well as those who have adequate prenatal care, all those who have poor care at delivery as well as those who have skilled care, all those who have an illness or defect during pregnancy, all those who have miscarriages or induced abortions as well as those who carry their babies to term, and those of all ages and all races, we find that in 1975 there were estimated to be 340 maternal deaths, and the maternal mortality rate (deaths due to complications of pregnancy and childbirth per 100,000 live births) was 10.8. Since there were estimated to be 3,149,000 live births in 1975 (U.S. Department of Health, Education, and Welfare, *Monthly Vital Statistics Reports*, 1976), the total of 340 suggests that there was one death for every 9,262 live births. In 1940, the maternal death rate was 376.0, about thirty-five times as high as in 1975; in 1950, it was 83.3, about eight times as high as in 1975 (U.S. Bureau of the Census, *Statistical Abstract*, 1975). Taken as a group, nonwhite women have a higher mortality rate than white women, and women having children in their teens have a higher rate than women in their twenties. Since World War II the rates for women of all races and ages have declined, but the disparities between whites and nonwhites and between women in their teens and those in their twenties still persist.

The reduction in the maternal mortality rate is one of the more dramatic but less publicized advances in modern medicine. In the decades immediately before the reader was born, when the rate was only beginning to decline, the reader's mother may have acquired attitudes which, in some cases, she passed on to her child.

Obstetrical practice is continually improving. Medical students and nurses are receiving better training. Refresher courses for physicians are growing in popularity. Hospital facilities are being improved and extended. One busy hospital reports only two maternal deaths in over 50,000 deliveries.

One of these was a woman who had been advised not to become pregnant because of kidney disease. The other was a woman who developed complications after leaving the hospital (*Ob. Gyn. News*, September 1, 1967).

Almost all births in the United States are delivered by physicians in hospitals (99.3 percent). Only 0.2 percent of births are delivered by physicians outside of hospitals, and only 0.5 percent are delivered by midwives or others (U.S. National Center for Health Statistics, 1975).

More and more agencies, both private and public, are directing their attention to better prenatal care and better care both during and after delivery. More people are being educated in the hygiene of pregnancy and are being taught both what to expect in pregnancy and what to seek in the way of care. Premarital examinations are increasing in both frequency and quality. Use of x-ray, ultrasound, and fetal heart monitors makes possible the detection of conditions that may give rise to difficulty in labor and delivery. Improved methods of diagnosis, immunization, and treatment make it possible to prevent more of the complications that arise during pregnancy as a result of diseases present before pregnancy began. More is being learned about antibiotics and other drugs. Anesthesia, analgesia, and methods of treating hemorrhage are being improved. All this plus the experience of some communities leads to the prediction that the maternal mortality rate can be still further reduced.

Most female readers will probably begin their childbearing in their early to middle twenties, a favorable time. Like most women who become mothers, they will be attended by a physician, perhaps by a specialist in obstetrics. Like most mothers, their children will be delivered in a hospital. They will have adequate prenatal and postnatal care. They will know enough about pregnancy and childbirth to follow their physician's instructions and to be cooperative. In short, in the light of what was said above, they will have childbirth almost without risk. They may, therefore, have childbirth completely without fear.

Perhaps by reading between the lines of a few letters written by women still in the hospital after the birth of their babies we may gain insight into the relative values of joy and pain. These letters express not exceptional but typical attitudes. The women who wrote them gave no indication of thinking of their recent experience as a forbidding "descent into the valley of the shadow." The reason there are not more such documents is that few women write them, not that only few women feel this way. The women who wrote these did not know at the time that they would be read by anyone except the friends to whom they were addressed. Hence there was no reason for being anything except straightforward and sincere. Personal details are omitted from these restatements; the rest is in the women's own words.

Mrs. A writes:

First I must apologize for staying away from the nice dinner you prepared for us Sunday. I really intended to come but I had other very important business on Sunday.

Now I can get down to business and *rave*! That boy is simply marvelous and I can see a new life for (the husband) and me. It's even more wonderful than I thought it would be and you know I've been thrilled for nine months.

The baby looks like _____ (husband), has black hair, big feet and big hands—and is the sweetest baby in town. I'm so happy I have to cry a little every once in a while. It still seems too good to be true. I only hope that someday you will celebrate a blessed event. It's worth all the pain and all the sacrifice; it's wonderful. And Dr. _____ is a great man and a great doctor. I almost felt like kissing him.

I am still on my back and writing is rather difficult. . . .

Mrs. B writes:

A week ago today I gave birth to a darling baby boy. I'm so thrilled about him that you'd think I was the first one ever to have a baby. I'm writing you about it now because I want to tell you how thankful I am for the discussions we had in class and for the opportunity of reading those letters from women who had just had babies. They made things so much easier for me mentally. I kept thinking of how they felt about it when untactful people would say to me, "You'll find out that it's not easy, etc., etc." One mother had the grace to say, "Oh, the pain—that's the first thing you forget." And that is what you can tell the girls that I say, too.

I'll admit that the first day I wondered whether I could ever have any playmates for my son (I'd like four, in all); but in another twenty-four hours I couldn't remember how terrible the pain was. Anyway, what's a half hour or so of pain when you get a lifetime of happiness for it? I don't think a child would want a woman for his mother if she couldn't stand that much for him. My son's daddy is in the Air Corps in Europe. It wasn't as nice having him gone at this time but at least he didn't have to pace the floor while he waited for me.

Mrs. C writes:

Before I became pregnant, my knowledge of the actual birth of a baby consisted of a few old wives' tales and bits of information from friends. After I was sure of my pregnancy, I became much more aware of the actual truth about childbirth. I realize that the more you know about something, the less you fear it, and believe that it is very important for a woman who is going to have a baby to know as much as possible about it.

My experience during labor and childbirth was a happy and somewhat humorous one. My labor began with the show of blood. As soon as I noticed it, I called my doctor and was told that labor would soon follow. Then I called my husband out of his Saturday morning class. He raced home as quickly as possible, and, like most expectant fathers, he was very excited. At this time my pains were not very severe. I was anxious but not afraid because I knew what to expect.

Sunday morning I felt fine and decided to go to church. I passed up Sunday School because I didn't feel like sitting through two services. The contractions continued during the service and were a little more painful. After church, we ate out since I didn't feel like cooking. We spent the afternoon timing the contractions and taking a long walk around the campus. By eight o'clock Sunday evening, after the pains had occurred at three-minute intervals for two hours, my husband called the doctor who agreed to meet us at the hospital.

My clothes for the hospital had been packed for two weeks, so we went directly to the hospital. By 1 A.M. Monday the pains were much more severe and labor progressed slowly and continued throughout the night. Monday morning I sat up, combed my hair, and fixed my face between contractions. I don't remember anything after that, but my precious son was born at 11:15 A.M. that Monday morning.

Mrs. D writes:

Our third little girl was born last Saturday night at 7:10 P.M. She weighed 6 lb. 5 oz. and looks just like her daddy. She is bald on top with a fringe of red fuzz, very much like Jiggs in the funny paper. Jennifer is another Read method baby—this time completely successful. I had her without anesthetic or sedative of any sort. I came to the hospital Friday night about 10 P.M., after my water broke, and then did nothing until Saturday afternoon about 2:30 P.M. Then my labor began. I called my husband and he came and stayed with me in my room during the first part. I relaxed easily with the pains and about 5:30 I went back to the labor ward. I relaxed well until the very end of the first stage when the pains became too strong to relax with. During the last few first stage pains, which were very sharp, I took a deep breath and held it till it passed. With the first second stage "pain" all pain ceased entirely and a new feeling began, a good "bearing down" feeling which was entirely painless. I was rushed to the delivery room after I announced that the second stage had begun and the baby was coming fast. The doctor asked me not to bear down while he rushed into his gloves, and I was surprised to find that I could control when the contractions would come. When he was ready I bore down good and the baby was born. I immediately popped up on an elbow and saw him lift her up. She made a few noises and was laid across my tummy and I watched while the cord was tied and cut. She was then carried to a table to be wrapped in a blanket and I was asked to lie back down and push once more. I popped up again to see the afterbirth and about that time the baby gave a good loud yell. The nurse brought her over for me to see once more before they took her to the nursery.

By that time I was cleaned up and ready to leave, so the doctor gave me a hand to sit up and I slipped off the table and walked out in the hall. I didn't feel at all weak and wanted to walk to my room; but my bed was already at the delivery room door so I climbed up and got a ride to my room. My husband was waiting there and as I rolled through the door I said, "Hi, honey. I'm hungry." Then I told him we had another daughter. While he went to round up some crackers for me to eat, I used the telephone by my bed to call some of my friends and tell them we had a girl. They were all amazed to hear me. I felt wonderful and got up several times during the night. I've been up and around ever since. I don't feel at all as if I'd had a baby and I am the happiest person in the world. The Read method worked so beautifully all the way that there was no need for fuss. There was nothing about any of it that I couldn't bear perfectly well and I was totally fascinated by every minute of it. I could have a dozen more just like it—but this is the end.

Lactation

For a brief period after the birth of the child the mother's breasts secrete colostrum, a substance that may have food value for the child and acts as a mild laxative but is not true milk. Colostrum is usually supplemented with water given by bottle. True milk appears in two to five days. Breast feeding was on the decline in this country following World War II (Eastman, 1963), but it appears to be regaining some of its popularity among young, educated mothers. Pediatricians are not as insistent upon it as they used to be. This is due in part to increased knowledge of infant nutrition and in part to improvement in prepared formulas. But breast feeding has by no means lost all of its proponents. Many pediatricians recommend it. Some psychologists, psychiatrists, anthropologists, and similar specialists feel that the method of infant feeding is influential in the psychosocial development of both mother and child (Newton, 1972). Montagu (Eastman, 1963), an anthropologist, in discussing breast feeding, men-

Breast feeding provides an opportunity for mothers to be very close to their infants. In earlier times most women breast-fed their children. Today's mother has the option, and a growing number of women are again choosing to breast-feed. (Susan Ylvisaker)

tions the "psychophysiological benefits" conferred upon mother and child by their "continuing symbiotic relationship" and calls breast feeding "very important for their further development." Some women derive a special satisfaction from breast feeding. Others do not. Some feel guilty when they cannot or do not nurse their babies. Such a feeling of guilt is unnecessary and inappropriate. It stems from attitudes of the past rather than from present-day knowledge of child rearing. Some mothers are reluctant to nurse their babies because they fear permanent breast enlargement and impairment of appearance. If a woman follows her physician's instructions, such a fear is groundless. Other women dislike being tied to their infants for feeding, and bottle feeding permits the mother to work and allows the father to play a greater role in child care.

Contrary to common assumption, it is possible for a woman to become pregnant while nursing. Ovulation or conception may occur without the reinstitution of the menses. In a study of 2,197 women it was found that among those who nursed their babies three or more months, menstruation had begun by the end of the third month in 26 percent. Among those who nursed their babies six or more months, menstruation had begun by the end of the sixth month in 60 percent. Among women who did not breast-feed their babies at all, menstruation had begun by the end of the third month in 90 percent and by the end of the sixth month in "virtually all" (Salber, Feinleib, and MacMahon, 1966). In a study of 2,885 patients of The Johns Hopkins Hospital it was found that one-fourth of the white women and one-third of the black women became pregnant within twelve months after delivery; 36 percent of the whites and 47 percent of the blacks were still nursing their babies when conception occurred (Guttmacher, 1937). In a recent study (Perez, Vela, Masnick, and Potter, 1972) it was found that the longer a woman nursed her baby the less was her chance of ovulating. "This implies a certain degree of protection against pregnancy. However, women do ovulate during full nursing and thus can become pregnant."

Multiple Births

Twins occur about once in eighty-eight live births. Three or more babies in one birth tend to occur as follows: If twins occur once in n births, triplets will occur once in n^2 births, quadruplets once in n^3 births, and quintuplets once in n^4 births (the Hellin-Zeleny hypothesis). In recent years in this country there have been two authenticated sets of quintuplets which survived beyond infancy.

Simultaneous births of more than five children occur rarely, and there is only one recorded case in which more than five children have survived. A woman in Capetown, South Africa had six children (three boys, three girls), all of whom survived, on January 11, 1974. Two medically recorded cases of nonuplets have been reported, one in Sydney, Australia, in 1971 and one in Philadelphia, Pennsylvania, in 1972. All of these children died (McWhirter and McWhirter, 1976). Multiple births of this magnitude are often associated with the use of fertility drugs to encourage ovulation. The twinning rate varies with the age of the mother. It is lowest in the teens, then the rate increases through the late thirties, after which it declines (*Statistical Bulletin*, 1972).

Twins are of two types: one-egg (monovular, monozygotic, so-called "identical") twins, and two-egg (binovular, dizygotic, so-called "fraternal") twins. About one-third of all twins are of the former type. One-egg twins are produced when the zygote has developed into a cluster of cells which breaks apart. Such twins are, in a sense, parts of the same individual. They have the same genetic constitution, are thus always of the same gender, and resemble each other very closely; but, being subject to prenatal and postnatal environmental influences, they are not so nearly identical in appearance and behavior that they cannot be distinguished by persons who know them well. Sometimes they are "identical" in the sense of being alike. At other times they are "mirror images" of each other; for example, one twin's right hand is like the other's left hand. Whether they are "identical" or "mirror image" depends upon factors involved in the twinning process, such as the time and plane of splitting in the cluster of cells. According to one point of view, the later the splitting occurs, the more different mirror-image twins are likely to be (Scheinfeld, 1967). According to another point of view, mirror imaging is unrelated to such splitting and occurs no more frequently than would be expected by chance (Bulmer, 1970).

When the splitting is incomplete, conjoined twins, commonly referred to as "siamese," result. Such twins are rare. In most cases they die before or soon after birth. If they live, they may or may not be separable through surgery, depending upon where and how they are joined and what organs they have in common. Most one-egg twins have one common placenta with two amnions and two cords (Hertig, 1960). A minority have two placentas, which may or may not be fused (see Exhibit 13-19). Very rarely one-egg twins are found in the same amniotic sac (Timmons and deAlvarez, 1963; Goplerud, 1964).

Two-egg twins are produced when two ova are released at one time and fertilized by two sperms. They are not produced by having two sperms fertilize one ovum, as is sometimes assumed. Two-egg twins may be of the same or of different gender. They have different genetic constitutions and are no more closely related than any two children having the same parents. They have two placentas, but these sometimes fuse, making classification difficult and at times leading to error. Two-egg twins have two amnions and two cords.

The individual children in a multiple birth are usually smaller than the child in a single birth, but their combined weight is often greater than that of a single child. The smaller size of the individuals is due in part to the fact that in the majority of cases multiple births occur prematurely.

There is evidence to indicate that the tendency for two-egg twinning is hereditary in the female, but the evidence is inconclusive relative to one-egg twinning. Not only daughters but also other female relatives—such as sisters—of women who have borne two-egg twins have a greater-than-average chance of bearing two-egg twins. Women who are themselves twins also are more likely to have twins. Furthermore, once a woman has borne twins, her chances of having twins in subsequent pregnancies are increased beyond the average rate (Scheinfeld, 1967; Bulmer, 1970). In 1961 a thirty-seven-year-old woman bore her seventh set of twins. In 1944 a Canadian woman bore her sixth set of all-surviving twins in eight years of marriage (Scheinfeld, 1967). A woman known to one of the authors had two sets of twins, one of triplets, and three singletons. The all-time reported record for childbearing, including multiple births, was of the first wife of Gyodor Vassilet, a peasant of Moscow, Russia, who in the nineteenth century had sixty-nine children, including sixteen pairs of twins, seven sets of triplets, and four sets of quadruplets (Gould and Pyle, 1896). These are, of course, extreme cases, but they support the assumption that a woman who has once borne twins is likely to do so again. The evidence does not suggest that "twinning skips generations," as is commonly believed, and multiple births still remain the exception rather than the rule, as indicated earlier.

It is ordinarily assumed that the sperms which fertilize the two ova in the production

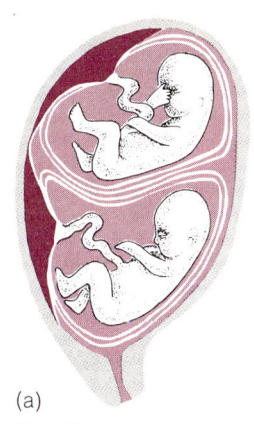

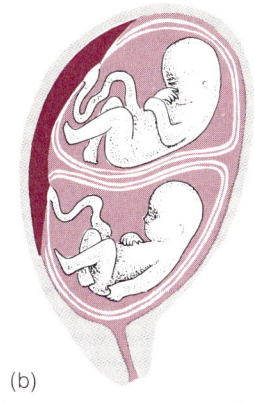

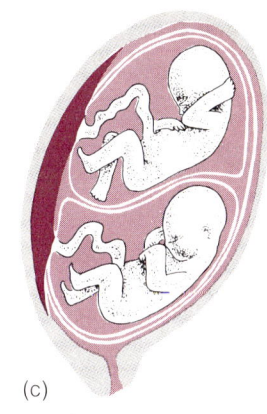

Exhibit 13-19 Twinning. (a) Two-egg twins: two placentas; each fetus with two sacs, amnion inside and chorion outside; sex may be different; fraternal twins. (b) Two-egg twins: two placentas have merged; each fetus has both membranes, amnion and chorion; sex may be different. (c) One-egg twins: one placenta; each fetus with inner sac (amnion); single outer membrane (chorion) envelops both; same sex; identical twins. (Adapted from sculptured birth series by Dickinson and Belskie in "Birth Atlas," Maternity Center Association, New York.)

of two-egg twins are deposited during the same act of insemination. Could such twins be produced by sperms from different acts of insemination, provided the inseminations occurred during the brief period in which the two ova released at one time of ovulation were fertilizable? This process is termed *superfecundation*, and the answer to the question is in the affirmative. Two-egg twins can even have different fathers if a woman has sexual intercourse with two men within a brief time span (Bulmer, 1970), or if, as discussed in Chapter 12, a mixture of the seminal fluid of the husband and that of a donor is used in artificial insemination.

An unusual case was taken to court in Baltimore in 1960 (Eastman, 1961). The man in question admitted intercourse with a woman who had borne twins but disclaimed paternity. Blood tests indicated that he could have been the father of one twin but not of the other. The woman claimed that she had had intercourse with no other man during the period in which the twins must have been conceived. The judge ruled that her statement was insufficient and that she must have been withholding evidence. Since the man could not have been the father of one twin, the final verdict was "not guilty," and he was ruled to be the father of neither twin.

The characteristics of the various forms of multiple births are summarized in Exhibit 13-20.

RH FACTOR

The Rh factor is a substance found in the blood. It derives its name from the fact that it was discovered during the course of experiments to learn what happened when the blood of one species was introduced into another. One type of animal used in the experiments was the Rhesus monkey. An individual in whose blood the Rh factor is present is designated as Rh-positive. One from whose blood it

Exhibit 13-20 Forms of multiple births

Type of Birth	Ovulations	Number of Ova	Inseminations	Number of Sperms
Identical twins	1	1	1	1
Fraternal twins	1	2	1	2
Superfecundation	1	2	2	2

is absent is designated as Rh-negative. Actually, there are several Rh factors. But we shall generalize and discuss them as if there were only one, and say that about 85 percent of the white population is Rh-positive. Nonwhite races appear to be almost entirely Rh-positive. There are also other types of mother-fetus blood incompatibility, but Rh incompatibility is the type of primary concern to most couples.

Whether an individual is Rh-positive or Rh-negative is determined by heredity. Rh-positive is dominant; Rh-negative is recessive. This means that one's blood will be Rh-positive if two positive genes are received from the parents (homozygous), or if one positive gene and one negative gene (heterozygous) are received. At the present stage of knowledge, there are no tests to distinguish with certainty between the two types of Rh-positive, though there are tests that make it possible to "guess" the more probable type of the husband (Queenan, 1967), and helpful evidence may sometimes be obtained from an analysis of an individual's family tree. Actually, there are more than one pair of genes involved, but again we shall generalize. In order to have Rh-negative blood, the individual must receive two negative genes. When sperms or ova are formed, the pairs of chromosomes, and hence pairs of genes, separate. Therefore, the combinations shown in Exhibit 13-21 are possible, letting a plus sign (+) indicate a positive gene and a minus sign (−) indicate a negative gene. The proportions given apply to large numbers of families. A particular couple of the type indicated in situation 6, for example, might, by chance, have all negative children.

The instance in which the Rh factor ordinarily can cause a problem is that indicated in situations 4 and 7 in Exhibit 13-21; that is, the mother is Rh-negative, and the father and child are Rh-positive. Generalizing, such a situation occurs in only about 10 percent of pregnancies, and sensitization of the mother occurs in only about 5 percent of these, or in about one pregnancy in two hundred. In other words, the incidence of sensitization among Rh-negative women is about 0.5 percent (Charles and Friedman, 1969; Clarke and McConnel, 1972). Many Rh-negative women who are married to homozygous (two genes for Rh-positive, as in situation 4 in Exhibit 13-21) Rh-positive husbands have several children without any of them being affected. However, if a woman gives birth to one baby that is affected, subsequent babies are likely to be affected.

Although it is generally true that there is no direct connection between mother and fetus, that the placental "roots" (villi) are part of a closed fetal circulatory system and merely extend into, but do not connect with, the mother's bloodstream, "the placenta is rarely, if ever, a completely tight seal" (Cohen, Zuelzer, Gustafson, and Evans, 1964). It is now established that fetal blood cells do "cross the placental barrier" and pass in minute quantities into the maternal circulation, at least in a considerable proportion of cases (Clayton, Feldhaus, and Whitacre, 1964; Turchetti, Palagi, and Lattanzi, 1965; Clayton, Feldhaus, Phythyon, and Whitacre, 1966;

Exhibit 13-21 Possible Rh-positive–Rh-negative combinations.

Father	Mother	Offspring
1. ++ (positive)	++ (positive)	all ++ (all positive)
2. ++ (positive)	+− (positive)	½ ++; ½ +− (all positive)
3. +− (positive)	++ (positive)	½ ++; ½ +− (all positive)
4. ++ (positive)	−− (negative)	all +− (all positive)
5. −− (negative)	++ (positive)	all +− (all positive)
6. +− (positive)	+− (positive)	¼ ++; ½ +−; ¼ −− (¾ positive; ¼ negative)
7. +− (positive)	−− (negative)	½ +−; ½ −− (½ positive; ½ negative)
8. −− (negative)	+− (positive)	½ +−; ½ −− (½ positive; ½ negative)
9. −− (negative)	−− (negative)	all −− (all negative)

McLarey and Fish, 1966). Fetal blood cells may also pass into the maternal circulation during the third stage of labor (when the placenta is separated from the uterine wall), during abortion, during amniocentesis, or during cesarean section (Zipursky, Pollack, Chown, and Israels, 1963; Clark and Jacobs, 1964; Dacie, 1967; Goldman and Eckerling, 1972). The amount of blood passing from fetus to mother need not be very great to produce an effect. In some cases 0.1 cubic centimeter of Rh-positive blood is sufficient (Queenan, 1967). In situations 4 and 7 in Exhibit 13-21, the Rh factor can cause a problem only if such passage occurs.

When an individual is vaccinated for smallpox, a small amount of vaccine, a foreign substance, is introduced into the bloodstream. The body reacts to this foreign substance and produces chemicals that are termed *antibodies*. The antibodies remain in the individual's bloodstream for some time. If the organisms that cause smallpox find their way into the bloodstream, the antibodies destroy them. Hence, the individual is immunized against the disease.

When an Rh-negative mother has an Rh-positive fetus and fetal blood cells pass into the maternal circulation, the mother's body may react to the Rh-positive blood of the child as to a foreign substance and produce antibodies. It is as if the mother were vaccinated against the blood of her baby. The result is a type of sensitization termed *isoimmunization*. When the antibodies from the mother pass back through the placenta into the blood of the fetus, having been formed to protect the mother from the fetus's Rh-positive blood, they damage red cells in that blood. Because of this damage, the condition in the child is termed *hemolytic* (blood-damaging) *disease of the newborn*. Since the part of the fetal blood damaged is the red cells and the condition causes the fetus to produce immature red cells (erythroblasts) at a rapid rate, the disease is also termed *erythroblastosis fetalis*.

Even when the mother is Rh-negative and the fetus is Rh-positive, and there is the passage of fetal blood cells into the maternal circulation such that the mother's body reacts to the baby's blood, she is not likely to produce enough antibodies in one pregnancy to affect the child. Or it may be that since it takes some time for antibodies to be produced, the first baby is born before it can be affected (Clarke and McConnell, 1972). The above statement must be qualified, however. It is the number of pregnancies, not the number of live-born children, that must be considered. For example, if a woman has two spontaneous abortions or stillbirths before she bears a live baby, so far as the Rh problem is concerned she would count three pregnancies. If an

Rh-negative woman had a transfusion of Rh-positive blood, antibodies would be produced that would give her a "head start" on her first pregnancy. Since the Rh factor was discovered in the early 1940s, there are women of childbearing age who may have had such a transfusion. In the absence of such transfusion the incidence of isoimmunization in a first pregnancy is very low, but it is not unknown (Queenan, 1967). In some cases this may possibly be due to the fact that the woman received an initial stimulus in antibody formation from her own mother's Rh-positive blood cells before birth (Taylor, 1967).

The antibodies produced by the mother damage the fetus's red blood cells. As a result of this damage, a chemical (*bilirubin*) is released and accumulates in the fetus's blood. This chemical is a pigment, and its presence produces a yellowish skin discoloration (jaundice). Since the red cells carry oxygen, damage to them reduces the oxygen-carrying capacity of the fetal blood. Hence the child may exhibit symptoms of anemia. The combined effect of the anemia and the chemical (bilirubin) may cause brain damage, with resultant mental retardation or cerebral palsy. It may even cause death. Since the red cells are formed in the liver of the fetus, this organ may enlarge in an effort to produce cells more rapidly than they are damaged. At the other extreme, the child's symptoms may be very mild and involve no more than a discoloration of the milk teeth which disappears when these teeth are replaced by permanent ones.

The Rh factor is something to be understood and taken into account when the blood types of parents are such that a problem may arise. This factor is, however, not as fearsome as was first thought. Part of the reason for this is that methods of both detecting the problem and preventing complications from it have been developed. Furthermore, should an Rh incompatibility develop, methods of treatment are available.

Since in so many cases Rh-positive fetal blood cells enter the maternal circulation late in pregnancy or during labor and delivery, a method has been devised for preventing isoimmunization in women who have not yet become sensitized. If Rh-positive fetal blood cells do pass into the Rh-negative maternal circulation, the woman's body reacts to them and forms antibodies, as explained previously. But this antibody formation takes some time. Therefore, within seventy-two hours after delivery (or abortion or cesarean section) the nonsensitized woman is injected (intramuscularly) with a special anti-Rh-gamma-globulin preparation, commercially called "RhoGAM" or "Gamulin Rh," procured from the blood plasma of Rh-negative women who have developed a high concentration of antibodies or from male volunteers who have been stimulated to produce antibodies (Friedman, 1969). Just how this preparation functions is not fully known. It may destroy Rh-positive fetal blood cells as antibodies formed in an Rh-negative woman's body during pregnancy damage the blood cells of an Rh-positive fetus. Hence, the woman does not produce antibodies against fetal blood, and isoimmunization is prevented (Freda, 1966; Hamilton, 1967; Queenan, 1967). Or it may be that the preparation suppresses the mother's antibody response to the Rh-positive fetal cells (Clarke, 1971). Apparently the antibodies introduced in the anti-Rh-gamma-globulin injection gradually disappear from the woman's blood, so that there are none left to pass into the blood of a fetus in a subsequent pregnancy.

Methods of treating an affected baby have also been developed. One method is an exchange transfusion by which the baby's Rh-positive blood is partially, or almost entirely, replaced with Rh-negative blood (Wu and Oh, 1969). A more recently developed method (Howell and Flowers, 1964) involves introducing a long needle through the abdominal wall of the mother, through the wall of the uterus, and into the abdominal cavity of the fetus. Then a fine plastic tube is introduced through the needle, and the latter is withdrawn. Through the plastic tube Rh-negative blood is transfused into the abdominal cavity of the fetus. From there it is absorbed via the baby's lymphatic system (Queenan, 1967). Intrauterine transfusion is ingenious and dramatic and has saved babies' lives.

If the use of Rh-negative blood in such cases is puzzling, several things might be kept in mind. The first problem is to give the baby blood that will function in the presence of the antibodies which passed to the child from the mother. Since the antibodies are designed to damage Rh-positive blood cells, the baby is given Rh-negative blood. The child will not react to this blood by the production of antibodies, since it is the Rh-negative individual who reacts to Rh-positive blood, not vice versa. Furthermore, the transfused Rh-negative blood will not produce antibodies in reaction with the baby's Rh-positive blood, since the antibodies are not formed in or by the blood but in the spleen, liver, bone marrow, and/or lymph nodes. The baby, Rh-positive by heredity, will continue to form Rh-positive blood which will gradually replace the Rh-negative blood with which it was transfused.

Several new approaches to the treatment of the baby give promise of reducing the need for exchange transfusions by increasing the baby's ability to excrete bilirubin. One method is the medication of the mother with phenobarbital for several weeks before delivery (Halpin, Jones, Bishop, and Lerner, 1972). Another is to subject the newborn infant to fluorescent light. Still another is early feeding of the newborn infant (within the first twelve hours after birth), which tends to decrease the absorption of bilirubin in the intestinal tract (Lucey, 1971). Fortunately, with the availability of RhoGAM, the need for such transfusions is rare.

If the situation discussed above is reversed, that is, if the mother is Rh-positive, the fetus is Rh-negative, and there is the passage of maternal blood cells into the fetal circulation, why is the mother not affected by antibodies produced by the fetus? There are several reasons. First, an immature organism usually has a lower capacity to produce antibodies than does a more mature one. Second, the difference in body size, and hence in quantity of blood (with resultant dilution), would make a difference. Third, there is no possibility of an accumulation of antibodies in the fetus through successive pregnancies.

CHOOSING AN OBSTETRICIAN

The importance of adequate prenatal care for the prospective mother cannot be overemphasized. Her health, both present and future, and her baby's well-being hinge in large measure upon her care during pregnancy. There are many useful books and pamphlets on this subject, and the reader is urged to refer to them. The woman must also choose a competent obstetrician. The latter should not be chosen only for ability to diagnose and treat disease. He or she should be chosen primarily for ability to handle cases of pregnancy.

Preferably the obstetrician should be equipped to handle the pregnancy from the first visit to the care of the mother after she leaves the hospital. The person chosen need not be able singlehandedly to meet all emergencies; that is too much to ask of any medical practitioner. But it is essential to be able to recognize and detect emergencies and be willing to call in a consultant if necessary. Some obstetricians work closely with a pediatrician, especially when a particular problem, such as that caused by the Rh factor, is anticipated.

The physician's personality is important, since contact with the prospective mother is so intimate. She should not be forced to have a physician whom she dislikes and with whom she cannot get along. Training is important. So is extent of experience. Does the person chosen have enough obstetric cases to gain experience? Does he or she become so busy that time-saving techniques, such as induction of labor or use of forceps for convenience rather than for patient good, are resorted to unnecessarily? Is there so much delegation to nurses that the peculiar relationship between obstetrician and mother is rendered unsatisfactory? "The obstetrician who depends upon the obstetrical nurse to follow his patients in labor and who wishes to be called only when delivery is imminent is not practicing obstetrics in the best sense of the term; he is a doctor who delivers babies. . . . No analgesia can take the place of considerate and conscientious care by the obstetrician" (Crampton, 1961). Does the physician keep abreast of new developments? Is obstetrics a special interest, or is it only incidental in a general practice? Will the physician, indeed may the physician, take patients to a reputable hospital? All these considerations are important.

A problem not infrequently faced by young couples is that of choosing an obstetrician soon after having settled in a new community, before sufficient time has elapsed to become thoroughly acquainted. In such cases, information may be gathered from friends or from persons at the husband's or wife's place of employment. The local hospital may yield some data. The couple may write to their physician in their home town and ask for recommendations. Learning which obstetricians the wives of other obstetricians choose for their own deliveries may be helpful.

Before the couple put their case in the obstetrician's hands, they may talk it over with him or her. Let them remember that they are employing the physician, not vice versa. They have a right to know what the doctor's techniques are, how many visits will be recommended before delivery, what care will be continued after delivery, to what hospital patients are taken, what the physician's attitude toward induced labor is, what will be done concerning relief of pain, what the total cost will be.

Once the obstetrician is chosen, everything relative to the case should be told. No detail, no matter how insignificant it may seem to the couple, should be withheld. Questions should be freely asked. Any obstetrician worth his or her salt would rather have the couple ask questions than let a clue remain hidden which, if revealed, might prevent complications.

Once the obstetrician is chosen, too, instructions should be followed faithfully, explicitly, and thoroughly. The couple should never let other people's advice supersede the doctor's instructions. If they do not like the way their case is being handled, they may change obstetricians. But as long as they accept a given obstetrician's services, they should cooperate to the utmost. Both the physician and the patient may play a part in establishing the rapport demanded by the nature of their relationship.

PREGNANCY AND THE COUPLE'S ADJUSTMENT

We are accustomed to saying that so-and-so is pregnant. In one sense that is correct; in another it is not. It would be more nearly accurate to say that there is pregnancy in the family. Pregnancy is in many ways a social condition. It certainly involves both husband and wife; it also involves their relatives, the mores of society, and the laws of the state.

Having a baby is a joint enterprise from the very beginning. The father's physiological role may not be so prominent as the mother's, but he has indispensable psychological and economic functions. The husband suffering the throes of becoming a parent is made the butt of many a joke. Much humorous discussion and literature are directed toward the "care and treatment" of expectant fathers. The father's situation is anything but a joke. A child needs two parents, and the father has a responsibility. There are many things that he may do to make the wife's nine months of pregnancy more enjoyable. He may assist with the housework. He may make certain that he and his wife do interesting things in their leisure time. He may prepare for the baby's coming by making things for the nursery. He should understand what is occurring so that he may help his wife follow the doctor's instructions and will know what to do in case an emergency arises. Together he and his wife may attend classes in infant care, which are becoming increasingly available in many communities. The wife is likely to be more than ordinarily dependent upon him, and he can do much to color her attitude, favorably or unfavorably, toward both the present and future pregnancies. Some pregnant women develop temporary personality traits that make them somewhat difficult to live with. It is important that the husband understand this fact.

Not the least of the father's functions is economic. Babies cost money. When the total cost of a child is taken into consideration, reckoning from early pregnancy through infancy, childhood, adolescence, to young adulthood, and including all expenses borne by parents from the initial doctor's fee to college education, the result is apt to take one's breath away. Each time a couple have a child, the financial responsibility they assume is roughly equivalent to that involved in purchasing a new home.

A question that often arises in connection with the prospective father, one which we raised earlier, is whether he should be in the delivery room (as distinguished from the labor room) when his baby is born. Some hospitals and obstetricians will permit him to be present; others will not. The trend is toward greater acceptability of fathers in the delivery room. Much depends upon the attitude of the wife. If his presence would reassure her, he may be useful. Some men want to witness the birth; others do not. Some feel that witnessing it makes the child seem more their own, since they are more nearly participators. "We have never had cause to regret the presence of a husband at his wife's delivery. Often, husbands lend much help in encouraging the vigorous physical efforts necessary for spontaneous birth," says one obstetrician (Margolis, 1970).

Unless her obstetrician advises to the contrary, a woman may with some exceptions pursue her regular activities, including housework or a job, during pregnancy. There are many sports in which she may engage, though she may not usually do things that are more or less violent in character (Hobbins, 1974). Sexual intercourse may be engaged in unless there are special considerations for which the obstetrician advises against it. In a healthy pregnancy where there is no abnormal condition of fetus, uterus, or placenta, the fetus is not readily dislodged, and spontaneous abortion is not brought about by the ordinary activities of life. "Nature has produced the safest packaging she can contrive and no ordinary thump or jar or blow can hurt the embryo. Harming it by external force is as difficult as rupturing the yolk of an egg without breaking the shell" (Fort, 1974).

Another question that is sometimes raised concerns the extent of the father's participation in infant care. Many modern fathers participate with enthusiasm. Others feel that infant care is the mother's responsibility. Still others, never having had experience with infants, are afraid of their own child. They feel awkward in holding it and fear that they will hurt it. The question of the father's participation in infant care is not one only of the contribution he can make to such care. It is also one of the contribution that such care can make to him. What will he miss if he does not participate? There is evidence to suggest that the human mother has no "maternal instinct" in the strict sense of the term, but that through handling, fondling, caring for, and nursing the baby she very quickly learns to love it. Of course, this process is greatly facilitated if the woman wants a baby very much and eagerly anticipates having it. Also, in every culture there is a pattern of expectation which colors the rearing of girls and orients them in the direction of motherhood. Certainly there is no paternal instinct. The father, too, learns to love the child through anticipation, caring for it, and fondling it. Furthermore, the day-to-day development of an infant is a fascinating process. As the baby's world expands and he or she becomes aware of more and more of the environment, many a modern father wants to be part of that world from the beginning with a strong affectional bond between himself and the child already established. He does not want to wait and then be introduced into the child's world later merely because infant care is time- and energy-consuming.

TERMS TO BE LEARNED

abdominal pregnancy
afterbirth
amnesic agent
amniocentesis
amnion (amniotic sac)
analgesic
anethesia (anesthetic)
anti-Rh gamma globulin
   (RhoGAM, Gamulin Rh)
ballottement
Barr body
bilirubin
binovular
Braxton-Hicks contractions
breech presentation
cesarean section
chorion
cilia
ciliary action
coccyx
colostrum
continuous conduction anesthesia
decidua basalis
decidua vera
dry birth
ectopic pregnancy
elective delivery
embryo
epididymis
episiotomy

erythroblastosis fetalis
fallopian tube
false labor
fertilization
fetal heart monitor
fetoscope
fetus
fimbriae
forceps
foreskin
gamete
genetic code
genital
glans
hemolytic disease
heterozygous
homozygous
human chorionic
   gonadotropin (HCG)
implantation
indication (medical)
induced labor
insemination
interstitial cells
isoimmunization
jaundice
labium (labia)
labor
lactation
lanugo

lightening
maternal impression
maternal mortality rate
meiosis
menstruation
mirror image
mitosis
molding
monovular
monozygotic
multiple birth
natural childbirth
navel
nidation
os (cervical)
ovary
ovulation (ovulate)
ovum (ova)
paracervical block
parthenogenesis
pelvis
penis
perineum
phocomelia
placenta
placental barrier
premature delivery
   (prematurity)
prenatal
prostate gland

pseudocyesis
pyschoprophylactic
pubic joint
pudendal block
reduction division
repercussion
Rh factor
Rh-negative
Rh-positive
rubella
saddle block
seminal fluid (semen)
seminal vesicle
sex chromatin
signs of pregnancy
  (positive, presumptive)
somatic cells
sperm (spermatozoa)
spinal anesthesia
superfecundation
term (full)
test for pregnancy
  (biologic, immunologic)
testis, testes (testicle, testicles)
testosterone
thalidomide
tranquilizer
trial labor
trimester
tubal pregnancy
twins (fraternal, identical)
ultrasound
umbilical cord
umbilicus
urethra
uterus
vagina
vernix caseosa
version
villi
viral
virgin
vulva
withdrawal symptoms
womb
yolk sac
zygote

SELECTED READINGS

AIMS, S.: *Immaculate Deception: A New Look at Women and Childbirth in America*, Houghton Mifflin Company, Boston, 1975. The author challenges current obstetric practices in examining what has happened to birth in American hospitals and what determinatives to current practice still exist.

APGAR, VIRGINIA, AND JOAN BECK: *Is My Baby All Right? A Guide to Birth Defects*, Pocket Books, New York, 1974. (Paperback.) Discussion of numerous birth defects, what causes them, what can be done about them. Answers many questions that concern parents and prospective parents. During her professional career Dr. Apgar was involved in the delivery of some 17,000 babies. She developed the "Apgar score" for evaluating the condition of the newborn.

BOSTON CHILDREN'S MEDICAL CENTER: *Pregnancy, Birth and the Newborn Baby*, Dell Publishing Co., Inc., New York, 1972. A nontechnical guide to pregnancy, birth, and the first six weeks of the baby's life. Discusses the psychological as well as the physiological aspects of childbearing; complications of pregnancy and childbirth; natural childbirth; care of the newborn.

BRADLEY, R. A.: *Husband-Coached Childbirth*, Harper & Row, Publishers, Inc., New York, 1974. An easy-to-read guide for men and women, intended for cases where the husband will assist in labor and delivery.

DICK-READ, GRANTLY: *Childbirth without Fear*, 4th ed., rev. and ed. by Helen Wessel and Harlan F. Ellis, Harper & Row, Publishers, Inc., New York, 1972. A discussion of natural childbirth by the man whose name has become almost a synonym for the term.

GADDIS, VINCENT, AND MARGARET GADDIS: *The Curious World of Twins*, Hawthorn Books, Inc., New York, 1972. (Paperback.) Multiple births; fertility drugs; life stories of twins, triplets, and other multiples; conjoined twins. Nontechnical. Many photographs.

GILBERT, MARAGRET SHEA: *Biography of the Unborn*, rev. ed., Hafner Press, New York, 1963. A detailed, nontechnical account of the development of the fetus.

GUTTMACHER, A.: *Pregnancy, Birth and Family Planning*, The Viking Press, New York, 1973. Basic but comprehensive discussion of pregnancy and childbirth by a noted expert and leader in family planning.

HAIRE, D.: *The Cultural Warping of Childbirth*, A special report of the International Childbirth Education Association, Seattle, Wash., 1972. A cross-cultural analysis of obstetric procedures; a critique of American practices.

HAMMER, SIGNE (ed.): *Women: Body and Culture*, Harper & Row, Publishers, Inc., New York, 1975. (See section IV: "Pregnancy, Birth, and Child Care".) A collection of articles dealing with the ways in which body and culture affect the sexual life of women in our society.

INGELMAN-SUNDBERG, AXEL, AND CLAES WIRSEN, WITH PHOTOGRAPHS BY LENNART NILSSON, BRITT WIRSÉN, AND CLAES WIRSÉN: *A Child Is Born*, translated by Annabelle MacMillan, Dell Publishing Co., Inc., New York, 1966. (Paperback.) Discusses prenatal development. Contains remarkable color photographs.

KARMEL, M.: *Thank You, Dr. Lamaze*, Doubleday & Company, Inc., Garden City, N.Y., 1965. Marjorie Karmel brings the Lamaze method of natural childbirth to America.

KITZINGER, S.: *The Experience of Childbirth*, Victor Gollancz Ltd., London, 1962. While the author is very much in favor of home births, she advises Americans of the risks because of the lack of a back-up system in America.

LAMAZE, F.: *Painless Childbirth*, trans. by L. R. Celestin, Henry Regnery Co., Chicago, 1970. The noted French physician explains the psychoprophylactic method of childbirth.

LEBOYER, F.: *Birth Without Violence*, Alfred A. Knopf, Inc., New York, 1975. A French physician explains the importance of focusing on the infant just born in providing for a gentle "entrance" into the world.

LILEY, H. M. I., AND BETH DAY: *Modern Motherhood*, Random House, Inc., New York, 1966. Discusses the unborn and the newborn and pregnancy and childbirth, not only from the point of view of the woman but also from that of the fetus; the development of the fetus and the young child as an individual; prenatal and postnatal care and hygiene. Includes an appendix of "practicalities" relating to diet, layette, etc. The main author is a pediatrician and mother of five children.

MEAD, M., AND N. NEWTON: "Pregnancy, Childbirth, and Outcome: A Review of Patterns of Culture and Future Research Needs," in S. A. Richardson and A. F. Guttmacher (eds.): *Childbearing: Its Social and Psychological Aspects*, The Williams and Wilkins Company, Baltimore, 1967. Fascinating explanation and description of child-rearing practices in different cultures.

MONTAGU, M. F. ASHLEY: *Prenatal Influences*, Charles C Thomas, Publisher, Springfield, Ill., 1962. A discussion of the factors that may possibly affect the fetus.

REED, SHELDON C.: *Counseling in Medical Genetics*, 2d ed., W. B. Saunders Company, Philadelphia, 1963. Material designed to answer frequently asked questions about human heredity.

RICHARDSON, S. A., AND A. F. GUTTMACHER (eds.): *Childbearing: Its Social and Psychological Aspects*, The Williams & Wilkins Company, Baltimore, 1967. An important book of readings by noted authors in the areas of sociology, psychology, and anthropology; discusses various aspects of pregnancy and childbirth.

SCHEINFELD, AMRAM: *Twins and Supertwins*, J. B. Lippincott Company, Philadelphia, 1967. Discusses the "inside view of the fascinating lives of the multiple-born"; the special characteristics, problems, and relationships of twins; suggestions for the parents of twins. "Supertwins" are triplets, etc. Includes case histories.

———: *Your Heredity and Environment*, J. B. Lippincott Company, Philadelphia, 1965. "A real encyclopedic discussion of what human beings are like and why."

SHAW, N. S.: *Forced Labor: Maternity Care in the U.S.*, Harper & Row, Publishers, Inc., New York, 1969. Based on field observation data collected by the author; the author examines the interaction of medical staff members, family members, and women in childbirth.

TANNER, JAMES M., AND GORDON RATTRAY TAYLOR: *Growth*, Time, Inc., New York, 1965. Discusses human growth and development, both prenatal and postnatal; changes at adolescence; the nature of genes and chromosomes.

WEBER, LAURA E.: *Between Us Women*, Doubleday & Company, Inc., Garden City, N.Y., 1962. Written by a woman physician for women. The objective is to answer women's questions about prenatal care, pregnancy, childbirth, and postnatal care.

WIEDENBACH, E.: *Family-Centered Maternity Nursing*, 2d ed., G. P. Putnam's Sons, New York, 1967. A text for nurses; the author outlines the goals and patient management techniques of a family-centered program.

Chapter 14

Child Rearing and Family Living

In fulfilling its functions the present-day American family is confronted by new conditions and new demands. With increased urbanization there has been extensive proliferation of the number and types of groups, or aggregates, with which an individual may be affiliated. Some of these compete with the family for time, interest, support, and loyalty. Individuals are drawn away from the family in a great variety of directions. Generalizing broadly, in earlier times there were more demands on the individual for the good of the family. Now there are more demands on the family, not only for the good of the individual, but also for the welfare of the many nonfamily clusters of which the individual is a member.

The family has several functions:

1 It is the basic, nuclear unit in society. A society is composed of individuals. These individuals, however, are

not entirely separate one from another. They occur and function as members of clusters of individuals. Some of these clusters are biologically produced and cohesive. Some are culturally produced and cohesive. The family is an outgrowth of both types of factors. The family is characterized by mutual aid and protection. It is an agency for the preservation and transmission of the cultural heritage of the group. In some cultures "family" suggests a structure different from that found in this country, but the central function is the same.

2   The family is a socially approved means for the production, nurture, rearing, and socialization of children. In our culture it is also a means of identifying children.

3   The family develops parents. As the family is a means of socializing children, so it is also a means of socializing parents. There are as great opportunities for personal growth in having children as there are in being children. In this "age of the child" there is some inclination to overlook the fact that parenthood as an end in itself is as important as parenthood as a means of child production and rearing. Parents are not merely adults who devote a part of their lives to the rearing of children who, in their turn, will devote their lives to the rearing of children, ad infinitum. Social theorists who speculate on the comparative values of child rearing in the family versus child rearing by the state often base their arguments only on the welfare of the child. They do not think of parents and forget what might happen to them under some untraditional scheme.

Despite modern-day mobility it is surprising to find how many young couples resist the forces that might move them away from their families. Most families live within a short driving distance of relatives, some within walking distance. Family sociologists have debated whether the modern nuclear family is isolated from its network of kin. Although there appears to be a trend in this direction, most families still reside near relatives, and the proximity of kin still appears to be a major consideration in determining where a couple will live. Research also points to the great reliance on relatives for services, financial assistance, and other forms of material and emotional support.

In earlier days, an individual was often appraised in part on the basis of his or her family membership. The reputation of the family was projected onto the person in a way that is now seldom found. Nowadays, especially in large metropolitan communities, there is so much acquaintance among individuals who know little or nothing about each other's families that such family-based evaluation is rarely possible. Family status is not "inherited" in the way it used to be.

One of the functions of the family is the transmission of the cultural heritage of the group from one generation to the next. But in rapidly changing times and amid the complexities and crosscurrents of present-day American society, what cultural patterns and values are to be transmitted? In the rearing of children, how insistent should parents be in adhering to the attitudes and standards of yesterday, how adaptive and permissive in accepting the shifting norms of today or anticipating the emerging patterns of tomorrow?

Contributing to this problem is the rapid evolution of new pressures being brought to bear on the processes of attitude formation and behavior pattern determination. In earlier times such pressures grew largely and more or less directly out of the life of the family and the community in which the family lived, with the addition, of course, of some ideas derived from reading, the mingling of people, immigration, travel, and social theorizing. The new and highly influential factor today is the introduction of mass media of communication that were hitherto unknown. Media such as movies, radio, and television in a sense make each family a miniature "melting pot" for the ideas, norms, and cultural patterns of the entire world, not just of the community in which the family is situated. But these media also present to the family pressures, suggestions, subtle germinal ideas, and behavior patterns which do not come from the life of the community in which the family lives but in many instances are artificial, synthetic, false, and at best presented for profit by a few individuals who are remote from the family and unconcerned about it. It is not surprising that parents wonder about child rearing and that some families fall short in performing their functions.

One function of the family which has come into prominence, but not into existence, in recent years is its contribution to the mental health of its members. The family more than any other single agency lays the foundation for mental health or illness, for good or poor adjustment to life. Therefore, in this discussion of child rearing considerable attention will be given to the role of the family in meeting children's psychological needs.

TRENDS IN PARENTHOOD

While it is still true that most Americans eventually become parents, there is an increasing number of young married women who are childless and intend to remain so. An analysis of United States Bureau of the Census sources indicates that before 1960 virtually all married women wanted children and had them, either through their own childbearing or adoption (DeJong and Sell, 1975). Since that time, however, an increase in voluntary childlessness among women under thirty has developed. This trend applies to both blacks and whites and can be tied to several social factors: an increasing age at marriage, an increase in marital disruption (and expectations that disruption may occur), increased educational attainment of women, increased school enrollment of women at the time they would be most likely to bear children, increased labor force participation of women, and the trend toward urbanization (DeJong and Sell, 1975). DeJong and Sell, in their analysis of trends in childlessness, conclude that a fundamental change is occurring and that young married women will be increasingly likely to remain voluntarily childless.

What about the overwhelming majority of couples who do become parents? A great deal of research indicates that young married couples desire fewer children than did couples in previous years, and that because of their more effective contraceptive use they are succeeding in reducing the size of their families. About three-fifths of all married women under the age of forty expect to have two or fewer children during their lifetime. This percentage is even higher for women who are now in their late teens and twenties (U.S. Bureau of the Census, *Current Population Reports*, 1975). In 1974, more than one out of

Exhibit 14-1 United States birth rates. (*Source*: U.S. Bureau of the Census, *Current Population Reports*, 1975.)

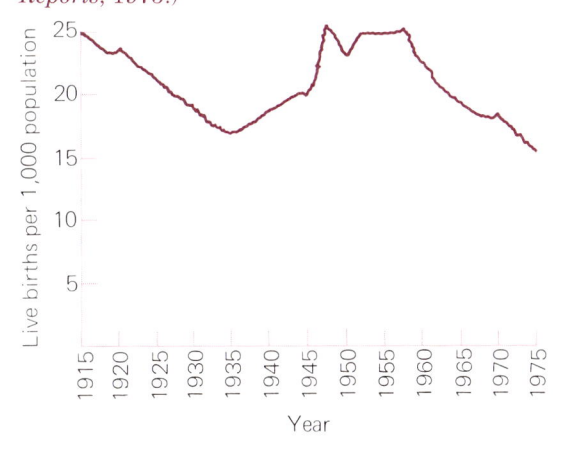

every six college-age American women stated that they expected to have only one child or none at all (U.S. Bureau of the Census, *Current Population Reports*, 1975).

The birth rate reached an all-time low in American history during the decade of the 1970s (U.S. Bureau of the Census, *Statistical Abstract*, 1976). (See Exhibit 14-1.) Although part of the dramatic decrease witnessed in the 1970s can be attributed to a delay in marriage and childbearing among some women, the greatest part of the decrease is undoubtedly due to an actual desire among women to have fewer children than did women in previous generations. It is probably safe to say that the two-child family is becoming the norm in America and will likely remain so for some years to come. There is increasing tolerance for childless marriages and one-child families. Only a very small number of young couples expect to have more than three children.

Part of the trend to smaller families may be due to the increased economic burden of child rearing. Since every decision to have an additional child means a decision to have a lower standard of living, many couples are weighing each childbearing decision very carefully. Based on an analysis of child-rearing costs (food, clothing, housing, medical care, education, transportation, recreation, and other expenses) for a typical urban two-child family in the North Central region of the United States, we can estimate that, in 1978 dollars, the eighteen-year costs of raising a child are approximately $53,000 (Pennock, 1970). If we were to include the income forgone by mothers who leave their jobs to raise children, the costs of medical care during pregnancy and childbirth, and the expense of a college education, the figure would be substantially higher.

Another trend that can be ascertained from research conducted by the census bureau is the postponement of childbearing after the wedding. In earlier times, couples were expected to begin their families shortly after they were married. If several years passed without a pregnancy, the couple was often subjected to pressures from within the family, or a fertility problem was suspected. In modern America, most couples who are not confronted with a premarital pregnancy decide to wait a while before beginning their family. This is easily accomplished through the use of effective contraception. It is not uncommon for couples to wait several years before beginning a family.

It has traditionally been true that blacks have higher fertility rates than whites, and that Roman Catholics have higher fertility rates than Protestants, who in turn have higher rates than Jews. These same comparisons also apply to the effectiveness of contraceptive use in these groups. Data from the National Fertility Studies suggest that while these differences still exist, they are diminishing. It is concluded that "American couples have changed their reproductive behavior radically . . . , adjusting their fertility goals sharply downward, and increasing substantially their ability to stop childbearing at the wanted level. All parts of the population have shared in these developments, particularly those whose performance previously deviated most from the national averages [blacks and Catholics]" (Ryder and Westoff, 1972).

FAMILY SIZE AND FAMILY INTERACTION

Although most of us have the impression that there are qualitative differences between small and large families, it is sometimes difficult to pinpoint what these differences are. Exhibit 14-2 presents a summary of the research on the relationship between family size and family interaction. It can readily be seen that small families seem to have a

Exhibit 14-2 Summary Of Variables Related To Family Size

Effects on Children	Small Families Favored	Large Families Favored
Intelligence	X	
Educational achievement	X	
Personality		
Personal ambition	X	
Independence	X	
Self-esteem	X	
Sociability	X	
Dominance	X	
Authoritarianism		X
Mental health		
Schizophrenia		X
Neurosis		X
Alcoholism		X
Behavioral disorders	X	
Physical health		
Physical development rate	X	
Obesity		X
Illness	X	
Infant mortality	X	
Satisfaction with family size		X
Effects on parents		
Mental health	X	
Physical health	X	
Time and freedom	X	
Effects on the family		
Maternal care and attention	X	
Excessive maternal concern		X
Interest in child's education	X	
Family closeness	X	
Family management		
Father involvement		X
Authoritarianism		X
Use of corporal punishment		X
Standard of living	X	
Social mobility		
Of head of household	X	
Of children	X	

Source: Adapted from Terhune, 1974.

number of advantages (Terhune, 1974). Family size seems to have an important effect on children's intelligence, educational achievement, behavioral disorders, physical development and obesity, parental interest in children's education, and on the family standard of living. Of course, these are generalizations based on a review of dozens of studies. It should not be concluded from this discussion that a particularly large family is destined to have problems. Indeed, each situation must be individually evaluated. The research suggests that *in general*, large families consistently exhibit tendencies in the direction of greater authoritarianism, both in family management by the parents and in personality development of the offspring. There is a greater reliance on corporal punishment in large families, and this appears to take its toll in parental physical and mental health. The evidence further suggests that parental interest and quality of child care diminish as family size increases (Terhune, 1974).

One factor which seems to complicate matters for large families is social class. Negative consequences due to low income and low education may result in particularly great burdens for large families. Financially, small families enjoy a better standard of living. The children receive better care and more interest from their parents. Family relations seem to be closer in small families, and these parents take a greater interest in their children. Children of small families have better social development (Terhune, 1974).

Another consequence of large family size is the amount of household work created. Exhibit 14-3 shows the total household work for families with differing numbers of children. As might be expected, the amount of household work increases as family size increases. For a family with four children, there is an average of twelve hours of household work accomplished each day.

A number of explanations have been advanced for the effects of family size on family interaction (Terhune, 1974). First, the lesser

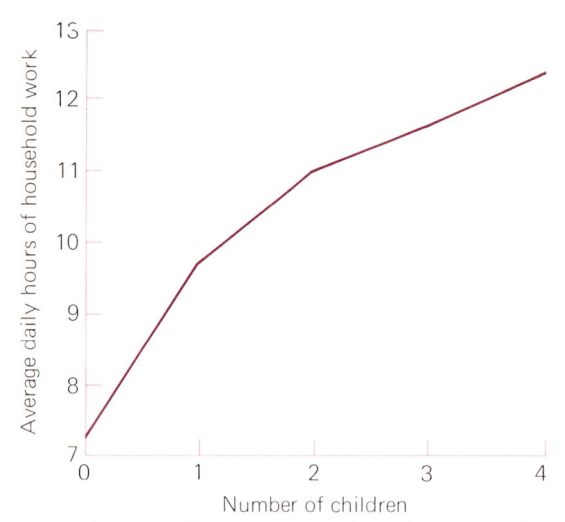

Exhibit 14-3 Family size and total household work. (Adapted from Terhune, 1974.)

amount of physical care of children in large families may account for some of the negative findings. Second, the greater focus of parental attention on each child in small families may contribute to better development, although there is some evidence that a too-concentrated focus can be an emotional stress. A third factor is the extent to which the family is likely to predominate in the world of the child. The individual from a small family is more likely to seek companionship outside the home, and this may contribute to social development.

Despite these findings, among the most important factors are parental desires and abilities. When parents *plan* and *desire* a large family (as opposed to it being a result of contraceptive accidents), some of the above effects may be mediated. Ability to afford several children is an important consideration, as is the couple's ability to manage a large family.

What about only children? There are a number of myths concerning "only children" and warnings to parents to avoid this situation. The data summarized in Exhibit 14-2 for small families include such children, and in most instances the positive effects of small families apply as much to the only-child situation as to the two-child situation. One author has concluded: "The differences between only children and those with siblings have been grossly exaggerated" (Udry, 1974). Some adults believe that only children are spoiled. If this means that they are dependent, lack ambition, and are unable to get along with others, the data do *not* confirm such a finding (Terhune, 1974). The conditions that are found in greater proportions among only children (compared to children with one sibling) are some mental health disorders, satisfaction with family size, and excessive maternal concern. In balance, in modern America the only child appears to have as good an opportunity for adequate emotional, physical, and social development as most other children from small (e.g., two-child) families, and may have better prospects for adjustment than many children from very large families.

TRANSITION TO PARENTHOOD

Parenthood is supposed to be a joyous experience, and for many couples it is so indeed (Russell, 1974). For many others, however, the joys of parenthood are at least partially overshadowed by the "crisis" it brings (LeMasters, 1957). No matter how well prepared they are, parenthood will present most couples with many challenges. It is also true, however, that this feeling of crisis usually subsides soon after the birth of the child, after the couple have adapted to their new life style (Hobbs and Cole, 1976). Much has been written by social scientists about "parenthood as crisis." Without reviewing the various debates about the extent to which couples are influenced by the birth of their first child, we would like to review some of the adjustments

Parent-child relationships change as society changes. The contemporary father shares in the life of his children; he is more than simply a disciplinarian. (*Chester Higgins, Jr., Rapho/Photo Researchers*)

that most couples must make when they become parents.

Parenthood has been described as a romantic myth. Most individuals are unprepared for parenthood and think only about its satisfactions—rarely its demands. The transition from the marital dyad to the family triad has several dimensions.

1   There tends to be a revised power structure, with the wife gaining more power in the marital relationship.

2   There is typically the loss of the wife's income from employment.

3   Extra expenses are created by the child, ranging from hospital and medical expenses to clothes, food, and furniture.

4   There tends to be a revision in the division of labor in the home.

5   Personal relationships are usually changed. For example, the amount of leisure time available decreases. Life-styles change, particularly since parental freedom and mobility is reduced.

6   There is a disruption of routines, since infants rarely conform to the parents' wishes about feeding, sleeping, and diapering.

7   There is an expansion of tasks, for example, more housekeeping.

8   Particularly with first children, parents often report anxiety about the child's welfare.

The birth of the first child represents a particularly drastic change in life-style for some women, although with increased participation in child rearing by fathers, the impact on women may decrease in the future. Research on the "transition to parenthood" indicates that men and women both report a number of personal adjustments following the birth of the first child. Some of the problems they reported are as follows (LeMasters, 1957):

MOTHERS	FATHERS
Loss of sleep	Decline in sexual response of wife
Confinement to the home	
Chronic tiredness and exhaustion	Economic pressure resulting from loss of wife's income
Reduction of social contacts	Expenditures for child
Loss of income	Worry about a second pregnancy

- Additional washing and ironing
- Long hours and a seven-day week
- Worry about being a good mother
- Decline in housekeeping standards
- Worry about increased weight after pregnancy
- Some disenchantment with the parental role

Couples need to be particularly conscious about jealousies which may develop if one spouse gives exclusive attention to the child at the expense of the other spouse. The husband especially may become jealous and feel neglected if his wife devotes all her attention to the child and none to him. Although the presence of the child will mean that the couple will have less time available for each other, they may share in some activities which involve both themselves and the child. The couple may also wish to set some time aside for themselves. This will necessitate budgeting for baby-sitters or soliciting the services of friends or relatives.

CHILD REARING

For several decades there has been so much said and written about the problems of child rearing, with much profit to be sure, that many parents have come to feel worried and harried. The pendulum of "the right way to do it" swings first one way then the other. Harassed parents try to keep pace with the changes or feel guilty when they fail to do so. Some have conflict with their own parents or parents-in-law because of differences in attitude and method that arise from generation to generation. "Pick up the child when it cries." "Don't pick up the child when it cries." "Show the child affection." "Don't show the child affection." Should there be scheduled feeding or demand feeding? Some modern young parents accept, rear, and enjoy their children with a natural but responsible casualness that would make the "patternizers" of the recent past throw up their hands in horror.

The rearing of children may be approached with greater confidence and relaxation and with less apprehension and tension if several points are recognized:

1 There is no single method of child rearing that is *the* way. Various methods are effective with different parents, different children, and under different circumstances. The method employed should be individualized. There is no overall or catchall method that applies equally well to all cases. One may readily note in observing children one knows that there may or may not be a complete correlation between quality of personality and the method of rearing which contributed to it. This generalization applies, of course, within reasonable limits and to more or less deliberately chosen methods of child rearing, not to every influence or condition under which children grow. Even when the latter is included, however, the correlation between quality of personality and the life conditions from which the personality emerged is far from complete.

2 No child is reared without some problems. The path of parent-child relationships is never perfectly smooth. It is never possible to predict in advance, and therefore to prepare for, every circumstance that will arise. Parents are called upon to do the best they can in a dynamic relationship involving ever-changing circumstances. Within these circumstances there is interaction between growing organisms each of which is in many ways unique. Much as the parents may know about children and family living through study or experience, part of the time they must "play it by ear." Study and experience are useful assets, but they are not guarantees of flawless child rearing.

Any problem that parents have with a particular child is in all probability not unique. It is almost certain to have been faced and solved—or lived with—by other parents. Sometimes an erroneous assumption of uniqueness leads parents to be unnecessarily pessimistic about a given problem.

The definition of a "problem" is ordinarily formulated by the person who has it rather than the person who is it. Parents speak of "problem children." But children refer to "problem parents." We may safely guess that there are as many of the latter as there are of the former. It depends from which side the issue is raised.

3 Usually to become seriously maladjusted a child must be subjected to a chronologically extended and circumstantially extensive distorted pattern of development. Serious maladjustment in children is not ordinarily produced by occasional, isolated parental mistakes that occur within a healthy pattern of parent-child relationships.

4 Someone has defined a child as "potential with a push." A personality has an "internal push" toward normal development, just as the body has a built-in "mechanism" which directs its changes toward physical health. One aspect of child rearing is to stay out of the way of the child's natural maturation. This does not imply letting the child "run wild." It implies only that personality develops by an "unfolding" as well as by an educative process.

5 Parents alone cannot provide everything a child needs for development. A child is reared by a multiplicity of agencies. The older the child becomes, the greater the number of these becomes. To some extent parents can control the selection of such agencies or modify their influence on the child. But the parents' possibilities in this regard are not limitless. This by no means implies lack of parental effort or concern. It does imply understanding and acceptance of the inevitable and the importance of providing a child early with a foundation of experience, learning, and security upon which such extraparental influences may be evaluated.

Children's Needs

With the above in mind let us turn our attention to some of the needs of children. Whether these are biologically or culturally determined will not be our concern. They are discussed because in the last analysis successful child rearing is the process of successfully meeting children's needs with reference to the needs of others and within the cultural framework of a given society.

In many respects the needs of children and the needs of adults are similar, at least insofar as verbal description of them is concerned. Hence in reading the following discussion of children's needs the reader may ask, "Which are also needs of adults? How can such needs be met in marriage? What contribution can one spouse make toward meeting the needs of the other?"

Some needs are universal. Others are individual. If a child's needs are not met in helpful, constructive ways, damaging, destructive ways may be resorted to in order to meet them.

Security If an infant is held and then suddenly deprived of support, it becomes terrified. This is one of human beings' partially "instinctive" reactions. It suggests that the need for security is present from the very beginning of life. "Insecurity" is used as a catchall explanation of numerous personality traits and types of behavior, especially when not all the factors in a given situation can be readily diagnosed. The concept has considerable usefulness and validity, nonetheless. Throughout life the individual does things which, according to a particular frame of reference, will produce security or avoid insecurity.

A young child's world is filled with the processes of functioning physiologically, growing, and learning. Because experiences are limited and the cumulative total is small, each separate experience constitutes a relatively larger part of the whole, so to speak, than is true with an adult. For example, eating is an insignificant part of an adult's total life activity, whereas it is a very significant part of a young child's. Similar experiences are not in the same proportion in child life as in adult life. Furthermore, both needs and behavior are more elemental in a child than in an adult. As a result, some things which adults take for granted are more fascinating, more poignant, and more meaningful to a young child and are therefore more likely to be a source of learning for the child than for the adult. In the light of this it may readily be seen that such things as feeding, fondling, cuddling, and holding a child, which an adult often mistakenly assumes are more or less incidental, may lay the groundwork for the child's feeling of security. Such experiences leave an indelible, though usually not recalled, impression on the child. Such a simple experience as being held snugly in its mother's or father's arms is one of the roots of a child's feeling of security.

A child may also develop a feeling of security through being trusted, being accepted, being recognized for achievement, and sharing in family activities and secrets, and in similar ways. Some of these will be discussed in the paragraphs which follow.

In order to have a feeling of security a child must be helped to develop it. It must emerge from activities which the parents initiate but through which the child responds to the parents and through which his or her response grows. It cannot be provided "second-hand." It cannot come through activities which the parents initiate but which the child resists or which deprive the child of the opportunity to grow. For example, parental overprotection, which is presumably designed to make the child secure, at least in the physical sense of the term, actually ultimately gives a feeling of insecurity. The reason is that when the parents are overprotective, the child is deprived of an opportunity to learn, and the parents, rather than the child, meet a present-life situation. Hence the child is not equipped to get along without the parents. Ultimately this eventuates in insecurity.

New experience In order to grow, and some would say in order to be happy, an individual needs new experience. In a way new experience and security may be at odds with each other. The individual grows and matures as he or she learns to feel secure in new experiences and new situations. It goes without saying that for some persons new experience adds zest to living. Others are content with a more nearly changeless status quo. One problem parents face in this age of passive recreation and the common question, "Where do we go?" rather than, "What do we do?" is that of how to provide a child with growth-producing new experience within limits of reasonable safety and control.

Self-preservation "Self-preservation," we say, "is the first law of life." In human beings it involves more than physical self-preservation. Self-preservation includes also preservation of the "self," the "I," which makes every person different from every other. Each person has a private world, partly of his or her own making, which that individual seeks to preserve and protect but may alter as interpretations of experience change. If life is found to be too complex, the person may manufacture an unreal "world" which, from that person's point of view, is a more satisfactory explanation of experience than is the world of reality.

Love The individual has a need to love and to be loved. In early years the individual's love in both the giving and the receiving is self-centered. As the individual matures, love more and more reflects concern for the "other than self." Children learn to love through being loved. But this does not happen through always being the center of attention and the recipient of love. Children must learn concern for others, for without such concern they cannot learn to love. All of us know of cases in which children have become so accustomed to receiving love without learning to give it that they remain self-centered all their lives.

Both boys and girls seek and need affection from parents of both genders. In our culture the major breakdown in this four-way giving and receiving of affection is often to be found in the relationship of father and son, especially after the latter has ceased to be a small child. The traditional standard of manliness in this country discourages kissing as an expression of affection between two postpubertal males. Some fathers are so sensitive to this prohibition that they are reluctant to kiss even very young sons.

But there are ways other than kissing through which father and son may show affection for one another. A paternal arm across a boy's shoulders, a slap on the back, or a son's hand upon his father's arm may express deep and warm affection. Some fathers and sons find a partial solution to the problem of expressing affection in acceptable masculine ways through what might be termed a playful or nonthreatening negative rather than a direct, positive approach, for example, wrestling and "horseplay." Some have worked out a special vocabulary of words which, though ordinarily used in a derogatory sense, become terms of endearment when used with each other, with a special meaning known to father and son. There are also, however, some fathers and sons who have retained kissing as an expression of affection even into the sons' adulthood. It is more likely to occur in private than in public. But the important point is that in some cases it does occur.

Belonging Human beings need to identify with others and have a sense of belonging to a group. The first and most natural group to which anyone belongs is the family. When this sense of belonging is undermined, a feeling of insecurity is produced and persons other than family members may be turned to for the satisfaction of needs. Unwanted children often exhibit such behavior. In disciplining a child, it is important that the impression be given that it is the act and not the person that is rejected by the parent.

As a child matures, affiliations with groups other than the family are formed. This is especially apparent in the teens, when the pressure of the peer group becomes almost irresistible. At this stage of development an individual is inclined to give more weight to the judgments of contemporaries than to those of parents. This may be carried to such an extreme that parents' judgments are given no weight at all. But if parents do not understand this phase of their child's development, they may accentuate the very process they deplore. The young adolescent is under tremendous pressure to conform to the ways of the peer group. If parents do not make some concessions in this process, they may "lose" the child completely. Perhaps the wisest plan is to make concessions on less important things and "hold the line" on a few essentials. In doing so, parents may well try to distinguish between those things the child wants to do which may be damaging or dangerous and those which are merely different from the way the parents think they should be done.

An individual can best achieve a sense of belonging by accepting responsibility in and for the group. In present-day America this is not always easy to arrange in the family. It may be accomplished, however, by such means as participation in household tasks, sharing family recreation and pleasures, and, within limits of understanding, sharing in family problems and troubles. In some cases parents deprive a child of an opportunity to share in the total life of the family by shielding him or her from the unpleasant aspects of family living.

Communication Human beings are

communicating mammals, and the individual's life is inextricably interwoven with those of others through communication. One aspect of belonging is communication. The fact that each person lives in a private world, as mentioned earlier, makes communication incomplete, but there is no way to solve this problem entirely. A problem that parents can solve is that which arises when they themselves arbitrarily thwart a child's communication because of their own lack of interest in what the child is trying to say or because they feel that the content of the communication is inappropriate, as, for example, when a child is rebuffed for asking a question regarding reproduction. Once the door of communication is closed, the latch and hinges soon become rusty, and in many cases it becomes difficult if not impossible to reopen it.

Keeping the door of communication open, however, is not always accomplished without problems. One father complained that his children had learned that he disciplined them for their misdeeds less severely or not at all when they told the truth. He felt that at times they "worked" him. But in weighing the pros and cons, he concluded that keeping the door of communication open, retaining good rapport with his children, and in this way having greater opportunity to help them think through their behavior and develop self-discipline were all more important than his disciplining them in every instance, even if they did "work" him on occasion.

Sense of achievement Typically, human beings have a desire for recognition. In children recognition and a sense of achievement are closely related. Mature persons more readily separate them. If children do not get the recognition they need under desirable auspices, they may seek it under undesirable auspices.

Because of this combination of needs—namely, for achievement and for recognition—the typical individual likes to feel useful. Sometimes helping a child to feel useful increases rather than decreases the work of the parent, for example, when a little girl wants to help her mother bake a cake. But it is worth an investment of time and effort, for in feeling useful the child not only satisfies a need per se but also strengthens ties with the family group.

Reaching out Human beings are the only organisms that reach out beyond their immediate experience. They do this in numerous ways, two of which are creative imagination and religious faith. As an individual matures, such reaching out should mature. One factor in the extension and maturing of faith is the process of probing the unknown with penetrating questions. When a child questions what parents assume to be established truth, the parents may well be assured that, if it is truth, the child, like themselves, will come to accept it; if it is not truth after all, the child has the right to discover this. Truth can be challenged, but it cannot be threatened. The more vigorously it is attacked, the more firmly established it becomes.

Children's creative imagination is sometimes not so carefully channeled as that of adults; and the children themselves cannot always distinguish between the imagined and the real. This leads some parents to confuse imaginings with dishonesty. They inflict punishment for the latter and eventually cripple the former.

In American culture conformity is considered a virtue. In some cases in which recognition and prestige are given to outstanding individuals, it is quantitative difference rather than qualitative difference that is recognized. The outstanding individual is "like everyone else, only more so." For example, the high school valedictorian, the beauty queen, the best of this or that is often basically a conformist; the individual may exhibit no true originality, no true creativity.

Parents are not free of pressure toward conformity where their children are concerned. Psychological tests, personality rating scales, tables of one sort or another, norms for children of a given age, the grade level system in schools, and so on, though useful, subtly suggest conformity. Hence parents sometimes sacrifice individuality by molding the child so that conformity rather than the release of creativity results. This does not imply letting the child become so out of step with peers that a social misfit is produced or personality becomes maladjusted. It does imply the development of the creativity inherent in every normal personality.

When we compare the number of young children who have insatiable curiosity, make crude but creative works of art, play-act, make up stories about imaginary characters, sing songs they have composed, beat out a rhythm, or dance spontaneously with the number of adults who are creative in similar ways, we realize that somewhere between childhood and adulthood conformity has overshadowed creativity and originality.

Growth and development We said earlier in this chapter that personality develops by an "unfolding" as well as by an educative process. This implies that the individual goes through stages of development. Within broad limits these stages are similar for everybody. Not all, however, pass through the same stage or reach the same point at exactly the same age. Each person has a unique pattern and rate of growth.

Generalizing somewhat, we can say that each stage of growth is typified by certain forms of behavior. For example, most children creep before they walk. Many suck their thumbs in their early years. Sometimes behavior at a given stage seems to the parents to represent retrogression, or backsliding, compared with a previous stage. For example, some children develop reasonably satisfactory table manners in their early years but revert to infantile eating habits temporarily at about the onset of adolescence, much to the despair of their parents. It would help parents to realize that, unless there are special factors at work to produce something in the nature of a fixation in the child, stage-typical behavior is ordinarily not habit-forming. This means that stage-typical behavior is something *into* which the child grows but *out of* which he or she also grows. Consider, for example, thumb-sucking. Parents torture their children with foul-tasting drugs, mechanical devices, threats, and punishment and torture themselves with concern and anxiety over this practice. Unless, as is true in some cases, the child is pressing thumb against palate in such a way that front teeth are pushed forward, the practice tends to be harmless. Almost all children grow out of it. Being stage-typical behavior, it is usually not habit-forming.

One of the reasons that parents often persist, even in the face of continual failure, in trying to alter stage-typical behavior through instruction, nagging, threat, punishment, and a free exuding of their own tension and anxiety is their fear that whatever is permitted in early years will continue throughout life. If the child runs out of the house unclothed, they fear exhibitionism. If a little boy wears his sister's clothes while play-acting, the parents wonder whether he will become a transvestite. If a child leaves toys lying around, the parents fear carelessness in leaving clothes strewn around after marriage. In many cases, it is not so much leaving things around at an early age that makes an adult careless but rather the fact that someone, either through constant haranguing or through picking up the things, teaches the child to have no responsibility in this regard, since somebody else will assume the responsibility.

The direction of development is determined in part by factors within the individual. But also development is determined in part by the pattern and framework of life into which the individual grows. This framework is provided partly by the family pattern. In a given respect a child may not at first conform to this family pattern. Since, however, the direction of growth is not predetermined, growth may occur in one direction as readily as in another. For example, a little child has no appreciation of courtesy. If the family provides a pattern of courtesy, the child is likely to become courteous. If, on the other hand, the family provides a pattern of habitual lack of courtesy, the child is likely to become discourteous. In order to accomplish the former, the family must begin and continue to provide the pattern of courtesy even while the child is too immature to be expected to exhibit the courtesy of an adult.

If parents are not consistent in establishing the pattern into which they expect their offspring to grow, it is not surprising when the child disappoints them. For example, some parents see no need to be courteous to a little child. Yet they become irritated when the child is discourteous to them. Some parents see nothing wrong in telling a child untruths. Some thoughtlessly embarrass a child in front of companions. Some are impatient when a child wants to talk with them and they say they do not have time to talk. Then when the child is reluctant to leave play when the parents want to talk, they consider this disobedience. Sometimes parents inflict punishment for honestly reporting some misdemeanor. Then they wonder why the child becomes dishonest. Some betray confidence. Then they wonder why the child ceases to confide in them. Some assure the child that he or she is trusted, then spy.

Inconsistency is also apparent in those instances in which parents disagree on the handling of a child. The child soon learns to "play" one parent against the other or to seek the approval of the parent who is more lax in giving permissions or meting out punishment.

Learning is the result of three processes, namely, experience, maturation, and instruction. Parents sometimes fail to distinguish between the last two processes, with the result that they expect learning through instruction before, through maturation, a point has been reached where this is possible. Instruction is to no avail until learning readiness has been achieved through growth. For example, a child aged six months could not be taught to read no matter how good the instruction. If instruction is started too early, that is, before learning readiness has been established, it will be ineffective; but if it is continued after readiness has been established, learning may occur quickly. It would probably have occurred by about the same time, however, if instruction had been delayed until readiness was established. Some things are learned without instruction—merely through maturation.

Being an individual No two persons are identical, not even "identical" twins. Each has a unique rate and pattern of growth, allowing for broad similarities at different stages of development, as mentioned above. Each has particular abilities and aptitudes. Yet these facts do not keep some parents from trying to make offspring alike, or from seeking to make one into a replica of a parent, or from attempting to squeeze a square peg into a round hole. Wise parents set their expectations according to a child's ability to achieve, not according to the achievements of other children or according to some arbitrary or unreasonable parent-imposed standard. For example, among the college-educated there is often such a premium put upon academic accomplishment that a child may be forced to attempt success in a field for which he or she has no apparent aptitude. A boy who might do very well as a mechanic is forced through parental pressure to work for a university degree, with the result that the son becomes an unhappy, maladjusted failure who is subtly rejected by the parents.

A similar problem is found in the situation where parents expect a child to enter a given occupation because of family tradition or parental leanings, or to serve as a vicarious success for a parent who was prevented by ability or circumstance from entering the occupation of choice. College and university counselors meet many of this type of student—a kind of living human sacrifice to thwarted parental ambitions.

Consider both the parental attempt to squeeze the square peg into the round hole and the effect of the parents' effort to keep their son immature in the following statement by a university senior, aged twenty-three, who was on scholastic probation. Said he, "I want to go into teaching. But my father is a physician, and his father was a physician. My parents insist that I go into medicine. I'm not interested in medicine, and I'm having trouble in my science and math courses. Mama says that if I don't make my grades, she won't let me use the car."

If a child is to be an individual, agreement with parents on everything cannot be expected. The right to make judgments, within, of course, limits of ability and safety, as mentioned earlier, must be recognized. Also, there should be no penalty for something that cannot possibly be controlled. Sometimes, for example, there is discrimination against the eldest child in the family or a less attractive child, or there is discrimination because of gender classification. For instance, the parents discipline a son severely but are more lenient with a daughter. One of the most devastating experiences in growing up is to be a second-class citizen in the family because parents consider another child their favorite.

A child is a child, not a small adult, and should not be expected to act like an adult. A child may be intelligent, but this fact does not necessarily result in reasonable behavior under given circumstances. Behavior cannot be expected to change suddenly merely because someone older suggests change. A child does not have, indeed cannot have, the foresight of an adult. A child is naturally selfish and cannot be expected suddenly to exhibit adult altruism.

Independence A child, like a ship, is to be launched. Some parents are like the proverbial man who carefully built a boat in his basement only to find that the boat was too large to pass through the basement door and hence never reached the water. Launching a child into adult independence is a prolonged, carefully planned process. It necessitates as much development on the part of the parent as on the part of the child. Many a parent is a "good" parent of an infant but remains the parent of an infant psychologically even when the offspring has grown to adulthood. The result is actual or attempted "apron strings." When the time comes that a child can get along without parents as an independent young adult, the parents may well take pride in a job well done. Yet some parents make this time one of sorrow.

Facing reality Insofar as it may be safe to do so, a child may be allowed to learn from experience rather than from instruction. One needs to learn to face the consequences of one's acts. For example, some individuals learn about the use of money only by spending money unwisely and thus being deprived of something. Children are sometimes allowed to evade reality in such a way that they are started on the road to emotional maladjustment; for instance, they may be permitted to rationalize, use alibis, or shirk responsibility to such an extent that they assume this is the way life is to be lived.

Discipline Children need discipline. It is one method of learning. It can provide a sense of security when it defines limitations, that is, the framework within which a child may operate. Many a parent has had the experience of being "pushed" to the point of exasperation. This is when the parent "blows up," the air is cleared, and the child settles down and accepts a definition of the area of operation as well as whatever limitations are to be observed. In this way peace and harmony are restored. Discipline can give a sense of security when it helps the child to get past previous misbehavior and to get rid of the sense of guilt growing out of it.

To fulfill its function, discipline need not always be negative; it may also be positive. In fact, whenever possible, it *should* be positive. One of the common errors in any area of life where one person seeks to modify the behavior of another is the assumption that the elimination of small faults results in the production of large virtues. A series of "don'ts" may be necessary on occasion, but it does not necessarily follow that in place of the behavior modified by the "don'ts" will be put behavior that is positive and constructive.

In order to accomplish its purpose and to be appreciated by a child, punishment must be fair and not too harsh. It should also be appropriate to the misdeed. Sometimes parents make a child dislike what is fundamentally a good thing because they use that good thing as punishment. For example, one of the greatest satisfactions in life is that which comes from work. Work, providing that it is honest and useful, deserves to be respected. If, however, parents impose work on a child as a means of punishment, it is not surprising that the child may grow to dislike it. This is especially true of certain household chores.

Nagging is ineffective as discipline for several reasons. It permits the child to evade the consequences of behavior with an easily ignored tongue-lashing as punishment, and immunization to the tongue-lashing may readily be developed. Nagging exposes the vulnerable spots of the nagger, providing an effective weapon for penalizing that person. It "tells" the child what is annoying to the parent. If, then, the child wants to annoy the parent, the means for doing it have been made clear.

To spank or not to spank—that is the perennial question in any discussion of discipline. On the one hand are those who deplore any suggestion of corporal punishment or penalizing physical contact between parent and child. On the other hand are those who consider spanking a form of communication. Some children, it is said, "respond" only to spanking. Arguments are presented on either side.

Evidence (Sears, Maccoby, and Levin, 1957) indicates that spanking often does not accomplish what it is intended to accomplish. Its good effects may be temporary; its harmful effects may be permanent. It is not a substitute for true discipline because it involves learning through fear rather than through trust. It is negative rather than positive. Not all children respond to spanking in the same way. Some are humiliated and embittered by it and become resentful. The parent-child relationship may break down.

On the other hand, many parents report good results with mild spanking which is administered fairly and only after verbal admonitions have failed to produce a change in behavior. In this instance, it is important that the child understand why he or she is being spanked, that the spanking be administered promptly, and that it not be harsh or abusive. If parents use spanking, it is important that they provide a context for its use. They must be careful to teach a child to differentiate between striking playmates and similar violence from the "violence" involved in spanking.

It is not uncommon for a mother to tell her young child that he or she will be disciplined when the father returns home at the end of the day. This is likely to be an ineffective and ill-advised method of punishment, since the father is continually put in the position of the ogre, and since the misbehavior is so removed from the punishment that the child may have forgotten what it was, remembering only the punishment. Punishment and misbehavior must always be tied together in order to have meaning to the child. This also suggests that spanking infants is of no value and may be very damaging. Some parents discipline babies, thinking that they are capable of modifying their baby's behavior by doing so. Infants are not mature enough to respond to such discipline and may become terrified of the parents as a result of it.

Spanking is often more a means of relieving parental feelings than an effective means of training a child. In some families it is a last resort, implying that it occurs when a parent is "at the end of the rope" because of tension, fatigue, or frustration. Spanking is often a reflection of ignorance; the parent knows no better form of discipline. It may be an expression of rejection of the child by the parent or an outgrowth of aggression. Spanking should not be the principal means of discipline used. If used at all, it should only supplement more verbally oriented discipline.

Parents, being human, have their "weak moments." In the complexities of family living they are not always free of fatigue and tension and do not always govern their every act by carefully considered theory. A happily

Discipline of children is a concern of parents beyond the early years of development. Parent-child conflict can be particularly troublesome during adolescence. (Julie Ann Low)

married couple may have a bitter quarrel, knowing that in so doing they fall short of their own ideal of marriage. They regret what has happened and try to avoid it in the future. In like manner a parent may have an occasional similar experience with a child. It is important that the parent realize that spanking falls short of the ideal. To assume that spanking is the *best* form of punishment is like assuming that quarreling is the best way to achieve adjustment in marriage.

Acceptance Overlapping several of the items already mentioned but deserving separate mention is the need for acceptance. Each individual wants to be accepted for what he or she is, if possible for what the self is conceived to be. Such acceptance is found in its purest form in the family, where a child is loved by parents without comparison with other children and without regard to whether or not love is deserved. Lack of such unqualified acceptance—for example, in the case of the mentally retarded—creates one of the most critical problems of childhood.

There is another aspect of acceptance, namely, acceptance of oneself. This implies learning to live with one's limitations. It also implies acceptance of one's gender classification and its attendant role. An individual cannot, of course, accept his or her own classification without simultaneously accepting the classification of the other gender. In learning to accept gender classification the individual develops a concept of gender role. Somehow, too, fitting sexual impulses into the social pattern must be learned. This suggests the need for education for sexuality.

EDUCATION FOR SEXUALITY

Nature and Objectives

Because of the traditionally narrow definition of "sex education" a new term, "education for sexuality," is coming into use. Education for sexuality is the process of teaching an individual to understand and accept self as a whole person and as such to relate self to other people in a healthy, constructive, and meaningful manner. It includes learning to fit sexuality into a satisfactory societal pattern. One of the central objectives of child rearing is the achievement of a balance between socialization and conformity to the societal structure on the one hand, and individual freedom, growth, and realization of innate potential on the other. Nowhere is the need for such a balance more apparent than in connection with education for sexuality.

In order to achieve the above, the individual needs factual information, to be sure. But much more than factual information, especially that minimum regarding genital anatomy and physiology commonly referred to as "the facts of life," is needed. The individual needs to understand sex not as a limited facet of life but rather as an integral part of life. In order to do this, in addition to acquiring sound factual information, healthy attitudes must be developed, values must be carefully weighed, meaning must be thoughtfully imputed to sexual behavior, and creative interpersonal relationships must be established. Whatever values are accepted relative to sex need to be consistent with the value system upon which individual life is being built and with the value structure of society.

Time to begin "When should I start to give my child sex education?" is a question often asked by parents. Actually, there is no time to "start," just as there is not a specific time to start to teach a child to be honest or to be a good citizen. We assume that the teaching of honesty and citizenship will be an integral part of the child's learning from birth onward. So it should be with education for sexuality.

If we may stretch a point for emphasis, we may say that education for sexuality begins before birth—not in the sense of verbal communication with the fetus, but in the sense of education for sexuality's having its roots in the attitudes of the parents toward the process by which the child was conceived.

Communication versus telling Some parents assume that they can avoid giving a child education for sexuality by telling nothing about sex. They assume that lack of verbal instruction means lack of communication. The opposite is true. When the parents give the child no verbal instruction, they communicate that sex is a topic so mysterious, so unpalatable, and so difficult to discuss—for them—that information had better be sought elsewhere.

Parental behavior in the home is also a means of communication whether or not anything specific is said about sex. The child soon learns through observation that there are differences between the genders both as to anatomy and as to role. Observation as to whether the parents are affectionate with one another, whether they accept their roles with enthusiasm or resistance, and a host of similar items are unavoidable. Such observations constitute part of education for sexuality.

Bodily Exposure

A young child takes anatomy for granted, at least until taught otherwise. Sooner or later genital organs are discovered. Such discovery is part of exploration of the world. To a little child everything encountered is new and interesting. Things and experiences no longer interesting to adults are fascinating to a young child because the entire world is new and is explored with all the equipment Nature provides for sensing and perceiving. Insofar as it is possible, the child uses all senses in observation. Touching the soft fur of a rabbit is responded to with exuberant delight. Listening to the ticking of a watch is done with rapt attention. Putting anything movable into the mouth strikes germ-conscious parents with horror. Curiosity is insatiable. Performing simple experiments, such as holding the family cat by the tail to see what happens, is not uncommon.

In the course of such observation and experimentation genital organs are discovered. The next step is to learn more about them, how they are constructed, what sensations occur when they are handled. When it is learned that there are two types of people in the world, male and female, interest and curiosity are extended to them. Since all normal children have such curiosity as to how boys and girls are constructed, it is not unusual for two children of opposite gender to make observations simultaneously. To them such a thing is as natural as tasting a new food.

Let us imagine two children, a boy and a girl, four years of age. They are playmates. They are curious about the differences in their genital organs. In a corner of the garage they set about satisfying their curiosity. By happenstance the mother of the little girl enters the garage to get something out of storage at just the moment that the two children are observing each other's genital organs. The mother becomes very upset. She sends the little boy home with an excited stream of invective following him like a swarm of angry bees. She hurries her daughter into the house. The little girl cannot avoid getting the impression that something terrible has occurred, that her mother is deeply disturbed, that she herself has committed an act which, at least in her mother's judgment, classifies her as "bad." There are girls who reach marriageable age still bearing the scars of such an experience.

How much better it would have been if the little girl's mother had treated the situation as natural and inoffensive. Perhaps the children need some help in understanding what is acceptable behavior in our society, what is "family" and what is not. But they are not to be condemned, frightened, and punished for adult fears and inhibitions projected onto the natural behavior of childhood. They are not to be traumatized through shock into acquiring a sense of guilt that is felt first only by the parent.

In connection with the question of bodily exposure on the part of family members within the home, opinions differ widely. There are parents who believe that every effort should be made to protect all family members, especially parents, from even the casual gaze of others. Such parents dress behind closed doors, bathe behind carefully inculcated "no trespassing" warnings, and become upset at accidental exposure. On the other hand there are parents who treat bodily exposure within the home as natural and to be taken for granted by family members. They draw a distinction, however, between observation of genital anatomy and observation of sexual behavior. When all the pros and cons are considered, and assuming that the parents do not make a cult of nudity, it seems clear that the more bodily exposure within the home is taken to be natural, the healthier the child's attitude toward such exposure will be. When parents are overly meticulous in preventing children from observing their bodies, the children's curiosity is increased, or at least certainly not decreased, and is more likely to lead to attempts to satisfy it outside the home under auspices unknown to parents and in situations permitting no questions to be asked.

Bodily exposure in the home can be just as "forced" as artificial barriers can be. There are times when any individual, child or adult, seeks privacy. Such privacy is to be respected by all family members. But an occasional demand for privacy is not the same as an overall fear of bodily exposure.

One problem giving concern to many women, even some of those who are relatively uninhibited in the matter of bodily exposure within the home, is that of whether a child, especially a boy, should be permitted to see

Children are naturally curious about pregnancy and childbirth. Sharing a new baby before its birth may be the first step toward family unity after the baby is born. (Ken Heyman)

the mother unclothed when she is wearing external menstrual protection. Menstruation is as natural as any other bodily function. In these presumably modern times there is no need to read into it the connotation of mystery, shame, and uncleanliness that was associated with the process in the past. Sooner or later the child will learn about menstruation. If the mother is sufficiently objective about it to permit him to do so, he can understand and accept it without emotion or undue curiosity even at an early age.

Children's Questions

There is widespread agreement to the effect that a child's questions concerning sex and reproduction should be answered, not evaded.

In no way, either by act or implication, should the child be made to feel that an honest question about something which is natural is inappropriate or "bad." One reason for which some parents avoid a child's questions, with a show of emotion on the part of the parent, is that the parent, not the child, is embarrassed to discuss the subject. To cover up this embarrassment the parent repulses the child with an assertion that that sort of question should not be asked.

Before a parent can answer a child's question intelligently, what has been asked must be ascertained. The real question may not be readily apparent in the verbal statement of it. This is illustrated in the well-worn story of the child who rushed up to the mother and said, "Mother, where did I come from?" The mother thought, "This is it," and launched into a long, previously prepared dissertation on reproduction. The child tried to interrupt but the mother would not permit it. When the mother finally finished, feeling that at last she had done successfully what she had long anticipated with apprehension, the child exclaimed, "But Mother, that's not what I meant. Billy down the street says he came from Chicago, and I wanted to know where I came from."

In answering a child's question, readiness to understand must be considered. A preschool child is not prepared to understand an explanation that would be more appropriate for a medical student. Only as much as can be absorbed needs to be told at the time. One is reminded of the little girl who said, "I don't like to ask Mother questions like that because she always tells me too much." If the parent keeps the door of communication open, the same questions will be asked over and over again as the child grows older. Each time further detail can be given. No matter how many times the same question is repeated, it should be answered.

There are some persons who feel that a child's questions concerning sex or reproduction should be answered immediately upon being asked. In general this is a satisfactory working principle. But in the complexity of family living it is not always possible to meet ideal standards, and parents should not feel guilty or inadequate, as some do, when they fall short, especially if the overall parent-child relationship is healthy. For instance, if we may exaggerate to make a point, a father need not feel guilty if he does not stop carving the Thanksgiving turkey and let the guests wait to be served just so he can answer the question of a child who has chosen this inopportune moment to ask why babies have fathers. He can tell the child that he will discuss the question later. Then he keeps his word and does discuss it later.

Vocabulary

There are different schools of thought regarding what vocabulary is best in teaching children about sex and reproduction. At one extreme are the advocates of technical, scientific, medical terminology. Every anatomical part, every physiological process is to be called by the correct technical term. At the other extreme are the adherents of the "do-do, da-da, tinkle, plunk" point of view. Everything is to be described in the most evasive type of "baby talk" so that camouflage of the natural is as nearly complete as human ingenuity in manufacturing new vocabulary will permit. Sometimes this process is carried to such an extreme that communication is limited to parent and child because no one else knows the meaning of the terms the two of them have concocted.

Neither of these extremes is entirely consistent with ordinary day-to-day living in our culture. Adults do not refer to every anatomical part and every physiological process by its correct technical term at all times regardless of circumstance. Neither do they use only substitute vocabulary. Common parlance represents a compromise, a combination of technical and substitute vocabulary.

The fundamental problem is one of communication, of imparting information, of imputing correct meaning, of facing rather than evading facts. There is also the correlative problem of avoiding giving the child a false impression. One of the commonest instances of such a false impression is using an unpalatable term to mean menstruation.

Masturbation

The day is past when masturbation was referred to as "self-abuse," just as nocturnal emissions are no longer termed "pollutions." Masturbation is such a widespread phenomenon of childhood and adolescence that attitudes toward it should be evaluated with this fact in mind. Studies show that in males masturbation is reported as being just short of universal, and an appreciable majority of young females are reported to have engaged in the practice at some time.

In view of the natural inclination to explore both their environment and their bodies, most children sooner or later discover that their genital organs are endowed with special sensitivity and that in the stimulation of these organs pleasurable sensation can be produced. If the child does not become acquainted with this fact through curiosity, it is likely to be learned from other children.

Contrary to common assumption, there is no evidence to prove that masturbation per se is physically harmful. Masturbation, as such, which involves only sexual self-stimulation, should be carefully distinguished from the dangerous practice of a girl's inserting some object into her vagina either in an attempt at masturbation or merely through curiosity. Among objects removed from girls' vaginas have been hairpins, safety pins, crayons, paper clips, beads, sand, stones, marbles, shells, nuts, corks, parts of toys, coins, and even a plastic pencil (Schneider and Geary, 1971). Anyone would agree that insertion of anything sharp or unclean is dangerous; and physicians are not infrequently called upon to remove such objects, sometimes after injury has caused infection or hemorrhage.

Masturbation may become psychologically damaging to the degree to which the child is led to develop a sense of guilt associated with it. Such a sense of guilt is instilled by parents or others who appraise the practice in terms of sin or immorality.

Parents have been known to try to prevent a child, especially a son, from masturbating by threatening the child with consequences that the parents know will not follow but which place upon the child an unbearable burden of fear and guilt. For example, one mother told her young son that, if he persisted in masturbating, his genital organs would fall off. Another told her son that masturbation would make him insane. A couple seen in counseling threatened to take their four-year-old daughter to the hospital to have her clitoris removed if she did not stop rubbing herself against the living-room couch. Such untruths and threats can do a child incalculable harm.

"What should I do if I discover that my child masturbates?" is a common question asked by parents. There are a number of things such parents might do.

1 Relax. The child will do no harm.

2 Do not make an issue of it. Do not "read into" it something which is not there. Do not connect in the child's mind the act of masturbation with parental emotional upset, threat, and condemnation.

3 Recognize that childhood masturbation tends to fall into the category of stage-typical behavior, which does not ordinarily result in permanent habits over which the individual has no control. Most persons modify its frequency and practice it through choice subject to voluntary control. They control it; it does not control them. It does not

dominate their lives, as parents often fear it will.

4 Sometimes masturbation is a symptom of a problem which does call for parental attention. For example, if a child masturbates excessively because of boredom and loneliness and has learned that masturbation is something that can be done with pleasure and alone, the provision of companionship and interesting activities may meet a need and make masturbation less "necessary." A counselor can be consulted if the parents feel a problem exists.

5 Do not drive the practice "under cover" by threat of punishment. If a child is inclined to masturbate, a time and place to do it will be found. If parents threaten the child for doing it in one place about which they know, the child will find another that is less likely to be discovered by them.

6 Do not expect a child to discontinue a pleasurable practice by an act of will, a level of determination and self-discipline that would do credit to an adult.

7 Keep the door of communication open. There is no reason why a child should not be able to discuss masturbation with parents just as any other type of behavior might be discussed. Such discussion should be permitted, not forced. The child, rather than the parents, should take the initiative, though the parents might suggest the possibility of discussion. Children in some families do take such initiative because parents have set up no barrier between themselves and the child. A child who voluntarily discusses masturbation with parents pays them a profound compliment. A child can hardly be expected to take the initiative in discussing with parents something that he or she knows in advance they will condemn.

Education for Sexuality Is Unavoidable

As suggested earlier in this chapter, education for sexuality is unavoidable. Parents cannot avoid giving a child education for sexuality by avoiding verbal instruction relative to sex. A child learns through other channels besides that of verbal instruction. There is a difference between instruction and communication. Parents' choice is not between education for sexuality and no education for sexuality. Their choice is between good education and poor education. No matter what they do or do not do, say or do not say, the child receives his or her first, and sometimes most indelible, education for sexuality from them.

FAMILY DEVELOPMENT

The family is a dynamic institution. It changes in slow, evolutionlike fashion as part of overall cultural change. Each family, too, is dynamic. It changes as the number, ages, needs, and behavior of family members change and as the family as a group adapts itself to fluid circumstances. No matter where the family is found, in whatever area, class, or culture, at whatever period in history, certain broad similarities are to be observed in the stages through which it passes, just as there are broad similarities in the stages through which individuals pass in their development from infancy to old age. This universal similarity among families has given rise to the concept of the *family life cycle*. The stages of this cycle overlap but are nonetheless distinguishable, much as the stages in the development of an individual overlap but are distinguishable; for example, infancy, childhood, adolescence, adulthood, middle age, and so on may be thought of as stages of development, even though each merges imperceptibly into the next and there is no clear-cut line of demarcation between them. In order for a family to move successfully through the several stages of the family life cycle, it must complete the *developmental tasks* at each stage. A developmental task, in the life of an individual or a family, is a task which arises at a given period of life, the successful completion of which leads to happiness and to success with later tasks, while the failure to complete it leads to unhappiness, social disapproval, and difficulty with later tasks (Havighurst, 1953).

Duvall (1971) discusses the several stages of the family cycle and the developmental tasks to be completed at each stage. The following is a very much condensed version of that discussion.

1 *The beginning family: establishment phase.* This stage starts with the wedding and continues until the first pregnancy. The developmental tasks of this stage include the establishment of a home and a pattern of living together as a couple and as members of an extended family and community.

2 *The beginning family: expectant phase.* This stage starts with the awareness of pregnancy and continues until the birth of the first child. The tasks of this stage include the reorganization of the home, the budget, the couple's various interpersonal relationships, and their philosophy of life to prepare for the arrival of the baby.

3 *The childbearing family.* This stage begins with the birth of the first child and continues until this child is thirty months old. Developmental tasks include adapting living arrangements to the needs of a young child. (Some refer to this process as "child-proofing" the home.) They also include meeting new expenses, reworking patterns of husband-wife responsibility, establishing new systems of communication and new interpersonal relationships with each other and with relatives, and fitting into the community as a young family.

4 *The family with preschool children.* This stage involves the couple learning to rear their children at the same time that they continue to develop as a couple, meeting new costs and new responsibilities.

5 *The family with school-age children.* This stage involves such developmental tasks as helping children to grow, providing for each family member's needs, learning to cooperate together as a family, and relating the family to a community.

6 *The family with teen-agers.* In this stage the needs of all members put new demands upon the family. Sometimes needs conflict. New patterns of money usage and communication must be worked out. Family responsibilities may be shared in a new way. The husband and wife, as well as each child, have need for continued development as persons. The parents also are called upon to develop a point of view consistent with teen-age values and activities.

7 *The family as a launching center.* This stage marks the beginning of family contraction. During this stage the children are prepared for leaving home to become independent and to establish new families. The parents must prepare themselves for this and for a renewal of their relationships as a couple.

8 *The family in the middle years.* In this stage the couple are called upon to readjust their living conditions, to adapt themselves to the "empty nest," to develop new, or pursue already established, interests and friendships. During this stage many couples draw closer together.

9 *The aging family.* This stage involves making satisfactory living arrangements, learning to live on retirement income, maintaining meaningful contacts with friends, children, and grandchildren, providing for illness, developing a philosophy that will enable the individual to face bereavement, and finding new meanings and reaffirming old meanings in life.

Our purpose in mentioning this succession of stages in the family life cycle with the developmental tasks of each stage has been to emphasize the importance of looking ahead. To make family life successful, parents as well as children must develop and mature. A "good" parent is actually a series of "good" parents, each having different responsibilities and performing different functions at various levels of development. Preparation for marriage means more than preparation for a wedding and for the first part of marriage. It means preparation for a way of life that in the great majority of cases characterizes a couple for as long as they both live.

TERMS TO BE LEARNED

birth rate	family life cycle	nuclear unit
developmental task	functions	parenthood as crisis
discipline	internal push	self-preservation
education for sexuality	launching center	sex education
family	masturbation	stage-typical
family interaction	maturation	behavior

SELECTED READINGS

ARNSTEIN, HELEN S.: *Your Growing Child and Sex*, The Bobbs-Merrill Company, Inc., Indianapolis, 1967. "A parent's guide to the sexual development, education, attitudes, and behavior of the child from infancy through adolescence." Describes general behavior patterns and attitudes at different stages and contains suggestions on how to deal with them.

BELL, R. Q.: "Contributions of Human Infants to Caregiving and Social Interaction," in M. Lewis and L. A. Rosenblum (eds.), *The Effect of the Infant on its Caregiver*, John Wiley & Sons, Inc., New York, 1974. Review of infant's contribution to parent-child interaction.

BENSON, L.: *Fatherhood: A Sociological Perspective*, Random House, Inc., New York, 1968. An "effort to place the useful theories and research knowledge about fatherhood into a coherent framework."

BERNARD, J.: *The Future of Motherhood*, Penguin Books, Inc., New York, 1974. Deals with motherhood as an institution and with the technological, political, economic, and ethical forces that shape the motherhood role.

BRAZELTON, T. B., B. KOSLOWSKI, AND M. MAIN: "The Origins of Reciprocity: The Early Mother-Infant Interaction," in Lewis and Rosenblum (eds.), op. cit. Description of the cyclical nature of mother-infant interaction; a major work.

CHESS, STELLA, ALEXANDER THOMAS, AND HERBERT G. BIRCH: *Your Child Is a Person*, The Viking Press, New York, 1965. "A psychological approach to parenthood without guilt." Material derived from a ten-year longitudinal study of 231 children.

CHILD STUDY ASSOCIATION OF AMERICA, INC.: *What to Tell Your Child about Sex*, rev. ed., Meredith Publishing Company, Des Moines, Iowa, 1968. Information for parents; answers to questions.

DEL SOLAR, CHARLOTTE: *Parents' Answer Book: What Your Child Ought to Know about Sex*, Grosset & Dunlap, Inc., New York, 1971. Produced by the Parent and Child Institute. Includes discussion of sex education and model answers to 100 questions which a parent can translate into language suitable for a given child.

DEMAREST, ROBERT J., AND JOHN J. SCIARRA: *Conception, Birth and Contraception*, McGraw-Hill Book Company, New York, 1969. A simple, clear explanation of anatomy and processes involved in conception, birth, and contraception, with many helpful illustrations. Suitable for reading by high school and college students, and also useful for parents contributing to the sex education of their children.

DOBSON, JAMES: *Dare to Discipline*, Tyndale House, Wheaton, Ill., 1970. The nature of effective discipline of children; illustrations of various methods.

GRUENBERG, SIDONIE MATSNER (ed.): *The New Encyclopedia of Child Care and Guidance*, Doubleday & Company, Inc., Garden City, N.Y., 1968. Covers a variety of topics and answers many questions.

ISCOE, IRA, AND HAROLD W. STEVENSON (eds.): *Personality Development in Children*, University of Texas Press, Austin, 1960. Penetrating observations on the personality development of children by six nationally known authorities.

JOHNSON, ERIC W.: *Love and Sex in Plain Language*, J. B. Lippincott Company, Philadelphia, 1967. "Modern parents who believe they can best help their children by telling them the whole truth about sex will be the audience for this book." Discusses love and sex, sexual intercourse, contraception, prenatal development and childbirth, and adolescent sex problems; presents "a constructive perspective on love and sex to which boys and girls may look forward."

JOHNSON, WARREN R.: *Human Sex and Sex Education*, Lea & Febiger, Philadelphia, 1963. The perspective and problems, rather than the curricula and techniques, of sex education; the language of sex.

LEMASTERS, E. E.: *Parents in Modern America*, The Dorsey Press, Homewood, Ill., 1970. A sociological analysis of the roles of modern American parents. Attention is given to the role of the father. A defense of parents; what happens to parents in the child-rearing process.

LESHAN, EDA J.: *The Conspiracy against Childhood*, Atheneum Publishers, New York, 1967. The author feels that too much pressure is put on children, that children should be allowed to grow and that individuality should be respected.

LEWIS, M., AND L. A. ROSENBLUM (eds.): *The Effect of the Infant on its Caregiver*, John Wiley & Sons, Inc., New York, 1974. Extensive review of animal and human studies of mother-infant interaction.

LYNN, D. B.: *The Father: His Role in Child Development*, Brooks/Cole Publishing Company, Monterey, Calif., 1974. Discusses the "father" cross-culturally and in America; examines theories on the father role and the father's impact on the development of the child.

MCBRIDE, A. B.: *The Growth and Development of Mothers*, Harper & Row, Publishers, Inc., New York, 1973. Parenthood as a role you "grow into by understanding your own behavior and learning how to handle your own needs." In going beyond the "motherhood mystique," the author examines the emotions both parents feel.

ROSSI, A. S.: "Transition to Parenthood," *Journal of Marriage and the Family*, vol. 30, pp. 20–39, 1968. The author considers what must be learned "in order to move smoothly through the transition from a childless married state to parenthood" as well as the effect of parenthood on the adult.

SALK, LEE, AND RITA KRAMER: *How to Raise a Human Being: A Parents' Guide to Emotional Health from Infancy through Adolescence*, Random House, Inc., New York, 1969. A guide for understanding the changing needs of children during critical periods of their maturation.

SCHWARTZ, ALVIN: *A Parent's Guide to Children's Play and Recreation*, Crowell-Collier Publishing Co., New York, 1963. A discussion of toys, games, etc.; use of trips in children's education; how to introduce a child to good music, etc.

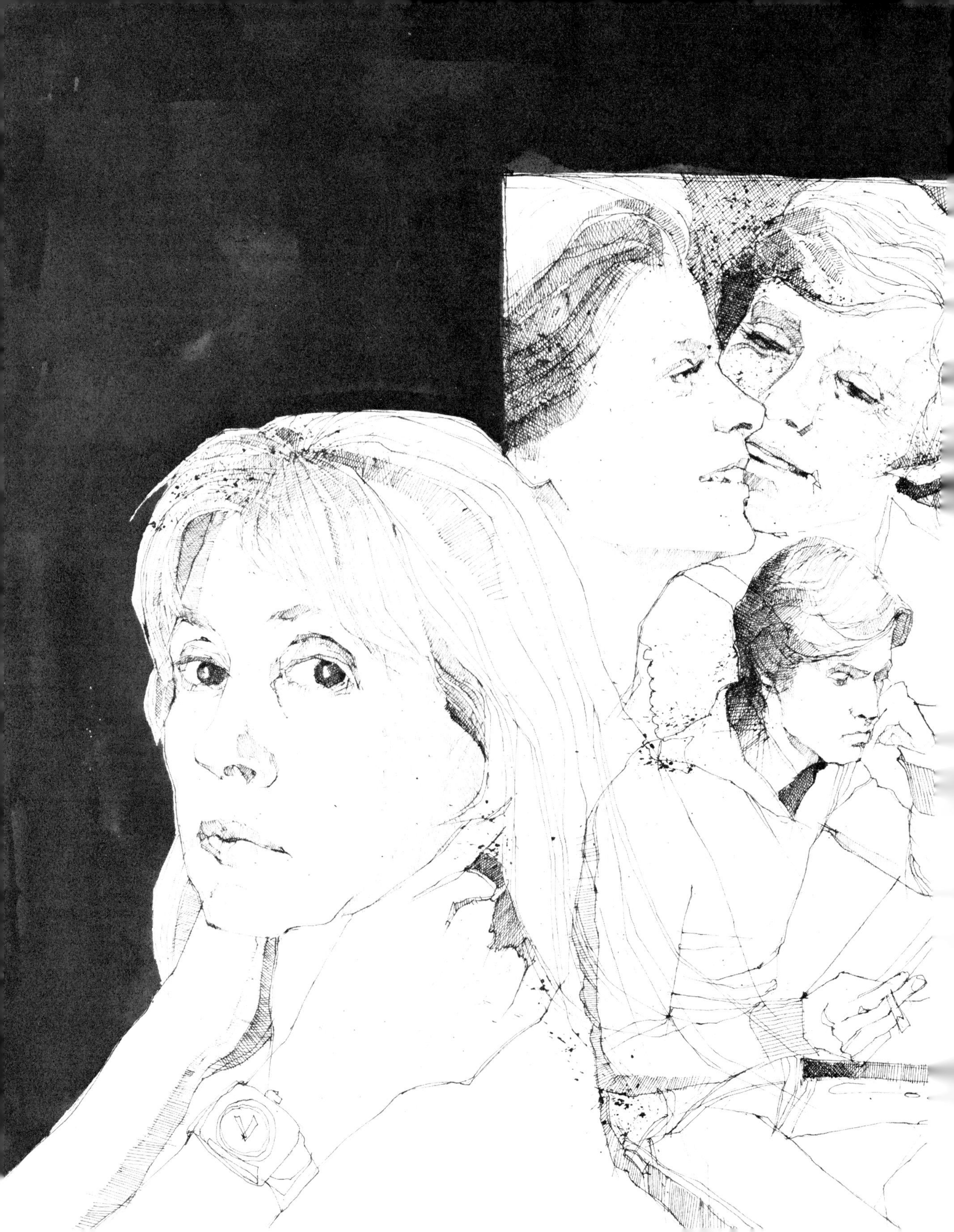

Part V
Beyond Marriage

Chapter 15

Marital Dissolution

Marriage is a human endeavor, and humans are fallible. Thus, there should be neither surprise nor pessimism when a certain proportion of marriages fail. Marriages can be described as "holy wedlock" or "holy deadlock." We may safely conclude that throughout history there have always been some marriages that failed. What stands out with regard to marital failure in this country today is not failure as such, but rather the fact that so many people escape from an unhappy marriage to try again, and that the cultural and legal doors are so widely open for that escape to occur. This does not mean that such escape may not be personally traumatic. It means only that it is readily possible and frequently occurs.

It is unrealistic to assume that all marriages will or should succeed. Yet this is an assumption that we are prone to make, an assumption made about no other human undertaking. But it is important to realize that it is individual marriages that fail. This does not indicate that the institution of marriage has failed. In college some students fail, but this is no indication that colleges have failed. In any profession, even with the best preparation, some individuals fail, but this is no reflection on the profession itself. Granted, it would be better if there were no failures in any human endeavor. However, the fact that some marriages fail is no argument against a couple committing themselves to marital success.

In various undertakings of life we act as if life were interminable, all the while knowing that it is not. We act as if life is going to go on from day to day much as we had hoped or planned. We even act as if we could foretell the future, when actually we are helpless to know what the next moment will bring. But we do not, therefore, conclude that life is not worth living, that it is an ironic, mocking trick of nature, that there is nothing to which we can commit ourselves. We do not hold that life is a failure. We know only that some individual lives, within the unchangeable framework of mortality, present opportunities and involve possibilities grasped by some but not reached by others.

There is a not uncommon assumption that the high divorce rate in this country indicates that marriages are poorer today than in earlier times. But is the divorce rate (an indication of *marital stability*) a fair indication of *marital quality*? Probably not. The liberalization of divorce laws, the tendency to divorce when things go wrong in a marriage, and society's greater tolerance of divorce and divorcing individuals have all inflated the American divorce rate in recent years. Thus, a marriage which might have remained intact but unhappy many years ago would be more likely to end in divorce today. No one knows how the *quality* of today's marriages compares to that of marriages of many years ago. We would speculate that the differences are not nearly as great as many are inclined to think. It is true, of course, that there are different pressures affecting modern marriages, many of which would tend to dissolve these unions. But there has really been no time in American history that was without imposing pressures.

In earlier times, too, standards of success and failure were different. Expectations and roles of husbands and wives were different. There was more emphasis on duty, a word unattractive to many contemporary Americans. Marital stability was considered to be a more reliable criterion of judgment than marital quality. In earlier days there was little for a couple to do about an unsuccessful marriage but "grin and bear it." Public opinion frowned upon divorce, and there was a stigma attached to divorced persons. There were few ways for a wife to support herself if she left her husband. Laws governing divorce were less permissive than they are today. Hence, we might guess that many couples remained together in a marriage that many present-day couples would seek to escape. One sociologist (Goode, 1956) has made the observation that Americans at all times in history have expressed the idea that they wished we could return the family to the way it was "in the good old days," as if there were some time in history when the family was the way everyone thought it should be. He called this notion "the classical family of Western nostalgia."

When a group of unsuccessful marriages in which there is no divorce is compared with a group ending in divorce, all the elements characteristic of the latter are found in the former, with one exception, namely, the willingness to terminate the marriage in court. Some marriages hold together in spite of elements contributing to failure because the couples are not willing to resort to divorce. How, then, can anyone determine how much marital failure there is today compared with years ago?

THE NATURE OF DIVORCE

Divorce is a symptom or an effect of marital failure. It is not a cause of such failure. Couples resort to the court after their marriages have disintegrated. In some cases, divorce is a secondary, rather than a primary, effect of failure. For instance, a couple are incompatible and consider their marriage a failure. This leads the husband to infidelity. The wife seeks a divorce on the ground of adultery. The adultery is a secondary cause of the marital failure and does not indicate why divorce occurred. It is interesting to note that a great number of both married and divorced persons report that they have had an adulterous relationship. Among divorcing couples where the incidence of adultery is higher, few individuals report that the third person was a factor in the main breakup. More often than not, adulterous relationships occurring near the termination of a marriage are a response to the faltering marriage, not a cause of its faltering. Among happily married couples, adultery represents no significant threat to some, while it may be very threatening to others.

In spite of the fact that divorce is a symptom or effect of failure rather than a cause of it, and in spite of the present-day high divorce rate, there are still persons who oppose or resist divorce and consider it a social evil. But when a marriage fails functionally, when it no longer contributes to the couple what they hoped for or expected, when it has become damaging to one or the other or both of the married persons, and when even counseling is unable to repair the dyad, there is highly questionable value in attempting to hold the marriage intact structurally.

Ideally, it would be better if no marriage ever had to be terminated in divorce. On the other hand, if no marriage, no matter what the degree of incompatibility between the spouses, could be terminated by a legal route of escape, life for many persons would become intolerable indeed. Individuals would be victimized by the relationships to which they were chained by law. Interpersonal relations that ought to be conducive to emotional health and personal happiness would be forced to remain rooted in bitterness, conflict, and frustration.

Americans are accustomed to asking about a recently divorced person, "What happened to cause the divorce?" Divorced persons themselves are often put in a position of explaining what the "cause" of the divorce was. Such questions and explanations tend to be simplistic, since it is rarely possible to specify a single cause or event which led to the divorce. Divorce occurs because a couple are no longer in love, their marriage has lost most of its meaning and luster, and in most cases there is a fair amount of conflict, hostility, and bitterness. It is unreasonable to expect or to give answers such as "he committed adultery," "she was a drunk," "their religious differences were too much to handle," or "she nagged him all the time." Such answers imply that there was one primary reason for the divorce, and this is rarely the case.

Actually, very few divorces are the result of one event, such as an act of adultery or cruelty, or one set of problems, such as religion or in-laws. Most marriages which fail do so because of a multitude of causes which influence the entire marital relationship. These problems tend to range from matters of great importance to the individuals to "tremendous trifles." Divorcing couples list as problematic virtually all areas that are suggested to them as possibilities. Such persons tend to let the negative feelings about their spouse carry over into virtually all areas of their relationship. This is understandable for a number of reasons.

First, couples having problems in some parts of their relationship may be unable to confine conflict about those matters to the issues at hand. Such conflict will often carry over into marginally related or unrelated areas of the marriage. A conflict over the influence of in-laws may create such bitterness that the couple use every occasion to vent their frustration about that matter. A "tremendous trifle" may set off an argument which blows some entire matter out of proportion. Second, as marital conflict and unhappiness increase, couples look for ways to justify their position. They become adversaries to each other and try to "prove their point" or "win the argument." The authors have had dozens of couples in counseling who actually keep mental or written notes about who said what in a given argument or on a given occasion. This is done for the purpose of "proving" that they were right and the other spouse was wrong. Some spouses say they wish they had a tape recorder to prove that they were right. Much counseling time is spent listening to angry couples telling the counselor in very precise detail the "wrongs" committed by their spouse. As the marital relationship accelerates into a conflict situation, the couples look for more faults in their spouse to justify their growing disenchantment. If unchecked, such accelerating conflict and bitterness makes the couple good candidates for divorce.

In rare cases, a single incident can be distasteful or threatening enough to lead to divorce. In other cases, a faltering marriage needs one dramatic incident to push one of the spouses to the point of initiating divorce actions. Most often, however, a spiraling effect is in operation in which the marital problems accelerate and begin to touch all parts of the relationship. At this point, one or both spouses may cross the "threshold" that makes them candidates for divorce.

In the typical case, divorce is preceded by separation. One spouse moves out of the household. The children, if there are any, stay with one parent. In many relationships there are a series of separations, with one spouse or the other walking out, coming back, and at some point walking out for good. In other marriages, the couple jointly realize that the marriage has failed and agree that they will separate. Of course, a peaceful separation is preferable to a hostile one, but many couples find the hostility difficult to avoid, despite their good intentions to do so. Since there is usually a period of at least a few months between separation and divorce, separation is really the event which signifies the beginning of the transition to the world of the formerly married. The divorce itself may be only a formality after a difficult separation.

DEFINITIONS

Many terms are used to refer to the ways in which marriages are dissolved. *Marital dissolution* is the most general term. It includes any circumstance in which a marriage may ultimately be terminated. Death of a spouse, divorce, annulment, separation, and desertion are the various forms of marital dissolution. *Divorce* refers to the legal termination of a marriage. Divorce is usually granted by a court or governmental agency to a couple who have been legally married but no longer wish to be so. *Annulment* refers to the legal termination of a relationship which may not have been a legal marriage. In some types of annulment (to be described later) it is said that a marriage never really existed, and thus the "marriage" is null and void. In another type, it is said that the marriage *may* have existed but the marriage is being declared null and void since marriage laws were violated. There are two kinds of separation. *Separation*, in the most general sense, refers to a situation where the marital partners are living apart by their choice, although still legally married. In most cases, a separation simply involves one partner moving out of the household. *Legal separation* is a court-ordered separation in which a couple are directed to live apart. The court will generally specify conditions under which the arrangement will exist. The couple are, however, still married. *Desertion* refers to the abandonment of one spouse by the other. In most states, desertion is a ground for divorce.

MARITAL DISSOLUTION IN HISTORICAL PERSPECTIVE

In the ancient Hebrew family divorce was rare, and solely in the hands of the male. A man could divorce his wife simply by saying that he no longer wanted her. Only public opinion and group pressure protected women from arbitrary decrees by their husbands. Under Christianity, divorce was extremely rare. Marriage came to be sacramental in nature and was dissoluble only through death. The Church wavered back and forth over the centuries about the conditions under which divorce could be allowed. The ecclesiastical courts sometimes granted a limited divorce (divorce from bed and board, now legal separation), recognizing that under certain conditions marriage might be intolerable. The Protestant Reformation led to a repudiation of the sacramental theory of marriage. As responsibility for marriage law was transferred from church to state, absolute divorce came to be recognized. During this time the notion developed that divorce could be granted only for serious violations of the marriage contract, and then only to the "innocent" party (Queen and Habenstein, 1974). In modern times, divorce has continued to be regulated by the state and is much more widespread than at any time in history.

MARITAL DISSOLUTION IN CROSS-CULTURAL PERSPECTIVE

In all modern societies, more marriages are terminated by the death of one spouse than by any other way. In other words, there is no modern nation in which divorce or separation is responsible for more marital dissolutions than is the natural death of one of the spouses. It should be pointed out, however, that data are not available for divorce rates in some of the more primitive, underdeveloped societies, and consequently we cannot make conclusions with certainty about the phenomenon of divorce in all cultures. Data available from the United Nations indicate that among modern nations, no country has a higher divorce rate than the United States (*United Nations Demographic Yearbook*, 1975).

Divorce laws vary from country to country, and in the United States, for example, divorce laws vary from state to state. Worldwide, there appear to be four primary types of divorce laws (Winch, 1971):

1 In some countries the law prohibits divorce and marriages can be terminated only by death. This is the policy of the Roman Catholic Church, and consequently the countries which have such laws are heavily Roman Catholic. Spain, Peru, Brazil, and Colombia are examples.

2 A divorce can be granted if one spouse has been found guilty of a violation of his or her marital obligations (for example, adultery, desertion, nonsupport, cruelty). This is one form of divorce in the United States and in many other countries of the world.

3 A divorce is granted if it is shown that the marriage is completely broken in fact—in other words, if there are signs of an "irretrievable breakdown" or "irreconcilable differences" in the marriage. This is the emerging "no-fault" type of divorce found in parts of the United States and in various forms in countries such as Switzerland, the U.S.S.R., Yugoslavia, Poland, Germany, and all the Scandinavian countries. It is expected to be the dominant form of American divorce in coming years.

4 Free power of the husband to terminate the marriage by repudiation of the wife. This is still the official law of Islam and of Judaism. It is not widely practiced in Israel, and there is a continuing movement to limit the husband's power and to allow the wife to initiate divorce. We may speculate that this form of divorce will all but vanish in the future.

The divorce *rates* of any given country are, of course, greatly influenced by the divorce *laws* of that country. Until a few years ago, being under the influence of Roman Catholic doctrine, Italy did not allow divorce under any circumstance. The low divorce rate in Italy did not, we may presume, indicate an absence of marital instability. There were many annulments, separations, and desertions. As might be expected, many divorces were granted following the legalization of divorce. The high United States divorce rates, then, may not necessarily suggest that American marriages are any more unhappy or unstable than those in any other country, but rather that our laws and the social attitudes surrounding divorce permit unhappy couples to resort to divorce more easily and with fewer consequences than couples in other countries. In assessing the total picture of marital instability, one must consider not only divorce but also separation, desertion, and annulment.

AMERICAN DIVORCE RATES

The divorce rate in the United States reached an all-time high in the 1970s. Exhibit 15-1 illustrates how the rate has fluctuated over the years. At the time of World War II, the divorce rate took a sharp upward turn, owing to the breakup of many "war marriages" and the effect of the war on other unstable marriages. In 1946, the rate reached what was then an all-time high—a level Americans never thought would be reached again. The pattern settled down somewhat after the war but never again reached the lower prewar rates. Beginning in the 1960s and continuing through the 1970s, the divorce rate increased dramatically and steadily until in 1975 it was the highest ever reached (U.S. Department of Health, Education, and Welfare, *Monthly Vital Statistics Report*, 1977). In 1976, for the first time in American history, more than one million divorces were granted in a single year (U.S. Bureau of the Census, *Statistical Abstract*, 1976).

The divorce rate may be expressed in various ways, some of which can be very misleading. One of the most common ways divorce rates are expressed is by calculating the ratio of divorces to weddings in a given year. In 1976, there were estimated to be 2,133,000 weddings and 1,077,000 divorces, a

Exhibit 15-1 Divorce rate in the United States, 1900–1975.

ratio of about one for every two weddings (U.S. Department of Health, Education, and Welfare, *Monthly Vital Statistics Report*, 1977). However, this is *not* equivalent to saying that one in two marriages ends in divorce, since the divorces granted in a given year represent marriages that, as a rule, began before that year. A better way of expressing the divorce rate is to look at the number of divorces per 1,000 population. In 1976 the divorce rate was 5.0 per 1,000 population (U.S. Department of Health, Education, and Welfare, *Monthly Vital Statistics Report*, 1977).

None of these figures are very helpful for determining the proportion of marriages which will ultimately fail. Since couples marrying in a given year may remain married for many years, may become widowed at any time, or may divorce early in the marriage or late in the marriage, it is very difficult to estimate how many of the marriages which are still intact may ultimately end in divorce. The problem is further complicated by the fact that the divorcing history of couples now marrying for the first time may turn out to be very different from that of couples who have married and divorced in the past. To estimate what proportion of marriages will ultimately end in divorce, we need to rely on methods of *demographic projection*, which allows social scientists to use mathematical formulas to predict, based on a series of assumptions, what *may* happen in the future.

Such an analysis (Glick and Norton, 1976) estimated that for persons born between 1940 and 1949, more than one in three are likely to experience at least one divorce during their lifetime. Moreover, more than one-third of those who obtain one divorce are likely to obtain a second one. If we took into account the continued high divorce rate, we could *estimate* that for individuals born between 1950 and 1960, between one-third and two-fifths of all first marriages will end in divorce. In addition, between 34 and 45 percent of those who obtain one divorce and remarry will be likely to obtain a second one. Combining the estimates for first marriages and remarriages, we estimate that for persons born between 1950 and 1960, *approximately 40 to 50 percent of all marriages will end in divorce.*

As Glick and Norton (1973) point out, such estimates may be too high if the upturn in divorce during the 1960s and 1970s turns out to have been largely attributed to the liberalization of divorce laws. In that case, the liberalization may have eased the divorce process and thereby had the effect of merely advancing the time when some of the divorces occurred. Divorce rates continue to remain high, however, and by 1977 had just begun to show signs of leveling off.

If we look at marital disruption in the broader sense, the extent of marital failure is even more dramatic. In 1975, for example, there were approximately 2,427,000 separated persons between 25 and 54 years of age. This was slightly more than half of the number of the persons in that age group who were divorced at that time (U.S. Bureau of the Census, *Current Population Reports*, 1975). In other words, among persons with disrupted marriages roughly one-third are separated and two-thirds are divorced. Separation, then, constitutes a major part of marital disruption. Of course, many of those who are separated eventually go on to divorce. If, however, we add to our estimate of divorces presented above a significant number of married couples who are separated, but not divorced, it would not be unreasonable to suggest that about half of all marriages among young American couples could be expected to be disrupted by divorce or separation. If we additionally consider that some couples continue to live together even though their marriages are unhappy, we may readily conclude that marital "failure" is more common than the divorce rate suggests. Unless factors contributing to the improvement of marriage and family life in American culture multiply, there is no reason to suppose that the incidence of marital disruption will not continue to be high.

Factors Affecting the Rate

The factors affecting the divorce rate are not necessarily the same as the ones that contribute to marital failure. We have said that divorce is a symptom of failure in the individual marriage. The rate is also a symptom of social change. Much of this change has been in the direction of removing some of the outside props that used to keep marriages intact even when they were disintegrating on the inside. Modern marriage is like a tent which has had its stakes pulled out one by one, each time making it more vulnerable to wind and storm. In earlier times marriages were held together in part by coercion from without. Now, when they hold together, it is largely through cohesion from within (recall our discussion of the various forces which act on the stability of a marriage in Chapter 10).

Some of the elements in the social situation that may contribute to the high divorce rate are a decreased tolerance of poor marital quality, the higher status of women, new standards of marital success and new ideals of married life, a decline of religious authority, more widespread liberalism of thought, changed ideas about masculine supremacy, the breakdown of primary group control owing to increased urbanization, the increased ability of women to support themselves following a divorce, the greater ease with which divorce may be obtained, the more widespread acceptance of divorce, and the mobility of the American population. In addition to these there are the following:

The decline in the death rate Since the death rate has declined and the average span of life has lengthened, some marriages that might have been broken by death end in divorce. A couple marrying in their early twenties and living until their early seventies are expected to remain married for over fifty years. Indeed, in 1971, 2.5 percent of the 49 million married women had already celebrated their fiftieth anniversary. There were 34,000 women who had been married sixty-five years or more (U.S. Bureau of the Census, *Current Population Reports*, 1972). It can be whimsically stated that marriage was never intended to last fifty years. Persons of previous generations and in previous eras were typically married for much shorter periods of time, simply because they did not live as long.

When a marriage ends in the death of one party, there is a not uncommon assumption that that marriage was at least passably successful. In some cases, there might have been a divorce had the deceased spouse lived longer. When both death and divorce are considered, we find that there were actually more "prematurely" broken homes in earlier days in this country than there are today.

Not everyone agrees that the decline in the death rate plays a significant role. Says Weiss (1975), "We can quickly reject the theory that increased longevity is to blame [for the high divorce rate]." He points out that although there have been substantial gains in increasing the length of life, the divorce rate has risen faster than life expectancy. Nevertheless, there is still the possibility that some marriages might have ended in divorce had the couple, or one of them, lived longer. Life expectancy cannot be considered the only reason for the high divorce rate, but it is probably one reason.

American attitudes relating to divorce Generalizing broadly, we may describe Americans as comfort-loving. They are impatient with discomfort and inconvenience.

They feel that whatever they do not like they have a right to change, either through established channels or by direct action. They are freedom-loving, and unhappy marriage may be interpreted as a form of restraint. "We have come . . . to regard the right of divorce as something like a civil liberty" (O'Neill, 1967). In spite of their sensitivity to group pressure, Americans are individualistic, and personal welfare is often given precedence over the welfare of the group. Americans are generally sympathetic with the "underdog," give help to someone in dire need, and lend support to a person or a group in time of unusual crisis or emergency. Such attitudes make us inclined to respond sympathetically to anyone who is the "victim" of a marital situation assumed to be caused largely by the other spouse.

The persistent popularity of weddings together with the high divorce rate raises the question: Do Americans say things they do not mean? As mentioned in an earlier chapter, some present-day couples write their own wedding ceremony, and in place of "till death do us part" or "so long as ye both shall live," or something to this effect, seeming to imply a promise to remain married no matter what, such couples include a conditional statement such as "so long as love lasts." But many couples still have a religious ceremony which includes the apparent promises of permanent fidelity. When such couples get divorces, do they exhibit lack of integrity and violation of solemn vows of lifelong unalterable union? Some would answer in the affirmative. But without stretching the meaning of the words of the ceremony, another conclusion may be reached.

In a typical, conventional Protestant wedding ceremony (different phraseology is used in the Jewish ceremony, and, of course, the Roman Catholic Church does not permit divorce), the expression "so long as ye both shall live" does not follow a statement of promise merely to stay married. It follows a statement of commitment to love, comfort, honor, protect, and be faithful to the other party. When in answer to the clergyman's question regarding this commitment each party says, "I will" (in some cases, "I do"), "will" need not be interpreted as the future tense of the verb. Rather, "will" may be interpreted as "I will to," an act of will. A person may make a commitment or express an intent to love another person for life, but no one can actually promise to do so. We know that in spite of commitment and all good intentions, love can, and sometimes does, change. It "dies." It cannot be forced or determined in advance.

War World War II brought in its wake a high marriage rate. Many of these marriages were hasty, poorly founded unions. War breeds many ill-chosen marriages. Also, many marriages collapsed, like poorly built houses during an earthquake, whereas they might have endured structurally had there been no war. Long separations during which husband and wife had different experiences, made new contacts, and lost interest in each other contributed to the breakup of many already existing marriages. With its necessary emphasis upon destruction and the insignificance of the individual, war changes the attitudes of some persons toward their responsibilities and toward the values by which they previously lived. The war also brought about great shifts in population and consequent increased breakdown of primary groups. High wages in war industries gave some persons the funds necessary to obtain divorces and gave others the quick money and, for them, unprecedentedly high income which often lead to loss of balance and perspective. War production provided many opportunities for wives who had not previously been employed to establish a new independence and escape the home.

Duration of Marriage Before Divorce

There is great variability among divorcing couples in the length of time between the wedding and divorce. This variability suggests that the factors which influence marital instability operate throughout marriage and that they may have their greatest toll at different times for different couples. The median number of years (middle point) dropped from 7.5 in 1963 to 6.5 in 1974 (U.S. Department of Health, Education, and Welfare, *Monthly Vital Statistics Report*, 1976). The interval decreases as the divorce rate increases (Plateris, 1973). The fact that the *median* interval has always been around seven years has led to the unfounded notion of a "seven-year itch." Actually, the *modal* (peak) interval between marriage and divorce is much shorter. As Exhibit 15-2 illustrates, the peak time of divorce action is between the second and fifth years of marriage. If we consider the fact that virtually all couples separate for at least a brief period before divorcing, the data are even more dramatic. An analysis conducted by the Division of Vital Statistics (Plateris, 1973) found that more couples separate in the first year of marriage than in any other year. Since the average length of time between separation and divorce, depending on the state, varies from a few months to about two years, marital disruption tends to occur earlier in marriage than most persons realize. The high incidence of separation leading to divorce in the early years of marriage indicates that *most marriages that fail show signs of this failure early in the relationship*. These data also indicate the lack of preparation for marriage that seems to characterize a great many couples.

Although many divorces occur early in the marriage, there is no evidence to suggest that couples make hasty decisions. In a study of 437 upper-middle-class Americans, Cuber and Harroff (1965) "found practically no evidence of impulsive decisions to seek divorce. The overwhelming impression is the reverse: when divorce occurred in these people's lives, it typically came as an 'end of the rope' decision."

Differentials in Divorce Rates

Divorce rates vary widely by social, economic, and geographical characteristics.

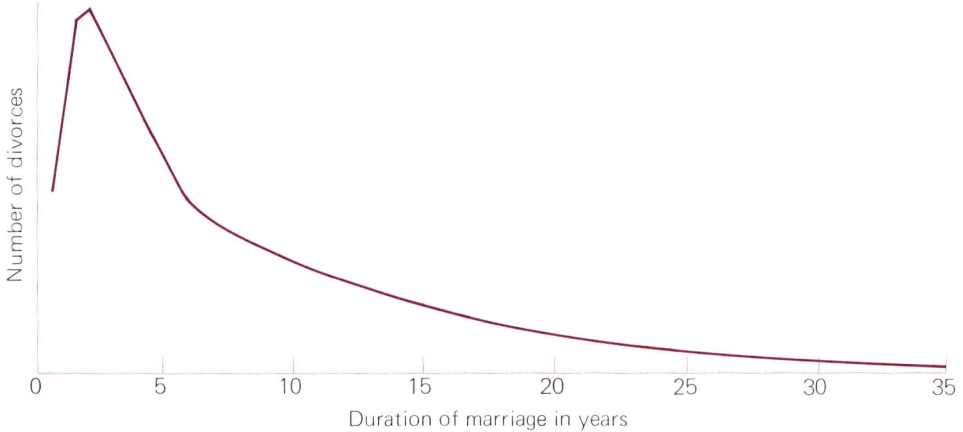

Exhibit 15-2 Duration of marriage to divorce 1969. (Adapted from Glick and Norton, 1976.)

Geographic Variation Divorce rates tend to increase going from east to west. The lowest divorce rates are in the Northeastern United States, whereas the highest are in the West. The divorce rate in a given state is likely to be influenced by the stringency of requirements for divorce in that state, the rural-urban balance, the religious affiliations of its residents, the proportion of young couples in the state, and the length of residency required for divorce.

Much is written about Nevada divorces. The laws there permit divorce after only a brief period of residence (six weeks). Nevada has become a haven for divorce seekers of the upper economic level, although with the liberalization of grounds in other states this may be changing. Even with its large and well-publicized divorce business, only about one American divorce in a hundred is granted there. On the other hand, with about 0.3 percent of the population, Nevada grants about 1.0 percent of the divorces. Its divorce rate is the highest in the nation (U.S. Bureau of the Census, *Statistical Abstract*, 1975). Nevada not only specializes in divorce; it also specializes in marriages. Its marriage rate per 1,000 population is the highest in the country (U.S. Bureau of the Census, *Statistical Abstract*, 1975). Of course, the reason for this is that many of the persons who obtain divorces there also marry there.

Racial variation Census data do not readily allow for an analysis of the independent effects of race on divorce rates. Blacks have higher divorce rates than do whites, but the precise extent of the differences have not been analyzed fully. In the 1970 census, about three-fifths of black men and more than three-fourths of white men were living with their first wives, while just under half of the black women and just under two-thirds of white women were living with their first husbands (U.S. Bureau of the Census, *Current Population Reports*, 1973). Since blacks tend to be of lower socioeconomic standing, part of the higher black divorce rate can be attributed to lesser economic resources. There is also geographical variation involved; Southern blacks have lower divorce rates than Southern whites, whereas blacks in the North have higher divorce rates than whites in the North (Plateris, 1973).

Educational variation There is an overall inverse relationship between divorce and educational level. In other words, the higher the educational level, the lower the divorce rate. There is, however, one interesting exception to this rule (Houseknecht and Spanier, 1976). Women with graduate training significantly increase their probability of divorce over women with just a bachelor's degree. Whereas the divorce rate among women declines as educational level increases up to the bachelor's degree, it almost doubles for that portion of the female population that venture on to graduate school. Furthermore, higher levels of graduate training involve even higher divorce rates. This exception to the general inverse relationship is related to the greater financial and social independence of these women, their greater participation in the labor force, and perhaps additional pressures which can be created in a dual-career marriage.

Social class variation There is an inverse relationship between social class and divorce rates. Those couples at the lower end of the socioeconomic ladder have the highest divorce rates, while persons in the upper middle and upper classes have significantly lower divorce rates. Perhaps more than any other social factor, financial hardship may cause severe strain on a marital relationship. Couples in the lowest socioeconomic strata often struggle to meet their day-to-day needs, and such a struggle can take a great toll. With greater income, a couple are more likely to be able to structure their lives in such a way as to avoid marital disruption (Scanzoni, 1968). Despite a higher divorce rate among persons of low social standing, there are also higher separation and desertion rates. Everything considered, there is a great amount of marital instability in the lower social strata, an understandable phenomenon.

Rural-urban variation Divorce rates are traditionally higher in urban areas, but the differences in recent years appear to be small (Bumpass and Sweet, 1972). The difference may be partially due to the complexities and pressures of urban life, but it is also likely that urban areas attract persons who are more prone to divorce. Furthermore, it is possible that persons who will soon divorce occasionally migrate to urban areas, where their adjustment to post-divorce life may be made more easily.

Variation in family stability Individuals whose parents have been divorced are considerably more likely to divorce themselves than individuals whose parents had an intact marriage (Bumpass and Sweet, 1972). This relationship has led some sociologists to remark that "divorce runs in families." While it would be oversimplifying to state that an individual is a likely candidate for divorce simply because his or her parents divorced, it appears that the tendency for divorce to occur from generation to generation exists even when other social factors are taken into account (Bumpass and Sweet, 1972). Thus, we must look for explanations for this occurrence. Tolerant attitudes toward divorce may be transmitted from parent to child. The child of a divorce may have a model of family life which defines divorce as a permissible remedy for an unhappy marriage. Or a number of other, as yet unanalyzed, social factors associated with divorce may simultaneously operate in conjunction with social class and family background variables (which are transmitted through families) to make such an individual a more likely divorce candidate.

Variation by number of times married Do persons who have remarried have higher divorce rates than persons marrying for the first time? The answer appears to be yes. Almost three-fourths of divorcing husbands and wives have been married only once, but 20 percent have been married twice and about 6 percent three times or more (Plateris, 1973). Various studies have found that couples in a second or subsequent marriage are particularly prone to divorce (Bumpass and Sweet, 1972; Monahan, 1958; Monahan, 1952; Monahan, 1959; Renne, 1970). There are two explanations for this finding. First, it should be noted that persons in a remarriage are a very select group. They have singled themselves out as persons who will, when a marriage fails, seek a divorce. Thus, they have already distinguished themselves from the rest of the population as persons who will resort to divorce if the marriage falters. There is, then, an attitudinal difference between first-marrieds and remarrieds. A second explanation is the obvious one—that persons who have divorced once may not be as good prospects for successful marriage as persons who have never been divorced. In other words, they may be predisposed to divorce because of a combination of personality, social, economic, and other factors. As we shall point out later, the former explanation probably accounts for a greater part of the difference in divorce rates than does the latter.

Other variations A number of other variables have already been mentioned as correlates of divorce. Divorce rates are higher among persons marrying at particularly young ages and when there has been a premarital pregnancy. Divorce rates are lower among Roman Catholics, undoubtedly a reflection of the strong stand against divorce taken by the Roman Catholic Church. Divorce rates are also especially low among Jews.

DIVORCE AND CHILDREN

Approximately 60 percent of divorces are granted to couples with children under 18 years of age (U.S. Department of Health, Education, and Welfare, *Monthly Vital Statistics Report*, 1976). Does the presence of children contribute to the stability of marriage? Statistical answers to this question must be interpreted with caution. The divorce rate for couples without children is higher than the rate for couples with children. Also, divorce rates tend to decline as the number of children increases. But the likelihood of divorce also declines with increasing age and with the duration of the marriage. Available data do not permit separating the effects of these three variables (U.S. Department of Health, Education, and Welfare, *Monthly Vital Statistics Report*, 1970).

In many cases in which there are no children the divorce occurred rather early in the marriage, when there was insufficient time to have offspring. There is no way of determining whether such couples would have had children or not. In some cases there is no doubt that children are the reason for a couple's continuing to live together after their marriage has failed. In others, too, children serve as a very absorbing common interest, one which binds the couple together and may counteract some of the factors operating to force them apart.

Scholars agree that couples should not consider having a child to prevent a failing marriage from ending in divorce. Children are not a remedy for marital ills.

Exhibit 15-3 shows that more and more children are involved in divorces every year. Children are becoming less of a deterrent to divorce in the United States, since increasing numbers of divorcing couples have children (Plateris, 1970). Should a couple remain married "for the sake of the children"? There are no conclusive answers, since every case is different. It is generally agreed, however, that children are likely to be better adjusted if they grow up in a peaceful home with one loving parent than if they grow up in a home filled with the turmoil created by two parents who do not love each other and who are constantly quarreling.

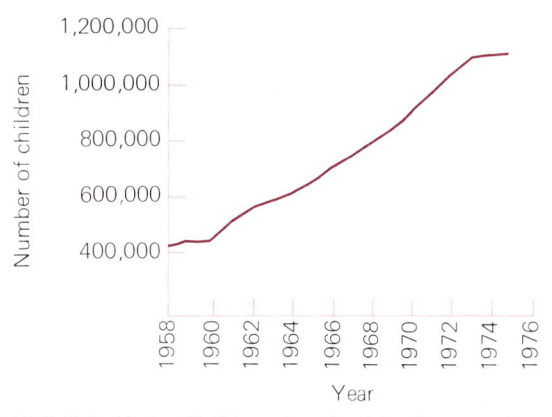

Exhibit 15-3 Children involved in divorces in the United States, 1958–1975. (Adapted from U.S. Department of Health, Education, and Welfare, *Monthly Vital Statistics Report*, 1976.)

Effects of Divorce upon Children

It is often impossible to separate the effects of divorce, as such, from the effects of the failing home situation, because divorce is preceded by marital breakdown. The child may not be aware of this, however, and sometimes the divorce brings to an unexpected end a relationship that had never been questioned. This happens even with persons of college age, who in many cases are taken aback when parents announce their intention of getting a divorce. Of course, in other cases the children urge the divorce and are relieved when it occurs.

The child of divorced parents is in a position somewhat akin to that of the middle horse in a three-horse team, pulled now in one direction, now in another as it attempts to accommodate itself to the movements of the other two horses. The child is torn between conflicting loyalties. It is difficult to cooperate with and understand two persons who are at odds and do not understand each other. If the child lives with each parent at different times, neither home may provide preparation for living in the other. If there is a leaning in the direction of one parent, and especially if there is an inclination to blame the other, there may be conflict and disappointment. The child may feel insecure and exhibit compensatory behavior. On the other hand, many children of divorced parents are well adjusted. "The evidence now available does not warrant the conclusion that children whose parents divorce are more likely later in their lives to have emotional problems than children whose parents do not divorce" (Weiss, 1975). There is much to be said for a child living in security and harmony with one parent rather than in an atmosphere of insecurity and conflict with two.

DIVORCE LAW

American divorce law is in a state of change. Traditional divorce law is based on an *adversary* system. The basic tenet of the adversary system of divorce is that in any marriage that fails, there must be one innocent party and one guilty party. The divorce can be granted only to the innocent party. Emerging divorce law, which now exists in many states, is commonly termed *no-fault* divorce law. The basic tenet of no-fault divorce is that marriage is a two-way street. If a marriage fails, it is likely that both spouses played some part in its failure. An alcoholic husband may have been drinking to excess to escape a nagging wife. An adulterous wife may have engaged in such activity because of a cruel and uncaring husband. No-fault divorce recognizes that both parties to a divorce had a part in it and, furthermore, that having to "prove" in a court of law that one's spouse is "guilty" of causing marital failure can be emotionally damaging to those involved, including children. No-fault divorce, then, provides a more realistic approach to marital failure. In the United States, marriage and divorce laws are created by the states. State legislatures make the laws, judges (courts) interpret them and rule on individual cases, and county or other local jurisdictions handle the administration of marriage and divorce procedures. The divorce laws of the fifty states are summarized in the Appendix.

The Adversary (Fault) System

In states with this form of divorce, an individual seeking a divorce must specify a *ground* for divorce. Grounds for divorce may be considered from two related points of view. They are the reasons alleged by a person seeking divorce on the basis of which injury is asserted and a claim is made that divorce should be granted. Grounds are also the categories of reasons for which the law permits divorce and the courts grant it. Grounds and causes are not necessarily the same, either for divorce in general or for the divorce of a specific couple. Usually what happens is something like this: A couple are incompatible, and their marriage is unsatisfactory. This leads one or both of them to commit some act—such as desertion, nonsupport, or adultery—which is a symptom of maladjustment but does fall within the categories of the law. On this basis one seeks divorce. Or, being incompatible, they may agree that they both want divorce. They then fit their situation into the most convenient legal category, often cruelty, so that the plea of one conforms to legal requirements and a divorce may be decreed. In many cases this amounts to a deliberate "trumping up" of grounds to satisfy the court. Hence statistics of divorce grounds do not present an accurate picture of conditions.

Grounds vary from state to state. They have been worked out with more regard for institutional considerations, such as status, support, and rights, than for problems of personality adjustment. We consider love to be one of the major bases for marriage, if not the primary basis. Yet lack of love passes unrecognized as a basis for divorce. In historical studies, contemporary discussions, or critical analyses of divorce, there is almost no mention of love. Its presence or absence is almost entirely disregarded in the rendering of court decisions.

Statistically the grounds are changing:

1 *As written in the laws of the several states*: The trend seems to be toward extending the number of grounds or toward eliminating all specific grounds in favor of one flexible one, as will be discussed later.

2 *As alleged in specific cases*: Desertion and adultery as grounds alleged have declined. Cruelty has increased. Nearly half the divorces granted under the adversary system nowadays are granted on the specific ground of cruelty. If such grounds as "indignities" and other grounds synonymous with cruelty are included, over two-thirds of all divorces would fall into this category (Plateris, 1973). The ten most common "fault" grounds for divorce, in order of their prevalence, are cruelty, neglect or nonsupport, indignities, desertion or abandonment, separation or absence, adultery, incompatibility, conviction of a crime, bigamy and fraud, and drunkenness. These grounds account for 95 percent of divorces under the adversary system (Plateris, 1973).

The definition of cruelty is constantly shifting. Cruelty ranges from physical violence (in some states specifically listed as physical cruelty) to simple nagging. Many cases are on record where cruelty has included such things as a wife's complaints about the food her husband prepared for dinner; one spouse's refusal to speak to the other; a husband's failure to make his children stop playing the saxophone; a wife's claim that a pet cat had deprived her of her husband's affection; and a man's use of biblical language to insult his wife. Of course, there were undoubtedly other factors involved in the failure of these marriages. There is a not uncommon tendency to construe cruelty as anything that a plaintiff alleges and a court will accept. This trend has occurred in recent years as couples have sought ways to circumvent outmoded divorce laws.

The statistical change in cruelty as an alleged ground for divorce may show one or more of several things: (1) That courts are becoming more lenient in granting divorce. (2) That divorce is being granted on less serious grounds. (3) That the true causes of marital failure are being recognized and their seriousness acknowledged. If this is true, it means that fewer couples are having to perjure themselves in order to obtain release. (4) That cruelty may be more readily established and proved than other grounds. The term is more flexible and permits broader interpretation by the court than, say, adultery or nonsupport. Most divorces are obtained on the grounds that are the least unpleasant to allege under the law. (5) That we are taking a more intelligent attitude toward divorce. (6) That courts and the general public are becoming more willing to have divorces granted for incompatibility. (7) That more is expected of marriage today, and that standards of success are rising. When expectations are not achieved, escape is permitted. The standards of success are becoming more personal and less institutional.

There are a variety of conditions that apply to each of the grounds for divorce. Although they vary widely from state to state, we can generalize about some of them. Desertion, for example, always has a specific time limit, usually one to two years. The spouse who leaves the home is considered the guilty party. There must be an intent to abandon the home. A husband called to military service, for example, is not guilty of desertion. The abandonment must be without justification. A woman who leaves home because her life is threatened by her husband would not be guilty of desertion. Grounds such as nonsupport must be considered in relation to what the husband (who is the stated breadwinner in most state marriage and divorce laws) can afford. The husband must provide reasonable support based on what he is able to earn. Adultery need not be categorically proved. It is usually sufficient to demonstrate that intent was present. To be "caught in the act" may mean only that a man and woman were found in bed together, were known to have stayed in the same hotel room, or were known to have had an affair. They need not be seen in the act of intercourse.

In most states, when one spouse sues the other for divorce under the adversary system, it is possible for the defendant to initiate a countercharge to the effect that the plaintiff has also been guilty of an offense that constitutes a ground for divorce. This is termed *recrimination*. In such cases the divorce may not be granted to either party. This means, in essence, that if one party has committed an offense, a divorce may be granted, but that if both parties have offended, neither can obtain a divorce. There are exceptions to this condition, however.

By and large, in order to obtain a divorce under the adversary system one party must prove injury by the other, and it must be injury of a type defined by the law of a particular state. If the couple themselves recognize that they have both been injured, they cannot get a divorce unless they conceal their understanding and perjure themselves in court to "prove" that one was innocent and the other guilty. Thus, in actual practice we already have divorce by mutual consent, but it has not been legalized.

Collusion is the circumstance of spouses cooperating in getting their divorce. Strictly speaking, collusion is not allowed, and a divorce cannot be given if collusion has occurred. In reality, however, collusion in some degree is almost universal, and courts ignore it. If, however, one party wanted to prevent a divorce from occurring, he or she could allege collusion. If this could be proved, the judge might not grant the divorce. The law states that a divorce suit is a legal contest, and collusion is any activity which would subvert the element of "contest." Collusion may occur if couples agree to submit false evidence regarding an offense that was not really committed, if an offense is committed solely for the purpose of creating a ground that will permit a divorce action to be filed, or if a legitimate defense to a divorce ground is suppressed by the defendant. Lawyers, judges, and divorcing parties all know that collusion exists—and as long as it is not brought to the attention of the court, it is usually ignored.

Connivance involves one spouse trying to create a ground for divorce by tricking the other spouse into committing an offense. For example, a husband who encourages another man to seduce his wife, so that he may charge her with adultery, is guilty of connivance.

Condonation is another defense to divorce which, if brought to the attention of the court, could prevent a divorce from going through. Condonation refers to the forgiveness of a wrongdoing on the part of one's spouse. If one spouse commits an offense which would be grounds for divorce, the "innocent" party is expected to file for divorce, stop living with the marital partner, and under no circumstances "forgive" the behavior. If the behavior is "forgiven," and the marriage continues with the couple living together, condonation has occurred and the previously "innocent" spouse may not be able to claim the wrongdoing as a ground for divorce.

Who Files For Divorce?

More women than men file for divorce under the adversary system. There are a number of possible reasons for this difference. (1) In some respects women have more at stake in marriage than do men. They are thus more inclined to feel the sting of failure. (2) There is still enough chivalry in the relationships of men and women so that when a couple agree together to get a divorce, the husband assumes the "blame" and lets the wife bring suit. (3) More grounds are available to women in some states. For example, the ground of nonsupport is seldom used by husbands. (4) Courts on the whole are inclined to be more sympathetic with women than with men. (5) If the couple agree upon alimony, child support, and custody of the children, the court will more readily stipulate it if the wife is the plaintiff. (6) It may still be somewhat easier for a man to face public opinion. (7) Women have greater freedom in seeking divorce now than formerly and are using this freedom.

An attorney reassures an anxious client before a divorce hearing. No-fault divorce laws have made legal proceedings a little easier. (Bruce Roberts, Rapho/Photo Researchers)

No-fault Divorce

One step in the direction of adapting divorce to present-day attitudes and needs is no-fault divorce. Most states now have one form or another of no-fault divorce. California was the first state, in 1970, to replace divorce with "dissolution of marriage." With the exception of incurable insanity, a ground rarely used and no longer necessary, the only ground for divorce in California is now "irreconcilable differences which have caused the irremediable breakdown of the marriage." Couples may jointly or singly initiate a divorce action; there is no accusation of specific divorce grounds; and there need be no lengthy testimony of who did what to whom on which occasion. Since California's new law went into effect, a number of states have followed, and no-fault divorce legislation has been introduced into virtually all of the fifty state legislatures, although it has met with resistance in some states. The legislation usually takes one of two general forms.

1 A period of separation without cohabitation

may be sufficient ground for divorce. In these states, the traditional divorce law may continue, but an amended or additional provision is allowed. Couples show that they have lived apart willingly because they are not suited for each other. These laws, then, allow a couple, by mutual agreement, to separate for a period and then divorce by virtue of passing through this time without reconciliation.

2 A general ground such as irreconcilable differences, irremediable breakdown, or incompatibility may be the only ground for divorce in a given state. If the court finds that this condition exists, it can order the marriage dissolved. During such proceedings, testimony or evidence about the wrongdoings of the spouses is inadmissible except where necessary to establish custody of the children.

In some of these no-fault states, judges are permitted to establish a counseling service as part of the divorce court, often referred to as reconciliation services. A couple then have the opportunity to attempt reconciliation if it is desired or suggested. This practice has not become widespread and is unlikely to, since such services are costly and virtually all couples who come for divorce have already made their decision. The most useful function of such a service could be in cases where one party wants the divorce and the other does not.

No-fault divorce is realistic. It recognizes the difficulty and the arbitrariness of attempting to assign specific causes for marital breakdown. It eliminates the destructive process of placing blame and proving fault. It does away with dishonesty, sometimes amounting to perjury, in making claims that have no real basis in fact but will be accepted by a court, especially if the defendant does not contest the divorce. It eliminates the false impression that one spouse is completely innocent while the other is completely guilty. "Pigeonholing cases into a few specific grounds leads the judge, the lawyers, and, most importantly, the parties to deal with the symptoms rather than the underlying causes of marital problems" (Wheeler, 1974). No-fault divorce involves no such pigeonholing.

The Future of Divorce Law

Before it is possible to talk intelligently about remedies for our high divorce rate, the objectives must be made clear. Is the objective to decrease divorce or to increase marital success? The latter would lead to the former, but the former would not produce the latter. If the aim is merely to reduce the number of divorces, this could be accomplished by making divorce more difficult through legal impediments. That would be to treat symptoms rather than the disease. More stringent divorce laws would not make marriages more successful; they would only prevent escape. "Arbitrary roadblocks cannot save dead marriages" (Wheeler, 1974).

In lieu of changed divorce laws some persons have suggested stricter marriage laws. The latter would no doubt prove the more effective, but there is a history of resistance to stricter marriage laws, since enacting them would take away some of our personal freedom. Furthermore, there is little agreement about what restrictions would be useful. Nevertheless, sentiment favoring legislation which would make couples meet more stringent marriage requirements exists. "So long as it is easier to get a marriage license than it is to get a driver's license, a high frequency of marital problems is inevitable" (Wheeler, 1974).

Uniform laws have also been suggested. Certainly even the proponents of variety for the sake of experimentation must admit that variety need not extend from one extreme to another. (There can be an approach to uniformity without identity.) The greatest danger in making marriage and divorce laws uniform in all states is that uniform laws would represent compromises. As it is, some states are more progressive than others. Compromise would mean the loss of some of the progress secured in the more advanced states. There is no hope of achieving uniformity through federal legislation, since the Constitution does not give the federal government authority to regulate marriage and divorce. All marriage and divorce laws are state laws. To get a federal law the Constitution would have to be amended, and the possibility of this happening is so remote that, at present at least, it is not worth considering.

In the last analysis, the most effective remedy for the current state of marriage and divorce is education—the gradual, slow, tedious education of the public, part of which is inert and apathetic and not even aware of the need for preparing people for marriage or for departing from timeworn and threadbare tradition. It is hoped that, coupled with education, counseling facilities will continue to increase and improve. The advancement of marriage depends also upon improving the emotional, social, and intellectual adjustment of the individual, for marriage can be no better than the people in it.

ANNULMENT

Annulments are not common, but they do occur. A couple might request an annulment for one of several reasons. Like divorce, grounds for annulment are determined by the states. In some states, an annulment is not mandatory because it is only a declaration that a marriage never existed. If, by law, the marriage never existed, that fact does not need to be declared. But an annulment decree is helpful for judicial certainty, and is recommended if the couple wish to know with certainty that they are not married. Annulments are granted, depending on the state, for the following reasons: one of the partners is already married to someone else (bigamy); the parties were insane, intoxicated, or just joking at the time of the wedding; force or duress was involved (e.g., shotgun weddings); one (or both) of the parties was not old enough to marry and did not have parental consent. These are perhaps the most common grounds, but there are others. The annulment laws of the fifty states are summarized in the Appendix.

There are two terms which apply to marriages which are being annulled: void and voidable. In law, any act which is void is null and ineffectual; it has no legal force or binding effect. In a marriage which is void, the union has never really existed. For instance, since laws do not permit bigamy, marriage to an already married person is void and never really existed. A marriage which is voidable is one which *may* be declared void. It is not void in and of itself. A voidable marriage has the potential of being declared void, but a proper court proceeding must declare it so. Non-age is the most common ground for declaring a marriage void. If one (or both) of the spouses was not of age, then there is the *option* of letting the marriage continue or annulling it. For instance, the parents might give their permission to the marriage, and it would be allowed to continue. Or perhaps by the time the non-age is discovered the couple are above the legal age and wish to continue the marriage.

SEPARATION

A legal separation, in contrast to an informal one arranged only by the couple, is much like a formal divorce. The only difference is that the couple are not divorced. They are still legally married and can terminate their separated status at any time by asking the appropriate judge for a change in status. Most legally separated couples do not remain in this status indefinitely, although it is possible to do so. A couple may wish to have a legal separation while they consider divorce or while they attempt reconciliation, or they may want it in order to avoid some of the effects of divorce. They may also request separation to protect financial and other interests while a divorce is pending, during a waiting period between filing and final decree, or while a contested divorce is under litigation. Whatever their reasons, to gain a legal separation one or both partners will need to retain an attorney(s) who will assist them in drawing up a separation agreement. Such an agreement will specify custody of the children, child support, visitation rights, handling of financial matters, custody of property, and perhaps temporary alimony.

CHILD SUPPORT AND ALIMONY

All states have some provision for the support of children whose parents are divorcing. Most, but not all, states also allow for alimony. *Child support* refers to monetary payment made by the parent who does not have custody of the children to the parent who does have custody. The money is intended to be used for the support of the children. Most women are awarded custody of their children. Although this is changing somewhat, it is likely to continue to be the rule rather than the exception for some time. Husbands, therefore, usually pay child support. Fathers usually will be given privileges of visitation or custody during parts of the year. The amount of child support is determined by the husband's income, the number of children, and the ability of the wife to contribute to the support of the children. The amount will be determined by the judge presiding over the divorce, but the judge will accept a reasonable recommendation by the couple and their attorney(s). Child support ordinarily is not tax deductible.

Alimony refers to payments made by an individual to his or her former spouse. Although most states allow for alimony, these payments are not customary following divorce. More common is what is known as a property or lump-sum settlement. At the time of divorce, assets are divided up according to arrangements worked out by the couple, their attorneys, and the judge. If the couple can agree on a fair settlement, the judge will usually approve it. If they cannot agree, the judge will, after hearing arguments on both sides, make a decision. A property settlement divides assets such as the home, automobile, furniture, and other possessions. A lump-sum settlement at divorce usually involves a "payment" from the husband to the wife of a lump sum of money, often substantial. Although the laws of many states now provide for lump-sum settlements favoring husbands over wives, it is usually the other way around since husbands tend to have greater earning power, and more of the savings have been accumulated by them. Alimony is tax deductible in some circumstances, but the tax laws are somewhat complicated in this regard.

POST-DIVORCE ADJUSTMENT

For some individuals divorce is jumping from the frying pan into the fire. It does not solve their problem. "Divorce is often the least harmful of all the available evils, but it is never the best of all conceivable worlds" (Wheeler, 1974). There is a difference between "solution" and "escape." After the decree and the removal of the immediately aggravating circumstances, the divorced person may feel that the situation was not so bad after all, that the divorce was too hasty, that the decree is regrettable, and that there was more love for the spouse than was realized.

One woman seen in counseling was married a total of four times, twice to the same man. Weiss (1975) refers to "the persistence of attachment." There are, too, of course, persons from whom divorces are obtained against their will. They may have committed some offense which gives the other person grounds for divorce, or they may be disinclined to use a defense, yet they do not want a divorce. For such persons a divorce may be profoundly disruptive.

The divorced person faces several problems. The conflict and rebellion (within self) must be settled. Wounded pride must be repaired. Habits must be readjusted. Such habits may have become more a part of the individual's life than was realized. Social relationships and friendships must be reorganized. A new relationship with the couple's children is necessary, no matter with which parent they live. Sexual life must be reoriented. A woman previously not employed may have to arrange for support. The individual is called upon to become accustomed to a change in identity.

Marriage, even a marriage that is not particularly satisfactory, has a way of becoming part of an individual's life and personality. Behavior patterns are not readily altered. Memories of the early years of marriage are not readily erased. The image of the spouse-that-used-to-be lingers. In the idealization lent by time and distance the unpleasant aspects of marriage may be forgotten and the pleasant aspects magnified. At best, the divorced individual must go through a period of readjustment. In few cases is it easy. In some instances divorce does solve problems or afford escape from those that are insoluble. In other instances the problems are too deep-set to be solved by court decree. The individual, though altering the type of problem confronted, does not decrease the intensity of the problem situation.

REMARRIAGE

This is a time when monogamous marriage is being called into question, when there are assertions on every hand that marriage and the nuclear family have failed, when some persons are experimenting with unconventional forms of relationships with the expectation that changing the structure of relationships will somehow change their functioning. Yet it is both interesting and significant that so many individuals, having experienced marriage and having had it fail, try it again. One would think that if the gloomy theorizers were correct, persons who had experienced monogamous marriage and the nuclear family and in one way or another had escaped would never allow themselves to make a mistake and be caught in the same dreadful trap again. But quite the contrary is true. The formerly married return to marriage. There must be profound values involved. How could those values be more dramatically indicated than in the remarriage rate? Not only do the formerly married return to marriage, but their return is characterized by a high rate of success.

Approximately one-fourth of all persons marrying have been married at least once before (Williams and Kuhn, 1973). As divorce rates increased during the 1960s, the tendency for divorced persons to remarry also increased, but the increase was more pronounced for men than women (U.S. Department of Health, Education, and Welfare, *Monthly Vital Statistics Report*, 1973). Although the increase appears to have leveled off in the 1970s, most divorced persons continue to remarry, and they do so within a remarkably brief span of time. One-sixth of previously divorced persons are remarried within one year of the divorce decree, and about half are remarried within three years. More than four out of every five divorced

About one in four marriages involves at least one person who is marrying for the second time. Remarriage following divorce or widowhood is common throughout the life cycle. (Myron Wood, Photo Researchers)

persons eventually remarry (Glick and Norton, 1976). Whereas divorced persons remarry on the average 3.2 years after the divorce, widowed persons take a longer time to remarry (Glick and Norton, 1976).

Remarriage is more common for divorced persons than for the widowed. The remarriage rates are higher for men than for women, probably because there are more widowed and divorced women than men. The increases in remarriage rates apply mainly to whites, not to blacks. The remarriage rates are highest at younger ages, with median ages of a first remarriage being 29.4 for females and 32.8 for males. Remarrying couples are more likely to have a civil ceremony, and their weddings are more likely to be seasonally dispersed—unlike first marriages which are disproportionately clustered in June and August (Williams and Kuhn, 1973; Glick and Norton, 1976).

If we compare two individuals of the same age, one who has never been married and one who has been divorced, regardless of the age the previously married person has a greater likelihood of marrying in a given time span than the never-married person.

Kephart (1973) interviewed women who had participated in discussion groups of divorced persons. He says, "A substantial majority—perhaps 80 to 90 percent—wish to remarry. The fact that their first marriages ended in divorce has by no means soured them on matrimony." Couples who divorce, therefore, are not rejecting marriage per se, but are rejecting a particular partner. The above evidence, considered together, indicates that our high divorce rate is not an indication of a declining marriage institution. As a social institution, marriage appears to be healthy and strong.

As we pointed out earlier in this chapter, remarried persons have higher divorce rates than do persons married for the first time. We explained that the difference may be due, in large part, to the propensity of these individuals to seek a divorce if the marriage should fail. It has been observed by social scientists (e.g., Leslie, 1973), however, that the *quality* of remarriages is no lower than the quality of first marriages. In fact, remarriages may be happier on the whole than are first marriages, since these individuals have the wisdom gained from a marriage that failed. They may have entered into the first marriage hastily or inadvisedly, but they entered the second marriage with less idealism and romanticism. The individual's expectations for the second marriage may be more realistic than his or her expectations were for the first. He or she may have gained from the experience of one bad marriage, and additional maturity may have been gained with age. Thus, we should not jump to the conclusion from the remarriage-divorce data that second or subsequent marriages are doomed to failure. Quite the contrary may be true.

TERMS TO BE LEARNED

adultery
adversary system
alimony
annulment
child support
collusion
comparative rectitude
condonation
connivance
defendant
demographic projection
desertion
divorce mill
divorce rate
ground for divorce
incompatibility
infidelity
marital dissolution
marital quality
marital stability
no-fault divorce
nonsupport
plaintiff
recrimination
remarriage
separation
separation ratio

SELECTED READINGS

BOHANNAN, P. (ed.): *Divorce and After*, Doubleday Company, Inc., Garden City, N.Y., 1970. Readings on the process and aftermath of divorce; includes cross-cultural comparisons.

CUSE, A.: *Financial Guideline: Divorce*, Guideline Publishing Co., Los Angeles, 1971. Initial look at points to consider before deciding on divorce and at current trends; covers financial and legal aspects of alimony, child support, hiring an attorney, attaining an adequate financial settlement, and other matters.

EPSTEIN, JOSEPH: *Divorced in America: Marriage in an Age of Possibility*, E. P. Dutton & Co., New York, 1974. Himself divorced, the author describes his experiences, feelings, and thoughts; what it means to go through the divorce process; law and social factors affecting divorce, alimony, and child custody; aftermath of divorce; problems to be faced. Author expresses bias toward the nuclear family.

GOODE, WILLIAM J.: *Women in Divorce*, The Free Press, New York, 1956. Analyzes the processes by which mothers are moved into a new position; deals with steps toward the divorce, the final dissolution, and post-divorce adjustment.

HUNT, M. M.: *The World of the Formerly Married*, McGraw-Hill Book Company, New York, 1966. A professional journalist delves into the social sciences by presenting the results of a large number of enlightening interviews with formerly married persons.

KRANTZLER, MEL: *Creative Divorce*, New American Library, New York, 1975. (Paperback.) Based on author's experience of divorce and a series of "divorce adjustment seminars" conducted by him. His objective is to present a positive program to help the individual accept divorce, get through the divorce crisis, and profit from the experience.

LOPATA, H. Z.: *Widowhood in an American City*, Schenkman Publishing Co., Cambridge, Mass., 1973. A sociological study of widowhood in Chicago based on a large number of personal interviews.

SHERESKY, N., AND M. MANNES: *Uncoupling: The Act of Coming Apart*, The Viking Press, New York, 1972. A practical guide to the emotional, as well as legal, complications of divorce; case study material used throughout the book.

SWITZER, E.: *The Law for a Woman*, Charles Scribner's Sons, New York, 1975. Explains various laws affecting women, including a state-by-state listing of the grounds for divorce.

WEISS, ROBERT S.: *Marital Separation: Coping with the End of Marriage and the Transition to*

Being Single Again, Basic Books, Inc., New York, 1975. Specific difficulties encountered by the separated; the decision to separate; the single parent; effect on children; steps leading to new attachments. Author organized a series of seminars for the separated and includes many direct quotations from the participants.

WHEELER, MICHAEL: *No-Fault Divorce*, Beacon Press, Boston, 1974. Discussion of no-fault divorce, its effects, advantages, and disadvantages; children in the divorce process; Nevada divorces; "quickie divorces"; migratory divorce.

WOMEN IN TRANSITION, INC.: *Women in Transition: A Feminist Handbook on Separation and Divorce*, Charles Scribner's Sons, New York, 1975. A guide to separation, divorce, child custody—the legalities and emotional trauma.

Chapter 16

Marriage and Family Counseling

In spite of their good intentions at the time of the wedding, most couples face problems of one sort or another as their marriage proceeds. Many of these problems, perhaps the majority, the couple themselves are able to solve—or live with. But in some cases a couple exhaust their own resources, and, though they have a will to succeed, they do not know the next steps to take. In many instances of this kind outside help may give them the suggestion, impetus, or reorientation needed. When home remedies fail in marriage, it is good sense to turn to someone qualified to provide assistance, just as one would in case of injury or disease. It is better to do that than to let a marriage atrophy or die in agony. Yet there are many people who hesitate to seek counseling. They do not want to admit that they cannot solve their problems by themselves, or they hesitate to divulge aspects of their private lives. Such reluctance seems to be more commonly found in men and in persons of lesser education than in college-educated individuals. Women are more accustomed than men to accept the help of others, and more highly educated persons may better understand the dynamics of counseling and what counseling can accomplish. Counseling also tends to attract people in younger rather than older age groups.

Who Should Visit a Counselor?

When there is a marital problem, it is important that both husband and wife seek counseling. It takes two persons to make a marriage, and it takes two to solve marital problems. One spouse alone cannot do it. Also, there are at least two aspects to marital situations. There are, of course, facts—circumstances and personalities as they actually are. But more importantly, there are interpretations of these circumstances and personalities. Only rarely can a husband and wife be completely objective about their marriage and keep their individual interpretations from coloring their reactions to it. Hence, only rarely can a marital problem be solved merely by altering facts. However, each spouse assumes that he or she interprets the facts as they are, while the other spouse's interpretation is biased. Hence, the counselor is confronted with the necessity of trying to make sense out of two interpretations. Resolution of the problem, then, comes more through changing the spouses' interpretations than through altering facts.

In some instances, one spouse is unwilling to come for counseling. When this is the case, the willing spouse may come alone. The counselor will discuss with his or her client whether or not it is necessary for the other spouse to be present in order for counseling to continue. In most cases, the counselor will see the willing spouse alone if the other spouse is not willing to be involved.

When Should Counseling Be Sought?

Ordinarily, marital problems develop over a period of time. Hence, a couple need not wait until their problems reach a crisis stage, until they are obviously insoluble, before counseling is sought. Unfortunately many couples do wait too long, and therefore the counseling has disappointing results. Also, counseling may be considered not only as a means of solving problems but also as a means of preventing them, or at least preventing them from reaching a critical stage. Counseling may be thought of as a type of education as well as a type of therapy. This is especially true of premarital counseling, as will be discussed later.

What May Counseling Be Expected to Accomplish?

It is very important for a person or a couple to realize that neither counseling nor a counselor can solve a marital problem. The couple must solve their own problem, but the counselor may help them do it. A counselor's function is different from that of a physician. A physician diagnoses an illness by means of an evaluation of symptoms, test results, and other reasonably objective evidence. Having diagnosed, the physician then prescribes a remedy which may be surgical, medicinal, or in the form of advice. If the patient wants to recover from the illness, no matter whether he or she fully understands it, doing what the physician says is presumably the way to get well. On the other hand, although a counselor may diagnose, the diagnosis rests on a mixture of both subjective and objective data. If the client wants to solve the problem, this is accomplished through counselor-guided client decisions, understanding, and motivation—not by simply doing what the counselor says. The physician tells the patient what the solution to the problem is, while the counselor helps the client find the solution to the problem. Although no two persons are exactly alike, the physician may assume that they are nearly enough alike to make a prescription reasonable. To some degree illnesses may be categorized relative to both cause and remedy. But there are more ramifications to marital problems, partly because they involve two complete individuals each of whom is unique. Therefore, they cannot be categorized relative to either cause or remedy.

Some persons say, "Why should we talk to a counselor when we can discuss our problems together?" In the first place, of course they can discuss their problems together. But why have they not done this? In the second place, discussing a problem with a third party may provide new perspective and may de-emotionalize the problem either through the process of discussion or through the provision of an outlet for feelings that may be otherwise restrained. It is often found that a couple can discuss a problem with a counselor in a reasonably controlled and objective manner, yet when they discuss it at home they become emotionally stirred up, sometimes to the point of irrationality.

There are no instant solutions to marital problems, and instant solutions should be

Marriage counseling may not succeed if a couple are not motivated to change or are resistive to the counselor. In their final session, this couple look with pride to their progress in counseling. (Bruce Roberts, Rapho/Photo Researchers)

neither expected nor anticipated in counseling. In most cases, several sessions are needed before a solution may be reached. In fact, some problems are insoluble, and the couple (or one of them) are faced with the alternatives of dissolving the marriage or continuing to live with the problem.

Some persons visit counselors hoping that an outsider will confirm their own judgment to the effect that they themselves are right and the other spouse is wrong. Strictly speaking, such persons do not want counseling because in their own minds they already have "all the answers." A counselor does not take sides or place blame. It may be true that one spouse is more at fault than the other, but it is not the counselor's function to declare this. The objective of counseling is to solve marital problems, not to judge spouses.

The counselor's function is to help people solve their problems within their own value structures, not to impose a value structure on them. There may be limitations on such a broad generalization in specific cases, but this is not equivalent to the counselor agreeing personally that "anything goes." The counselor may recognize that a client's values may need reexamination and reassessment, but this is accomplished through the client's efforts, not by counselor decree. The counselor does not make moral judgments. Moralizing is not counseling.

A counselor should not be expected to take the initiative in suggesting a conference, although the counselor may make it known that such a conference is available. People are not helped through counseling, marital or individual, unless they want to be helped. The motivation to take the first step toward counseling is equivalent to taking the first step toward problem solving.

Whatever is said during a counseling conference is considered strictly confidential. The counselor does not divulge to any other person, even to the other spouse, what is said, unless permission to do so is obtained from the client. Sometimes, after one spouse has visited a counselor, the other spouse does so, too, and expects the counselor to divulge what has been said by the first spouse. Since competent counselors do not violate confidentiality without permission, an individual may speak freely. Without confidentiality counseling would lose most of its effectiveness.

Through counseling, situational or relationship problems can more effectively be modified or solved. Personality problems are more complex, elusive, and less amenable to change. Of course, some personality problems may be approached through psychiatric or psychological counseling; most marriage counselors have some training in these areas, but tend to focus their practice on marriage and family relationships.

Types of Counseling

Marriage counseling, broadly defined, is any consultation of a married person with anyone else about his or her marriage. Marriage counseling with a trained and licensed professional usually involves both spouses. There may be variation, however, in how the counseling is conducted. The format used will depend on the counselor and his or her approach but also on the specific situation presented by the couple. Both spouses may be seen together in all sessions. The counselor may want to see each spouse individually once and then together after those initial sessions, or spouses may be seen individually on a more regular basis. The counselor may also use techniques which involve alternatives between individual and joint sessions. Other variations are used depending on the circumstances.

Family counseling is consultation involving family problems which may extend beyond the marriage relationship. There is a very fine line between marriage and family counseling, since children, parents, and other family members are likely to have an influence on any problems which may have developed. In both marriage and family counseling, counselors sometimes ask a colleague to participate in the counseling process. For example, a child may be seen by one counselor while parents are seen by another. In some cases, different counselors see each spouse, and in still other cases, two counselors work together in all sessions.

Family therapy is a specialized form of treatment in which all family members are involved in the counseling and are seen together regardless of what the problem is or who is involved. The basic theory behind family therapy is that no matter who seems to have the problem, the entire family is probably involved in creating it, since they form such a powerful reference group for each other. Family therapy is often used when there are particular problems evident with one child.

The Nature of Marriage and Family Counseling

Marriage and family counselors deal with a range of problems including premarital counseling, sexual adjustment and dysfunction, family financial management, conflict, communication, in-law problems, family decision making, problems in child rearing or parent-child relationships, divorce and post-divorce adjustment, and other matters which relate to the marital relationship, the family situation, or personal-emotional matters that are closely tied to marital and family relationships. Marriage and family counseling is different from *psychotherapy* or *psychoanalysis*, forms of treatment directed more to the individual and his or her emotional or psychological adjustment. Problems such as anxiety, depression, inability to adapt to one's environment, and difficulty in dealing with other persons are more routinely seen by persons who practice psychotherapy and psychoanalysis. Marriage and family counselors, social workers, psychologists, clergymen, physicians, psychiatrists, and members of other "helping" professions often work together or consult with each other about their work. In most communities, counselors will refer a client to another professional if they feel that he or she could better be helped by someone with a different type of training or specialization. In actuality, many marriage and family counselors are also psychotherapists or psychiatrists or have training in related areas.

The Counselor

Friends and relatives ordinarily do not function effectively as counselors. Often they freely give advice, which tends to fall on deaf ears. They may have deep concern for the couple or one of them. But it is difficult for such persons to be objective, since they are to some degree emotionally involved, and usually they do not have the training, background, or experience upon which effective counseling is based. They all too often look at the couple's problem through their own eyes rather than the couple's, and their suggestions tend to be of the "if I were you" variety.

Physicians may serve effectively as counselors on marital problems if they have the necessary personal qualifications and understanding. But, as mentioned earlier, physicians are accustomed to diagnosing and prescribing; they are inclined by training to impose what they think is the solution to the problem on the couple instead of helping the couple to reach their own solution. And most physicians have no formal training in counseling. Also, many physicians are very busy. They may not be inclined to devote the time to counseling that effective counseling requires. A physician may be more than amply qualified to practice medicine and yet not have an understanding of personality or of marital problems. Some physicians are cognizant of human anatomy and physiology but lack an adequate understanding of human sexuality. Only in recent years has the study of human sexuality been introduced into the curricula of some medical schools.

Clergymen of all faiths commonly serve as counselors on marital problems. Some of them do very well. Others are too busy with church affairs to give the necessary time. Still others tend to moralize. Some even use a counseling conference as an opportunity to deliver a miniature sermon. Like physicians, most clergymen have background and training in their particular profession (for example, theology, ethics, pastoral care) but lack specific training in marriage and family counseling.

Marriage and family counseling—or at least advice giving—is probably as ancient as marriage itself. But in recent years there has emerged a specific profession, that of marriage and family counselor, involving special training and special qualifying assessment of practitioners by professional organizations or state licensing boards, or both. In some states, marriage counselors are licensed. But even such qualifying assessment does not guarantee that all counselors are equally competent, just as similar assessment in other professions does not guarantee that all professionals are equally competent. Counselors, like their clients, are individuals and should be evaluated and selected as such. Every counselor, just as every individual in any profession, should (ideally) be aware of his or her own limitations and should not go beyond his or her competence. No counselor is equally competent to discuss all possible problems; clients should be freely referred to other counselors as situations indicate. It is not a symptom of incompetence for a counselor to say, "I don't know." It may rather be a symptom of competence.

Counselors range in competence from highest to lowest. Some are so low on the competence scale and so lacking in certain characteristics desirable in counselors or, conversely, so endowed with characteristics undesirable in counselors that they may be classified as quacks or charlatans. Some of these are not only incompetent but even downright unscrupulous. How may they be recognized? The following are possible clues:

▶ They make extravagant claims. They do not recognize or admit their own limitations and make much of asserting that they can handle a great variety of problems.

▶ They advertise. The fact that a counselor is listed in the yellow pages of a telephone book is permissible, however, since this type of listing is not considered advertising.

▶ Their fees are excessively high. Some persons who do marriage counseling do not charge fees, for example, clergymen. But most professional counselors for whom counseling is a major part or all of their professional activity do of necessity charge fees. Fees for such counseling vary just as do fees for medical, dental, or legal services. By and large these fees are reasonable.

▶ They sometimes demand payment in advance for service not yet rendered. The impression given is that they are more interested in the fees than in the counselee.

▶ When asked about their training and experience, they are vague and evasive. In some cases they fabricate training and experience which they have not had.

▶ They make "snap" diagnoses. They may have one solution to all problems or may resort to highly oversimplified solutions to complex problems.

▶ They put excessive pressure on the counselee to return for more counseling.

▶ They divulge confidential information.

How May Competent Counselors Be Located?

College and university students are particularly fortunate, first, because so many college and university communities have available a multiplicity of professional services, and second, because so often within the school there are persons who are competent counselors themselves or can recommend someone to the individual seeking help. Once the initial contacts are made in the school community, referral may be made to other off-campus counselors when the student leaves school.

Of course, many individuals develop marital problems after leaving school and while living in a community where professional personnel are not known or may not be found. The American Association of Marriage and Family Counselors (AAMFC) is the primary professional association in this field. Applicants for membership are carefully screened before counselors are certified and admitted. Members are found throughout the country. An individual seeking a marriage counselor may write or telephone the Association's Headquarters (Executive Director, 225 Yale Avenue, Claremont, CA 91711, telephone 714-621-4749). The individual will be referred to a qualified counselor available in his or her community or some other community within travel distance. The counselor may then be contacted. Marriage and family counseling may also be obtained through many community or family service agencies.

Training of Marriage and Family Counselors

The American Association of Marriage and Family Counselors has rigorous standards for certification. A member must have recognized graduate professional education with a minimum of an earned master's degree from an accredited educational institution in an appropriate behavioral science field, mental health discipline, or recognized helping profession. For example, marriage and family counselors may be clinical or counseling psychologists, physicians (usually psychiatrists), sociologists, social workers, or clergymen (trained in pastoral counseling).

Of course much of this graduate training is expected to be related to marriage and the family. Thus, certification as a marriage and family counselor entails more than the usual requirements for such professions: (1) The counselor must have 200 hours of approved supervision in the practice of marriage and family counseling, ordinarily to be completed in a two- to three-year period. Supervision means that the student counselor works under the careful guidance of a very experienced counselor and has meetings with that person at least weekly to discuss the student counselor's cases and to evaluate his or her personal and professional growth. (2) Following this intensive period of supervision, the counselor must have 1,000 hours of clinical experience in the practice of marriage and family counseling under approved supervision, involving at least fifty different cases. Variations in these requirements are allowed depending on the applicant's type of academic background and training.

Some Basic Principles

The first principle used in counseling is the necessity of establishing *rapport*. Without rapport between counselor and client, little communication would result, and little progress would be made. Individuals sometimes say, "Why should I pay all that money just to have someone listen to me talk for an hour?" Is it a fact that counselors don't say much, or is it just a myth? It is true that counselors do a lot of listening, and in some sessions they may hardly say anything at all. But there is a reason for this. Following the establishment of rapport, the counselor needs to listen. He or she needs to hear the problem in the words of the client. The counselor may probe by asking questions, or may ask the client to elaborate on some points but not others. This is an important early step in any kind of counseling. This principle is called *ventilation*. Persons in distress usually have a need to ventilate their feelings, conflicts, hostilities, aggressions, or whatever else is on their mind. Ventilation may be in and of itself therapeutic. A third important principle is *interpretation*. After hearing about the problem and evaluating it, the counselor may make certain interpretations of what dynamics may be involved in the problem. The counselor often strives to encourage *insight development*. This is a fourth principle in counseling and has as its purpose encouraging the clients themselves to understand the source of the problem and what part they have in the dynamics of the situation. *Support* is a fifth principle. Counselors often take a major role in providing support for their clients. Many clients are dejected or frustrated because of the problem at hand. They need to be told that the problem can be solved if they are motivated to do so. The counselor has a role, then, in providing the couple with the emotional and intellectual support they need to get back on their feet.

Motivation is probably the single most important ingredient in the success of counseling. In marriage counseling, this means that both partners must want to work at the problem. Unsuccessful marital counseling often has as its cause the unwillingness of one or both partners to work at improving the marriage. Do marriage counselors disapprove of divorce? Do they encourage or discourage it? Actually, most marriage counselors are neither for nor against divorce. When it is warranted, when all else has failed, when the best efforts of the couple and counselor indicate that the marriage cannot succeed, most counselors will help a couple make a satisfactory adjustment to divorce. The actual decision to divorce, however, can only be the couple's. In some cases, counseling which ends in divorce for the couple can be considered successful counseling.

Some counselors are more *behaviorally* oriented than others. Behaviorally oriented therapy is directed to changing the actual day-to-day behaviors of the spouses. It is reasoned that all the talk in the world and all the understanding developed will not solve a problem unless actual behaviors are changed. Other counselors rely almost exclusively on insight development, reasoning that this should be the main focus of the counseling since no problem can be adequately solved unless the clients understand why it exists and how the individuals contribute to it. Most counselors use a combination of these two strategies. Thus, couples who seek marriage counseling will often spend considerable time talking about the problems at hand, but they may also be given "homework" assignments and activities to work on between sessions.

Premarital and Postmarital Counseling

Some marital problems may be prevented if counseling is sought before the wedding. The subject of such counseling may be a specific premarital problem, or it may be a checkup before marriage is undertaken. Students may say something to this effect: "We plan to marry, and marriage is going to be very important to us. We want to enter it with as much insight as we can get. We'd like to talk it over with you just to make sure that we have not overlooked anything." Such a premarital checkup makes every bit as much sense as an annual medical examination or a checkup on a new car.

Divorced or widowed persons frequently face problems as critical, complex, and traumatic as those faced by married persons. They, too, may be helped through counseling.

The Responsibility of the Prospective Counselee

When an individual or a couple visit a counselor, it is not a matter of transferring the problem to the counselor's shoulders and waiting for a ready-made solution. There is a responsibility to enter the counseling relationship intending to talk freely and candidly, to keep an open mind and work through to a solution (if possible) with the counselor, to persist until a solution is found or the impossibility of a solution is admitted.

Couples should feel free to inquire about counseling without any obligation whatsoever. In the first session, they may ask about fees and about the counselor's qualifications. They have the right to be fully informed about what is involved. They may want to make an initial agreement that they will evaluate their progress after a certain number of sessions to determine whether counseling should continue or terminate. They should be as open and straightforward as possible with the counselor and have the right to expect the same in return from the counselor. However, they must respect the counselor's profession and not try to undermine what he or she is trying to do. Some individuals tend to "intellectualize," always claiming to have all the answers and know more than the counselor. Clients should work with the counselor, not against him or her. Above all, it must be remembered that every counselor is different, as is every couple. Consequently, there are no pat answers or formulas for success in counseling, since every case will also be different.

TERMS TO BE LEARNED

behaviorally
charlatan
counseling
counselor
family counseling
family therapy
insight development
interpretation
marriage counseling
motivation
psychoanalysis
psychotherapy
rapport
situational problem
support
therapy
value structure
ventilation

SELECTED READINGS

KNOX, D.: *Marriage Happiness: A Behavioral Approach to Counseling*, Research Press Company, Champaign, Ill., 1971. Discusses marital problems and one particular set of approaches for solving them.

KOCH, JOANNE, AND LEW KOCH: *The Marriage Savers*, Coward, McCann & Geoghegan, Inc., New York, 1976. This book is addressed to people who need or who are seeking help. Based on over 100 interviews with therapists and 200 individuals and couples. Discusses types of counselors and therapists, clergymen, social service agencies; kinds of therapy; sex clinics—values, drawbacks, limitations; encounter groups; controversial procedures; competent and incompetent counselors and therapists—how to recognize quacks and exploiters; how to find a competent counselor or therapist. Lists many names and addresses.

SATIR, V.: *Conjoint Family Therapy*, Science and Behavior Books, Palo Alto, Calif., 1964. Intended to prepare students for effective family therapy work; emphasizes use of the family as therapeutic unit.

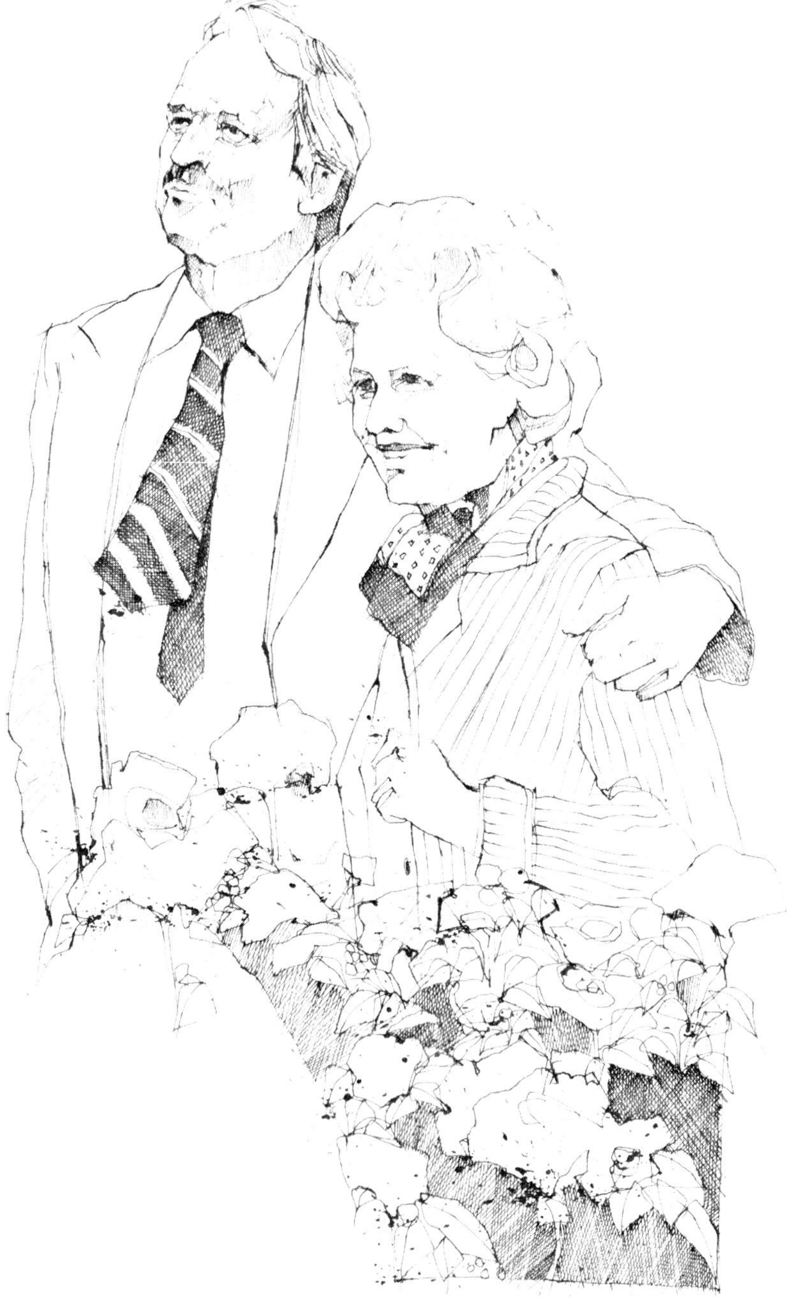

Epilog

If, as authors of this text, we were required to identify a theme which guided the preparation of this book, we would acknowledge our belief that marriage is an institution of great personal interest to most Americans which deserves—indeed requires—the attention of scholars, researchers, and students. The primary objective of this book, therefore, has been to present an organized body of factual information which is based on the best available research data and scholarly analysis, on our experience in teaching and counseling, and on our own thinking about the issues, problems, realities, and personal concerns relating to marriage. Marriage can and should be a topic for study; and we have endeavored to present a comprehensive but useful discussion of the topics which our readers might find relevant.

We should like to conclude our presentation by making three points. First, the institution of marriage has changed throughout history, it differs from culture to culture, and it varies from couple to couple. Marriage is a dynamic institution which has lasted through periods when other social institutions have not endured. Furthermore, each couple who marry find that their own marriage changes throughout its unique history, sometimes culminating in a lifelong relationship, sometimes culminating in separation or divorce. Regardless of the nature and extent of changes in the marital institution or changes in a given couple's marriage, it is evident that in the years ahead most individuals are likely to marry, as did the men and women of previous generations. It is also true, however, that some individuals will choose not to marry and others will design their own marriage relationships to suit their particular needs. This conclusion leads us to our second point.

As our society has become more open to new life-styles, more tolerant of individual variation, and more willing to accept individuals with values and attitudes different from those of the majority, so has marriage changed. Many of the changes which we have discussed in this book point to the great freedom that individuals have in structuring their contemporary marriages in ways that are best for them. Not only can we say that no two marriages are alike, we can also say that no two marriages need be alike. We are of the opinion that the freedom and independence which are available to modern couples can be used to maximize the rewards of marriage. Social change and change in marriage are not incompatible. On the contrary, they may complement each other in advantageous ways.

Our third point is a simple one. No book contains all the answers nor even asks all the questions. This book should be considered no more than the first step in education about marriage. The reader will find, as the authors have, that there is much more to be learned about the topics presented in this book through both reading and the continuous evaluation of personal experience—and, fortunately, the field is a growing one which makes this continued education possible.

Appendix

Marriage and Divorce Laws in the Fifty States

Appendix

Divorce Laws

	No-fault grounds only	Mixed grounds: Fault	Mixed grounds: No-fault	Fault grounds only	Residence required	Time between interlocutory and final decree
Alabama		a-k	x		6 months	none
Alaska		a-i;k	x		1 year	none
Arizona	x				90 days	none
Arkansas		a-f;h,i,k	3-year separation		60 days	none
California	x (plus insanity)				6 months	6 months
Colorado	x				90 days	none
Connecticut		a-d;f;h,k	x plus 3-year separation		1 year	none
Delaware		a-h;i,k	x plus 18-month separation		2 years	3 months
District of Columbia		a,b,d	1-year separation		1 year	none
Florida	x (plus insanity)				6 months	none
Georgia		a-h;j,k	x		6 months	none
Hawaii	x				1 year	
Idaho		a-d;f,h,i	x plus 5-year separation		6 weeks	none
Illinois				a-g;k	6 months	none
Indiana		c,d,h	x		6 months	none
Iowa	x				1 year	none
Kansas		a-d;f;h,i	x		60 days	none
Kentucky	x				180 days	none
Louisiana		a,d	2-year separation		1 year	none
Maine		a-c;e-g;i	x		6 months	none
Maryland		a,b,d,e,h	1-year separation		1 year	none
Massachusetts		a-g;i	x		2 years	6 months
Michigan	x				1 year	none
Minnesota	x				1 year	none
Mississippi		a-h;j,k	x		1 year	none
Missouri	x				90 days	none
Montana	x				1 year	none
Nebraska	x				1 year	6 months
Nevada	x (plus insanity)				6 weeks	none
New Hampshire		a-f;i,k	x plus 2-year separation		1 year	none
New Jersey		a-d;f-h	18-month separation		1 year	none
New Mexico		a-c	x		6 months	none
New York		a-d	1-year separation		1 year	none
North Carolina		a,d,e,h,j,k	1-year separation		6 months	none

North Dakota	a-d;f,h,i	x	1 year	none
Ohio	a-f;i,k	2-year separation	6 months	none
Oklahoma	a-f;h-k	x	6 months	none
Oregon		x	6 months	90 days
Pennsylvania			1 year	none
Rhode Island	a-g;i,k	x plus 5-year separation	2 years	6 months
South Carolina	a-c;f,g	3-year separation	1 year	none
South Dakota			1 year	none
Tennessee	a-g;i-k	2-year separation	6 months	none
Texas	a-d;h	x plus 3-year separation	1 year	none
Utah	a-f;h,i	3-year separation	3 months	3 months
Vermont	a-d;h,i,k	6-month separation	6 months	3 months
Virginia	a-e;j,k	1-year separation	1 year	none
Washington	x	a-e;h,k	6 months	none
West Virginia	a-d;f-h	2-year separation	1 year	none
Wisconsin	a-d;f,h,i	1-year separation	6 months	none
Wyoming	a-f;h-k	2-year separation	60 days	none

Notes:

x indicates no-fault grounds, including irreconcilable differences, irretrievable breakdown of marriage, insupportable marriage, or incompatibility

Fault grounds are indicated by:
a—adultery
b—desertion; abandonment
c—cruelty
d—conviction; felony; imprisonment
e—impotence; physical incapacity
f—habitual drunkenness; intemperance
g—habitual use of drugs; addiction
h—insanity
i—nonsupport; willful neglect
j—woman pregnant (by another man) at marriage
k—other fault grounds (for example, unnatural behavior; indignities; bigamy; fraud; void or voidable marriage; disappearance)

Sources:

Alexander, S., *State-by-state Guide to Women's Legal Rights*. Wollstonecraft Incorporated, Los Angeles, 1975.
The Family Law Reporter, The Bureau of National Affairs, Inc., Washington, D.C., 1974-1976.
Sell, K. D., Personal communication, Dec. 20, 1976.
World Almanac and Book of Facts, 1976. Newspaper Enterprise Association, Inc., New York, 1975, p. 970.

Marriage Information

Compiled by William E. Mariano: Council on Marriage Relations, Inc., 110 East 42 St., New York, N.Y. 10017 (as of Nov. 1, 1975)

Marriageable age, by states, for both males and females with and without consent of parents or guardians. But in most states, the court has authority, in an emergency, to marry young couples below the ordinary age of consent, where due regard for their morals and welfare so requires. In many states, under special circumstances, blood test and waiting period may be waived.

State	With consent Men	With consent Women	Without consent Men	Without consent Women	Blood test Required	Other state accepted *	Wait for license	Wait after license
Alabama (b)	17	14	21	18	Yes	Yes	None	None
Alaska	18	16	19	18	Yes	No	3 days	None
Arizona	16^2	16	18	18	Yes	Yes	None	None
Arkansas	17	16^4	18	18	Yes	No	3 days	None
California	$—^2$	$—^2$	18	18	Yes	Yes	None	None
Colorado	16	16	18	18	Yes	....	None	None
Connecticut	16	16(q)	18	18	Yes	Yes	4 days	None
Delaware	—(q)	16^4	18	18	Yes	Yes	None	24 hrs. (c)
District of Columbia	18	16	21	18	Yes	Yes	3 days	None
Florida	18	16	21	21	Yes	Yes	3 days	None
Georgia	18	16	18	18	Yes	Yes	None (b)	None (o)
Hawaii	17(e)	16	18	18	Yes	Yes	None	None
Idaho	16	16	18	18	Yes	Yes	None (p)	None
Illinois (a)	—(e)	15(e)	18	18	Yes	Yes	None	None
Indiana	17	17	18	18	Yes	No	3 days	None
Iowa	16(e)	16(e)	18	18	Yes	Yes	3 days	None
Kansas	$—(e)^2$	$—(e)^2$	18	18	Yes	Yes	3 days	None
Kentucky	18	16	18	18	Yes	No	3 days	None
Louisiana (a)	18	16	18	18	Yes	No	None	72 hours
Maine	16	16	18	18	No	No	5 days	None
Maryland	18	16	21	18	None	None	48 hours	None
Massachusetts	$—^2$	$—^2$	18	18	Yes	Yes	3 days	None
Michigan (a)	—	16	18	18	Yes	No	3 days	None
Minnesota	—	16(e)	18	18	None	....	5 days	None
Mississippi (b)	17	15	21	21	Yes	....	3 days	None
Missouri	15	15	18	18	Yes	Yes	3 days	None
Montana	$—^2$	$—^2$	18	18	Yes	Yes	5 days	None
Nebraska	18	16	18	18	Yes	Yes	5 days	None
Nevada	—	16	18	18	None	None	None	None
New Hampshire (a)	14(e)	13(e)	18	18	Yes	Yes	5 days	None
New Jersey (a)	—	16	18	18	Yes	Yes	72 hours	None
New Mexico	16	16	21	21	Yes	Yes	None	None
New York	16	14	18	18	Yes	No	None	24 hrs.(h)
North Carolina (a)	16	16	18	18	Yes	Yes	None	None
North Dakota (a)	$—^2$	15	18	18	Yes	....	None	None
Ohio (a)	18	16	18	18	Yes	Yes	5 days	None
Oklahoma	16	16	18	18	Yes	No	None (f)	....
Oregon	18(e)	15(e)	18	18	Yes	No	7 days	None
Pennsylvania	16	16	18	18	Yes	Yes	3 days	None

451
Appendix

	With consent		Without consent		Blood test		Wait for license	Wait after license
State	Men	Women	Men	Women	Required	Other state accepted *		
Rhode Island (a) (b)	18	16	18	18	Yes	No	None	None
South Carolina	16	14	18	18	None	None	24 hrs.	None
South Dakota	18	16	18	18	Yes	Yes	None	None
Tennessee (b)	16	16	21	21	Yes	Yes	3 days	None
Texas	16	16	18	18	Yes	Yes	None	None
Utah (a)	16	14	21	18	Yes	Yes	None	None
Vermont (a)	18	16	18	18	Yes	....	None	5 days
Virginia (a)	16	16	18	18	Yes	Yes(r)	None	None
Washington	17	17	18	18	(d)	....	3 days	None
West Virginia	18[2]	16	18	18	Yes	No	3 days	None
Wisconsin	18	16	18	18	Yes	Yes	5 days	None
Wyoming	18	16	21	21	Yes	Yes	None	None
Puerto Rico	16	16	21	21	(f)	None	None	None
Virgin Islands	16	14	21	18	None	None	8 days	None

*Many states have additional special requirements; contact individual state.

(a) Special laws applicable to non-residents. (b) Special laws applicable to those under 21 years; Alabama: bond required if male is under 21, female under 18. (c) 24 hours if one or both parties resident of state; 96 hours if both parties are non-residents. (d) None, but male must file affidavit. (e) Parental consent plus Court's consent required. (f) None, but a medical certificate is required. (g) Wait for license from time blood test is taken; Arizona, 48 hours. (h) Marriage may not be solemnized within 10 days from date of blood test. (j) If either under 21; Idaho, 3 days; Oklahoma, 72 hrs. (x) May be waived. (l) 3 days if both applicants are under 18 or female is pregnant. (2) Statute provides for obtaining license with parental or court consent with no state minimum age. (3) If either party is under 18, 3 days. (4) Under 16, with parental and court consent. Delaware: Female under 18. (o) All those between 19-21 cannot waive 3 day waiting period. (p) If either under 18— wait full 3 days. (q) If under stated age court consent required. (r) Virginia blood test form must be used.

Source: *The World Almanac and Book of Facts, 1976.* Newspaper Enterprise Association, Inc., New York, 1975.

Appendix

Annulment Grounds

	Fraud	Force—duress	Insanity—feeble-mindedness	Impotence—physical incapacity	Nonage*	Prohibited degree of relationship	Previous existing marriage	Color—race**	Under influence of alcohol, drugs, incapacitating substances at time marriage solemnized	Married as a jest or dare	Other grounds
Alabama	x		x			x	x	x			
Alaska	x	x	x		x	x	x				
Arizona			x			x	x				
Arkansas	x	x		x	x	x		x			
California	x	x	x	x	x		x				
Colorado	x	x	x	x	x	x	x		x	x	
Connecticut						x					
Delaware	x	x	x	x	x	x	x		x	x	
District of Columbia	x	x	x	x	x	x	x				
Florida†	x	x					x				
Georgia	x		x		x	x	x		x		
Hawaii	x	x	x	x	x	x	x				A
Idaho	x	x	x	x	x	x	x				
Illinois	x	x	x			x					
Indiana	x		x		x	x	x				B
Iowa		x		x	x	x	x				
Kansas	x			x	x	x	x				C
Kentucky	x	x	x	x	x	x	x		x		
Louisiana	x	x				x	x				
Maine		x			x	x	x				D
Maryland						x	x				
Massachusetts			x		x	x	x				
Michigan	x	x	x		x	x	x				
Minnesota	x	x	x		x	x	x				
Mississippi	x		x	x	x	x	x	x			C–E
Missouri	x	x	x	x		x	x				E
Montana	x	x	x	x	x	x	x		x		
Nebraska	x	x	x	x	x	x	x				
Nevada	x		x		x	x	x				
New Hampshire				x	x	x	x				
New Jersey	x	x	x	x	x	x	x		x		
New Mexico					x	x	x				
New York	x	x	x	x	x	x	x				D
North Carolina	x		x	x	x	x	x	x			F
North Dakota	x	x	x	x	x	x	x				
Ohio	x	x	x	x	x	x	x				G
Oklahoma		x			x	x	x				
Oregon	x	x	x		x	x	x				
Pennsylvania		x				x	x		x		

Annulment Grounds

	Fraud	Force–duress	Insanity—feeble-mindedness	Impotence—physical incapacity	Nonage*	Prohibited degree of relationship	Previous existing marriage	Color–race**	Under influence of alcohol, drugs, incapacitating substances at time marriage solemnized	Married as a jest or dare	Other grounds
Rhode Island#			x		x	x	x				
South Carolina		x	x	x	x	x	x	x			
South Dakota	x	x	x	x	x	x	x				
Tennessee	x	x	x		x	x	x	x			
Texas	x	x	x	x	x	x	x		x		
Utah		x	x		x	x	x				E–B
Vermont	x	x	x	x	x	x	x				
Virginia	x	x	x	x	x	x					C–H–I
Washington	x	x	x		x	x	x		x		
West Virginia	x	x	x	x	x	x	x	x			C–H–B–I–J
Wisconsin	x	x	x	x	x	x	x				
Wyoming	x	x	x	x	x	x	x				

Notes:

*Nonage, without parental consent; **As a result of the Supreme Court decision and a precedent set in Virginia, this ground, while still on the books of the listed states, would not be seen as valid; #In Rhode Island the courts have no jurisdiction to annul marriages. The remedy is by divorce which may be granted for any prohibited marriage; A–Leprosy; loathsome disease; B–Venereal disease; C–Concealment of pregnancy; D–Life imprisonment; E–Not married by proper authority, failure to obtain license; F–Misrepresentation of condition of life, belief that woman is pregnant; G–Epilepsy; H–Unchastity, prostitution prior to marriage of either party; I–Felony conviction; J–Mistaken identity. †Circuit court has jurisdiction.

Sources:

Alexander, S. *State-by-state Guide to Women's Legal Rights*. Los Angeles: Wollstonecraft Incorporated, 1975.
Family Law Reporter, The. The Bureau of National Affairs, Inc., Washington, D.C., 1974–1976.
Martindale-Hubbell Law Directory (vol. VI). Martindale-Hubbell, Inc., Summit, New Jersey, 1974.

References

Abdul-Karim, Raja W., and Samir N. Beydoun: "Growth of the Human Fetus," pp. 37–52 in Raja W. Abdul-Karim (ed.), "Human Fetal Medicine," *Clinical Obstetrics and Gynecology*, vol. 17, no. 3, pp. 33–193, September 1974.
Ackerman, Nathan W.: *The Psychodynamics of Family Life*, Basic Books, Inc., New York, 1958.
Albert, A.: "The Mammalian Testis," in William C. Young (ed.), *Sex and Internal Secretions*, 3d ed., The Williams & Wilkins Company, Baltimore, 1961, chap. 5.
Allan, Malcolm S.: "Husband-attended Deliveries," *Obstetrics and Gynecology*, vol. 27, no. 1, pp. 146–148, January 1966.
Allen, Fred H., Jr., and Louis K. Diamond: *Erythroblastosis Fetalis*, Little, Brown and Company, Boston, 1957.
American Medical Association: *What you should know about "the pill"* (pamphlet), Chicago, 1970.
American Medical Association Committee on Human Sexuality: *Human Sexuality*, American Medical Association, Chicago, 1972.
American Social Health Association: *Today's VD Control Problem*, New York, 1971 and 1975.
Anderson, Gerald: "Prostaglandin vs. Saline for Midtrimester Abortion," *Contemporary OB/GYN*, vol. 4, no. 1, pp. 91–95, July 1974.
—— **and Leon Speroff:** "Prostaglandins and Abortion," pp. 245–257 in George Schaefer (ed.), "Legal Abortions in New York State: Medical, Legal, Nursing, Social Aspects (July 1–December 31, 1970)," *Clinical Obstetrics and Gynecology*, vol. 14, no. 1, pp. 1–324, March 1971.
Aronson, Howard G., and Carl F. Glienke: "A Study of the Incidence of Pregnancy following Adoption," *Fertility and Sterility*, vol. 14, no. 5, pp. 547–553, September-October 1963; abstracted in *Obstetrical and Gynecological Survey*, vol. 19, no. 1, pp. 158–159, February 1964.
Aronson, Marvin E.: "Fatal Air Embolism Caused by Bizarre Sexual Behavior during Pregnancy," *Medical Aspects of Human Sexuality*, vol. 3, no. 12, pp. 33–39, December 1969.
—— **and Philip K. Nelson:** "Fatal Air Embolism in Pregnancy Resulting from an Unusual Sex Act," *Obstetrics and Gynecology*, vol. 30, no. 1, pp. 127–130, July 1967.
Arrata, W. S. M., and L. Iffy: "Normal and Delayed Ovulation in the Human," *Obstetrical and Gynecological Survey*, vol. 26, no. 10, pp. 675–689, October 1971.
Arronet, George H., Carol A. Bergquist, and Mahendra C. Parekh: "The Influence of Adoption on Subsequent Pregnancy in Infertile Marriage," *International Journal of Fertility*, vol. 19, p. 159, 1974; abstracted in *Obstetrical and Gynecological Survey*, vol. 31, no. 1, pp. 30–31, January 1976.
Ayre, J. Ernest, Franklin C. Reyner, Wilma B. Fagundes, and J. Maurice LeGuerrier: "Oral Progestins and Regression of Carcinoma in

Situ and Cervical Dysplasia: Cytologic Evaluation," *Obstetrics and Gynecology*, vol. 34, no. 4, pp. 545–560, October 1969.

Aznar-Ramos, Ramon: "Side Effects Utilizing Placebo," in Edward T. Tyler (ed.), *Progress in Conception Control, 1969*, J. B. Lippincott Company, Philadelphia, 1969, pp. 54–60.

Bahr, S. J.: "Effects on Power and Division of Labor in the Family," in L. W. Hoffman and F. I. Nye (eds.), *Working Mothers*, Jossey-Bass, Inc., San Francisco, 1974.

Baker, T. G.: "A Quantitative Cytological Study of Germ Cells in Human Ovaries," *Proc. Soc. Roy. Med.*, vol. 56, p. 417, 1963; abstracted in *Obstetrical and Gynecological Survey*, vol. 19, no. 4, pp. 700–701, August 1964.

Bakker, Cornelis B., and Cameron R. Dightman: "Side Effects of Oral Contraceptives," *Obstetrics and Gynecology*, vol. 28, no. 3, pp. 373–379, September 1966.

Ballard, Charles A., and Francis E. Ballard: "Four Years' Experience with Midtrimester Abortion by Amnioinfusion," *American Journal of Obstetrics and Gynecology*, vol. 114, no. 5, pp. 575–581, Nov. 1, 1972.

Barber, Hugh R. K., Edward A. Graber, and James J. O'Rourke: *Are the Pills Safe?* Charles C Thomas, Publisher, Springfield, Ill., 1969.

Bardwick, Judith M.: "Psychological Conflict and the Reproductive System," in Judith M. Bardwick, Elizabeth Douvan, Matina S. Horner, and David Gutmann, *Feminine Personality and Conflict*, Brooks/Cole Publishing Company, Monterey, Calif., 1970.

———: *Psychology of Women*, Harper & Row, Publishers, Inc., New York, 1971.

Barnett, L. D.: "Research on International and Interracial Marriages," *Marriage and Family Living*, vol. 25, pp. 105–107, 1963.

Barron, Donald H.: "The Placenta as Fetal Lung," in Claude A. Villee (ed.), *The Placenta and Fetal Membranes*, The Williams & Wilkins Company, Baltimore, 1960, chap. 4.

Barron, M.: *The Blending American*, Quadrangle Press, Chicago, 1972.

Bartell, G. D.: *Group Sex: An Eyewitness Report on the American Way of Swinging*, New American Library, New York, 1971.

Barton, John J.: "Laparoscopy in Gynecological Practice," in Ralph M. Wynn (ed.), *Obstetrics and Gynecology Annual 1972*, Appleton-Century-Crofts, New York, 1972, pp. 351–372.

Bauman, K. E.: "Selected Aspects of the Contraceptive Practices of Unmarried University Students," *American Journal of Obstetrics and Gynecology*, vol. 108, no. 2, pp. 203–209, 1970. Also in *Medical Aspects of Human Sexuality*, vol. 5, no. 8, pp. 76–89, August 1971.

Bayer, A. E.: "Early Dating and Early Marriage," *Journal of Marriage and the Family*, vol. 30, pp. 628–632, 1968.

Beach, Frank A. (ed.): *Sex and Behavior*, John Wiley & Sons, Inc., New York, 1965.

Beacham, Daniel Winston, and Woodard Davis Beacham: *Synopsis of Gynecology*, 8th ed., The C. V. Mosby Company, St. Louis, 1972.

Bednarik, Karl: *The Male in Crisis*, trans. by Helen Sebba, Alfred A. Knopf, Inc., New York, 1970.

Beer, Alan E.: "Differential Diagnosis and Clinical Analysis of Dysfunctional Uterine Bleeding," pp. 434–450 in Edward S. Wallach (ed.), "Dysfunctional Uterine Bleeding," *Clinical Obstetrics and Gynecology*, vol. 13, no. 2, pp. 361–488, June 1970.

Behrman, S. J., and Yoshiaki Sawada: "Heterologous and Homologous Inseminations with Human Semen Frozen and Stored in Liquid-Nitrogen Refrigerator," *Fertility and Sterility*, vol. 17, pp. 457–466, July-August 1966.

Bell, Robert: *Marriage and Family Interaction*, 4th ed., The Dorsey Press, Homewood, Ill., 1975.

——— **and Shelli Balter:** "Premarital Sexual Experiences of Married Women," *Medical Aspects of Human Sexuality*, vol. 7, no. 11, pp. 111–123, November 1973.

——— **and Phyllis L. Bell:** "Sexual Satisfaction among Married Women," *Medical Aspects of Human Sexuality*, vol. 6, no. 12, pp. 136–144, December 1972.

——— **and Jay B. Chaskes:** "Premarital Sexual Experience among Coeds, 1958 and 1968," *Journal of Marriage and the Family*, vol. 32, no. 1, pp. 81–84, February 1970.

——— **and D. Peltz:** "Extramarital Sex Among Women," *Medical Aspects of Human Sexuality*, vol. 8, pp. 10–31, 1974.

Benjamin, Harry: *The Transsexual Phenomenon*, Julian Press, Inc., New York, 1966.

Benson, Ralph.: *Handbook of Obstetrics and Gynecology*, 4th ed., Lange Medical Publications, Los Altos, Calif., 1971.

Benzie, R. J., and T. A. Doran: "The 'Fetoscope'—A New Clinical Tool for Prenatal Genetic Diagnosis," *American Journal of Obstetrics and Gynecology*, vol. 121, no. 4, pp. 460–464, Feb. 15, 1975.

Berger, B., B. Hackett, and R. M. Millar: "The Communal Family," *The Family Coordinator*, vol. 21, pp. 419–427, 1972.

Berlind, Melvyn: "The Contralateral Corpus Luteum: An Important Factor in Ectopic Pregnancy," *Obstetrics and Gynecology*, vol. 16, no. 1, pp. 51–52, July 1960.

Bernard, Jessie: "The Fourth Revolution," in Ruth E. Albrecht and E. Wilbur Bock (eds.), *Encounter: Love, Marriage, and Family*, Holbrook Press, Inc., Boston, 1972*a*.

———: *The Future of Marriage*, World Publishing Company, New York, 1972*b*.

———: *Women, Wives, Mothers: Values and Options*, Aldine Publishing Company, Chicago, 1975.

Berscheid, E., and E. Walster:

"Physical Attractiveness," in L. Berkowitz (ed.), *Advances in Experimental Social Psychology*, vol. 7, Academic Press, New York, 1972.

Besanceney, P. H.: *Interfaith Marriages: Who and Why*, College and University Press, New Haven, Conn., 1970.

Bishop, David W.: "Biology of Spermatozoa," in William C. Young (ed.), *Sex and Internal Secretions*, 3d ed., The Williams & Wilkins Company, Baltimore, 1961, chap. 13.

Blazer, John A.: "Married Virgins: A Study of Unconsummated Marriages," *Journal of Marriage and the Family*, vol. 26, no. 2, pp. 213–214, May 1964.

Blood, R. O., Jr.: "A Retest of Waller's Rating Complex," *Marriage and Family Living*, vol. 17, pp. 41–47, 1955.

———: *Marriage*, 2d ed., The Free Press, Glencoe, Ill., 1969.

——— and D. M. Wolfe: *Husbands and Wives*, Free Press of Glencoe, Inc., New York, 1960.

Boggs, Thomas R.: "Mortality and Morbidity from Hemolytic Disease of the Newborn," pp. 933–944 in Edward A. Banner (ed.), "Rh Factor," *Clinical Obstetrics and Gynecology*, vol. 7, no. 4, pp. 901–1055, December 1964.

Bolognese, Ronald J., and Stephen L. Corson: *Interruption of Pregnancy: A Total Patient Approach*, The Williams & Wilkins Company, Baltimore, 1975.

Bolton, C. D.: "Mate Selection as the Development of a Relationship," *Marriage and Family Living*, vol. 23, pp. 234–240, 1961.

Bosmajian, Hamida, and Haig Bosmajian (eds.): *This Great Argument: The Rights of Women*, Addison-Wesley Publishing Company, Inc., Reading, Mass., 1972.

Bourke, Geoffrey J., and Richard J. Whitty: "Smallpox Vaccination in Pregnancy: A Prospective Study," *British Medical Journal*, vol. 1, pp. 1544–1546, June 13, 1964.

Bourne, Aleck W., and Leslie H. Williams: *Recent Advances in Obstetrics and Gynecology*, McGraw-Hill Book Company, New York, 1953.

Böving, Bent G.: "Anatomy of Reproduction," in J. P. Greenhill, *Obstetrics*, 13th ed., W. B. Saunders Company, Philadelphia, 1965, chap. 1.

Bowes, Kenneth (ed.): *Modern Trends in Obstetrics and Gynecology*, Paul B. Hoeber, Inc., New York, 1956.

Bowman, Henry A.: Unpublished study, Columbia, Mo., 1950.

Bradley, R. A.: *Husband-Coached Childbirth*, Harper & Row, Publishers, Inc., 1974.

Brandling-Bennett, A. D., John F. Modlin, and Kenneth Herrmann: "The Risks of Rubella Vaccination in Pregnancy," *Contemporary OB/GYN*, vol. 4, no. 1, pp. 77–80, July 1974.

Brasch, R.: *How Did It Begin?* David McKay Company, Inc., New York, 1965.

Breckinridge, Sophonisba: "The Activities of Women outside the Home," in *Report of the President's Research Committee on Social Trends*, McGraw-Hill Book Company, New York, 1933, pp. 709–750.

Bremer, Johan: *Asexualization*, The Macmillan Company, New York, 1959.

Brenner, Paul F., Donna L. Cooper, and Danial R. Mishell, Jr.: "Clinical Study of a Progesterone-releasing Intrauterine Contraceptive Device," *American Journal of Obstetrics and Gynecology*, vol. 121, no. 5, pp. 704–706, March 1, 1975.

Brim, O. G., Jr.: "Socialization Through the Life Cycle," in O. G. Brim, Jr., and S. Wheeler: *Socialization After Childhood: Two Essays*, John Wiley & Sons, Inc., New York, 1966.

British Medical Journal, vol. 2, no. 5599, pp. 187–188, Apr. 27, 1968.

———: "Pregnancy without a Uterus," vol. 5946, no. 4, p. 677, Dec. 21, 1974.

Broderick, Carl B. (ed.): *A Decade of Family Research and Action*, National Council on Family Relations, Minneapolis, 1971.

Bromley, Dorothy Dunbar, and Florence Haxton Britten: *Youth and Sex*, Harper & Row, Publishers, Inc., New York, 1938.

Brotherton, Janet, and I. L. Craft: "A Clinical and Pathologic Study of 91 Cases of Spontaneous Abortion," *Fertility and Sterility*, vol. 23, no. 4, pp. 289–294, April 1972.

Brown, Barbara A., Thomas I. Emerson, Gail Falk, and Ann E. Freedman: "The Equal Rights Amendment: A Constitutional Basis for Equal Rights for Women," *The Yale Law Journal*, vol. 80, no. 5, pp. 872–985, April 1971.

Brown, Edward, and Peter Barglow: "Pseudocyesis: A Paradigm for Psychophysiologic Reactions." *Archives of General Psychiatry*, vol. 24, no. 3, pp. 221–229, March 1971.

Bruce, Joan, and G. F. M. Russell: "Premenstrual Tension: A Study of Weight Changes and Balances of Water, Sodium, and Potassium," *The Lancet*, vol. 2, pp. 267–271, Aug. 11, 1962.

Brueschke, Erich E., and Lourens J. D. Zaneveld: "Development and Evaluation of Reversible Vas Occlusive Devices," in John J. Sciarra, Colin Markland, and J. Joseph Speidel (eds.), *Control of Male Fertility*, Harper & Row, Publishers, Inc. (Medical Department), Hagerstown, Md., 1975, pp. 112–123.

Bulmer, M. G.: *The Biology of Twinning in Man*, Oxford University Press, New York, 1970.

Bumpass, L.: "The Trend of Interfaith Marriage in the United States," *Social Biology*, vol. 17, pp. 253–259, 1970.

——— and J. A. Sweet: "Differentials in Marital Instability: 1970," *American Sociological Review*, vol. 37, pp. 754–766, 1972.

Bunge, R. G.: "Some Observations on the Male Ejaculate," *Fertility and*

Sterility, vol. 21, no. 9, pp. 639–644, September 1970.

Burchinal, L. G.: "Adolescent Role Deprivation and High School Age Marriage," *Marriage and Family Living*, vol. 21, pp. 378–384, 1959.

———**and L. E. Chancellor:** "Ages of Marriage, Occupations of Grooms and Interreligious Marriage Roles," *Social Forces*, vol. 40, pp. 348–354, 1962.

———**and**———: "Social Status, Religious Affiliation, and Ages at Marriage," *Marriage and Family Living*, vol. 25, pp. 219–221, 1963.

Burgess, E. W., and L. S. Cottrell, Jr.: *Predicting Success or Failure in Marriage*, Prentice-Hall, Inc., Englewood Cliffs, N.J., 1939.

———**and H. J. Locke:** *"The Family: From Institution to Companionship,"* American Book Company, New York, 1945.

———**and Paul Wallin:** *Engagement and Marriage*, J. B. Lippincott Company, Philadelphia, 1953.

Busselen, Harry J., Jr., and Carroll Kincaid Busselen: "Adjustment Differences between Married and Single Undergraduate University Students: An Historical Perspective," *The Family Coordinator*, vol. 24, no. 3, pp. 281–287, July 1975.

Butler, N. R., H. Goldstein, and E. M. Ross: "Cigarette Smoking in Pregnancy: Its Influence on Birth Weight and Perinatal Mortality," *British Medical Journal*, vol. 2, no. 5806, pp. 127–130, Apr. 15, 1972.

Calderone, M. S.: "Family Planning: Its Role in Human Cost Accounting," *Pennsylvania Medical Journal*, vol. 66, no. 10, pp. 31–34, October 1963.

———**(ed.):** *Manual of Contraceptive Practice*, The Williams and Wilkins Company, Baltimore, 1964.

Calhoun, A. W.: *A Social History of the American Family*, Barnes and Noble, Inc., New York, 1945.

Cannon, K. L., and R. Long: "Premarital Sexual Behavior in the Sixties," *Journal of Marriage and the Family*, vol. 33, no. 1, pp. 36–49, February 1971.

Cantor, B., R. Jewelewicz, M. Warren, I. Dyrenfurth, A. Patner, and R. L. Vande Wiele: "Hormonal Changes during Induction of Midtrimester Abortion by Prostaglandin $F_{2\alpha}$," *American Journal of Obstetrics and Gynecology*, vol. 113, no. 5, pp. 607–615, July 1, 1972.

Capraro, Vincent J.: "Diagnosis and Management of Ambiguous Sexual Development," in Duncan E. Reid and C. D. Christian (eds.), *Controversy in Obstetrics and Gynecology, II*, W. B. Saunders Company, Philadelphia, 1974.

———, **William P. Dillon, and Marcos B. Gallego:** "Microperforate Hymen: A Distinct Clinical Entity," *Obstetrics and Gynecology*, vol. 44, no. 6, pp. 903–905, December 1974.

Carns, D. E.: "Religiosity, Premarital Sexuality and the American College Student: An Empirical Study," unpublished doctoral dissertation, Indiana University, Bloomington, 1969.

———: "Talking About Sex: Notes on First Coitus and the Double Sexual Standard," *Journal of Marriage and the Family*, vol. 35, pp. 677–688, 1973.

Carr, David H.: "Chromosome Studies in Spontaneous Abortions," *Obstetrics and Gynecology*, vol. 26, no. 3, pp. 308–326, September 1965.

Carter, H., and P. C. Glick: *Marriage and Divorce: A Social and Economic Study*, Harvard University Press, Cambridge, Mass., 1970.

———**and Alexander Plateris:** "Trends in Divorce and Family Disruption," *Indicators*, U.S. Department of Health, Education, and Welfare, August 1963.

Cates, W., Jr., and Roger W. Rochat: "Illegal Abortions in the United States: 1972–1974," *Family Planning Perspectives*, vol. 8, pp. 86–92, March/April 1976.

Cavanagh, John R.: "Rhythm of Sexual Desire in Women," *Medical Aspects of Human Sexuality*, vol. 3, no. 2, pp. 29–39, February 1969.

Cawood, C. David: "Petting and Prostatic Engorgement," *Medical Aspects of Human Sexuality*, vol. 5, no. 2, pp. 204–218, February 1971.

Center for Disease Control, H. E. W.: *Abortion Surveillance, Annual Summary, 1974*, Atlanta, 1976.

Cervenka, Jaroslav, Robert J. Gorlin, and Richard P. Bendel: "Prenatal Sex Determination," *Obstetrics and Gynecology*, vol. 37, no. 6, pp. 912–915, June 1971.

Chard, T., C. N. Hudson, C. R. W. Edwards, and N. R. H. Boyd: "Release of Oxytocin and Vasopressin by the Human Foetus during Labour," *Nature*, vol. 234, no. 5328, pp. 352–353, Dec. 10, 1971.

Charles, Allan G., and Emanuel A. Friedman, *Rh Isoimmunization and Erythroblastosis Fetalis*, Appleton-Century-Crofts, New York, 1969.

Charny, Charles W., Ramon Suarez, and Nader Sadoughi: "Castration in the Male," *Medical Aspects of Human Sexuality*, vol. 4, no. 5, pp. 80–83, May 1970.

Chin, James, Allan J. Ebbin, Miriam G. Wilson, and Edwin H. Linnette: "Avoidance of Rubella Immunization of Women During or Shortly Before Pregnancy," *Journal of the American Medical Association*, vol. 215, no. 4, pp. 632–634, Jan. 25, 1971.

Christensen, Harold T.: *Marriage Analysis: Foundations for Successful Family Life*, The Ronald Press, New York, 1958.

———: "Child Spacing Analysis via Record Linkage: New Data plus a Summing Up of Earlier Reports," *Marriage and Family Living*, vol. 25, no. 3, pp. 272–380, August 1963.

———: "Studies in Child Spacing: I—Premarital Pregnancy as Measured by the Spacing of the First Birth from Marriage," *American Sociological Review*, vol. 18, no. 1, pp. 53–59, February 1953.

———, **Robert Andrews, and Sophie Freiser:** "Falsification of Age at

Marriage," *Marriage and Family Living*, vol. 15, no. 4, pp. 301–304, November 1953.

——— and K. E. Barber: "Interfaith Versus Intrafaith Marriage in Indiana," *Journal of Marriage and the Family*, vol. 29, pp. 461–469, 1967.

——— and Christina F. Gregg: "Changing Sex Norms in America and Scandinavia," *Journal of Marriage and the Family*, vol. 32, no. 4, pp. 616–627, November 1970.

——— and Hanna H. Meissner: "Studies in Child Spacing: III—Premarital Pregnancy as a Factor in Divorce," *American Sociological Review*, vol. 18, no. 6, pp. 641–644, December 1953.

Christenson, C. V., and J. H. Gagnon: "Sexual Behavior in a Group of Older Women," *Journal of Gerontology*, vol. 20, pp. 351–355, 1965.

Clark, Alexander, and Paul Wallin: "Women's Sexual Responsiveness and the Duration and Quality of their Marriages," *American Journal of Sociology*, vol. 71, pp. 187–196, 1965.

Clark, Thomas L., and Warren M. Jacobs: "Isoimmunization of the Rh-negative Mother during the Third Stage of Labor," *Obstetrics and Gynecology*, vol. 23, no. 5, pp. 764–767, May 1964.

Clarke, C. A.: The Mechanism of Action of Rh-Immune Globulin," pp. 611–624 in John T. Queenan (ed.), "The Rh Problem," *Clinical Obstetrics and Gynecology*, vol. 14, no. 2, pp. 491–646, June 1971.

——— and Richard B. McConnell: *Prevention of Rh-Hemolytic Disease*, Charles C Thomas, Publisher, Springfield, Ill., 1972.

Clayton, Everett M., Jr., William Feldhaus, James M. Phython, and Frank E. Whitacre: "Transplacental Passage of Fetal Erythrocytes during Pregnancy," *Obstetrics and Gynecology*, vol. 28, no. 2, pp. 194–197, August 1966.

———, ———, and Frank E. Whitacre: "Fetal Erythrocytes in the Maternal Circulation of Pregnant Women," *Obstetrics and Gynecology*, vol. 23, no. 6, pp. 915–919, June 1964.

Clayton, R. R.: *The Family, Marriage, and Social Change*, D. C. Heath and Company, Lexington, Mass., 1975.

——— and H. L. Voss: "Shacking Up: Cohabitation in the 1970s," *Journal of Marriage and the Family*, vol. 39, no. 2, pp. 273 283, May 1977.

Clemens, Alphonse H.: *Design for Successful Living*, 2d ed., Prentice-Hall, Inc., Englewood Cliffs, N.J., 1964.

Coffey, Donald S., and Coy Freeman: "Vas Injection: A New Nonsurgical Procedure to Induce Sterility in Human Males," in John J. Sciarra, Colin Markland, and J. Joseph Speidel (eds.), *Control of Male Fertility*, Harper & Row, Publishers, Inc. (Medical Department), Hagerstown, Md., 1975.

Cohen, Flossie, Wolf W. Zuelzer, David Gustafson, and Margaret M. Evans: "Mechanisms of Isoimmunization I: The Transplacental Passage of Fetal Erythrocytes in Homospecific Pregnancies," *Blood*, vol. 23, no. 5, pp. 621–646, May 1964.

Committee on Maternal Health, Food and Nutrition Board, National Research Council: *Maternal Nutrition and the Course of Pregnancy*, National Academy of Sciences, Washington, 1970.

Comstock, G. W., F. K. Shah, M. B. Meyer, and H. Abbey: "Low Birth Weight and Neonatal Mortality Rate Related to Maternal Smoking and Socioeconomic Status," *American Journal of Obstetrics and Gynecology*, vol. 111, no. 1, pp. 53–59, Sept. 1, 1971.

Connell, Elizabeth: *Science News*, May 21, 1966, pp. 12–14.

———: "The Pill Revisited," *Family Planning Perspectives*, vol. 7, pp. 62–71, March/April 1975.

Constantine, L., and J. Constantine: "Where Is Marriage Going?" *The Futurist*, April 1970.

——— and ———: "Report on Ongoing Research in Group Marriage," paper presented to January meeting, Society for the Scientific Study of Sex, New York, 1971.

——— and ———: "The Group Marriage," in M. Gordon (ed.), *The Nuclear Family in Crisis: The Search for an Alternative*, Harper & Row, Publishers, Inc., New York, 1972.

——— and ———: *Group Marriage: A Study of Contemporary Multilateral Marriage*, The Macmillan Company, New York, 1973.

Coombs, R. H.: "A Value Theory of Mate Selection." *The Family Life Coordinator*, vol. 10, pp. 51–54, 1961.

Cooper, Donna L., Anita K. Millen, and Daniel R. Mishell, Jr.: "The Copper T 220C: A New Long-acting Copper Intrauterine Contraceptive Device," *American Journal of Obstetrics and Gynecology*, vol. 124, no. 2, pp. 121–124, Jan. 15, 1976.

Coser, Rose Laub (ed.): *The Family: Its Structure and Functions*, St. Martin's Press, Inc., New York, 1964.

Cottrell, Ann Baker: "Outsiders' Inside View: Western Wives' Experience in Indian Joint Families," *Journal of Marriage and the Family*, vol. 37, no. 2, pp. 400–407, May 1975.

Crampton, C. B.: "Uncomplicated Obstetrics: A Reevaluation," *Connecticut Medicine*, vol. 25, no. 5, pp. 279–283, May 1961.

Crist, Takey: "Contraceptive Practices among College Women," *Medical Aspects of Human Sexuality*, vol. 5, no. 11, pp. 168–176, November 1971.

———: "Assistance for the Sexually Active Female," reprinted from the *Journal of Gynecological and Neonatal Nursing*, vol. 2, no. 2, p. 5, 1973.

Crosby, Warren M.: "Trauma during Pregnancy: Maternal and Fetal Injury," *Obstetrical and Gynecological Survey*, vol. 29, no. 10, pp. 683–699, October 1974.

Csapo, A. I., J. P. Sauvage, and W. G. Wiest: "The Efficacy and Acceptability of Intravenously Administered Prostaglandin $F_{2\alpha}$ as an Abortifacient," *American Journal of Obstetrics and Gynecology*, vol. 111, no. 8, pp. 1059–1063, Dec. 15, 1971.

Cuber, J. F., and Peggy B. Harroff: *The Significant Americans*, Appleton-Century-Crofts, New York, 1965.

Cutright, P.: "Income and Family Events: Marital Stability," *Journal of Marriage and the Family*, vol. 33, pp. 291–306, 1971.

Cutter Laboratories, Inc.: *Treatment of Female Infertility with Pergonal (Menotropins)*, Berkeley, Calif.

Dacie, J. V.: *The Haemolytic Anaemias, Part IV*, 2d ed., Grune & Stratton, Inc., New York, 1967.

Dalton, Katharina: *The Premenstrual Syndrome*, William Heinemann Ltd., London, 1964.

———: *The Menstrual Cycle*, Warner Books, Inc., New York, 1969.

Daly, Michael J.: "Evaluation of Preferred Management of Premenstrual Tension—Pelvic Congestive Syndrome and Allied States," in Duncan E. Reid and C. D. Christian (eds.), *Controversy in Obstetrics and Gynecology II*, W. B. Saunders Company, Philadelphia, 1974, pp. 753–759.

D'Augelli, J. F.: "The Relationship of Moral Reasoning, Sex Guilt, and Interpersonal Interaction to Couple's Premarital Sexual Experience," unpublished doctoral dissertation, University of Connecticut, 1972.

———and H. J. Cross: "Relationship of Sex Guilt and Moral Reasoning to Premarital Sex in College Women and in Couples," *Journal of Consulting and Clinical Psychology*, vol. 43, pp. 40–47, 1975.

Davis, Hugh J.: "Status of Intrauterine Devices in Clinical Practice," *Current Medical Digest*, vol. 33, no. 6, pp. 873–879, June, 1966.

———: *Intrauterine Devices for Contraception: The IUD*, The Williams & Wilkins Company, Baltimore, 1971.

———: "Intrauterine Contraceptive Devices: Present Status and Future Prospects," *American Journal of Obstetrics and Gynecology*, vol. 114, no. 1, pp. 134–151, Sept. 1, 1972.

———and John Lesinski: "Mechanism of Action of Intrauterine Contraceptives in Women," *Obstetrics and Gynecology*, vol. 36, no. 3, pp. 350–358, September 1970.

Davis, Katherine B.: *Factors in the Sex Life of Twenty-two Hundred Women*, Harper & Row, Publishers, Inc., New York, 1929.

Davis, Kingsley: "Sexual Behavior," in Robert K. Merton and Robert A. Nesbit, (eds.), *Contemporary Social Problems*, Harcourt, Brace and World, New York, 1971, pp. 313–360.

———: "The American Family in Relation to Demographic Change," in C. F. Westoff and R. Parke, Jr. (eds.), *Demographic and Social Aspects of Population Growth*, vol. 1 of U.S. Commission on Population Growth and the American Future research reports, Government Printing Office, 1972.

Dean, D. G., and G. B. Spanier: "Commitment: An Overlooked Variable in Marital Adjustment?" *Sociological Focus*, vol. 7, pp. 113–118, Spring 1974.

Debrovner, Charles H.: "Vaginal Lubrication," *Medical Aspects of Human Sexuality*, pp. 32–42, November 1975.

Deep, Anthony A., and Ivan Jacobson: "Soap-induced Abortion," *Obstetrics and Gynecology*, vol. 25, no. 2, pp. 241–244, February 1965.

DeJong, Gordon F., and Ralph R. Sell: "Childlessness: A Demographic Path Analysis of Changes among Married Women," paper presented at the annual meeting of the Southern Sociological Society, Washington, D.C., 1975.

Denfeld, D.: "Dropouts from Swinging," *The Family Coordinator*, vol. 23, pp. 45–50, 1974.

———and M. Gordon: "The Sociology of Mate Swapping, or The Family that Swings Together Clings Together," *Journal of Sex Research*, vol. 6, pp. 85–100, 1970.

Dewhurst, Christopher J., and Ronald R. Gordon: *The Intersexual Disorders*, Bailliere, Tindall & Cassell, Ltd., London, 1969.

Dickinson, Robert Latou, and Lura Beam: *The Single Woman*, The Williams & Wilkins Company, Baltimore, 1934.

DiSaia, Philip J., Clarence D. Davis, and Ben Z. Taber: "Continuous Tablet Therapy for Oral Contraception," *Obstetrics and Gynecology*, vol. 31, no. 1, pp. 119–124, January 1968.

Donald, Ian: *Practical Obstetric Problems*, 3d ed., Year Book Medical Publishers, Inc., Chicago, 1964.

Donnelly, James F., Jr.: "Etiology of Prematurity," pp. 647–657 in Edward H. Bishop (ed.), "Prematurity," *Clinical Obstetrics and Gynecology*, vol. 7, no. 3, pp. 641–748, September 1964.

Drill, Victor A.: *Oral Contraceptives*, McGraw-Hill Book Company, New York, 1966.

Dubin, Lawrence: "Various Sexual Problems Blamed for Male Infertility," *Journal of the American Medical Association*, vol. 220, no. 6, pp. 780–781, May 8, 1972.

Duenhoelter, Johann H., and Norman F. Grant: "Complications following Prostaglandin $F_{2\alpha}$-Induced Midtrimester Abortion," *Obstetrics and Gynecology*, vol. 46, no. 3, pp. 247–250, September 1975.

———and Jack A. Pritchard: "Human Fetal Respiration," *Obstetrics and Gynecology*, vol. 42, no. 5, pp. 746–750, November 1973.

Duffy, Benedict J., Jr., and Sister M. Jean Wallace: *Biological and Medical Aspects of Contraception*, University of Notre Dame Press, Notre Dame, Ind., 1969.

Durrell, L.: *Clea*, E. P. Dutton & Co., New York, 1961.

Duvall, Evelyn Mills: *Family Development*, 4th ed., J. B. Lippincott Company, Philadelphia, 1971.

Eastman, Nicholson J. (ed.): editor's comments, *Obstetrical and Gynecological Survey*, vol. 16, no. 1, February 1961; vol. 17, no. 1, February

1962; vol. 18, no. 3, June 1963; vol. 19, no. 6, December 1964.

Eastman, William F.: "First Intercourse," *Sexual Behavior*, vol. 2, no. 3, pp. 22–27, March 1972.

Eckstein, P., Margaret Whitby, K. Fortherby, Christine Butler, T. K. Mukherjee, J. B. C. Burnett, D. J. Richards, and T. P. Whitehead: "Clinical and Laboratory Findings in a Trial of Norgestrel, a Low-dose Progestogen-only Contraceptive," *British Medical Journal*, vol. 3, no. 5820, pp. 195–200, July 22, 1972.

Edgren, Richard A.: "The Biology of Steroidal Contraceptives," in Daniel Lednicer (ed.) *Contraception: The Chemical Control of Fertility*, Marcel Dekker, Inc., New York, 1969, pp. 23–68.

Ehrlich, Shirley Stendig: "The Psychological Impact of New Parenthood," in Boston Children's Medical Center, *Pregnancy, Birth and the Newborn Baby*, Dell Publishing Co., Inc., New York, 1972, pp. 223–229.

Ehrmann, Winston: *Premarital Dating Behavior*, Holt, Rinehart and Winston, Inc., New York, 1959.

Eichler, Lillian: *The Customs of Mankind*, Doubleday & Company, Inc., Garden City, N.Y., 1925.

Eisner, Thomas, Ari Van Tienhoven, and Frank Rosenblatt: "Population Control, Sterilization, and Ignorance," *Science*, vol. 167, no. 3917, p. 337, Jan 23, 1970.

Ejlersen, Mette: *Sexual Liberation*, trans. by Marianne Kold Madsen, Award House, Universal Publishing & Distributing Corporation, New York, 1969.

Elias, James E.: "Teenage Sexual Patterns: An Examination of the Risk-Taking Behavior of Youth," *Social Health Papers No. 5*, pp. 10–14, American Social Health Association, New York, 1969.

Engle, Earl T. (ed.): *Studies on Testis and Ovary, Eggs and Sperm*, Charles C Thomas, Publisher, Springfield, Ill., 1952.

Enovid Bulletin no. 7, G. D. Searle & Company, Chicago, October 1961.

Ersek, Robert A.: "Frozen Sperm Banks," *Journal of the American Medical Association*, vol. 220, no. 10, p. 1365, June 5, 1972.

Eshleman, J. R.: "Mental Health and Marital Integration in Young Marriages," *Journal of Marriage and the Family*, vol. 27, pp. 255–262, 1965.

Exner, Max Joseph: *Problems and Principles of Sex Education: A Study of 948 College Men*, Association Press, New York, 1915.

Fairfield, R.: *Communes, U.S.A.: A Personal Tour*, Penguin Books, Inc., Baltimore, 1971.

Farris, Edmond J.: *Human Ovulation and Fertility*, J. B. Lippincott Company, Philadelphia, 1956.

Feldman, Joseph G., and Jack Lippes: "A Four-year Comparison between the Utilization and Use-Effectiveness of Sequential and Combined Oral Contraceptives," *Contraception*, vol. 3, p. 93, 1971; abstracted in *Obstetrical & Gynecological Survey*, vol. 28, no. 8, pp. 594–595, August 1971.

Fernandez, Carlos M., and Julio J. Barbosa: "Primary Ovarian Pregnancy and the Intrauterine Device," *Obstetrics and Gynecology*, vol. 47, no. 1, pp. 9s–11s, January 1976 (supplement).

Ferreira, Antonio J.: *Prenatal Environment*, Charles C Thomas, Publisher, Springfield, Ill., 1969.

Ferriss, Abbott L.: *Indicators of Trends in the Status of American Women*, Russell Sage Foundation, New York, 1971.

Findley, Palmer: *The Story of Childbirth*, Doubleday & Company, Inc., Garden City, N.Y., 1933.

Finegold, Wilfred J.: *Artificial Insemination*, Charles C Thomas, Publisher, Springfield, Ill., 1964.

Finger, F. W.: "Sex Beliefs and Practices among Male College Students," *Journal of Abnormal and Social Psychology*, vol. 42, pp. 57–67, 1947.

Fisher, Seymour: *The Female Orgasm*, Basic Books, Inc., New York, 1973.

Fiumara, Nicholas J.: "Ineffectiveness of Condoms in Preventing Venereal Disease," *Medical Aspects of Human Sexuality*, vol. 6, no. 10, pp. 146–150, October 1972.

Fleet, William F., Jr., Edmund W. Benz, Jr., David T. Karson, Lewis B. Lefkowitz, and Kenneth L. Herrmann: "Fetal Consequences of Maternal Rubella Immunization," *Journal of the American Medical Association*, vol. 227, no. 6, pp. 621–627, February 11, 1974.

Flowers, Charles E., Jr.: *Obstetric Analgesia and Anesthesia*, Paul B. Hoeber, Inc., New York, 1967.

———: "Systemic Medication," in Sol M. Shnider (ed.), *Obstetrical Anesthesia*, The Williams & Wilkins Company, Baltimore, 1970, pp. 60–70.

———**and Sol M. Shnider:** "Effects of Labor, Delivery and Drugs on the Fetus and Newborn" in Shnider, *op. cit.*, 1970, pp. 37–48.

Fluhmann, C. Frederic: *The Management of Menstrual Disorders*, W. B. Saunders Company, Philadelphia, 1956.

Food and Drug Administration: *FDA Consumer*, December 1972–January 1973.

———: *Papers*, vol. 5, no. 6, July–August 1971; vol. 5, no. 7, September 1971; vol. 5, no. 9, November 1971; vol. 6, no. 6, July–August 1972.

Forfar, John O.: "Drugs That Cause Birth Defects," *Contemporary OB/GYN*, vol. 4, no. 1, pp. 61–65, July 1974.

Fort, Arthur T.: "Management of the Injured Gravida," *Contemporary OB/GYN*, vol. 3, no. 2, pp. 41–46, February 1974.

Foy, Felician A. (ed.): *1973 Catholic Almanac*, Our Sunday Visitor, Inc., Huntington, Ind., 1972.

———: *1976 Catholic Almanac*, Our Sunday Visitor, Inc., Huntington, Ind. 1975.

Freda, Vincent J.: "Prevention of Isoimmunization to the Rh Factor in Obstetrics," in J. P. Greenhill (ed.), *The Year Book of Obstetrics and Gynecology* (1966–67 Year Book Series),

Year Book Medical Publishers, Inc., Chicago, 1966, pp. 275–289.

Freedman, Mervin B.: *The College Experience*, Jossey-Bass, Inc., San Francisco, 1967. Chap. 7, "The Sexual Behavior of American College Woman: An Empirical Study and an Historical Survey," is also found in Ailon Shiloh (ed.), *Studies in Human Sexual Behavior: The American Scene*, Charles C Thomas, Publisher, Springfield, Ill., 1970, chap. 13.

Freedman, Ronald, Pascal K. Whelpton, and Arthur A. Campbell: *Family Planning, Sterility, and Population Growth*, McGraw-Hill Book Company, New York, 1959.

Freeman, Roger K.: "Pneumoperitoneum from Oral-genital Insufflation," *Obstetrics and Gynecology*, vol. 36, no. 1, pp. 162–164, July 1970.

Freund, M., and J. Wiederman: "Factors Affecting the Dilution, Freezing and Storage of Human Semen," *Journal of Reproduction and Fertility*, vol. 11, no. 1, 1966; abstracted in *Obstetrical and Gynecological Survey*, vol. 21, no. 4, pp. 655–656, August 1966.

Fried, Paul H., A. E. Rakoff, R. R. Schopbach, and Albert J. Kaplan: "Pseudocyesis—A Psychosomatic Study in Gynecology," *Journal of the American Medical Association*, vol. 145, no. 17, pp. 1329–1335, Apr. 28, 1951.

Friedman, Emanuel A.: "Analgesia," in J. P. Greenhill, *Obstetrics*, 13th ed., W. B. Saunders Company, Philadelphia, 1965, pp. 378–385.

——: "Prevention of Rh Isoimmunization," in Allan G. Charles and Emanuel A. Friedman (eds.), *Rh Isoimmunization and Erythroblastosis Fetalis*, Appleton - Century - Crofts, New York, 1969, pp. 203–218.

Friedman, Leonard J.: *Virgin Wives*, Tavistock Publications, Ltd., London, 1962.

Fromme, Allan: *The Ability to Love*, Farrar, Straus & Giroux, Inc., New York, 1965.

Fujita, Byron N., Nathaniel N. Wagner, and Ronald J. Pion: "Contraceptive Use among Single College Students," *American Journal of Obstetrics and Gynecology*, vol. 109, no. 5, pp. 787–793, Mar. 1, 1971.

Gage, M. G.: "Economic Roles of Wives and Family Economic Development," *Journal of Marriage and the Family*, vol. 37, pp. 121–129, 1975.

Gambrell, Richard D.: "Immediate Postpartum Oral Contraception," *Obstetrics and Gynecology*, vol. 36, no. 1, pp. 101–106, July 1970.

Garcia, Celso-Ramon: "Detection and Diagnosis of Ovulation," pp. 380–389 in Luigi Mastroianni, Jr. (ed.), "Ovulation," *Clinical Obstetrics and Gynecology*, vol. 10, no. 2, pp. 343–430, June 1967.

——(ed.): "Oral Contraception," *Clinical Obstetrics and Gynecology*, vol. 11, no. 3, pp. 623–752, September 1968.

——: "Clinical Aspects of Oral Hormonal Contraception," in Mary Steichen Calderone (ed.), *Manual of Family Planning and Contraceptive Practice*, 2d ed., The Williams & Wilkins Company, Baltimore, 1970, pp. 283–330.

——**and Gregory Pincus:** "Clinical Considerations of Hormonal Control of Human Fertility," pp. 844–856 in C. Lee Buxton (ed.), "Medical Practice and Population Control," *Clinical Obstetrics and Gynecology*, vol. 7, no. 3, pp. 749–875, September 1964.

Garcia-Bunuel, Rafael: "New and Experimental Methods of Fertility Control," *Current Medical Digest*, vol. 33, no. 6, pp. 889–899, June 1966.

Gebhard, Paul H.: "Factors in Marital Orgasm," in Ailon Shiloh (ed.), *Studies in Human Sexual Behavior: The American Scene*, Charles C Thomas, Publisher, Springfield, Ill., 1970a, chap. 23.

——: "Female Sexuality," in Paul H. Gebhard, Jan Raboch, and Hans Giese, *The Sexuality of Women*, trans. by Colin Bearne, Stein and Day, Inc., New York, 1970b, pp. 10–43.

Gilbert Youth Research: "How Wild Are College Students?" *Pageant*, vol. 7, pp. 10–21, 1951.

Gill, Merton M.: "Functional Disturbances of Menstruation," *Bulletin of the Menninger Clinic*, vol. 7, no. 1, pp. 6–14, January 1943.

Gillespie, Luke: "Smoking and Low Birth Weight," pp. 658–665 in Edward H. Bishop (ed.), "Prematurity," *Clinical Obstetrics and Gynecology*, vol. 7, no. 3, pp. 641–748, September 1964.

Gillett, P. G., R. A. H. Kinch, L. S. Wolfe, and C. Pace-Asciak: "Therapeutic Abortion with the Use of Prostaglandin $F_{2\alpha}$," *American Journal of Obstetrics and Gynecology*, vol. 112, no. 3, pp. 330–338, Feb. 1, 1972.

Glass, Robert H., and Nathan G. Kase: *Woman's Choice*, Basic Books, Inc., New York, 1970.

Glick, P. C.: "Intermarriage and Fertility Patterns Among Persons in Major Religious Groups," *Eugenics Quarterly*, vol. 7, pp. 31–38, 1960.

——: "A Demographer Looks at American Families," *Journal of Marriage and the Family*, vol. 37, pp. 15–26, 1975.

——**and A. J. Norton:** "Perspectives on the Recent Upturn in Divorce and Remarriage," *Demography*, vol. 10, pp. 301–314, 1973.

——**and**——: "Number, Timing, and Duration of Marriages and Divorces in the United States: June 1975," U.S. Bureau of the Census, *Current Population Reports*, Series P-20, No. 297, Government Printing Office, 1976.

Golden, Boris A.: "Honeymoon Sexual Problems," *Medical Aspects of Human Sexuality*, vol. 5, no. 5, pp. 139–152, May 1971.

Goldfarb, Alvin F.: *Advances in the Treatment of Menstrual Dysfunction*, Lea & Febiger, Philadelphia, 1964.

——: "Clomiphene Citrate: Its Effect in Some Ovulatory Defects," pp. 390–400 in Luigi Mastroianni, Jr. (ed.), "Ovulation," *Clinical Obstetrics and Gynecology*, vol. 10, no. 2, pp. 343–417, June 1967.

———, Antonio Morales, Abraham E. Rakoff, and Peter Protos: "Critical Review of 160 Clomiphene-related Pregnancies," *Obstetrics and Gynecology*, vol. 31, no. 3, pp. 342–345, March 1968.

Goldman, George D., and Donald S. Milman (eds.): *Modern Woman: Her Psychology and Sexuality*, Charles C Thomas, Publisher, Springfield, Ill., 1969.

Goldman, Jack A., and Benjamin Eckerling: "Prevention of Rh Isoimmunization after Abortion with Anti-Rh$_0$(D)-Immunoglobin," *Obstetrics and Gynecology*, vol. 40, no. 3, pp. 366–370, September 1972.

Goldsmith, Sadja, and Alan J. Margolis: "Aspiration Abortion without Cervical Dilation," *American Journal of Obstetrics and Gynecology*, vol. 110, no. 4, pp. 580–582, June 15, 1971.

Goldstein, B.: *Human Sexuality*, McGraw-Hill Book Company, New York, 1976.

Goldzieher, Joseph, Louis E. Moses, Eugene Averkin, Cora Scheel, and Ben Z. Taber: "Nervousness and Depression Attributed to Oral Contraceptives: A Double-blind Placebo-controlled Study," *American Journal of Obstetrics and Gynecology*, vol. 111, no. 8, pp. 1013–1020, Dec. 15, 1971.

——— and Edris Rice-Wray: *Oral Contraception: Mechanism and Management*, Charles C Thomas, Publisher, Springfield, Ill., 1966.

Good, Frederick L., and Otis F. Kelly: *Marriage, Morals, and Medical Ethics*, P. J. Kenedy & Sons, New York, 1951.

Goode, W. J.: *After Divorce*, The Free Press of Glencoe, Inc., Glencoe, Ill., 1956.

———: "The Theoretical Importance of Love," *American Sociological Review*, vol. 24, pp. 39–47, 1959.

———: *World Revolution and Family Patterns*, The Free Press, New York, 1963.

Goodlin, Robert C., David W. Keller, and Margaret Raffin: "Orgasm during Late Pregnancy," *Obstetrics and Gynecology*, vol. 38, no. 6, pp. 916–920, December 1971.

Goplerud, Clifford P.: "Monoamniotic Twins with Double Survival," *Obstetrics and Gynecology*, vol. 23, no. 2, pp. 289–290, February 1964.

Gorbach, Arthur: "A Healthy Pregnancy," in The Boston Children's Medical Center, *Pregnancy, Birth and the Newborn Baby*, Dell Publishing Co., Inc., New York, 1972, pp. 73–93.

Gordon, Albert I.: *Intermarriage*, Beacon Press, Boston, 1964.

Gordon, Michael, and M. Charles Bernstein: "Mate Choice and Domestic Life in the Nineteenth-Century Marriage Manual," *Journal of Marriage and the Family*, vol. 32, no. 4, pp. 665–674, November 1970.

Grabill, W. H.: "Premarital Fertility," U.S. Bureau of the Census, *Current Population Reports*, Series P-23, No. 63, August 1976.

Granfield, David: *The Abortion Decision*, rev. ed., Image Books, Doubleday & Company, Inc., Garden City, N.Y., 1971.

———: "A Catholic Lawyer's View," in Robert E. Hall (ed.), *Abortion in a Changing World: I*, Columbia University Press, New York, 1970, pp. 149–156.

Grant, Alan: "Spontaneous Cure Rate of Various Infertility Factors or Post Hoc and Propter Hoc," *Australian & New Zealand Journal of Obstetrics and Gynaecology*, vol. 9, pp. 224–227, November 1969.

Graves, Lester R., Jr., and J. T. Francisco: "Medicolegal Aspects of Rape," *Medical Aspects of Human Sexuality*, vol. 4, no. 4, pp. 109–120, April 1970.

Green, H. Gordon: "Infants of Alcoholic Mothers," *American Journal of Obstetrics and Gynecology*, vol. 118, no. 5, pp. 713–716, March 1, 1974.

Green, Richard, and John Money (eds.): *Transsexualism and Sex Reassignment*, The Johns Hopkins Press, Baltimore, 1969.

Greenblatt, Robert B.: "Menstrual Physiology," in Alvin F. Goldfarb (ed.), *Advances in the Treatment of Menstrual Dysfunction*, Lea & Febiger, Philadelphia, 1964, pp. 13–25.

Greenhill, J. P. (ed.): *The 1943 Year Book of Obstetrics and Gynecology*, Year Book Medical Publishers, Inc., Chicago, 1944.

———: *Obstetrics in General Practice*, 3d ed., Year Book Medical Publishers, Inc., Chicago, 1945; 4th ed., 1948.

———(ed.):*The Year Book of Obstetrics and Gynecology*, 1954–55, Year Book Medical Publishers, Inc., Chicago, 1954; 1957–58 (1957); 1960–61 (1960); 1961–62 (1961); 1962–63 (1962b); 1963–64 (1963); 1964–65 (1964); 1965–66 (1965b); 1966–67 (1966); 1972 (1972).

———: *Analgesia and Anesthesia in Obstetrics*, 2d ed., Charles C Thomas, Publisher, Springfield, Ill., 1962a.

———: *Obstetrics*, 13th ed., W. B. Saunders Company, Philadelphia, 1965a.

Grold, L. James: "Patterns of Jealousy," *Medical Aspects of Human Sexuality*, vol. 6, no. 5, pp. 118–126, May 1972.

Group for the Advancement of Psychiatry: *The Right of Abortion: A Psychiatric View*, Charles Scribner's Sons, New York, 1970.

Groves Conference on Marriage and the Family, Myrtle Beach, S.C., unpublished manuscript, 1974.

Guttmacher, Alan Frank: *Life in the Making*, Garden City Books, New York, 1933.

———: *Into This Universe*, The Viking Press, New York, 1937.

———: *Pregnancy and Birth*, Signet Books, New York, 1962.

———, Robert E. Hall, Christopher Tietze, and Harriet Pilpel: "Legal Abortion," *Medical Aspects of Human Sexuality*, vol. 5, no. 8, pp. 50–75, August 1971.

Guyton, Arthur C.: *Textbook of Medical Physiology*, 4th ed., W. B.

Saunders Company, Philadelphia, 1971.

Hack, M., M. Brish, M. Serr, V. Insler, and B. Lunenfeld: "Outcome of Pregnancy after Induced Ovulation," *Journal of the American Medical Association*, vol. 211, no. 5, pp. 791–797, Feb. 2, 1970.

Hacker, Helen Mayer: "The New Burdens of Masculinity," *Marriage and Family Living*, vol. 19, no. 3, pp. 227–233, August 1957.

———: "Women as a Minority Group," *Social Forces*, vol. 30, no. 1, pp. 60–69, October 1951. Also in Hamida Bosmajian and Haig Bosmajian (eds.), *This Great Argument: The Rights of Women*, Addison-Wesley Publishing Company, Inc., Reading, Mass., 1972, pp. 127–145. Excerpts in Nona Glazer-Malbin and Helen Youngelson Waehrer (eds.), *Woman in a Man-made World*, Rand McNally & Company, Chicago, 1972, pp. 39–44.

Hall, Robert E.: "A Comparative Evaluation of Intrauterine Contraceptive Devices," *American Journal of Obstetrics and Gynecology*, vol. 94, no. 1, pp. 65–77, Jan. 1, 1966.

———: "A Three Year Study of the Lippes Loop," *Bulletin of the Sloane Hospital for Women*, vol. 13, no. 1, pp. 1–5, Spring 1967.

———: "Intrauterine Devices: Clinical Aspects," in Mary Steichen Calderone, *Manual of Family Planning and Contraceptive Practice*, 2d ed., The Williams & Wilkins Company, Baltimore, 1970.

Halpin, Thomas F., Albert R. Jones, H. Lee Bishop, and Saul Lerner: "Prophylaxis of Neonatal Hyperbilirubinemia with Phenobarbital," *Obstetrics and Gynecology*, vol. 40, no. 1, pp. 85–90, July 1972.

Hamblen, E. C.: *Endocrinology of Women*, Charles C Thomas, Publisher, Springfield, Ill., 1945.

Hamblin, Robert L., and Robert O. Blood, Jr.: "Premarital Experience and the Wife's Sexual Adjustment," *Social Problems*, vol. 4, no. 2, pp. 122–130, October 1956.

Hamilton, Eugene G.: "Prevention of Rh Isoimmunization by Injection of Anti-D Antibody," *Obstetrics and Gynecology*, vol. 30, no. 6, pp. 812–815, December 1967.

Hamilton, G. V.: *A Research in Marriage*, Albert & Charles Boni, Inc., New York, 1929.

Hampson, Joan G.: "The Case Management of Somatic Sexual Disorders in Children: Psychologic Considerations," in Charles W. Lloyd (ed.), *Human Reproduction and Sexual Behavior*, Lea & Febiger, Philadelphia, 1964, chap. 13.

Hampson, John L.: "Determinants of Psychosexual Orientation," in Frank A. Beach (ed.), *Sex and Behavior*, John Wiley & Sons, Inc., New York, 1965, pp. 108–132.

———: "Deviant Sexual Behavior; Homosexuality; Transvestism," in Charles W. Lloyd, 1964, chap. 28.

Hanson, James W., Kenneth L. Jones, and David W. Smith: "Fetal Alcohol Syndrome: Experience with 41 Patients," *Journal of the American Medical Association*, vol. 235, no. 14, pp. 1458–1460, Apr. 5, 1976.

Hardy, Janet B.: "Fetal Consequences of Maternal Viral Infections in Pregnancy," *Archives of Otolaryngology*, vol. 98, p. 218, 1973; abstracted in *Obstetrical and Gynecological Survey*, vol. 29, no. 4, 265–268, April 1974.

Harper, Fowler V.: "Sex and the Law," in Charles W. Lloyd, 1964, chap. 25.

Harper, Robert A.: "Communication Problems in Marriage and Marriage Counseling," *Marriage and Family Living*, vol. 20, no. 2, pp. 107–112, May 1958.

———**and Walter Stokes:** *45 Levels to Sexual Understanding and Enjoyment*, Prentice-Hall, Inc., Englewood Cliffs, N.J., 1971.

Hart, Gavin: "Role of Preventive Methods in the Control of Venereal Disease," *Clinical Obstetrics and Gynecology*, vol. 18, no. 1, pp. 243–253, March 1975.

Hartman, Carl G.: *Science and the Safe Period*, The Williams & Wilkins Company, Baltimore, 1962.

Haskins, Arthur L.: "Oviduct Sterilization with Tantalum Clips," *American Journal of Obstetrics and Gynecology*, vol. 114, no. 3, pp. 370–377, October 1972.

Hatch, Merton C.: "Maternal Deaths Associated with Induction of Labor," *New York Journal of Medicine*, vol. 69, no. 4, pp. 599–602, Feb. 15, 1969.

Hatcher, R. A., G. K. Stewart, F. Guest, R. Finkelstein, and C. Godwin: *Contraceptive Technology, 1976–1977*, Irvington Publishers, Inc., New York, 1976.

Havighurst, Robert J.: *Human Development and Education*, Longmans, Green & Company, Ltd., London, 1953.

Heer, David M.: "The Prevalence of Black-White Marriage in the United States, 1960 and 1970," *Journal of Marriage and the Family*, vol. 36, no. 2, pp. 246–258, May 1974.

Hepker, Wilma, and Jerry S. Cloyd: "Role Relationships and Role Performance: The Male Married Student," *Journal of Marriage and the Family*, vol. 36, no. 4, pp. 688–696, November 1974.

Hertig, Arthur Y.: "Pathological Aspects," in Claude A. Villee (ed.), *The Placenta and Fetal Membranes*, The Williams & Wilkins Company, Baltimore, 1960, chap. 8.

Herzig, Norman: "Air Embolism Caused by Oral-genital Acts," *Medical Aspects of Human Sexuality*, vol. 6, no. 4, pp. 84–85, April 1972.

Hetzel, A. M., and M. Cappetta: "Marriages: Trends and Characteristics, United States," U.S. Department of Health, Education, and Welfare, *Vital and Health Statistics*, Publication no. (HSM) 72-1007, Rockville, Md., 1971.

Hibbard, Lester T.: "Abortion, Gas Embolus, and Sudden Death," *California Medicine*, vol. 110, p. 305, 1969; abstracted in *Obstetrical and Gynecological Survey*, vol. 24, no. 11, pp. 1368–1370, November 1969.

Hirsh, Harold L.: "Legal Guidelines for the Performance of Abortions," *American Journal of Obstetrics and Gynecology*, vol. 122, no. 6, pp. 679–682, July 15, 1975.

Hobbins, John C.: "Sports during Pregnancy," *Contemporary OB/GYN*, vol. 3, no. 4, pp. 36–38, April 1974.

Hobbs, D. F., and S. P. Cole: "Transition to Parenthood: A Decade Replication," *Journal of Marriage and the Family*, vol. 38, no. 3, pp. 723–732, 1976.

Hobbs, Lisa: *Love and Liberation*, McGraw-Hill Book Company, New York, 1970.

Hodgson, Jane E.: "The Physician's Role in Abortion Counseling," in Ronald J. Bolognese and Stephen L. Corson (eds.), *Interruption of Pregnancy: A Total Patient Approach*, The Williams & Wilkins Company, Baltimore, 1975, pp. 35–59.

———**and Kathey C. Portmann:** "Complications of 10,453 Consecutive First-trimester Abortions: A Prospective Study," *American Journal of Obstetrics and Gynecology*, vol. 120, no. 6, pp. 802–807, Nov. 15, 1974.

Hoffman, Jacob: *Female Endocrinology*, W. B. Saunders Company, Philadelphia, 1944.

Hoffman, L. W., and F. I. Nye: *Working Mothers*, Jossey-Bass, Inc., San Francisco, 1974.

Hohman, Leslie B., and Bertram Schaffner: "The Sex Lives of Unmarried Women," *American Journal of Sociology*, vol. 52, no. 6, pp. 501–507, May 1947.

Hollender, Marc H.: "Women's Wish to Be Held: Sexual and Nonsexual Aspects," *Medical Aspects of Human Sexuality*, vol. 5, no. 10, pp. 12–26, October 1971.

Hollingshead, A. B.: "Cultural Factors in the Selection of Marriage Mates," *American Sociological Review*, vol. 15, pp. 619–627, 1950.

Holmberg, A. R.: *Nomads of the Long Bow: The Siriono of Eastern Bolivia*, Publication No. 10, Smithsonian Institute, Institute of Social Anthropology, Washington, D.C., 1950.

Holtzman, Lester: "Medical-legal Considerations of Abortion in New York State under the New Abortion Law," pp. 36–47 in George Schaefer (ed.), "Legal Abortions in New York State: Medical, Legal, Nursing, Social Aspects (July 1–December 31, 1970)," *Clinical Obstetrics and Gynecology*, vol. 14, no. 1, pp. 1–324, March 1971.

Hon, Edward H.: *A Manual of Pregnancy Testing*, J. & A. Churchill, Ltd., London, 1961.

Horton, F. W.: *Prostaglandins*, Springer Verlag, Berlin, 1972.

Houseknecht, Sharon, and Graham B. Spanier: "Marital Disruption among Highly Educated Women: An Exception to the Rule." Paper presented at the Conference on Women in Midlife Crises. Ithaca, New York, 1976.

Howell, Doris A., and Charles E. Flowers: "Recent Advances in the Treatment of Hemolytic Disease of the Newborn," pp. 945–956 in Edward A. Banner (ed.), "Rh Factor," *Clinical Obstetrics and Gynecology*, vol. 7, no. 4, pp. 901–1055, December 1964.

Huffman, John W.: "Principles of Adolescent Gynecology," in Ralph M. Wynn (ed.), *Obstetrics and Gynecology Annual: 1975* (vol. 4), Appleton-Century-Crofts, New York, 1975, pp. 287–308.

Hunt, Morton: *Sexual Behavior in the 1970s*, Playboy Press, Chicago, 1974.

Huston, Ted L.: "Ambiguity of Acceptance, Social Desirability, and Dating Choice," *Journal of Experimental Social Psychology*, vol. 9, pp. 32–42, 1973.

———**(ed.):** *Foundations of Interpersonal Attraction*, Academic Press, New York, 1974.

Hutchinson, Donald L.: "Amniotic Fluid," in Stewart L. Marcus and Cyril C. Marcus (eds.), *Advances in Obstetrics and Gynecology*, vol. 1, The Williams & Wilkins Company, Baltimore, 1967, chap. 8.

Hyams, Leonard L.: "Coital Induction of Labor," *Medical Aspects of Human Sexuality*, vol. 6, no. 4, p. 90, April 1972.

Hyatt, Herman W., Sr.: "Relationship of Maternal Mumps to Congenital Defects and Fetal Deaths, and to Maternal Morbidity and Mortality," *American Practitioner*, vol. 12, no. 5, pp. 359–363, May 1961.

Hytten, F. E., and A. M. Thomson: "Maternal Physiological Adjustments," in Committee on Maternal Nutrition, Food and Nutrition Board, National Research Council, *Maternal Nutrition and the Course of Pregnancy*, National Academy of Sciences, Washington, 1970, pp. 41–73.

Illsley, Raymond: "The Sociological Study of Reproduction and Its Outcome," in Stephen A. Richardson and Alan F. Guttmacher (eds.), *Childbearing: Its Social and Psychological Aspects*, The Williams & Wilkins Company, Baltimore, 1967, pp. 75–141.

Ingraham, Hollis S., and Robert J. Longood: "Abortion in New York State since July, 1970," pp. 5–24 in George Schaefer (ed.), "Legal Abortions in New York State: Medical, Legal, Nursing, Social Aspects (July 1–December 31, 1970)," *Clinical Obstetrics and Gynecology*, vol. 14, no. 1, pp. 1–324, March 1971.

Inselberg, R.: "Marital Problems and Satisfaction in High School Marriages," *Marriage and Family Living*, vol. 24, pp. 71–77, 1962.

Israel, S. Leon: *Diagnosis and Treatment of Menstrual Disorders and Sterility*, 5th ed., Harper & Row, Publishers, Incorporated, New York, 1967.

Ivey, Melville E., and Judith M. Bardwick: "Patterns of Affective Fluctuation in the Menstrual Cycle," *Psychosomatic Medicine*, vol. 30, no. 3, pp. 336–345, May–June 1968.

Jacobson, Benjamin D., and Merle B. Davis: "A Simple and Rapid Immunologic Test for Pregnancy, Based on Agglutination-Inhibition," *Obstetrics and Gynecology*, vol. 25, no. 2, pp. 192–196, February 1965.

Jacobson, P. and A. Matheny: "Mate Selection in Open Marriage Systems," *International Journal of Comparative Sociology*, vol. 3, pp. 98–124, 1962.

Jaffe, F. S., and J. G. Dryfoos: "Fertility Control Services for Adolescents: Access and Utilization," *Family Planning Perspectives*, vol. 8, no. 4, pp. 167–175, 1976.

Janowsky, David S., and Roderic Gorney: "The Curse, I: Vicissitudes and Variations in Female Fertility Cycle," *Psychosomatics*, vol. 7, pp. 242–246, July–August 1966.

Jensen, Oliver: *The Revolt of American Women*, rev. ed., Harcourt Brace Javanovich, Inc., New York, 1971.

Johnson, Virginia, and William H. Masters: "Sexual Incompatibility: Diagnosis and Treatment," in Charles W. Lloyd (ed.), *Human Reproduction and Sexual Behavior*, Lea & Febiger, Philadelphia, 1964, chap. 26.

Johnson, Wayne L., H. Fred Stegall, John N. Lein, and Robert F. Rushmer: "Detection of Fetal Life in Early Pregnancy with an Ultrasonic Doppler Flowmeter," *Obstetrics and Gynecology*, vol. 26, no. 3, pp. 305–307, September 1965.

Jolly, Hugh: *Sexual Precocity*, Charles C Thomas, Publisher, Springfield, Ill., 1955.

Jones, Howard W., Jr., and William Wallace Scott: *Hermaphroditism, Genital Anomalies and Related Endocrine Disorders*, 2d ed., The Williams & Wilkins Company, Baltimore, 1971.

Josselyn, Irene M.: "Sexual Identity Crises in the Life Cycle," in Georgene H. Seward and Robert C. Williamson (eds.), *Sex Roles in Changing Society*, Random House, Inc., New York, 1970.

Journal of American Medical Association, vol. 212, no. 7, p. 1137, May 18, 1970; vol. 212, no. 12, p. 2029, June 22, 1970; vol. 220, no. 11, pp. 1419–1420, June 12, 1971.

Kaats, Gilbert F., and Keith E. Davis: "The Dynamics of Sexual Behavior of College Students," *Journal of Marriage and the Family*, vol. 32, no. 3, pp. 390–399, August 1970.

Kane, Francis J., Morris A. Lipton, and John A. Ewing: "Hormonal Influences in Female Sexual Response," *Archives of General Psychiatry*, vol. 20, no. 2, pp. 202–209, 1969.

Kanin, Eugene J.: "Premarital Sex Adjustments, Social Class, and Associated Behaviors," *Marriage and Family Living*, vol. 22, no. 3, pp. 258–262, August 1960.

———: "Sex Aggression by College Men," *Medical Aspects of Human Sexuality*, vol. 4, no. 9, pp. 25–40, September 1970.

——— **and David H. Howard:** "Postmarital Consequences of Premarital Sex Adjustments," *American Sociological Review*, vol. 23, no. 5, pp. 556–562, October 1958.

Kanowitz, Leo: *Women and the Law: The Unfinished Revolution*, University of New Mexico Press, Albuquerque, 1969.

———: *Sex Roles in Law and Society*, University of New Mexico Press, Albuquerque, 1973.

Kanter, R. M.: *Communes: Creating and Managing the Collective Life*, Harper & Row, Publishers, Inc., New York, 1973.

Kaplan, Helen Singer: *The New Sex Therapy*, A Brunner/Mazel Publication published in cooperation with Quandrangle/The New York Times Book Co., New York, 1974.

Karim, Sultan M. M.: "Prostaglandins and Human Reproduction: Physiological Roles and Clinical Uses of Prostaglandins in Relation to Human Reproduction," in S. M. M. Karim (ed.), *The Prostaglandins: Progress in Research*, Wiley-Interscience, John Wiley & Sons, Inc., New York, 1972, pp. 71–164.

Karow, William G., William C. Gentry, and Sheldon Payne: "Artificial Insemination: Indications and Rationale," *Lying-in (Chicago)*, vol. 2, pp. 34–38, January 1969, abstracted in J. P. Greenhill (ed.), *The Year Book of Obstetrics and Gynecology 1969*, Year Book Medical Publishers, Inc., Chicago, 1969, pp. 410–411.

Katz, A. W. and R. Hill: "Residential Propinquity and Marital Selection: A Review of Theory, Method, and Fact," *Marriage and Family Living*, vol. 20, pp. 27–36, 1958.

Katz, Joseph: "Four Years of Growth, Conflict, and Compliance," in Joseph Katz, et al., *No Time for Youth*, Jossey-Bass, Inc., San Francisco, 1968, pp. 3–73.

Kaye, Bernard M., and Burnell V. Reaney: "Viral Diseases in Pregnancy: Prevention and Fetal Effects." *Obstetrics and Gynecology*, vol. 19, no. 5, pp. 618–621, May 1962.

Kegel, Arnold H.: "Sexual Functions of the Pubococcygeus Muscle," *The Western Journal of Surgery, Obstetrics and Gynecology*, vol. 60, no. 10, pp. 521–524, October 1952.

Kennedy, Eugene C.: *The New Sexuality: Myths, Fables, and Hang-ups*, Doubleday & Company, Inc., Garden City, N.Y., 1972.

Kephart, William M.: *The Family, Society, and the Individual*, 3d ed., Houghton Mifflin Company, Boston, 1972.

———: "Sexual Activity of Divorced Women," *Medical Aspects of Human Sexuality*, vol. 7, no. 10, pp. 146–160, October 1973.

Kerckhoff, A. C., and K. E. Davis: "Value Consensus and Need Complementarity in Mate Selection," *American Sociological Review*, vol. 27, pp. 395–403, 1962.

Kerenyi, Thomas D., Nathan Mandelman, and David S. Sherman: "Five Thousand Consecutive Saline Abortions," *American Journal of Obstetrics and Gynecology*, vol. 116, no. 5, pp. 593–600, July 1, 1973.

Kessel, Neil, and Alec Coppen: "The Prevalence of Common Menstrual Symptoms," *The Lancet*, vol. 2, no. 7298, pp. 61–64, July 13, 1963.

Khudr, Gabriel, and Kurt Benirschke: "Fluorescence of the Y Chromosome: A Rapid Test to Determine Fetal Sex," *American Journal of Obstetrics and Gynecology*, vol. 110, no. 8, pp. 1091–1095, Aug. 15, 1971.

Kinsey, Alfred C., Wardell B. Pomeroy, and Clyde E. Martin: *Sexual Behavior in the Human Male*, W. B. Saunders Company, Philadelphia, 1948.

———, ———, ———**and Paul H. Gebhard:** *Sexual Behavior in the Human Female*, W. B. Saunders Company, Philadelphia, 1953.

Kirkendall, Lester A.: *Premarital Intercourse and Interpersonal Relationships*, Julian Press, Inc., New York, 1961.

Kirkpatrick, C.: *The Family as Process and Institution*, 2d ed., The Ronald Press, New York, 1963.

Kirshen, Edward J., Frederick Naftolin, and Kenneth J. Ryan: "Intravenous Prostaglandin $F_2 \alpha$ for Therapeutic Abortion," *American Journal of Obstetrics and Gynecology*, vol. 113, no. 3, pp. 340–344, June 1, 1972.

Kistner, Robert W.: *Gynecology Principles and Practice*, Year Book Medical Publishers, Inc., Chicago, 1964.

———: "Induction of Ovulation with Clomiphene Citrate (Clomid)," *Obstetrical and Gynecological Survey*, vol. 20, no. 6, pp. 873–900, December 1965.

———: "The Use of Clomiphene Citrate, Human Gonadotropin, and Human Menopausal Gonadotropin for Induction of Ovulation in the Human Female," in *Advances in Gynecological Endocrinology, Proceedings of the Symposium*, Charleston, S.C., 1965, Excerpta Medica Foundation, New York, 1966, pp. 12–23.

———: *The Pill: Facts and Fallacies about Today's Oral Contraceptives*, Dell Publishing Co., Inc., New York, 1969a.

———: *The Use of Progestins in Obstetrics and Gynecology*, Year Book Medical Publishers, Inc., Chicago, 1969b.

Klemer, R. H.: "What Has Happened to Marriages?" in Richard H. Klemer (ed.), *Counseling in Marital and Sexual Problems*, The Williams & Wilkins Company, Baltimore, 1965, chap. 2.

———: *Marriage and Family Relationships*, Harper & Row, Publishers, Inc., New York, 1970.

Knight, James A.: "Sexual Implications of Money," *Medical Aspects of Human Sexuality*, vol. 3, no. 6, pp. 29–35, June 1969.

———: "Unusual Case: False Pregnancy in a Male," *Medical Aspects of Human Sexuality*, vol. 5, no. 3, pp. 58–71, March 1971.

Knopf, Olga: *The Art of Being a Woman*, Doubleday & Company, Inc., Garden City, N.Y., 1932.

Koedt, Anne: "The Myth of Vaginal Orgasm," in Leslie B. Tanner (ed.), *Voices from Women's Liberation*, New American Library, Inc., New York, 1971, pp. 158–166.

Krause, Harry D.: "Scientific Evidence and the Ascertainment of Paternity," *Family Law Quarterly*, vol. 5, no. 2, pp. 252–281, June 1971.

Kroger, W. S.: "Psychophysiologic Aspects of Oral Contraception," in Dean L. Moyer (ed.), *Progress in Conception Control 1968*, J. B. Lippincott Company, Philadelphia, 1968, chap. 8.

———**and S. Charles Freed:** *Psychosomatic Gynecology*, The Free Press of Glencoe, Inc., Chicago, 1956.

Lamb, Wanda M., George A. Ulett, William H. Masters, and Donald W. Robinson: "Premenstrual Tension: EEG, Hormonal and Psychiatric Evaluation," *American Journal of Psychiatry*, vol. 109, pp. 840–848, May 1953.

Landis, Carney, et al.: *Sex in Development*, Paul B. Hoeber, Inc., New York, 1940.

Landis, Judson T.: "Social Correlates of Divorce or Nondivorce Among the Unhappily Married," *Marriage and Family Living*, vol. 25, pp. 178–180, 1963.

———**and Mary G. Landis:** *Building a Successful Marriage*, 4th ed., Prentice-Hall, Inc., Englewood Cliffs, N.J., 1963.

Lane, Mary E.: "Sex during Menstruation," *Medical Aspects of Human Sexuality*, pp. 143–144, October 1974.

Lav, H. Lorrin: "A New Simple Immunassay for Human Chorionic Gonadotropin," *American Journal of Obstetrics and Gynecology*, vol. 109, no. 1, pp. 29–31, Jan. 1, 1971.

Lehfeldt, Hans: "Psychology of Contraceptive Failure," *Medical Aspects of Human Sexuality*, vol. 5, no. 5, pp. 68–77, May 1971.

Lehtinen, Marlene: "Incidence of Intercourse among College Students," *Medical Aspects of Human Sexuality*, vol. 8, no. 1, pp. 223–224, January 1974.

LeMasters, E. E.: "Parenthood as Crisis," *Marriage and Family Living*, vol. 19, pp. 352–355, November 1957.

Leon, J. J.: "Sex-Ethnic Marriage in Hawaii: A Nonmetric Multidimensional Analysis," *Journal of Marriage and the Family*, vol. 37, pp. 775–781, 1975.

Leslie, G.: *The Family in Social Context*, 2d ed., Oxford University Press, New York, 1973.

Levin, Max, Albert Ellis, Judith Bardwick, Richard C. Robertiello, Leah C. Schaefer, and Mary Boulton: "Is There Any Difference between 'Vaginal' and 'Clitoral' Orgasm?" *Sexual Behavior*, vol. 2, no. 3, pp. 41–45, March 1972.

Levin, Robert J., and Amy Levin: "The Redbook Report: A Study of Female Sexuality," *Redbook*, September, October 1975.

Levine, Seymour: "Sex Differences in the Brain," in *The Nature and Nurture of Behavior (Developmental Psychobiology)*, readings from the *Scientific American*, introductions by William T. Greenough, W. H. Freeman and Company, San Francisco, 1973, pp. 49–54.

Lewis, R. A.: "A Longitudinal Test of a Developmental Framework for Premarital Dyadic Formation," *Journal of Marriage and the Family*, vol. 35, pp. 16–26, 1973.

——— **and G. B. Spanier:** "Syndiasmos: Married and Unmarried Cohabitation," unpublished manuscript, The Pennsylvania State University, University Park, Pa., 1975.

———**and**———: "Theorizing About the Quality and Stability of Marriage," in W. Burr, R. Hill, I. Nye, and I. Reiss (eds.), *Contemporary Theories About the Family*, The Free Press, Glencoe, Ill., 1978.

———,———, **V. Storm, and C. Lehecka:** "Commitment in Married and Unmarried Cohabitation," paper presented at the annual meeting of the American Sociological Association, San Francisco, 1975.

Leyburn, James G.: *Frontier Folkways*, Yale University Press, New Haven, Conn., 1935.

Lidz, Ruth W.: "Emotional Factors in the Success of Contraception," *Fertility & Sterility*, vol. 20, no. 5, pp. 761–771, September–October 1969.

Life, vol. 58, no. 17, Apr. 30, 1965, p. 68.

Liley, A. W.: "Amniocentesis and Amniography in Hemolytic Disease," in J. P. Greenhill (ed.), *The 1964–65 Year Book of Obstetrics and Gynecology*, Year Book Medical Publishers, Inc., Chicago, 1964, pp. 256–265.

Linton, Eugene B.: "Honeymoon Cystitis," *Medical Aspects of Human Sexuality*, vol. 5, no. 8, pp. 111–116, August 1971.

Linton, R.: *The Study of Man*, Appleton-Century-Crofts, New York, 1936.

Lloyd, Charles W. (ed.): *Human Reproduction and Sexual Behavior*, Lea & Febiger, Philadelphia, 1964.

———: "Infertility," in Charles W. Lloyd, *op. cit.*, 1964b, chap. 21.

———: "Problems Associated with the Menstrual Cycle," in Charles W. Lloyd, *op. cit.*, 1964c, chap. 15.

———**and James H. Leathem:** "Fertilization, Implantation and Pregnancy," in Charles W. Lloyd, *op. cit.*, 1964, chap. 7.

———**and**———: "Reproductive Cycles, Oogenesis, Ovulation and Conception," in Charles W. Lloyd, *op. cit.*, 1964, chap. 6.

Locke, Harvey J.: *Predicting Adjustment in Marriage*, Holt, Rinehart and Winston, Inc., New York, 1951.

Lopata, Helena Znaniecki: *Occupation: Housewife*, Oxford University Press, New York, 1971.

Loraine, John A., and E. Trevor Bell: *Fertility and Contraception in the Human Female*, E. & S. Livingstone, Ltd., Edinburgh and London, 1968.

Loung, K. C., A. E. R. Buckle, and Mary M. Anderson: "Results in 1,000 Cases of Therapeutic Abortion Managed by Vacuum Aspiration," *British Medical Journal*, vol. 4, no. 5785, pp. 477–479, Nov. 20, 1971.

Lowrie, Samuel H.: "Early and Late Dating: Some Conditions Associated with Them," *Marriage and Family Living*, vol. 23, pp. 284–291, 1961.

———: "Early Marriage: Premarital Pregnancy and Associated Factors," *Journal of Marriage and the Family*, vol. 27, no. 1, pp. 48–56, February 1965.

Lubin-Finkel, M., and D. J. Finkel: "Sexual and Contraceptive Knowledge, Attitudes and Behavior of Male Adolescents," *Family Planning Perspectives*, vol. 7, pp. 256–260, November, December 1975.

Luce, Gay Gaer: *Biological Rhythms in Psychiatry and Medicine*, National Institute of Mental Health, Washington, 1970.

Lucey, Jerold F.: "Changing Concepts Regarding Exchange Transfusions and Neonatal Jaundice," pp. 586–596 in John T. Queenan (ed.), "The Rh Problem," *Clinical Obstetrics and Gynecology*, vol. 14, no. 2, pp. 491–646, June 1971.

Lurie, Harry L. (ed.): *Encyclopedia of Social Work*, 15th issue, National Association of Social Workers, New York, 1965.

Maas, J. M.: "The Use of Sequential Therapy in Contraception," in Robert Greenblatt (ed.), *Ovulation*, J. B. Lippincott Company, Philadelphia, 1966, pp. 206–215.

McCammon, Robert E.: "The Birnberg Bow as an Intrauterine Contraceptive Device," *Obstetrics and Gynecology*, vol. 29, no. 1, pp. 67–70, January 1967.

McCary, James Leslie: *Human Sexuality*, 2d ed., D. Van Nostrand, New York, 1973.

McDermott, Sandra: *Female Sexuality: Its Nature and Conflicts*, Simon & Schuster, Inc., New York, 1970.

MacDonald, John M.: "False Accusations of Rape," *Medical Aspects of Human Sexuality*, vol. 7, no. 5, pp. 170–194, May 1973.

McDonald, Robert L.: "The Role of Emotional Factors in Obstetric Complications: A Review," *Psychosomatic Medicine*, vol. 30, no. 2, pp. 222–237, March–April 1968.

———**and Cecil F. Lanford:** "Effects of Smoking on Selected Clinical Obstetric Factors," *Obstetrics and Gynecology*, vol. 26, no. 4, pp. 470–475, October 1965.

MacDonald, Ronald R.: "Clinical Pharmacology of Progestogens," in Ronald R. MacDonald (ed.), *Scientific Basis of Obstetrics and Gynaecology*, J. and A. Churchill, London, 1971.

McGuire, Therence F., and Richard M. Steinhilber: "Sexual Frigidity," *Mayo Clinic Proceedings*, vol. 39, no. 6, pp. 416–426, June 1964.

———**and**———: "Frigidity, the Primary Female Sexual Dysfunction," *Medical Aspects of Human Sexuality*, vol. 4, no. 10, pp. 108–123, October 1970.

Mackenzie, John M., Arnold Roufa, and Harold M. M. Tovell: "Midtrimester Abortion: Clinical Experience with Amniocentesis and Hypertonic Installation in 400 Patients," pp. 107–123 in George Schaefer (ed.), "Legal Abortions in New York State: Medical, Legal, Nursing, Social Aspects (July 1–December 31, 1970)," *Clinical Obstetrics and Gynecology*,

vol. 14, no. 1, pp. 1–324, March 1971.
McLarey, Don C., and Stewart A. Fish: "Fetal Erythocytes in the Maternal Circulation," *American Journal of Obstetrics and Gynecology*, vol. 95, no. 6, pp. 824–830, July 15, 1966.
McWhirter, Norris, and Ross McWhirter: *Guinness Book of World Records*, 1976 ed., Bantam Books, New York, 1976.
Maccoby, Eleanor Emmons, and Carol Nagy Jacklin: *The Psychology of Sex Differences*, Stanford University Press, Stanford, Calif., 1974.
Mace, David R.: "Acceptable Sexual Variety in Marriage," *Medical Aspects of Human Sexuality*, vol. 6, no. 6, pp. 153–157, June 1972 (*a*).
———: *Sexual Difficulties in Marriage*, Fortress Press, Philadelphia, 1972 (*b*).
Macklin, E. D.: "Unmarried Heterosexual Cohabitation on the University Campus," unpublished manuscript, Cornell University, Ithaca, N.Y., 1974.
———: *Cohabitation Research Newsletter, Issue 5*, State University College, Oswego, N.Y., April 1976.
Maeck, John Van S., and Charles A. Phillips: "Rubella Vaccine Program: Its Implications in Obstetric Practice," *American Journal of Obstetrics and Gynecology*, vol. 112, no. 4, pp. 513–518, Feb. 15, 1972.
Mahan, Charles S., and Carlfred B. Broderick: *Human Reproduction*, in Carlfred B. Broderick and Jessie Bernard (eds.), *The Individual, Sex and Society*, The Johns Hopkins Press, Baltimore, 1969.
Mann, Edward C., and Gary Cunningham: "Coital Cautions in Pregnancy," *Medical Aspects of Human Sexuality*, vol. 6, no. 10, pp. 14–25, October 1972.
Margolis, Alan J.: "Preparation of the Obstetrical Patient," in Sol M. Shnider (ed.), *Obstetrical Anesthesia*, The Williams & Wilkins Company, Baltimore, 1970, pp. 51–56.
Margulies, Lazar C.: "Intrauterine Contraception: A New Approach," *Obstetrics and Gynecology*, vol. 24, no. 4, pp. 515–520, October 1964.
Marshall, Sumner: "Cystitis and Urethritis in Women Related to Sexual Activity," *Medical Aspects of Human Sexuality*, vol. 8, no. 5, pp. 165–176, May 1974.
Martin, Chester B., Jr., and Eugene M. Long, Jr.: "Sex during the Menstrual Period," *Medical Aspects of Human Sexuality*, vol. 3, no. 6, pp. 37–49, June 1969.
Martinson, F. M.: "Ego Deficiency as a Factor in Marriage," *American Sociological Review*, vol. 20, pp. 161–164, 1955.
———: "Ego Deficiency as a Factor in Marriage—A Male Sample," *Marriage and Family Living*, vol. 21, pp. 48–52, 1959.
Masters, William H.: "The Sexual Response Cycle in the Human Female: Vaginal Lubrication," *Annals of the New York Academy of Sciences*, vol. 83, art. 2, pp. 301–317, Nov. 18, 1959.
———: "The Sexual Response Cycle of the Human Female: I. Gross Anatomic Considerations," *The Western Journal of Surgery, Obstetrics and Gynecology*, vol. 68, no. 1, pp. 57–72, January–February 1960.
———**and Virginia E. Johnson:** "The Human Female: Anatomy and Sexual Response," *Minnesota Medicine*, vol. 43, pp. 31–36, January–December 1960.
———**and**———: "Anatomy and Physiology," in Charles W. Lloyd (ed.), *Human Reproduction and Sexual Behavior*, Lea & Febiger, Philadelphia, 1964, part II, chap. 25.
———**and**———: "The Sexual Response Cycles of the Human Male and Female: Comparative Anatomy and Physiology," in Frank A. Beach (ed.), *Sex and Behavior*, John Wiley & Sons, Inc., New York, 1965.
———**and**———: *Human Sexual Response*, Little, Brown and Company, Boston, 1966.
———**and**———: *Human Sexual Inadequacy*, Little, Brown and Company, Boston, 1970.
———**and**———: *The Pleasure Bond*, Little, Brown and Company, Boston, 1975.
Mayes, Bruce: "The Effect of Rubella on the Fetus," in R. J. Kellar (ed.), *Modern Trends in Obstetrics*, Butterworth, Inc., Washington, 1963, chap. 11.
Mead, M.: "Introduction," in W. Ehrman, *Premarital Dating Behavior*, Holt, Rinehart and Winston, New York, 1959.
———: "Marriage in Two Steps," in Herbert A. Otto (ed.), *The Family in Search of a Future*, Appleton-Century-Crofts, New York, 1970, chap. 7. (Reprinted from *Redbook*, July 1966.)
Mears, Eleanor: *International Journal of Fertility*, vol. 13, pp. 340–345, October–December 1968; abstracted in J. P. Greenhill (ed.), *The Year Book of Obstetrics and Gynecology, 1969*, Year Book Medical Publishers, Inc., Chicago, 1969, pp. 404–405.
———**, M. P. Vessey, Lidija Andolsek, and Antonija Oven:** "Preliminary Evaluation of Four Oral Contraceptives Containing Only Progestogens," *British Medical Journal*, vol. 2, no. 5659, pp. 730–734, June 21, 1969.
Medical News: "Children of Alcoholic Mothers Fail to Thrive Physically and Mentally," vol. 229, no. 1, p. 9, July 1, 1974.
———: "Defects Studied in Infants of Alcoholic Mothers," vol. 226, no. 5, pp. 520–521, Oct. 29, 1973.
Medical Research Council: "Risk of Thromboembolic Disease in Women Taking Oral Contraceptives," a preliminary communication by a subcommittee, *British Medical Journal*, vol. 2, no. 5548, pp. 355–359, May 6, 1967.
Melody, George F.: "Behavioral Implications of Premenstrual Tension," *Obstetrics and Gynecology*, vol. 17, no. 4, pp. 439–441, April 1961.
Merit Publishing Company: *National Survey of High School High Achievers*, Northfield, Ill., 1970, 1971.

Meyer, Henry M., Jr., and Paul D. Parkman: "Rubella Vaccination: A Review of Practical Experience," *Journal of the American Medical Association*, vol. 215, no. 4, pp. 613–619, Jan. 25, 1971.

Meyer, Robert: "The Male Pill?" in David Charles (ed.), *Progress in Conception Control 1967*, J. B. Lippincott Company, Philadelphia, 1967, chap. 10.

Millett, Kate: *Sexual Politics*, Doubleday & Company, Inc., Garden City, N.Y., 1970.

Mills, C. Wright: "Methodological Considerations of the Sociology of Knowledge," *American Journal of Sociology*, vol. 46, no. 3, pp. 316–330, November 1940.

Mishell, Daniel R., Jr., Robert Israel, and Norman Freid: "A Study of the Copper T Intrauterine Contraceptive Device (TCu 200) in Nulliparous Women," *American Journal of Obstetrics and Gynecology*, vol. 116, no. 8, pp. 1092–1096, Aug. 15, 1973.

──, **Mary Lumkin, and Sergio Stone:** "Inhibition of Ovulation with Cyclic Use of Progestogen-impregnated Intravaginal Devices," *American Journal of Obstetrics and Gynecology*, vol. 113, no. 7, pp. 927–932, Aug. 1, 1972.

Mitsuya, Hideo, Jun Asai, Keiji Suyama, Takao Ushida, and Kenzo Hosoe: "Application of X-ray Cinematography in Urology. I. Mechanism of Ejaculation," *Journal of Urology*, vol. 83, no. 1, pp. 86–92, January 1960.

Mofid, M., M. W. Rhee, and M. Lankerani: "Ovarian Pregnancy with Delivery of a Live Baby," *Obstetrics and Gynecology*, vol. 47, no. 1, pp. 5s–8s, January 1976 (supplement).

Moghissi, Kamran S.: "Prostaglandins in Reproduction," in Ralph M. Wynn (ed.), *Obstetrics and Gynecology Annual 1972*, Appleton-Century-Crofts, New York, 1972.

Moloshok, Ralph E.: "Fetal Risk Associated with Maternal Systemic Injections," pp. 608–622 in Elsie R. Carrington (ed.), "Teratology," *Clinical Obstetrics and Gynecology*, vol. 9, no. 3, pp. 593–706, September 1966.

Monahan, T. P.: "How Stable Are Remarriages?" *American Journal of Sociology*, vol. 57, pp. 280–288, 1952.

──: "Changing Nature and Instability of Remarriages," *Eugenics Quarterly*, vol. 5, pp. 73–85, 1958.

──: "The Duration of Marriage to Divorce: Second Marriages and Migratory Types," *Marriage and Family Living*, vol. 21, pp. 134–138, 1959.

──: "When Married Couples Part: Statistical Trends and Relationships in Divorce," *American Sociological Review*, vol. 27, no. 5, pp. 625–633, October 1962.

Money, John: "Factors in the Genesis of Homosexuality," in George Winokur (ed.), *Determinants of Human Sexual Behavior*, Charles C Thomas, Publisher, Springfield, Ill., 1963, chap. 2.

──(ed.): *Sex Research: New Developments*, Holt, Rinehart and Winston, Inc., New York, 1965.

──: "Sexually Dimorphic Behavior, Normal and Abnormal," in Norman Kretchmer and Dwain H. Walcher (eds.), *Environmental Influences on Genetic Expression: Biological and Behavioral Aspects of Sexual Differentiation* (Fogarty International Center Proceedings, no. 2), National Institutes of Health, Bethesda, Md., 1969, pp. 201–212.

──: "Sexual Dimorphism and Homosexual Gender Identity," in Nathaniel N. Wagner (ed.), *Perspectives on Human Sexuality*, Behavioral Publications, Inc., New York, 1974, pp. 42–79.

──**and Anke A. Ehrhardt:** *Man & Woman, Boy & Girl*, The Johns Hopkins University Press, Baltimore, 1972.

──**and Patricia Tucker:** *Sexual Signatures: On Being a Man or a Woman*, Little, Brown and Company, Boston, 1975.

Montagu, M. F. Ashley: *Adolescent Sterility*, Charles C Thomas, Publisher, Springfield, Ill., 1946.

Morris, John McLean, and Gertrude Van Wagenen: "Interception: Use of Postovulatory Estrogens to Prevent Implantation," *American Journal of Obstetrics and Gynecology*, vol. 115, no. 1, pp. 101–106, Jan. 1, 1973.

Moss, J. J., F. Apolonio, and M. Jensen: "The Premarital Dyad During the Sixties," *Journal of Marriage and the Family*, vol. 33, pp. 50–59, 1971.

──**and R. Gingles:** "The Relationship of Personality to the Incidence of Early Marriage," *Marriage and Family Living*, vol. 21, pp. 373–377, 1959.

Moyer, Dean L., and Daniel R. Mishell: "Reactions of Human Endometrium to the Intrauterine Foreign Body," *American Journal of Obstetrics and Gynecology*, vol. 111, no. 1, pp. 66–80, Sept. 1, 1971.

Mueller, S. A.: "The New Triple Melting Pot: Herberg Revisited," *Review of Religious Research*, vol. 13, pp. 18–33, 1971.

Munro, Alistair: "Human Sexual Behavior," in Ronald R. MacDonald (ed.), *Scientific Basis of Obstetrics and Gynaecology*, J. and A. Churchill, London, 1971.

Murdock, G. P.: *Social Structure*, The Macmillan Company, New York, 1949.

Murphy, John F., and Risteard Mulcahy: "The Effect of Age, Parity, and Cigarette Smoking on Baby Weight," *American Journal of Obstetrics and Gynecology*, vol. 111, no. 1, pp. 22–25, Sept. 1, 1971.

Murray, R. Richard: "Abortion in an Upstate Community Hospital," pp. 141–148 in George Schaefer (ed.), "Legal Abortions in New York State: Medical, Legal, Nursing, Social Aspects (July 1–December 31, 1970)," *Clinical Obstetrics and Gynecology*, vol. 14, no. 1, pp. 1–324, March 1971.

Murstein, B. I.: "Stimulus-Value-

Role: A Theory of Marital Choice," *Journal of Marriage and the Family*, vol. 32, pp. 465–481, 1970.

Nathanson, Bernard N.: "Drugs for the Production of Abortion: A Review," *Obstetrical and Gynecological Survey*, vol. 25, no. 8, pp. 727–731, August 1970.

———: "Suction Curettage for Early Abortion: Experience with 645 Cases," in Schaefer, 1971, pp. 99–106.

———**and George Lawrence:** "Should Abortion Be Available on Request?" *Sexual Behavior*, vol. 1, no. 7, pp. 64–71, October 1971.

Neu, Carlos, and Alberto Di Mascio: "Variations in the Menstrual Cycle," *Medical Aspects of Human Sexuality*, vol. 8, no. 2, pp. 164–191, February 1974.

Neubardt, Selig: *A Concept of Contraception*, Simon & Schuster, Inc., New York, 1967.

Neumann, Hans H., and Janet M. Baecker: "Treatment of Gonorrhea: Penicillin or Tetracyclines?" *Journal of the American Medical Association*, vol. 219, no. 4, pp. 471–474, Jan. 24, 1972.

A New Catechism, Herder and Herder, Inc., New York, 1967.

Newton, John, Julian Elias, John McEwan, and George Mann: "Intrauterine Contraception with the Copper-7; Evaluation after Two Years," *British Medical Journal*, no. 5938, vol. 3, pp. 447–450, Aug. 17, 1974.

Newton, Niles: "The Point of View of the Consumer," paper presented at the American Medical Association Congress on the Quality of Life, Chicago, March 1972.

Niebyl, Jennifer Robinson: "Pregnancy following Total Hysterectomy," *American Journal of Obstetrics and Gynecology*, vol. 119, no. 4, pp. 512–515, June 15, 1974.

Noonan, John T., Jr.: *Contraception*, The Belknap Press, Harvard University Press, Cambridge, Mass., 1966.

———(ed.): *The Morality of Abortion: Legal and Historical Perspectives*, Harvard University Press, Cambridge, Mass., 1970.

Novak, Edmund R., Georgeanna Seegar Jones, and Howard W. Jones, Jr.: *Novak's Textbook of Gynecology*, 8th ed., The Williams & Wilkins Company, Baltimore, 1970.

Novak, Emil: *Textbook of Gynecology*, The Williams & Wilkins Company, Baltimore, 1944.

Nye, F. I.: "Husband-Wife Relationship," in L. W. Hoffman and F. I. Nye (eds.), *Working Mothers*, Jossey-Bass, Inc., San Francisco, 1974.

———**and F. M. Berardo:** *The Family: Its Structure and Interaction*, The Macmillan Company, New York, 1973.

———**and Lois W. Hoffman (eds.):** *The Employed Mother in America*, Rand McNally & Company, Chicago, 1963.

Ob. Gyn. News, vol. 2, no. 19, p. 38, Oct. 15, 1967; vol. 2, no. 16, p. 27, Sept. 1, 1967.

Ochsner, Alton: "Influence of Smoking on Sexuality and Pregnancy," *Medical Aspects of Human Sexuality*, vol. 5, no. 11, pp. 78–92, November 1971.

Odell, William D., and Dean L. Moyer: *Physiology of Reproduction*, The C. V. Mosby Company, St. Louis, 1971.

Oettinger, Katherine Brownell: "Illegitimacy Problems: A 1962 Priority," in *Proceedings of the Conference on Unwed Mothers*, The Social Hygiene Society of D.C. and Mt. Vernon Place Methodist Church, Washington, 1962, pp. B-1–B-8.

Oliven, John F.: *Sexual Hygiene and Pathology*, 2d ed., J. B. Lippincott Company, Philadelphia, 1965.

———: *Clinical Sexuality*, 3d ed., J. B. Lippincott Company, Philadelphia, 1974.

O'Neill, William L.: *Divorce in the Progressive Era*, Yale University Press, New Haven, Conn., 1967.

Osofsky, Joy D., Howard J. Osofsky, Renga Rajan, and Michael R. Fox: "Psychologic Effects of Legal Abortion," pp. 215–234 in George Schaefer (ed.), "Legal Abortions in New York State: Medical, Legal, Nursing, Social Aspects (July 1–December 31, 1970)," *Clinical Obstetrics and Gynecology*, vol. 14, no. 1, pp. 1–324, March 1971.

Ostergard, Donald R.: "The Physiology and Clinical Importance of Amniotic Fluid: A Review," *Obstetrical and Gynecological Survey*, vol. 25, no. 4, pp. 297–319, April 1970.

Otto, Herbert A. (ed.): *The New Sexuality*, Science and Behavior Books, Inc., Palo Alto, Calif., 1971.

Packard, Vance: *The Sexual Wilderness*, David McKay Company, Inc., New York, 1968.

Page, Ernest W., Claude A. Villee, and Dorothy B. Villee: *Human Reproduction: The Core Content of Obstetrics, Gynecology and Perinatal Medicine*, W. B. Saunders Company, Philadelphia, 1972.

Pakter, Jean, David Harris, and Frieda Nelson: "Surveillance of the Abortion Program in New York City: Preliminary Report," in Schaefer, 1971, pp. 267–299.

Palti, Z.: "Clomiphene Therapy in Defective Spermatogenesis," *Fertility and Sterility*, vol. 21, no. 12, pp. 838–843, December 1970.

Panner, Reuben, Fred Massarik, and Byron Evans: *The Unmarried Father*, Springer Publishing Co., Inc., New York, 1971.

Papp, Z., S. Gardo, G. Herpay, and A. Arvay: "Prenatal Sex Determination by Amniocentesis," *Obstetrics and Gynecology*, vol. 36, no. 3, pp. 429–432, September 1970.

Parkman, M. A., and J. Sawyer: "Dimensions of Ethnic Intermarriage in Hawaii," *American Sociological Review*, vol. 32, pp. 593–607, 1967.

Paschkis, Karl E., Abraham E. Rakoff, Abraham Cantarow, and Joseph J. Rupp: *Clinical Endocrinology*, 3d ed., Paul B. Hoeber, Inc., New York, 1967.

Pasnau, Robert O.: "Psychiatric Complications of Therapeutic Abortion," *Obstetrics and Gynecology*, vol. 40, no. 2, pp. 252–256, August 1972.

Patterns of Disease, Parke, Davis and Company, Detroit, September 1964.

Pavela, Todd H.: "An Exploratory Study of Negro-White Intermarriage in Indiana," *Journal of Marriage and the Family*, vol. 26, no. 2, pp. 209–211, May 1964.

Pearlin, Leonard I.: "Status Inequality and Stress in Marriage," *American Sociological Review*, vol. 40, no. 3, pp. 344–357, June 1975.

Peck, N. W., and F. L. Wells: "On the Psycho-sexuality of College Graduate Men," *Mental Hygiene*, vol. 7, no. 4, pp. 697–714, October 1923.

———— and ————: "Further Studies in Psycho-sexuality of College Graduate Men," *Mental Hygiene*, vol. 9, no. 3, pp. 502–520, July 1925.

Peel, John, and Malcolm Potts: *A Textbook of Contraceptive Practice*, Cambridge University Press, London, 1969.

Pennock, J. L.: "Cost of Raising a Child," *Family Economics Review*, ARS, 62-5, pp. 13–17, March 1970.

Pennsylvania Bar Institute: *Pennsylvania Family Law*, PBI Publication No. 66, Harrisburg, Pa., 1976.

Peretti, Peter O.: "Premarital Sexual Behavior between Females and Males of Two Middle-sized Midwestern Cities," *Journal of Sex Research*, vol. 5, no. 3, pp. 218–225, August 1969.

Perez, Alfredo, Patricio Vela, George S. Masnick, and Robert G. Potter: "First Ovulation after Childbirth: The Effect of Breast-feeding," *American Journal of Obstetrics and Gynecology*, vol. 114, no. 8, pp. 1041–1047, Dec. 15, 1972.

Perkins, H. F.: "Adoption and Fertility," *Eugenical News*, vol. 21, pp. 95–101, 1936.

Perlmutter, Johanna F.: "Heroin Addiction and Pregnancy," *Obstetrical and Gynecological Survey*, vol. 29, no. 7, pp. 439–446, July 1974.

Peterman, D., C. A. Ridley, and S. M. Anderson: "A Comparison of Cohabiting and Noncohabiting College Students," *Journal of Marriage and the Family*, vol. 36, pp. 344–354, 1974.

Peterson, K. M.: *Early Sex Information and Its Influence on Later Sex Concepts*, unpublished M.A. thesis, University of Colorado, 1938. (Mentioned in Winston Erhmann, *Premarital Dating Behavior*, Holt, Rinehart and Winston, Inc., New York, 1959.)

Peterson, William F.: "Pregnancy Following Oral Contraceptive Therapy," *Obstetrics and Gynecology*, vol. 34, no. 3, pp. 363–367, September 1969.

————, **Kenneth N. Morese, and D. Frank Kaltreider:** "Smoking and Prematurity," *Obstetrics and Gynecology*, vol. 26, no. 6, pp. 775–779, December 1965.

Pillay, A. P., and Albert Ellis: "Sex, Society and the Individual," *The International Journal of Sexology*, Bombay, India, 1953.

Pincus, Gregory: *The Control of Fertility*, Academic Press, Inc., New York, 1965.

Piver, M. Steven, and Robert A. Johnston, Sr.: "The Safety of Multiple Cesarean Sections," *Obstetrics and Gynecology*, vol. 34, no. 5, pp. 690–693, November 1969.

Plateris, A. A.: "Children of Divorced Couples: United States, Selected Years," U.S. Department of Health, Education and Welfare, *Vital and Health Statistics*, Government Printing Office, 1970.

————: "Divorces: Analysis of Changes, U.S. 1969," Department of Health, Education, and Welfare, *Vital and Health Statistics*, Publication no. (HSM) 73-1900, Rockville, Md., 1973.

Pope Paul VI: "An Apostolic Letter Issued 'Motu Proprio' Determining Norms of Mixed Marriages, March 31, 1970," National Conference of Catholic Bishops, Washington, 1970.

————: *Humanae vitae*, July 29, 1968.

Pope Pius XII: *Moral Questions Affecting Married Life: the Apostolate of the Midwife* (pamphlet), Paulist Press, New York, 1951.

Porterfield, Austin L., and H. Ellison Salley: "Current Folkways of Sexual Behavior," *American Journal of Sociology*, vol. 52, no. 3, pp. 209–216, November 1946.

Potter, A. L.: "Cesareans Galore," *Rhode Island Medical Journal*, vol. 52, no. 2, pp. 106–116, February 1967.

Potter, Edith L.: "Defective Babies Who Die before Birth," *Clinical Pediatrics*, vol. 1, no. 2, pp. 73–74, November 1962.

Pratt-Thomas, H. R., Lawrence White, and H. H. Messer: "Primary Ovarian Pregnancy: Presentation of Ten Cases, including One Full-term Pregnancy," *Southern Medical Journal*, vol. 67, p. 920, 1974; abstracted in *Obstetrical and Gynecological Survey*, vol. 30, no. 2, pp. 106–109, February 1975.

President's Commission on the Status of Women: *American Women* (report), Washington, 1963.

Price, Dorothy, and H. Guy Williams-Ashman: "The Accessory Reproductive Glands of Mammals," in William C. Young (ed.), *Sex and Internal Secretions*, The Williams & Wilkins Company, Baltimore, 1961, chap. 6.

Pritchard, Jack A.: "Deglutition by Normal and Anencephalic Fetuses," *Obstetrics and Gynecology*, vol. 25, no. 3, pp. 289–297, March 1965.

Queen, S. A., and R. W. Habenstein: *The Family in Various Cultures*, 4th ed., J. B. Lippincott Company, Philadelphia, 1974.

Queenan, John T.: *Modern Management of the Rh Problem*, Paul B. Hoeber, Inc., New York, 1967.

Raboch, Jan: "Studies in the Sexuality of Women," in Paul H. Gebhard, Jan Raboch, and Hans Giese, *The Sexuality of Women*, trans. by Colin Bearne, Stein and Day, Inc. New York, 1970, pp. 48–94.

Ramey, Irene G.: "Clitoral versus Vaginal Orgasm—Women Dispute Researchers," *Medical Aspects of*

Human Sexuality, vol. 8, no. 5, pp. 215–216, May 1974.

Ramey, J. W.: "Emerging Patterns of Innovative Behavior in Marriage," *The Family Coordinator*, vol. 21, pp. 435–456, 1972.

Ramsey, Glenn V., Bert Kruger Smith, and Bernice Milburn Moore: *Women View Their Working World*, The Hogg Foundation for Mental Health, University of Texas, Austin, 1963.

Reeves, Billy D., James E. Garvin, and Thomas W. McElin: "Premenstrual Tension: Symptoms and Weight Changes Related to Potassium Therapy," *American Journal of Obstetrics and Gynecology*, vol. 109, no. 7, pp. 1036–1041, Apr. 1, 1971.

Reevy, William Robert: *Marital Prediction Scores of College Women Relative to Behavior and Attitudes*, unpublished Ph.D. dissertation, The Pennsylvania State University, 1954. (Mentioned in Winston Erhmann, *Premarital Dating Behavior*, Holt, Rinehart and Winston, Inc., New York, 1959.)

Reid, Duncan E., and C. D. Christian (eds.): *Controversy in Obstetrics and Gynecology II*, W. B. Saunders Company, Philadelphia, 1974.

Reiss, Ira L.: *Premarital Sexual Standards in America*, The Free Press of Glencoe, Inc., New York, 1960a.

———: "Toward a Sociology of the Heterosexual Love Relationship," *Marriage and Family Living*, vol. 22, pp. 139–145, 1960b.

———: "Social Class and Campus Dating," *Social Problems*, vol. 13, pp. 193–205, 1965.

———(ed.): "The Sexual Renaissance in America," *Journal of Social Issues*, vol. 22, no. 2, pp. 1–137, April 1966a.

———: "The Sexual Renaissance: A Summary and Analysis," *Journal of Social Issues*, vol. 22, no. 2, pp. 123–137, April 1966b.

———: *The Social Context of Premarital Sexual Permissiveness*, Holt, Rinehart and Winston, Inc., New York, 1967.

———: "Premarital Sexual Standards," in Carlfred B. Broderick and Jessie Bernard (eds.), *The Individual, Sex, and Society*, The Johns Hopkins Press, Baltimore, 1969, pp. 109–118.

———: "How and Why America's Sexual Standards Are Changing," in John H. Gagnon and William Simon (eds.), *The Sexual Scene*, Trans-Action Books, Aldine Publishing Company, Chicago, 1970a, pp. 43–57. Also in Ailon Shiloh (ed.), *Studies in Human Sexual Behavior: The American Scene*, Charles C Thomas, Publisher, Springfield, Ill., 1970b, pp. 200–209.

———: *The Family System in America*, Holt, Rinehart and Winston, Inc., New York, 1971.

Renne, K. S.: "Correlates of Dissatisfaction in Marriage," *Journal of Marriage and the Family*, vol. 32, pp. 54–67, 1970.

Riemer, Svend: "Married Students Are Good Students," *Marriage and Family Living*, vol. 9, no. 1, pp. 11–12, February 1947.

Riley, Gardner M.: *Gynecologic Endocrinology*, Paul B. Hoeber, Inc., New York, 1959.

Roberts, R. E.: *The New Communes*, Prentice-Hall, Inc., Englewood Cliffs, N.J., 1971.

Robinson, Ira E., Karl King, and Jack O. Balswick: "The Premarital Sexual Revolution among College Females," *The Family Coordinator*, vol. 21, no. 2, pp. 189–194, April 1972.

Robinson, S. C.: "Pregnancy Outcome Following Oral Contraceptives," *American Journal of Obstetrics and Gynecology*, vol. 109, no. 3, pp. 354–358, Feb. 1, 1971.

Rock, John: "Calendar Rhythm: General Considerations," in Mary Steichen Calderone (ed.), *Manual of Family Planning and Contraceptive Practice*, 2d ed., The Williams & Wilkins Company, Baltimore, 1970, pp. 376–381.

———, **Christopher Tietze, and Helen B. McLaughlin:** "Effect of Adoption on Fertility," *Fertility and Sterility*, vol. 16, no. 3, pp. 305–312, May–June 1965.

Rockwell, R. C.: "Historical Trends and Variations in Educational Homogamy," *Journal of Marriage and the Family*, vol. 38, pp. 83–95, 1976.

Rogers, E. M., and E. Havens: "Prestige Rating and Mate Selection on a College Campus," *Marriage and Family Living*, vol. 22, pp. 55–59, 1960.

Rosenthal, E.: "Divorce and Religious Intermarriage: The Effect of Previous Marital Status upon Subsequent Marital Behavior," *Journal of Marriage and the Family*, vol. 32, pp. 435–440, 1970.

Ross, Robert T.: "Measures of the Sex Behavior of College Males Compared with Kinsey's Results," *Journal of Abnormal and Social Psychology*, vol. 45, pp. 753–755, 1950.

Roth, J., and R. F. Peck: "Social Class and Social Mobility Factors Related to Marital Adjustment," *American Sociological Review*, vol. 16, pp. 478–487, 1951.

Rovinsky, Joseph J.: "Abortion in New York City: Preliminary Experience with a Permissive Abortion Statute," *Obstetrics and Gynecology*, vol. 38, no. 3, pp. 333–342, September 1971.

Roy, Subir, Donna Cooper, and Daniel R. Mishell, Jr.: "Experience with Three Different Models of the Copper T Intrauterine Contraceptive Device in Nulliparous Women," *American Journal of Obstetrics and Gynecology*, vol. 119, no. 3, pp. 414–417, June 1, 1974.

Rudolph, Andrew H.: "Control of Gonorrhea: Guidelines for Antibiotic Treatment," *Journal of the American Medical Association*, vol. 220, no. 12, pp. 1587–1589, June 19, 1972.

Rush, David: "Examination of the Relationship between Birth Weight, Cigarette Smoking during Pregnancy and Maternal Weight Gain," *Journal of Obstetrics and Gynaecology of the British Commonwealth*, vol. 81, p. 746, 1974; abstracted in *Obstetrical*

References

and Gynecological Survey, vol. 30, no. 6, pp. 363–364, June 1975.

——— **and Edward H. Kass:** "Maternal Smoking: A Reassessment of the Association with Perinatal Mortality," *American Journal of Epidemiology*, vol. 96, p. 183, 1972; abstracted in *Obstetrical and Gynecological Survey*, vol. 28, no. 3, pp. 186–188, March 1973.

Russell, C. S.: "Transition to Parenthood: Problems and Gratifications," *Journal of Marriage and the Family*, vol. 36, no. 2, pp. 294–303, 1974.

Ryder, N. B., and C. F. Westoff: "Wanted and Unwanted Fertility in the United States: 1965–1970," in C. F. Westoff and Robert Parke, Jr. (eds.), *Demographic and Social Aspects of Population Growth*, vol. 1 of the Commission on Population Growth and the American Future, Government Printing Office, 1972.

Salber, E. J., M. Feinleib, and B. MacMahon: "The Duration of Postpartum Amenorrhea," *American Journal of Epidemiology*, vol. 82, no. 2, pp. 347–358, November 1966.

Samenfink, J. Anthony, and Robert L. Milliken: "Marital Status and Academic Success: A Reconsideration," *Marriage and Family Living*, vol. 23, no. 3, pp. 226–227, August 1961.

Sandberg, Eugene C., and Ralph I. Jacobs: "Psychology of the Misuse and Rejection of Contraception," *Medical Aspects of Human Sexuality*, vol. 6, no. 6, pp. 34–70, June 1972. Also in *American Journal of Obstetrics and Gynecology*, vol. 110, no. 2, pp. 227–242, May 15, 1971.

Savel, Lewis, E., and Edward Roth: "Effects of Smoking in Pregnancy: A Continuing Retrospective Study," *Obstetrics and Gynecology*, vol. 20, no. 3, pp. 313–319, September 1962.

Saxton, Lloyd: *The Individual, Marriage, and Family*, 2d ed., Wadsworth Publishing Company, Inc., Belmont, Calif., 1972.

Scanzoni, J.: "A Social System Analysis of Dissolved and Existing Marriages," *Journal of Marriage and the Family*, vol. 30, pp. 452–461, 1968.

Schaefer, George (ed.): "Legal Abortions in New York State: Medical, Legal, Nursing, Social Aspects (July 1–December 31, 1970)," *Clinical Obstetrics and Gynecology*, vol. 14, no. 1, pp. 1–324, March 1971.

Scheinfeld, Amram: *Twins and Supertwins*, J. B. Lippincott Company, Philadelphia, 1967.

Schneider, George T., and William L. Geary: "Vaginitis in Adolescent Girls," pp. 1057–1076 in John W. Huffman (ed.), "Gynecology of Adolescence," *Clinical Obstetrics and Gynecology*, vol. 14, no. 4, pp. 961–1108, December 1971.

Schroder, Ralph: "Academic Achievement of the Male College Student," *Marriage and Family Living*, vol. 25, no. 4, pp. 420–423, November 1963.

Schroeter, Arnold L., and James B. Lucas: "Gonorrhea: Diagnosis and Treatment," *Obstetrics and Gynecology*, vol. 39, no. 2, pp. 274–285, February 1972.

Schwarz, Richard H.: *Septic Abortion*, J. B. Lippincott Company, Philadelphia, 1968.

Scommegna, Antonio, Theresita Avila, Manual Luna, Ramaa Rao, and W. Paul Dmowski: "Fertility Control by Intrauterine Release of Progesterone," *Obstetrics and Gynecology*, vol. 43, no. 5, pp. 769–779, May 1974.

Scott, James S.: "Developments in Haemolytic Disease of the Foetus and Newborn," in R. J. Kellar (ed.), *Modern Trends in Obstetrics*, Butterworth, Inc., Washington, 1963, chap. 5.

Scott, L. Stuart: "Unilateral Cryptorchidism: Subsequent Effects on Fertility," *Journal of Reproduction and Fertility*, vol. 2, pp. 54–60, February 1961.

Scott, Roger D.: "Critical Illnesses and Deaths Associated with Intrauterine Devices," *Obstetrics and Gynecology*, vol. 31, no. 3, pp. 322–327, March 1968.

Sears, Robert R.: "Development of Gender Role," in Frank A. Beach (ed.), *Sex and Behavior*, John Wiley & Sons, Inc., New York, 1965.

———, **Eleanor E. Maccoby, and Harry Levin:** *Patterns in Child Rearing*, Harper & Row, Publishers, Inc., New York, 1957.

Seymour, R. J., and L. C. Powell: "Depomedroxyprogesterone Acetate as a Contraceptive," *Obstetrics and Gynecology*, vol. 36, no. 4, pp. 589–596, October 1970.

Shah, F., M. Zelnik, and J. F. Kantner: "Unprotected Intercourse among Unwed Teenagers," *Family Planning Perspectives*, vol. 7, pp. 39–43, January/February 1975.

Shainess, Natalie: "Locus of Orgasmic Sensation in Women," *Medical Aspects of Human Sexuality*, p. 107, October 1975.

Shearman, Rodney, P. *Induction of Ovulation*, Charles C Thomas, Publisher, Springfield, Ill., 1969.

Sherfey, Mary Jane: *The Nature and Evolution of Female Sexuality*, Random House, Inc., New York, 1972.

Sherman, J. K.: "Research on Frozen Human Semen: Past, Present and Future," *Fertility and Sterility*, vol. 15, no. 5, pp. 485–499, September–October 1964.

Shettles, L. B.: "Predetermining Children's Sex," *Medical Aspects of Human Sexuality*, vol. 6, pp. 172ff, June 1972.

Shipman, Gordon, and H. Yuan Tien: "Nonmarriage and the Waiting Period," *Journal of Marriage and the Family*, vol. 27, no. 2, pp. 277–280, May 1965.

Sickels, Robert J.: *Race, Marriage, and the Law*, University of New Mexico Press, Albuquerque, 1972.

Sjövall, Elisabet: "Coitus Interruptus," in Mary Steichen Calderone (ed.), *Manual of Family Planning and Contraceptive Practice*, 2d ed.,

The Williams & Wilkins Company, Baltimore, 1970, pp. 433–437.

Skipper, J. K., and G. Nass: "Dating Behavior: A Framework for Analysis and an Illustration," *Journal of Marriage and the Family*, vol. 28, pp. 412–420, 1966.

Sklare, M.: "Intermarriage and the Jewish Future," *Commentary*, vol. 37, pp. 46–52, 1964.

Sloan, R. Bruce (ed.): *Abortion: Changing Views and Practice*, Grune & Stratton, Inc., New York, 1971.

Smith, Reginald A., and Richard E. Symmonds: "Vaginal Salpingectomy (Fimbrectomy) for Sterilization," *Obstetrics and Gynecology*, vol. 38, no. 3, pp. 400–402, September 1971.

Smith, W. J., Jr.: "Rating and Dating: A Restudy," *Marriage and Family Living*, vol. 14, pp. 312–317, 1952.

Smithells, R. W.: "The Prevention and Prediction of Congenital Abnormalities," in Ronald R. MacDonald (ed.), *Scientific Basis of Obstetrics and Gynaecology*, J. and A. Churchill, London, 1971, chap. 10.

Sorensen, Robert C.: *Adolescent Sexuality in Contemporary America*, World Publishing Company, New York, 1973.

Southam, Anna L.: "Intrauterine Devices," pp. 814–828 in C. Lee Buxton (ed.), "Medical Practice and Population Control," *Clinical Obstetrics and Gynecology*, vol. 7, no. 3, pp. 749–875, September 1964.

———, **and F. P. Gonzoga:** "Systemic Changes during the Menstrual Cycle," *American Journal of Obstetrics and Gynecology*, vol. 91, no. 1, pp. 142–165, Jan. 1, 1965.

Spanier, G. B.: "A Study of the Relationship Between and Social Correlates of Romanticism and Marital Adjustment," unpublished master's thesis, Iowa State University, 1971.

———: "Romanticism and Marital Adjustment," *Journal of Marriage and the Family*, vol. 34, pp. 481–487, 1972.

———: "Sexual Socialization and Premarital Sexual Behavior: An Empirical Investigation of the Impact of Formal and Informal Sex Education," unpublished doctoral dissertation, Northwestern University, Evanston, Ill., 1973.

———: "Formal and Informal Sex Education as Determinants of Premarital Sexual Behavior," *Archives of Sexual Behavior*, vol. 5, pp. 39–67, 1976a.

———: "Measuring Dyadic Adjustment: New Scales for Assessing the Quality of Marriage and Similar Dyads," *Journal of Marriage and the Family*, vol. 38, pp. 15–28, 1976b.

———: "Perceived Sex Knowledge, Exposure to Eroticism and Premarital Sexual Behavior: The Impact of Dating," *Sociological Quarterly*, vol. 17, pp. 247–261, 1976c.

———: "Use of Recall Data in Survey Research on Human Sexual Behavior," *Social Biology*, vol. 23, pp. 244–253, 1976d.

———: "Sex Education and Premarital Sexual Behavior among American College Students," *Adolescence*, 1977a.

———: "Sources of Sex Information and Premarital Sexual Behavior," *Journal of Sex Research*, vol. 13, 1977b.

———: *Human Sexuality in a Changing Society*, Burgess Publishing Company, in press, 1978.

——— **and C. L. Cole:** "Mate Swapping: Perceptions, Value Orientations and Participation in a Midwestern Community," *Archives of Sexual Behavior*, vol. 4, pp. 143–159, 1975.

———**and**———: "Toward Clarification and Investigation of Marital Adjustment," *International Journal of Sociology of the Family*, vol. 6, pp. 121–146, Spring 1976.

———, **R. A. Lewis, and C. L. Cole:** "Marital Adjustment over the Family Life Cycle: The Issue of Curvilinearity," *Journal of Marriage and the Family*, vol. 37, pp. 263–275, 1975.

Speert, Harold, and Alan F. Guttmacher: *Obstetrical Practice*, Landsberger Medical Books, New York, 1956.

Statistical Bulletin, vol. 44, May 1963; vol. 48, July 1967; vol. 48, September 1967; vol. 49, December 1968; vol. 51, January 1970; vol. 51, June 1970; vol. 51, October 1970; vol. 52, July 1971; vol. 52, December 1971; vol. 53, April 1972; vol. 53, June 1972; vol. 55, August 1974, Metropolitan Life Insurance Company, New York.

Steinberger, Emil, and Keith D. Smith: "Artificial Insemination with Fresh or Frozen Semen," *Journal of the American Medical Association*, vol. 223, no. 7, pp. 778–783, Feb. 12, 1973.

Stoller, Robert J.: *Sex and Gender*, Science House, Inc., New York, 1968.

Stone, L. Joseph, and Joseph Church: *Childhood and Adolescence*, Random House, Inc., New York, 1957.

Stone, Martin L., Louis J. Solerno, Marvin Green, and Carl Zelson: "Narcotic Addiction in Pregnancy," *American Journal of Obstetrics and Gynecology*, vol. 109, no. 5, pp. 716–723, Mar. 1, 1971.

Strausz, Ivan K., and Harold Schulman: "500 Outpatient Abortions Performed under Local Anesthesia," *Obstetrics and Gynecology*, vol. 38, no. 2, pp. 199–205, August 1971.

Sumner, William Graham, and Albert Galloway Keller: *The Science of Society*, Yale University Press, New Haven, Conn., 1927.

Surgeon General: "Smoking and Pregnancy," from "The Health Consequences of Smoking, 1971," U.S. Department of Health, Education, and Welfare.

———: "The Health Consequences of Smoking," *A Report of the Surgeon General, 1972*, U.S. Department of Health, Education, and Welfare.

Sutherland, Hamish, and Iain Stewart: "A Critical Analysis of the Premenstrual Syndrome," *The Lan-*

cet, vol. 1, pp. 1180–1183, June 5, 1965.

Tanner, James M., and Gordon Rattray Taylor: *Growth*, Time-Life Books, a division of Time, Inc., New York, 1965.

Tatum, Howard J.: "Intrauterine Contraception," *American Journal of Obstetrics and Gynecology*, vol. 112, no. 7, pp. 1000–1023, Apr. 1, 1972.

———: "Metallic Copper as an Intrauterine Contraceptive Agent," *American Journal of Obstetrics and Gynecology*, vol. 117, no. 5, pp. 602–618, Nov. 1, 1973.

———: "Copper-Bearing Intrauterine Devices," *Clinical Obstetrics and Gynecology*, vol. 17, no. 1, pp. 93–119, March 1974.

Tauber, Oscar E., Robert E. Haupt, and Hester Fassel: *Zoology 358: Physiology of Reproduction. A Laboratory Guide*, Iowa State University, Ames, Iowa, 1970.

Taussig, Helen B.: "A Study of the German Outbreak of Phocomelia," *Journal of the American Medical Association*, vol. 180, no. 13, pp. 1106–1114, June 30, 1962.

Taylor, E. Stewart: editor's comments, *Obstetrical and Gynecological Survey*, vol. 22, no. 4, p. 610, August 1967; vol. 23, no. 1, p. 92, January 1968; vol. 24, no. 8, p. 1092, August 1969.

Terhune, K. W.: *A Review of the Actual and Expected Consequences of Family Size*, U.S. Department of Health, Education, and Welfare, Public Health Service, National Institutes of Health Publication No. (NIH) 75-779, Government Printing Office, 1974.

Terman, Lewis: *Psychological Factors in Marital Happiness*, McGraw-Hill Book Company, New York, 1938.

Tietze, Christopher: "Probability of Pregnancy Resulting from Single Unprotected Coitus," *Fertility & Sterility*, vol. 11, no. 5, pp. 485–488, 1960.

———: "Intra-uterine Contraceptive Rings: History and Statistical Appraisal," in Christopher Tietze and Sarah Lewit (eds.), "Intra-uterine Contraceptive Devices," *Proceedings of the Conference, April 30–May 1, 1962, International Congress Series No. 54*, Excerpta Medica Foundation, New York, pp. 9–20.

———: "Effectiveness and Acceptability of Intrauterine Contraceptive Devices," *American Journal of Public Health*, vol. 55, p. 1874, 1965; abstracted in *Obstetrical and Gynecological Survey*, vol. 21, no. 3, pp. 483–486, June 1966.

———: "Intra-uterine Contraception," in Stewart L. Marcus and Cyril C. Marcus (eds.), *Advances in Obstetrics and Gynecology*, vol. 1, The Williams & Wilkins Company, Baltimore, 1967, chap. 35.

———: "The Condom," in Mary Steichen Calderone (ed.), *Manual of Family Planning and Contraceptive Practice*, 2d ed., The Williams & Wilkins Company, Baltimore, 1970*a*, pp. 424–428.

———: "Relative Effectiveness," in Calderone, op. cit., pp. 268–275 (1970*b*).

Time, Aug. 31, 1970, pp. 15–23; Dec. 14, 1970, p. 50; Dec. 28, 1970, pp. 22, 34–39; Mar. 20, 1972 (special issue).

Timmons, J. Daniel, and Russell R. de Alvarez: "Monoamniotic Twin Pregnancy," *American Journal of Obstetrics and Gynecology*, vol. 86, no. 7, pp. 875–881, Aug. 1, 1963.

Timonen, Henri, Juhani Toivonen, and Tapani Luukkainen: "Use-effectiveness of the Copper-T 300 during the First Year," *American Journal of Obstetrics and Gynecology*, vol. 120, no. 4, pp. 466–469, Oct. 15, 1974.

Trethowan, W. H.: "Pregnancy Symptoms in Men," *Sexual Behavior*, vol. 2, no. 11, pp. 23–27, November 1972.

Trythall, Sylvester W.: "The Premarital Law," *Journal of the American Medical Association*, vol. 187, no. 12, pp. 900–903, Mar. 21, 1964.

Turchetti, G., R. Palagi, and E. Lattanzi: "Anemia in the New Born Due to Transplacental Fetal Hemorrhage," *Obstetrics and Gynecology*, vol. 26, no. 5, pp. 698–701, November 1965.

Turnbull, A. C., and Anne B. M. Anderson: "Uterine Function in Human Pregnancy and Labour," in Ronald R. MacDonald (ed.), *Scientific Basis of Obstetrics and Gynaecology*, J. and A. Churchill, London, 1971, chap. 3.

Udry, J. R.: "Marital Instability by Race, Sex, Education, and Occupation Using 1960 Census Data," *American Journal of Sociology*, vol. 72, pp. 203–209, 1966.

———: "Marital Instability by Race and Income Based on 1960 Census Data," *American Journal of Sociology*, vol. 72, pp. 673–674, 1967.

———: *The Social Context of Marriage*, 3d ed., J. B. Lippincott Company, Philadelphia, 1974.

Underwood, Paul B., Kelvin F. Kesler, John M. O'Lane, and Dwight A. Callagan: "Prenatal Smoking Empirically Related to Pregnancy Outcome," *Obstetrics and Gynecology*, vol. 29, no. 1, pp. 1–8, January 1967.

United Nations: *Demographic Yearbook*, New York, 1975.

U.S. Bureau of the Census: *Current Population Reports*, Ser. P-20, P-23, P-25, 1966–1976.

———: "Social and Economic Variations in Marriage, Divorce, and Remarriage: 1967," *Current Population Reports*, Ser. P-20, no. 223, 1971.

———: *Census of the United States*, 1970.

———: *Statistical Abstract of the United States*, 1972 (93d ed.), 1975 (96th ed.), and 1976 (97th ed.), 1972, 1975, 1976.

———: "Marital Status and Living Arrangements: March, 1975," *Current Population Reports*, Ser. P-20, no. 287, 1975.

U.S. Department of Health, Education, and Welfare: *Infant, Fetal, and Maternal Mortality, United States, 1963*, National Center for Health Statistics, ser. 20, no. 3, September 1966.

———: "Projections of the Population of the United States by Age, Sex and

Color to 1990, with Extensions of Population by Age and Sex to 2015," *Current Population Reports*, ser. 25, no. 381, 1967*a*.

———: *Vital Statistics Report*, vol. 15, no. 13, July 26, 1967*b*.

———: *Vital Statistics of the United States, 1968*, vol. 2, sec. 5, 1968.

———: *Monthly Vital Statistics Report*, 1970–1977.

———: *Vital and Health Statistics*, ser. 20, 21, 1971–1977.

———: *Vital Statistics of the United States*, 1973, vol. 2, sec. 5, 1975.

U.S. Department of Labor: *1969, Handbook on Women Workers*, Bulletin no. 294.

———: "Dual Careers, *Manpower Research Monograph*, 1970, vol. I, no. 21.

———, Bureau of Labor Statistics, 1976.

U.S. National Center for Health Statistics: "Summary Report, Final Natality Statistics, 1973," *Monthly Vital Statistics Report*, vol. 23, no. 11, Supplement, 1975.

———: "Final Divorce Statistics, 1974," *Monthly Vital Statistics Report*, vol. 25, no. 1, Supplement, 1976.

U.S. Supreme Court: *Jane Roe et al. v. Henry Wade*, no. 70-18, Jan. 22, 1973; *Mary Doe et al. v. Arthur K. Bolton*, no. 70-40, Jan. 22, 1973.

———: *Planned Parenthood of Central Missouri et al. v. Danforth, Attorney General of Missouri et al.*, no. 74-1151, July 1, 1976; *Danforth, Attorney General of Missouri v. Planned Parenthood of Central Missouri et al.*, no. 74-1419, July 1, 1976.

Valenti, C., C. C. Lin, A. Baum, M. Massobrio, and A. Carbonara: "Prenatal Sex Determination," *American Journal of Obstetrics and Gynecology*, vol. 112, no. 7, pp. 890–895, Apr. 1, 1972.

van Niekerk, William A.: *True Hermaphroditism: Clinical, Morphologic and Cytogenic Aspects*, Harper & Row, Publishers, Inc., New York, 1974.

Vener, A. M., and C. S. Stewart: "Adolescent Sexual Behavior in Middle America Revisited: 1970–1973," *Journal of Marriage and the Family*, vol. 36, pp. 728–735, 1974.

Verkauf, Barry Stephen: "Acquired Clitoral Enlargement," *Medical Aspects of Human Sexuality*, pp. 134–151, April 1975.

Vessey, Martin P., Richard Doll, and Peter M. Sutton: "Oral Contraceptives and Breast Neoplasia: A Retrospective Study," *British Medical Journal*, vol. 3, no. 5829, pp. 719–724, Sept. 23, 1972.

———, ———, **R. Peto, B. Johnson, and P. Wiggins:** "A Long-Term Follow-Up Study of Women Using Different Methods of Contraception—An Interim Report," *Journal of Biosocial Science*, vol. 8, p. 373, 1976.

Villee, Claude A. (ed.): *The Placenta and Fetal Membranes*, The Williams & Wilkins Company, Baltimore, 1960.

Wakin, Edward, and Joseph F. Scheuer: *The De-Romanization of the American Catholic Church*, The Macmillan Company, New York, 1966.

Wall, Roscoe L., Jr.: "Evaluation and Management of Infertility," *Clinical Obstetrics and Gynecology*, vol. 12, no. 4, pp. 851–926, December 1969.

Wallach, Edward E.: "Breast and Reproductive System Effects of Oral Contraceptives," pp. 645–668 in Celso-Ramon Garcia (ed.), "Oral Contraception," *Clinical Obstetrics and Gynecology*, vol. 11, no. 3, pp. 623–752, September 1968.

Waller, Willard: "The Rating and Dating Complex," *American Sociological Review*, vol. 2, pp. 727–734, 1937.

———: *The Family: A Dynamic Interpretation*, rev. by Reuben Hill, Holt, Rinehart and Winston, Inc.,

Wallin, Paul, and Alexander L. Clark: "A Study of Orgasm as a Condition of Women's Enjoyment of Coitus in the Middle Years of Marriage," *Human Biology*, vol. 35, no. 2, pp. 131–139, May 1963.

Walster, E., V. Aronson, D. Abrahams, and L. Rottman: "Importance of Physical Attractiveness in Dating Behavior," *Journal of Personality and Social Psychology*, vol. 4, pp. 508–516, 1966.

Walter, George S.: "Psychologic and Emotional Consequences of Elective Abortion," *Obstetrics and Gynecology*, vol. 36, no. 3, pp. 482–491, September 1970.

Washington, Joseph R., Jr.: *Marriage in Black and White*, Beacon Press, Boston, 1970.

Weinstein, Eugene A.: "Adoption and Fertility," *American Sociological Review*, vol. 27, no. 3, pp. 408–412, June 1962.

Weinstock, E., C. Tietze, F. S. Jaffe, and J. G. Dryfoos: "Legal Abortions in the United States Since the 1973 Supreme Court Decisions," *Family Planning Perspectives*, vol. 7, pp. 23–31, January/February 1975.

Weiss, R. S.: *Marital Separation: Coping with the End of Marriage and the Transition to Being Single Again*, Basic Books, Inc., New York, 1975.

Werner, Arnold: "Sex Questions Asked by College Students," *Medical Aspects of Human Sexuality*, pp. 32–61, May 1975.

Wershub, Leonard Paul: *Sexual Impotence in the Male*, Charles C Thomas, Publisher, Springfield, Ill., 1959.

———: *The Human Testis: A Clinical Treatise*, Charles C Thomas, Publisher, Springfield, Ill., 1962.

Westoff, Charles F.: "Coital Frequency and Contraception," *Family Planning Perspectives*, vol. 3, pp. 136–141, Summer 1974.

———: "Trends in Contraceptive Practice: 1965–1973," *Family Planning Perspectives*, vol. 8, pp. 54–57, 1976.

——— **and Larry Bumpass:** "The Revolution in Birth Control Practices of U.S. Roman Catholics," *Science*, vol. 179, p. 41ff., Jan. 5, 1973; abstracted in *Obstetrical and Gynecological Survey*, vol. 28, no. 7, pp. 494–496, July 1973.

Westoff, L. A., and C. F. Westoff:

From Now to Zero, Little, Brown and Company, Boston, 1971.

Wharton, Lawrence R.: *The Ovarian Hormones*, Charles C Thomas, Publisher, Springfield, Ill., 1967.

Wheeler, M.: *No-Fault Divorce*, Beacon Press, Boston, 1974.

Wile, Ira S., and Mary Day Winn: *Marriage in the Modern Manner*, Appleton-Century-Crofts, Inc., New York, 1929.

Wilkins, Lawson: *The Diagnosis and Treatment of Endocrine Disorders in Childhood and Adolescence*, Charles C Thomas, Publisher, Springfield, Ill., 1965.

Williams, H. Stephen, and Mary B. Meyer: "Cigarette Smoking, Infant Birth Weight, and Perinatal Mortality Rates," *American Journal of Obstetrics and Gynecology*, vol. 116, no. 6, pp. 890–892, July 15, 1973.

Williams, K. M., and R. P. Kuhn: "Remarriages, United States," U.S. Department of Health, Education, and Welfare, *Vital and Health Statistics* Publication no. (HRA), 74-1903, Rockville, Md., 1973.

Willocks, James, Ian McDonald, T. C. Duggan, and N. Day: "Fetal Cephalometry by Ultrasound," *Journal of Obstetrics and Gynecology of the British Commonwealth*, vol. 71, no. 1, pp. 11–20, February 1964.

Willson, J. Robert: "Contraceptive Devices: Their Effectiveness in Controlling Fertility and Their Effects on Uterine Tissue," *Pacific Medicine and Surgery*, vol. 73, no. 1A, pp. 44–51, February 1965.

Winch, Robert F.: *Mate-Selection: A Study of Complementary Needs*, Harper & Row, Publishers, Inc., New York, 1958.

———: *The Modern Family*, 2d ed., Holt, Rinehart and Winston, Inc., New York, 1963.

———: "Another Look at the Theory of Complementary Needs in Mate-Selection," *Journal of Marriage and the Family*, vol. 29, pp. 756–762, 1967.

———: *The Modern Family*, 3d ed., Holt, Rinehart and Winston, Inc., New York, 1971.

———: "Theorizing About the Family," in R. F. Winch and G. B. Spanier, (eds.), *Selected Studies in Marriage and the Family*, 4th ed., Holt, Rinehart and Winston, New York, 1974a, pp. 21–30.

———: "Complementary Needs and Related Notions about Voluntary Mate-Selection," in Winch and Spanier, 1974b.

———, T. Ktsanes, and V. Ktsanes: "The Theory of Complementary Needs in Mate-Selection: An Analytic and Descriptive Study," *American Sociological Review*, vol. 19, pp. 241–249, 1954.

———and Graham Spanier (eds.): *Selected Studies in Marriage and the Family*, Holt, Rinehart and Winston, Inc., New York, 4th ed., 1974.

Winokur, George (ed.): *Determinants of Human Sexual Behavior*, Charles C Thomas, Publisher, Springfield, Ill., 1963.

Wu, Paul Y. K., and William Oh: "Management of the Newborn," in Allan G. Charles and Emanuel A. Friedman, *Rh Immunization and Erythroblastosis Fetalis*, Appleton-Century-Crofts, New York, 1969, chap. 14.

Wyll, Shelby A., and Kenneth L. Herrmann: "Inadvertent Rubella Vaccination of Pregnant Women," *Journal of the American Medical Association*, vol. 225, p. 1472, 1973; abstracted in *Obstetrical and Gynecological Survey*, vol. 29, no. 3, pp. 188–190, March 1974.

Yahia, Clement, and Melvin L. Taymor: "A 3-Minute Immunologic Pregnancy Test," *Obstetrics and Gynecology*, vol. 23, no. 1, pp. 37–40, January 1964.

Yankowski, John S.: *The Yankowski Report on Premarital Sex*, Holloway Publishing Company, Los Angeles, 1965.

Young, William C.: "The Mammalian Ovary," in William C. Young (ed.), *Sex and Internal Secretions*, 3d ed., The Williams & Wilkins Company, Baltimore, 1961, chap. 7.

———: "The Organization of Sexual Behavior by Hormonal Action during the Prenatal and Larval Periods in Vertebrates," in Frank A. Beach (ed.), *Sexual Behavior*, John Wiley & Sons, Inc., New York, 1965, chap. 5.

———, **Robert W. Goy, and Charles H. Phoenix:** "Hormones and Sexual Behavior," *Science*, vol. 143, no. 3603, pp. 212–218, Jan. 17, 1964.

Zañartu, Juan, and Rudolfo Guerrero: "Steroid Release from Polymer Vaginal Devices: Effect on Fertility Inhibition," *Steroids*, vol. 21, p. 325, 1973; abstracted in *Obstetrical and Gynecological Survey*, vol. 29, no. 1, pp. 52–54, January 1974.

Zelnik, Melvin, and John F. Kantner: "Sexuality, Contraception and Pregnancy among Young Unwed Females in the United States," in Charles F. Westoff and Robert Parke, Jr. (eds.), Commission on Population Growth and the American Future, Research Reports, vol. 1, *Demographic and Social Aspects of Population Growth*, Washington, D.C., pp. 357–374, 1972.

———: "Sexual and Contraceptive Experience of Young Unmarried Women in the United States, 1976 and 1971," *Family Planning Perspectivs*, vol. 9, no. 2, pp. 55–71, March/April 1977.

Zelson, Carl, Estrellita Rubio, and Edward Wasserman: "Neonatal Narcotic Addiction: 10 Year Observation," *Pediatrics*, vol. 48, no. 2, pp. 178–189, August 1971.

Zielske, F., U. J. Koch, R. Badura, and H. Ladeburg: "Studies on Copper Release from Copper-T Devices (T-Cu200) and Its Influence on Sperm Migration In Vitro," *Contraception*, vol. 10, p. 651, 1974; abstracted in *Obstetrical and Gynecological Survey*, vol. 30, no. 5, pp. 340–342, May 1975.

Zipursky, Alvin, Janet Pollack, Bruce Chown, and L. G. Israels: "Transplacental Foetal Haemorrhage after Placental Injury during Delivery or Amniocentesis," *The Lancet*, vol. 2, no. 7306, pp. 493–494, 1963.

Name Index

Abbey, H., 349, 459
Abdul-Karim, R. W., 350, 455
Abrahams, D., 477
Abt, L. E., 165
Ackerman, N. W., 455
Aims, S., 379
Albert, A., 455
Albert, E. M., 215
Albrecht, R. E., 456
Ald, R., 53
Aldous, J., 82
Alexander, S., 215, 449
Allan, M. S., 455
Allen, F. M. J., 455
Altbach, E. H., 215
Altman, D., 29
Altman, I., 81
Amundsen, K., 215
Anderson, A. B. M., 356, 476
Anderson, G., 329, 330, 455
Anderson, M. M., 329, 468
Anderson, S. M., 38, 472
Andolsek, L., 469
Andreas, C., 215
Andrews, R., 212, 458
Apgar, V., 379
Apolonio, F., 470
Aries, P., 9
Arisian, K., 191
Arnstein, H. S., 405
Aronson, H. G., 321, 455
Aronson, M. E., 270, 455
Aronson, V., 477
Arrata, W. S. M., 340, 352, 455
Arronet, G. H., 321, 455
Arvay, A., 352, 471
Asai, J., 338, 470
Astin, H. S., 29
Averkin, E., 303, 463
Avila, T., 307, 474
Ayre, J. E., 302, 455
Aznar-Ramos, R., 303, 456

Bach, G. K., 81, 250

Badura, R., 307, 478
Baecker, J. M., 111, 471
Baer, J., 164
Bahr, S. J., 205, 456
Bailard, T. E., 250
Baker, T. G., 340, 456
Bakker, C. B., 302, 456
Ballard, C. A., 239, 456
Ballard, F. E., 329, 456
Balswick, J. O., 29, 473
Balter, S., 90, 456
Banner, E. A., 457, 465
Banowsky, W. S., 114
Barber, H. R. K., 305, 456
Barber, K. E., 162, 163, 459
Barbosa, J. J., 344, 461
Bardwick, J. M., 19, 20, 29, 70, 71, 274, 456, 465, 467
Barglow, P., 352, 457
Barnett, L. D., 147, 456
Barr, J., 55
Barron, D. M., 348, 456
Barron, M. L., 155, 164, 456
Bartell, G. D., 279, 287, 456
Barton, J. J., 316, 456
Baum, A., 352, 477
Bauman, K. E., 107, 456
Bayer, A. E., 80, 456
Beach, F. A., 266, 456, 464, 469, 474, 478
Beacham, D. W., 300, 456
Beacham, W. D., 300, 456
Beam, L., 88, 460
Bearne, C., 462, 472
Beck, J., 379
Bednarik, K., 26, 210, 215, 456
Beer, A. E., 296, 456
Behrman, S. J., 322, 456
Bell, E. T., 302, 304, 308, 319, 468
Bell, P. L., 254, 258, 456
Bell, R., 7, 75, 77, 80, 89, 90, 254, 258, 277, 456
Bell, R. Q., 405
Belliveau, F., 287
Bendel, R. P., 352, 458

Benirschke, K., 352, 466
Benjamin, H., 456
Benson, L., 405
Benson, R., 456
Benz, E. W., 349, 461
Benzie, R. J., 345, 456
Berardo, F., 9, 206, 471
Berger, B., 48, 53, 456
Berger, M. E., 53
Bergquist, C. A., 321, 455
Berkowitz, L., 477
Berlind, M., 343, 456
Berman, L. A., 164
Bernard, J., 53, 96, 215, 250, 405, 456, 469, 473
Berne, E., 250
Bernstein, M. C., 194, 463
Berscheid, E., 76, 77, 81, 456
Besanceney, P. H., 155, 164, 456
Beydoun, S. N., 350, 455
Biehl, D. L., 250
Birch, H. G., 405
Bird, C., 215
Bird, J., 250
Bird, L., 250, 287
Bishop, D. W., 338, 457
Bishop, E. H., 460, 462
Bishop, H. L., 375, 464
Blackburn, C. W., 250
Blazer, J. A., 262, 272, 457
Blood, R. O., Jr., 62, 77–79, 100, 151, 225, 457, 464
Bock, E. W., 456
Boggs, T. R., 457
Bohannan, P., 433
Bolognese, R. J., 329, 330, 457, 465
Bolton, C. D., 128, 457
Bosmajian, H., 215, 457, 464
Boulton, M., 467
Bourke, G. J., 349, 457
Bourne, A. W., 350, 457
Böving, B. G., 305, 457
Bowes, K., 274, 275, 457
Bowman, H. A., 135, 457

Name Index

Boyd, N. R. H., 356, 458
Bradley, R. A., 359, 379, 457
Brandling-Bennett, A. D., 349, 457
Brannon, R., 216
Brasch, R., 181, 457
Brazelton, T. B., 405
Brecher, E. M., 114
Breckinridge, S., 200, 457
Bremer, J., 23, 457
Brenner, P. F., 307, 457
Brenton, M., 215
Brill, M., 165
Briller, S. W., 215
Brim, O. G., Jr., 59, 457
Brish, M., 463
Britten, F. H., 88, 457
Broderick, C. B., 114, 268, 457, 469, 473
Bromley, D. D., 88, 457
Brotherton, J., 323, 457
Brown, B. A., 207, 457
Brown, E., 352, 457
Bruce, J., 275, 457
Brueschke, E. E., 315, 457
Buckle, A. E. R., 329, 468
Bulmer, M. G., 370, 371, 457
Bumpass, L., 143, 144, 151, 155, 160, 162, 163, 422, 457, 477
Bunge, R. G., 322, 457
Burchinal, L. G., 144, 156, 162, 163, 458
Burgess, E. W., 88, 135, 139, 458
Burnett, J. B. C., 461
Burr, W., 468
Busselen, C. K., 187, 458
Busselen, H. J., Jr., 187, 458
Butler, C., 461
Butler, N. R., 349, 458
Buxton, C. L., 462, 475

Calderone, M. S., 294, 333, 458, 462, 464, 473, 474, 476
Calhoun, A. W., 71, 458
Callagan, D. A., 349, 476
Campbell, A. A., 312, 462
Cannon, K. L., 92, 93, 114, 458
Cantarow, A., 274, 471
Cantor, B., 330, 458
Cappetta, M., 144, 464
Capraro, V. J., 263, 266, 458
Carbonara, A., 352, 477
Carden, M. L., 53, 215
Carns, D. E., 14, 89, 92, 93, 458
Carr, D. H., 323, 458
Carr, W. R., 218
Carrington, E. R., 470
Carter, H., 147, 458
Cates, W., Jr., 326, 458
Catlin, N., 53

Cavanagh, J. R., 274, 458
Cawood, C. D., 103, 458
Celestin, L. R., 380
Cervenka, J., 352, 458
Chafetz, J. S., 29
Chancellor, L. E., 156, 162, 163, 458
Chard, T., 356, 458
Charles, A. G., 372, 458, 462, 478
Charles, D., 470
Charny, C. W., 24, 458
Chaskes, J. B., 75, 80, 89, 456
Chess, S., 405
Chin, J., 349, 458
Chown, B., 373, 478
Christensen, H. T., 78, 87–89, 109, 114, 162, 163, 212, 250, 458, 459
Christenson, C. V., 133, 459
Christian, C. D., 458, 460, 473
Clark, A. L., 254, 258, 276, 459, 477
Clark, T. L., 373, 459
Clarke, C. A., 372–374, 459
Clatworthy, N. M. K., 217
Clayton, E. M., Jr., 372, 459
Clayton, R. R., 38, 139, 459
Clemens, A. H., 459
Cloyd, J. S., 189, 464
Coffrey, D. S., 315, 459
Cohen, F., 372, 459
Cole, C. L., 132, 226, 279, 475
Cole, S. P., 386, 465
Comstock, G. W., 349, 459
Connell, E., 30, 302, 303, 314, 459
Constantine, J., 49, 50, 53, 459
Constantine, L., 49, 50, 53, 459
Coombs, R. H., 128, 459
Cooper, D. L., 307, 308, 457, 459, 473
Coppen, A., 274, 466
Corson, S. L., 329, 330, 457, 465
Coser, R. L., 459
Cotton, D. W., 215
Cottrell, A. B., 145, 459
Cottrell, L. S., 458
Craft, I. L., 232, 457
Crampton, C. B., 376, 459
Crandall, E. W., 250
Crist, T., 106, 343, 459
Croake, J. W., 53
Cromwell, R. E., 250
Crosby, W. M., 459
Cross, H. J., 94, 460
Csapo, A. I., 329, 459
Cuber, J. F., 164, 287, 420, 460
Cudlipp, E., 216
Cunningham, G., 273, 469
Cuse, A., 433
Cutright, P., 114, 150, 460

Dacie, J. V., 373, 460
Dalton, K., 274, 275, 460
Daly, M. J., 274, 460
D'Antonio, W. V., 288
D'Augelli, J. F., 94, 460
David, D. S., 216
Davis, C. D., 300, 460
Davis, H. J., 306, 308, 460
Davis, K., 143, 278, 460
Davis, K. B., 88, 100, 460
Davis, K. E., 89, 93, 128, 129, 466
Davis, M. B., 355, 465
Day, B., 380
Day, N., 360, 478
deAlvarez, R. R., 370, 476
Dean, D. G., 42, 460
De Beauvoir, S., 216
Debrouner, C. H., 264, 460
Decrow, K., 216
Decter, M., 216
Deep, A. A., 328, 460
De Jong, G. F., 293, 383, 460
Del Solar, C., 405
Demarest, R. J., 405
Denfeld, D., 279, 280, 460
Denmark, F., 216
Deutsch, R. M., 81
Dewhurst, C. J., 26, 460
Diamond, L. K., 455
Dickinson, R. L., 88, 460
Dick-Read, G., 363, 379
Dightman, C. R., 302
Dillon, W. P., 263, 458
Di Mascio, A., 274, 471
Di Saia, P. J., 300, 460
Dizard, J., 216
Dmowski, W. P., 307, 474
Dobson, J., 405
Doll, R., 302, 477
Donald, I., 460
Donnelly, C., 191
Donnelly, J. F., Jr., 349, 460
Doran, T. A., 345, 456
Doten, D., 81
Douvan, E., 29, 456
Drill, V. A., 301, 302, 317, 460
Dryfoos, J. G., 105, 109, 323, 466, 477
Dubin, L., 272, 460
Duenhoelter, J. H., 345, 460
Duffy, B. J., Jr., 161, 460
Duggan, T. C., 360, 478
Durrell, L., 460
Duvall, E. M., 404, 460
Dyrenfurth, I., 330, 458

Eastman, N. J., 368, 371, 460
Eastman, W. F., 90, 107, 461
Ebbin, A. J., 349, 458

Name Index

Eckerling, B., 373, 463
Eckstein, P., 461
Edgren, R. A., 461
Edwards, C. R. W., 356, 458
Ehrhardt, A. A., 23, 24, 30, 470
Ehrlich, S. S., 185, 461
Ehrmann, W., 81, 89, 92, 93, 95, 96, 114, 461, 472, 473
Eichler, L., 181, 183, 461
Eisenman, R., 55
Eisner, T., 316, 461
Ejlersen, M., 267, 461
Elias, J., 307, 471
Elias, J. E., 89, 461
Ellis, A., 467, 472
Ellis, H. F., 379
Ellis, J., 216
Emerson, T. I., 207, 457
Engle, E. T., 341, 461
Epstein, C. F., 216
Epstein, J., 433
Ersek, R. A., 322, 461
Eshleman, J. R., 144
Evans, B., 115, 471
Evans, M. M., 372, 459
Ewing, J. A., 320, 466
Exner, M. J., 88, 461

Fagundes, W. R., 302, 455
Fairfield, R., 45, 53, 461
Falk, G., 207, 457
Farber, S. M., 215
Farrell, W., 216
Farris, E. J., 298, 461
Fassel, H., 15, 476
Fasteau, M. F., 30
Feinleib, M., 369, 474
Feldhaus, W., 372, 459
Feldman, J. G., 461
Fernandez, C. M., 344, 461
Ferreira, A. J., 345, 350, 461
Ferriss, A. L., 201, 202, 461
Filene, P. G., 216
Findley, P., 264, 461
Finegold, W. J., 322, 333, 461
Finger, F. W., 88, 461
Finkelstein, R., 334, 464
Finkle, D. J., 91, 468
Firestone, S., 216
Fish, S. A., 373, 469
Fisher, A., 29
Fisher, E. O., 250
Fisher, S., 267, 287, 461
Fitzgerald, G. R., 53
Fiumara, N., 111, 461
Fleet, W. F., Jr., 349, 461
Flowers, C. E., Jr., 362, 374, 461, 465
Fluhmann, C. F., 274, 275, 461

Folkman, J. D., 217
Forfar, J. O., 349, 461
Fort, A. T., 377, 461
Foulks, E., 55
Fox, D. J., 219
Fox, M. K., 471
Foy, F. A., 159, 160, 461
Francisco, J. T., 105, 463
Freda, V. J., 374, 461
Freed, S. C., 274, 467
Freedman, A. E., 207, 457
Freedman, M. B., 89, 257, 462
Freedman, R., 312, 462
Freeman, C., 315, 459
Freeman, R. K., 270, 462
Freid, N., 308, 470
Freiser, S., 212, 458
Freund, M., 322, 462
Fried, P. H., 352, 462
Friedan, B., 217
Friedman, E. A., 372, 374, 458, 462, 478
Friedman, L. J., 343, 462
Fromm, E., 81
Fromme, A., 255, 462
Frotherby, K., 461
Fujita, B. N., 90, 106, 108, 462
Furlong, W. B., 164

Gaddis, M., 379
Gaddis, V., 379
Gage, M. G., 204, 462
Gager, N., 217
Gagnon, J. H., 114, 133, 459, 473
Gallego, M. B., 263, 458
Gambrell, R. D., 301, 462
Garcia, C., 298, 300, 302, 314, 462, 477
Garcia-Bunnel, R., 314, 462
Gardo, S., 355, 471
Garvin, J. E., 274, 473
Geary, W. L., 402, 474
Gebhard, P. H., 85, 92, 93, 100, 254, 267, 462, 467, 472
Genné, W. H., 165
Gentry, W. C., 322, 466
Giese, H., 462, 472
Gilbert, M. S., 379
Gill, M. M., 274, 462
Gillespie, L., 349, 462
Gillett, P. G., 329, 462
Gillette, P. J., 333
Gingles, R., 144, 470
Gittelson, N., 287
Glass, R. H., 343, 462
Glazer-Malbin, N., 464
Glick, P. C., 6, 9, 33, 36, 41, 51, 142, 147, 155, 417, 420, 432, 458, 462

Glienke, C. F., 321, 455
Godwin, C., 334, 464
Goldberg, L., 217
Goldberg, S., 30
Golden, B. A., 191, 258, 264, 273, 343, 462
Goldfarb, A. F., 305, 319, 462, 463
Goldman, A., 55
Goldman, G. D., 269, 463
Goldman, J. A., 373, 463
Goldsmith, S., 329, 463
Goldstein, B., 110–112, 463
Goldstein, H., 349, 458
Goldzieher, J. W., 30, 302, 303, 305, 463
Gonzoga, F. P., 274, 475
Good, F. L., 161, 463
Goode, W. J., 9, 62, 82, 118, 150, 194, 216, 217, 412, 433, 463
Goodlin, R. C., 273, 463
Goplerad, C. P., 370, 463
Gorbach, A., 273, 463
Gordon, A. I., 155, 162–164, 463
Gordon, M., 53, 194, 279, 459, 460, 463
Gordon, R. R., 26, 460
Gordon, S., 29, 114
Gorlin, R. J., 352, 458
Gorney, R., 274, 466
Gornick, V., 217
Goslin, D. A., 30
Gough, K., 9
Goy, R. W., 24, 478
Graber, E. A., 305, 456
Grabill, W. H., 105, 463
Granfield, D., 327, 463
Grant, A., 321, 463
Grant, N. F., 460
Graves, L. R., Jr., 105, 463
Green, H. G., 349, 463
Green, M., 349, 475
Green, R., 26, 30, 463
Greenblatt, R. B., 463, 468
Greenhill, J. P., 18, 273, 274, 296, 298, 321, 323, 341, 343, 346, 349, 352, 354, 357, 358, 360, 457, 461–463, 466, 468, 469
Greenough, W. T., 467
Greer, G., 217, 219
Gregg, C. F., 87–89, 459
Grold, L. J., 244, 463
Gross, M. I., 250
Gruenberg, S. M., 405
Guerrero, R., 314, 478
Guest, F., 334, 464
Gustafson, D., 372, 459
Gutmann, D., 29, 456
Guttmacher, A. F., 350, 351, 362, 369, 379, 463, 465, 475
Guyton, A. C., 268, 338, 463

Name Index

Habenstein, R. W., 9, 118, 415, 472
Hack, M., 463
Hacker, H. M., 207, 210, 464
Hackett, B., 48, 53, 456
Haire, D., 379
Hall, R. E., 308, 463, 464
Halpin, T. F., 375, 464
Halsell, G., 165
Hamblen, E. C., 274, 464
Hamblin, R. L., 100, 464
Hamilton, E. G., 374, 464
Hamilton, G. V., 88, 100, 464
Hammer, S., 30, 380
Hampson, J. G., 26, 464
Hampson, J. L., 26, 464
Hanson, J. W., 349, 464
Hardin, G., 333
Hardy, J. B., 348, 464
Harper, F. V., 464
Harper, R. A., 243, 267, 272, 464
Harris, D., 326, 471
Harroff, P. B., 287, 420, 460
Hart, G., 111, 464
Hart, H. H., 54
Hartman, C. G., 296–298, 312, 337, 338, 464
Haskins, A. L., 316, 464
Hastings, D. W., 287
Hatch, M. C., 346, 464
Hatcher, R. A., 300, 301, 305, 307, 313, 317, 334, 464
Hathorn, R., 165
Haupt, R. E., 15, 476
Havens, E., 78, 473
Havighurst, R. J., 404, 464
Heer, D. M., 146, 464
Henslin, J. M., 288
Hepker, W., 189, 464
Herpay, G., 352, 471
Herrmann, K. L., 349, 457, 461, 478
Hertig, A. Y., 370, 464
Herzig, N., 270, 464
Hettlinger, R. F., 114
Hetzel, A. M., 144, 464
Hibbard, L. T., 328, 464
Hilgers, T. W., 334
Hill, R., 82, 142, 466, 468, 477
Hirsh, H. L., 464
Hobbins, J. C., 377, 465
Hobbs, D. F., 386, 465
Hobbs, L., 217, 267, 465
Hodgson, J. E., 328, 329, 465
Hoffman, H., 114
Hoffman, J., 274, 465
Hoffman, L. W., 202, 206, 217, 456, 465, 471
Hoffman, M., 30
Hohman, L. B., 88, 465
Hollender, M. H., 258, 465

Hollingshead, A. B., 139, 465
Holmberg, A. R., 352, 465
Holtzman, L., 465
Holzman, G. B., 464
Hon, E. H., 355, 465
Horan, D. J., 334
Horner, M. S., 29, 456
Horton, F. W., 329, 465
Hosoe, K., 338, 470
Houriet, R., 54
Houseknecht, S., 151, 421, 465
Howard, D. H., 100, 466
Howell, D. A., 374, 465
Hudson, C. N., 356, 458
Huffman, J. W., 343, 465, 474
Hunt, M., 90, 277, 278, 433, 465
Huston, T. L., 76, 77, 138, 465
Hutchinson, D. L., 351, 352, 465
Hutt, C., 30
Hyams, L. L., 273, 465
Hyatt, H. W., Sr., 348, 465
Hyde, J. S., 30
Hytten, F. E., 350, 465

Iffy, L., 340, 352, 455
Illsley, R., 349, 465
Ingelman-Sundberg, A., 380
Ingraham, H. S., 329, 465
Inselberg, R., 143, 465
Insler, V., 463
Iscoe, I., 405
Israel, R., 308, 470
Israel, S. L., 274, 352, 465
Israels, L. G., 373, 478
Ivey, M. E., 274, 465

Jacklin, C. N., 16, 30, 469
Jacobs, R. I., 107, 474
Jacobs, W. M., 373, 459
Jacobson, B. D., 355, 465
Jacobson, I., 328, 460
Jacobson, P., 139, 466
Jaffe, F. S., 105, 109, 325, 466, 477
Janeway, E., 217
Janowsky, D. S., 274, 466
Jensen, M., 470
Jensen, O., 207, 217, 466
Jewelewicz, R., 330, 458
Johnson, B., 477
Johnson, E. W., 405
Johnson, R. E., 287
Johnson, V., 19, 20, 24, 100, 243, 255, 257, 260, 263, 265–269, 273, 281, 285, 287, 288, 312–314, 343, 466, 469
Johnson, W. L., 354, 466
Johnson, W. R., 406
Johnston, R. A., Sr., 361, 472
Jolly, H., 18, 466

Jones, A. R., 375, 464
Jones, G. S., 274, 298, 322, 471
Jones, H. W., Jr., 23, 266, 267, 274, 298, 322, 466, 471
Jones, K. L., 349, 464
Josselyn, I. M., 26, 466
Juhasz, A. M., 114

Kaats, G. F., 89, 93, 466
Kaiser, R. W., 250
Kaltreider, D. F., 349, 472
Kane, F. J., 320, 466
Kanin, E. J., 89, 100, 102, 466
Kanowitz, L., 51, 466
Kanter, R. M., 46, 48, 54, 466
Kantner, J. F., 14, 90–93, 106–108, 474, 478
Kaplan, A. J., 352, 462
Kaplan, H. S., 100, 265, 268, 270, 274, 281, 285, 466
Kapstein, R., 165
Karim, S. M. M., 329, 330, 466
Karmel, M., 380
Karow, W. G., 322, 466
Karson, D. T., 349, 461
Kase, N. G., 343, 462
Kasirsky, G., 334
Kass, E. H., 349, 473
Katchadourian, H. A., 287
Katz, A. W., 142, 466
Katz, J., 89, 466
Kaye, B. M., 348, 466
Kegel, A. H., 266, 466
Kellar, R. J., 469, 474
Kelleher, S. J., 165
Keller, A. G., 182, 255, 475
Keller, D. W., 273, 463
Keller, J. F., 53
Kelly, O. F., 161, 463
Kennedy, E. C., 60, 86, 114, 466
Kephart, W. M., 142, 432, 466
Kerckhoff, A. C., 128, 129, 466
Kerenyi, T. D., 329, 466
Kesler, K. F., 349, 476
Kessel, N., 274, 466
Khudr, G., 352, 466
Kinch, R. A. H., 330, 462
King, K., 473
Kinkade, K., 54
Kinsey, A. C., 14, 85, 86, 88, 92, 93, 100, 270, 277, 284, 467, 473
Kirkendall, L., 100, 101, 467
Kirkpatrick, C., 139, 467
Kirschenbaum, H., 191
Kirshen, E. J., 330, 467
Kistner, R. W., 266, 302, 319, 341, 343, 467
Kitzinger, S., 380
Klemer, R. H., 241, 467

Name Index

Knight, J. A., 352, 467
Knoll, M. W., 250
Knopf, O., 245, 467
Knox, D., 443
Koch, J., 443
Koch, L., 443
Koch, U. J., 306, 478
Koedt, A., 267, 467
Komisar, L., 217
Korda, M., 218
Koslowski, B., 405
Kraditor, A. S., 218
Kramer, R., 406
Krantzler, M., 433
Krause, H. D., 106, 467
Kretchmer, N., 470
Kreykamp, A. M. J., 165
Kroger, W. S., 274, 303, 467
Ktsanes, T., 125, 478
Ktsanes, V., 125, 478
Kuhn, R. P., 154, 431, 432, 478

Ladeburg, H., 306, 478
Lader, L., 334
Lamaze, F., 363, 380
Lamb, W. M., 274, 467
Landis, C., 88, 467
Landis, J. T., 88, 143, 151, 163, 467
Landis, M. G., 88
Lane, M. E., 273, 467
Lanford, C. F., 349, 468
Lankerani, M., 344, 470
Larsson, C. M., 165
Lasagna, L., 114
Lattanzi, E., 372, 476
Lau, H. L., 355, 467
Lawrence, G., 471
Leach, W. H., 191
Leathem, J. H., 468
Le Boyer, F., 364, 380
Lednicer, D., 461
Lefkowitz, L. B., 349, 461
Le Guerrer, J. M., 302, 455
Lehecka, C., 41, 42, 468
Lehfeldt, H., 107, 467
Lehrman, N., 287
Lehtinen, M., 90, 467
Lein, J. N., 354, 466
Le Masters, E. E., 386, 387, 406, 467
Leon, J. J., 146, 467
Lerner, S., 375, 464
Leshan, E. J., 406
Lesinski, J., 306, 460
Leslie, G., 139, 432, 467
Levin, A., 7, 91, 276–278, 467
Levin, H., 396, 474
Levin, M., 467

Levin, R. J., 7, 91, 276–278, 287, 467
Levine, S., 24, 467
Levinger, G., 82
Lewis, E. C., 30
Lewis, M., 405, 406
Lewis, R. A., 38, 41, 42, 118, 128, 129, 132, 139, 151, 165, 222, 223, 226, 276, 468, 475
Lewit, S., 476
Leyburn, J. G., 194, 468
Libby, R. W., 54
Lidz, R. W., 303, 468
Lifton, R. J., 218
Liley, A. W., 464
Liley, H. M. I., 380
Lin, C. C., 352, 477
Lincoln, J., 55
Lindemann, C., 114
Linnette, E. H., 349, 458
Linton, E. B., 273, 468
Linton, R., 61, 468
Lipmann-Blumen, J., 30
Lippes, J., 461
Lipton, M. A., 320, 466
Lloyd, C. W., 274, 297, 320, 464, 466, 468, 469
Lobsenz, N. M., 250
Locke, H. J., 132, 139, 458, 468
Long, E. M., Jr., 273, 469
Long, R., 92, 93, 114, 458
Longood, R. J., 329, 465
Lopata, H. Z., 183, 204, 218, 433, 468
Loraine, J. A., 302, 304, 308, 319, 468
Loung, K. C., 329, 468
Lowrie, S. H., 80, 468
Lubin-Finkle, M., 91, 468
Lucas, J. B., 111, 474
Luce, G. G., 242, 468
Luker, K., 334
Lumkin, M., 314, 470
Luna, M., 307, 474
Lunde, D. T., 287
Lunenfeld, B., 463
Lurie, H. L., 468
Luukkainen, T., 307, 476
Lynn, D. B., 406

Maas, J. M., 468
McBride, A. B., 406
McCammon, R. E., 308, 468
McCary, J. L., 287, 352, 468
Maccoby, E. E., 16, 30, 396, 469, 474
McConnell, R. B., 372, 373, 459
McDermott, S., 268, 287, 468
McDonald, I., 360, 478
MacDonald, J. M., 105, 468

McDonald, R. L., 349, 352, 468
MacDonald, R. R., 304, 468, 470, 475, 476
Mace, D. R., 191, 250, 270, 287, 334, 469
Mace, V., 250
McElin, T. W., 274, 473
McEwan, J., 307, 471
McGinnis, R., 478
McGinnis, T., 250
McGuire, T. F., 258, 267, 468
Mackenzie, J. M., 329, 468
Macklin, E. D., 6, 38, 39, 41, 54, 469
McLarey, D. C., 373, 469
McLaughlin, H. B., 321, 473
MacMahon, B., 369, 474
McWhirter, N., 369, 469
McWhirter, R., 369, 469
Madsen, M. K., 461
Maeck, J. V. S., 349, 469
Mahan, C. S., 268, 469
Main, M., 405
Mandelman, N., 329, 466
Mann, E. C., 273, 469
Mann, G., 307, 471
Mannes, M., 433
Marcus, C. C., 465, 476
Marens, S. L., 465, 476
Margolis, A. J., 329, 377, 463, 469
Margulies, L. C., 307, 469
Mariano, W. E., 450
Marine, G., 218
Markland, C., 457, 459
Marshall, S., 272, 469
Martin, C. B., Jr., 273, 469
Martin, C. E., 85, 92, 93, 100, 467
Martinson, F. M., 144, 469
Masnick, G. S., 369, 472
Massarik, F., 115, 471
Massey, C., 54
Massobrio, M., 352, 477
Masters, W. H., 19, 20, 24, 100, 243, 255, 257, 260, 263, 265–269, 273, 274, 280, 285, 287, 288, 312–314, 343, 466, 467, 469
Mastroianni, L., Jr., 462
Matheny, A., 139, 466
Mayes, B., 348, 469
Mazur, R. M., 115
Mead, M., 42, 43, 54, 71, 380, 469
Mears, E., 302, 469
Meissner, H. H., 459
Melody, G. F., 274, 469
Melville, K., 54
Merton, R. K., 460
Messer, H. H., 344, 472
Meyer, H. M., Jr., 349, 470
Meyer, M. B., 349, 459, 478
Meyer, R., 314, 470

Name Index

Mill, J. S., 218
Millar, R. M., 48, 53, 456
Millen, A. K., 307, 459
Miller, J. B., 30
Millett, K., 207, 218, 219, 267, 470
Milliken, R. L., 187, 474
Mills, C. W., 96, 470
Milman, D. S., 269, 463
Mishell, D. R., Jr., 306–308, 314, 457, 459, 470, 473
Mitchell, H. E., 250
Mitsuya, H., 338, 470
Modlin, J. F., 349, 457
Mofid, M., 344, 470
Moghissi, K. S., 329, 330, 470
Moloshok, R. E., 349, 470
Monahan, T. P., 422, 470
Money, J., 22–24, 26, 30, 31, 115, 463, 470
Montagu, M. F. A., 18, 138, 368, 380, 470
Moore, B. M., 202, 473
Morales, A., 319, 463
Moran, B. K., 217
Morese, K. N., 349, 472
Morgan, R., 218
Mornell, P., 288
Morris, J. M., 294, 470
Moses, L. E., 303, 463
Moss, J. J., 144, 155, 470
Moyer, D. L., 306, 338, 342, 467, 470, 471
Mudd, E. H., 250
Mueller, S. A., 470
Mukherjee, T. K., 461
Mulcahy, R., 349, 470
Munro, A., 470
Murdock, G. P., 49, 59, 278, 470
Murphy, J. F., 349, 470
Murray, R. R., 470
Murstein, B. I., 82, 128, 470

Naftolin, F., 330, 467
Nass, G., 73, 474
Nathanson, B. N., 328, 329, 471
Nelson, F., 326, 471
Nelson, P. K., 370, 455
Nesbit, R. A., 460
Neu, C., 274, 471
Neubardt, S., 343, 471
Neubeck, B., 288
Neumann, H. H., 111, 467, 471
Newman, C., 191
Newton, J., 307, 471
Newton, N., 350, 368, 380, 471
Nichols, J., 218
Niebyl, J. R., 343, 471
Nilsson, L., 345, 380
Noonan, J. T., Jr., 159, 327, 471

Norton, A. J., 6, 33, 36, 417, 420, 432, 462
Novak, E., 274, 471
Novak, E. K., 274, 298, 322, 471
Noyes, J., 54
Nye, I. F., 9, 202, 205, 206, 217, 456, 465, 468, 471

Ochsner, A., 349, 471
Odell, W. D., 338, 342, 471
Oettinger, K. B., 109, 471
Oh, W., 374, 478
O'Lane, J. M., 349, 476
Oliven, J. F., 23, 320, 338, 343, 471
Olson, D. H., 250
O'Neill, G., 54
O'Neill, N., 54
O'Neill, W. L., 218, 419, 471
O'Rourke, J. J., 305, 456
Osofsky, H. J., 471
Osofsky, J. D., 471
Ostergard, D. R., 348, 471
Otto, H. A., 54, 469, 471
Oven, A., 469

Pace-Asciak, C., 330, 462
Packard, V., 89, 115, 471
Page, E. W., 275, 299, 350, 471
Pakter, J., 326, 471
Palagi, R., 372, 476
Palti, Z., 319, 471
Panner, R., 115, 471
Papp, Z., 352, 471
Parekh, M. C., 321, 455
Parelman, A., 29
Parke, R., Jr., 460, 474, 478
Parkman, M. A., 146, 471
Parkman, P. D., 349, 470
Parshley, H. M., 216
Paschkis, K. E., 274, 471
Pasnau, R. O., 327, 471
Patner, A., 330, 458
Pavela, T. H., 147, 472
Payne, S., 322, 466
Pearlin, L. I., 149, 472
Peck, C. W., 29
Peck, N. W., 88, 472
Peck, R. F., 150, 473
Peel, J., 300, 302, 308, 472
Peltz, D., 7, 277, 456
Pennock, J. L., 384, 472
Peretti, P. O., 90, 472
Perez, A., 369, 472
Perkins, M. F., 321, 472
Perlmutter, J. F., 349, 472
Perntz, K., 218
Perrucci, C. C., 218

Peterman, D., 38, 472
Peterson, K. M., 88, 472
Peterson, W. F., 302, 349, 472
Peto, R., 477
Phillips, C. A., 349, 469
Phoenix, C. H., 24, 478
Phythyon, J. M., 372, 459
Pierce, R., 115
Pierson, E. C., 288
Pillay, A. P., 472
Pilpel, H., 463
Pineus, G., 296, 305, 317, 462, 472
Pion, R. J., 106, 108, 462
Piver, M. S., 361, 472
Plateris, A. A., 72, 144, 420–423, 425, 458, 472
Pollack, J., 373, 478
Pomeroy, W. B., 85, 92, 93, 100, 115, 467
Pope Paul VI, 160, 161, 472
Pope Pius XII, 161, 472
Porter, S., 250
Porterfield, A. L., 88, 472
Portmann, K. C., 329, 465
Potter, A. L., 472
Potter, E. L., 323, 472
Potter, R. G., 369, 472
Potts, M., 300, 302, 308, 472
Powell, L. C., 474
Pratt-Thomas, H. R., 344, 472
Price, D., 338, 472
Pritchard, J. A., 345, 460, 472
Protos, P., 319, 463
Pyle, L., 165

Queen, S. A., 9, 118, 415, 472
Queenan, J. T., 372–375, 459, 468, 472

Raboch, J., 258, 462, 472
Raffin, M., 273, 463
Rajan, R., 471
Rakoff, A. E., 274, 319, 352, 462, 463, 471
Ramey, I. G., 267, 472
Ramey, J. W., 49, 54, 473
Ramsey, G. V., 202, 473
Ramsey, P., 334
Rao, R., 307, 474
Reaney, B. V., 348, 466
Reed, E., 218
Reed, S. C., 380
Reeves, B. D., 274, 473
Reeves, N., 218
Reevy, W. R., 88, 473
Reid, D. E., 458, 460, 473
Reining, P., 334

Name Index

Reiss, I. L., 63, 64, 78, 86, 92–96, 115, 288, 468, 473
Renne, K. S., 422, 473
Reyner, F. C., 302, 455
Rhee, M. W., 344, 470
Rice-Wray, E., 302, 305, 463
Richards, D. J., 461
Richardson, S. A., 380, 465
Richter, L., 287
Ridley, C. A., 38, 472
Riemer, S., 187, 473
Riley, G. M., 18, 473
Robertiello, R. C., 467
Roberts, R. E., 48, 54, 473
Roberts, R. W., 115
Robertson, C. N., 54
Robinson, D. W., 274, 467
Robinson, I. E., 89, 90, 473
Robinson, S. C., 302, 473
Rochat, R. W., 326, 458
Rock, J., 165, 321, 473
Rockwell, R. C., 150, 152, 473
Rodman, H., 334
Rogers, C. R., 54
Rogers, E. M., 78, 473
Rosenberg, B. G., 30
Rosenblatt, F., 316, 461
Rosenblum, L. A., 405, 406
Rosenthal, E., 156, 473
Ross, E. M., 349, 458
Ross, R. T., 88, 473
Rossi, A. S., 406
Roth, E., 349, 474
Roth, J., 150, 473
Rothchild, J., 55
Rottman, L., 477
Roufa, A., 329, 468
Routtenberg, L. S., 192
Rovinsky, J. J., 327, 473
Roy, S., 308, 473
Rubin, W. S., 334
Rubin, Z., 82
Rubio, E., 349, 478
Rudolph, A. H., 111, 473
Rupp, J. J., 274, 471
Rush, D., 349, 473
Rushmer, R. F., 354, 466
Russell, C. S., 386, 474
Russell, G. F. M., 275, 457
Ryan, K. J., 330, 467
Ryder, N. B., 384, 474
Sadoughi, N., 24, 458
Safilios-Rothschild, C., 218
Sakol, J., 217
Salber, E. J., 369, 474
Salk, L., 406
Salley, H. E., 88, 472
Samenfink, J. A., 187, 474
Sandberg, E. C., 107, 474
Sarvis, B., 334

Satir, V., 443
Sauvage, J. P., 329, 459
Savel, L. E., 349, 474
Sawada, Y., 322, 456
Sawyer, J., 146, 471
Saxton, L., 73, 76, 474
Scanzoni, J., 149, 150, 250, 422, 474
Schaefer, G., 455, 465, 468, 470, 471, 474
Schaeffer, L. C., 288, 467
Schaffner, B., 88, 465
Scheel, C., 303, 463
Scheinfeld, A., 138, 370, 380, 474
Schellevis, L., 165
Scheuer, J. F., 161, 477
Schneider, G. T., 402, 474
Schopback, R. R., 352, 462
Schroder, R., 187, 474
Schroeter, A., 111, 474
Schulman, H., 329, 475
Schwartz, A., 406
Schwarz, R. H., 328, 474
Sciarra, J. J., 405, 457, 459
Scommegna, A., 307, 474
Scott, J. S., 474
Scott, L. S., 320, 474
Scott, R. D., 308, 474
Scott, W. W., 23, 266, 267, 466
Seaman, B., 288
Sears, R. R., 26, 396, 474
Sebba, H., 456
Seldin, R. R., 192
Seligson, M., 192
Sell, K. D., 449
Sell, R., 293, 383, 460
Serr, M., 463
Seymour, R. J., 474
Shah, F., 106–108, 349, 459, 474
Shainess, N., 474
Shaw, N. S., 380
Shearman, R. P., 319, 474
Sheresky, N., 433
Sherfey, M. J., 267, 474
Sherman, D. S., 329, 466
Sherman, J. A., 31
Sherman, J. K., 322, 474
Shettles, L. B., 352, 474
Shiloh, A., 462, 473
Shipman, K. J., 212, 474
Shnider, S. M., 461, 469
Shorter, E., 219
Sickels, R. J., 165, 176, 474
Simon, J., 165
Simon, P., 165
Simon, W., 114, 473
Singer, I., 288
Sjovall, E., 313, 343, 474
Skinner, B. F., 46, 54
Skipper, J. K., 73, 474

Sklare, M., 155, 475
Sloan, R. B., 475
Smith, B. K., 202, 473
Smith, D. W., 349, 464
Smith, J. R., 288
Smith, K. D., 322, 475
Smith, L. G., 288
Smith, R. A., 316, 475
Smith, W. J., Jr., 78, 475
Smithells, R. W., 349, 475
Snoek, J. D., 82
Solerno, L. J., 349, 475
Sorensen, R. C., 90, 92, 106, 115, 475
Southam, A. L., 274, 307, 475
Spanier, G. B., 7, 9, 10, 12, 14, 38, 41, 42, 80, 81, 85, 92, 93, 97, 118, 127, 132, 139, 151, 162, 165, 222, 223, 226, 228, 232, 276, 279, 421, 460, 465, 468, 475, 478
Speck, R. V., 55
Speert, H., 475
Speidel, J. J., 457, 459
Speroff, L., 329, 455
Spiro, M. E., 55
Sprague, W. D., 55
Stassinapoulos, A., 219
Stegall, H. F., 354, 466
Steinberger, E., 322, 475
Steinhilber, R. M., 258, 267, 468
Steinmann, A., 219
Steinmetz, S. K., 251
Stembler, S., 219
Stensund, R., 191
Stevenson, H. W., 405
Stewart, C. S., 90, 477
Stewart, G. K., 334, 464
Stewart, I., 274, 475
Stokes, W., 267, 272, 464
Stoller, R. J., 25, 475
Stone, A., 288
Stone, G., 288
Stone, H. M., 288
Stone, M. L., 349, 475
Stone, S., 314, 470
Storm, V., 41, 42, 468
Straus, M., 251
Strausz, I. K., 329, 475
Stuart, I. R., 165
Suarez, R., 24, 458
Summer, W. G., 182, 225, 475
Sutherland, H., 274, 475
Sutton, P. M., 302, 477
Suyama, K., 338, 470
Sweet, J. A., 143, 144, 151, 162, 163, 422, 457
Switzer, E., 433
Symmonds, R. E., 316, 475
Symonds, C., 288

Name Index

Taber, B. Z., 300, 303, 460, 463
Tanner, J. M., 345, 380, 475
Tanner, L., 467
Targ, D. B., 218
Tatum, H. J., 306, 307, 476
Tauber, O. E., 15, 476
Taubin, S. B., 250
Taussig, H. B., 349, 476
Taylor, D., 81
Taylor, E. S., 346, 374, 476
Taylor, G. R., 345, 380, 475
Taymor, M. L., 355, 478
Terhune, K. W., 385, 386, 476
Terman, L., 88, 100, 476
Thomas, A., 405
Thompson, A. M., 350, 465
Thompson, M. L., 219
Tien, H. Y., 212, 474
Tietze, C., 108, 308, 321, 325, 463, 473, 476, 477
Timmons, J. D., 370, 476
Timonen, H., 307, 476
Tinker, I., 334
Toivonen, J., 307, 476
Tovell, H. M. M., 329, 468
Trainer, J. B., 288
Trethowan, W. H., 476
Troelstrup, A. W., 251
Trythall, S. W., 476
Tucker, P., 22–24, 31, 470
Turchetti, G., 372, 476
Turnbull, A. C., 356, 476
Tyler, E. T., 456

Udry, J. R., 150, 155, 386, 476
Ulett, G. A., 274, 467
Underwood, P. B., 349, 476
Ushida, T., 338, 470

Valenti, C., 352, 477
van Niekerk, W. A., 23, 477
Van Noort, L. G. A., 165
Van Tienhoven, A., 316, 461
van Wagenen, G., 294, 470
Vande Wiele, R. L., 330, 458
Vela, P., 369, 472
Vener, A. M., 90, 477
Verkauf, B. S., 266, 477
Vessey, M. P., 302, 304, 469, 477
Villee, C. A., 275, 299, 348, 350, 456, 471, 477

Villee, D. B., 275, 299, 350, 471
Vincent, C. E., 115
Voss, H. L., 38, 459

Waehrer, H. Y., 464
Wagner, N. N., 106, 108, 462, 470
Wahlrous, S., 251
Wakin, E., 161, 477
Walcher, D. H., 470
Wall, R. L., Jr., 477
Wallace, E. Z., 30
Wallace, M. J., 161, 460
Wallach, E. E., 302, 477
Wallach, E. S., 456
Waller, W., 77–79, 249, 477
Wallin, P., 88, 135, 139, 254, 258, 276, 458, 459, 477
Walster, E., 76, 77, 81, 456, 477
Walter, G. S., 327, 477
Ware, C., 219
Warner, R., 54
Warren, M., 330, 458
Washington, J. R., Jr., 144, 165, 477
Wasserman, E., 349, 478
Weber, L. E., 380
Weinberg, M., 31
Weinstein, E. A., 321, 477
Weinstock, E., 325, 477
Weiss, R. S., 418, 424, 431, 433, 477
Wells, F. L., 88, 472
Werner, A., 272, 477
Wershub, L. P., 477
Wessel, H., 379
Westoff, C. F., 7, 160, 275, 276, 315, 318, 384, 460, 474, 477, 478
Westoff, L. A., 275, 276, 477
Wharton, L. R., 18, 478
Wheeler, M., 428, 430, 434, 478
Wheeler, S., 457
Whelpton, P. K., 312, 462
Whitacre, F. E., 372, 459
Whitby, M., 461
White, L., 344, 472
Whitehead, T. P., 461
Whitehurst, R. N., 54, 288
Whitty, R. J., 349, 457
Wiedenbach, E., 380
Wiederman, J., 322, 462
Wiest, W. G., 329, 459

Wiggins, P., 477
Wile, I. S., 245, 478
Wilkens, L., 18, 478
Williams, C. J., 31
Williams, H. S., 349, 478
Williams, K. M., 154, 431, 432, 478
Williams, L. H., 350, 457
Williams-Ashman, H. G., 338, 472
Willocks, J., 360, 478
Willson, J. R., 306, 478
Wilson, M. G., 349, 458
Wilson, R. H. L., 215
Winch, R. F., 5, 9, 10, 35, 36, 62, 73, 118, 125, 126, 128, 138, 139, 415, 478
Winn, M. D., 245, 478
Winokur, G., 22, 266, 320, 470, 478
Wirsén, B., 380
Wirsén, C., 380
Wolf, S., 55
Wolfe, D. M., 151, 457
Wolfe, L. S., 330, 462
Wood, H. C., 334
Wrenn, L. G., 166
Wu, P. Y. K., 374, 478
Wyden, P., 250
Wylie, E. M., 334
Wyll, S. A., 349, 478
Wynn, R. M., 456, 465, 470

Yahia, C., 355, 478
Yankelovich, D., 55
Yankowski, J. S., 89, 478
Yorburg, B., 31
Young, L., 115
Young, W. C., 24, 26, 297, 319, 455, 457, 472, 478

Zañartu, J., 314, 478
Zaneveld, L. J. D., 315, 457
Zelnick, M., 14, 90–93, 106–108, 474, 478
Zelson, C., 349, 475, 478
Zielske, F., 307, 478
Zipursky, A., 373, 478
Zubin, J., 115
Zuelzer, W. W., 372, 459

Subject Index

Abortion, 7, 323–330
  deaths from, 326
  definition of, 294, 323
  fetus, nature of, 326–327
  future of, 330
  incidence among unmarried females, 7, 105
  induction of, 328–330
    amnioinfusion, 329
    dilatation & curettage (D & C), 328–329
    hysterectomy, 330
    menstrual extraction, 328
    prostaglandins, use of, 329–330
    saline injection, 329
    self-induction, 328
    vacuum-aspiration, 329
  legal, number of, 325–326
  liberalization, effects of, 327
  Supreme Court decision, 325, 327
  types of, 323–326
    on request, 324–326
      man, rights of, 327
    spontaneous, 323
      defective fetus in, 323
      genders, differences between, 26
      silent, 323
    therapeutic, 323–324
Adoption, 330–332
  black market, 332
  infertility, as a cure for, 321
Adultery (see Sex, extramarital)
Afterbirth, 346, 361–362
Afterglow, 258
Age:
  of consent, 105
  at first marriage, 142–143
  and marriage, stability of, 143–144

Age:
  for marriage, legal, 172–173, 450–451
  mixed marriage, difference in, 144–145
Alcohol, effect on fetus, 349
Alternative lifestyles (see Marriage, alternatives to)
Amenorrhea, 19
American Association of Marriage and Family Counselors, 441
Amniocentesis and ascertaining gender of fetus, 351–352
Amnioinfusion, abortion, as means of inducing, 329
Amnion, fetus, development of, 343
Androgen, secretion by embryonic testes, 23
  grounds for, 452–453
Annulment:
  nature of, 173, 414–415, 429
Artificial insemination (see Insemination, artificial)

Ballottement as sign of pregnancy, 354
Barr body, 351
Basal body temperature:
  ovulation, relation to, 297–298
  pregnancy, presumptive sign of, 354
Behavior, aspects of, 229–234
Bigamy, annulment, as ground for, 173
Bilirubin, 374
Birth control, 293–332
  definition of, 294
  methods of, 298–318
    coitus reservatus, 313

Birth control:
  methods of: comparative effectiveness of, 316–318
    condom, 310
    diaphragm, 309–310
    douching, 313–314
    incomplete intercourse (withdrawal), 312–313
    intrauterine device (IUD, IUCD), 306–309
      action of, 306–307
      expulsion of, 307
      failure rate of, 308
      insertion of, 306
      nature of, 306
      side effects of, 308
    intravaginal device (IVD), 314
    mini-pill, 305
    morning-after pill (DES), 314
    oral contraceptives, 298–306
      and cancer, 302
      contraindications for, 301–302
      effects of, 299–302
      and fertility, 302
      risk/benefit ratio and, 304
      side effects of, 302–305
        beneficial, 305
      and thromboembolic disease, 304–305
    progesterone, injection of, 305–306
    progestin only pills, 305
    safe period or rhythm, 311–312
    salpingectomy (tubal ligation), 316
    spermicide, 310–311
    sperms, preventing formation of, 314
    sterilization, 314–316
    vasectomy, 315

Subject Index

Birth control:
  practice of, trends in, 318
  requirements for, 294–295
Birth rate, 26, 383–384
  decrease in, 7
Breast feeding, 368–369
  and menstruation, 369
  and pregnancy, 369
Bride price, 117
Bundling, 71

Caesarean section, 360–361
Campus marriage (*see* Marriage, college)
Castration, effects of, 23
Catholic–non-Catholic marriage (*see* Marriage, mixed, Catholic–non-Catholic)
Child, birth of first, effect on marriage, 386–388
Childbirth, 355–378
  afterbirth, 361–362
  caesarean section, 360–361
  dry birth, 356
  episiotomy during, 360
  fetus, identification of, 361
  labor: duration of, 356–357
    stages of, 356
  lightening, 355
  molding of head of fetus, 359
  natural, 363–364
  pain, relief of, 362–363
    drugs used for, 362–363
  pelvis during, 359
  version, 359
Childlessness, voluntary, 6, 7, 383
  (*See also* Infertility)
Children:
  and divorce, 423–424
    custody and support of, after, 430
  of employed mothers, 202, 206
  rearing of, 388–403
    cost, 384
    discipline, 396–398
    men, participation in, 14–15, 377–378
    needs of, 389–398
    stage-typical behavior, 393
    women, responsibility for, 14–15
Choice, freedom of, 85, 98–99
Chromosomes, 22, 336–337
Cilia, 341
Clitoris, 266–267
  nature of, 266
  role in orgasm, 266–267
  stimulation of, 266
Cohabitation, 38–44
  advantages, 39

Cohabitation:
  common-law marriage, not same as, 43, 45
  forms of, 38–39
  frequency of, 38, 40
  and marital quality, 42
  and marriage of participants, 41–43
  as permanent alternative to marriage, 6, 43–44
  problems, 43
  persons involved, 40
  problems, 39–40
  reasons for, 39–40
  suggested policies for, 40–41
Coitus interruptus as method of conception control, 312–313
Coitus reservatus as method of conception control, 313
College marriage (*see* Marriage, college)
Collusion and divorce, 426
Colostrum:
  after childbirth, secretion of, 368
  pregnancy, as presumptive sign of, 353
Common-law marriage, 44–45
  definition of, 44
  reasons for, early, 44
Communes as alternative to marriage, 6, 45–48
  types of, 45–46
Communication:
  child's need for, 391–392
  in marriage, 241–243
Complementary needs, theory of, in choice of marriage partner, 125–126
Conception:
  and insemination, 342
  meaning of, 294
Conception control, 294
  (*See also* Birth control)
Condom:
  as method of birth control, 310
  and venereal disease, prevention of, 111
Conflict in marriage:
  boredom as cause of, 239–240
  focal points of, 237–238
Congenital traits, 122
Consanguineous relationships, prohibited by law, 172
Contraception (contraceptives):
  increase in use of, 7
  and premarital sexual intercourse, inadequate use during, 106–108
  reasons for, 107–108
  use of: by Catholic women, 160

Contraception (contraceptives):
  use of: by unmarried women, 7
  (*See also* Birth control)
Corpus luteum, 295, 296
  hormones secreted by, 340–341
Counseling:
  marriage and family, 435–443
    basic principles, 441–442
    counselee, responsibility of, 443
    qualifications of counselor, 439–441
    premarital and postmarital, 442
    types of, 438–439
Cryptorchidism, infertility, as cause of, 320

Date, qualities of, 75–76
Dating, 71–81
  changes in, 7, 71–72
  decreasing formality of, 74
  definition of, 72–73
  early, trends toward, 80–81
  failures in, and marriage failure, 72
  functions of, 73
  gender differences in, 77
  group activities, increase in, 74
  importance of, 71
  initiated by females, 73–74
  and marital stability, 80
  and physical attractiveness, 76–77
  as preparation for marriage, 7
  rating and, complex, 77–79
  and social change, 73–75
  social skills developed in, 79
  steady, 80–81
    and sexual activity, 81
    trends towards, 80–81
Death rate, 27
  decline of, and divorce, 418
  maternal, 365
Determinism, 8
Diaphragm as method of birth control, 309–310
Dilatation and curettage (D & C) as means of inducing abortion, 328–329
Diminishing returns, law of, and marriage adjustment, 248–249
Discipline in child rearing, 396–398
Divorce, 413–429
  adjustment after, 430–431
  adversary (fault) system, 424–427
  and age of first marriage, 422

Subject Index

Divorce:
  Catholic Church's attitude toward, 160
  causes of, 413–414
  child support and alimony, 430
  and children, 423–424
  collusion, 426
  condonation, 426–427
  connivance, 426
  and death rate, decline of, 418
  definition of, 414
  duration of marriage before, 420
  grounds for, 424–427, 448–449
  law, 424–429
    future of, 428–429
  laws, of fifty states, 448–449
  no-fault, 427–428
  of one partner in mixed marriage, 153–154
  rate, 6, 33, 416–423
    differentials in, 420–423
    factors affecting, 418–419
  recrimination, 426
  and remarriage, 422, 431–433
  and separation, 414, 429–430
  as symptom of failure, 413
  who files for, 427
Double standard, 99
Douching as method of birth control, 313–314
Dowry, 118
Dry birth, 356
Dyspareunia, 284

Education, and mixed marriage, difference in, 150–151
Ejaculation:
  orgasm, relation to, 257, 270–271
  premature, 282–283
    and feelings of failure, 20
  retarded, 283
Embryo, 344
Endogamy, 147
Engagement, 131–137
  broken, 135–137
  length of, 132
  questions to be discussed during, 133–134
  revealing past during, 134
  rings, pins, etc., 133
  as transition to marriage, 132–133
Episiotomy during childbirth, 360
Erythroblastosis fetalis, 373
Estrogen, secreted by Graafian follicle, 295–340
Ethnocentrism, 7

Eunuch, 23
Exogamy, 147
Extramarital sex (*see* Sex, extramarital)

Family:
  definition of, 3
  development, 403–404
  developmental tasks, 403–404
  domestic, 35
  equalitarian, 197
  functions of, 381–383
    changing, 9
  life cycle, 403
  nuclear, 35
  of orientation, 6
  of procreation, 6
  size, interaction, relation to, 384–386
Family planning, 294
Father:
  in delivery room during childbirth, 377
  participation of, in infant care, 377–378
Fear:
  as jealousy, 243–244
  of pain during sex, 261–264
Female orgasm, capacity and frequency, 257–258, 266–270
Female sexual desire, reasons for lack of, 256
Female sexual response, nature of, 265–270
Femininity, 24
Fertility, 293–332
  drugs, 319–320
  menarch, relation to, 18
  menopause, relation to, 320
Fertilization, 342
  definition of, 294
Fetus:
  appearance in X-ray, as positive sign of pregnancy, 354–355
  development of, 343–346
  factors affecting: alcohol, 349
    anesthesia, 349
    bacteria and viruses, 348
    maternal impressions, 350
    narcotic drugs, 349
    rubella, 348–349
    smoking, mother's, 349
    thalidomide, 349
  gender of, 351–352
    ascertainment of, 351–352
    amniocentesis, 351–352
    Barr body, 351
    sex chromatin, 351–352
    controlling, 352

Fetus:
  gender of: determination of, 351–352
  head of, molding of, 359
  heartbeat of, as positive sign of pregnancy, 354
  identification of, 361
  movement of, as positive sign of pregnancy, 354
  nature of, and abortion, 326–327
  protection, food, and oxygen supply, 346–350
  shape of, as positive sign of pregnancy, 354
Fimbriae, 341
Follicle-stimulating hormone (FSH), 340
Forceps, obstetrical, 360
Frigidity (*see* Orgasmic dysfunction)

Gametes, 336–338
Gender:
  definition of, 12
  determination of, 351–352
  differences, 11–28
    in androgen secretion of embryonic testes, 23
    birth rate, 26
    causes, 22–26
      culture and experience, 24–26
      physiological processes (glands), 23–24
    death rate, 27
      as homicide victims, 27
      suicide rates, 27
    erotic movies, reaction to, 22
    freedom, 18
    life expectancy, 16, 27
    occupational opportunities and expectations, 17–18
    physiological, 16
    at puberty, 20
    sex ratio, 27–28
    visual experience, 20, 22
    widows and widowers, 28
  identity, 12–13
    age at establishment of, 23
    clinics, 13
    definition of, 12
    development of, 12–13
  role, 12–13, 26
    definition of, 12
    development of, 13
  similarities, 12, 15–26
    causes of, 22–26
Genders:
  complementarity of, 28

Subject Index

Genders:
    equality of, 28
    overlapping attributes of, 15–16
Genes, 22, 336–337
Graafian follicle, 295, 340
Group marriage, 48–50
    definition of, 4

Hemolytic disease of newborn, 373
    (*See also* Rh factor)
Hereditary traits, 122
Heredity:
    and choice of marriage partner, 122–123
    determiners of, 336–338
Hermaphroditism, 23
Heterosexuality, 12
Homemaker, value of service performed, 204
Homogamy, 118
    and choice of marriage partner, 139–140
Homosexuality, 12
Honeymoon, 183
    cystitus, 272
Household, nature of, 36
Human chorionic gonadotropin (HCG) and pregnancy tests, 355
Humanae vitae, 160
Husband, role of, 197–199
Hymen, 262–263
    and first sexual intercourse, 262–263
    intact, and pregnancy, 343
    and premarital medical examination, 263
    virginal forms of, 262–263

Illegitimacy, incidence of, 7, 108–109
    (*See also* Pregnancy, premarital)
Implantation, 342
    definition of, 294
Impotence, sexual, 281–282
    and feelings of failure, 20
Infatuation and love, 66–68
Infertility, 318–321
    and adoption, 321
    correction of, 320–321
    definition of, 318
    factors contributing to, 318–319
    male, cryptorchidism as cause of, 320
In-laws, 247–248
Insemination:
    artificial, 321–323
        Catholic attitude toward, 160–161

Insemination:
    artificial: and legitimacy of child, 322
    and conception, 342
Interception, 294
Intercourse (*see* Sexual intercourse)
Interest, least, principle of, 79–80
Interfaith marriage (*see* Marriages, mixed, religion, difference in)
Intermenstrual bleeding, 297
Interstitial cells and testosterone secretion, 338
Intrauterine device (IUD, IUCD) (*see* Birth control, methods of, intrauterine device)
Intravaginal device (IVD) as method of birth control, 314
Isoimmunization and Rh factor, 373

Jealousy, 243–244
Jewish–non-Jewish marriage, 161–162

Kinsey studies, 85–86

Labia, tumscence of, 263–265
Labor (*see* Childbirth, labor)
Lactation, 368–369
Lacunae, 295–347
Lanugo, 345
Laparoscopy and tubal ligation, 316
Law of divorce, future of, 428–429
Law and framework for marriage, 172–177
Least interest, principle of, 249
Leisure time in marriage, use of, 239–240
Life expectancy:
    gender differences, 16, 27–28
    racial differences, 27
Lightening in pregnancy, 355
Love:
    child's need for, 390–391
    definitions of, 62–63
    dual, 64
    falling in, stages of, 62–64
    at first sight, compulsive, 66
    and infatuation compared, 66–68
    meanings of, 61
    misconceptions concerning, 64–66
    questions for self-evaluation, 68–70
    romantic, 62
    wheel theory of, 63–64

Luteinizing hormone (LH), production of, 340

Male and female, prenatal development of, 15
Marriage:
    adjustment in: decline in early years, 226–227
    definition of, 221–249
    factors affecting: acceptance, 240–241
        communication, 241–243
        conflict, 225–226
        conflict resolution, 225–226
        diminishing returns, law of, 248–249
        domination, 244–245
        failure, publicizing of, 214
        fear, (jealousy), 243–244
        first child, birth of, 386–388
        focal points, 237–238
        homeopathic remedies, 245–246
        in-laws, 247–248
        least interest, principle of, 249
        legislation, 211–212
        leisure time, use of, 239–240
        money, use of, 238–239
        motivation, 240
        obscurantism, 212–213
        overdependence, 245
        perspective, 234–236
        pregnancy, 376–378
        preparation for marriage, lack of, 212
        quarreling, 246–247
        romance, premarital, 213
        serious attitude, lack of, 213
        sex, 213
        stereotypes, 213–214
        tension, 246–247
        tremendous trifles, 236–237
        understanding personality and behaviors, 228–238
    over life cycle, 226–228
    measurement of, 227–228
    wedding, implied in, 180
    of aliens, 175
    alternatives to, 5–6, 33–52
        cohabitation, 6, 38–44
        communes, 6, 45–48
        group marriage, 4, 48–50
        homosexual marriage, 38, 50–51
        singleness, 6
        trial marriage, 41–43
    arrangement of, 4
    change of status, 175
    changes in, 195–200
    college, 186–192

Subject Index

Marriage:
    college: role reversal in, 189
        students involved, 186–187
        success in, 190
    common law, 44–45
        cohabitation versus, 43
        definition of, 44
        reasons for early, 44
    contracts, 176–177
    definition of, 3, 35, 59
    dissolubility of, and wedding, 180
    dissolution of, 411–433
        cross-cultural perspective, 415–416
        definition of, 414
        historical perspective, 415
        and separation, 414
        (*See also* Divorce)
    in earlier times, 193–195
    failure in, 411–413
    forms of, 3–4
    function of, 5
    group, 4, 48–50
    homosexual, 38, 50–51
    importance of, 4–5
    instability of, 6
    institutional aspects of, 193
    interpersonal aspects of, 195–197
    launching of, 171–190
    love, as basis for, 195
    mixed, 139–164
        age difference, 144–145
        Catholic–non-Catholic, 158–161
            preparation for, 161
        definition of, 140
        difference in education, 150–151
        endogamy, 147
        exogamy, 147
        factors associated with success or failure, 140–141
        family background, 148–149
        and intelligence, difference in, 151–152
        interracial, 146–148
            incidence of, 148
            increase, factors contributing to, 147
        Jewish–non-Jewish, 161–162
        nationality differences, 145–146
        previous marital status, difference in, 153–154
        religion: difference in, 154, 163
            trends, 155–156
        social class, difference in, 149–150

Marriage:
    multilateral, 48
    popularity of, 3
    by proxy, 175
    quality of, 222–225, 412
        definition of, 222
        factors affecting, 222
            external, 222
            internal, 222
    rate, 33, 141–142
    readiness for, factors in, 177–178
    reasons for, 4, 60–61
        love, 61–71
        rebound, 60
    repudiation of, as reason for singleness, 38
    research on, 8
    on shipboard, 175
    and social change, 6, 7
    and social climate, 193–214
    socialization for, 3–4, 59–81
    stability of, 222–225, 412
        definition of, 222
        and education, 151
        and religion, 162–163
        and social class, 150
    success, prediction of, 8
    transition to, from singleness, 183–186
    in two steps, 42–43
    universality of, 3, 59
    values, found in, 60–61
Marriage laws, 172–177
    age for marriage, 172–173
    and antenuptial contracts, 176
    capacity to marry, 172–173
    consensus, 174
    divorce, remarriage after, 176
    of fifty states, 450–451
    health certificate, 173–174
    interracial marriage, 176
    license, 174
    officiant, 174
    reciprocity, 176
    residency, 174–175
    void and voidable marriages, 173
    waiting period, 173
Marriage partner:
    choice of, 117–137
        background factors, 121
        common interests, 123–124
        complementary needs, theory of, 125–126
        developmental theories of, 128–130
        differentials in, 152–153
        economic elements, 124–125
        escalators, theory of, 128–129
        field of eligibles, 118

Marriage partner:
    choice of: filter theory, 129
        hereditary traits, 122–123
        homogamy, 118
        length of acquaintance, 127–128
        likes and opposites, 125–126
        parent, similarity to, 126–127
        parental objections to, 131
        physical health, 121–122
        poor, reasons for, 130–131
        principles guiding, 118–119
        propinquity, 142
        sexual attraction, 121
        standards of behavior, 124
    qualities of, 119–120
    surrogate, 285
Masculinity:
    meaning of, 24
    new burdens of, 210
Masturbation and education for sexuality, 402–403
Mate swapping (*see* Swinging)
Maternal mortality, 365
Meiosis, 337
Men, position of, 210–211
Menarche:
    definition of, 18
    and fertility, 18
Menopause:
    fertility, relation to, 320
    and ovariectomy (oophorectomy), 320
Menotropins, 319
Men's liberation movement, 210
Menstrual cycle, 295–298
    intermenstrual bleeding, 297
    length of, 296–297
Menstrual extraction (*see* Abortion, induction of, menstrual extraction)
Menstruation, 295–298
    anovulatory, 296
    and blood clotting, 298
    cause of, 295–296
    cessation of, as sign of pregnancy, 353
    nature of, 295–298
    ovulation, relation to, 296–298
    ovulatory, 295–296
    painful, causes of, 298
    sexual intercourse during, 273
Miscarriage, 346
    (*See also* Abortion, types of, spontaneous)
Mitosis, 336
Mittelschmerz, 297
Mixed marriage (*see* Marriage, mixed)
Molding of head of fetus, 359

Subject Index

Money:
    and marriage partner, choice of, 124–125
    use of, in marriage, 238–239
Monogamy, 4
Morality, new, 85
Motherhood, earliest case of, 18
Multiple births, 369–371
    and fertility drugs, 319
    incidence of, 369
    superfecundation, 371
    types of, 369
Myotonia as response to sexual stimulation, 265–266

Nagging:
    and child rearing, 396
    in marriage, 233–234
New morality, 85
Nidation, 294–342
Nocturnal emission, 18

Obscurantism, 212–213
Obstetrician, choice of, 375–376
Oophorectomy, 24
    menopause, as cause of, 320
Orchialgia, 103
Orgasm:
    concern for, 19
    female, nature of, 257–258, 266–270
    lack of, and enjoyment of sexual intercourse, 19–20
    multiple, 19
    pretense of, 20
    and sexual performance, 19–20
    simultaneous, 270
Orgasmic dysfunction, 283–284
Ova (see Ovum)
Ovarectomy, 24
    menopause, as cause of, 320
Ovaries:
    and gender difference, 23
    and ovum production, 339–340
Ovulation, 298–299
    and basal body temperature, 297–298
    induction of, 319
        clomiphene, use of, 319
        menotropins, use of, 319
    menstruation, relation to, 296–298
    pain associated with, 297
    time of, ascertaining, 297–298, 311–312
Ovum:
    life of, 341

Ovum:
    movement of, 341
    nature of, 337–338
    number of, 340
    production of, 339–342
    release at puberty, 18

Papanicolaou (Pap) smear, 301–302
Parenthood:
    single, frequency, 51
    transition to, 386–388
    trends in, 383–384
Parents:
    and college marriage: attitude toward, 188
        subsidy of, 188–189
    objections to choice of marriage partner, 131
Parthenogenesis, 342–343
Paternity, accusation of, 105–106
Paternity tests, 105–106
Pelvic examination, 264–265
Periodicity of sexual desire, 273–274
Personality, understanding of, 228–238
Perspective in marriage adjustment, 234–236
Petting, 102–103
Phocomelia, 349
Placenta:
    development of, 343
    nature and function of, 346–347
    passage of viruses through, 348
Polyandry, 4
Polygamy, 3
Polygyny, 3
Preejaculation and assumption of parthenogenesis, 342
Pregnancy, 355–378
    breast feeding, relation to, 369
    and couples' adjustment, 376
    duration of, 346
    ectopic, 343–344
    false, 352
    premarital, 104–105
        frequency of, 106, 108–109
        legitimized by wedding, 175–176
    sexual intercourse during, 273
    signs of, 352–355
        positive, 354–355
            definition of, 352
            fetal heart beat, 354
            fetus: appearance in X-ray, 354–355
            movement of, 354

Pregnancy:
    signs of: positive: fetus: shape of, 354
    presumptive, 352–354
        ballottement, 354
        basal body temperature, 354
        definition of, 352
        menstruation, cessation of, 353
        morning sickness, 353
        repercussion, 354
    tests for, 355
    tubal, 343–344
    weight gain during, 349–350
Premarital medical examiniation, 263–265
Premarital pregnancy (see Pregnancy, premarital)
Premarital sexual intercourse (see Sexual intercourse, premarital)
Premenstrual syndrome, 274–275
    incidence of, 274
    symptoms of, 274
Premenstrual tension (see Premenstrual syndrome)
Probabilism, definition of, 8
Progesterone, 295
Prostaglandins as means of inducing abortion, 329–330
Prostate gland and secretion of seminal fluid, 338
Pseudocyesis, 352
Puberty:
    adjustments called for, 18
    changes at, 18–20
Pubococcygeus muscle and sexual stimulation, 266

Quarreling, marriage role in, 246–247

Race, difference in mixed marriage, 146–148
Rape:
    accusation of, 105
    statutory, 105
Rating and dating complex, 77–79
Reduction division, 349
Religion:
    difference in mixed marriage, 154–163
    and marriage stability, 162–163
Remarriage:
    and divorce, 422
    and mixed marriage, 153–154

Subject Index

Remarriage:
　rate, 6, 33, 431–432
Rh factor, 371–375
　and antibody formation, 372–373
　and bilirubin formation, 374
　and erythroblastosis fetalis, 373
　　treatment of, 374–375
　　　exchange transfusion, 374–375
　　　feeding baby, 375
　　　fluorescent light, use of, 375
　　　intrauterine transfusion, 374–375
　　　phenobarbitol, use of, 375
　and hemolytic disease of newborn, 373
　and isoimmunization, 373
　　prevention of, 374
　nature of, 371–372
Rhythm (*see* Safe period)
Ring:
　engagement, meaning of, 133
　wedding, significance of, 181

Safe period as method of birth control, 311–312
Salpingectomy, 316
Scrotum, temperature and sperm formation, 338
Semen (*see* Seminal fluid)
Seminal fluid:
　ejaculation of, 257
　　in nocturnal emissions, 18
　　premature, 282
　　retarded, 283
　frozen, 322–328
　　children born when used, 322
　　sperm banks, 322–323
　nature of, 338
　secretion of, at puberty, 18
Separation, 415, 429–430
Sex:
　of assignment and rearing, 26
　co-marital (*see* Swinging)
　definition of, 12
　drive: differences between men and women, 19
　　female, after ovariectomy (oophorectomy), 320
　education (*see* Sexuality, education for)
　extramarital, 7, 277–281
　　incidence of, 277–278
　　increase in, 7
　　and marriage adjustment, 278
　　swinging (*see* Swinging)
　group (*see* Swinging)
　and love: combining, by women, 20

Sex:
　and love: separation of, by men, 20
　in marriage, 253–286
　　bodily exposure, inhibitions concerning, 261
　　intercourse, frequency of, 275–276
　　and marriage adjustment, 276
　　mutuality of, 255–257
　　pain, fear of, 261–264
　　periodicity of desire, 273–274
　　success or failure in, 258–260
　　vaginal lubrication, 263–264
　nature of, 255
　psychologic, 26
　ratio, 27–28
　variables of, 26
Sex-object preference, development of, 12
Sexual adequacy, concern for, 256
Sexual dimorphism, 11
Sexual dysfunctions, 281–286
　in female, 283–285
　　dyspareunia, 284
　　orgasmic dysfunction, 283–284
　　vaginismus, 284–285
　in male, 281–283
　　impotence, 281–282
　　premature ejaculation, 282–283
　　retarded ejaculation, 283
　treatment of, 285–286
Sexual evolution, 84–85, 112
Sexual intercourse:
　acceptable behavior, 271
　difficulty in, 258–261
　and female: need for, 100
　　orientation, 95–96
　　preparation for, 270
　　reactions in, 257–258
　first, fear of pain in, 261–264
　frequency of, in marriage, 275–276
　incomplete, as means of birth control, 312–313
　and male: need for, 100
　　orientation, 95–96
　　reactions in, 257–258
　during menstruation, 273
　painful, 284
　positions for, 271
　during pregnancy, 273
　premarital, 83–113
　　age, relation to, 93
　　class, relation to, 93
　　and contraception, 106–108
　　　inadequate use of, 106–108
　　double standard, 99
　　education, relation to, 93

Sexual intercourse:
　premarital: emotional attachment, relation to, 93
　　female, possible consequences for, 104–105
　　freedom of choice, 98–99
　　and goal orientation, 99–100
　　incidence, 87–91
　　　active, 87
　　　cumulative, 87
　　increase in, 7
　　　among females, 7
　　male, possible consequences for, 105–106
　　male-female differences, 92–93
　　marriage, effect on, 99–100
　　physical attractiveness, relation to, 93
　　racial differences, 93
　　recent trends, 91–92
　　relationship between male and female, effect on, 100–102
　　religiosity, relation to, 93
　　research on, 87–91
　　　findings, summary of, 92–93
　　　methodological problems of, 96–97
　　risks in, 103–112
　　and sexual socialization, 97–98
　　venereal disease, 109–112
Sexual permissiveness, 94–95
Sexual reaction, male-female differences, 257–258
　nature of, 257–258
Sexual response, 265–275
　male-female differences in, 266–272
　phases of, 269–270
　stimulation for, 270–271
　　acceptable and unacceptable means, 270–271
Sexual revolution, 84–85, 112–113
Sexual socialization, 12–13, 20–22
　components of, 12–13
　　acquiring skills, knowledge, and values, 13
　　disposition to act in sexual contexts, development of, 13
　　gender identity, development of, 12–13
　　gender role, development of, 13
　　sex-object preference, development of, 12
　definition of, 12
　genders, differences between, 20–22

Subject Index

Sexual standards, 94–95
Sexual tension, effect of, 103
Sexuality:
  definition of, 12
  education for, 398–403
    bodily exposure, 399–400
    children's questions about, 400–401
    masturbation, 402–403
Signs of pregnancy (*see* Pregnancy, signs of)
Singleness:
  as alternative to marriage, 6
  frequency of, 36
  and parenthood, 51–52
  reasons for, 36–38
    homosexuality and, 37–38
    repudiation of marriage, 38
Socialization, 59
Sperm, 338–339
  frozen (*see* Seminal fluid, frozen)
  life of, 339
  nature of, 338
  number of, 338–339
    and fertilization, 342
  preventing formation of, as method of birth control, 314
  release at puberty, 18
  and seminal fluid, 338
Sperm banks (*see* Seminal fluid, frozen, sperm banks)
Spermatozoa (*see* Sperm)
Sterilization, 314–316
Superfecundation, 371
Supreme Court decision on abortion, 325, 327
Swinging, 279–281
  incidence of, 279

Temperature, basal body (*see* Basal body temperature)
Tension as affecting marriage adjustment, 246–247

Testalgia, 103
Testes:
  and gender differences, 23
  and sperm production, 338
  testosterone, production by interstitial cells, 338
Test-tube baby, 321
Testicles (*see* Testes)
Thalidomide, effect on fetus, 349
Thermal shift, 298
Thrombophlebitis and contraceptive pills, 304–305
Transsexual, 13
Transvestite, 13
Trial marriage, 41–43
  problems of, 41–42
Tubal ligation, 316
  and laparoscopy, 316
Tumescence of labia, 263–265
Twins, types of, 369–370

Umbilical cord, development from zygote, 343

Vagina:
  role in orgasm, 266–267
  sensitivity to stimuli and pain, 266
Vaginismus, 284–285
Vas deferens (vasa deferentia) and sperm storage, 338
Vasectomy, 315
Vasocongestion, 103, 265
Venereal disease, 109–112
  and condom as preventative, 111
  incidence of, 110
  rate of, 110
  risk of, in premarital sexual intercourse, 109–112
Vernix caseosa, 345
Version, 359
Villi, 347

Wedding, 178–183
  ceremony, 178–179
  customs, 180–183
  functions of, 178
  homosexual, 38
  meaning of term, 180–181
  number of, 141
  and premarital pregnancy, legitimizing of, 175–176
  ring, 181
Wife, role of, 199, 200
Withdrawal as means of birth control, 312–313
Women:
  and employment, 15
  employment of married, 200–206
    breakdown of division of labor, 202–204
    and children, 202
      effect on, 206
    and comparative prestige, 204
    and marriage, effect on, 205–206
    number, 200–201
    problems, 202–205
  freedom in initiating dating, 73–74
  as minority group, 207–208
  position of, 206–210
Women's liberation movement, 208–209

Yellow body (*see* Corpus luteum)

Zygote:
  development of, 343
  implantation of, 342
  nidation of, 342
  potential of, 335–336